# CENSUS OF INDIA 1911

## Census of India 1871-1951, 9 Sets In 384 Bindings (9788121258876) Rs. 700000

## Census of India 1911, 23 Vols. In 41 Bindings (9788121271271) Rs. 69000

1. India - Report (9788121275071) Rs. 2475 (Vol. I, Pt. 1)
2. India - Tables (9788121275057) Rs. 2225 (Vol. I, Pt. 2)
3. Andaman and Nicobar Islands - Report & Tables (9788121275033) Rs. 900 (Vol. II, Pt. 1 & 2)
4. Assam - Report (9788121275019) Rs. 1000 (Vol. III, Pt. 1)
5. Assam - Tables (9788121274999) Rs. 1300 (Vol. III, Pt. 2)
6. Baluchistan - Report & Tables (9788121274975) Rs. 950 (Vol. IV, Pt. 1 & 2)
7. Bengal, Bihar And Orissa And Sikkim - Report (9788121274951) Rs. 3100 (Vol. V, Pt. 1)
8. Bengal - Tables (9788121274937) Rs. 2250 (Vol. V, Pt. 2)
9. Bihar And Orissa - Tables and Bengal And Sikkim - Chapter I of Administrative Volume (9788121274913) Rs. 1800 (Vol. V, Pt. 3 & 4)
10. City of Calcutta - Report and Tables and Administrative (9788121274876) Rs. 1300 (Vol. VI, Pt. 1 & 2 & 3)
11. Bombay - Report (9788121274814) Rs. 1950 (Vol. VII, Pt. 1)
12. Bombay - Imperial Tables and Administrative Report (9788121274791) Rs. 3300 (Vol. VII, Pt. 2 & 3)
13. Bombay (Town And Island) - Report And Tables (9788121274753) Rs. 1250 (Vol. VIII, Pt. 1 & 2)
14. Burma - Report (9788121274739) Rs. 2250 (Vol. IX, Pt. 1)
15. Burma - Tables (9788121274715) Rs. 1480 (Vol. IX, Pt. 2)
16. Central Provinces And Berar - Report (9788121274692) Rs. 1475 (Vol. X, Pt. 1)
17. Central Provinces And Berar - Tables (9788121274678) Rs. 1900 (Vol. X, Pt. 2)
18. Coorg - Report And Tables Madras - Report (9788121274630) Rs. 1740 (Vol. XI & Vol. XII, Pt. 1)
19. Madras - Imperial And Provincial Tables (9788121274616) Rs. 1500 (Vol. XII, Pt. 2)
20. Madras - Administrative Report and city of Madras (9788121274593) Rs. 630 (Vol. XII, Pt. 3 & 4)
21. North - West Frontier Province - Report & Tables (9788121274579) Rs. 2150 (Vol. XIII, Pt. 1 & 2)
22. Punjab - Report (9788121274555) Rs. 3000 (Vol. XIV, Pt. 1)
23. Punjab - Tables (9788121274531) Rs. 2200 (Vol. XIV, Pt. 2)
24. Punjab - Appendices To The - Imperial Tables (9788121274517) Rs. 950 (Vol. XIV, Pt. 3)
25. United Provinces of Agra And Oudh - Report (9788121274494) Rs. 2225 (Vol. XV, Pt. 1)
26. United Provinces of Agra And Oudh - Tables (9788121274470) Rs. 4000 (Vol. XV, Pt. 2)
27. United Provinces of Agra And Oudh - Provincial Tables And Appendices (9788121274456) Rs. 570 (Vol. XV, Pt. 3)
28. Baroda - Report (9788121274432) Rs. 2000 (Vol. XVI, Pt. 1)
29. Baroda State - The Imperial Tables (9788121274418) Rs. 850 (Vol. XVI, Pt. 2)
30. Central India Agency - Report And Tables (9788121274395) Rs. 1470 (Vol. XVII)
31. Cochin - Report And Imperial Tables (9788121274371) Rs. 1150 (Vol. XVIII, Pt. 1 & 2)
32. Hyderabad State - Report (9788121274357) Rs. 890 (Vol. XIX, Pt. 1)
33. Hyderabad State - Imperial And Provincial Tables (9788121274333) Rs. 1750 (Vol. XIX, Pt. 2)
34. Kashmir - Report (9788121274319) Rs. 950 (Vol. XX, Pt. 1)
35. Kashmir - Tables (9788121274296) Rs. 1170 (Vol. XX, Pt. 2)
36. Mysore - Report (9788121274272) Rs. 1200 (Vol. XXI, Pt. 1)
37. Mysore - Tables (9788121274258) Rs. 1500 (Vol. XXI, Pt. 2)
38. Rajputana And Ajmer-Merwara - Report (9788121274234) Rs. 1470 (Vol. XXII, Pt. 1)
39. Rajputana And Ajmer-Merwara - Tables (9788121274210) Rs. 1700 (Vol. XXII, Pt. 2)
40. Travancore - Report (9788121274197) Rs. 1870 (Vol. XXIII, Pt. 1)
41. Travancore - Imperial Tables (9788121274173) Rs. 870 (Vol. XXIII, Pt. 2)

Owing to the antiquity and rarity of this book, certain pages are regrettably absent, and readability is compromised due to the blurring of the original text. If you possess any insights regarding the availability of these missing sections, kindly inform us. Your assistance is crucial in ensuring the completion of this significant work for the benefit of future generations.

# CENSUS OF INDIA, 1911

## VOLUME - XVII

# CENTRAL INDIA AGENCY

## REPORT AND TABLES

**MAJOR C. E. LUARD**

GYAN

*Published by*

Gyan Publishing House
5, Ansari Road
Daryaganj, New Delhi-110002
Phone: 011-47034999, 9811692060
E-mail: books@gyanbooks.com

*Distribution Network*
gyanbooks.com
India, USA, Canada, UK, Australia



ISBN: 978-81-212-7127-1 (Set) 23 Vols. In 41 Bindings

ISBN: 978-81-212-7439-5 (PB) Vol. XVII

First Published, 1913

2nd Impression 2024

*Printed at:* Gyan Press, Delhi.



**CENSUS OF INDIA 1911**

# CENSUS OF INDIA, 1911

## VOLUME XVII

# CENTRAL INDIA AGENCY

## Part I—REPORT
## Part II—TABLES

## *Agents for the Sale of Books published by the Superintendent of Government Printing, India, Calcutta.*

### In the United Kingdom.

Messrs Constable & Co., 10, Orange Street, Leicester Square, London, W.C.
Messrs. Kegan Paul, Trench, Trübner & Co., 68-74, Carter Lane, E.C.
Mr. Bernard Quaritch, 11, Grafton Street, New Bond Street, London, W.
Messrs. P. S. King & Son, 2 and 4, Great Smith Street, Westminster, London, S.W.
Messrs. H. S. King & Co., 65, Cornhill, and 9, Pall Mall, London.
Messrs. Grindlay & Co., 54, Parliament Street, London, S.W.
Mr. T. Fisher Unwin, 1, Adelphi Terrace, London, W.C.
Messrs. W. Thacker & Co., 2, Creed Lane, London, E.C.
Messrs. Luzac & Co., 46, Great Russell Street, London, W.C.
Mr. B. H. Blackwell, 50 and 51, Broad Street, Oxford.
Messrs. Deighton, Bell & Co., Cambridge.
Messrs. Oliver & Boyd, Tweeddale Court, Edinburgh.
Messrs. E. Ponsonby, Ld., 116, Grafton Street, Dublin.

### On the Continent.

Mr. Otto Harrassowitz, Leipzig.
Mr. Karl W. Hiersemann, Leipzig.
Messrs. R. Friedlander & Sohn, Berlin, W. N., Carlstrasse, 11.
Mr. Ernest Leroux, 28, Rue Bonaparte, Paris, France.
Mr. Martinus Nijhoff, The Hague, Holland.

### In India and Ceylon.

Messrs. Thacker, Spink & Co., Calcutta and Simla.
Messrs. Newman & Co., Calcutta.
Messrs. R. Cambray & Co., Calcutta.
Messrs. S. K. Lahiri & Co., Calcutta.
Messrs. B. Banerjee & Co., Calcutta.

### In India and Ceylon—*contd.*

The Calcutta School Book and Useful Literature Society, 309, Bow Bazar Street, Calcutta.
Messrs. Butterworth & Co. (India), Ld., Calcutta.
The Weldon Library, 18-5, Chowringhee, Calcutta.
Messrs. M. C. Sircar & Sons, 75, Harrison Road, Calcutta.
Messrs. Higginbotham & Co., Madras.
Messrs. V. Kalyanarama Iyer & Co., Madras.
Messrs. G. A. Natesan & Co., Madras.
Messrs. S. Murthy & Co., Madras.
Messrs. Thompson & Co., Madras.
Messrs. Temple & Co., Madras.
Messrs. Combridge & Co., Madras.
Messrs. P. R. Rama Iyer & Co., Madras.
Messrs. Thacker & Co., Ld., Bombay.
Messrs. A. J. Combridge & Co., Bombay.
Messrs. D. B. Taraporevala, Sons & Co., Bombay.
Mrs. Radhabai Atmaram Sagoon, Bombay.
Mr. Sundar Pandurang, Bombay.
Messrs. Gopal Narayan & Co., Bombay.
Messrs. Ram Chandra Govind & Son, Kalbadevi, Bombay.
Mr. N. B. Mathur, Superintendent, Nazir Kanun Hind Press, Allahabad.
Rai Sahib M. Gulab Singh & Sons, Mufid-i-Am Press, Lahore and Calcutta.
Messrs. A. Chand & Co., Punjab.
Superintendent, American Baptist Mission Press, Rangoon.
Babu S. C. Talukdar, Proprietor, Students and Co., Cooch Behar.
Messrs. A. M. & J. Ferguson, Colombo, Ceylon.
Manager, Educational Book Depôts, Nagpur and Jubbulpur.*
Manager of the Imperial Book Depôt, 63, Chandney Chauk Street, Delhi.*
Manager, *East Coast News*, Vizagapatam.*
Manager, "The Agra Medical Hall and Co-operative Association, Limited" (Successors to A. John & Co., Agra).*
Superintendent, Basel Mission Book and Tract Depository, Mangalore.*
Messrs. P. Varadachary & Co., Madras.*
Mr. H. Liddell, Printer, etc., 7, South Road, Allahabad.*
Messrs. D. C. Anand & Sons, Peshawar.*

*N.B.*—[Those marked with an asterisk (*) are agents for sale of Legislative Department publications only.]

# CENSUS OF INDIA, 1911

## VOLUME XVII

# CENTRAL INDIA AGENCY

## REPORT AND TABLES

BY

Major C. E. LUARD, M.A. (Oxon.), I.A.

*Superintendent of Census Operations*

CALCUTTA

SUPERINTENDENT GOVERNMENT PRINTING, INDIA

1913

# TABLE OF CONTENTS.

## Part I.—REPORT.

### Introduction.


| | Para. | Page. |
|---|---|---|
| Past and Present Census | 1 | i |
| Arrangement for Enumeration | 2 | *ib.* |
| Code of Census Procedure | 3 | *ib.* |
| Appointment of Census Officers | 4 | *ib.* |
| Census Divisions | 5 | *ib.* |
| House numbering | 6 | ii |
| Instructions, Schools and Conference | 7 | *ib.* |
| Census Calendar | 8 | iii |
| Preliminary Enumeration | 9 | *ib.* |
| Notice to Public | 10 | *ib.* |
| Closing of Public Offices | 11 | *ib.* |
| Special Arrangements | 12 | *ib.* |
| The Census | 13 | *ib.* |
| Recount | 14 | iv |
| Provisional Totals | 15 | *ib.* |
| Final Totals | 16 | *ib.* |
| Special Industrial Schedule | 17 | v |
| Special forms for Railway, Post, Telegraph and Irrigation Departments | 18 | *ib.* |
| Census Act and Regulations | 19 | *ib.* |
| Certificates of Merits or Sanads | 20 | *ib.* |
| Accommodation | 21 | *ib.* |
| Preparation of Final Totals | 22 | vi |
| Code of Abstraction, Sorting, Tabulating and Compilation | 23 | *ib.* |
| Slip System | 24 | *ib.* |
| Checking of entries | 25 | vii |
| Slip Copying | 26 | *ib.* |
| The Staff | 27 | *ib.* |
| Sorting | 28 | *ib.* |
| Tabulation and Compilation | 29 | *ib.* |
| Imperial Tables | 30 | *ib.* |
| The Report | 31 | viii |
| Cost | 32 | *ib.* |
| Acknowledgments | 33 | ix |


### Chapter I.—Distribution of the Population.

#### *I.—General Description of Central India Agency.*


| | | |
|---|---|---|
| Area, Population and Boundary | 1 | 1 |
| Variations in area since 1901 | 2 | *ib.* |
| Difficulty in obtaining correct areas | 3 | *ib.* |
| Natural Divisions adopted | 4 | *ib.* |


#### *II.—Area, Population and Density.*


| | | |
|---|---|---|
| General | 5 | 2 |
| Relation of Area and Population | 6 | *ib.* |
| Density in Natural Divisions | 7 | 3 |


#### *III.—Towns and Villages.*


| | | |
|---|---|---|
| Definition | 8 | 4 |
| Towns | 9 | *ib.* |
| The Village | 10 | 6 |


#### *IV.—Houses and Families.*


| | | |
|---|---|---|
| Definition | 11 | 7 |
| Subsidiary Tables | ... | *ib.* |

| CHAPTER II.—MOVEMENT OF POPULATION. | PARA. | PAGE. |
|---|---|---|
| Introductory | 12 | 10 |
| Variations since 1881 | 13 | 11 |
| Examination of Results | 14 | *ib.* |
| Natural Population | 15 | 13 |
| Summary | 16 | *ib.* |
| Subsidiary Tables | ... | 15 |
| **CHAPTER III.—MIGRATION.** | | |
| Classes of Migration | 17 | 16 |
| Conditions affecting Migration | 18 | *ib.* |
| Results of Migration | 19 | *ib.* |
| Central India and Foreign Countries | 20 | *ib.* |
| Movement in India | 21 | *ib.* |
| United Provinces | 22 | 17 |
| Rajputana | 23 | *ib.* |
| The Central Provinces and Berars | 24 | *ib.* |
| Other Provinces and States | 25 | *ib.* |
| Internal Movements | 26 | *ib.* |
| Summary | 27 | 19 |
| Subsidiary Tables | ... | 21 |
| **CHAPTER IV.—RELIGION.** | | |
| Introductory | 28 | 23 |
| Hindus—(General) | 29 | 24 |
| Definition of Hindu | 30 | *ib.* |
| Animists | 31 | 26 |
| Variation among Hindus and Animists | 32 | 27 |
| Musalmans | 33 | *ib.* |
| Jains | 34 | 28 |
| Christians | 35 | 29 |
| Missions (General) | 36 | 30 |
| Canadian Presbyterian Mission | 37 | *ib.* |
| Roman Catholic Mission | 38 | *ib.* |
| Friends Foreign Mission | 39 | 31 |
| American Friends Mission | 40 | *ib.* |
| Conversion | 41 | *ib.* |
| Other Religious Beliefs | 42 | *ib.* |
| Race and Sect | 43 | *ib.* |
| Summary | 44 | 32 |
| Subsidiary Tables | .. | 34 |
| **CHAPTER V.—AGE.** | | |
| Statistics | 45 | 37 |
| Inaccuracy | 46 | *ib.* |
| Detailed Examination | 47 | 38 |
| Mean Age | 48 | *ib.* |
| Religion and Age | 49 | *ib.* |
| Caste and Age | 50 | 39 |
| Fecundity | 51 | *ib.* |
| Subsidiary Tables | ... | 40 |
| **CHAPTER VI.—SEX.** | | |
| General | 52 | 50 |
| Sex and Locality | 53 | 51 |
| Sex and Religion | 54 | *ib.* |
| Sex and Age | 55 | 52 |
| Proportion of the Sexes | 56 | *ib.* |
| Sex and Caste | 57 | *ib.* |
| Sex and Ceremony | 58 | 53 |
| Subsidiary Tables | ... | 55 |
| **CHAPTER VII.—CIVIL CONDITION.** | | |
| Introductory | 59 | 59 |
| General Statistics | 60 | *ib.* |
| Marriage and Religion | 61 | 60 |
| Religion and Locality | 62 | 61 |
| Child Marriage | 63 | 62 |
| Caste and Marriage | 64 | *ib.* |
| Birth Customs | 65 | 63 |
| Terms of Relationship | 66 | 64 |
| Subsidiary Tables | ... | 69 |

| Chapter VIII.—Education. | Para. | Page. |
|---|---|---|
| Scope of Return | 67 | 76 |
| English | 68 | *ib.* |
| Religious Distribution | 69 | *ib.* |
| Locality | 70 | 77 |
| Comparative | 71 | 78 |
| Education by Caste | 72 | 79 |
| Comparison of Castes | 73 | *ib.* |
| Subsidiary Tables | ... | 80 |

| Chapter IX.—Language. | | |
|---|---|---|
| Statistics | 74 | 86 |
| Details of Dialects | 75 | *ib.* |
| Distribution | 76 | 87 |
| Classification | 77 | 88 |
| Province of Aryan Tongues | 78 | *ib.* |
| Local Shibboleths | 79 | 89 |
| Subsidiary Tables | ... | 90 |

| Chapter X.—Infirmities. | | |
|---|---|---|
| Statistics | 80 | 94 |
| Accuracy of Return | 81 | *ib.* |
| Classes of Infirmities | 82 | *ib.* |
| Insanity | 83 | 95 |
| Deaf-Mutism | 84 | 96 |
| Blindness | 85 | 97 |
| Leprosy | 86 | 98 |
| Caste and Infirmity | 87 | 99 |
| Subsidiary Tables | ... | 100 |

| Chapter XI.—Caste, Tribe or Race. | | |
|---|---|---|
| Statistics | 88 | 102 |
| Accuracy of Return | 89 | *ib.* |
| Caste | 90 | *ib.* |
| Distribution | 91 | *ib.* |
| Hindu Castes | 92 | *ib.* |
| Kachhi | 93 | 103 |
| Ahir and Bharud | 94 | *ib.* |
| Bagri | 95 | *ib.* |
| Baiga | 96 | *ib.* |
| Balai | 97 | *ib.* |
| Bansphor | 98 | *ib.* |
| Beldar | 99 | *ib.* |
| Deswali | 100 | 104 |
| Gusain | 101 | *ib.* |
| Khati | 102 | *ib.* |
| Korku | 103 | *ib.* |
| Gahalot | 104 | *ib.* |
| Raghubansi | 105 | *ib.* |
| Rawat | 106 | *ib.* |
| Tambat | 107 | *ib.* |
| Brahman | 108 | *ib.* |
| Rajput | 109 | *ib.* |
| Bania | 110 | *ib.* |
| Other Castes | 111 | *ib.* |
| Animist | 112 | *ib.* |
| Musalman | 113 | 105 |
| Caste and Traditional Occupation | 114 | *ib.* |
| New Castes | 115 | *ib.* |
| Caste Government | 116 | *ib.* |
| Caste Control by Hindu Rajas | 117 | 106 |
| Caste Restrictions | 118 | *ib.* |
| Caste and Occupation | 119 | 107 |
| Herdsmen | 120 | *ib.* |
| Craftsmen | 121 | 108 |
| Traders | 122 | *ib.* |
| Warrior Classes | 123 | *ib.* |
| Priests and Devotees | 124 | *ib.* |
| Bards and Astrologers | 125 | 109 |
| Depressed Classes | 126 | *ib.* |
| Subsidiary Tables | ... | 110 |

## CHAPTER XII—OCCUPATION OR MEANS OF LIVELIHOOD.


| | PARA. | PAGE. |
|---|---|---|
| Statistics | 127 | 114 |
| Scheme of Classification | 128 | *ib.* |
| M. Bertillon's Scheme | 129 | 115 |
| Accuracy of Record | 130 | *b.* |
| Limitation of the Return | 131 | *ib.* |
| General Conclusion | 132 | 116 |
| General Discussion of the Result | 133 | *ib.* |
| Natural Divisions and Occupations | 134 | *ib.* |
| Comparison between the Occupations of Cities and Villages | 135 | 117 |
| Workers and Dependents | 136 | 118 |
| Agricultural Occupation | 137 | *ib.* |
| Landlords | 138 | *ib.* |
| Cultivators | 139 | 119 |
| Pasture | 140 | *ib.* |
| Fishing and Hunting | 141 | *ib.* |
| Mining | 142 | *ib.* |
| Industry | 143 | 120 |
| Textile | 144 | *ib.* |
| Hides, Skins, etc. | 145 | *ib.* |
| Bone | 146 | *ib.* |
| Wood | 147 | *ib.* |
| Metal | 148 | *ib.* |
| Ceramics | 149 | *ib.* |
| Chemical Products | 150 | *ib.* |
| Food Industries | 151 | *ib.* |
| Industries of Dress and the Toilet | 152 | *ib.* |
| Furniture Industries | 153 | *ib.* |
| Building | 154 | *ib.* |
| Construction of Means of Transport | 155 | *ib.* |
| Production and Transmission of Physical Forces | 156 | *ib.* |
| Industries of Luxuries | 157 | *ib.* |
| Industries connected with refuse matter | 158 | 121 |
| Transport | 159 | *ib.* |
| Trade | 160 | *ib.* |
| Public Administration | 161 | *ib.* |
| Professions | 162 | *ib.* |
| Persons with Private Incomes | 163 | *ib.* |
| Domestic Service | 164 | *ib.* |
| Insufficiently described Occupations | 165 | *ib.* |
| Unproductive | 166 | *ib.* |
| Factory Statistics | 167 | *ib.* |
| Occupation and Religion | 168 | *ib.* |
| Caste and Occupation | 169 | 122 |
| Decaying Industries | 170 | 123 |
| Female Occupations | 171 | *ib.* |
| Subsidiary Tables | .. | 125 |

## LIST OF DIAGRAMS AND MAPS.


| | PAGE. |
|---|---|
| Map of Central India Agency . . . . . . . . . . | Frontispiece. |
| Diagram showing the Relation of Area and Population . . . . . | 2 |
| Diagram showing the density of population in the Agency, a few States and British contiguous districts . . . . . . . . . | 3 |
| Maps showing the density of the population in different Natural Divisions . | 3, 4, 5 |
| Diagram showing the total Urban and Rural population of the Central India Agency in the different Natural Divisions . . . . . . | 11 |
| Maps showing the Variations in the different Natural Divisions . . . | 12, 13, 14 |
| Diagram showing the Variation since 1901 per 1,000 of the population of each Natural Division . . . . . . . . . . . . | 14 |
| Diagram showing the proportion of Immigrants in each Natural Division . | 18 |
| Map showing the ebb and flow of Migration between adjacent Provinces and States and Central India Agency . . . . . . . . . | 19, 20 |
| Maps showing the distribution of Hindus in Central India Agency . . | 24 |
| Maps showing the distribution of Animists in Central India Agency . . | 26 |
| Maps showing the distribution of Muhammadans in Central India Agency . | 28 |
| Diagram showing the actual number of Males returned of each age per 100,000 . . . . . . . . . . . . . . | 37 |
| Diagram showing the distribution of Corrected age periods of 100,000 persons of each Sex . . . . . . . . . . . . . | *ib.* |
| Maps showing the Proportion of Males and Females in different Natural Divisions . . . . . . . . . . . . . . | 50, 51 |
| Diagram showing the number of Females to 1,000 Males at each age period . | 52 |
| Diagram showing the Compartments of Horoscope . . . . . . | 53 |
| Diagram showing the number per 1,000 aged 0-10 who are Married (by religion) . . . . . . . . . . . . . . | 60 |
| Diagram showing the number per 1,000 aged 15-40 who are Widowed (by religion) . . . . . . . . . . . . . . | *ib.* |
| Diagram showing the proportion of the Married per 1,000 of each age period by Natural Divisions . . . . . . . . . . | 61 |
| Maps showing the amount of Literacy in the different Natural Divisions . | 76 |
| Diagram showing the number of persons per 1,000 in each Natural Division who are Literate . . . . . . . . . . . . | 77 |
| Diagram showing the number per 1,000 of each Main Religion who are Literate | *ib.* |
| Maps showing the extent to which Eastern Hindi, Western Hindi and Rajasthani Languages are spoken in Central India Agency . . . | 87, 88 |
| Maps showing the prevalence of Insanity in Central India Agency . . | 95 |
| Diagram showing the number of the Insane per 100,000 persons of each age period . . . . . . . . . . . . . . . | *ib.* |
| Maps showing the prevalence of Deaf-Mutism in Central India Agency . | 96 |
| Diagram showing the number of Deaf-Mutes per 100,000 of persons of each age period . . . . . . . . . . . . . . | *ib.* |
| Maps showing the prevalence of Blindness in Central India Agency . . | 97 |
| Diagram showing the number of the Blind per 100,000 of each age period . | 98 |
| Maps showing the prevalence of Leprosy in Central India Agency . . | *ib.* |
| Diagram showing the number of Lepers per 100,000 persons of each age period . . . . . . . . . . . . . . . | 99 |
| Diagram showing the relative strength of Hindu Castes . . . . . | 103 |
| Diagram showing the relative strength of Animists . . . . . . | 104 |
| Diagram showing the relative strength of Musalman Castes . . . . | 105 |
| Diagram showing the General Distribution of the population by Occupation (Sub-Classes) . . . . . . . . . . . . . | 116 |
| Diagram showing the Distribution of the Population by Occupation (Classes) in each Natural Division . . . . . . . . . . | 117 |
| Diagram showing the Main Distribution by Occupation (Sub-Classes) for Religion . . . . . . . . . . . . . . | 122 |
| Maps showing the Proportion of Female to Male Workers in each Natural Division . . . . . . . . . . . . . . | 123, 124 |

# INTRODUCTION.

There have been in all four Censuses of the population of Central India, the first being that of 1881.

| | | |
|---|---|---|
| First | 17th February | 1881. |
| Second | 26th February | 1891. |
| Third | 1st March | 1901. |
| Fourth | 10th March | 1911. |

The actual date of each Census is given in the inset.

**Past and Present Censuses.**

All four enumerations have been synchronous with those taken in British India. In the first two, however, a modified form of the schedule was adopted, while in the last two the British India schedule was used. The night of the 10th March was selected for the final census on the present occasion from the fact that the moon's light would be sufficient for the enumerators to carry out their work, at the same time allowing a margin of time for the check by Supervisors and other Inspecting Officers. Moreover, on this date there were no marriages, important religious festivals or large fairs to disturb the population. The dates of some small fairs (chiefly in the Bhil country) were altered so as to avoid this day. All States agreed to this date being fixed.

**Arrangement for Enumeration.**

2. The present census was taken on lines similar to those of 1901. The method adopted for the taking of the census and the compilation of the results are mainly those embodied in the Imperial Census Code, Parts I and II, of which a short account will be found in the Administrative Volume. The more noticeable features connected with the operations are briefly as under.

As soon as it was decided that a decennial census should be taken, the preparation of the Village Registers and the collection of information regarding persons available as Supervisors and Enumerators was commenced. The model form received from the Census Commissioner for India was modified to suit local convenience and was issued to all concerned with translations in the local vernaculars.

**Code of Census Procedure.**

3. The census office was opened on the 1st of April 1910 after which detailed instructions for the taking of the census were issued. These were embodied in the form of a Code to facilitate each stage of the operations. The instructions were based generally on those of the Imperial Code adopted for British India, with such alterations as were required to suit local conditions. A *Manual of Instructions* for Supervisors and Charge Superintendents was also compiled and issued in advance. All these were translated into the local vernaculars. These instructions were further supplemented by the issue of Circulars on points which, practice proved, were not sufficiently explained in the Code or Manual.* A *Specimen Enumeration Book* with typical entries was also issued for instruction to each enumerator who carried it about with him.

**Appointment of Census Officers.**

4. Early in March 1910 all the States were requested to appoint their own Census Officers and place them in direct correspondence with the Provincial Superintendent of Census. For each group of small States and guaranteed holdings in the Political Charges a common Census Officer was appointed working under the supervision of the Political Officers. The Census Officers in the States were either Revenue Officers or Officers with previous experience; the Charge Superintendents were Pargana or Tahsil Officers; the Supervisors, subordinate revenue or police officers, head clerks in offices and school masters; the Enumerators, the village *Patwaris*, school masters, clerks, senior students and the like.

**Census Divisions.**

5. On their appointment the Census Officers started the formation of the necessary census divisions of Charges, Circles and Blocks. Villages and towns were first divided into one or more Blocks, each containing ordinarily not more than 40 to 50 houses, and placed in charge of an official called the Enumerator; a group of Blocks, ordinarily 10 to 15, into a Circle, the official in charge being designated Supervisor; and a number of Circles into a Charge, the official responsible being known as the Charge Superintendent. In most cases the Charge corresponded to a revenue unit, *viz.*, a Tahsil, a Pargana, a Thana, a Tappa, etc. In the case of large States Charges were often sub-divided into two or more. A Town usually formed a separate Charge being sub-divided where necessary for efficiency. Small States and Guaranteed Holdings

---

* NOTE.—Instructions regarding the entry of castes, tribes or races in column 8, the entry of dialects in column 13 and with respect to the census in areas affected by plague were the only Circulars required.

were made into independent Charges, irrespective of the number of houses they contained, and the local Kamdars were appointed Charge Superintendents.

On Railways, each section of a line passing through the Agency constituted a Charge, an officer of the line such as an Assistant Engineer, a Traffic Superintendent, or Loco Superintendent, being appointed Charge Superintendents. Traffic Inspectors were appointed Supervisors for groups of minor stations and Station Masters of important stations for their own premises, the Station Masters of small stations and clerks of others being appointed Enumerators. Each Railway Company appointed its own Chief Census Officer for the line passing through Central India, who was responsible to the Provincial Superintendent of Census.

Important Municipalities such as Lashkar, Indore, Ujjain and Bhopal were formed into Special Charges under the Chief Municipal Officer of the place.

British Cantonments and Civil Stations were treated as Charges on the above lines.

**House numbering.**

6. The next step taken was the numbering of houses. The definition of a House adopted in 1901 was altered to make it more precise and illustrated by diagrams :—

(*i*) Any structure other than a dwelling house, such as tent, pavilion, temple, *sarai*, etc., or a site, camping ground, *ghat*, etc., to which a separate number has been affixed.

(*ii*) The dwelling place of one or more families with their dependants and resident servants having an independent entrance, whether that entrance be from a road, gallery, balcony, corridor, courtyard or otherwise.

Each such house was given a separate number. The numbering ran in a consecutive series for each village, a division of a town, cantonment, civil station, or railway station premises, etc., to avoid the mistake of double numbering the same premises and to guide the Enumerator. When all the houses had been numbered a statement showing the number of houses was prepared and an indent for the requisite number of census forms made.

The work of house numbering was started in villages after 15th October 1911, and completed by 15th November.

**Instructions, Schools, Conference.**

7. A Conference of all Census Officers was held early in May 1910. Each Census Officer was asked to bring two supervisors and three or four Enumerators to receive practical training in the work of enumerating and compiling Circle and Charge Summaries. A part of the Indore Residency was made into a typical Charge, houses were numbered, census divisions were formed and those present were taken round by the Head Clerk and made to fill up blank schedule forms printed for the purpose. The entries made were carefully scrutinised by the Provincial Superintendent of Census.

This opportunity was also utilised to read through the provisional issue of the Census Code, the Manual of Instructions for Charge Superintendents and Supervisors and Instructions to Enumerators on the cover of the Enumeration book in the presence of all the Census Officers, both in English and the Vernaculars, and all doubtful points raised were satisfactorily settled. The Census Officers and others present were asked to criticise freely from their practical experience and knowledge of the locality they came from. After receiving this training the Census Officials returned to their States and opened local classes at convenient centres. The Chief Census Officers imparted instruction to the Charge Superintendents and selected Supervisors, on the above lines, these in their turn opened training schools in their own Charges making the Enumerators fill up schedule forms. The instructions thus filtered down from the Chief Census Officers to the Enumerators. Too great stress cannot be laid on the early institution of such classes which are worth reams of printed instructions.

The Bombay, Baroda and Central India Railway very kindly furnished free passes in order to enable the Provincial Superintendent of Census to depute an official to give the necessary instruction to their employés. In other cases the Head Clerk while on tour gave detailed instructions and checked the entries made by the railway enumerators.

8. A Census Calendar was prepared and printed and copies circulated, showing the dates on which the different stages of the operations had to be begun and completed, up to the 17th March 1911. Political Officers and Inspecting Officers in each State were also supplied with these calendars and specially requested to check operations during the course of their ordinary tours. **Census Calendar.**

9. The census divisions being thus marked out, the machinery put in working order and house numbering checked with the Block and House Lists, the Preliminary Census was started on 15th January in villages and on the 15th February in towns. This consisted of the writing up by the Enumerator in the enumeration schedule for each numbered house all the necessary particulars regarding each person ordinarily resident in the house. The information then recorded in the 14 out of the 16 columns (3-16) was, Name, Religion (in the case of Christians the religious sect also), Sex, Civil Condition, Age, Caste, Tribe or Race, Principal occupation, Subsidiary occupation, Actual occupation of the person on whom dependent, Birth-place (Province or State and district), Dialect spoken in the household, Literate or illiterate, Knowledge of English and certain Infirmities. The Preliminary record in village areas was finished by February 15th and in towns by March 1st, 1911. **Preliminary Enumeration.**

The interval between these dates and the census date was utilised by Supervisors and Charge Superintendents in checking and correcting the entries.

Independent efforts were also made to check the completion of the different operations and examine the entries of the enumerators. Inspecting Officers and touring officers were kind enough to spare time and trouble in examining the work, thus keeping the District Census Officers on the alert.

10. After the completion of the Preliminary Enumeration the village and town dwellers were warned by printed notice and by proclamation to remain in their houses on the night of the 10th March 1911 until the enumerator came, to give all particulars asked for, and to mention all persons who were enumerated before but had left or died since and supply particulars for all new comers and newly born children. This notice in the Bhil tract and forest areas was given by the headman of the village, where the final census was carried out before dark or the next morning. **Notice to the Public.**

11. To allow all officials who could be spared to assist in the Final Enumeration and accelerate the compilation of the Provisional Totals all public offices, schools, etc., were either closed from the 9th to 11th March 1911 or such officials as were actually engaged in the carrying out of the census were allowed leave. **Closing of Public Offices.**

12. Special arrangements were made for the enumeration of fairs, camping grounds, road *chaukis*, railway travellers, hospitals and dispensaries, and jails and lock-ups. Special men were appointed to deal with fairs and camping grounds; roadside *chaukis* were included in the villages within whose boundaries they were situated. Hospitals and jails were enumerated by their own officials. **Special Arrangements.** *Fairs, Camping Grounds, etc.*

As the Bhaguria fair in the Bhil tract, always attended by large numbers of Bhils and Bhilalas, was likely to interfere with the progress of the Final Enumeration, the State officials in that tract had the fair held a week in advance. *Bhaguria Fair.*

All travellers by road and by rail were provided with Travellers' Tickets showing that they had been enumerated, to avoid double counting. *Travellers' Tickets.*

13. In the Final Enumeration or the Census Proper each Enumerator went round his Block after sunset on March 10th with the Enumeration Book in his hand and a pen and ink, checking and correcting the entries made in the Preliminary Enumeration as compared with the actual facts existing on the census night, by striking out the entries for persons who had left or died and recording information in the different columns of the Schedule for all new comers or newly born children. It was commenced at 7 P.M. and completed at midnight excepting in certain jungle areas. Practically all the hilly and jungle tracts in the Agency lying between 21° 15′ and 23° 15′ N. L. and 74° 5′ and 75° 15′ E.L. and all parts of Rewah south of the Kaimur range were treated as non-synchronous areas. The former, which comprises the Bhil country in the Bhopawar Agency, the States of Jhabua, Barwani, Ali-Rajpur, Jobat, the Petty Estates round them and the Petlawad and **The Census.**

Sendhwa Parganas of Indore State, were enumerated by daylight on the 10th March or on the morning of 11th March. The huts of the Bhils and Gonds being scattered over large mountainous and forest areas coupled with the danger of wild beasts made it impossible for the Enumerator to go about at night.

To secure reasonable expedition and minimise the troubles of the Enumerator two guns were ordered to be fired where this was possible, the first as a warning to the public to be in their houses and to officials to stop traffic on roads and the other to indicate the commencement of the Final Counting.

**Re-count.**

14. The towns of Lashkar, Lashkar-Brigade, Morar, Gwalior, Indore, Sanawad, Bhopal and Dhar were affected with plague at the time of the Final Enumeration. These places were re-counted as shown in the inset. The result is shown on the fly-leaf of Imperial Table IV.

| Name. | Date. |
|---|---|
| Lashkar | 8th July 1911. |
| Lashkar-Brigade | do. |
| Morar | do. |
| Gwalior | do. |
| Indore | 20th July 1911. |
| Sanawad | do. |
| Bhopal | 10th July 1911. |
| Dhar | 2nd July 1911. |

**Provisional Totals.**

15. After completing the Final Census on the night of the 10th March 1911 the Enumerators and Supervisors met at centres previously selected on the morning of 11th March to make up their totals. The Enumerators prepared the abstracts at the end of the Enumeration Book showing the number of Occupied Houses and the total number of Persons, Males and Females in their Blocks. These abstracts were checked by others and then posted up by the Supervisor for his Circle Summary. The Circle Summaries were in their turn similarly tested and combined into a Charge Summary after which the totals were wired or sent by post or special messenger with all possible despatch to the Chief Census Officer concerned. These Officers on receipt of Summaries for all Charges made up their totals for the State as a whole and communicated them by telegram direct to the Census Commissioner for India and to the Provincial Superintendent of Census at Indore.

The Provisional Totals in the different areas were in most States in Central India collected by special messengers, on horse-back or camels who carried the totals to the Charge Superintendents by whom the figures were either telegraphed to the Census Officer or again despatched by similar special arrangements. In the wild tracts of Bhopal the totals were carried from the Supervisors' headquarters by messengers who were given guards to accompany them at night as a precaution against dangers. In the jungle tracts of Rewah particular care was necessary in traversing the passes in the hills, and the heavily wooded tracts where wild animals are numerous. In these districts special runners were posted at short distances who travelled by night attended by guides with burning torches, and an escort of six or eight men to protect them and show them the ill-defined paths. This action of the Rewah Darbar resulted in complete success, their totals being the third to arrive. In none of the previous censuses had it been possible for the Rewah Darbar to send the Provisional Totals in time for publication, while the difference was only 1 per 10,000 between their Final and Provisional Totals.

The first totals were received from the Baoni State on the 11th March, the last from Gwalior State on the 15th. Special arrangements were made in the headquarter office for combining and wiring the Provisional Totals for each Political Charge and the Agency as a whole to the Census Commissioner for India. The first of these for Baghelkhand was wired on the 13th and the last for Gwalior Residency on the 16th March 1911. The total population for the Agency as a whole, according to these Provisional Totals, numbered 9,365,165 of whom 4,804,914 were males and 4,560,251 females.

It should be remarked that the taking of the Census up to the submission of the Provisional Totals was carried out in the Gwalior State by Mr. J. W. D. Johnstone, C.I.E., who received instructions from the Census Commissioner direct. I am much indebted to him for the assistance he rendered me.

**Final Totals.**

16. After going through various processes of sorting and tabulating the Final Totals were obtained, which gave 9,369,067 persons, consisting of 4,807,711 males and 4,561,356 females. This final figure showed an increase of 3,902

persons, being a difference of only 0·04 per cent. which speaks well for general efficiency of the Census arrangements. The Census Commissioner to whom final figures for individual States were from time to time communicated wrote as follows :—

"The extreme accuracy of the Provisional Totals sent up from the States reflects the greatest credit on all concerned."

**Special Industrial Schedule.**

17. A Special Census was taken of persons employed in industries in which the workers in factories did not number less than 20 persons. This was taken simultaneously with the census of the general population on March 10th in order to collect correct information regarding recent developments. The form of this Special Schedule, received from the Census Commissioner, was printed locally in English and Vernacular with instructions for filling it up at the back, and distributed on the 5th March 1911 to the owners, agents and managers of mines, factories, works, mills, etc., through departmental heads and collected on the morning of the 16th March to obviate all danger of confusion with the ordinary schedules. The result of these enquiries are embodied in Table XV-E. Under the orders of the Census Commissioner a Register of all mines, factories, mills, etc., was compiled before the issue of the schedules and checked with the return of factories received periodically in the Central India Agency Office and sent to the Director General of Commercial Intelligence, Calcutta.

**Special forms for Railway, Post, Telegraph and Irrigation Departments.**

18. Simultaneously with the general census, information regarding the number of Europeans, Anglo-Indians and Indians employed on Railways, and in the Post, Telegraph and Irrigation Departments, also on a special form, was collected through their Departmental Officers. The results were compiled and submitted to the Census Commissioner.

**Census Act and Regulations.**

19. In a preliminary circular the obligations of all public servants and loyal subjects to assist in the taking of the census was made known and published in local State gazettes or otherwise. No necessity arose for a regular Census Act. All concerned cordially helped in the operations. The demeanour of the people throughout was excellent. Even the most backward and wild sections of the population, such as Bhils, Bhilalas, Gonds, and Kols, etc., have now become familiar with the object for which the census is being taken and have no dread of its resulting in enhanced taxation or a call for fighting men, as was the impression on previous occasions. These tribes not only gladly replied to whatever was asked of them but cordially co-operated with the census staff by remaining at home when the Final Enumeration was being made, and where night counting was possible kept a light burning till the Enumerator's arrival at their huts.

**Certificates of Merit or Sanads.**

20. For good services rendered in the taking of the census all census officials were granted Certificates of Merit or Sanads. The Enumerators and Supervisors received these from the Chief Census Officers of the area in which they worked; the Charge Superintendents and Census Officers of smaller States from the Provincial Superintendent of Census in Central India under the direction of the Local Government, while the Chief Census Officers of the large States, and others whose work was specially commendable, received these Sanads with the signature of the Hon'ble the Agent to the Governor-General in Central India.

Those of the unpaid Enumerators and Supervisors and certain selected permanent employés who showed unusual zeal and energy in the work were afterwards employed in the central office at Indore.

**Accommodation.**

21. Some difficulty in obtaining accommodation for the Tabulation Office had been anticipated. It was, however, successfully overcome.

Besides the Opium Godown, the old police lines, now dismantled, and the Jaora bungalow just outside the compound, the Kothis of Rai Bahadur Kesri Singh on the main road, the Ratlam and Dewas Junior Branch Kothis and the Residency School building were, through the kindness of those with whom permission to use them rested, made available for the accommodation of the Abstraction Office Staff. The Rajgarh State made its own arrangements by placing its clerks in the Rajgarh house opposite the Ratlam Kothi. No rent was demanded for the use of these buildings except the Jaora bungalow. Before the clerks could be located in them these houses had to be provided with latrines and thoroughly repaired for which some expenditure was incurred.

**Preparation of Final Totals.**

22. After the Provisional Totals were despatched the Enumeration Books for all the States, the Military and Civil areas under the British Government and the Railway Sections were carefully packed by Charges and other units and sent with Summaries for the subsequent purposes of Abstraction, Tabulation and Compilation to the Central India Census Office at Indore. On arrival the books were checked with the Circle, Charge and State Summaries in the presence of the Head Clerk and entered in the record register which was opened for each State and other independent areas, so as to enable them to be issued for abstraction, systematically. A certain number of record clerks was entertained one month in advance of the Final Census for the purpose.

**Code of Abstraction, Sorting, Tabulating, and Compilation.**

23. The Code of Instructions for copying on slips the particulars of each person enumerated, for sorting the written up slips and tabulating and compiling the results was issued by the Census Commissioner for India. This was followed in all the processes and no need arose for compiling one locally. A few supplementary instructions were issued now and then by the Provincial Superintendent and the Head Clerk in the course of their daily rounds of inspection. Immense advantage was derived from there being only one Central Office as all correspondence was avoided and uniformity ensured.

**Slip System.**

24. The system of abstracting entries from the schedule form which was worked in 1901 was followed on the present occasion with this exception that instead of two slips only *one* was written up for each person giving all particulars. The size of the slips was somewhat smaller (2 inches by 4½) and the numbers of the columns of the schedule from which the information was to be recorded were printed in English and Vernacular on one side only. Religion was indicated by the colour, while Sex and Civil Condition were indicated by symbols printed on the slip.

Five colours were used to denote the five main religions and green was used to indicate other religions. The symbols were printed in the right hand top corner of the slip. These together with the slip used are shown below :—

(Slip.)

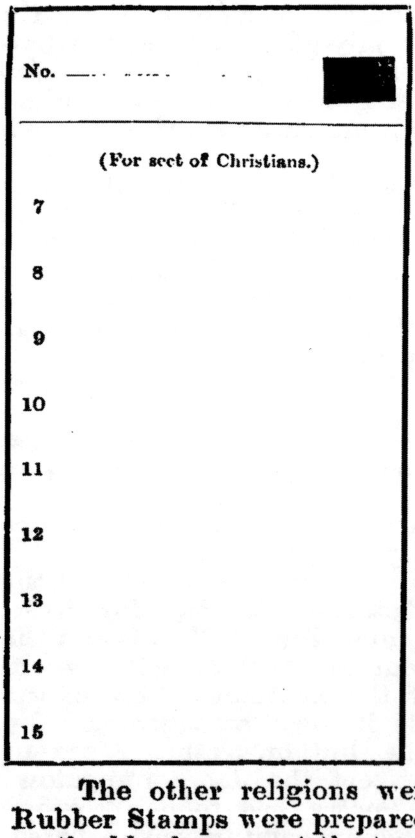


| Religion. | Colour. |
|---|---|
| 1. Hindu . . | Badami |
| 2. Jain . . . | Yellow |
| 3. Animist . . | Blue . |
| 4. Musalman . . | Red . |
| 5. Christian . . | White . |
| 6. Other religions . | Green . |

(Symbols.)

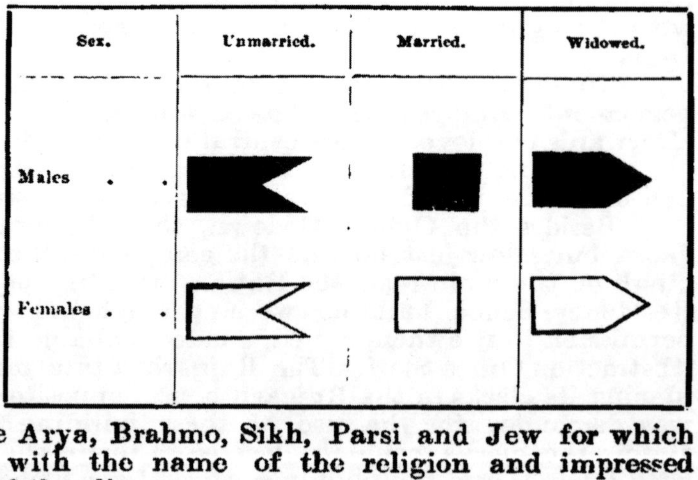


The other religions were Arya, Brahmo, Sikh, Parsi and Jew for which Rubber Stamps were prepared with the name of the religion and impressed on the blank space at the top of the slip.

25. Before actually issuing the Enumeration Books for the work of copying on to the slips, all the entries in the schedules were carefully examined by a special staff of examiners and all obvious errors or omissions were rectified and supplied. Very little correction was needed except unfortunately in Gwalior State where the schedules for many districts showed gross carelessness and indifference to orders, necessitating the employment of a large special staff to correct and check the books. **Checking of Entries.**

26. Before the actual work was started an experimental abstraction and tabulation office, on a small scale, had been opened at Indore, in November 1910, to give training to a certain number of persons and see what practical difficulties were met with. Those trained in their turn imparted instruction to others. **Slip Copying.**

The regular Abstraction Office was actually opened on the 22nd March 1911, this process being completed on 20th May. The number of copyists employed in the first week was 422 and the average number of slips copied daily by a copyist was 244. When the office was in full swing the number of copyists was 898 (not counting the Checkers and Supervisors) and the daily outturn of each copyist totalled 424 slips. The clerks deputed from Dewas J.B., Rajgarh and Ratlam wrote up the greatest number, averaging over 1,000 at this stage.

The slips for Infirmities were written up separately as were also those for the abstraction of entries from the Industrial Schedules.

27. The staff of the office of the Provincial Superintendent, and the establishment for abstracting and tabulating the census schedules for the British Pargana of Manpur, Cantonments and Railways, and compiling the Imperial Tables for the Agency was paid for by Government. For the work of the States all States of any size supplied their own men. The Datia, Panna and Ajaigarh States sent their Census Officers also to conduct the operations. The Gwalior, Indore, Bhopal and Rewah States supplied Special Officers to control their establishments; these officers remained in charge from start to finish and assisted in compiling the report and tables for their States. **The Staff.**

28. No sorting was required for Tables I-VI, which were compiled by the Supervisors from Register A, maintained during the slip copying period, but only from Table VII onwards. **Sorting.**

The sorting of the slips was begun on 22nd May 1911 and finished on 31st August, the number of sorters reaching a maximum of 574 when this process was in full swing. The unit of sorting was a small estate, group of minor holdings or a Pargana of a large State. All the railway stations and British areas were treated as independent units. The figures for the former were incorporated in the States in which they were situated.

29. The work of tabulating the results was carried on simultaneously with the sorting. As soon as a unit was sorted, the result was entered in a sorter's ticket. All such tickets were combined by districts for the big States, and for whole States in the case of smaller units. As soon as a State was completed these were combined in their turn for each Political Charge by special compilers appointed and paid for by Government for the compilation of the Central India Imperial Tables. These were sent to the Census Commissioner in manuscript and simultaneously to the Press. The first Imperial Tables sent to the Census Commissioner were Tables XVII and XVIII on the 25th August 1911. Tables I-VI were next sent on the 7th September 1911. The task of adjusting Table II for 1901 and 1891 was very arduous. Alterations had taken place in every State of any size and also in the Political Charges and these alterations had, in a very large number of cases, been effected by the transfer of groups of villages or isolated villages necessitating a re-adjustment through the village list. Fresh changes, moreover, took place after the census was taken, indeed after sorting was completed. By 9th October 1912 the last of the Tables—Table XVI—was despatched to the Census Commissioner for India. All these Tables were examined in the Census Commissioner's office and no mistakes were found. All the Obligatory and Optional Tables prescribed were compiled. **Tabulation and Compilation.**

30. Besides the regular Tables which actually numbered 23, three Provincial Tables were also compiled giving leading Census statistics for all States and Estates and British Areas. **Imperial Tables.**

The units for compilation were 51, all States of any size forming independent units.

**The Report.**

31. A complete alteration has been made on this occasion in the form of the Report.

In 1901 all Tables were compiled by Political Charges, a procedure which entailed much waste of time and unnecessary expense. The Political Charge is not an administrative unit, but merely an artificial and constantly varying unit, created for the convenience of political control. In no case does a charge comprise only one State, while large States are often split up between several Political Charges. It is, therefore, clear that statistics given by Charges are of little or no real value and to give a whole series of costly Tables based on this arrangement is waste of money. On the submission of this view to the Hon'ble the Agent to the Governor-General he decided that only the first six Tables which might *possibly* be of use, should be given by Charges. Imperial Tables I-VI are accordingly given by Political Charges, while the remaining Tables have been given for the Central Indial Agency as a whole. This has reduced the amount of printed matter by over 200 pages. On the other hand statistics by States, which were most inadequately dealt with in 1901, are very fully treated in the Imperial Volume.

The bulk of the Table Volume having been reduced to the minimum by this arrangement, it was decided to print the Report and Statistics in one Volume to make the book of some size.

The writing up of the Report was commenced when compilation work was well advanced. The first Chapter was sent in manuscript to the Census Commissioner for India on the 6th April 1912. Each Chapter on completion was sent to the Census Commissioner for his information and to the Superintendent Government Printing at Calcutta simultaneously.

Besides the Imperial Report all the Principal States and a few Minor States (29 in all) shown in the margin received separate Reports containing —

| | |
|---|---|
| 1. Gwalior. | 16. Bijawar. |
| 2. Indore. | 17. Baoni. |
| 3. Bhopal. | 18. Chhatarpur. |
| 4. Rewah. | 19. Sitamau. |
| 5. Orchha. | 20. Sailana. |
| 6. Datia. | 21. Rajgarh. |
| 7. Dhar. | 22. Narsinghgarh. |
| 8. Dewas S. B. | 23. Maihar. |
| 9. Dewas J. B. | 24. Jhabua. |
| 10. Samthar. | 25. Barwani. |
| 11. Jaora. | 26. Ali-Rajpur. |
| 12. Ratlam. | 27. Khilchipur. |
| 13. Panna. | 28. Jobat. |
| 14. Charkhari. | 29. Alipura. |
| 15. Ajaigarh. | |

(i) A brief report dealing with all essential points such as variations since 1901, etc., and necessary Subsidiary or Inset Tables.

(ii) Tabular matter, adjusted to the size of the States, smaller States getting only the more important Tables. The headings of all Tables were given bi-lingually, in English and Hindi or Urdu, but only English figures were used.

(iii) A Village List for the State giving the total number of occupied houses and of persons, males and females, by religions.

(iv) Where possible Maps were given.

(v) Guaranteed Villages, in accordance with the orders, were shown both in the accounts for the States to which they belong as also in the two Provincial Tables in the Imperial Volume where each estate appears as a complete unit.

These State Reports were compiled by the Provincial Census Superintendent except that for Gwalior which was written by Mr. H. M. Bull, Inspector General of Education for that State.

**Cost.**

32. As accounts are not yet finally made up, only approximate figures can be given for the cost. The figures given below may, however, be taken as correct for all practical purposes :—

COST OF CENSUS.

| Year. | Departmental Accounts. | Treasury Accounts. | Cost per head. Departmental. | Cost per head. Treasury. |
|---|---|---|---|---|
| | Rs. | Rs. | Pies. | Pies. |
| Imperial 1901 | 77,683 | ... | ... | ... |
| States 1901 | 116,377 | ... | ... | ... |
| Imperial 1911 | 65,357 | 37,232 | ... | ... |
| States 1911 | 87,500 | ... | ... | ... |
| TOTAL 1901 | 196,060 | ... | 4·3 | ... |
| TOTAL 1911 | 152,857 | 37,232 | 3·0 | 0·8 |

33. It would be impossible to specify by name all the persons who have co-operated in the different stages of the operations. The Census Officers, who worked immediately under me, have, without exception, done most extraordinarily well and my warmest thanks are due to each and all of them for the zeal and energy with which they carried out the troublesome duties of the Enumeration. A list of these gentlemen is given below :— **Acknowledgments.**

1. Mr. J. W. D. Johnstone, C.I.E., (Gwalior).
2. Mr. K. G. Reshimwale, (Indore).
3. Munshi Saiyad Kudrat Ali, (Bhopal).
4. Lal Beni Bahadur Singh, (Rewah).
5. Lala Ujagar Chand, (Orchha).
6. Pandit Ram Ratan Tiwari, (Datia).
7. Mr. K. G. Nadkar, (Dhar).
8. Mr. M. N. Phadnis, (Dewas S. B).
9. Mr. V. R. Deo, (Dewas J. B.).
10. Munshi Habib Hassan, (Samthar).
11. Mirza Muhammad Said, B.A., (Jaora).
12. Mr. Dorabji F. Vakil, B.A. (Ratlam).
13. Lala Sital Parshad, (Panna).
14. Pandit Ram Datta, (Charkhari).
15. Bakshi Thakur Parshad, (Ajaigarh).
16. Munshi Debi Parshad, (Bijawar).
17. Munshi Muhammad Said. (Baoni).
18. Munshi Sohan Lal, (Chhatarpur).
19. Mr. Naulakha Lal Singh, (Sitamau).
20. Mr. Kothari Hari Singh, (Sailana).
21. Pandit Jisukhram, (Rajgarh).
22. Munshi Parmanand, (Narsinghgarh).
23. Munshi Bala Parshad, (Nagod).
24. Lala Gur Dayal, (Maihar).
25. Pandit B. Damodar Rao, (Jhabua).
26. Mr. Meherjibhoy Hormasji, (Barwani).
27. Pandit R. G. Phadnis, (Ali-Rajpur).
28. Babu Ram Parshad, (Khilchipur).
29. Rai Sahib Babu Kedarnath, (Korwai, etc.).
30. Pandit Ramlal, (Jobat).
31. Munshi Nanne Khan, (M. S. Baghelkhand).
32. Babu Balkrishna Kapur, (M. S. Gwalior).
33. Rai Sahib Munshi Kashi Parshad, (M. S. Bundelkhand).
34. Munshi Enayat Husen, (M. S. Bhopawar).
35. Jamadar Mohan Singh, (Malwa Minor holdings).
36. Panda Shankar Lal, (M. H. Bhopal).
37. Baba Mulsingh, Sadar Kanungo, (Manpur Pargana).
38. The Assistant Agent to the Governor-General, (Indore Residency).
39. The Cantonment Magistrate, (Mhow).
40. „ „ „ (Nimach).
41. „ „ „ (Nowgong).
42. „ Officer Commanding (at Agar).
43. „ „ „ (at Guna).
44. „ Superintendent and Magistrate, (Sehore).
45. Census Officers in Charge of C. I. Sections of E. I. R., B. N. R., G. I. P. R., and B. B. & C. I. R.

I wish, however, to offer my particular thanks to Lal Beni Bahadur Singh, Census Commissioner for Rewah State, and his Assistant Pandit Bhawani Datta Joshi, B.A., Head Master of the Venkat High School at Satna. The enormous advance shown by the work of this State in the present census is entirely due to the exceptional pains taken by these officers to make all the arrangements as perfect as possible. To Pandits Purushottam Joshi of Old Indore and Shastri Damodar Tryambak Joshi of Ujjain I am obliged for information on sex at birth and castes.

I must not omit to mention my obligations to the Chiefs and the Residents, Political Agents and other Officials of the Political Department whose ready help was always at my disposal, without which indeed I should have often found my duties very difficult to carry out.

The Headquarter staff worked admirably, and I cannot too highly praise the industry, care and energy shown by my Head Clerk Pandit Shridhar Rao in the arduous task of controlling the large Abstraction Office as well as the ordinary correspondence work and the extra responsibilities which my transfer to other duties latterly threw upon him.

In November 1911 I was transferred to other duties and the Census work had to be completed as a *paraergon*. This has not, however, materially delayed the work as the Press has never been left idle.

I would express my thanks to the Superintendent, Government Printing, India, Calcutta, for the excellent proofs sent me and the rapid way in which the work has been done.

Finally to the Census Commissioner for India my warm thanks are due for his ready help in all my difficulties.

C. E. LUARD, *Major*,

*January 1913.* *Superintendent of Census.*

# CENTRAL INDIA AGENCY

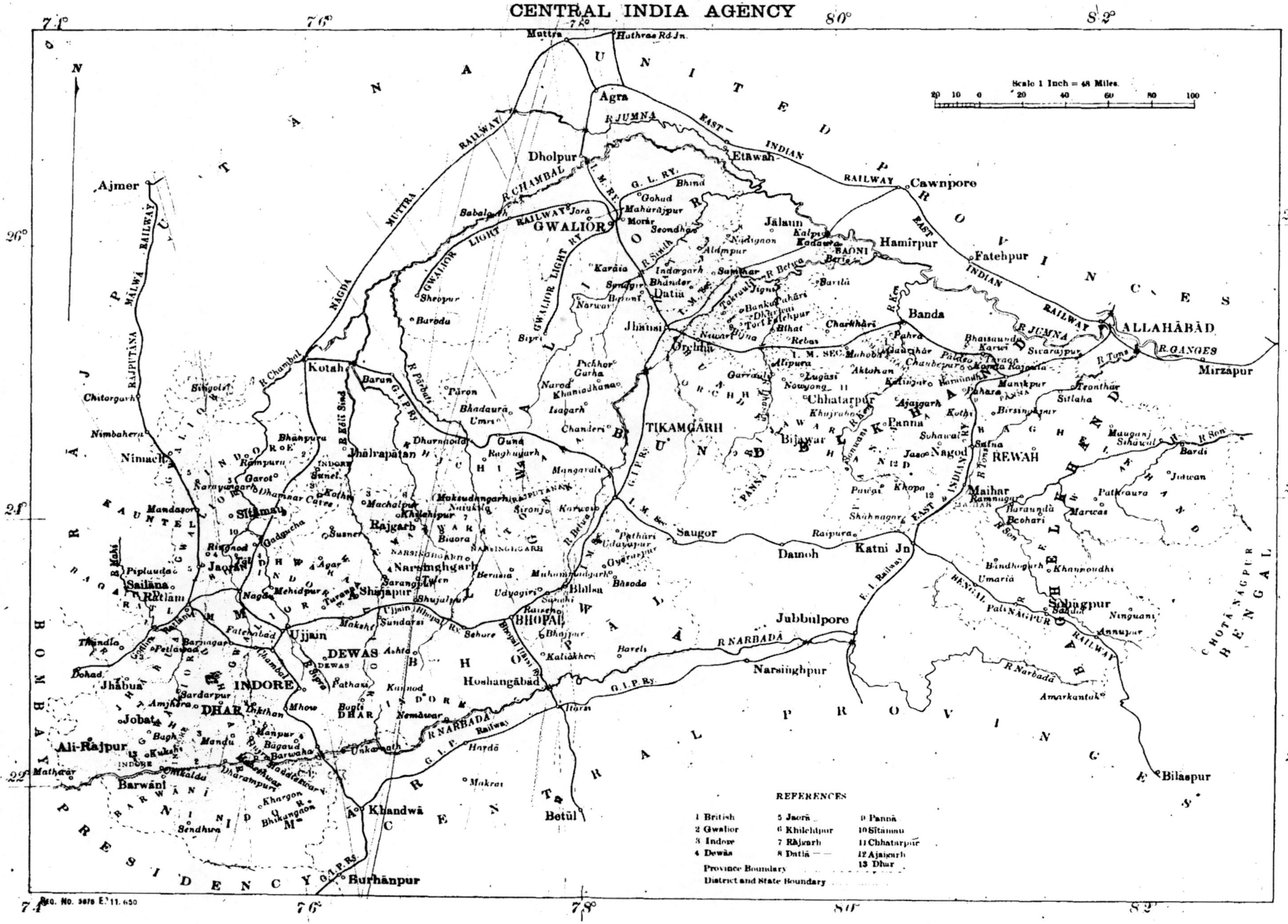

# CHAPTER I.

---

## Distribution of the Population.

### *I.—General Description of Central India Agency.*

**Area, Population and Boundary.** THE tract known as the Central India Agency is composed of a number of Native States and Estates under the general political control of the Agent to the Governor General in Central India whose head-quarters are at Indore. The tract, which lies between 21°—22′ and 26°—52′ N. and 74°—0′ and 83°—0′ E. has an area of 77,367 square miles, and a population of just over nine millions. This area may be compared to the combined areas of Belgium (11,373), Denmark (14,844), Holland (12,582), Greece (24,977) and Switzerland (15,469).

On the north and north-east, the Agency is bounded by the Chambal river which separates it from the United Provinces and the Rajputana Agency; on the east and along its southern boundary lie the Central Provinces, beyond the Vindhya and Satpura Ranges; the south-western boundary is formed by the Khandesh, Rewa-Kantha, and Panch-Mahal Districts of the Bombay Presidency, while various States of Rajputana enclose it on the west.

**Variations in area since 1901.** 2. The area dealt with in 1901 was 78,772 square miles. The transfer of certain isolated Rajputana portions, then under the political control of this Agency, to Rajputana and the inclusion of island tracts of Central India lying outside its borders, excluded in the last Census, have altered the area to that shown in the inset table.

| | |
|---|---|
| Area in 1901 . . . | 78,772 |
| *Deduct*—Tonk (Rajputana portions) . | 1,439 |
| | 77,333 |
| *Add*—Island tracts of Central India . | 34 |
| | 77,367 |

**Difficulty in obtaining correct areas.** 3. The greatest difficulty still arises in adjusting internal areas. Various transfers have taken place between the Political Charges, but the lack of surveys, the tendency of Darbars to exaggerate their possessions and the fact that surveys made for revenue purposes commonly omit waste and forest areas and the lands of feudatories and are, therefore, incomplete, makes adjustment very unsatisfactory.

While the political control of the Agency lies with the Government of India working through its political officers, the actual administrative units are the States and Estates comprised in the Agency, numbering in all about 130 from Gwalior with 25,000 square miles in area, equal to that of Greece, to tiny holdings of one or two villages. The political relations existing between the different States and between individual States and the Government of India are very diverse.

### *Natural Divisions.*

4. Natural divisions are required to bring out the effects of locality on the figures. The Natural Divisions adopted on this occasion are the same as those of 1901—the Plateau, Low-lying and Hilly.

The Plateau tract includes the Malwa Plateau, the highland tract stretching from the great wall of the Vindhyas to about Narwar or from 22°—34′ to 25°—39′ north latitude, a land of open rolling plains dotted with low flat-topped hills of basaltic formation. On the east it touches Bundelkhand and on the west Rajputana; possessing soil of great fertility, produced by the disintegration of the basalt, with a moderate rainfall of 30 inches per annum. It grows all the ordinary crops without irrigation and has long been famous for its poppy and the opium obtained from it. The inhabitants belong to the regular cultivating classes. Its climate is unusually temperate and equable, due to its elevation above sea level which averages 1,600 feet and rises in places to over 2,000. The Low-lying tract embraces northern Gwalior and stretches across into Bundelkhand and Baghelkhand up to the Kaimur Range. It differs from the Plateau in being only some 700 feet above sea level, possessing a climate more subject to extremes, and a rainfall of 45 inches per annum; the soil is good, but its fertility is not so great as that of the Plateau. The country is generally flatter and in parts is typical of an alluvial spread.

The Hilly tract, as its name implies, lies along the ranges of the Vindhyas and Satpuras and their offshoots. Here agriculture is little practised, the inhabitants being mostly members of the wild tribes and the country largely covered with forest and cut up by numerous ravines. These Natural Divisions, while they adequately express the general lie of the land, are necessarily drawn on broad lines and the figures for each Division are, therefore, in part affected by the overlapping of tracts; where this is noticeable attention will be drawn to it.

## *II.—Area, Population and Density.*

5. Statistics of area and population are given in Imperial Table I for the Agency and for the Political Charges or units of political control, and in Provincial Table I for the principal administrative units, the States. As already noted in the Introduction, figures for Political Charges are not given after Table VI.

Proportional figures will be found in the Subsidiary Tables at the end of this Chapter.

| Locality. | Area. | Population. | Density by square mile. |
|---|---|---|---|
| **Central India** | **77,367** | **9,357,000** | **121** |
| Plateau . . | 30,813 | 3,683,000 | 120 |
| Low-lying . . | 21,118 | 3,311,000 | 157 |
| Hilly . . | 25,436 | 2,363,000 | 93 |

The inset table shows the density of the population.

In no case is the pressure at all severe, the Low-lying Natural Division showing only 157 persons per square mile.

**Relation of Area and Population.**

6. The inset diagram illustrates the relative area and population of the three Natural Divisions into which the Agency has been divided. Each white and black diamond represents one per cent. of the total area and population, respectively.

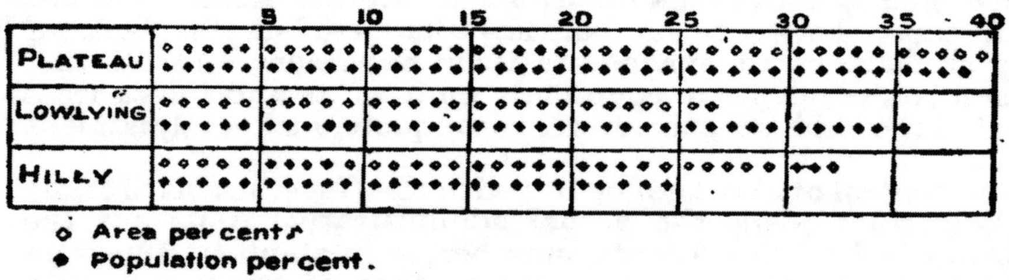


The Plateau has the largest area and population; the Hilly tract stands next in area but with less population, the Low-lying has least area but most population.

An examination of the density in contiguous portions of the Agency and of British India shows in most cases how much greater the pressure in British India is. In a small isolated tract of Indore, Alampur, which lies far from the rest of the State the density rises to 426 per square mile, due to its peculiar position. Similarly a high density, 353 per square mile, is met with in the isolated tract of Gangapur in Gwalior which lies in Rajputana far from its parent State.

In no cases, save those of Alampur and Gangapur, does the density ordinarily rise to even 250 per square mile, including towns. The Huzur Tahsil of Rewah

*Diagram showing the density of population in the Agency a few states and British contiguous districts.*

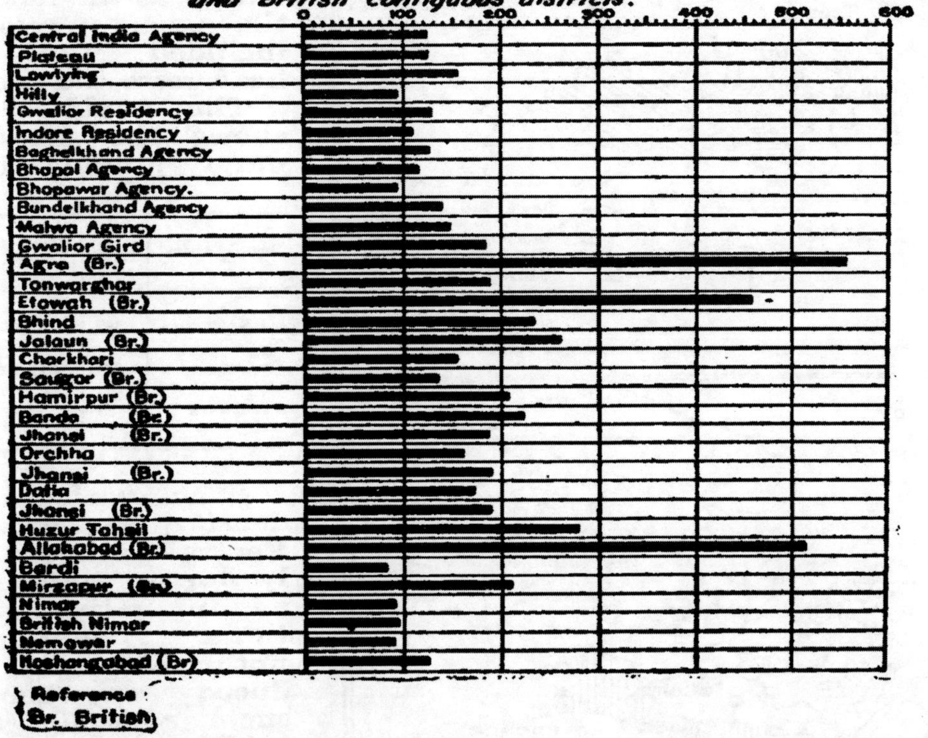


alone, with the town of Rewah, has a density of 282 persons to the square mile.

7. The highest density in the three Natural Divisions is in the Low-lying tract with 157 persons to the square mile or if the urban area is excluded 104, the Plateau coming next with 120. The highest ratio on the Plateau is 144 in the Mehidpur Zila of the Indore State, including the towns of Tarana and Mehidpur, with 130 for the rural area only. The Mandasor Zila in Gwalior comes next with 127 or for the rural area 112. **Natural Divisions.**

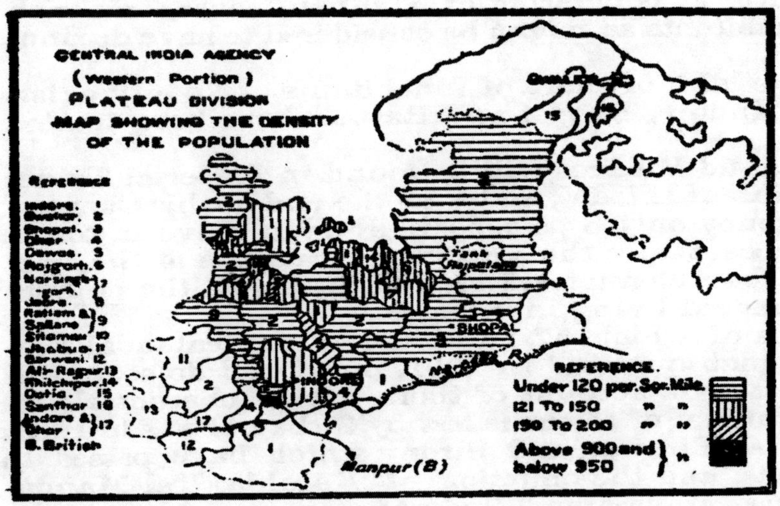


It is clear that this tract with its high class soils could easily support a larger population. Comparison is not, however, possible with any contiguous British area, though Saugor may be taken as approximating to the same conditions.

The Low-lying tract has, as mentioned above, a density of 157 to the square mile, or excluding the urban area 104. There is little doubt, however, that many parts of this tract could even now bear a far greater population, if irrigation was systematically introduced. Hamirpur, Banda, Etawah and Agra, with which the northern part of this tract is interlaced, have a much higher density as the diagram above shows.

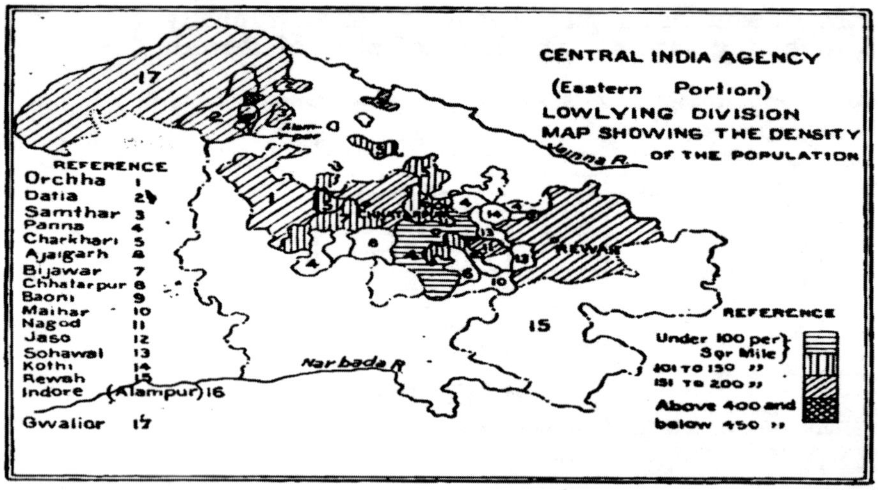


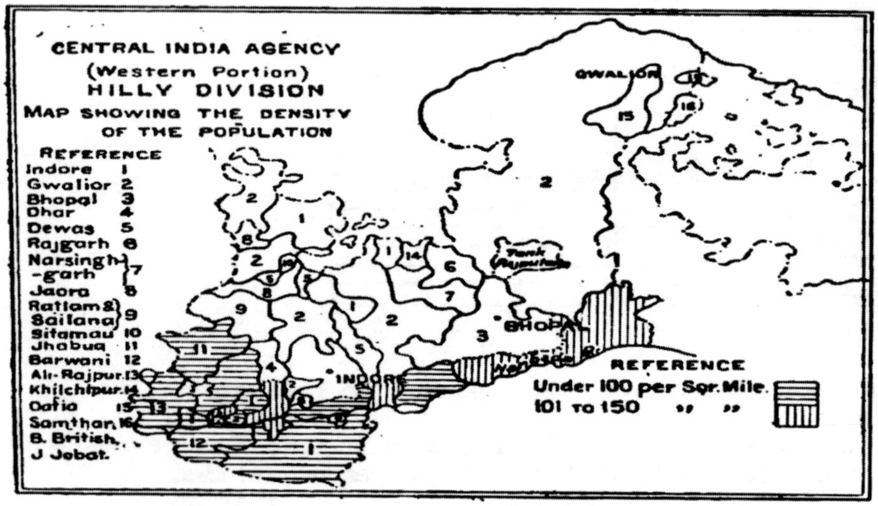


The Hilly tract while it shows the lowest density gives a higher figure than the truth, as the more fertile parts unavoidably included under this head raise the average.

The table below shows the density in purely jungle tracts :—

| Jungle tract. | Area. | Population. | Density per square mile. |
|---|---|---|---|
| Ali Rajpur . | 836 | 72,454 | 87 |
| Jhabua . | 1,336 | 111,292 | 83 |
| Kathiwara . | 71 | 3,837 | 54 |

Such variations in density as occur in Central India are mainly due to natural and administrative conditions. Irrigation has not yet been introduced anywhere on such a scale as to modify ordinary climatic conditions, though several large projects are being carried out in Gwalior.

### *III.—Town and Village.*

8. For Census purposes a "Town" was held to include all municipalities and cantonments, every place with a population of 5,000 and over, and such other places of less than 5,000 inhabitants as might be considered to have distinot urban characteristics.

A "City" is a town with one lakh or more of inhabitants. No city exists in the Agency, although Lashkar, Indore, Bhopal and Ratlam have been treated as cities for local purposes.

The statistics regarding Towns and Villages will be found in Imperial Tables III, IV and V and in Subsidiary Tables III, IV, and V at the end of this Chapter. Of the total population of the Agency only 8 persons in every 100 live in towns while 92 inhabit villages. This accentuates the agricultural nature of the tract and if the places with genuine urban characteristics are subtracted, the population shows 98 persons in every hundred living in villages.

9. There are in all 77 towns of which 57 fulfil the numerical qualifications. Among the towns are 7 which qualified in 1901, but do not do so on this occasion, while 13 have been selected on account of their urban characteristics or local importance. The total number of towns is less by 3 than it was in 1901, owing to the exclusion of Chhabra, Pirawa, and Sironj which have passed to Rajputana with the Tonk Districts, and the omission of Karahia, Tal-Mandawal, Mungaoli, Sunel, Gautampura, Manasa and Nadigaon.

Seven new towns have been added—Sipri, Morena, Sanawad, Raisen, Maharajpur, Rajnagar and Nagod. Mhow, Nimach and Nowgong are British cantonments. Agar, Guna and Sehore are Military stations, the last being also the headquarters of a Political Charge. The Agent to the Governor

General's camp (commonly known as the "Indore Residency") is the head-quarters of the local administration and of the Resident at Indore.

Many of these places have municipalities, so called, but they are in fact merely town committees.

Plague has dislocated the urban figures especially in the larger towns. The table below shows the variation due to this cause :—

| Town. | 1911. | 1901. | Decrease per cent. |
|---|---|---|---|
| Lashkar | 46,900 | 89,000 | 47 |
| Indore | 44,900 | 86,000 | 48 |
| Bhopal | 56,000 | 77,000 | 27 |
| Mhow Cantonment | 29,800 | 36,000 | 17 |
| Ratlam | 27,900 | 36,300 | 23 |
| Jaora | 18,000 | 23,800 | 24 |
| Mandasor | 16,700 | 20,900 | 20 |
| Gwalior | 14,600 | 16,800 | 13 |
| Morar | 13,500 | 19,100 | 29 |
| Nimach | 12,300 | 15,300 | 20 |
| Lashkar (Brigade) | 9,200 | 13,400 | 31 |
| Indore Residency | 9,100 | 11,100 | 18 |
| Dhar | 7,400 | 17,700 | 58 |
| Sanawad | 3,500 | 7,800 | 55 |

This has reduced the maximum figure from three towns to one town, *viz.*, Bhopal, in the "over 50,000" class, whereas in 1901 all the first three towns in the list fell in this category. The towns between 5,000 and 10,000 have risen by two, between 10,000 and 20,000 fallen by three and between 20,000 and 50,000 by one.

Of the urban population again 35 per cent. live in towns of over 20,000 and 36 per cent. in towns of 5,000 to 10,000, the average population of a town being 10,200 persons.

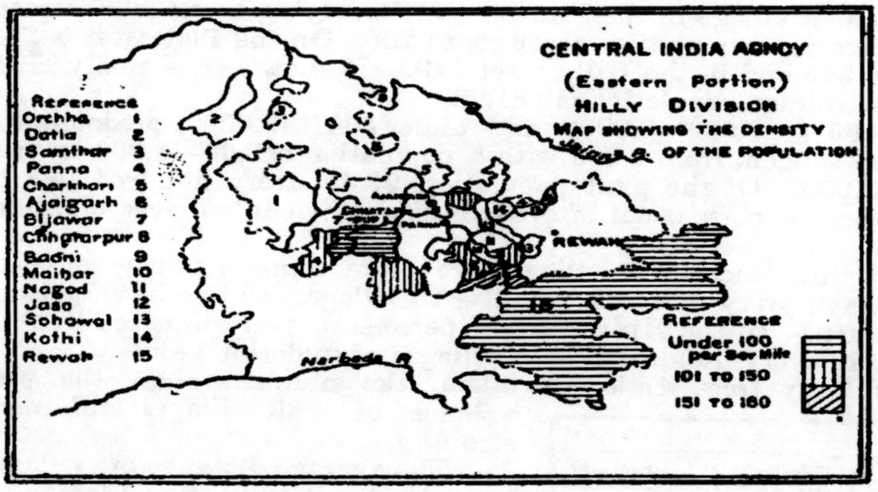


That the Agency is almost entirely agricultural is shown by the fact that only 8 persons in every 100 live in towns, while it should also be borne in mind that decided urban characteristics are really lacking, except in the four largest towns, the rest are only semi-urban, the last twenty indeed being little more than over-grown villages.

Industries are in their infancy, while administrative conditions are not generally favourable and until they develop there is little likelihood of any real increase in the genuine urban population. Of the Natural Divisions the Plateau stands first with 5 per cent. more dwelling in towns and mainly in towns of over 20,000 population. Expansion, it will be seen, is met with only in State capitals, and in a few favoured spots, such as Biaora and Sanawad, the last a rapidly growing town temporarily affected by plague, where peculiar conditions have made them commercial centres on trade routes. In early days towns were either political capitals, military posts or religious centres. Such settlements naturally decline under modern conditions, unless fresh life is given to them, and such life can come from one source only, the increase of industrial and commercial activity. In the Agency, little development has taken place in this direction owing mainly to political and administrative conditions. Hence, towns of importance in former days, such as Bhilsa, Chanderi, Gohad, Gwalior, Narwar, Ujjain, and others are falling behind in the race. Ujjain, a trading centre of some importance, even in Buddhist days, has lost ground, under modern conditions in spite of its position as a junction on three lines of Railway and its claims as a sacred city. Mandasor is declining and the approaching abolition of the opium trade will probably hit it still more severely in the near future; Gwalior has been killed by its modern neighbour Lashkar; Sehore, as is always the case, has lost its position owing to the foundation of the neighbouring British civil station of the same name.

Subsidiary Table V shows that there has been a fall of 18 per cent. in the urban population dealt with on the same basis as 1901. The big towns, owing to plague, show a serious diminution, while a large rise has taken place in small towns.

Plague has, however, vitiated figures so that no accurate idea of the variation can be obtained. If the population of 1901 is taken in the case of plague-stricken towns the result gives 960,000 inhabitants, which shows that the population is stationary.

The Village.

10. The Census village corresponds to revenue village, a village with attendant hamlets being considered as a single unit.

The difficulty in obtaining correct lists of villages is almost inconceivable until the task is attempted. Departmental lists and maps invariably disagree in names and numbers, and these are often both at variance with the actual settlements to be found on the spot. It is hoped that the present lists (except in Gwalior) are now perfect. The larger the State the greater the difficulty. The Central India village, outside jungle tracts, is a compact collection of houses. In the centre come those of the better classes, the landlord's residence often being conspicuous in the centre of all; on the outskirts are the huts of cultivators and beyond at a little distance the low castes. In the jungle tracts it is far otherwise. The Bhil avoids his neighbour and a village in such cases will often cover several miles, although the population is insignificant; one such village stretches for close on seven miles along the line of a high road. The average area of a village in the Plateau and Low-lying tracts is 2·1 square miles while the average population amounts to 260. On the Plateau it is 226, on the Low-lying 319 and in the Hilly tract 249. If, however, a really Hilly tract is taken, the average population is only 83.

Villages of 500 to 1,000 (2,890) and "under 500" (29,000) predominate, the fall being very sudden, from 2,800 with a population of 500—1,000 to only 900 with over 1,000. Of the total population 92 in every hundred live in villages, while over 50 persons out of every hundred live in villages of under 500 people.

In the Low-lying tract large villages are more common, but even here out of 93 persons in every hundred, who live in villages, 40 live in villages of under 500 population. In the Hilly tract 97 persons in every hundred live in villages, while 60 in every hundred live in villages of under 500 souls.

If a strictly Hilly tract section is taken, the numbers show the prevalence of small villages still more strongly.

| Hilly tracts. | Number per cent. in villages of | |
|---|---|---|
| | 500—5,000 | Under 500 |
| Ali Rajpur | 28 | 72 |
| Jhabua | 12 | 88 |

The average distance of villages apart is 1½ miles; in the Plateau it is 1·4, in the Low-lying tract 1·5 and in the Hilly tract 1·6 miles.

## IV.—Houses and Families.

11. The question "What is a house?" is always a difficult one to answer. The definition given in 1901 was not found by Census Officers sufficiently precise for their assistants, and on this occasion the following definition was, therefore, given and illustrated by diagrams.

A house for Census purposes is defined as follows :—

(*i*) Any structure other than a dwelling house, such as tent, pavilion, temple, serai, etc., or a site, camping ground, ghat, etc., to which a separate number has been affixed.

(*ii*) The dwelling place of one or more families with their dependents and resident servants having an independent entrance, whether that entrance be from a road, gallery, balcony, corridor, courtyard, or otherwise.

It will be seen, however, that no material difference from the results of 1901 has arisen in the figures in Subsidiary Table VII. The house in Central India, except in the larger towns, is almost invariably a separate entity which can be easily distinguished, occasionally several lie in one courtyard but even this is not usual.

Houses vary in their appearance with the materials of which they are constructed and these again vary with the locality. Along the ranges, where limestone and sandstone abound, the houses are constructed and roofed with stone as in Gwalior and Bhopal where even small huts are largely made of this material. In Gwalior and some other places the better houses are in such cases decorated with fine pierced stone work screens. Where stone is not found brick is used in the better class of house, carved wooden balconies, door-frames and windows being common, as at Ujjain and Indore.

Houses of more than one storey are not often met with except in towns, though the more important villages, which are the residences of the local Thakurs, occasionally have one or two-storeyed houses. A courtyard is often enclosed by prolonging the outer walls of the house and is used for the cattle to herd in.

For the rest small huts with frames of bamboo or the commoner kinds of tree either roofed with sunbaked tiles, grass or mud or regularly thatched form the homes of the agricultural population. In the jungle tract wattle or *chhappar* huts are the only habitations. In Ali-Rajpur and the south-west corner of the Agency the Bhil huts are usually built on piles, the cattle herding below while the inhabitants live above them.

SUBSIDIARY TABLE I.—**Density, Water Supply and Crops.**

| Natural Division. | Mean density per square mile in 1911. | Percentage of total area. | | Percentage to cultivable area. | | Percentage of cultivated area which is irrigated. | Normal rain fall. | Percentage of gross cultivated area under. | | | | | | | | | | | | | |
|---|---|---|---|---|---|---|---|---|---|---|---|---|---|---|---|---|---|---|---|---|---|
| | | Cultivable. | Net cultivated. | Net cultivated. | Double cropped. | | | Rice. | Wheat. | Gram. | Jowar. | Bajra. | Maize. | Kodon. | Other food-grains and pulses. | Oilseeds. | Sugar-cane. | Poppy. | Cotton. | Tobacco. | Miscellaneous. |
| 1 | 2 | 3 | 4 | 5 | 6 | 7 | 8 | 9 | 10 | 11 | 12 | 13 | 14 | 15 | 16 | 17 | 18 | 19 | 20 | 21 | 22 |
| Central India . . . . | 121 | 46·63 | 24·65 | 52·86 | 2·03 | 5·87 | 33 | 4·71 | 11·25 | 11·39 | 17·33 | 0·55 | 3·37 | 1·0 | 18·83 | 2·77 | 0·06 | 0·37 | 4·71 | 0·02 | 28·65 |

SUBSIDIARY TABLE II.—**Distribution of the Population classified according to Density.**

| Political Charge and Natural Division. | UNITS WITH A POPULATION PER SQUARE MILE OF | | | |
|---|---|---|---|---|
| | UNDER 150. | | 150—300. | |
| | Area. | Population 000's omitted. | Area. | Population 000's omitted. |
| 1 | 2 | 3 | 4 | 5 |
| **Central India** | **77,367** | **9,357** | ... | ... |
| 1 Gwalior Residency | 24,384<br>*31·6* | 3,091<br>*33·0* | ... | ... |
| 2. Indore Residency | 9,004<br>*11·7* | 979<br>*10·5* | ... | ... |
| 3. Baghelkhand Agency | 14,706<br>*19·0* | 1,773<br>*19·0* | ... | ... |
| 4. Bhopal Agency | 9,154<br>*11·8* | 1,051<br>*11·3* | ... | ... |
| 5. Bhopawar Agency | 7,274<br>*9·3* | 698<br>*7·5* | ... | ... |
| 6. Bundelkhand Agency | 10,118<br>*13·0* | 1,375<br>*14·5* | ... | ... |
| 7. Malwa Agency | 2,727<br>*3·6* | 390<br>*4·2* | ... | ... |
| ***Natural Divisions.*** | | | | |
| Plateau | 30,813<br>*39·8* | 3,683<br>*39·3* | ... | ... |
| Low-lying Tract | ... | ... | 21,118<br>*27·3* | 3,311<br>*35·4* |
| Hilly Tract | 25,436<br>*32·9* | 2,363<br>*25·3* | ... | ... |

NOTE.—The figures below the absolute ones represent the proportion per cent. which the area and population of each density group bear to the total area.

SUBSIDIARY TABLE III.—**Distribution of the Population between Towns and Villages.**

| Political Charge and Natural Division. | AVERAGE POPULATION PER | | NUMBER PER MILLE RESIDING IN | | NUMBER PER MILLE OF URBAN POPULATION RESIDING IN TOWNS WITH A POPULATION OF | | | | NUMBER PER MILLE OF RURAL POPULATION RESIDING IN VILLAGES WITH A POPULATION OF | | | |
|---|---|---|---|---|---|---|---|---|---|---|---|---|
| | Town. | Village. | Towns. | Villages. | 20,000 and over. | 10,000 to 20,000. | 5,000 to 10,000. | Under 5,000. | 5,000 and over. | 2,000 to 5,000. | 500 to 2,000. | Under 500. |
| 1 | 2 | 3 | 4 | 5 | 6 | 7 | 8 | 9 | 10 | 11 | 12 | 13 |
| **Central India** | **10,209** | **260** | **84** | **916** | **345** | **198** | **356** | **101** | **1** | **65** | **376** | **558** |
| 1. Gwalior Residency | 9,921 | 273 | 90 | 910 | 310 | 245 | 347 | 98 | 2 | 62 | 401 | [illegible] |
| 2. Indore Residency | 12,583 | 245 | 141 | 859 | 540 | ... | 435 | 25 | ... | 69 | 318 | 613 |
| 3. Baghelkhand Agency | 8,571 | 267 | 34 | 966 | 438 | ... | 338 | 224 | ... | 36 | 407 | 558 |
| 4. Bhopal Agency | 10,124 | 205 | 106 | 894 | 505 | ... | 322 | 173 | ... | 37 | 283 | 675 |
| 5. Bhopawar Agency | 7,000 | 211 | 30 | 970 | ... | ... | 1,000 | ... | ... | 93 | 226 | 681 |
| 6. Bundelkhand Agency | 8,984 | 339 | 72 | 928 | ... | 546 | 332 | 122 | ... | 115 | 479 | 406 |
| 7. Malwa Agency | 13,122 | 237 | 202 | 798 | 355 | 428 | 167 | 55 | ... | 84 | 307 | 609 |
| ***Natural Divisions.*** | | | | | | | | | | | | |
| Plateau | 11,199 | 226 | 124 | 876 | 432 | 159 | 332 | 77 | 2 | 61 | 294 | 643 |
| Low-lying Tract | 10,240 | 319 | 74 | 926 | 298 | 291 | 277 | 134 | ... | 79 | 487 | 434 |
| Hilly Tract | 6,767 | 249 | 34 | 966 | ... | 132 | 725 | 143 | ... | 54 | 343 | 603 |

SUBSIDIARY TABLE IV.—**Number per mille of the Total Population and of each Main Religion who live in Towns.**

| Political Charge and Natural Division. | NUMBER PER MILLE WHO LIVE IN TOWNS. | | | | | | |
|---|---|---|---|---|---|---|---|
| | Total Population. | Hindu. | Musalman. | Animist. | Jain. | Christian. | Others. |
| 1 | 2 | 3 | 4 | 5 | 6 | 7 | 8 |
| **Central India** | **84** | **66** | **402** | **7** | **240** | **822** | **807** |
| 1. Gwalior Residency | 90 | 71 | 391 | 11 | 213 | 928 | 892 |
| 2. Indore Residency | 141 | 111 | 435 | 27 | 345 | 935 | 807 |
| 3. Baghelkhand Agency | 34 | 28 | 262 | ... | 350 | 528 | 297 |
| 4. Bhopal Agency | 106 | 71 | 460 | 1 | 221 | 964 | 839 |
| 5. Bhopawar Agency | 30 | 38 | 155 | 4 | 55 | 153 | 383 |
| 6. Bundelkhand Agency | 72 | 61 | 389 | 16 | 75 | 800 | 761 |
| 7. Malwa Agency | 202 | 152 | 586 | 11 | 574 | 801 | 953 |
| ***Natural Divisions.*** | | | | | | | |
| Plateau | 125 | 91 | 468 | 16 | 331 | 909 | 899 |
| Low-lying Tract | 74 | 61 | 414 | 11 | 109 | [illegible] | 712 |
| Hilly Tract | 34 | 32 | 177 | 4 | 85 | 11 | 222 |

SUBSIDIARY TABLE V.—**Towns classified by Population.**

| CLASS OF TOWN. | Number of towns in each class in 1911. | Proportion to total Urban population per mille. | Number of females per 1,000 males. | Increase per cent. in the population of towns as classed at previous censuses. | | | Increase per cent. in Urban population of each class from 1881—1911. | |
|---|---|---|---|---|---|---|---|---|
| | | | | 1901 to 1911. | 1891 to 1901. | 1881 to 1891. | (a) In towns as classed in 1881. | (b) In the total of each class in 1911 as compared with the corresponding total in 1881. |
| 1 | 2 | 3 | 4 | 5 | 6 | 7 | 8 | 9 |
| ***Total*** | ***77*** | ***1,000*** | ***904*** | ***—18·1*** | ***—3·7*** | ***+9·3*** | ***—16·8*** | ***—11·6*** |
| I. 100,000 and over | ... | ... | ... | ... | —14·3 | ... | ... | ... |
| II. 50,000—100,000 | 1 | 71 | 935 | —41·4 | +6·8 | +17·6 | —32·3 | —74·4 |
| III. 20,000—50,000 | 6 | 274 | 852 | —14·7 | +5·4 | +5·1 | —9·1 | +0·1 |
| IV. 10,000—20,000 | 11 | 198 | 913 | —19·1 | —7·7 | +5·0 | —17·7 | +9·1 |
| V. 5,000—10,000 | 39 | 356 | 920 | —0·5 | —9·2 | +7·1 | —5·4 | +32·7 |
| VI. Under 5,000 | 20 | 101 | 935 | —2·1 | +3·0 | ... | ... | ... |

SUBSIDIARY TABLE VI.—**City.**

| CITY. | Population in 1911. | Number of persons per square mile. | Number of females to 1,000 males. | Proportion of foreign born per mille. | Percentage of Variation. | | | |
|---|---|---|---|---|---|---|---|---|
| | | | | | 1901—1911. | 1891—1901. | 1881—1891. | Total 1881—1911. |
| 1 | 2 | 3 | 4 | 5 | 6 | 7 | 8 | 9 |
| Bhopal | 56,204 | 7,114 | 935 | 324 | —27·0 | +9·5 | +27·0 | +1·4 |
| Lashkar | 46,952 | 11,738 | 937 | 50 | —47·3 | —14·3 | +18·2 | —46·7 |
| Indore | 44,947 | 8,171 | 813 | 296 | —48·2 | +4·5 | +10·1 | —40·4 |
| Ratlam | 27,957 | 23,298 | 960 | 147 | —23·0 | +21·8 | —4·0 | —10·0 |

SUBSIDIARY TABLE VII.—**Persons per House and Houses per Square Mile.**

| Political Charge and Natural Division. | Average Number of Persons per House. | | | | Average Number of Houses per Square Mile. | | | |
|---|---|---|---|---|---|---|---|---|
| | 1911. | 1901. | 1891. | 1881. | 1911. | 1901. | 1891. | 1881. |
| 1 | 2 | 3 | 4 | 5 | 6 | 7 | 8 | 9 |
| ***Central India.*** | ***5*** | ***5*** | ***5*** | ... | ***26*** | ***21*** | ***25*** | ... |
| 1. Gwalior Residency | 5 | 5 | 6 | ... | 27 | 23 | 24 | ... |
| 2. Indore Residency | 4 | 5 | 5 | ... | 26 | 20 | 24 | ... |
| 3. Baghelkhand Agency | 5 | 5 | 5 | ... | 25 | 21 | 23 | ... |
| 4. Bhopal Agency | 4 | 5 | 5 | ... | 26 | 19 | 27 | ... |
| 5. Bhopawar Agency | 5 | 5 | 5 | ... | 20 | 15 | 20 | ... |
| 6. Bundelkhand Agency | 5 | 5 | 5 | ... | 30 | 24 | 27 | ... |
| 7. Malwa Agency | 4 | 4 | 5 | ... | 34 | 30 | 34 | ... |
| ***Natural Divisions.*** | | | | | | | | |
| Plateau | 4 | 5 | ... | ... | 28 | 22 | ... | ... |
| Low-lying Tract | 5 | 6 | ... | ... | 32 | 28 | ... | ... |
| Hilly Tract | 5 | 5 | ... | ... | 19 | 15 | ... | ... |

# CHAPTER II.

## Movement of Population.

Introductory.

12. The results dealt with in this Chapter are administratively of great importance. In Central India, however, the absence of vital statistics of any reliability whatsoever deprives the discussion of much of its value.

Having dealt with the condition of the population on March 10th, 1911, the variations since 1881 have now to be considered.

It would be interesting to form some idea of the condition of the territories now comprised in the Agency in early days, but materials are scanty and vague and, at the best, the following sketch is little more than guess work.

The earliest days of which any definite record exists are those of the Buddhist period. In the early books of the followers of this faith describing conditions about B. C. 700—600 various petty kingdoms are noticed showing the existence of regular settlements, while great trade routes are mentioned as passing through this region. One led from Paithan *viâ* Maheshwar, Ujjain and Bhilsa eastwards to Shravasti, while another appears to have passed in the direction of Ashta, Sehore, and Bhilsa to Bharhut in Nagod State. This, at any rate, shows that there was movement across the country, and to enable such movement to be possible there must have been settlements of some kind at intervals. Heavy forests, wild animals and wilder men are mentioned. Later comes the account of the adventurous Chinaman, Hiuen Tsiang (A. D. 630—45), who visited Malwa and describes the country as noted for its fertility, with a soil specially suited to crops of winter wheat; the inhabitants are, he adds, docile, virtuous, and of remarkable intelligence; their educated people being noted for their great learning. Vague as this is it points to a certain settled standard of civilisation. But a more certain indication of the suitability of the tract for settlement and of its being, for those days, populous, is the attraction it had for the invader. From the time of Asoka (B.C. 250) to the days of Baber (A.D. 1527) Malwa in particular was always the promised land to the invader. From the 9th to the 12th century it was cut up into numerous Rajput kingdoms of which the most famous was that of the Malwa Paramaras. The large number of buildings of this period of which remains are still standing testifies to a population of some size and of general distribution. In Mughal days Malwa was one of the most important provinces of the Empire with an income of 5,900,000 Dams or R1,470,500. Its fertility and climate were famous and it was the great centre of a famous weaving industry of fine cloths and muslins, an industry that still languishes at Chanderi. All this points to a well populated tract. At the same time the Mughal Emperors were able to hunt lions and elephants within its limits showing that heavy forests still covered large areas.

A *very* rough estimate for Malwa based on the area as returned by Abul Fazl points to a population of 643,208 persons for 8,040,104 *bighas* or a density of 81·9 per square mile.

In the east of the Agency the country was less inviting, more rugged with less fertile soil and heavier forests. Although there are references to this region they are much briefer and point to far less developed conditions. A striking instance of this is Baghelkhand which was known to the Mughals as Bhatghora, their knowledge of the tract ending with this piece of information, Abul Fazl having nothing further to say about it.

On the fall of the Mughal Empire anarchy followed and from 1717 for one hundred years Maratha and Pindari worked their will on the western section of the Agency until almost every village was deserted and the peasants had either been killed or had fled. The few of stouter heart who remained did but little cultivation and jungle soon hid many districts previously covered with corn and poppy. The accounts of the campaign of 1818-19 carried out by Lord Hastings, show how great the devastation was, how many tracts had become overgrown with jungle, how many villages lay without inhabitants. The population in these days can have been little more than one-third of what it was in Mughal days. Recovery was rapid and, as soon as peace was restored, the old inhabitants and their descendants returned to occupy their old haunts. From 1820 onwards seasons alone have been responsible for general changes, though here and there political conditions have temporarily affected the population of individual States.

**Variation since 1881.**

13. The first Census was taken in 1881. In this enumeration as in that of 1891 the information collected was not complete. In 1901 and on the present occasion the Census has followed that of British India in all details.

The total population on the present occasion amounts to 9,357,000, an increase of 859,000 since 1901 and of 95,000 since 1881; between 1891 and 1901 there was a fall of 1,600,000.

As, however, variations may be due to (*a*) the inclusion of new areas, (*b*) greater accuracy of enumeration, or (*c*) a real increase, it is necessary to consider these factors. In Subsidiary Table I the areas have been adjusted so as to be comparative.

As regards variation due to increased accuracy, it is certain that the figures for the two earlier enumerations suffered from lack of experience and the system followed, but as between 1901 and 1911, although there are indications of local variations that are probably in part accounted for by this cause, they are not such as to materially affect the figures of the Agency as a whole; this source of variation may, therefore, be eliminated in considering the figures of the last two Censuses which are alone strictly comparable.

There remains the last cause—actual increase; this will be now considered.

**1901 to 1911.**

The Census of 1901 followed on the heels of a very severe famine which seriously affected the west of the Agency, and especially the Hilly tract causing heavy mortality among the old and the young—among those, that is, at the two extremes of life. The absence of any vital statistics makes actual check impossible, but it may be assumed that an abnormally high birth rate and a low death rate resulted from these conditions. So far as is possible this question has been dealt with in Chapter V on Age.

The decade has been characterised by several severe but localised visitations of plague for which the returns give an approximate figure of 40,000 deaths. On these returns no great reliance can, however, be placed, and the true figure is probably considerably higher. The effects of plague are not, however, so far-reaching as those of famine, and except here and there have been mainly confined to urban areas.

Some local distress was caused by bad seasons but it amounted only to scarcity of a more or less severe type, no general famine appeared and agricultural conditions were on the whole good.

There have been no artificial stimulants to increase the population such as extensive irrigation projects, industrial developments or the like. In all Central India there are only 144 factories, mines, etc., employing 16,000 people.

**Examination of Results.**

14. It remains to examine the results in detail so far as is feasible without vital statistics. It may be remarked at the outset that figures for Agencies will be found in the Subsidiary Tables. These being purely artificial units will not be further considered.

*Diagram showing the total urban and rural population of the Central India Agency in the different natural divisions*

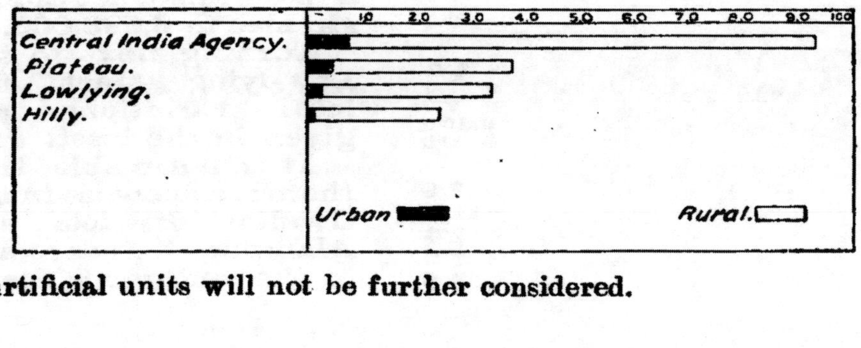

Surveying the Agency as a whole the first point that appears is that the increase is practically restricted to the west of the tract and the hills, the Plateau showing a rise of 11 per cent. and Hilly tract of 24 per cent. From the remarks made above this is what would be expected from the rebound after the losses caused by the famine of 1900.

Examining figures for the principal units on the Plateau in detail, the increase between 1901-11 is as given in the inset.

It is difficult to account always for the variation in contiguous districts. Thus, the contiguous districts of Ujjain and Mehidpur show a difference of 21 per cent., Bhilsa and Isagarh of 19, Diwanganj and Berasia, bordering on Bhilsa, show a much smaller rise, but the larger rise in the Gwalior district is, no doubt, due to the fact that the eastern part of Bhilsa is in reality hilly as the neighbouring hilly districts of Bhopal, Garhi, and Raisen also show a very large increase. Part of the increase may be due to better enumeration, but the actual loss in the Bhopal State in the famine of 1899-1900 was nearly 40 per cent., and the increase must be practically wholly due to the rebound.

The natural population of this tract approximates to 3,593,000.

Turning next to the Low-lying tract, the local variations are given in the inset.

It is noticeable that there is a decrease in the Gwalior districts and Alampur of Indore and in the contiguous States

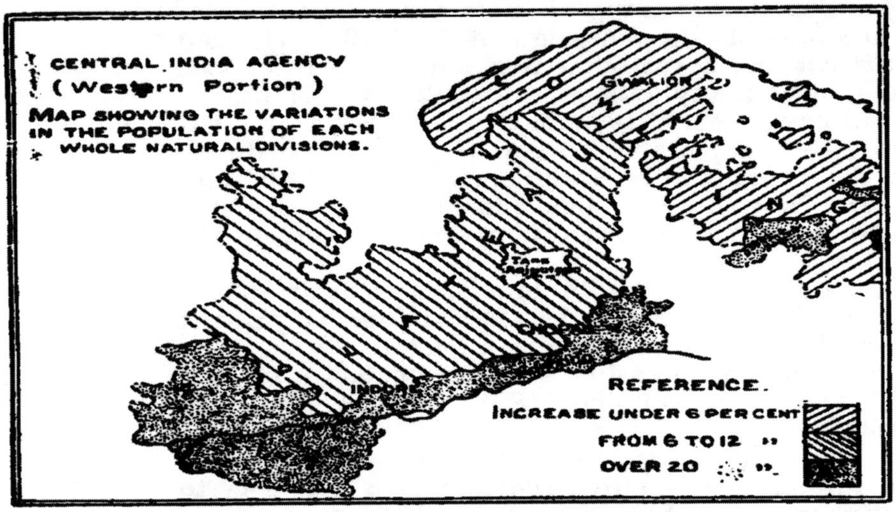


| State and District. | Percentage. Variation. | State and District. | Percentage. Variation. |
|---|---|---|---|
| **Gwalior State** | + **14·6** | **Indore State—** | |
| Bhilsa | + 38·0 | Rampura-Bhanpura | + 23·0 |
| Isagarh | + 19·0 | **Bhopal State** | + **6·8** |
| Narwar | + 12·0 | Diwanganj | + 5·0 |
| Ujjain | + 11·0 | Berasia | + 19·0 |
| Mandasor | + 11·5 | Ashta | + 34·0 |
| Shajapur | + 8·0 | Doraha | + 24·0 |
| **Indore State** | + **9·0** | Nazirabad | + 37·0 |
| Indore (rural) | + 12·6 | **Other States** | + **9·0** |
| Mehidpur | + 32·0 | | |

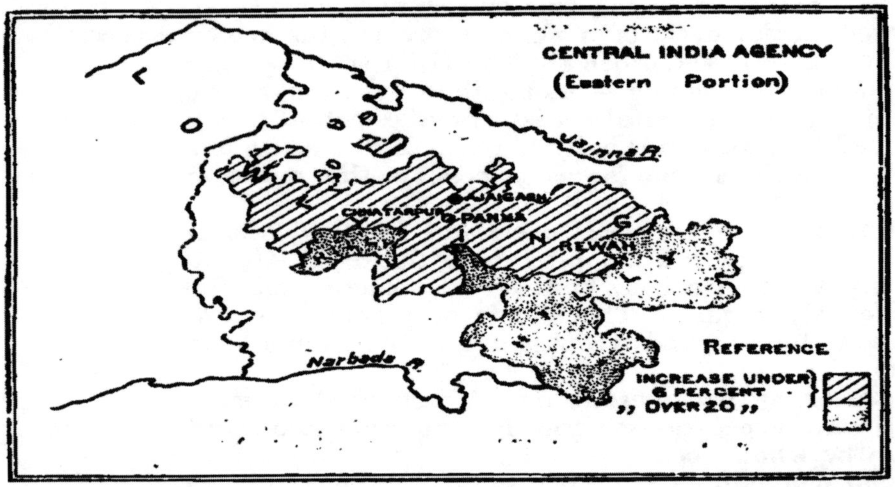


| State and District. | Percentage. Variation. |
|---|---|
| **Gwalior State** | — **7·3** |
| Gird (rural) | + 9·4 |
| Tonwarghar | + 0·6 |
| Bhind | — 4·5 |
| Sheopur | — 8·0 |
| **Indore State** | ... |
| Alampur | — 6·0 |
| **Rewah State** | + **8·0** |
| Huzur Tahsil | + 7·0 |
| Raghurajnagar | + 7·0 |
| Sitlaha | + 10·0 |
| Mauganj | + 9·0 |
| **Orchha State** | + **3·0** |
| **Datia State** | —**11·0** |
| **Charkhari State** | + **7·0** |
| **Chhatarpur State** | + **7·0** |
| **Maihar State** | + **14·0** |

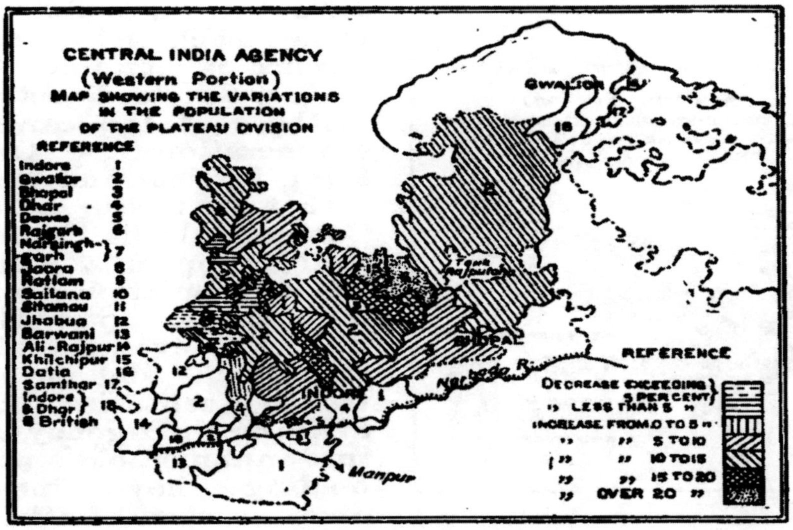


| State and District. | | Percentage, Variation. |
|---|---|---|
| **Gwalior State** | . | + **24·0** |
| Amjhera . | . | + 24·0 |
| **Indore State** | . | + **33·0** |
| Nemawar . | . | + 27·0 |
| Nimar . | . | + 35·0 |
| **Bhopal State** | . | + **13·5** |
| Bamhori . . | . | + 18·6 |
| Garhi . . | . | + 111·0 |

| State and District. | Percentage, Variation. |
|---|---|
| **Bhopal State—** | |
| Raisen . . . . | + 65·0 |
| Mardanpur . . . | + 45·0 |
| **Rewah State** . | + **20·5** |
| Bardi . . . . | + 16·0 |
| Beohari and Bandogarh . | + 49·0 |
| **Barwani State** . | + **43·0** |
| **Ali-Rajpur State** | + **44·0** |
| **Jhabua State** . | + **37·0** |

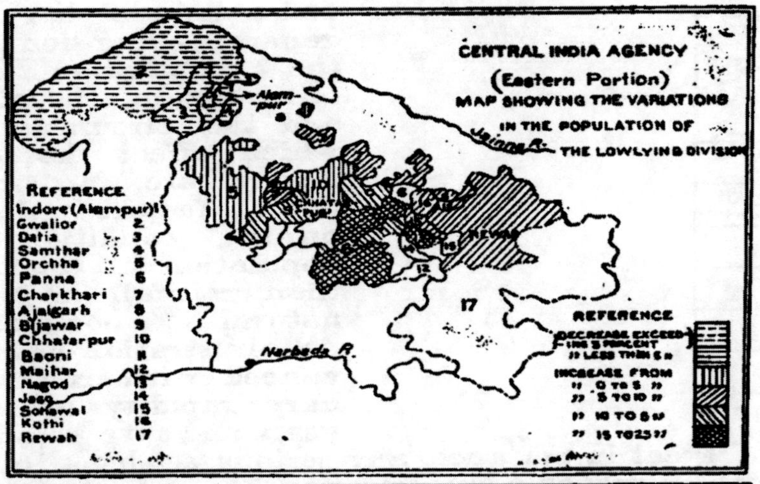


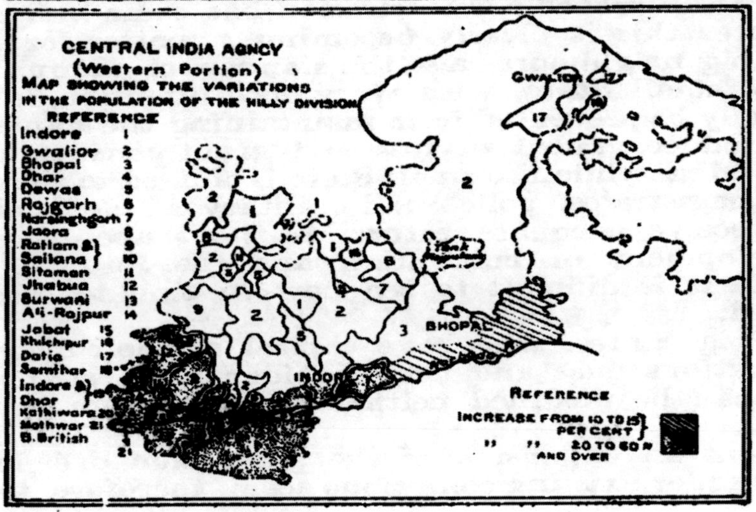


of Datia and Samthar. On the other hand in the more eastern portion of this Natural Division there is an average rise of 8 per cent. This is to be accounted for partly by the leanness of the years 1907 to 1909 which affected Datia, Samthar and the surrounding country.

The Hilly tract figures examined in detail show that the rise has been everywhere considerable, especially along the actual ranges where there is little land not genuinely Hilly, as in Beohari, Barwani and Ali-Rajpur. The high figures for Garhi and Raisen are not easy to explain.

**Natural Population.**

15. The natural population of each Natural Division is given in the inset, that is to say, the actual population and those born in the tract but enumerated outside *less* immigrants. It will be seen that the Plateau and Hilly areas gain by immigration while the Low-lying tract loses. It is not possible to distinguish immigration of a temporary or permanent character, and there is thus a slight error which is unavoidable.

### *Summary.*

16. The inferences to be deduced from the figures here discussed are that the population has recovered rapidly from the effects of the great famine of 1899-1900. The large rise in the Plateau and Hilly tracts with the small increase in the Low-lying area clearly demonstrate this. Has the population reached its normal? The figure is still 7·7 per cent. below that of

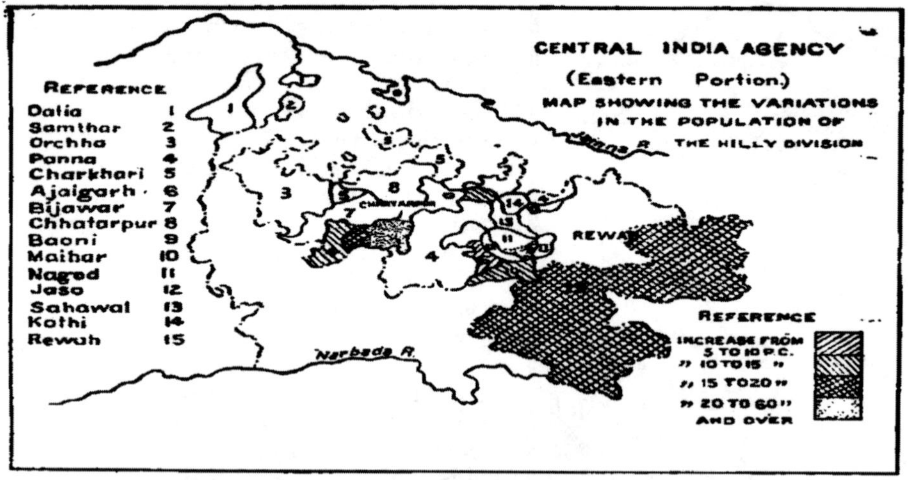


| | Plateau. | Low-lying. | Hilly. |
|---|---|---|---|
| Actual population . . . . | 3,683,491 | 3,310,703 | 2,362,786 |
| Immigrants . . . . | 199,297 | 160,650 | 114,308 |
| Emigrants . . . . . | 109,678 | 424,702 | 1,696 |
| Natural population . . . | 3,593,872 | 3,574,755 | 2,250,174 |

*Diagram showing the variation since 1901 per 1000 of the population in each natural division.*

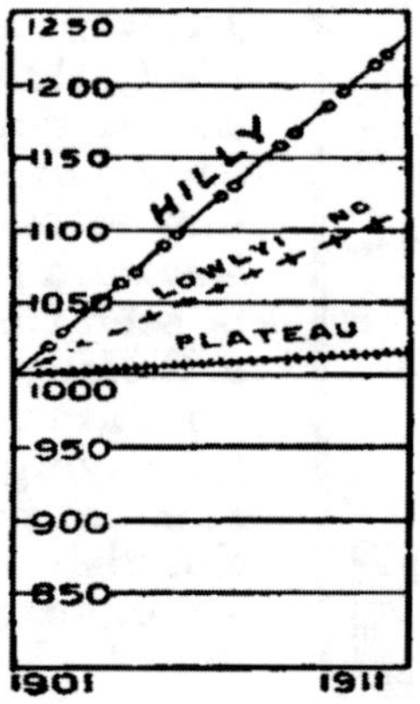


1891, and it is difficult to say whether that difference is genuine or mainly due to defective methods at the earlier enumeration. One thing is clear and that is that the fertile soil of Central India could easily support a much larger population; will it ever do so? The historical events of the eighteenth and nineteenth centuries by dividing the Agency up into innumerable small holdings have introduced a state of affairs which militates very seriously against any considerable rise in numbers. Excluding natural calamities, which after all are only temporary in their effect, political conditions are in Central India the real bar to a general expansion of the population. Administration, therefore, and the circumstances which affect its efficiency are far more potent factors in determining conditions of population in this area than rainfall or other natural conditions. Administration has advanced with extraordinary rapidity of late years and save possibly, in a few cases, unlikely to be of great importance, any serious set-back in this direction is improbable. But with improved administration has come increased cost. To all but the largest States this is clearly becoming a matter for very serious consideration. As their big neighbours raise the standard of administration they raise the cost, and the small State, with every good intention, is not only left behind but may eventually be prevented from maintaining the standard. The big States raise salaries, introduce graded services and grant pensions thus absorbing all the best material. Meanwhile the small State is obliged to raise its expenditure—revenue officers, magistrates, police and military all demanding higher pay—while it does not receive adequate return in the shape of good officials. Capital for the development of cultivation and the fostering of industry is not forthcoming, and it is difficult to see how in time to come a retrograde motion is to be avoided.

Even in the cases of the big States, who have capital at their disposal, development is arrested by vexatious dues and taxes incident to a stringent border system, and until this can be modified neither cultivator nor trader will ever be able to do his best.

All this will tend to prevent an expansion of the population over large tracts and any considerable rise under existing conditions seem, therefore. to be impossible.

SUBSIDIARY TABLE I.—**Variation in relation to Density since 1881.**

| Political Charge and Natural Division. | Percentage of Variation, Increase (+) Decrease (—). | | | Net Variation. | | Mean density per square mile. | | | |
|---|---|---|---|---|---|---|---|---|---|
| | 1901-1911. | 1891-1901. | 1881-1891. | 1891-1911. | 1881-1911. | 1911. | 1901. | 1891. | 1881. |
| 1 | 2 | 3 | 4 | 5 | 6 | 7 | 8 | 9 | 10 |
| **Central India** . . . . . | **+10·1** | **−16·2** | **+9·4** | **−7·7** | **+1·0** | **121** | **+ 110** | **131** | **120** |
| 1. Gwalior Residency . . . | +4·7 | −12·6 | ... | −8·5 | ... | 127 | 121 | 138 | ... |
| 2. Indore Residency . . . | +16·3 | −20·6 | ... | −7·7 | ... | 109 | 93 | 118 | ... |
| 3. Baghelkhand Agency . . | +14·1 | −13·0 | ... | −0·8 | ... | 121 | 106 | 122 | ... |
| 4. Bhopal Agency . . . . | +13·4 | −27·9 | ... | −18·2 | ... | 115 | 101 | 140 | ... |
| 5. Bhopawar Agency . . . | +27·3 | −23·1 | ... | −2·1 | ... | 96 | 75 | 98 | ... |
| 6. Bundelkhand Agency . . . | +5·1 | −10·2 | ... | −5·6 | ... | 136 | 129 | 144 | ... |
| 7. Malwa Agency . . . . | +6·5 | −19·6 | ... | −14·4 | ... | 143 | 134 | 167 | ... |
| ***Natural Divisions.*** | | | | | | | | | |
| Plateau . . . . . . | +10·7 | ... | ... | ... | ... | 120 | 108 | ... | .. |
| Low-lying Tract . . . | +1·5 | ... | ... | ... | ... | 157 | 154 | ... | ... |
| Hilly Tract . . . . | +23·8 | ... | ... | ... | ... | 93 | 75 | ... | ... |

SUBSIDIARY TABLE II.—**Variation in Natural Population.**

| Natural Division. | Population in 1911. | | | | Population in 1901. | | | | Variation per cent (1901-1911) in natural population, Increase (+) Decrease (—) |
|---|---|---|---|---|---|---|---|---|---|
| | Actual Population. | Immigrants. | Emigrants. | Natural Population. | Actual Population. | Immigrants. | Emigrants. | Natural Population. | |
| 1 | 2 | 3 | 4 | 5 | 6 | 7 | 8 | 9 | 10 |
| **Central India** . | **9,356,980** | **474,255** | **536,076** | **9,418,801** | **8,628,781** | **672,263** | **453,660** | **8,410,178** | **+12·0** |
| Plateau . . | 3,683,491 | 199,297 | 109,678 | 3,593,872 | ... | ... | ... | ... | ... |
| Low-lying Tract | 3,310,703 | 160,650 | 424,702 | 3,574,755 | ... | ... | ... | ... | ... |
| Hilly Tract . | 2,362,786 | 114,308 | 1,696 | 2,250,174 | ... | ... | ... | ... | ... |

SUBSIDIARY TABLE IV.—**Variation by Natural Division classified according to Density.**

***(a) Actual Variation. (b) Proportional Variation.***

| Natural Division. | Decade. | Variation in Natural Division with a population per square mile at commencement of decade of | | Natural Division. | Decade. | Variation in Natural Division with a population per square mile at commencement of decade of | |
|---|---|---|---|---|---|---|---|
| | | Under 150. | 150—300 | | | Under 150. | 150—300. |
| 1 | 2 | 3 | 4 | 1 | 2 | 3 | 4 |
| **Central India** . | **1901-1911** | **+859,175** | ... | **Central India** . | **1901-1911** | **+10·1** | ... |
| Plateau . | 1901-1911 | +355,658 | ... | Plateau . . | 1901-1911 | +10·7 | ... |
| Low-lying Tract | 1901-1911 | +50,433 | −613 | Low-lying Tract | 1901-1911 | +4·3 | −0·08 |
| Hilly Tract . | 1901-1911 | +453,697 | ... | Hilly Tract . | 1901-1911 | +23·8 | ... |

# CHAPTER III.

## Migration.

17. The Table dealt with in this Chapter is Table XI recording the birth-places of those enumerated. At the end of the Chapter are certain Subsidiary Tables dealing with the subject.

Migration, it may be remarked, is usually divided into five classes.

I. *Casual.*—Movements between adjacent tracts and villages is ordinarily of this kind. It is chiefly due to the custom of seeking a wife in another village and females preponderate among the migrants. In the Agency this is much the commonest class.

II. *Temporary.*—Caused by pilgrimages, fairs such as that of Khajaraho in Chhatarpur and temporary employment on works. In the former case females are apt to be in excess, but on works men preponderate.

III. *Periodic.*—Due to migration for harvest work at stated seasons. Men ordinarily preponderate in this case. It is not a common form in Central India.

IV. *Semi-permanent.*—This form is not common in the Agency. It is caused by men living in one place, where they earn their livelihood, while their families live elsewhere. In former days this was a common form in Maratha States, where the large following of Dakshni officials kept up a close touch with their homes south of the Narbada. Now, however, these families have to a very great extent become localised.

V. *Permanent.*—This is caused by overcrowding or attraction to other districts. This is only met with in Central India as the result of the latter cause in places where better administration attracts cultivators from one State to another or bad administration has driven the people away.

**Conditions affecting Migration.**

18. The last Census following on the heels of a severe famine found a sadly diminished population. Since then, while there have been local lean years leading in some parts to distress, no famine has attacked the Agency sufficient to cause any marked exodus, nor has any severe distress outside caused a great flow inwards.

Trade, while it has on the whole progressed, has not made any gigantic strides. Harvesting was over before the Census took place and no influx occurred on this account.

Disease in the form of plague has been the most disturbing factor, but while it causes temporary movement it does not have any permanent effect, and its influence was in this instance mainly felt in big towns.

No large public works have been opened sufficient to very materially affect results.

Improved means of communication and administrative improvements have to some extent affected movement between States.

The only large fair held during the Census was that of Khajaraho in Chhatarpur held from 27th February to 20th March. Special arrangements were made, as in 1901, for dealing with this concentration of people. Large numbers came from the United Provinces to attend the fair.

**Migration.**

19. It may be remarked before proceeding to discuss results that the Census makes no real distinction between the various kinds of migrations, and except for the partial indication afforded by the relative proportions of the sexes it is not possible to distinguish them.

Of the 9,356,980 persons enumerated in the Agency, over 8,880,000 were born within its limits, leaving only 5 per cent. born outside, of whom 3·4 were born in the contiguous districts.

**Central India and Foreign Countries.**

20. The figures for those born beyond India may be briefly dismissed as they are of no particular interest. Of the 3,864 persons so born, 3,283 were born in Europe, 3,171 being chiefly officials in civil and military employ; 355 were born in other Asiatic countries, of whom 178 were Afghans, for the most part in military employ.

**Movement in India.**

21. The total number of immigrants from India into the Agency was 470,000 in 1911 as compared with 668,000 in 1901, emigrants amounting to 536,000 as compared with 454,000.

The larger number of immigrants in 1901 was due to the influx of famine-stricken, especially from the United Provinces, Rajputana and Bombay. The increase of 82,000 among emigrants on this occasion occurs in Rajputana, the Central Provinces and Bombay. This movement was temporary and caused by the exodus on account of plague from towns on the Plateau.

**United Provinces.**

22. The greatest number of immigrants come from this Province amounting to 36 per cent. of the total immigrants, while the Agency sends 37 per cent. of its emigrants to it. The intermingling of the boundaries of several of the districts with those of the States is responsible for this; throughout females are in excess, the movement being almost wholly due to the custom of seeking a wife in a distant village. The greater part of the movement takes place in the Low-lying Natural Division in which tract this intermingling of territories mainly occurs, Jhansi alone sending any considerable number to the Plateau Division, chiefly to Gwalior territory.

| District. | Emigration from the United Provinces. | | | |
|---|---|---|---|---|
| | Total. | Males. | Females. | Chiefly to |
| Agra | 9,800 | 3,900 | 5,900 | Gwalior. |
| Allahabad | 8,200 | 4,500 | 3,700 | Rewah. |
| Banda | 21,300 | 7,500 | 13,800 | Baghelkhand and Bundelkhand. |
| Hamirpur | 32,000 | 12,000 | 20,000 | Bundelkhand. |
| Jhansi | 36,600 | 9,900 | 26,700 | Gwalior and Bundelkhand. |
| Others | 61,100 | 30,200 | 30,900 | |
| Total | 169,000 | 68,000 | 101,000 | |

The disparity between males and females is greatest in the movement to the Low-lying tract, which agrees with the view that marriage is the cause.

**Rajputana.**

23. Rajputana followed the United Provinces in importance sending 149,000 or 32 per cent., it receiving in return 101,000 from the Agency. Women are here also in excess except in the case of Jaipur and is due to marriage transactions between Rajputs and Marwaris. A considerable increase of emigrants to Rajputana has taken place. This is explained by the fall in immigrants as compared with 1901. Most of these people had entered Malwa in 1900 in hopes of relief from famine. They later on returned home. A certain number, no doubt, were also recent refugees from plague-stricken localities in Malwa.

| State. | Emigration from Rajputana. | | | |
|---|---|---|---|---|
| | Total. | Males. | Females. | Chiefly to |
| Jaipur | 26,000 | 14,000 | 12,000 | Gwalior and Indore. |
| Jhalawar | 8,800 | 3,700 | 5,100 | Indore and Malwa. |
| Kotah | 16,200 | 6,800 | 9,400 | Gwalior and Indore. |
| Tonk | 16,000 | 7,000 | 9,000 | Gwalior. |
| Others | 77,000 | 35,500 | 41,500 | |
| Total | 144,000 | 67,000 | 77,000 | |

**The Central Provinces and Berars.**

24. The Central Provinces send 80,000 persons to the Agency and receive in return 198,000.

Most of the movement is from border districts. The immigrants pass mainly into the Hilly tracts of Bundelkhand and Baghelkhand while Saugor sends a considerable number into Gwalior, Bhopal and Panna. Females are here also in excess.

| District. | Emigration from Central Provinces and Berars. | | | |
|---|---|---|---|---|
| | Total. | Males. | Females. | Chiefly to |
| Hoshangabad | 18,500 | 6,700 | 11,800 | Bhopal and Indore. |
| Jubbulpore | 15,500 | 5,400 | 10,100 | Rewah, Maihar and Panna. |
| Saugor | 15,600 | 6,200 | 9,400 | Gwalior Bhopal and Panna. |
| Nimar | 4,800 | 1,400 | 3,400 | Indore. |
| Others | 25,600 | 11,500 | 14,100 | |
| Total | 80,000 | 31,200 | 48,800 | |

**Other Provinces and States.**

25. Of the remaining Provinces Bombay sends 54,000 and receives 19,000. Here also most of the movement is between the neighbouring districts of Khandesh and the Panch Mahals, those concerned being mainly Bhils and kindred tribes. Females are in excess only in the Hilly tract where the Bhils move to and fro in search of wives.

**Internal Movements.**

26. An analysis of the internal movement between the three Natural Divisions proves that 66 per cent. of the immigrants were persons born in the Agency who passed to and fro, while 24 per cent. came from just over the borders.

Subsidiary Table IV shows that in the Plateau out of every 100 persons born within its limits 94 still resided there while 5 in every 100 were born within the Hilly tract which adjoins it; in the Low-lying area out of every 100 of the home-born 86 were still within the tract, while 7 were enumerated in the contiguous Hilly tract; in the Hilly tract out of every 100 born within its limits 92 were enumerated locally and 8 in the Plateau area. This shows that movement is more common in the Low-lying area than it is in the other two

DIAGRAM

SHOWING THE PROPORTION OF IMMIGRANTS IN EACH NATURAL DIVISION:

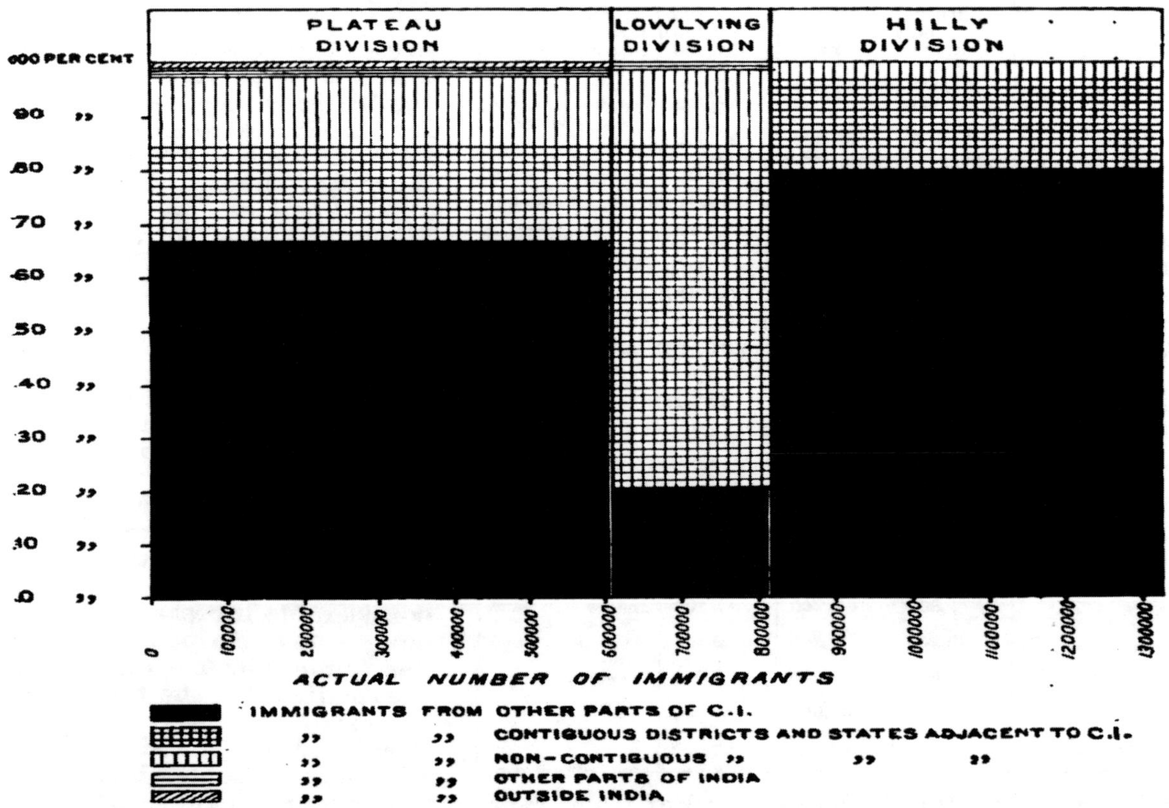


Natural Divisions. An examination of the figures for the States shows that this movement depends almost wholly on the nature of the borders. When there is much intermingling of boundaries movement appears greater and where areas are compact it is less. Thus Bhopal, Rewah, Orchha and Jhabua show a home-born percentage of over 90, Datia, Panna and Chhatarpur of over 80, while in the case of Charkhari and the Malwa States of Indore, Dhar, Ratlam, etc., the percentage of home-born falls to 70 and below. The Gwalior district figures also illustrate this. In Northern Gwalior, which is a large compact area with well defined borders, the percentage of home-born is higher than in the Malwa districts where the Zilas are not defined by well marked boundaries and State areas are much intermingled. Emigration to a distance takes place very little. Out of 536,000 emigrants only 20,900 or 39 in every 1,000 persons went to non-contiguous areas. The most important figures are given in the inset. To Assam and Bihar and Orissa men go to work in the tea gardens. They belong mainly to the agricultural classes and come principally from districts of Rewah, Bhopal and Gwalior. Those who go to the Punjab are chiefly members of the families of men employed in the Settlement Department and State forces.

| Percentage of home-born. | |
|---|---|
| **Northern Gwalior** | **89** |
| Gwalior Gird | 91 |
| Bhind | 89 |
| Tonwarghar | 90 |
| Sheopur | 89 |
| Narwar | 87 |
| **Malwa Districts** | **77** |
| Ujjain | 77 |
| Mandasor | 69 |
| Shajapur | 85 |
| Amjhera | 76 |

| EMIGRATION | | | |
|---|---|---|---|
| To | | Mainly from | |
| Bengal | 2,700 | Gwalior | 1,600 |
| | | Rewah | 500 |
| Assam | 7,000 | Rewah | 5,000 |
| | | Bhopal | 1,700 |
| Bihar and Orissa | 3,600 | Gwalior | 1,300 |
| | | Rewah | 900 |
| | | Bundelkhand | 700 |
| Punjab | 3,000 | Gwalior | 2,300 |

The immigrants from the Punjab are mainly soldiers and show an excess of males. The 3,600 emigrants are from Gwalior, Indore, Bhopal and Bundelkhand.

Of the immigrants from Baroda 73 per cent. go to the Maratha States of Gwalior (315), and Indore (1,339), here they are largely men employed by the State Public Works Department, Dhar (69) and the two Dewas States (99) with which it has political relations. The curious figures are those of Barwani (268). The reason for the unusually large number in this case is due to Kolis and Bhils who have migrated to Barwani in search of employment; most of them were working as labourers and some as cultivators.

Bengal takes 2,700 and sends 1,000. The movement is mainly with Gwalior, Rewah, Indore and Bundelkhand, where there are Bengali communities who keep up connection with their Province.

Of the 2,000 sent by Hyderabad 936 are employed in the British army and are found in the Cantonments of Nimach and Mhow, the rest being in Gwalior and Indore where they number 219 and 258, Bhopal and Rewah also returning 185 and 131.

The other figures are unimportant.

### *Summary.*

27. The results here discussed disclose the actual state of affairs on 10th March 1911, which depends on the local conditions then prevailing—a loss as between immigrants and emigrants of 65,000 persons is recorded as compared with a gain, in 1901, of 215,000. This was expected as the number of immigrants in 1901 was swelled by the famine-stricken from Rajputana and United Provinces who came into the Agency, especially into Malwa, hoping for relief. Added to this, a certain exodus was caused on this occasion by plague. The loss is, therefore, not a genuine fall in the indigenous population.

As elsewhere in India the salient features of the migratory movements are the smallness of the number which moves and the limited area within which the movement takes place. The map in the inset gives the ebb and flow between

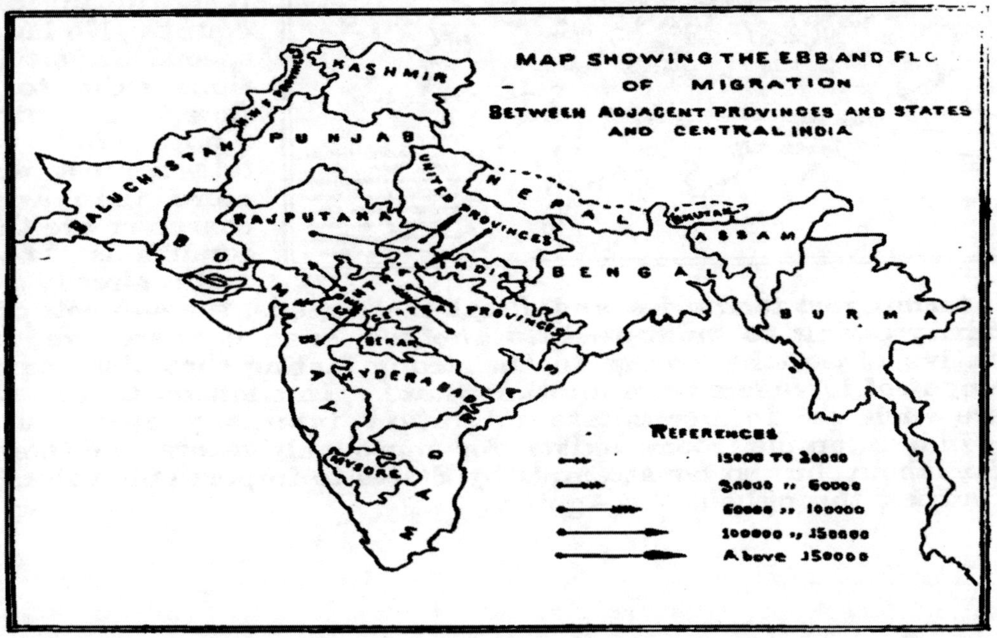


the chief States and contiguous tracts outside the Agency. Of every 1,000 persons in Central India 949 were born within its borders while 34 were born in contiguous areas. Migration, therefore, in the true sense of the term, does not exist, the movements responsible for these figures being due mainly to marriage customs among Hindus which usually require a man to seek a wife outside the village in which he resides, and also necessitate the return of the bride to her parents' house for the first confinement. The extent of this movement as has been duly noted depends very largely on the nature of the border line. In Bundelkhand where the British India districts are intermingled with the States and the boundaries are purely political, there is much freer intercourse between those living in British India and the States while in Malwa and Northern Gwalior where the boundaries are better defined, the movement is less. The main causes of fluctuation are alterations in the mutual conditions of the community which in an agricultural tract like Central India depends on the seasons. This fact is very clearly brought out by the figures on this occasion. A serious epidemic such as plague, though also a disturbing factor, is only temporary while its effects are not so far-reaching. Except for certain communities, such as that of the Marwari merchants, those who leave their homes on account of plague seldom move far, and though, owing to the interlacing of State boundaries, such movement may cause a considerable fall in some particular district or State, the diminution in the population of the Agency as a whole is insignificant on this account. No large works or special industrial attractions exist to induce a flow of immigrants. Another force which militates against movement of more than a temporary character are the peculiar conditions of Central India already referred to with its intermingled territories and fiscal restrictions, the subjects of one State not ordinarily caring to migrate into another even if there are no serious administrative objections, owing to the strong feeling that often exists against the settlement of intruders from another State. In addition to this the density is nowhere such as to necessitate migration internally owing to the overpressure; indeed ample room exists for more cultivators and there is a great demand for labour, but so far attempts by States to import cultivators have had but little success throughout the Agency.

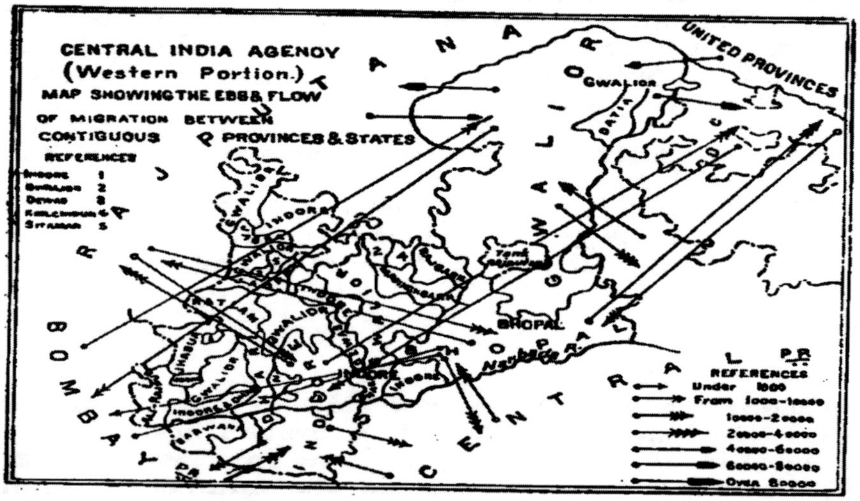


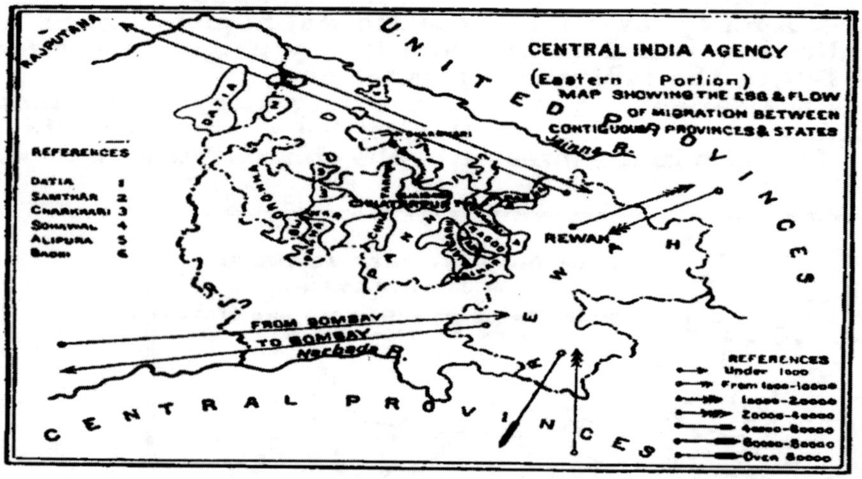

## SUBSIDIARY TABLE I.—Immigration. (Actual figures.)

| Natural Division where enumerated. | Born in (000's omitted). | | | | | | | | | | | | | | | | | |
|---|---|---|---|---|---|---|---|---|---|---|---|---|---|---|---|---|---|---|
| | Natural Division. | | | Contiguous district in Central India. | | | Other parts of Central India. | | | Contiguous parts of other Provinces, etc. | | | Non-contiguous parts of other Provinces, etc. | | | Outside India. | | |
| | Total. | Males. | Females. | Total. | Males. | Females. | Total. | Males. | Females. | Total. | Males. | Females. | Total. | Males. | Females. | Total. | Males. | Females. |
| 1 | 2 | 3 | 4 | 5 | 6 | 7 | 8 | 9 | 10 | 11 | 12 | 13 | 14 | 15 | 16 | 17 | 18 | 19 |
| **Central India** | **8,882** | **4,586** | **4,296** | ... | ... | ... | ... | ... | ... | **321** | **131** | **190** | **149** | **80** | **69** | **4** | **3** | **1** |
| Plateau | 3,073 | 1,597 | 1,476 | ... | ... | ... | 411 | 203 | 208 | 104 | 49 | 55 | 93 | 52 | 41 | 3 | 3 | ... |
| Low-lying tract | 3,110 | 1,638 | 1,472 | ... | ... | ... | 40 | 18 | 22 | 128 | 42 | 86 | 31 | 15 | 16 | 1 | 1 | ... |
| Hilly tract | 1,822 | 917 | 905 | ... | ... | ... | 427 | 214 | 203 | 89 | 40 | 49 | 25 | 13 | 12 | ... | ... | ... |

## SUBSIDIARY TABLE II.—Emigration. (Actual figures.)

| Natural Division of Birth. | Enumerated in (000's omitted). | | | | | | | | | | | | | | | | | |
|---|---|---|---|---|---|---|---|---|---|---|---|---|---|---|---|---|---|---|
| | Natural Division. | | | Contiguous district in Central India. | | | Other parts of Central India. | | | Contiguous parts of other Provinces, etc. | | | Non-contiguous parts of other Provinces, etc. | | | Outside India. | | |
| | Total. | Males. | Females. | Total. | Males. | Females. | Total. | Males. | Females. | Total. | Males. | Females. | Total. | Males. | Females. | Total. | Males. | Females. |
| 1 | 2 | 3 | 4 | 5 | 6 | 7 | 8 | 9 | 10 | 11 | 12 | 13 | 14 | 15 | 16 | 17 | 18 | 19 |
| **Central India** | **8,882** | **4,586** | **4,296** | ... | ... | ... | ... | ... | ... | **515** | **218** | **297** | **20** | **12** | **8** | ... | ... | ... |
| Plateau | 3,073 | 1,597 | 1,476 | ... | ... | ... | 201 | 100 | 101 | 104 | 46 | 58 | 5 | 3 | 2 | ... | ... | ... |
| Low-lying tract | 3,110 | 1,638 | 1,472 | ... | ... | ... | 510 | 250 | 260 | 409 | 172 | 237 | 15 | 9 | 6 | ... | ... | ... |
| Hilly tract | 1,822 | 917 | 905 | ... | ... | ... | 167 | 85 | 82 | 2 | 1 | 1 | ... | ... | ... | ... | ... | ... |

## SUBSIDIARY TABLE III.—Proportional Migration to and from each Natural Division.

| Natural Division. | Number per mille of actual population of | | | | | | Number of females to 100 males amongst | | | |
|---|---|---|---|---|---|---|---|---|---|---|
| | Immigrants. | | | Emigrants. | | | Immigrants. | | Emigrants. | |
| | Total. | From contiguous district. | From other places. | Total. | To contiguous district. | To other places. | From contiguous district. | From other places. | To contiguous district. | To other places. |
| 1 | 2 | 3 | 4 | 5 | 6 | 7 | 8 | 9 | 10 | 11 |
| **Central India** | **51** | **34** | **17** | **57** | **55** | **2** | **144** | **86** | **136** | **65** |
| Plateau | 166 | 28 | 138 | 84 | 28 | 56 | 111 | 97 | 128 | 101 |
| Low-lying tract | 61 | 39 | 22 | 282 | 123 | 159 | 204 | 115 | 138 | 103 |
| Hilly tract | 229 | 38 | 191 | 71 | 1 | 70 | 122 | 99 | 228 | 96 |

## SUBSIDIARY TABLE IV.—Migration between Natural Division (actual figures) compared with 1901.

| Natural Division in which born. | | Number enumerated (000's omitted) in Natural Division. | | |
|---|---|---|---|---|
| | | Plateau. | Low-lying tract. | Hilly tract. |
| 1 | | 2 | 3 | 4 |
| Plateau | 1911 | 3,073 | 31 | 179 |
| | 1901 | ... | ... | ... |
| Low-lying tract | 1911 | 253 | 3,110 | 257 |
| | 1901 | .. | ... | ... |
| Hilly tract | 1911 | 158 | 9 | 1,893 |
| | 1901 | ... | ... | ... |
| | Total | 3,484 | 3,150 | 2,349 |

Note.—Natural Division figures for 1901 are not available.

SUBSIDIARY TABLE V.—**Migration between Central India and other parts of India.**

| Province or State. | Immigrants to Central India. | | | Emigrants from Central India. | | | Excess (+) or deficiency (—) of Immigration over Emigration. | |
|---|---|---|---|---|---|---|---|---|
| | 1911. | 1901. | Variation. | 1911. | 1901. | Variation. | 1911. | 1901. |
| 1 | 2 | 3 | 4 | 5 | 6 | 7 | 8 | 9 |
| **Total** | **470,391** | **668,525** | **—198,134** | **536,076** | **453,660** | **+82,416** | **—65,685** | **+214,865** |
| **British Territory** | **464,979** | **661,120** | **—196,141** | **533,709** | **448,426** | **+85,283** | **—68,730** | **+212,694** |
| United Provinces of Agra and Oudh | 168,736 | 319,694 | — 150,959 | 195,815 | 199,319 | — 3,377 | — 27,080 | + 120,840 |
| Do. States | 395 | 465 | — 70 | 127 | | | + 268 | |
| Central Provinces and Berar | 80,057 | 66,978 | + 13,083 | 179,479 | 148,618 | + 49,942 | — 99,422 | — 81,640 |
| Do. States | 4 | | | 19,081 | | | — 19,077 | |
| Bombay Presidency including Aden. | 47,165 | 70,119 | — 22,954 | 15,133 | 11,528 | + 7,716 | + 32,032 | + 63,865 |
| Do. States | 6,946 | 5,274 | + 1,672 | 4,111 | | | + 2,835 | |
| Ajmer-Merwara | 5,226 | 1,266 | + 3,960 | 2,046 | 56,471 | + 44,904 | + 3,180 | + 118,131 |
| Rajputana States | 144,401 | 173,336 | — 28,935 | 99,329 | | | + 45,072 | |
| Punjab | 7,859 | 14,664 | — 5,819 | 3,127 | 3,692 | + 29 | + 4,732 | + 10,972 |
| Do. States | 423 | | | 503 | | | — 80 | |
| North-West Frontier Province | 563 | | | 91 | | | + 472 | |
| Assam | 8 | 5,039 | — 2,912 | 7,102 | 23,117 | — 9,264 | — 7,094 | — 18,078 |
| Do. States | ... | | | 2 | | | — 2 | |
| Bihar and Orissa | 1,047 | | | 3,058 | | | — 2,011 | |
| Do. States | 68 | | | 530 | | | — 462 | |
| Bengal | 1,004 | | | 2,659 | | | — 1,655 | |
| Do. States | ... | | | 14 | | | — 14 | |
| Eastern Bengal | ... | | | 464 | | | — 464 | |
| Do. States | ... | | | 24 | | | — 24 | |
| Madras | 1,033 | 1,026 | + 9 | 503 | 479 | + 25 | + 530 | + 547 |
| Do. States | 2 | | | 1 | | | + 1 | |
| Baluchistan | 20 | ... | + 20 | 133 | ... | + 133 | — 113 | ... |
| Do. States | 10 | ... | + 10 | ... | ... | ... | +10 | ... |
| Burma | 13 | ... | + 13 | 221 | 218 | + 3 | — 208 | — 218 |
| Andamans and Nicobars | ... | ... | ... | 156 | ... | + 156 | — 156 | ... |
| British India, unspecified | ... | 3,259 | — 3,259 | ... | 4,984 | — 4,984 | ... | — 1,725 |
| **Native States** | **5,220** | **7,087** | **— 1,867** | **2,100** | **5,234** | **— 3,134** | **+ 3,120** | **+ 1,853** |
| Baroda | 2,482 | 4,452 | — 1,970 | 1,413 | 819 | + 594 | + 1,069 | + 3,633 |
| Hyderabad | 2,177 | 2,627 | — 450 | 565 | 4,347 | — 3,782 | + 1,612 | — 1,720 |
| Mysore | 491 | ... | + 491 | 85 | 39 | + 46 | + 406 | — 39 |
| Kashmir and Jammu | 70 | 8 | + 62 | 35 | 29 | + 6 | + 35 | — 21 |
| Sikkim | ... | ... | ... | 2 | ... | + 2 | — 2 | ... |
| **Foreign Settlements** | **192** | **318** | **— 126** | ... | ... | ... | **+ 192** | **+ 318** |
| Portuguese Settlement | 177 | 318 | — 141 | ... | ... | ... | + 177 | + 318 |
| French Settlement | 15 | ... | + 15 | ... | ... | ... | + 15 | ... |
| **Foreign British Colonies** | ... | ... | ... | **267** | ... | **+ 267** | **— 267** | ... |
| Fiji | ... | ... | ... | 259 | ... | + 259 | — 259 | .. |
| Uganda | ... | ... | ... | 5 | ... | + 5 | — 5 | ... |
| Ceylon | ... | ... | ... | 1 | ... | + 1 | — 1 | ... |
| Federated Malay States | ... | ... | ... | 2 | ... | + 2 | — 2 | ... |

# CHAPTER IV.

## Religion.

### *Introductory.*

28. The results dealt with in this Chapter are collected in the Tables VI, XVII and XVIII and in the Subsidiary Tables at the end of the text.

| Religion. | Number in 1911. | Number in 1901. |
|---|---|---|
| *Total* | *9,357,000* | *8,498,000* |
| Hindus | 8,263,000 | 6,868,000 |
| Musalmans | 511,000 | 515,000 |
| Jains | 88,000 | 112,000 |
| Animists | 483,000 | 992,000 |
| Christians | 9,000 | 8,000 |
| Others | 3,000 | 3,000 |

The record of sects in 1901 furnished only a wilderness of names and the inquiry was, therefore, not repeated on this occasion.

The enormous predominance of Hindus in Central India is clearly shown here, the next most important community forming only $\frac{1}{18}$ of the total population.

The general distribution by religions in the last two enumerations is given in the inset.

The most noticeable points in these figures are that Hindus have risen by 20 per cent. while Animists have fallen by 51 per cent. This is mainly due to more accurate recording of religions in all parts but especially in the Gwalior and Rewah States. In 1901, owing to the want of schools of instruction for enumerators all classes met with in jungle tracts, and in the Baghelkhand Political Charge in particular, were indiscriminately returned as Animists. The other causes influencing results are actual increase or decrease, migration and conversion. In the Bhopawar Agency and in the Indore State districts along the line of the Vindhyas and Satpuras the Bhils, who suffered severely in the famine of 1899-1900, have recovered and a rise averaging 30 per cent. has taken place in the population of this area. A similar rise is met with in Khandesh and other neighbouring districts of British India.

***Increase in Jungle tract in general population and Jungle tribes:***

| Locality. | Increase per cent. General population. | Increase per cent. Jungle tribes. |
|---|---|---|
| **Central India—** | | |
| Jhabua | 37 | 72 |
| Barwani | 43 | 55 |
| Ali Rajpur | 44 | 69 |
| **British Districts—** | | |
| Panch Mahals | 24 | 39 |
| Rewa Kantha | 39 | 70 |
| Khandesh | 13 | 26 |

While the effects of migration are negligible in the Agency as a whole, Hinduism on the other hand continues the steady process of gathering the jungle tribes within her pale. During the actual census a somewhat unfortunate tendency to return as many persons as possible as Hindus was caused by the manifesto issued by the All-India Moslem League. This manifesto dealt with the raising of the submerged classes of India, but gave rise to the idea that all such persons would be converted to Muhammadanism.

The Musalman population has fallen 0·8 per cent., an unimportant variation. Jains have fallen by 21 per cent. In each of these cases, but especially in the latter, the fact that many of the largest towns were half empty owing to plague is the main cause of the fall.

Christians show a rise of 15 per cent. which includes a rise of over 34 per cent. in the Bundelkhand and of 160 per cent. in the Bhopawar Agency. This rise in the Bundelkhand Agency is among the Christians in the Nowgong Cantonment and is fortuitous. In the Bhopawar Agency and the Hilly tract it is due to the great rise in the number of Christians among the Bhils due to conversions by the Roman Catholic and the Presbyterian Missions.

| Christian population in | | |
|---|---|---|
| State. | 1911. | 1901. |
| Dhar . . . . . | 71 | 58 |
| Jhabua . . . . . | 110 | 76 |
| Ali Rajpur . . . . | 187 | 18 |
| Jobat . . . . . | 8 | 0 |
| Barwani . . . . | 12 | 9 |

The urban and rural figures show that Jains, Musalmans and Christians are mainly town dwellers, the Jains being traders and the Musalmans either in military service or the police, or shopkeepers. The Christians are almost all Europeans or Anglo-Indians. The country is thus peopled almost wholly by Hindus, even Animists forming only 5 per cent.

### *Hindus.*

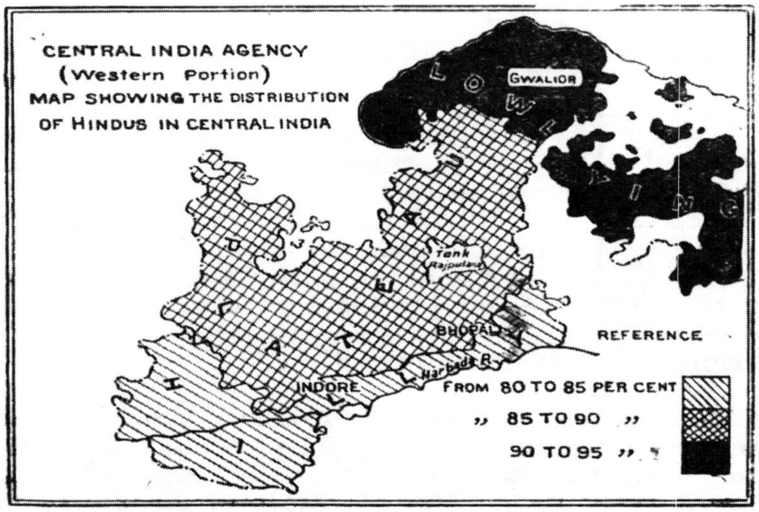


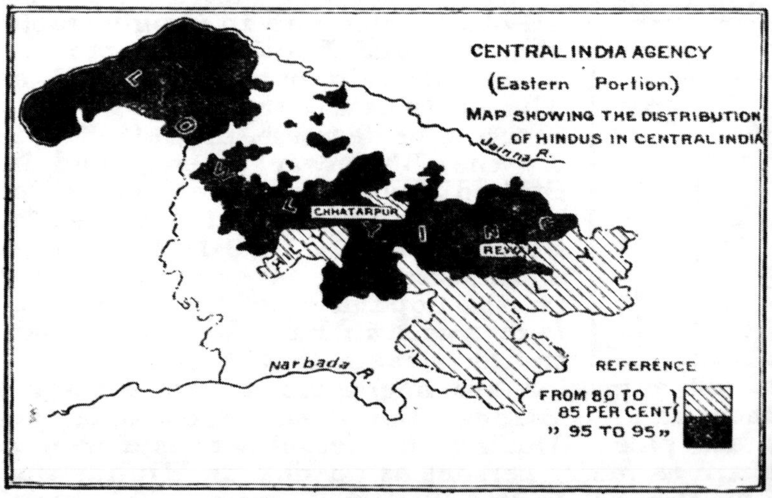


29. Of the total population nearly 90 per cent. are Hindus. They predominate, as is natural, in the Plateau and Low-lying areas with their highly cultivated tracts. In urban areas their superiority is diminished by an increase of the Musalman population, a ratio more emphasised in the Plateau than in the Low-lying area, the ratio in the latter case rising to 96 per cent., and falling to 80 per cent. only, even in the Hilly tracts, where the Animistic classes are met with.

Of the political charges, Gwalior Residency has the largest population of Hindus. Malwa, now a very small charge, stands last, the existence of the Jaora State raising the proportion of Musalmans, while Ratlam town as the principal Jain centre in Central India causes a predominance of this religion. Save in the Hilly tract the distribution is identical, 38 per cent. throughout the Agency.

Definition of Hindu.

30. The Census Commissioner pointed out that the Census return for Hindus was considered misleading by certain authorities inasmuch as many were included under this term who were not strict Hindus. Careful inquiries were made from the larger States which elicited practically the unanimous opinion that every person calling himself a Hindu who did not profess some definite faith other than Hinduism in its widest sense was a Hindu. The Census

Commissioner also proposed certain tests which he considered might prove useful in differentiating Hindus and Non-Hindus, *viz.* :—

i. Do members of the caste or tribe worship the great Hindu deities ?
ii. Are they allowed to enter Hindu temples or make offerings at the shrine ?
iii. Will good Brahmans act as their priests* ?
iv. Will degraded Brahmans do so ? In that case are they recognised as Brahmans by persons outside the caste or are they Brahmans only in name ?
v. Will clean castes take water from them ?
vi. Do they cause pollution (*a*) by touch, (*b*) by proximity ?

These tests were rejected entirely as being capable of distinguishing castes and social grades but assisting in no way whatsoever towards the differentiation of Hindus and Non-Hindus. Thus the application of tests 2, 5 and 6 would exclude all unclean castes (*ati-shudra*) while 1, 3, and 4 would exclude practically all *shudras*.

It was held that the worship of minor deities only by the members of any caste or tribe in no way debars them from being Hindus, even when such worship is frankly animistic. Such persons are considered as being still uneducated and ignorant and uninstructed in the best forms of devotion, but are none the less Hindus and as soon as knowledge is imparted to them will turn to the more orthodox deities, their local gods being relegated to a less important position but still being recognised as deities with local power whom the most orthodox Hindu would admit had claims to consideration. Permission to enter a shrine is governed rather by local custom than ordinance. Thus the Mahars worship Vithoba in the temple at Pandharpur, but are not allowed to approach nearer than a certain flight of steps to their god ; at Dattatreya's temple at Wadi near Kolhapur no Panch Gaud Brahman is allowed to enter although the Panch Dravids may do so freely, yet both are admittedly Brahmans of good class. In southern India in particular, Brahmans are debarred from entering many parts of temples. Generally speaking Dhobis, Kalars, Balais, Kumhars, Mochis, Kanjars, Kolis and others are excluded from temples owing to the nature of their occupations and their mode of living. But in Gujarat certain Kumhars, held elsewhere as unclean, are considered clean, while in parts of Bundelkhand Khangars, Balais, Baris and Chhipis (tailors) are admitted to temples, although no high caste man will accept water from their hands. The employment of Brahmans is also only a test of status as is also the acceptance of water. These customs often vary locally. Thus in Central India Audich Brahmans living beyond the southern border within Khandesh will not accept water from any but Brahmans, but as soon as they cross over into the Agency they will dine with other Audich families and will accept water drawn by Kachhis and Ahirs. Brahmans of the same class in Malwa and Nimar differ in that the former refuse to accept water drawn by Kahars while the latter drink it, a local distinction. Till quite lately Audich and Malwi Brahmans would not accept *kachchi* from each other, now they have commenced to dine together freely.

Pollution by proximity merely is not known in Central India, and that by touch is only a caste matter.

Many of the great saints of India have been of the unclean castes as for instance Rohidas and Sajjan Kasai who were Chamars and Chaukamela a Mahar.

Dhobis, Mochis, Chamars, Balais, etc., who follow Hindu rites and customs have an undisputed claim to be considered Hindus and the extension of the claim to lower and less sophisticated classes is not illogical.

Even those professing reformed or connected faiths are held to come within the pale of Hinduism such as Sikhs, Jains, Brahmos, Aryas, Dhamis, etc., who have creeds based more or less on Hindu scriptures, and who follow rites and customs modified from those observed by the orthodox.

Definition under these circumstances is scarcely possible and there is, moreover, a distinct general *Indian* idea attaching to the term Hindu. The nearest definition for a Hindu derivable from these views would perhaps be "Every native of India whose ancestors have always been recognised as Hindus, and who does not profess a faith deliberately antipathetic to doctrines based, to however small a degree, on Hindu sentiment and who follows rites and customs derived from or tinged by orthodox Brahmanical practices."

* Exception was taken to the use of terms good and degraded.

The idea of India is essential as it is most deliberately stated that no non-Indian,* however strict in adhering to the minutest Hindu rites and observances, can ever become a Hindu.

One or two Darbars sent short lists of those who might possibly not be deemed Hindus including most of the unclean castes and jungle tribes, but even in these cases they were diffident regarding the classification.

### *Animists.*

31. The Animist class, so called for want of a better name, included all persons who, when asked to state their religion, replied that they were not Hindus, Musalmans, etc., and belonged in fact to none of the recognised forms of faith. All Animists are members of jungle tribes such as the Bhil. Not a very exact or happy term, the name Animist serves to denote a person who believes in the existence and omnipresence of spirit bodies or souls, of whom the most powerful are considered divine beings with powers for good and evil in this world. These spirits are untrammeled in their movements and at will enter into and abide temporarily or permanently in some object living or lifeless which then becomes an object of awe and worship. It is clear that Animism has not only played an important part in all faiths but may also be detected more or less concealed in the most advanced religions of to-day.

To obtain a really correct return of so nebulous a form of belief is no easy matter, and necessarily much must be left, in spite of careful instructions, to the idiosyncracy of the enumerator. It becomes indeed for census purposes a mere negation of connection with any recognised faith, the enumerator in all such cases entering the Tribal name in the 4th column in place of that of a religion.

The Animistic tribes, as the representatives of an early civilisation which was forced to retreat before the streams of immigrants from the north and take refuge in the wildest parts of the tract, are met with mainly along the Vindhya and Satpura ranges and include Bhils, Patlias, Gonds, etc. They are, therefore, most numerous in the Bhopawar Political Charge and the Hilly tract Natural Division.

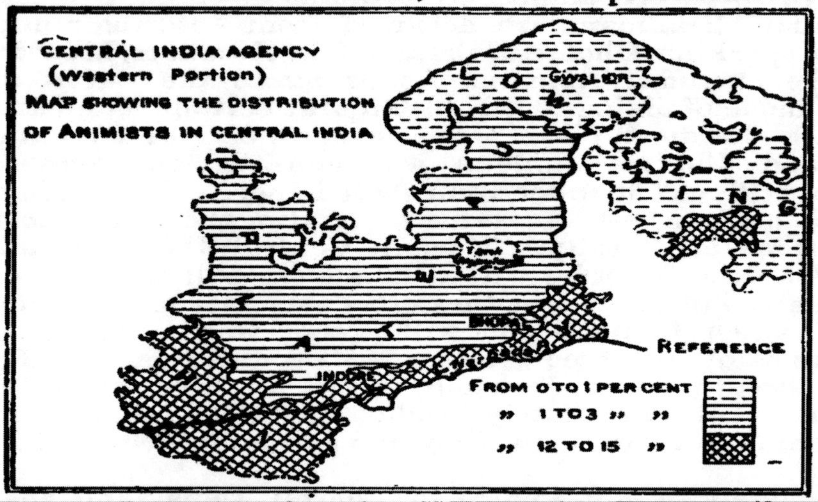


Indeed the greater number live in the States of Jhabua, Ali Rajpur and Barwani which possess 39 per cent. of the total Animistic population of Central India.

Better enumeration has caused a very striking fall of over 50 per cent. in the number of Animists, of which most occurs in the Baghelkhand Political Charge.

To a certain extent the ever increasing tendency of the jungle tribes to enrol themselves as Hindus is also responsible for this fall.

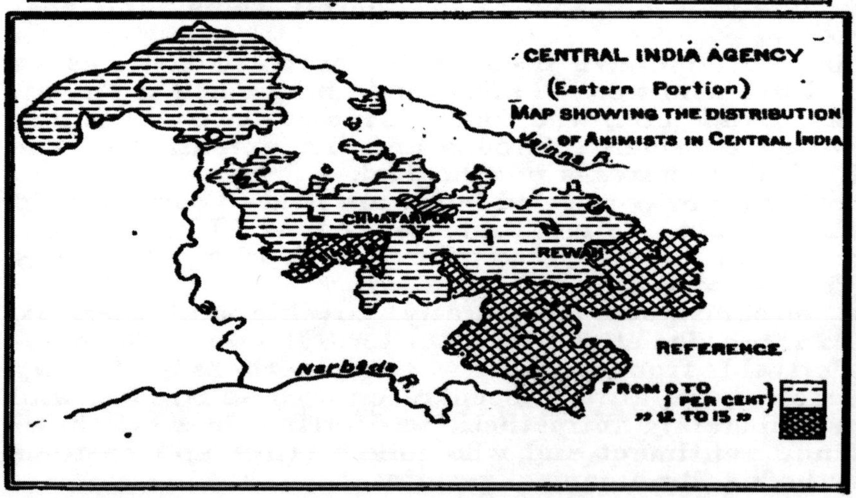


---

* Mrs. Besant was instanced.

It is unnecessary to deal at length with this well known process. Regular settlements are becoming the order of the day, schools increase yearly in number and roads and railways are opening out the forest tracts, thus raising the standard of civilisation, making the members of the jungle tribes realise the semi-outcaste position they hold and rendering them more prone to enter the Hindu fold; ten years hence the figures should fall still further, while it will be interesting to note how far the further extension of Hinduism into this field will tend to restrict the success of missionaries. The number of Indian Christians drawn from this class has increased by 140 per cent. but their number is not yet sufficient to make any material difference.

On the other hand better enumeration has raised the numbers in the Bhopal Agency where in 1901 the enumeration in the south of that State was indifferent. Another cause of the rise is a genuine increase of the jungle population averaging 30 per cent. in the country south of the Vindhyas, an increase shared by the British Districts just over the border. The famine of 1899-1900 hit the inhabitants of this region very hard and the figures in the 1901 census clearly proved its effect. A series of good years has resulted in the natural rebound. This cause is also partly responsible for the rise in the Bhopal State.

The numbers of the important jungle tribes returned as Hindus and Animists is given on the fly sheet to Table VI which shows that Bhils and Bhilalas alone return more Animists than Hindus and the difference in favour of Hindus is certain to increase every decade.

A general rise in the Hindu population has taken place.

The greatest increase is shown in the Baghelkhand Political Charge and in the Hilly tract. Migration plays so small a part in Central India as a whole that its effects may be neglected.

**Variation among Hindus and Animists.**

32. The variation between Hindus and Animists in the Census of 1901 and 1911 is so remarkable as to require special mention. In 1901 no schools of instruction were held until very late when it was impossible to train the enumerators fully. The result was that the rule regarding the record of a man's religion was often disregarded, especially in Rewah where all those living in the hilly districts were returned indiscriminately as "Animists."

The insct shows the percentage of variation for the largest states as a whole and for the Hilly tract, in the case of these two religions. In Gwalior the greatest fall in the Animistic figures took place among the Saharias, Kirars and Minas met with in the hilly country in Northern Gwalior where a fall of 95 per cent. is recorded. In Indore the Nimar and Nemawar districts shew respectively a rise of 63 and 55 per cent. among Hindus and a fall of 51 and 80 per cent. among Animists, chiefly Bharuds, Patlias and Korkus, while the Mehidpur district shews a rise of 34 per cent. among Hindus and a fall of 77 per cent. in its Animistic population chiefly Bharuds and Korkus.

| | VARIATION PER CENT AMONG HINDUS AND ANIMISTS. | | | | | | | |
|---|---|---|---|---|---|---|---|---|
| | Gwalior. | | Indore. | | Bhopal. | | Rewah. | |
| | State. | Hilly. | State. | Hilly. | State. | Hilly. | State. | Hilly. |
| Hindus | +14 | +51 | +30 | +60 | +20 | +35 | +46 | +73 |
| Animists | —73 | —16 | —53 | —70 | —36 | -71 | —100 | —100 |

In Bhopal the variation is similar, chiefly among Gonds and Korkus.

Turning to Rewah the source of the great fall in the Animistic population of the Agency is at once discovered. In 1901 Rewah returned 280,000 Animists mainly Gonds and Kols but on this occasion only 10! This variation is wholly due to a careful adherence to the rule by which every main religion was to be recorded exactly as a man stated it, irrespective of his caste or tribe. This caused a fall of about cent. per cent. among the Kols (170,000) and Gonds (153,000) who form the bulk of the jungle population.

## *Musalmans.*

33. In 1901 Musalmans stood third in order of numerical importance but the reduction in the Animistic population already noted has brought them into the second place in spite of a fall of just under 1 per cent.

Though the greatest number of Musalmans is met with in the Gwalior Residency with its 28 towns; the effect of a single Muhammadan State is clearly shown in the figures for the Bhopal Political Charge where the Musalmans number only 68,000 less than in Gwalior Residency, even making allowances for an exodus on account of plague.

The urban population claims most of them as they form only 3 per cent. of the rural inhabitants. Their predominance on the Plateau is due primarily to historical conditions prevailing in former days, many families dating from the time of the Mughal rule, a few even from before that period and others from the days of the Pindari hordes; to the greater number of towns in this tract; and to the large Musalman State of Bhopal.

The slight fall recorded, less than 1 per cent., is due mainly to the deserted condition of the most important urban centres owing to plague. The rise noticeable in the Hilly tract is reported from the Bhopal Agency and was due to the families which had left the city (where a fall of 8,000 was recorded) on account of plague and were living in the districts.

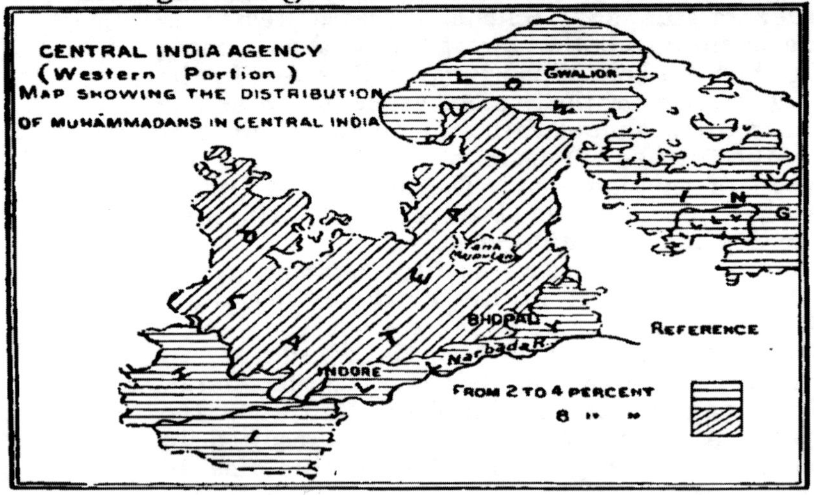


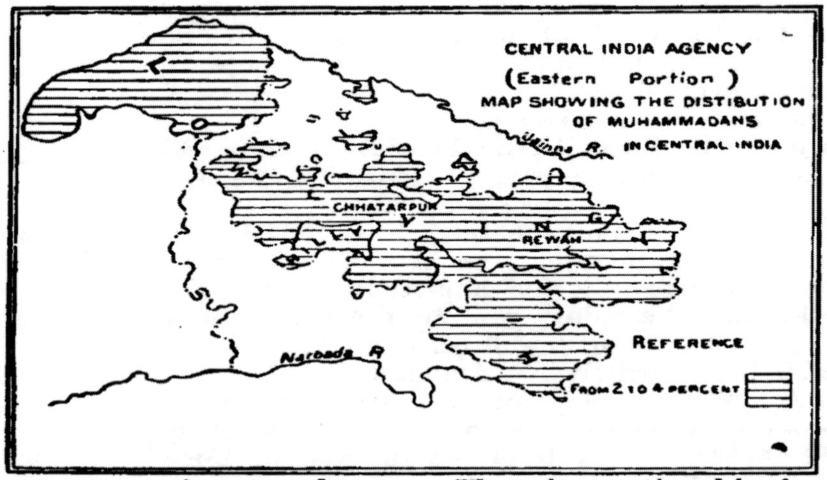


The Indore Residency and Bhopawar Political Charge show a slight increase. But the variations are small and detailed examination reveals no special causes.

An examination of the district figures for the four chief States shows that a fall of 3 per cent. took place in Gwalior chiefly in the city and surrounding districts where a decrease of 18 per cent. was recorded, balanced somewhat by a rise of 15 per cent. in the Amjhera district. This apparently large increase is merely due to the addition of a few families to the usually small Musalman population in this area owing to plague in Dhar town and the presence of settlement officials. The actual increase is only 782.

In Indore a rise of 3 per cent. is mainly due to the increase in the Nimar and Nemawar districts of 25 per cent. attributable to the same causes.

Plague was responsible for a fall of 2 per cent. in Bhopal.

Rewah records a rise of 2 per cent. caused by the very large increase in Bandhogarh, due to the railway population containing members of this class.

### *Jains.*

34. Forming about 1 per cent. of the population of the Agency, the Jains are town-dwellers contributing less than 1 per cent. to the rural area. Drawn chiefly from the Marwari trader class they are mainly met with in western Central India, nearly 40 per cent. more inhabiting the Plateau than the Lowlying area. The 42 per cent. in the Gwalior Political Charge are found chiefly in those districts of this Charge which lie topographically in Malwa.

The fall of 21 per cent. is due mainly to the exodus from large towns caused by plague. The Marwari is ever the first to move out into the land of his origin or elsewhere on the advent of this epidemic. Another cause is the absence of a record of sect by which in 1901 a number of Jains who called themselves Hindus were added to the Jain total during compilation. Instructions, however, were much better carried out on this occasion although there was undoubtedly an increased tendency, amounting in some localities almost to insistence, that the Jain is merely, like the Vaishnava or Shaivite, a sectarian division of the great Hindu faith, and this is in spite of the somewhat importunate asseverations and demands for distinction made by a certain Jain Sabha.

The political charges show no variation of any importance.

The district figures for the four principal States show a large fall of 29 per cent. in Gwalior, mainly in the city and surrounding districts where it amounts to 36 per cent. and in the Plateau districts of 28 per cent. Plague was responsible for this.

Indore shows a fall of 24 per cent. due to the same cause, the deficiency rising to 47 per cent. in the Indore district including the city. The Nemawar and Alampur districts each show a rise of about 40 per cent. but the large percentage rise is actually represented by an addition of only a few individuals of this faith.

Bhopal owes its fall of 20 per cent. to plague, the Western district showing a decrease of 30 per cent.

Rewah alone shows an increase. This amounts to 14 per cent. in the State as a whole but in the Beohari and Bandhogarh districts rises to 70 per cent. and in the Sohagpur to 96 per cent. owing to the opening of new bazars.

### *Christians.*

35. The Christian community is mainly European and Anglo-Indian. Separation of the figures for those two classes is never complete, as many in the latter class return themselves in the former. The Europeans are chiefly officers and soldiers in the cantonments and military stations, civil officials of Government and a few missionaries. The Anglo-Indian section is composed of officials on the railways and clerks in the offices of various departments of the Government and State administrations. The number of Christians in the service of the Native States is comparatively unimportant.

The total number of Christians has risen by 15 per cent. in the last decade. Examination of the figures shows that the changes as regards political charges are insignificant except in the Bhopawar Agency, where a rise of 160 per cent. has taken place and in the Bundelkhand Charge where a rise of 34 per cent. has occurred.

The rise in Bundelkhand is artificial being due to the presence of more British troops in the Nowgong cantonment. In the Bhopawar Agency it is due to the increase among Indian Christians, Roman Catholics showing an increase of 30 per cent. and Presbyterians of 57 per cent., these accretions being due to the Roman Catholic Mission stations in Manpur and the Jhabua State and the Canadian Presbyterian Mission in Dhar and Ali-Rajpur.

This rise also accounts for the increase in the Hilly tract Natural Division in which most of the Bhopawar Political Charge lies.

Of the chief States Gwalior records a loss of 29 per cent. due to the transfer of the Christian colony from the Nimach *pargana* boundary into cantonment limits. Indore shows a rise of 119 per cent., 118 per cent., in the Indore district and 100 in Mehidpur and Rampura-Bhanpura. The increase in the first case is due to the opening of a new industrial settlement at Kasalpura near Mhow and the latter to the fortuitous presence of two Christians where none were returned previously. The establishment of a district headquarters at Garoth and of a railway centre at Shamgarh has caused the rise in Rampura-Bhanpura.

A small rise of 10 per cent. is recorded by Bhopal State amounting to 100 per cent. in the jungle tracts balanced by a fall of 81 per cent. in the Western Nizamat, due to the exodus caused by plague in the city.

Rewah shows the enormous rise of 138 per cent., Sohagpur showing 96 per cent., due to railway employés.

### *Missions.*

36. The Missions working now in Central India are the Canadian Presbyterian Mission with stations at Indore, opened in 1887, where a college, theological seminary, high schools, primary schools, industrial homes and a hospital are maintained. Mhow opened in 1877, schools; Nimach opened in 1885, a girls' orphanage, schools and hospital for women; Ratlam opened in 1886, with girls' orphanage, men's hospital and press; Ujjain opened in 1887, men's hospital; Dhar opened in 1895, women's hospital and schools; Amkhut (Ali-Rajpur) opened in 1897, industrial farm and school; Kharua (Panth-Piploda) opened in 1910, dispensary; Rasalpura (Mhow) opened in 1902 and separated from Mhow, in 1910, boys' school and work-shops; Barwaha (Indore) opened in 1911, dispensary. The Roman Catholics at Mariapur in Manpur Pargana, Thandla and Jhabua, the Friends Foreign (Quaker) Mission Association at Sehore, and the Friends American Mission at Nowgong. Generally speaking although they do not restrict themselves to any class only the lower classes and jungle tribes are reached by the Missions. Indeed except the Canadian Presbyterian Mission, which works mainly among the Bhils and cognate tribes of the Vindhyas and Satpura ranges, conversion is very rarely effected in Central India although the educational and medical facilities offered by these Missions are freely accepted.

**Canadian Presbyterian Mission.**

37. This is by far the most important Mission in Central India and working as it does chiefly among the jungle tribes its success in converting is far greater than that of other Missions. The famines of 1897 and 1900, moreover, assisted materially as a large number of orphans passed into the care of the Mission.

The number of Presbyterian Indians, who, it may be safely taken, are all connected with this Mission, is 1,277 in excess of the figures of 1901 – a rise of 123 per cent. The Mission books, however, returned nearly double that number as actually baptised. Some of these may have been absent at the census but no doubt a considerable number who had returned to live in villages were entered as Bhils, etc. The Mission also claims that many who shrink from the rite of baptism privately profess and follow the Christian religion.

Converts have usually been individuals but in a few cases whole families have joined.

The educational side is supported by a college at Indore teaching up to the M. A. Standard. High schools for boys, one high school at Indore (the only institution of the kind in Central India) for girls, and many other schools, industrial homes, and orphanages. Books and tracts are disseminated and an Anglo-Vernacular periodical is issued.

Numerous medical institutions are also maintained.

**Roman Catholic Mission.**

38. The Roman Catholics have besides a convent at Mhow three regular Mission stations.

1. *Mariapur*, near Khurda-Khedi, in the Manpur British Pargana. A colony of 66 families, with 73 children (44 boys and 29 girls) is settled here. Out of 114 children born between 1901 and 1911 there were 67 males and 47 females. This colony has been formed with famine orphans rescued in 1896-1897 (Guna-Bhopal) and 1899-1900 (Ajmer-Ujjain). Boys and girls were brought up, and trained by the Fathers and Nuns of the Mission and married, no account whatever being taken of the castes they respectively belonged to. They now form a community of their own being on good terms with their neighbours, the Gujars and Bhils. The land granted by Sir David Barr in 1898 measuring 387½ acres, is divided between them. The Mission is responsible for the payment of Government taxes, but every cultivator has to pay his own share to the Mission. On marriage they are given a house, a pair of bullocks and the ordinary agricultural implements. Then they are left to themselves and have nothing to expect from the Mission except a certain supervision of their work, together with advice, praise or blame as the case may be, and the loan of a few rupees (*takkavi*) during the monsoon, to prevent them from falling into the hands of the village money-lenders.

2. *Thandla*, in Jhabua State was started in 1896. Famine-stricken children (exclusively Bhils) were received in 1900 and 1902 and brought up in Christianity. Some are still in the orphanage. Up to date the result is 41 families settled on fields, on their own responsibility, in various villages near Thandla. They keep up *social* intercourse, just as they did before they joined the Mission, with their non-Christian relatives and other Bhils and so are gradually influencing them. There are 309 Christian Bhils in Thandla and nineteen surrounding villages. There are also a few Balai converts, 35 in number, who socially associate with the non-Christians of their own caste but not with the Christian Bhils.

3. *Jhabua* has had since 1905 a dispensary and a school for Bhil boys. A few converts have been made.

**Friends Foreign Mission.**

39. The Friends Foreign Association began operations at Sehore in 1890, working only within the limits of the station and at the Leper Asylum.

In 1900 during the great famine the Mission worked in the States of Bhopal, Rajgarh, and Narsinghgarh and employed on one day in June as many as 11,000 persons in sinking wells, making roads, etc., while a poor house was opened. Loans of seed and cattle were made and *pardanashin* women were assisted. One lakh was spent in relieving distress. Evangelistic tours commenced ten years ago while since 1904 a mission station has been started in Bhopal City. Very few converts have been made. Schools, reading rooms and orphanages are maintained and medical aid is given.

**American Friends Mission.**

40. The American Friends Mission (Quaker) at Nowgong works among all classes. In 15 years, however, only 75 conversions have taken place and several of the converts have returned to their original faith. Some 700 villages are worked in and schools are maintained while industrial training is also given.

41. It is thus clear that in Central India except among the Bhils and similar tribes little or no conversion work takes place, and it will be interesting to note what success is obtained in the next decade should no famine arise to swell the numbers by means of orphan children, as the opening up of the hilly tracts is causing a rapid spread of Hinduism which must militate against the extension of Christian tenets.

### *Others.*

42. Under this denomination come Aryas, Brahmo Samajists, Sikhs, Parsis and Jews, in all 2,919. Of this community the Sikhs are soldiers serving in British and State regiments, and the Parsis traders and clerks, mainly in cantonments. The number of Brahmos returned is too small, and that of the Arya-Samajists is below the truth, due to their returning themselves in almost every case as Hindus, while no sect being recorded, it was not possible to rectify the return.

| Religion. | Total. | Males. | Females. |
|---|---|---|---|
| Arya | 139 | 90 | 49 |
| Brahmo Samajists | 9 | 6 | 3 |
| Sikh | 1,384 | 953 | 431 |
| Parsis | 1,330 | 689 | 641 |
| Jews | 57 | 34 | 23 |

A return of these two classes for Indore City and the Indore Residency (Agent to the Governor General's Camp) as obtained from the heads of the two communities, is given in the inset.

| Class. | Total. | Males. | Females. |
|---|---|---|---|
| Aryas | 164 | 140 | 24 |
| Brahmos | 67 | 38 | 29 |

**Race and Sect.**

43. Europeans are in the majority, but they are nearly equalled by Indian Christians. It will be noticed, moreover, that owing to the preponderance of the soldier class in this division males far exceed females, while among Indian Christians the figures are nearly equal.

As remarked above the return for Anglo-Indians is certainly below the mark some having entered themselves as pure Europeans.

The Indian Christian community has largely increased. For this the famine of 1899-1900 is in part responsible. Large numbers of destitute children and infants, who have since become Christians, were taken in by Missions. The record of sect even in the Christian community is not so simple as might be expected. The return, however, shews only 249 persons who gave no sect and 473 "Protestants," and may be considered as fairly successful.

The Missions on this occasion were requested to instruct their converts how to answer the enumerator and the return is certainly more accurate on that account though the Missions claim a much larger number. On the other hand possibly a few, but not many, have been omitted purposely, as it was reported that some landholders had issued orders that no Christians were to be returned from their villages. When information of such an order was received steps were at once taken to see that the entries were correctly made.

Of the sects the Anglican communion stands first, owing chiefly to the European troops in cantonments, the same disproportion of males and females does not, however, appear as the Anglo-Indian and Indian Christian females raise the figures. Next in importance come the Roman Catholics with a considerable proportion of Indian communicants while the Presbyterians follow, most of the members of this sect being the pupils of the Canadian Presbyterian Mission.

Of the other sects none is of importance numerically, though the presence of Quaker Missions at Sehore and Nowgong may be noted as responsible for the Quaker community.

The inset shows that Europeans are mostly of the Anglican community, Anglo-Indians and Indian Christians of the Roman Catholic. The Presbyterians draw most of their members from the jungle communities among whom their Mission works.

| Sect. | Percentage of each sect per race. | | | Percentage of each race per sect. | | | Total. |
|---|---|---|---|---|---|---|---|
| | Europeans. | Anglo-Indians. | Indian Christians. | Europeans. | Anglo-Indians. | Indian Christians. | |
| Anglican | 70 | 26 | 8 | 87 | 4 | 9 | 100 |
| Roman Catholics | 20 | 62 | 46 | 29 | 11 | 60 | 100 |
| Presbyterian | 4 | 2 | 30 | 12 | 1 | 87 | 100 |
| Other sects | 6 | 10 | 16 | ... | ... | ... | ... |
| Total | 100 | 100 | 100 | ... | ... | ... | ... |

## *Summary.*

44. The general deductions to be made from the results discussed in this Chapter are that Hinduism by its steady absorption of the jungle tribes must continue to increase its numbers, and will do so even if a severe famine again causes a temporary set-back and throws the forest clans into the arms of the missionaries. It can scarcely be doubted that the census of 1921 will show very few, if any, Animists.

With the Musalman population it is far otherwise. Any considerable rise in their numbers is improbable, and there are even signs that a decline may be expected in the next decade.

The Jain community should certainly increase as the States develop their commercial and industrial undertakings.

The most interesting point for consideration is the probable effect in Central India of modern tendencies on the great western faith. Any large increase in the indigenous Christian community seems impossible, the large rise in the figures on this occasion being due to the unusual facilities for conversion given by the famine of 1900. The opening up and general civilisation of the forest tracts which is yearly increasing must clear the way for the advance of Hinduism and so restrict the field from which converts are now chiefly made.

While on the one hand circumstances militate against the rapid extension of Christianity through the Agency as an active religion, the extension of civilisation will tend to facilitate the spread of its educating influence, already more apparent every year. Although the States of Central India are very conservative and are more slowly permeated than British India by the influence of western ideas and ideals yet the steady raising of the ethical plane due to this influence is sufficiently obvious.

If a comparison is made between the present day administration of almost any State in the Agency, certainly of any important State, and that of twenty or thirty years ago the advance is enormous. This is due mainly to the higher ethical standard reached and the consequent greater purity of administrative methods. The material advantages of this improvement soon manifest themselves and lead to a further advance along the same lines.

This moral influence is not of course due entirely to missionary enterprise but mainly to the general spread of education, a far more constant contact with Europeans and a much closer touch with the methods of practical administration followed in British India, than obtained formerly. It is, moreover, not sectarian and is derived from the laymen of the younger generation and not from the priest. The change also so far from causing any general abandonment of the old faiths appears to be leading laymen to form a more intimate acquaintance with the foundations of their religions resulting in a careful search for the highest moral teaching which they contain.

So long as this path is followed the spread of Christian religious doctrine in the states is unlikely though the spread of its moral ideals will increase.

It will be interesting to see ten or twenty years hence how far these predictions have been fulfilled and their effect on the general prosperity of the States, the tone of the administration and the conditions of society.

SUBSIDIARY TABLE I.—**General Distribution of the Population by Religion.**

| Religion and locality. | Actual number in 1911. | Proportion per 10,000 of the Population. | | | | Variation per cent Increase (+) Decrease (—). | | | Net Variation. |
|---|---|---|---|---|---|---|---|---|---|
| | | 1911 | 1901 | 1891 | 1881 | 1901-1911 | 1891-1901 | 1881-1891 | 1881-1911 |
| 1 | 2 | 3 | 4 | 5 | 6 | 7 | 8 | 9 | 10 |
| HINDU. | | | | | | | | | |
| **Central India** . | **8,262,638** | **8,830** | **8,081** | **7,468** | **8,422** | **+20·3** | **—9·3** | **—2·9** | **+5·9** |
| Plateau . . . | 3,213,388 | 8,724 | 8,166 | ... | ... | +18·2 | ... | ... | ... |
| Low-lying Tract . . | 3,136,307 | 9,473 | 8,939 | ... | ... | + 7·6 | ... | ... | ... |
| Hilly Tract . . | 1,912,943 | 8,097 | 6,470 | ... | ... | +54·9 | ... | ... | ... |
| MUSALMAN. | | | | | | | | | |
| **Central India** . | **511,200** | **546** | **606** | **546** | **551** | **—0·8** | **—6·9** | **+8·3** | **+0·1** |
| Plateau . . . | 297,238 | 807 | 909 | ... | ... | — 1·7 | ... | ... | ... |
| Low-lying Tract . . | 121,077 | 366 | 412 | ... | ... | — 9·9 | ... | ... | ... |
| Hilly Tract . . | 92,885 | 393 | 411 | ... | ... | +18·4 | ... | ... | ... |
| ANIMIST. | | | | | | | | | |
| **Central India** . | **483,394** | **517** | **1,168** | **1,890** | **962** | **—51·3** | **—48·2** | **+115·0** | **—45·8** |
| Plateau . . . | 110,312 | 300 | 684 | ... | ... | —51·5 | ... | ... | ... |
| Low-lying Tract . . | 30,857 | 93 | 563 | ... | ... | —83·2 | ... | ... | ... |
| Hilly Tract . . | 342,225 | 1,448 | 3,045 | ... | ... | —41·1 | ... | ... | ... |
| JAIN. | | | | | | | | | |
| **Central India** . | **87,471** | **94** | **131** | **87** | **54** | **—21·6** | **+27·1** | **+76·2** | **+75·6** |
| Plateau . . . | 52,839 | 143 | 214 | ... | ... | —25·9 | ... | ... | ... |
| Low-lying Tract . . | 21,085 | 64 | 82 | ... | ... | —21·1 | ... | ... | ... |
| Hilly Tract . . | 13,547 | 57 | 71 | ... | ... | — 0·1 | ... | ... | ... |
| CHRISTIAN. | | | | | | | | | |
| **Central India** . | **9,358** | **10** | **10** | **6** | **8** | **+15·3** | **+35·4** | **—15·2** | **+32·5** |
| Plateau . . . | 7,368 | 20 | 20 | ... | ... | + 9·3 | ... | ... | ... |
| Low-lying Tract . . | 1,137 | 3 | 3 | ... | ... | + 5·1 | ... | ... | ... |
| Hilly Tract . . | 853 | 4 | 2 | ... | ... | +178·8 | ... | ... | ... |
| OTHERS. | | | | | | | | | |
| **Central India** . | **2,919** | **3** | **4** | **3** | **3** | **—3·0** | **+10·0** | **+10·2** | **+17·7** |
| Plateau . . . | 2,346 | 6 | 7 | ... | ... | — 0·9 | ... | ... | ... |
| Low-lying Tract . . | 240 | 1 | 1 | ... | ... | —41·9 | ... | ... | ... |
| Hilly Tract . . | 333 | 1 | 1 | ... | ... | +46·1 | ... | ... | ... |

SUBSIDIARY TABLE II.—**Distribution by Political Charges and Natural Division of the Main Religion.**

| Political Charge and Natural Division. | Number per 10,000 of the Population who are | | | | | | | | | | | | | | | | | | | | | | | |
|---|---|---|---|---|---|---|---|---|---|---|---|---|---|---|---|---|---|---|---|---|---|---|---|---|
| | Hindu. | | | | Musalman. | | | | Animist. | | | | Jain. | | | | Christian. | | | | Others. | | | |
| | 1911 | 1901 | 1891 | 1881 | 1911 | 1901 | 1891 | 1881 | 1911 | 1901 | 1891 | 1881 | 1911 | 1901 | 1891 | 1881 | 1911 | 1901 | 1891 | 1881 | 1911 | 1901 | 1891 | 1881 |
| 1 | 2 | 3 | 4 | 5 | 6 | 7 | 8 | 9 | 10 | 11 | 12 | 13 | 14 | 15 | 16 | 17 | 18 | 19 | 20 | 21 | 22 | 23 | 24 | 25 |
| **Central India** . . | **8,830** | **8,081** | **7,468** | **8,422** | **546** | **606** | **546** | **551** | **517** | **1,168** | **1,890** | **962** | **94** | **131** | **87** | **54** | **10** | **10** | **6** | **8** | **3** | **4** | **3** | **3** |
| 1. Gwalior Residency . | 9,187 | 8,525 | ... | ... | 546 | 596 | ... | ... | 138 | 692 | ... | ... | 121 | 180 | .. | ... | 5 | 5 | ... | ... | 3 | 2 | ... | ... |
| 2. Indore Residency . | 8,659 | 7,961 | ... | ... | 805 | 930 | ... | ... | 369 | 880 | ... | ... | 106 | 162 | ... | ... | 49 | 55 | ... | ... | 12 | 13 | ... | ... |
| 3. Baghelkhand Agency | 9,744 | 7,742 | ... | ... | 239 | 253 | ... | ... | 22 | 1,009 | ... | .. | 4 | 5 | ... | ... | 1 | 1 | ... | ... | ... | ... | ... | ... |
| 4. Bhopal Agency . | 8,415 | 7,697 | ... | ... | 958 | 1,093 | ... | ... | 559 | 1,113 | ... | ... | 61 | 87 | ... | ... | 3 | 3 | ... | ... | 4 | 7 | ... | ... |
| 5. Bhopawar Agency . | 5,296 | 4,710 | ... | ... | 468 | 547 | ... | .. | 4,094 | 4,557 | ... | ... | 124 | 177 | ... | ... | 15 | 8 | ... | ... | 3 | 1 | ... | ... |
| 6. Bundelkhand Agency | 9,355 | 9,369 | .. | ... | 342 | 354 | .. | ... | 202 | 175 | ... | ... | 94 | 93 | ... | ... | 6 | 5 | ... | ... | 1 | 4 | ... | ... |
| 7. Malwa Agency . . | 7,885 | 7,651 | .. | ... | 1,094 | 1,198 | .. | ... | 726 | 749 | ... | ... | 280 | 386 | .. | ... | 12 | 13 | ... | ... | 3 | 3 | ... | ... |
| NATURAL DIVISIONS. | | | | | | | | | | | | | | | | | | | | | | | | |
| Plateau . . . | 8,724 | 8,163 | ... | ... | 807 | 909 | ... | ... | 300 | 684 | ... | ... | 143 | 214 | ... | ... | 20 | 20 | ... | ... | 6 | 7 | ... | ... |
| Low-lying Tract . | 9,473 | 8,939 | ... | ... | 366 | 412 | . | ... | 93 | 563 | ... | ... | 64 | 82 | ... | ... | 3 | 3 | ... | ... | 1 | 1 | ... | ... |
| Hilly Tract . . | 8,097 | 6,470 | ... | ... | 393 | 411 | ... | ... | 1,448 | 3,045 | ... | ... | 57 | 71 | ... | ... | 4 | 2 | ... | ... | 1 | 1 | ... | ... |

SUBSIDIARY TABLE III.—**Christians. Number and Variation.**

| Political Charge and Natural Division. | Actual number of Christians in 1911. | Actual number of Christians in 1901. | Variations per cent. 1901—1911. |
|---|---|---|---|
| 1 | 2 | 3 | 4 |
| **Central India** | **9,358** | **8,113** | **+15·3** |
| 1. Gwalior Residency | 1,670 | 1,530 | +9·2 |
| 2. Indore Residency | 4,824 | 4,597 | +4·9 |
| 3. Baghelkhand Agency | 163 | 165 | —1·2 |
| 4. Bhopal Agency | 331 | 319 | +3·8 |
| 5. Bhopawar Agency | 1,084 | 417 | +160·0 |
| 6. Bundelkhand Agency | 812 | 608 | +33·6 |
| 7. Malwa Agency | 474 | 477 | —0·6 |
| NATURAL DIVISIONS. | | | |
| Plateau | 7,368 | 6,725 | +9·6 |
| Low-lying Tract | 1,137 | 1,082 | +5·1 |
| Hilly Tract | 853 | 306 | +178·8 |

SUBSIDIARY TABLE IV.—**Races and Sects of Christians (Actual Numbers).**

| Sect. | European. Males. | European. Females. | Anglo-Indian. Males. | Anglo-Indian. Females. | Indian. Males. | Indian. Females. | Total. 1911. | Total. 1901. | Variation + or —. |
|---|---|---|---|---|---|---|---|---|---|
| 1 | 2 | 3 | 4 | 5 | 6 | 7 | 8 | 9 | 10 |
| **Central India** | **3,716** | **866** | **296** | **269** | **2,158** | **2,053** | **9,358** | **8,113** | **+1,245** |
| Anglican Communion | 2,682 | 514 | 77 | 70 | 118 | 202 | 3,663 | 2,815 | +848 |
| Armenian | 2 | ... | ... | ... | ... | ... | 2 | ... | +2 |
| Baptist | 32 | 1 | ... | ... | 27 | 15 | 75 | 16 | +59 |
| Greek | 1 | ... | 1 | ... | ... | ... | 2 | 3 | —1 |
| Lutheran | 1 | ... | ... | 1 | ... | ... | 2 | | +2 |
| Methodist | 100 | ... | ... | ... | 13 | 11 | 124 | 47 | +77 |
| Presbyterian | 145 | 36 | 5 | 7 | 537 | 740 | 1,470 | 627 | +843 |
| Protestant | 21 | 8 | 4 | 4 | 305 | 131 | 473 | ... | +473 |
| Quaker | 1 | 2 | ... | ... | 20 | 25 | 48 | 68 | —20 |
| Roman Catholic | 655 | 271 | 183 | 169 | 1,090 | 873 | 3,241 | 4,031 | —790 |
| Salvationists | 2 | ... | ... | ... | ... | ... | 2 | ... | +2 |
| Sect not returned | 67 | 34 | 26 | 18 | 48 | 56 | 249 | 496 | —247 |
| Indefinite Beliefs | 7 | ... | ... | ... | ... | ... | 7 | 10 | —3 |

SUBSIDIARY TABLE V.—**Distribution of Christians per Mille (*a*) Races by Sects and (*b*) Sects by Races.**

| Sect. | Races distributed by Sect. | | | | Sects distributed by Race. | | | |
|---|---|---|---|---|---|---|---|---|
| | European. | Anglo-Indian. | Indian. | Total. | European. | Anglo-Indian. | Indian. | Total. |
| 1 | 2 | 3 | 4 | 5 | 6 | 7 | 8 | 9 |
| Anglican Communion | 698 | 260 | 76 | 392 | 873 | 40 | 87 | 1,000 |
| Armenian | ... | ... | ... | ... | 1,000 | ... | ... | 1,000 |
| Baptist | 7 | ... | 10 | 8 | 440 | ... | 560 | 1,000 |
| Greek | ... | 2 | ... | ... | 500 | 500 | ... | 1,000 |
| Lutheran | ... | 2 | ... | ... | 500 | 500 | ... | 1,000 |
| Methodist | 22 | ... | 6 | 13 | 806 | ... | 194 | 1,000 |
| Presbyterian | 40 | 21 | 303 | 157 | 123 | 8 | 869 | 1,000 |
| Protestant | 6 | 14 | 104 | 51 | 61 | 17 | 922 | 1,000 |
| Quaker | 1 | ... | 10 | 5 | 63 | ... | 937 | 1,000 |
| Roman Catholic | 202 | 623 | 466 | 346 | 286 | 109 | 605 | 1,000 |
| Salvationists | ... | ... | ... | ... | 1,000 | ... | ... | 1,000 |
| Sect not returned | 22 | 78 | 25 | 27 | 406 | 177 | 417 | 1,000 |
| Indefinite Beliefs | 2 | ... | ... | 1 | 1,000 | ... | ... | 1,000 |
| Total | 1,000 | 1,000 | 1,000 | 1,000 | 489 | 61 | 450 | 1,000 |

SUBSIDIARY TABLE VI.—**Religions of Urban and Rural Population.**

| Natural Division. | Number per 10,000 of Urban Population who are | | | | | | Number per 10,000 of Rural Population who are | | | | | |
|---|---|---|---|---|---|---|---|---|---|---|---|---|
| | Hindu. | Musalman. | Animist. | Jain. | Christian. | Others. | Hindu. | Musalman. | Animist. | Jain. | Christian. | Others. |
| 1 | 2 | 3 | 4 | 5 | 6 | 7 | 8 | 9 | 10 | 11 | 12 | 13 |
| **Central India** | **6,946** | **2,614** | **46** | **266** | **98** | **30** | **9,003** | **357** | **560** | **77** | **2** | **1** |
| Plateau | 6,360 | 3,027 | 40 | 381 | 146 | 46 | 9,060 | 491 | 336 | 110 | 2 | 1 |
| Low-lying Tract | 7,812 | 2,038 | 14 | 93 | 36 | 7 | 9,606 | 232 | 100 | 61 | 1 | ... |
| Hilly Tract | 7,636 | 2,021 | 179 | 143 | 12 | 9 | 8,113 | 335 | 1,494 | 54 | 3 | 1 |

# CHAPTER V.

## Age.

**45.** The Tables discussed in this Chapter are Table VII giving the distribution of the whole population by age, sex and religion, and Table XIV giving similar statistics for selected castes. The Subsidiary Tables are given at the end of the text.

**Inaccuracy.**

**46.** Of all the data collected in the Census those of age are undoubtedly the least reliable. A progressive age table should, of course, show the highest figure for children under 1 year and a steady decrease from that point onwards. Knowledge of age is uncertain while other factors tend to cause a concealment of the truth. Even in Europe with its more general spread of education, the proportion of those who have but a vague idea of the year of their birth is very large. In India this ignorance is far more general. The tendency to "lump" on round figures is, therefore, very great, and this is accentuated by the daily use of many common expressions of a collective class, such as, *das-pandra :* ten or fifteen, *tis-chālis :* thirty or forty. Among females there is also a deliberate tendency to understate the age of unmarried girls who are nearing or have reached the age of puberty. The diagram given shows the actual number of males at each age as shown in Subsidiary Table I.

*Diagram showing the actual number of males returned at each age per 100000*

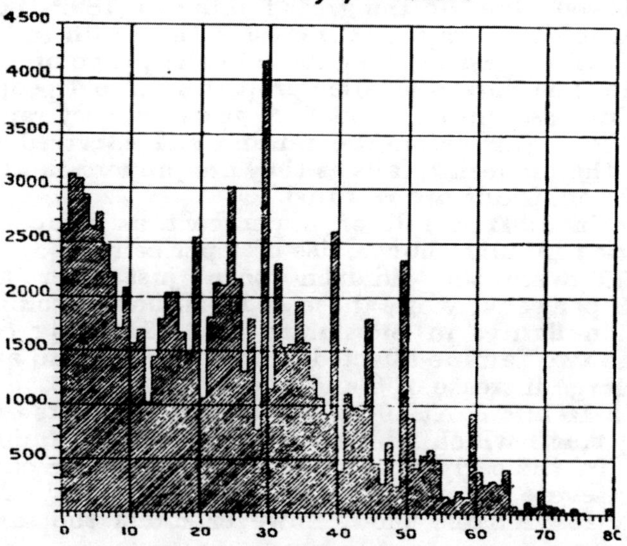


From this it would appear that colloquial expressions have more influence than even multiples of ten and five in causing lumping. Here the effect of *do tīn baras ka hoga, das bārah baras ka, solāh satra baras ka, bīs pachīs baras ka* and *chālis pachās baras ka,* is clearly shown. The figures are also similar.

A smoothed table, of ages arrived at by the approximate method

*Diagram showing the distribution of corrected age periods of 100000 persons of each sex.*

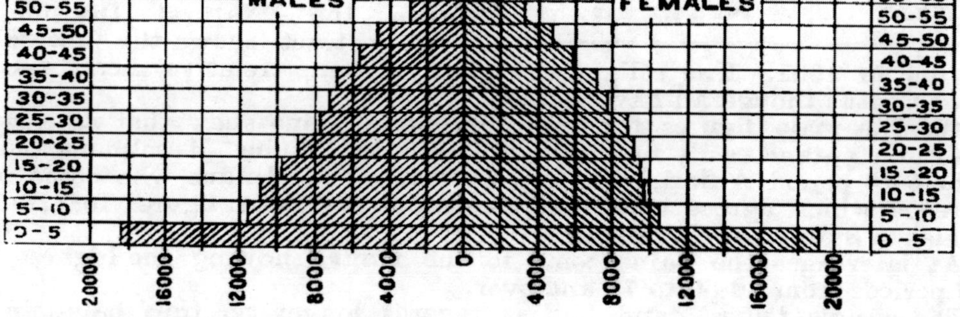


known as "Bloxam's" is appended and the diagram above illustrates the result of the correction. Another custom which increases the difficulty of accurate record is the use of the current year in stating the age, by which a man of 29 is called 30. In the case of children the enumerator was instructed to record all under 1 year as "infant," but children who have remained at the breast long after this age are apt to be still returned as "bachha." The use of *arhai* and *derh* for $2\frac{1}{2}$ and $1\frac{1}{2}$ is not sufficiently common among the uneducated to ensure that children of over one or two years who are still suckling will be correctly entered.

Those who are in the prime of life understate ages and those who are over 50 exaggerate them.

Admittedly these figures would be of no use were it not that the sources of error may be considered constant and the figures at different enumerations, therefore, comparable.

Vital statistics of any value whatsoever there are none in the Agency, from which a check could be applied.

Before proceeding to discuss the results it should be remarked that figures for migration may be discarded as their influence on the figures for the whole Agency is negligible.

**Detailed Examination.**

47. The male figures only will be discussed as being more reliable.

In comparing the figures with those of 1901 it is to be borne in mind that that enumeration followed close on the great famine of 1899-1900. Famine affects a population in an unequal way. It increases the death roll of the very young and the very old, while passing over those in the prime of life. The figures at the end of a famine thus show a smaller proportion of old people and children. The consequent increase in the next few years is very rapid. When, however, those who were born just before the famine and survived its effects reach the reproducing age, the birth-rate falls as they are proportionately few in number. In time normal conditions are restored.

The children of 5-10 show in 1901 a fall of 3 per cent. as compared with 1891, while those of this period in 1911 show a rise of 1 per cent.

The boys of 10-15 in 1911 were the children born just after the famine, and they show a fall of 3 per cent., while those at 15-20 have declined 2 per cent. The Natural Division figures in Subsidiary Table II bring out this fact more strongly. Here the two famine-affected tracts, the Plateau and the Hilly, show respectively the large increase of 6 and 4 per cent. at 0-5, and the Hilly a rise of 2 per cent. at 5-10 also. At 10-15 the decline amounts to 3 and 4 per cent. The Low-lying tract, which did not suffer in that famine, shows no such violent variations in the early years, but a fall of 2 per cent. at 20-40 corresponds with the severe famine in that area in 1897. The female figures which are generally less reliable show, however, much the same variations.

**Mean Age.**

48. The mean age, as given here, is based on the rough method of calculation described in the last Census Report for India. This is necessarily the mean age of those living at the Census and does not refer to duration or expectation of life. It is thus affected by the death and birth-rate of the decade which cannot unfortunately be ascertained.

| | 1911. | 1901. |
|---|---|---|
| Hindu | 29·2 | 30·0 |
| Musalman | 30·7 | 31·0 |
| Jain | 31·7 | 32·0 |
| Animist | 27·0 | 27·9 |
| Plateau | 29·4 | 30·0 |
| Low-lying | 29·6 | 30·0 |
| Hilly | 28·3 | 29·0 |
| Central India | 29·2 | 29·9 |

The figures point to a fall of nearly one year in the mean age for the Agency, which may be accounted for by the large increase which has taken place this decade. There is little to choose between the Natural Divisions, but the Hilly tract shows the lowest figure as it did in 1901. The religions show the same relative mean ages as at the last Census though all have fallen.

**Religion and Age.**

49. The male figures for the different religions show that at early ages the Animists stand easily first, being followed by Hindus, Musalmans and Jains. At the 5-10 period Animists are 2 per cent. above Hindus who come next, a difference which agrees with that shown by the caste figures for Bhils and Bhilalas in Subsidiary Table IV.

At later ages the Jains come to the front, showing the highest figures at all periods from 40-50 to 70 and over.

The jungle tribes stand last as regards longevity, thus balancing their more rapid birth-rate.

The female figures show similar differences, but being less reliable may be passed over without discussion.

Locality, apparently, has an effect on the figures. Hindus on the Plateau and on the Hilly tract show 2 per cent. more children under 5 than in the Low-lying area, but at 60 and over the Low-lying tract shows 1 per cent. more. Jains also show the highest figures at 0-5 in the Hills, and most old people in the Low-lying area. Musalmans show least children and fewest old people in the Low-lying tract.

The remarks previously made on the effects of famine in the Natural Divisions should be borne in mind, however, as regards these local variations.

50. To discuss these figures in great detail is not necessary and only males need be considered. Of the three conventional groups of Brahmans, Rajputs and Traders, it will be seen that Brahmans show at 40 and over 233 living to 221 among Rajputs and 220 among Traders. Musalman sections of the community show 237. Among individual castes, Bhadauria Rajputs (86) stand first, being followed by Dhangars (104), Bhils (144), and Bhilalas (155). The reverse is observed as regards children. In the groups themselves among Brahmans the Sanadhyas (289) show most persons over 40, Shrigaud (253) following; among Rajputs Gahalot (277) and Ponwar (252) come first; while Agarwal (236) and Oswal (232) stand first among Traders. **Caste and Age.**

51. Subsidiary Table V gives the proportion of children under 10 to 100 married females of 15-40 and VI the variation since 1901. The number of children at 0-10 has risen by 36 per cent., due to the increased fecundity which followed on the famine of 1900, the number of children under 10 to every 100 married women of 15-40 has risen by 21 per cent. It will be seen that in the number of children the Hilly tract stands first, the Plateau last and this may possibly be in part due to the later age of marriage among the jungle tribes which causes greater prolificness in spite of poorer material conditions. As regards the proportion of elderly people the Low-lying tract stands first, while the two other tracts differ little, but their females live longer than their males, while in the Low-lying tract the reverse is the fact. There is little to choose in regard to married females aged 15-40, but the Low-lying tract shows fewest married at this age. **Fecundity.**

The two inset tables below give the relative fecundity by religion. The Animistic tribes stand first with 6 per cent. more children than Hindus, while the Jains come last, the Animists also showing least difference in the sex figures. The higher figure for Hindus in the Hilly tract is due to the inclusion of large numbers of the jungle tribes in this denomination. In the case of Muhammadans and Jains it is due to the fact that there are few families of these denominations in the tracts and those who live there are chiefly officials and others in good circumstances.

| Religion. | Proportion of children under 10 per 10,000. | |
|---|---|---|
| | Male. | Female. |
| Hindu | 2,703 | 2,802 |
| Musalman | 2,479 | 2,672 |
| Animist | 3,372 | 3,316 |
| Jain | 2,185 | 2,352 |

| Natural Division. | Proportion of male children under 10 per 10,000. | | | |
|---|---|---|---|---|
| | Hindu. | Musalman. | Animist. | Jain. |
| Plateau | 2,720 | 2,489 | 3,294 | 2,183 |
| Low-lying | 2,524 | 2,333 | 3,032 | 2,159 |
| Hilly | 2,974 | 2,641 | 3,448 | 2,239 |

SUBSIDIARY TABLE I.—**Age Distribution of 100,000 of each Sex by Annual Periods.**

| Age. | Hindu. | | Age. | Hindu. | | Age. | Hindu. | |
|---|---|---|---|---|---|---|---|---|
| | Males. | Females. | | Males. | Females. | | Males. | Females. |
| 1 | 2 | 3 | 1 | 2 | 3 | 1 | 2 | 3 |
| **Total** | **100,000** | **100,000** | 33 | 1,530 | 1,261 | 67 | 48 | 79 |
| 0 | 3,796 | 4,067 | 34 | 1,565 | 1,577 | 68 | 122 | 51 |
| 1 | 2,639 | 2,790 | 35 | 1,956 | 1,733 | 69 | 69 | 94 |
| 2 | 3,133 | 3,520 | 36 | 1,578 | 1,496 | 70 | 234 | 282 |
| 3 | 3,095 | 3,182 | 37 | 1,268 | 744 | 71 | 86 | 134 |
| 4 | 2,929 | 3,128 | 38 | 1,064 | 1,198 | 72 | 69 | 73 |
| 5 | 2,639 | 2,672 | 39 | 920 | 883 | 73 | 39 | 58 |
| 6 | 2,771 | 2,837 | 40 | 2,625 | 3,864 | 74 | 27 | 15 |
| 7 | 2,499 | 1,863 | 41 | 391 | 890 | 75 | 42 | 44 |
| 8 | 2,211 | 2,020 | 42 | 1,107 | 1,643 | 76 | 20 | 18 |
| 9 | 1,684 | 1,960 | 43 | 988 | 1,040 | 77 | 17 | 24 |
| 10 | 2,082 | 1,678 | 44 | 985 | 840 | 78 | 14 | 12 |
| 11 | 1,569 | 1,448 | 45 | 1,809 | 1,824 | 79 | 9 | 7 |
| 12 | 1,715 | 1,178 | 46 | 482 | 536 | 80 | 57 | 78 |
| 13 | 1,010 | 690 | 47 | 287 | 325 | 81 | 8 | 10 |
| 14 | 1,450 | 1,183 | 48 | 671 | 539 | 82 | 12 | 14 |
| 15 | 1,818 | 1,624 | 49 | 286 | 287 | 83 | 12 | 7 |
| 16 | 2,023 | 1,790 | 50 | 2,856 | 2,591 | 84 | 9 | 9 |
| 17 | 2,023 | 1,017 | 51 | 896 | 795 | 85 | 17 | 12 |
| 18 | 1,682 | 1,822 | 52 | 435 | 769 | 86 | 11 | 11 |
| 19 | 1,494 | 1,096 | 53 | 537 | 694 | 87 | 11 | 8 |
| 20 | 2,536 | 2,688 | 54 | 607 | 679 | 88 | 9 | 9 |
| 21 | 1,087 | 1,883 | 55 | 595 | 717 | 89 | 7 | 9 |
| 22 | 1,822 | 1,828 | 56 | 181 | 240 | 90 | 11 | 9 |
| 23 | 2,133 | 1,281 | 57 | 142 | 124 | 91 | 9 | 8 |
| 24 | 2,123 | 1,383 | 58 | 217 | 164 | 92 | 10 | 9 |
| 25 | 3,003 | 3,934 | 59 | 170 | 160 | 93 | 7 | 6 |
| 26 | 2,152 | 2,143 | 60 | 905 | 1,303 | 94 | 6 | 4 |
| 27 | 1,303 | 1,224 | 61 | 396 | 416 | 95 | 6 | 4 |
| 28 | 1,805 | 1,958 | 62 | 284 | 385 | 96 | 6 | 5 |
| 29 | 753 | 962 | 63 | 303 | 322 | 97 | 5 | 3 |
| 30 | 4,179 | 3,499 | 64 | 290 | 307 | 98 | 6 | 2 |
| 31 | 1,156 | 1,415 | 65 | 421 | 357 | 99 | 3 | 2 |
| 32 | 2,322 | 2,394 | 66 | 97 | 77 | 100 | 2 | 3 |

**SUBSIDIARY TABLE II.—Age Distribution of 10,000 of each Sex in Central India and each Natural Division.**

| Age. | 1911. | | 1901. | | 1891. | | 1881. | |
|---|---|---|---|---|---|---|---|---|
| | Males. | Females. | Males. | Females. | Males. | Females. | Males. | Females. |
| 1 | 2 | 3 | 4 | 5 | 6 | 7 | 8 | 9 |
| **Central India—** | | | | | | | | |
| 0—1 | 346 | 358 | 207 | 193 | 275 | 296 | Not available. | Not available. |
| 1—2 | 220 | 240 | 190 | 194 | 142 | 161 | Not available. | Not available. |
| 2—3 | 280 | 320 | 238 | 246 | 234 | 272 | Not available. | Not available. |
| 3—4 | 313 | 362 | 205 | 231 | 280 | 340 | Not available. | Not available. |
| 4—5 | 299 | 305 | 228 | 243 | 293 | 322 | Not available. | Not available. |
| **Total 0—5** | **1,458** | **1,585** | **1,068** | **1,107** | **1,225** | **1,391** | Not available. | Not available. |
| 5—10 | 1,258 | 1,233 | 1,159 | 1,085 | 1,449 | 1,453 | Not available. | Not available. |
| 10—15 | 1,008 | 835 | 1,272 | 1,020 | 1,188 | 939 | Not available. | Not available. |
| 15—20 | 843 | 733 | 1,015 | 917 | 798 | 719 | Not available. | Not available. |
| 20—25 | 902 | 1,005 | 942 | 1,050 | 799 | 892 | Not available. | Not available. |
| 25—30 | 974 | 1,010 | 936 | 954 | 893 | 946 | Not available. | Not available. |
| 30—35 | 989 | 955 | 949 | 927 | 1,008 | 993 | Not available. | Not available. |
| 35—40 | 620 | 563 | 621 | 637 | 622 | 582 | Not available. | Not available. |
| 40—45 | 687 | 692 | 696 | 733 | 763 | 738 | Not available. | Not available. |
| 45—50 | 339 | 316 | 373 | 432 | 322 | 277 | Not available. | Not available. |
| 50—55 | 425 | 477 | 448 | 499 | 433 | 456 | Not available. | Not available. |
| 55—60 | 140 | 133 | 200 | 214 | 115 | 112 | Not available. | Not available. |
| 60—65 | 221 | 307 | | | | | Not available. | Not available. |
| 65—70 | 56 | 57 | 326 (60 and over) | 425 (60 and over) | 385 (60 and over) | 502 (60 and over) | Not available. | Not available. |
| 70 and over | 80 | 99 | | | | | Not available. | Not available. |
| MEAN AGE | 29·21 | 29·63 | 29·85 | 31·02 | 29·25 | 29·31 | Not available. | Not available. |
| ***Plateau—*** | | | | | | | | |
| 0—5 | 1,585 | 1,662 | 908 | 875 | Not available. | Not available. | Not available. | Not available. |
| 5—10 | 1,171 | 1,127 | 1,186 | 1,034 | Not available. | Not available. | Not available. | Not available. |
| 10—15 | 890 | 728 | 1,328 | 945 | Not available. | Not available. | Not available. | Not available. |
| 15—20 | 816 | 749 | 1,036 | 904 | Not available. | Not available. | Not available. | Not available. |
| 20—40 | 3,618 | 3,652 | 3,677 | 4,000 | Not available. | Not available. | Not available. | Not available. |
| 40—60 | 1,622 | 1,641 | 1,569 | 1,830 | Not available. | Not available. | Not available. | Not available. |
| 60 and over | 348 | 441 | 306 | 412 | Not available. | Not available. | Not available. | Not available. |
| MEAN AGE | 29·44 | 29·76 | 30·0 | 32·0 | Not available. | Not available. | Not available. | Not available. |
| ***Low-lying—*** | | | | | | | | |
| 0—5 | 1,272 | 1,378 | 1,181 | 1,270 | Not available. | Not available. | Not available. | Not available. |
| 5—10 | 1,246 | 1,258 | 1,088 | 1,081 | Not available. | Not available. | Not available. | Not available. |
| 10—15 | 1,129 | 928 | 1,207 | 1,030 | Not available. | Not available. | Not available. | Not available. |
| 15—20 | 921 | 746 | 1,004 | 908 | Not available. | Not available. | Not available. | Not available. |
| 20—40 | 3,411 | 3,452 | 3,244 | 3,326 | Not available. | Not available. | Not available. | Not available. |
| 40—60 | 1,646 | 1,727 | 1,912 | 2,012 | Not available. | Not available. | Not available. | Not available. |
| 60 and over | 375 | 511 | 364 | 473 | Not available. | Not available. | Not available. | Not available. |
| MEAN AGE | 29·59 | 30·38 | 30·0 | 31·0 | Not available. | Not available. | Not available. | Not available. |
| ***Hilly—*** | | | | | | | | |
| 0—5 | 1,607 | 1,749 | 1,182 | 1,365 | Not available. | Not available. | Not available. | Not available. |
| 5—10 | 1,414 | 1,362 | 1,230 | 1,184 | Not available. | Not available. | Not available. | Not available. |
| 10—15 | 1,022 | 870 | 1,277 | 1,141 | Not available. | Not available. | Not available. | Not available. |
| 15—20 | 767 | 690 | 994 | 953 | Not available. | Not available. | Not available. | Not available. |
| 20—40 | 3,374 | 3,461 | 3,359 | 3,336 | Not available. | Not available. | Not available. | Not available. |
| 40—60 | 1,460 | 1,486 | 1,661 | 1,749 | Not available. | Not available. | Not available. | Not available. |
| 60 and over | 356 | 482 | 297 | 372 | Not available. | Not available. | Not available. | Not available. |
| MEAN AGE | 28·29 | 28·44 | 29·0 | 30·0 | Not available. | Not available. | Not available. | Not available. |

SUBSIDIARY TABLE III.—**Age Distribution of 10,000 of each Sex in Main Religion.**

| Age. | 1911. | | 1901. | | 1891. | | 1881. | |
|---|---|---|---|---|---|---|---|---|
| | Males. | Females | Males. | Females. | Males. | Females. | Males. | Females. |
| 1 | 2 | 3 | 4 | 5 | 6 | 7 | 8 | 9 |
| **ALL RELIGIONS—** | | | | | | | | |
| 0—1 | 346 | 358 | 207 | 193 | 275 | 296 | | |
| 1—2 | 220 | 240 | 190 | 194 | 142 | 161 | | |
| 2—3 | 280 | 320 | 238 | 246 | 234 | 272 | | |
| 3—4 | 313 | 362 | 205 | 231 | 281 | 340 | | |
| 4—5 | 299 | 305 | 228 | 243 | 293 | 322 | | |
| **Total 0—5** | **1,458** | **1,585** | **1,068** | **1,187** | **1,225** | **1,391** | | |
| 5—10 | 1,258 | 1,233 | 1,159 | 1,085 | 1,449 | 1,453 | | |
| 10—15 | 1,008 | 835 | 1,272 | 1,020 | 1,188 | 939 | | |
| 15—20 | 843 | 733 | 1,015 | 917 | 798 | 719 | | |
| 20—25 | 902 | 1,005 | 942 | 1,050 | 799 | 892 | | |
| 25—30 | 974 | 1,010 | 936 | 954 | 893 | 946 | | |
| 30—35 | 989 | 955 | 949 | 927 | 1,008 | 993 | | |
| 35—40 | 620 | 563 | 621 | 637 | 622 | 582 | | |
| 40—45 | 687 | 692 | 696 | 733 | 763 | 738 | | |
| 45—50 | 339 | 316 | 373 | 432 | 322 | 277 | | |
| 50—55 | 425 | 477 | 443 | 499 | 433 | 456 | | |
| 55—60 | 140 | 133 | 200 | 214 | 115 | 112 | | |
| 60—65 | 221 | 307 | } 326 | 425 | 385 | 502 | | |
| 65—70 | 56 | 57 | | | | | | |
| 70 and over | 80 | 99 | | | | | | |
| MEAN AGE | **29·21** | **29·63** | **29·85** | **31·02** | **29·25** | **29·31** | | |
| ***Hindu—*** | | | | | | | | |
| 0—1 | 344 | 356 | 211 | 193 | 272 | 288 | | |
| 1—2 | 218 | 238 | 192 | 195 | 142 | 159 | | |
| 2—3 | 277 | 317 | 235 | 242 | 228 | 262 | | |
| 3—4 | 309 | 358 | 200 | 223 | 273 | 330 | | |
| 4—5 | 297 | 301 | 220 | 234 | 286 | 312 | | |
| **Total 0—5** | **1,445** | **1,570** | **1,058** | **1,087** | **1,201** | **1,351** | Not available. | Not available. |
| 5—10 | 1,257 | 1,232 | 1,143 | 1,048 | 1,426 | 1,429 | | |
| 10—15 | 1,017 | 827 | 1,275 | 993 | 1,194 | 930 | | |
| 15—20 | 851 | 731 | 1,025 | 907 | 812 | 728 | | |
| 20—25 | 903 | 999 | 940 | 1,051 | 807 | 894 | | |
| 25—30 | 972 | 1,007 | 928 | 963 | 898 | 951 | | |
| 30—35 | 987 | 956 | 944 | 927 | 1,008 | 995 | | |
| 35—40 | 618 | 567 | 626 | 655 | 627 | 587 | | |
| 40—45 | 689 | 696 | 690 | 744 | 763 | 749 | | |
| 45—50 | 338 | 321 | 374 | 454 | 328 | 285 | | |
| 50—55 | 426 | 483 | 419 | 510 | 434 | 468 | | |
| 55—60 | 141 | 135 | 242 | 221 | 119 | 117 | | |
| 60—65 | 220 | 310 | } 336 | 440 | 383 | 516 | | |
| 65—70 | 55 | 57 | | | | | | |
| 70 and over | 81 | 99 | | | | | | |
| MEAN AGE | **29·21** | **29·73** | **29·98** | **31·38** | **29·36** | **29·80** | | |
| ***Musalman—*** | | | | | | | | |
| 0—1 | 325 | 354 | 201 | 211 | 275 | 307 | | |
| 1—2 | 198 | 214 | 171 | 194 | 126 | 147 | | |
| 2—3 | 262 | 301 | 220 | 253 | 213 | 264 | | |
| 3—4 | 286 | 339 | 197 | 233 | 238 | 299 | | |
| 4—5 | 253 | 288 | 216 | 243 | 242 | 279 | | |
| **Total 0—5** | **1,324** | **1,491** | **1,005** | **1,134** | **1,094** | **1,296** | | |

SUBSIDIARY TABLE III.—**Age Distribution of 10,000 of each Sex in Main Religion**—contd.

| Age. | 1911. | | 1901. | | 1891. | | 1881. | |
|---|---|---|---|---|---|---|---|---|
| | Males. | Females. | Males. | Females. | Males | Females. | Males. | Females. |
| 1 | 2 | 3 | 4 | 5 | 6 | 7 | 8 | 9 |
| 5—10 | 1,154 | 1,181 | 1,082 | 1,145 | 1,231 | 1,320 | Not available. | Not available. |
| 10—15 | 973 | 859 | 1,144 | 1,078 | 1,074 | 911 | | |
| 15—20 | 841 | 740 | 923 | 878 | 781 | 733 | | |
| 20—25 | 919 | 1,043 | 926 | 1,044 | 851 | 976 | | |
| 25—30 | 988 | 1,002 | 983 | 961 | 950 | 972 | | |
| 30—35 | 975 | 957 | 991 | 951 | 1,074 | 1,026 | | |
| 35—40 | 631 | 532 | 634 | 571 | 642 | 536 | | |
| 40—45 | 707 | 733 | 816 | 768 | 841 | 783 | | |
| 45—50 | 394 | 296 | 420 | 339 | 334 | 252 | | |
| 50—55 | 498 | 503 | 502 | 514 | 517 | 505 | | |
| 55—60 | 154 | 122 | 192 | 169 | 126 | 110 | | |
| 60—65 | 281 | 332 | | | | | | |
| 65—70 | 83 | 62 | 382 | 458 | 485 | 580 | | |
| 70 and over | 83 | 147 | | | | | | |
| MEAN AGE | 30·65 | 30·26 | 31·03 | 31·87 | 30·63 | 30·38 | | |
| ***Animist—*** | | | | | | | | |
| 0—1 | 418 | 423 | 185 | 179 | 293 | 324 | | |
| 1—2 | 294 | 311 | 190 | 184 | 151 | 173 | | |
| 2—3 | 368 | 401 | 266 | 272 | 270 | 316 | | |
| 3—4 | 439 | 467 | 253 | 293 | 328 | 399 | | |
| 4—5 | 411 | 400 | 298 | 303 | 344 | 378 | | |
| **Total 0—5** | **1,930** | **2,002** | **1,192** | **1,234** | **1,386** | **1,590** | | |
| 5—10 | 1,441 | 1,315 | 1,351 | 1,308 | 1,637 | 1,599 | | |
| 10—15 | 906 | 782 | 1,371 | 1,184 | 1,212 | 984 | | |
| 15—20 | 719 | 742 | 1,004 | 999 | 746 | 675 | | |
| 20—25 | 786 | 1,058 | 939 | 1,046 | 731 | 857 | | |
| 25—30 | 967 | 1,077 | 947 | 894 | 841 | 920 | | |
| 30—35 | 1,041 | 942 | 951 | 917 | 989 | 981 | | |
| 35—40 | 632 | 521 | 567 | 556 | 595 | 570 | | |
| 40—45 | 647 | 574 | 660 | 630 | 744 | 677 | | |
| 45—50 | 270 | 240 | 328 | 385 | 283 | 249 | | |
| 50—55 | 316 | 342 | 347 | 406 | 397 | 387 | | |
| 55—60 | 83 | 89 | 132 | 188 | 91 | 92 | | |
| 60—65 | 169 | 213 | | | | | | |
| 65—70 | 37 | 42 | 211 | 303 | 348 | 419 | | |
| 70 and over | 56 | 61 | | | | | | |
| MEAN AGE | 27·01 | 27·07 | 29·94 | 28·74 | 28·09 | 28·03 | | |
| ***Jain—*** | | | | | | | | |
| 0—1 | 294 | 287 | 202 | 210 | 250 | 278 | | |
| 1—2 | 157 | 190 | 162 | 192 | 129 | 130 | | |
| 2—3 | 235 | 262 | 192 | 233 | 194 | 216 | | |
| 3—4 | 233 | 258 | 177 | 197 | 195 | 233 | | |
| 4—5 | 235 | 239 | 181 | 233 | 198 | 233 | | |
| **Total ū—5** | **1,154** | **1,236** | **914** | **1,065** | **966** | **1,090** | | |
| 5—10 | 1,032 | 1,116 | 954 | 1,033 | 1,069 | 1,153 | | |
| 10—15 | 998 | 846 | 1,051 | 967 | 1,055 | 906 | | |
| 15—20 | 874 | 803 | 927 | 926 | 864 | 832 | | |
| 20—25 | 965 | 1,016 | 1,061 | 1,059 | 931 | 952 | | |
| 25—30 | 942 | 931 | 952 | 894 | 949 | 918 | | |
| 30—35 | 959 | 932 | 1,024 | 920 | 1,006 | 970 | | |
| 35—40 | 671 | 625 | 683 | 611 | 708 | 680 | | |
| 40—45 | 709 | 759 | 766 | 841 | 795 | 860 | | |
| 45—50 | 454 | 393 | 460 | 411 | 464 | 368 | | |
| 50—55 | 524 | 565 | 572 | 582 | 544 | 572 | | |
| 55—60 | 225 | 204 | 237 | 208 | 196 | 159 | | |
| 60—65 | 285 | 361 | | | | | | |
| 65—70 | 95 | 89 | 399 | 483 | 453 | 587 | | |
| 70 and over | 113 | 124 | | | | | | |
| MEAN AGE | 31·69 | 31·81 | 31·99 | 31·79 | 31·90 | 31·89 | | |

SUBSIDIARY TABLE III.—**Age Distribution of 10,000 of each Sex in Main Religion**—*contd.*

| Age. | 1911. | | 1901. | | 1891. | | 1881. | |
|---|---|---|---|---|---|---|---|---|
| | Males. | Females. | Males. | Females. | Males. | Females. | Males. | Females. |
| 1 | 2 | 3 | 4 | 5 | 6 | 7 | 8 | 9 |
| ***Christian—*** | | | | | | | | |
| 0—1 | 224 | 402 | 139 | 210 | 148 | 407 | | |
| 1—2 | 143 | 279 | 120 | 125 | 103 | 285 | | |
| 2—3 | 164 | 332 | 102 | 199 | 126 | 285 | | |
| 3—4 | 185 | 386 | 115 | 214 | 148 | 356 | | |
| 4—5 | 154 | 238 | 168 | 265 | 103 | 420 | | |
| **Total 0—5** | **870** | **1,637** | **644** | **1,013** | **628** | **1,753** | | |
| 5—10 | 215 | 1,032 | 646 | 1,544 | 420 | 1,144 | | |
| 10—15 | 347 | 806 | 685 | 1,791 | 285 | 821 | | |
| 15—20 | 564 | 1,496 | 552 | 1,940 | 382 | 834 | | |
| 20—25 | 3,293 | 1,346 | 1,713 | 868 | 3,432 | 1,273 | | |
| 25—30 | 1,165 | 1,220 | 2,459 | 987 | 2,595 | 1,299 | | |
| 30—35 | 812 | 747 | 1,059 | 781 | 840 | 840 | | |
| 35—40 | 525 | 546 | 554 | 435 | 440 | 614 | | |
| 40—45 | 337 | 383 | 463 | 668 | 362 | 511 | | |
| 45—50 | 220 | 222 | 515 | 479 | 247 | 155 | | |
| 50—55 | 152 | 267 | 296 | 247 | 160 | 310 | | |
| 55—60 | 65 | 94 | 182 | 210 | 81 | 129 | | |
| 60—65 | 83 | 107 | | | | | | |
| 65—70 | 20 | 31 | 232 | 217 | 128 | 317 | | |
| 70 and over | 32 | 66 | | | | | | |
| MEAN AGE | **29·53** | **26·65** | **30·06** | **27·30** | **30·55** | **27·51** | | |
| ***Others—*** | | | | | | | | |
| 0—1 | 181 | 262 | 202 | 200 | 212 | 313 | | |
| 1—2 | 124 | 166 | 138 | 150 | 87 | 168 | | |
| 2—3 | 198 | 270 | 227 | 130 | 119 | 413 | Not available. | Not available. |
| 3—4 | 147 | 296 | 173 | 319 | 147 | 302 | | |
| 4—5 | 152 | 340 | 187 | 389 | 114 | 247 | | |
| **Total 0—5** | **802** | **1,334** | **927** | **1,188** | **679** | **1,443** | | |
| 5—10 | 830 | 1,160 | 592 | 1,088 | 614 | 1,128 | | |
| 10—15 | 784 | 715 | 794 | 948 | 658 | 961 | | |
| 15—20 | 914 | 968 | 888 | 1,267 | 1,115 | 994 | | |
| 20—25 | 1,422 | 1,107 | 1,198 | 1,148 | 1,974 | 1,408 | | |
| 25—30 | 1,473 | 1,360 | 1,312 | 1,088 | 1,539 | 927 | | |
| 30—35 | 1,196 | 907 | 1,040 | 858 | 1,136 | 950 | | |
| 35—40 | 801 | 540 | 818 | 559 | 707 | 369 | | |
| 40—45 | 570 | 453 | 557 | 549 | 560 | 519 | | |
| 45—50 | 406 | 410 | 493 | 200 | 294 | 279 | | |
| 50—55 | 339 | 401 | 449 | 479 | 321 | 346 | | |
| 55—60 | 152 | 113 | 316 | 309 | 109 | 201 | | |
| 60—65 | 158 | 253 | | | | | | |
| 65—70 | 51 | 96 | 621 | 369 | 294 | 480 | | |
| 70 and over | 102 | 183 | | | | | | |
| MEAN AGE | **31·62** | **30·19** | **33·73** | **29·72** | **31·34** | **28·82** | | |
| PLATEAU. ***All Religions—*** | | | | | | | | |
| 0—5 | 1,535 | 1,662 | 908 | 875 | | | | |
| 5—10 | 1,171 | 1,127 | 1,186 | 1,034 | | | | |
| 10—15 | 890 | 728 | 1,328 | 945 | | | | |
| 15—20 | 816 | 749 | 1,036 | 904 | | | | |
| 20—40 | 3,618 | 3,652 | 3,677 | 4,000 | | | | |
| 40—60 | 1,622 | 1,641 | 1,559 | 1,830 | | | | |
| 60 and over | 348 | 441 | 306 | 412 | | | | |
| MEAN AGE | **29·44** | **29·76** | **30·0** | **32·0** | Not available. | Not available. | | |
| ***Hindu—*** | | | | | | | | |
| 0—5 | 1,546 | 1,670 | 899 | 830 | | | | |
| 5—10 | 1,173 | 1,125 | 1,192 | 998 | | | | |
| 10—15 | 890 | 721 | 1,352 | 1,010 | | | | |
| 15—20 | 820 | 744 | 1,050 | 894 | | | | |
| 20—40 | 3,619 | 3,656 | 3,681 | 4,095 | | | | |
| 40—60 | 1,615 | 1,647 | 1,519 | 1,854 | | | | |
| 60 and over | 337 | 437 | 307 | 319 | | | | |
| MEAN AGE | **20·34** | **29·77** | **30·0** | **32·0** | | | | |

SUBSIDIARY TABLE III.—**Age Distribution of 10,000 of each Sex in Main Religion**—*contd.*

| | Age. | 1911. | | 1901. | | 1891. | | 1881. | |
|---|---|---|---|---|---|---|---|---|---|
| | | Males. | Females. | Males. | Females. | Males. | Females. | Males. | Females. |
| | 1 | 2 | 3 | 4 | 5 | 6 | 7 | 8 | 9 |
| PLATEAU | ***Musalman—*** | | | | | | | | |
| | 0—5 | 1,365 | 2,003 | 969 | 1,062 | Not available. | Not available. | Not available. | Not available. |
| | 5—10 | 1,124 | 1,205 | 1,094 | 1,188 | | | | |
| | 10—15 | 937 | 656 | 1,186 | 1,067 | | | | |
| | 15—20 | 801 | 740 | 905 | 856 | | | | |
| | 20—40 | 3,498 | 3,783 | 3,632 | 3,608 | | | | |
| | 40—60 | 1,775 | 1,316 | 1,824 | 1,779 | | | | |
| | 60 and over | 500 | 297 | 390 | 440 | | | | |
| | MEAN AGE | **30·80** | **30·14** | **31·0** | **31·0** | | | | |
| | ***Animist—*** | | | | | | | | |
| | 0—5 | 1,938 | 2,003 | 951 | 1,123 | | | | |
| | 5—10 | 1,355 | 1,205 | 1,332 | 1,224 | | | | |
| | 10—15 | 888 | 656 | 1,326 | 1,168 | | | | |
| | 15—20 | 705 | 740 | 1,098 | 1,065 | | | | |
| | 20—40 | 3,636 | 3,783 | 3,564 | 3,562 | | | | |
| | 40—60 | 1,343 | 1,316 | 1,563 | 1,575 | | | | |
| | 60 and over | 239 | 297 | 166 | 283 | | | | |
| | MEAN AGE | **27·31** | **27·55** | **29·0** | **29·0** | | | | |
| | ***Jain—*** | | | | | | | | |
| | 0—5 | 1,141 | 1,253 | 854 | 980 | | | | |
| | 5—10 | 1,042 | 1,068 | 958 | 1,068 | | | | |
| | 10—15 | 963 | 783 | 1,120 | 1,006 | | | | |
| | 15—20 | 860 | 840 | 935 | 954 | | | | |
| | 20—40 | 3,569 | 3,580 | 3,696 | 3,537 | | | | |
| | 40—60 | 1,945 | 1,922 | 2,031 | 2,002 | | | | |
| | 60 and over | 480 | 554 | 406 | 453 | | | | |
| | MEAN AGE | **31·78** | **31·84** | **32·0** | **32·0** | | | | |
| | ***Christian—*** | | | | | | | | |
| | 0—5 | 820 | 1,579 | Not available. | Not available. | | | | |
| | 5—10 | 469 | 965 | | | | | | |
| | 10—15 | 329 | 838 | | | | | | |
| | 15—20 | 571 | 1,669 | | | | | | |
| | 20—40 | 6,900 | 3,840 | | | | | | |
| | 40—60 | 708 | 937 | | | | | | |
| | 60 and over | 118 | 172 | | | | | | |
| | MEAN AGE | **29·32** | **26·51** | | | | | | |
| | ***Others—*** | | | | | | | | |
| | 0—5 | 767 | 1,200 | Not available. | Not available. | | | | |
| | 5—10 | 823 | 1,027 | | | | | | |
| | 10—15 | 704 | 713 | | | | | | |
| | 15—20 | 957 | 1,027 | | | | | | |
| | 20—40 | 4,989 | 3,968 | | | | | | |
| | 40—60 | 1,457 | 1,503 | | | | | | |
| | 60 and over | 303 | 562 | | | | | | |
| | MEAN AGE | **31·81** | **31·15** | | | | | | |
| LOW-LYING. | ***All Religions—*** | | | | | | | | |
| | 0—5 | 1,272 | 1,378 | 1,181 | 1,270 | | | | |
| | 5—10 | 1,246 | 1,258 | 1,088 | 1,081 | | | | |
| | 10—15 | 1,129 | 928 | 1,207 | 1,030 | | | | |
| | 15—20 | 921 | 746 | 1,004 | 908 | | | | |
| | 20—40 | 3,411 | 3,452 | 3,244 | 3,226 | | | | |
| | 40—60 | 1,646 | 1,727 | 1,912 | 2,012 | | | | |
| | 60 and over | 375 | 511 | 364 | 473 | | | | |
| | MEAN AGE | **29·59** | **30·38** | **30·0** | **31·0** | | | | |

SUBSIDIARY TABLE III.—**Age Distribution of 10,000 of each Sex in Main Religion.**—*contd.*

LOW-LYING.

| Age. | 1911. | | 1901. | | 1891. | | 1881. | |
|---|---|---|---|---|---|---|---|---|
| | Males. | Females. | Males. | Females. | Males. | Females. | Males. | Females. |
| 1 | 2 | 3 | 4 | 5 | 6 | 7 | 8 | 9 |
| ***Hindu—*** | | | | | Not available. | Not available. | Not available. | Not available. |
| 0—5 | 1,273 | 1,376 | 1,174 | 1,274 | | | | |
| 5—10 | 1,251 | 1,258 | 1,091 | 1,077 | | | | |
| 10—15 | 1,135 | 929 | 1,205 | 1,020 | | | | |
| 15—20 | 926 | 748 | 1,003 | 906 | | | | |
| 20—40 | 3,403 | 3,455 | 3,245 | 3,213 | | | | |
| 40—60 | 1,611 | 1,725 | 1,913 | 2,033 | | | | |
| 60 and over | 371 | 509 | 369 | 477 | | | | |
| MEAN AGE | **29·54** | **30·37** | **30·0** | **31·0** | | | | |
| ***Musalman—*** | | | | | | | | |
| 0—5 | 1,181 | 1,345 | 1,107 | 1,240 | | | | |
| 5—10 | 1,152 | 1,211 | 1,068 | 1,066 | | | | |
| 10—15 | 1,028 | 900 | 1,007 | 1,080 | | | | |
| 15—20 | 848 | 725 | 969 | 873 | | | | |
| 20—40 | 3,588 | 3,425 | 3,191 | 3,391 | | | | |
| 40—60 | 1,775 | 1,790 | 2,250 | 1,822 | | | | |
| 60 and over | 428 | 604 | 408 | 528 | | | | |
| MEAN AGE | **30·68** | **31·14** | **31·0** | **31·0** | | | | |
| ***Animist—*** | | | | | | | | |
| 0—5 | 1,734 | 1,852 | 1,397 | 1,212 | | | | |
| 5—10 | 1,297 | 1,367 | 1,086 | 1,179 | | | | |
| 10—15 | 970 | 847 | 1,472 | 1,182 | | | | |
| 15—20 | 765 | 675 | 1,064 | 967 | | | | |
| 20—40 | 3,353 | 3,390 | 3,211 | 3,316 | | | | |
| 40—60 | 1,479 | 1,480 | 1,534 | 1,786 | | | | |
| 60 and over | 400 | 389 | 236 | 358 | | | | |
| MEAN AGE | **28·49** | **28·10** | **28·0** | **29·0** | | | | |
| ***Jain—*** | | | | | | | | |
| 0—5 | 1,153 | 1,200 | 1,052 | 1,238 | | | | |
| 5—10 | 1,006 | 1,206 | 903 | 1,005 | | | | |
| 10—15 | 1,114 | 1,010 | 989 | 885 | | | | |
| 15—20 | 896 | 718 | 887 | 922 | | | | |
| 20—40 | 3,386 | 3,304 | 3,624 | 3,294 | | | | |
| 40—60 | 1,928 | 1,981 | 2,163 | 2,133 | | | | |
| 60 and over | 517 | 581 | 382 | 523 | | | | |
| MEAN AGE | **31·70** | **31·61** | **32·0** | **32·0** | | | | |
| ***Christian—*** | | | Not available. | Not available. | | | | |
| 0—5 | 593 | 1,304 | | | | | | |
| 5—10 | 417 | 1,131 | | | | | | |
| 10—15 | 265 | 754 | | | | | | |
| 15—20 | 366 | 1,246 | | | | | | |
| 20—40 | 7,147 | 3,855 | | | | | | |
| 40—60 | 985 | 1,188 | | | | | | |
| 60 and over | 227 | 522 | | | | | | |
| MEAN AGE | **32·32** | **29·58** | | | | | | |
| ***Others—*** | | | | | | | | |
| 0—5 | 397 | 1,798 | | | | | | |
| 5—10 | 1,126 | 2,247 | | | | | | |
| 10—15 | 927 | 674 | | | | | | |
| 15—20 | 795 | 449 | | | | | | |
| 20—40 | 5,099 | 3,708 | | | | | | |
| 40—60 | 1,457 | 899 | | | | | | |
| 60 and over | 199 | 225 | | | | | | |
| MEAN AGE | **30·98** | **33·29** | | | | | | |

SUBSIDIARY TABLE III.—**Age distribution of 10,000 of each Sex in Main Religion**—*concld.*

| Age. | 1911. | | 1901. | | 1891. | | 1881. | |
|---|---|---|---|---|---|---|---|---|
| | Males. | Females. | Males. | Females. | Males. | Females. | Males. | Females. |
| 1 | 2 | 3 | 4 | 5 | 6 | 7 | 8 | 9 |
| **HILLY.** | | | | | | | | |
| ***All Religions*—** | | | | | | | | |
| 0—5 . . . | 1,607 | 1,749 | 1,182 | 1,265 | | | | |
| 5—10 . . . | 1,414 | 1,362 | 1,230 | 1,184 | | | | |
| 10—15 . . . | 1,022 | 870 | 1,277 | 1,141 | | | | |
| 15—20 . . . | 767 | 690 | 994 | 953 | | | | |
| 20—40 . . . | 3,374 | 3,461 | 3,359 | 3,336 | | | | |
| 40—60 . . . | 1,460 | 1,436 | 1,661 | 1,749 | | | | |
| 60 and over . . | 356 | 432 | 297 | 372 | | | | |
| MEAN AGE . . . | **28·29** | **28·44** | **29·0** | **30·0** | | | | |
| ***Hindu*—** | | | | | | | | |
| 0—5 . . . | 1,560 | 1,714 | 1,163 | 1,256 | | | | |
| 5—10 . . . | 1,413 | 1,370 | 1,151 | 1,100 | | | | |
| 10—15 . . . | 1,037 | 879 | 1,243 | 1,122 | | | | |
| 15—20 . . . | 776 | 680 | 1,021 | 943 | | | | |
| 20—40 . . . | 3,369 | 3,437 | 3,322 | 3,307 | | | | |
| 40—60 . . . | 1,480 | 1,472 | 1,771 | 1,868 | | | | |
| 60 and over . . | 365 | 448 | 329 | 404 | | | | |
| MEAN AGE . . . | **28·44** | **28·66** | **30·0** | **30·0** | | | | |
| ***Musalman*—** | | | | | | | | |
| 0—5 . . . | 1,386 | 1,545 | 1,052 | 1,255 | | | | |
| 5—10 . . . | 1,255 | 1,286 | 1,058 | 1,096 | | | | |
| 10—15 . . . | 1,017 | 888 | 1,196 | 1,088 | | | | |
| 15—20 . . . | 750 | 664 | 921 | 924 | | | | |
| 20—40 . . . | 3,464 | 3,582 | 3,701 | 3,471 | | | | |
| 40—60 . . . | 1,621 | 1,524 | 1,767 | 1,745 | | | | |
| 60 and over . . | 507 | 511 | 305 | 421 | | | | |
| MEAN AGE . . . | **30·13** | **29·52** | **30·0** | **30·0** | | | | |
| ***Animist*—** | | | | | | | | |
| 0—5 . . . | 1,946 | 2,015 | 1,248 | 1,286 | | | | |
| 5—10 . . . | 1,482 | 1,345 | 1,430 | 1,376 | | | | |
| 10—15 . . . | 940 | 817 | 1,365 | 1,191 | | | | |
| 15—20 . . . | 719 | 749 | 945 | 979 | Not available. | Not available. | Not available. | Not available. |
| 20—40 . . . | 3,363 | 3,558 | 3,383 | 3,377 | | | | |
| 40—60 . . . | 1,293 | 1,200 | 1,404 | 1,495 | | | | |
| 60 and over . . | 257 | 316 | 225 | 296 | | | | |
| MEAN AGE . . . | **26·78** | **26·32** | **28·0** | **25·0** | | | | |
| ***Jain*—** | | | | | | | | |
| 0—5 . . . | 1,203 | 1,224 | 965 | 1,183 | | | | |
| 5—10 . . . | 1,036 | 1,164 | 1,032 | 899 | | | | |
| 10—15 . . . | 953 | 843 | 1,140 | 913 | | | | |
| 15—20 . . . | 890 | 790 | 962 | 783 | | | | |
| 20—40 . . . | 3,653 | 3,514 | 3,705 | 3,570 | | | | |
| 40—60 . . . | 1,756 | 1,830 | 1,796 | 2,089 | | | | |
| 60 and over . . | 509 | 635 | 400 | 563 | | | | |
| MEAN AGE . . . | **31·36** | **31·87** | **31·0** | **32·0** | | | | |
| ***Christian*—** | | | | | | | | |
| 0—5 . . . | 1,868 | 2,286 | | | | | | |
| 5—10 . . . | 1,187 | 1,[illegible]57 | | | | | | |
| 10—15 . . . | 681 | 653 | | | | | | |
| 15—20 . . . | 885 | 653 | | | | | | |
| 20—40 . . . | 4,088 | 3,970 | | | | | | |
| 40—60 . . . | 1,187 | 955 | | | | | | |
| 60 and over . . | 154 | 126 | | | | | | |
| MEAN AGE . . . | **26·94** | **24·95** | Not available. | Not available. | | | | |
| ***Others*—** | | | | | | | | |
| 0—5 . . . | 1,359 | 1,955 | | | | | | |
| 5—10 . . . | 650 | 1,354 | | | | | | |
| 10—15 . . . | 1,250 | 752 | | | | | | |
| 15—20 . . . | 700 | 902 | | | | | | |
| 20—40 . . . | 4,050 | 3,684 | | | | | | |
| 40—60 . . . | 1,550 | 827 | | | | | | |
| 60 and over . . | 450 | 526 | | | | | | |
| MEAN AGE . . . | **30·78** | **27·05** | | | | | | |

SUBSIDIARY TABLE IV.—**Age Distribution of 10,000 of each Sex in certain Castes.**

| Caste. | Males. Number per mille aged | | | | | Females. Number per mille aged | | | | |
|---|---|---|---|---|---|---|---|---|---|---|
| | 0—5 | 5—12 | 12—15 | 15—40 | 40 and over. | 0—5 | 5—12 | 12—15 | 15—40 | 40 and over. |
| 1 | 2 | 3 | 4 | 5 | 6 | 7 | 8 | 9 | 10 | 11 |
| Brahman | 118 | 151 | 86 | 412 | 233 | 137 | 164 | 76 | 385 | 238 |
| „ Shrigaud | 104 | 129 | 66 | 448 | 253 | 144 | 154 | 104 | 383 | 215 |
| „ Shrimali | 83 | 118 | 77 | 488 | 234 | 195 | 154 | 81 | 378 | 192 |
| „ Sarwaria | 128 | 172 | 91 | 404 | 205 | 138 | 181 | 76 | 383 | 222 |
| „ Sanadhya | 101 | 119 | 81 | 410 | 289 | 136 | 137 | 72 | 390 | 265 |
| „ Jijhotia | 130 | 147 | 85 | 415 | 223 | 135 | 148 | 79 | 332 | 256 |
| „ Bhagor | 110 | 136 | 85 | 457 | 212 | 121 | 161 | 81 | 395 | 242 |
| Rajput | 121 | 137 | 100 | 421 | 221 | 141 | 148 | 84 | 399 | 228 |
| „ Chauhan | 142 | 140 | 89 | 409 | 220 | 146 | 139 | 97 | 366 | 252 |
| „ Tonwar | 99 | 161 | 112 | 428 | 200 | 180 | 173 | 73 | 404 | 170 |
| „ Ponwar | 129 | 117 | 75 | 427 | 252 | 130 | 125 | 70 | 420 | 255 |
| „ Kachhwaha | 81 | 67 | 206 | 465 | 181 | 127 | 150 | 95 | 427 | 201 |
| „ Rathod | 133 | 132 | 82 | 431 | 222 | 149 | 140 | 75 | 406 | 230 |
| „ Gahalot | 145 | 117 | 93 | 368 | 277 | 174 | 119 | 106 | 326 | 275 |
| „ Bhadauria | 124 | 193 | 130 | 467 | 86 | 113 | 199 | 79 | 386 | 223 |
| „ Bundela | 45 | 136 | 99 | 444 | 206 | 119 | 150 | 100 | 418 | 213 |
| „ Baghel | 127 | 148 | 75 | 430 | 220 | 135 | 164 | 56 | 332 | 212 |
| Maratha | 109 | 111 | 66 | 467 | 247 | 110 | 116 | 93 | 410 | 271 |
| Ajna | 122 | 107 | 67 | 424 | 280 | 123 | 126 | 75 | 469 | 207 |
| Bhat | 130 | 130 | 92 | 408 | 240 | 145 | 150 | 113 | 364 | 228 |
| Gujar | 127 | 128 | 80 | 441 | 224 | 136 | 154 | 82 | 401 | 227 |
| Dhangar | 152 | 181 | 179 | 303 | 185 | 122 | 164 | 108 | 420 | 186 |
| Sondhia | 148 | 131 | 61 | 438 | 222 | 110 | 108 | 100 | 419 | 263 |
| Bania | 121 | 143 | 86 | 430 | 220 | 136 | 148 | 100 | 393 | 223 |
| „ Agarwal | 115 | 134 | 89 | 426 | 236 | 134 | 157 | 108 | 375 | 226 |
| „ Mahesri | 103 | 113 | 84 | 474 | 226 | 119 | 127 | 142 | 377 | 235 |
| „ Oswal | 118 | 133 | 75 | 442 | 232 | 153 | 139 | 86 | 408 | 214 |
| „ Porwal | 120 | 140 | 81 | 437 | 222 | 136 | 142 | 87 | 416 | 219 |
| „ Gahohi | 119 | 160 | 89 | 425 | 207 | 112 | 148 | 80 | 395 | 265 |
| Khangar | 165 | 155 | 91 | 368 | 221 | 126 | 159 | 109 | 395 | 211 |
| Kachera | 136 | 182 | 94 | 421 | 167 | 131 | 159 | 73 | 354 | 278 |
| Bhilala | 197 | 182 | 79 | 387 | 155 | 209 | 172 | 77 | 397 | 145 |
| Saharia | 195 | 153 | 77 | 412 | 163 | 212 | 150 | 74 | 451 | 113 |
| Bhil | 193 | 157 | 77 | 429 | 144 | 200 | 162 | 48 | 405 | 185 |
| Gond | 172 | 174 | 91 | 374 | 189 | 175 | 168 | 72 | 368 | 217 |
| Kol | 166 | 176 | 84 | 270 | 204 | 156 | 168 | 76 | 397 | 203 |
| Musalman | 131 | 147 | 64 | 421 | 237 | 146 | 149 | 70 | 407 | 228 |
| „ Shaikh | 138 | 148 | 59 | 410 | 245 | 144 | 145 | 70 | 405 | 236 |
| „ Sayad | 138 | 133 | 80 | 420 | 229 | 159 | 155 | 76 | 389 | 221 |
| „ Pathan | 121 | 148 | 67 | 433 | 231 | 146 | 155 | 68 | 413 | 218 |

SUBSIDIARY TABLE V.—**Proportion of Children under 10 and of Persons over 50 to those aged 15—40; also of Married Females aged 15—40 per 1,000 Females.**

| Natural Division. | Proportion of children under 10 both sexes per 100. | | | | Proportion of persons over 50 per 100 aged 15—40. | | | | Number of married females aged 15-40 per 100 females of all ages. | |
|---|---|---|---|---|---|---|---|---|---|---|
| | Persons aged 15—40. | | Married females aged 15—40. | | 1911. | | 1901. | | | |
| | 1911. | 1901. | 1911. | 1901. | Males. | Females. | Males. | Females. | 1911. | 1901 |
| 1 | 2 | 3 | 4 | 5 | 6 | 7 | 8 | 9 | 10 | 11 |
| **Central India** | **68** | **49** | **158** | **139** | **24** | **25** | **22** | **25** | **36** | **33** |
| Plateau | 62 | Not available. | 154 | Not available. | 20 | 24 | Not available. | Not available. | 37 | Not available. |
| Low-lying Tract | 70 | | 151 | | 31 | 28 | | | 35 | |
| Hilly Tract | 74 | | 172 | | 20 | 23 | | | 36 | |

SUBSIDIARY TABLE VI.—**Variations in Population at certain Age Periods.**

| Agency. | Period. | Variation per cent. in population (increase + decrease —). | | | | | |
|---|---|---|---|---|---|---|---|
| | | All ages. | 0—10 | 10—15 | 15—40 | 40—60 | 60 and over. |
| 1 | 2 | 3 | 4 | 5 | 6 | 7 | 8 |
| Central India | 1891—1901 | —16·3 | —33·92 | —10·10 | —9·35 | —6·79 | —28·99 |
| | 1901—1911 | +10·1 | +35·71 | —12·88 | +4·44 | -3·00 | +18·87 |

# CHAPTER VI.

## Sex.

General.

52. The record of sex is one of the most important in the Census, but in Central India the absence of vital statistics detracts somewhat from the value of discussion.

In Europe females everywhere outnumber males, the proportion for England and Wales being 1,068 females to 1,000 males, but in Central India as in India generally males are in excess.

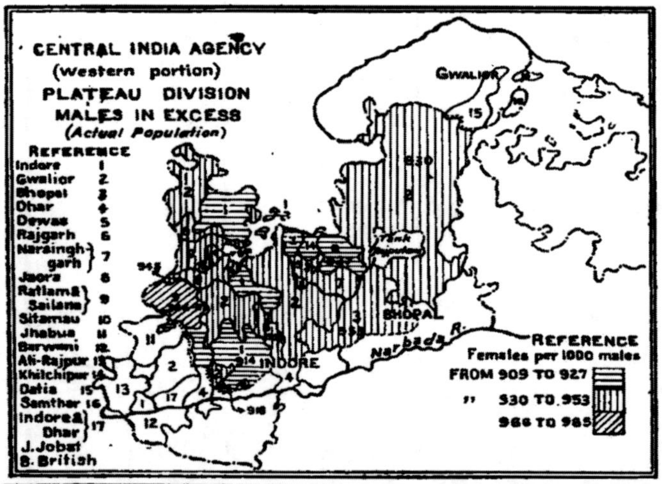


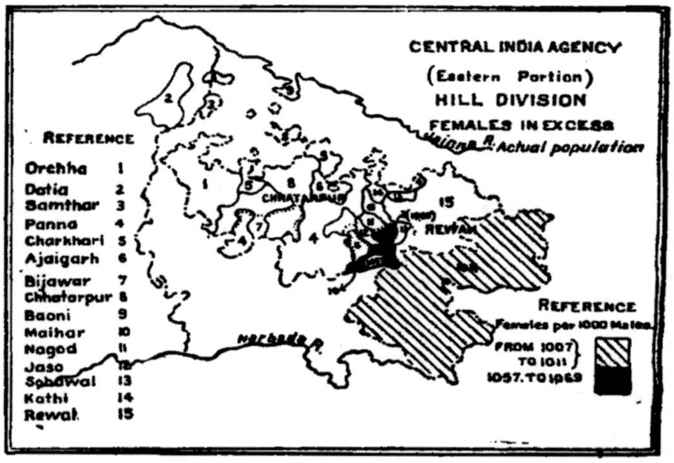


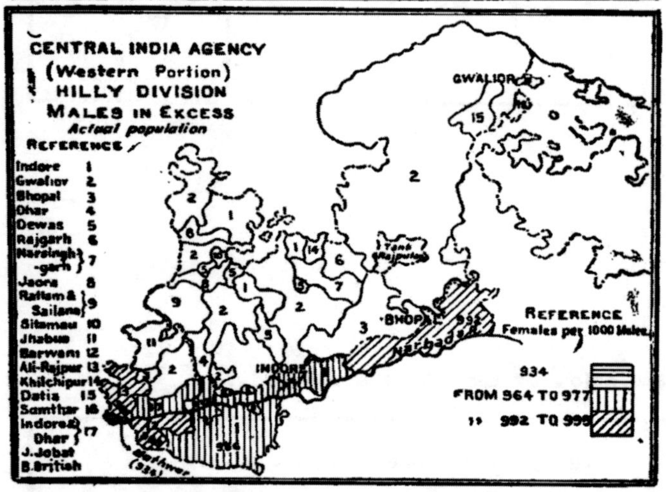


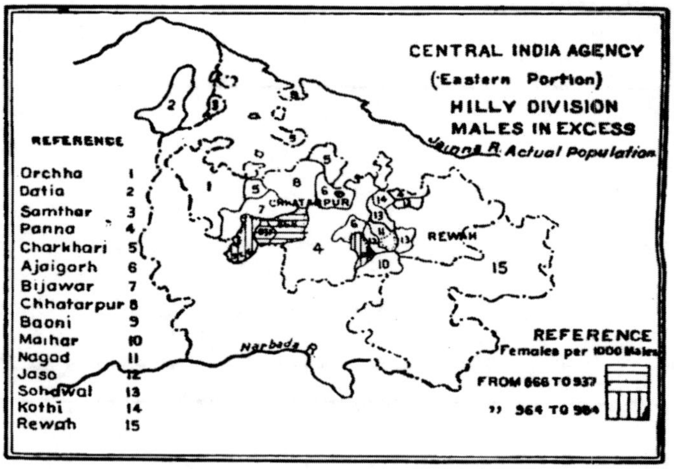


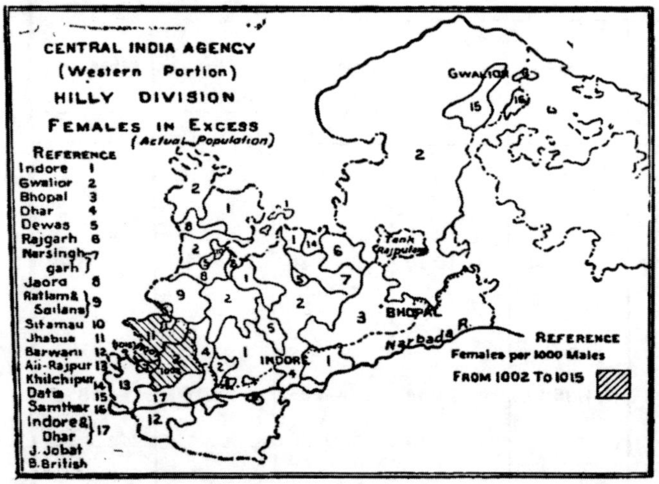


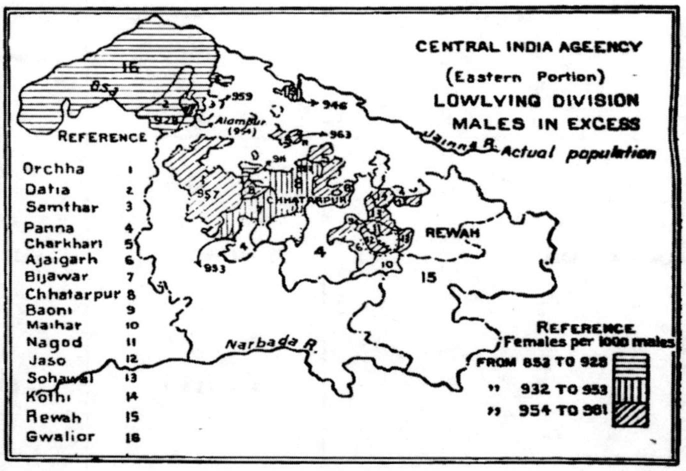

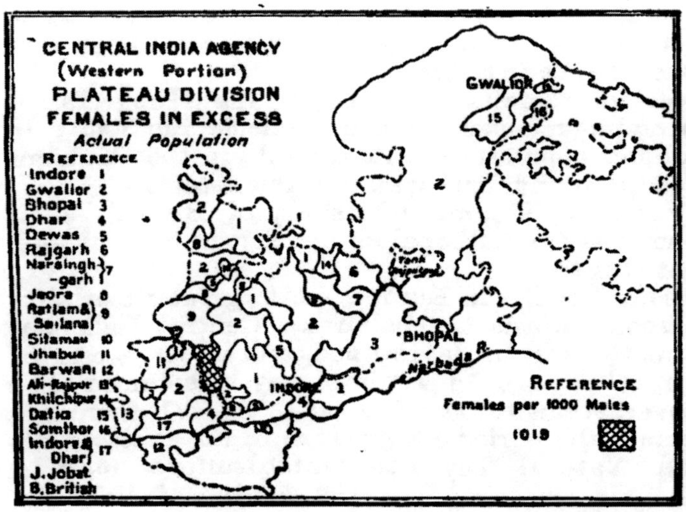


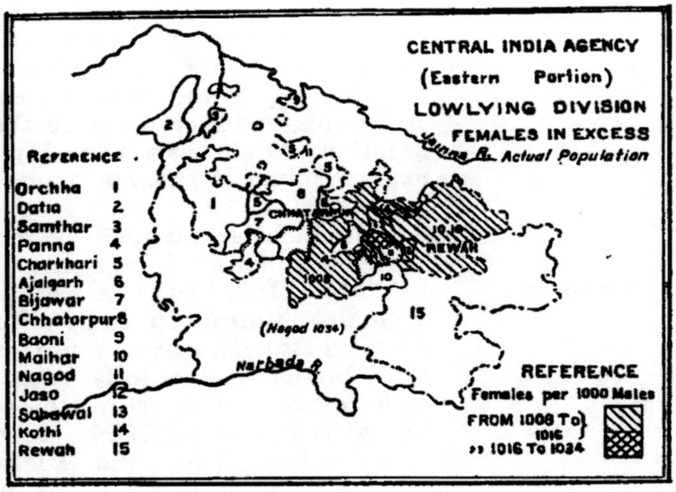


On this occasion males numbered 4,800,000, females 4,500,000, or stated otherwise in every 1,000 persons 514 were males and 486 females. This figure includes all immigrants and excludes persons born in Central India absent on March 10th. If the natural population is taken, that is the total number of those born in Central India whether enumerated within the Agency or without, *less* those born elsewhere but enumerated in the Agency, the proportion rises to 955 females to every 1,000 males

In the Agency as a whole the effect of migration is not great, as can be seen in the inset. When, however, smaller units are taken the effects are more noticeable.

| Locality. | Sex and Migration. Females to 1,000 males. | |
|---|---|---|
| | Actual population. | Natural population. |
| **Central India** . | **949** | **955** |
| Gwalior . | 903 | 924 |
| Indore . | 948 | 949 |
| Bhopal . | 971 | 993 |
| Rewah . | 1,014 | 1,022 |

**Sex and Locality.**

53. While the Agency as a whole shows a proportion of 949 females to 1,000 males the figure in the Hilly tract rises to 995, the Plateau showing 935 and the Low-lying tract 932.

In smaller areas this is not the case. Thus Rewah state shows an excess of 10,000 females on its total population, giving a proportion of 1,014 females to 1,000 males, while the individual Tahsils of Mauganj and Beohari in this State give a proportion of 1,022 and 1,040 respectively. Other States show a high figure also, as for instance, Jhabua, Jaso, Sohawal and most of the Bhumia Estates in the Bhopawar Political Charge. All these units, it should be remarked, lie in jungle-covered areas inhabited by Bhils, Gonds and kindred tribes who invariably have a large proportion of females.

The disturbance caused by plague in the urban figures makes it valueless to discuss the proportions of females in towns.

**Sex and Religion.**

54. Among the religions the Animists alone show a general excess of women, 243,700 females to 239,600 males or 1,017 females to every 1,000 males. Hindus give a ratio of 948, Musalmans of 918, and Jains of 914. The proportion has risen since 1901 except among Jains and Musalmans.

Locality has an effect on the proportions, Animists showing the highest ratio in the Low-lying tract and the others in the Hilly.

When smaller units are examined it is clear that the proportion of women varies inversely with the civilisation of the tract. In the previous section the excess of females in the jungle areas was commented on. In Rewah, where on this occasion the Gonds and Kols insisted on being classed as Hindus, the proportion of women in this region amounts to 1,014.

An excess of females is met with only in tracts where the tribes are found as in the Amjhera (*Bhil*) district of Gwalior, the Nemawar (*Gond*) and Nimar (*Bhil*) districts of Indore, all the Rewah districts save three (*Gond and Kol*), Dhar (*Bhil*), Jhabua (*Bhil*), Barwani (*Bhil*), Ali-Rajpur (*Bhil*), and the minor States of the Baghelkhand (*Gond and Kol*) and Bhopawar (*Bhil*), Political Charges.

It is thus clear that an excess of females points to an excess of those whose methods of living, whether the faith they returned was Hindu or Animistic, are akin to those of the Animistic tribes.

Among Musalmans an excess of females is found in the Huzur Tahsil of Rewah, owing mainly to the employment of the males outside the State; in Samthar which has a large Musalman population in its capital; in the Muhammadan States of Basoda, Muhamadgarh and Pathari and a few estates.

Jains show an excess only in the Nizamat-i-Mashriq of Bhopal. This was artificial and caused by the exodus from Bhopal city on account of plague, the men alone having returned at this time.

**Sex and Age.**

55. Male births exceed those of females in Europe but the greater mortality of male children in early life soon adjusts the balance. Central India has no vital statistics by which this matter can be determined, but as an excess of male births appears to be usual in other parts of India it may be assumed to be so here also. The return, moreover, seems to bear this out. At 0-1 there are 984 girls to every 1,000 boys, while in the period 0-5 girls are in an excess of 31.

In the Hilly and Plateau Natural Divisions which suffered most in the famine of 1900 the excess of girls is very marked. The concealment of females at this early age is not likely and the errors in recording the sexes may be considered equal in each case. At the middle ages (except for lumping) boys are generally in excess until old age is reached, when females take the lead. This may be in part due to greater longevity but mis-statement of age is certainly mainly responsible.

| Locality. | Number of girls to 1,000 boys at 0-5. |
|---|---|
| **Central India** | **1,031** |
| Plateau | 1,013 |
| Low-lying | 1,009 |
| Hilly | 1,083 |

*Diagram showing the number of females to 1000 males at each age period.*

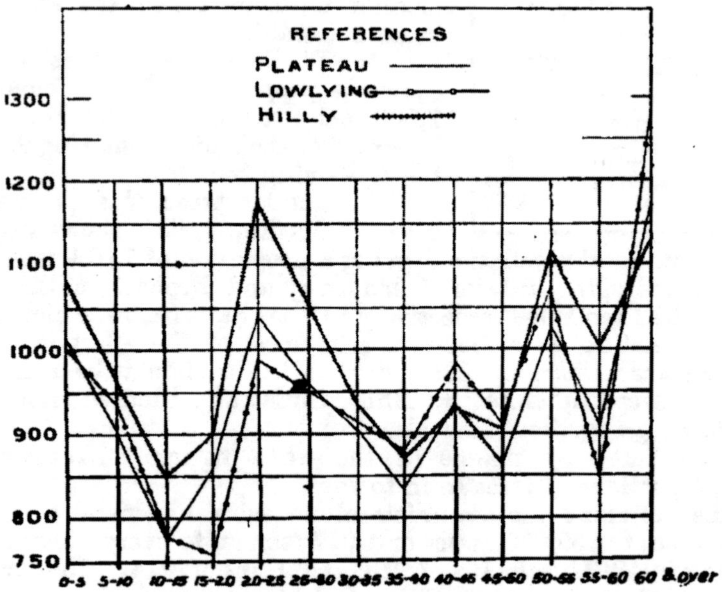


**Proportion of the Sexes.**

56. No increase has taken place since 1901 in the proportion of the sexes though the figures rose from 911 females to 1,000 males in 1891 to 949 in 1901 and 1911.

The excess of males has been attributed to various causes but so far no really satisfactory answer is forthcoming. Briefly the causes tending to produce an excess of males in later years is the mis-statement of female ages at 10-15, neglect of girls resulting in sickness and death, early cohabitation and unscientific midwifery, and the hard lives led by married women and widows of the labouring classes. No traces of female infanticide can be found. It is, therefore, probable that a real deficiency exists among females, exaggerated to some extent by mis-statement of age and possibly also to some omissions.

57. The figures in this case require to be taken with caution as there are clear signs of imperfect returns in some castes, and it would be unprofitable to base any theories on them. The highest proportion is given by the trader group, 1,032 females to 1,000 males, Brahmans (994), and Rajputs (822) following.

**Sex and Caste.**

Among the individual castes Shrimali Brahmans (1,346) of Malwa stand first, the semi-Rajput Sondhias (1,160) coming next, while Maheshri

Banias (1,139), Gonds (1,107), Agarwal Banias (1,103), Chauhan Rajputs (1,098), Kols (1,080), Oswal Banias (1,067), Sarwaria Brahmans (1,050) Bhilalas (1,017), and Bhils (1,002) all show an excess of females. The age figures will not bear scrutiny.

**Sex and Ceremony.**

58. The imperative necessity of having a son causes Hindus to resort to various ceremonial practices in order to increase the probability of male issue.

The usual ceremony consists in placing a girl immediately at the first menses in a specially decorated room made for the occasion known as *makhar* where she is fed on every delicacy by relatives and friends for several days. This is followed within 16 days by the Garbhadhan (*garbha*=conception+ *dhan*=to bear) or fœtus-bearing rite, which is supposed to ensure conception. On an auspicious day, which must be on the 6th, 8th, 10th, 12th, 14th, or 16th as the even numbers favour male issue, after the menses first appear a *Hom* or sacrifice is made during which the husband places his right hand on his wife's body just above the right thigh. The Punsavan (*puman*= male+*suyate*=produced) or male-making ceremony which usually follows, consists in the husband's taking his wife's head between his knees and dropping the juice of Dubha (*Cynodon dactylon*) grass down her right nostril. This is believed to ensure male issue. On the failure of these regular rites the advice of priests and Sadhus is sought and penances and offerings as suggested by these authorities are resorted to, many being of a fantastic and even irksome nature. Later on *dhais* are called in to give their views as to the sex of the child in the womb and various indications are sought. Those usually relied on are :—

(1) If the child lies to the right of the womb it will be a male.

(2) If the woman's eyes have a faded or whitish look, the palms of the hands are reddish, and she appears abnormally weak, a male is indicated.

(3) In the case of a female the child lies on the left while the woman's eyes and the palms of her hands have a yellow tint.

(4) Pregnancy lasting over 9 months is an indication of male issue.

(5) If the pregnancy commences in the dark half (*badi*) of a month a male child will be conceived, if in the light half a female.

(6) General horripilation of the mother is supposed to accompany male conception.

(7) In a case of male conception the pains are in the womb, but those of female conception are felt in the intestines.

(8) If the woman dreams of male things, such as cocoanuts, plantains, snakes, etc., a male child will be born, but if the articles are of feminine gender, such as cucumbers, oranges and the like, a girl will appear.

(9) A desire for sweet things indicates a male child, salt things a female.

(10) If the womb is unusually distended and the face looks young and fresh while the woman walks with energy, lifting her feet high, a girl will be born, while the opposite signs indicate a boy.

(11) A feeling of obstruction in the intestines on the right side indicates a boy, on the left a girl.

The Jyotishi is also an important person in such cases.

The horoscope ( कुंडली ) of a man contains 12 compartments and the planets ( ग्रहा: ) occupying these compartments are 9 *viz.*, Ravi (*Sun*), Chandra (*Moon*), Mangal (*Mars*), Budha (*Mercury*), Guru (*Jupiter*), Shukra (*Venus*), Shani (*Saturn*), Rahu and Ketu (Ascending and Descending nodes). When the horoscope is to be examined in connection with progeny ( सुत ) and prosperity ( लाभ ) two compartments, *viz.*, the fifth and the eleventh have to be studied respectively for these two objects. Shlokas referring to this are given below :—

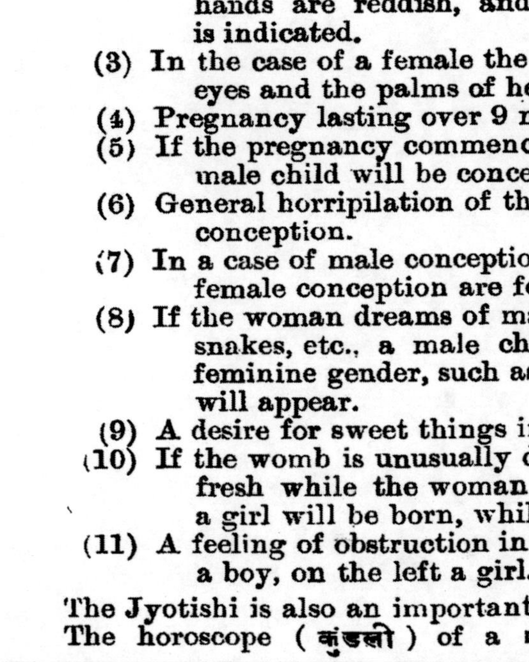

(1) पंचमस्थो यदा शुक्रो भौमयुक्तो निरीक्षितः।
तदा वर्षे विजानीयात् गर्भपुत्रसमुद्भवं ॥ १ ॥

(2) लाभे सुतेच शुक्रेंदू सुतलाभेऽथवा क्रमात्।
शुक्रेंदू पश्यतः पुत्रो वर्षेस्मिन् संतति र्ध्रुवम ॥ २ ॥

इति वर्ष लग्न फलम्

(1) When Shukra (*Venus*) is seen with Mangal (*Mars*) in compartment 5 of a yearly horoscope ( वर्ष कुंडली ) it is probable that there will be male issue that year.

(2) When Shukra (*Venus*) and Chandra (*Moon*) are in the eleventh and fifth compartments respectively or *vice versá* there is *certainty* of male issue that year.

These Shlokas are applicable to the (वर्ष कुंडली) yearly horoscope and have to be worked out every year from the horoscope made at birth (जन्म कुंडली)

(1) पुत्रस्थाने गते भौमे मेषसिंहालिमीनगे।
जीवदृष्टियुते वापि पुत्रप्राप्तिं विनिर्दिशेत् ॥ १ ॥

(2) नवमे पंचमे राहौ नवमे पंचमे शनौ।
नवमे पंचमे भौमे पुत्रः स्वप्ने न दृश्यते ॥ २ ॥

(3) पंचमस्थाः शुभाः सर्वे पुत्रसंतानकारकाः।
क्रूराः संततिमृत्युंच कुपुत्रंच धरासुतः ॥ ३ ॥

(4) बालस्य जन्मकाले तु पंचमे धरणीसुतः।
अपुत्रश्च भवेत् बालो नारी चैव विशेषतः ॥ ४ ॥

(5) अपुत्रं कुरुते भानुः पुत्रमेकं निशाकरः।
सशोकं पुत्रहीनंच पंचमे धरणीसुतः ॥ ५ ॥

(6) एकः पुत्रो रवौ वाच्यश्चंद्रे चैव सुताद्वयं।
भौमे पुत्रा त्रयो वाच्या बुधे पुत्रीचतुष्टयं ॥
गुरौ गर्भे सुताः पंच षटपुत्रा भृगुनंदने।
शनौच गर्भपातः स्यात् राहौ गर्भो भवेन्नहि ॥ ६ ॥

(7) सुतस्थाने द्विपापौ वा त्रिपापाश्चत्र संस्थिताः।
तदा स्त्री पुरुषो वंध्या विज्ञेयो ऽसुतपुत्रकः ॥ ७ ॥

(8) पुत्रे रविः प्रचुरकोपसुतं बुधश्च।
स्वस्थात्मजं शशिधरात्तनुजावपुत्रं ॥
शुक्रेंदुदेवगुरवः सुतसद्मसंस्थाः।
कुर्वंति पुत्रबहुलं सुखिनं पुमांसं ॥ ८ ॥

(1) When Mangal (*Mars*), in compartment 5, is connected with any of the following four Rashis (signs of the Zodiac), *viz.*, Mesh (*Aries*), Sinha (*Leo*), Vrishchik (*Scorpio*) and Mīna (*Pisces*) and is in opposition to Guru (*Jupiter*), there will be male issue.

(2) If Shanī (*Saturn*), Rāhu (*Ascending node*) or Mangal (*Mars*) stand in compartment 9 or 5 there is no hope of having male issue, or even of dreaming of it.

(3) When compartment 5 is occupied by an auspicious planet ( शुभग्रहाः) *Shubhagraha, i.e.*, Shukra (*Venus*), Chandra (*Moon* between the 5th day of the bright half and that of the dark one), Budha

(*Mercury*), and Guru (*Jupiter*), male issue is expected, and when occupied by inauspicious planets ( पापग्रहाः ) *papagrahas, i.e.,* Shani (*Saturn*), Surya (*Sun*), Rahu and Ketu (*Ascending and Descending nodes*), the progeny will die in at birth, while if Mangal occupies the same column the issue will be male but of bad character.

(4) When in a (*Kundali*) horoscope diagram prepared at the birth of a child the star Mangal (*Mars*) lies in the fifth compartment, that child will probably never have male issue, specially if it is a female child.

(5) When compartment 5 is occupied by Ravi (*Sun*) there will certainly be no male issue, when occupied by Chandra (*Moon*) there will be one male issue, and in the case of its being occupied by Mangal (*Mars*) no male issue is likely.

(6) When the following Grahas ( ग्रहाः ) *planets* are in compartment 5 the results will be as stated below:—

| | Name of Graha. | Particulars of issue to be expected. |
|---|---|---|
| 1 ( रवि ) | Sun . . . . | Gives one male issue. |
| 2 ( चंद्र ) | Moon . . . . | Gives two females. |
| 3 ( मंगल ) | Mangal (Mars) . . | Gives three males. |
| 4 ( बुध ) | Budha (Mercury) . . | Gives four females. |
| 5 ( गुरु ) | Guru (Jupiter) . . | Gives five males. |
| 6 ( शुक्र ) | Shukra (Venus) . . | Gives six males. |
| 7 ( शनी ) | Shani (Saturn) . . | Causes untimely delivery. |
| 8 ( राहु ) | Rahu (Ascending node) . | Obstructs child bearing altogether. |

(7) When two or three of the ( पापग्रहाः ) *papagrahas* stand in compartment 5 no male issue is expected if the horoscope is of a male and if it is a female, she will be a barren woman.

(8) If Ravi (*Sun*) stands in compartment 5, very hot tempered male issue is expected, if Budah (*Mercury*) stands there, only a few. If compartment 5 is occupied by Shani (*Saturn*) and Mangal (*Mars*) there will be no male issue and if occupied by Shukra (*Venus*), Chandra (*Moon*) and Deva guru (*Jupiter*), there will be many good male issues.

All these Shlokas are applicable to the horoscope drawn up at birth (*Janma Kundali.*)

SUBSIDIARY TABLE I.—**General proportion of the sexes by Natural Division.**

| Natural Division. | Number of females to 1,000 males. | | | | | | | |
|---|---|---|---|---|---|---|---|---|
| | 1911. | | 1901. | | 1891. | | 1881. | |
| | Actual population. | Natural population. | Actual population. | Natural population. | Actual population. | Natural population. | Actual population. | Natural population. |
| 1 | 2 | 3 | 4 | 5 | 6 | 7 | 8 | 9 |
| **Central India . .** | **949** | **955** | **949** | **954** | **912** | **921** | **897** | **903** |
| Plateau . . . | 935 | 944 | 943 | ... | ... | ... | ... | ... |
| Low-lying Tract . . | 932 | 946 | 128 | ... | ... | ... | .. | ... |
| Hilly Tract . . | 995 | 989 | ... | ... | ... | ... | ... | ... |

SUBSIDIARY TABLE II.— **Number of females per 1,000 males at different age periods by religions at each of the last 3 Censuses.**

| Age. | All Religions. | | | Hindu. | | | Musalman. | | |
|---|---|---|---|---|---|---|---|---|---|
| | 1891. | 1901. | 1911. | 1891. | 1901. | 1911. | 1891. | 1901. | 1911. |
| 1 | 2 | 3 | 4 | 5 | 6 | 7 | 8 | 9 | 10 |
| **Central India.** | | | | | | | | | |
| 0—1 | 980 | 884 | 984 | 960 | 867 | 981 | 991 | 967 | 1,000 |
| 1—2 | 1,093 | 966 | 1,035 | 1,020 | 959 | 1,034 | 1,031 | 1,045 | 992 |
| 2—3 | 1,058 | 982 | 1,083 | 1,039 | 973 | 1,084 | 1,104 | 1,009 | 1,055 |
| 3—4 | 1,108 | 1,068 | 1,096 | 1,093 | 1,051 | 1,097 | 1,120 | 1,094 | 1,089 |
| 4—5 | 1,003 | 1,010 | 965 | 989 | 1,003 | 960 | 1,023 | 1,039 | 1,025 |
| *Total 0—5* | *1,036* | *980* | *1,031* | *1,019* | *970* | *1,029* | *1,053* | *1,030* | *1,033* |
| 5—10 | 915 | 888 | 930 | 908 | 866 | 929 | 953 | 978 | 940 |
| 10—15 | 721 | 761 | 786 | 706 | 737 | 780 | 754 | 865 | 810 |
| 15—20 | 822 | 857 | 827 | 813 | 836 | 814 | 837 | 869 | 846 |
| 20—25 | 1,019 | 1,058 | 1,059 | 1,004 | 1,056 | 1,049 | 1,018 | 1,039 | 1,042 |
| 25—30 | 967 | 966 | 983 | 960 | 980 | 982 | 909 | 901 | 931 |
| *Total 0—30* | *911* | *910* | *943* | *898* | *898* | *938* | *923* | *945* | *941* |
| 30—40 | 882 | 945 | 895 | 877 | 951 | 899 | 809 | 868 | 852 |
| 40—50 | 854 | 1,034 | 932 | 859 | 1,063 | 939 | 783 | 828 | 858 |
| 50—60 | 945 | 1,049 | 1,024 | 958 | 1,045 | 1,032 | 850 | 907 | 888 |
| 60 and over | 1,190 | 1,287 | 1,223 | 1,213 | 1,285 | 1,241 | 1,062 | 1,087 | 1,180 |
| *Total 30 and over* | *916* | *1,007* | *959* | *919* | *1,027* | *966* | *838* | *886* | *901* |
| **Total All Ages (Actual population)** | 911 | 949 | 949 | 906 | 945 | 948 | 888 | 922 | 918 |
| **Total All Ages (Natural population)** | 921 | 954 | 955 | ... | ... | ... | ... | ... | ... |

SUBSIDIARY TABLE II.—**Number of females per 1,000 males at different age periods by religions at each of the last 3 Censuses.**

| Age. | Animist. | | | Jain. | | | Christian. | | | Others. | | |
|---|---|---|---|---|---|---|---|---|---|---|---|---|
| | 1891. | 1901. | 1911. | 1891. | 1901. | 1911. | 1891. | 1901. | 1911. | 1891. | 1901. | 1911. |
| 1 | 11 | 12 | 13 | 14 | 15 | 16 | 17 | 18 | 19 | 20 | 21 | 22 |
| **Central India—** | | | | | | | | | | | | |
| 0—1 | 1,061 | 966 | 1,080 | 1,008 | 954 | 893 | 955 | 760 | 928 | 718 | 486 | 938 |
| 1—2 | 1,091 | 964 | 1,074 | 908 | 1,089 | 1,107 | 957 | 528 | 1,011 | 986 | 596 | 864 |
| 2—3 | 1,114 | 1,028 | 1,110 | 1,010 | 1,111 | 1,019 | 786 | 982 | 1,060 | 1,653 | 365 | 986 |
| 3—4 | 1,126 | 1,154 | 1,081 | 1,085 | 1,019 | 1,013 | 832 | 985 | 1,079 | 1,000 | 914 | 1,308 |
| 4—5 | 1,048 | 1,038 | 988 | 1,067 | 1,176 | 988 | 1,413 | 791 | 800 | 1,046 | 1,026 | 1,444 |
| *Total 0—5* | *1,091* | *1,034* | *1,055* | *1,093* | *1,068* | *979* | *968* | *790* | *974* | *1,039* | *633* | *1,077* |
| 5—10 | 938 | 968 | 928 | 976 | 992 | 987 | 947 | 1,201 | 1,085 | 896 | 908 | 905 |
| 10—15 | 772 | 863 | 877 | 777 | 812 | 774 | 1,000 | 1,314 | 1,301 | 711 | 590 | 590 |
| 15—20 | 860 | 994 | 1,060 | 872 | 915 | 840 | 759 | 856 | 1,371 | 434 | 706 | 685 |
| 20—25 | 1,113 | 1,114 | 1,370 | 926 | 915 | 962 | 139 | 261 | 311 | 347 | 475 | 504 |
| 25—30 | 1,089 | 943 | 1,134 | 874 | 861 | 603 | 174 | 203 | 291 | 298 | 353 | 598 |
| *Total 0—30* | *961* | *979* | *1,051* | *908* | *993* | *911* | *316* | *509* | *503* | *507* | *578* | *691* |
| 30—40 | 930 | 970 | 890 | 845 | 842 | 873 | 395 | 379 | 499 | 348 | 377 | 469 |
| 40—50 | 857 | 977 | 902 | 882 | 936 | 905 | 380 | 487 | 561 | 453 | 353 | 606 |
| 50—60 | 990 | 1,240 | 1,100 | 892 | 895 | 938 | 636 | 471 | 858 | 630 | 510 | 690 |
| 60 and over | 1,148 | 1,448 | 1,290 | 1,172 | 1,108 | 1,063 | 880 | 476 | 783 | 798 | 308 | 1,109 |
| *Total 30 and over* | *930* | *1,043* | *947* | *798* | *907* | *917* | *443* | *439* | *566* | *447* | *359* | *575* |
| **Total All Ages (Actual population)** | 950 | 990 | 1,017 | 985 | 916 | 914 | 347 | 508 | 517 | 487 | 354 | 647 |
| **Total All Ages (Natural population)** | ... | ... | ... | ... | ... | ... | ... | ... | ... | ... | ... | ... |

SUBSIDIARY TABLE III.—**Number of females per 1,000 males at different age-periods by religions and by natural divisions.**

| Age. | All Religions. | Hindu. | Musalman. | Animist. | Jain. | Christian. | Others. |
|---|---|---|---|---|---|---|---|
| 1 | 2 | 3 | 4 | 5 | 6 | 7 | 8 |
| **Plateau** | | | | | | | |
| 0—1 | 992 | 994 | 993 | 960 | 905 | 978 | 846 |
| 1—2 | 1,030 | 1,020 | 1,032 | 1,091 | 1,089 | 1,033 | 933 |
| 2—3 | 1,062 | 1,064 | 1,028 | 1,090 | 1,027 | 948 | 958 |
| 3—4 | 1,062 | 1,058 | 1,104 | 1,069 | 1,072 | 1,070 | 1,043 |
| 4—5 | 930 | 923 | 1,000 | 964 | 983 | 716 | 1,833 |
| ***Total 0—5*** | ***1,013*** | ***1,012*** | ***1,031*** | ***1,030*** | ***1,005*** | ***955*** | ***1,018*** |
| 5—10 | 901 | 898 | 928 | 886 | 937 | 1,022 | 812 |
| 10—15 | 766 | 759 | 816 | 834 | 743 | 1,265 | 660 |
| 15—20 | 859 | 850 | 833 | 1,047 | 893 | 1,458 | 699 |
| 20—25 | 1,044 | 1,045 | 947 | 1,302 | 979 | 183 | 513 |
| 25—30 | 965 | 969 | 908 | 1,087 | 905 | 290 | 581 |
| ***Total 0—30*** | ***935*** | ***928*** | ***953*** | ***1,024*** | ***914*** | ***478*** | ***678*** |
| 30—40 | 906 | 873 | 847 | 822 | 887 | 602 | 474 |
| 40—50 | 912 | 920 | 846 | 897 | 888 | 604 | 631 |
| 50—60 | 1,008 | 1,023 | 855 | 1,164 | 927 | 806 | 758 |
| 60 & over | 1,184 | 1,218 | 962 | 1,238 | 1,056 | 724 | 1,210 |
| ***Total 30 & over*** | ***936*** | ***944*** | ***863*** | ***941*** | ***915*** | ***569*** | ***608*** |
| **Total All Ages (Actual population)** | 935 | 937 | 918 | 997 | 914 | 497 | 651 |
| **Total All Ages (Natural population)** | 944 | ... | ... | ... | ... | ... | ... |
| **Low-lying** | | | | | | | |
| 0—1 | 945 | 945 | 915 | 1,008 | 927 | 500 | 1,000 |
| 1—2 | 1,051 | 1,058 | 927 | 1,240 | 1,195 | 727 | 1,000 |
| 2—3 | 1,087 | 1,088 | 1,074 | 1,152 | 910 | 2,333 | 3,000 |
| 3—4 | 1,062 | 1,059 | 1,155 | 1,107 | 939 | 800 | 5,000 |
| 4—5 | 928 | 925 | 1,000 | 1,068 | 801 | 1,000 | 5,000 |
| ***Total 0—5*** | ***1,009*** | ***1,008*** | ***1,016*** | ***1,099*** | ***930*** | ***957*** | ***2,667*** |
| 5—10 | 940 | 938 | 938 | 1,085 | 1,071 | 1,182 | 1,176 |
| 10—15 | 766 | 764 | 781 | 899 | 802 | 1,238 | 429 |
| 15—20 | 755 | 754 | 762 | 909 | 715 | 1,483 | 333 |
| 20—25 | 991 | 994 | 891 | 1,291 | 990 | 208 | 310 |
| 25—30 | 953 | 959 | 810 | 1,100 | 834 | 151 | 778 |
| ***Total 0—30*** | ***906*** | ***909*** | ***999*** | ***1,067*** | ***893*** | ***409*** | ***719*** |
| 30—40 | 908 | 912 | 860 | 880 | 829 | 419 | 333 |
| 40—50 | 960 | 964 | 876 | 1,004 | 935 | 418 | 333 |
| 50—60 | 1,005 | 1,008 | 938 | 1,081 | 858 | 783 | 429 |
| 60 & over | 1,272 | 1,278 | 1,260 | 1,002 | 1,005 | 1,000 | 667 |
| ***Total 30 & over*** | ***979*** | ***982*** | ***922*** | ***958*** | ***982*** | ***500*** | ***364*** |
| **Total All Ages (Actual population)** | 932 | 939 | 892 | 1,030 | 890 | 436 | 589 |
| **Total All Ages (Natural population)** | 946 | ... | ... | ... | ... | ... | ... |
| **Hilly** | | | | | | | |
| 0—1 | 1,018 | 1,008 | 1,119 | 1,056 | 799 | 867 | 1,500 |
| 1—2 | 1,026 | 1,023 | 953 | 1,057 | 1,057 | 1,125 | 667 |
| 2—3 | 1,115 | 1,116 | 1,128 | 1,113 | 1,139 | 1,056 | 500 |
| 3—4 | 1,185 | 1,220 | 968 | 1,088 | 935 | 1,278 | 2,500 |
| 4—5 | 1,062 | 1,077 | 1,139 | 989 | 947 | 1,000 | 1,200 |
| ***Total 0—5*** | ***1,083*** | ***1,089*** | ***1,063*** | ***1,059*** | ***958*** | ***1,071*** | ***963*** |
| 5—10 | 958 | 962 | 978 | 920 | 1,058 | 1,000 | 1,385 |
| 10—15 | 847 | 841 | 832 | 889 | 833 | 837 | 400 |
| 15—20 | 897 | 870 | 844 | 1,065 | 836 | 684 | 854 |
| 20—25 | 1,187 | 1,158 | 1,143 | 1,403 | 860 | 1,196 | 667 |
| 25—30 | 1,059 | 1,043 | 1,055 | 1,153 | 1,000 | 806 | 615 |
| ***Total 0—30*** | ***1,006*** | ***1,015*** | ***924*** | ***1,059*** | ***928*** | ***957*** | ***760*** |
| 30—40 | 1,007 | 918 | 862 | 897 | 881 | 632 | 548 |
| 40—50 | 912 | 930 | 875 | 894 | 927 | 488 | 235 |
| 50—60 | 922 | 1,098 | 934 | 1,077 | 1,069 | 1,385 | 500 |
| 60 & over | 1,088 | 1,216 | 963 | 1,259 | 1,175 | 714 | 778 |
| ***Total 30 & over*** | ***971*** | ***980*** | ***890*** | ***947*** | ***964*** | ***667*** | ***493*** |
| **Total All Ages (Actual population)** | 995 | 992 | 954 | 1,023 | 942 | 875 | 665 |
| **Total All Ages (Natural population)** | 989 | ... | ... | ... | ... | ... | ... |

SUBSIDIARY TABLE IV.—**Number of females per 1,000 males for certain selected castes.**

| CASTE. | NUMBER OF FEMALES PER 1,000 MALES. | | | | | | |
|---|---|---|---|---|---|---|---|
| | All Ages. | 0—5 | 5—12 | 12—15 | 15—20 | 20—40 | 40 and over |
| 1 | 2 | 3 | 4 | 5 | 6 | 7 | 8 |
| Brahman | 994 | 1,150 | 1,078 | 881 | 792 | 986 | 1,066 |
| „ Shrigand | 932 | 1,286 | 1,118 | 1,466 | 1,149 | 681 | 798 |
| „ Shrimali | 1,346 | 3,161 | 1,753 | 1,413 | 1,062 | 1,033 | 1,105 |
| „ Sarwaria | 1,050 | 1,140 | 1,098 | 880 | 833 | 1,059 | 1,137 |
| „ Sanadhya | 950 | 1,272 | 1,097 | 849 | 786 | 952 | 871 |
| „ Jijhotia | 897 | 933 | 902 | 833 | 633 | 915 | 1,031 |
| „ Bhagor | 907 | 995 | 1,072 | 866 | 642 | 843 | 1,036 |
| Rajput | 822 | 958 | 890 | 692 | 747 | 793 | 848 |
| „ Chauhan | 1,098 | 1,133 | 1,093 | 1,199 | 972 | 986 | 1,252 |
| „ Tonwar | 498 | 913 | 536 | 321 | 511 | 452 | 420 |
| „ Ponwar | 777 | 784 | 827 | 720 | 667 | 808 | 787 |
| „ Kachhwaha | 946 | 1,473 | 2,140 | 437 | 1,219 | 745 | 1,049 |
| „ Rathod | 807 | 901 | 856 | 742 | 799 | 746 | 837 |
| „ Gahalot | 651 | 787 | 667 | 747 | 968 | 446 | 650 |
| „ Bhadauria | 729 | 664 | 751 | 451 | 452 | 844 | 1,886 |
| „ Bundela | 976 | 1,010 | 1,083 | 979 | 669 | 1,056 | 1,009 |
| „ Baghel | 956 | 1,020 | 1,052 | 713 | 796 | 1,081 | 921 |
| Maratha | 890 | 898 | 929 | 1,248 | 803 | 772 | 981 |
| Ajna | 744 | 749 | 875 | 827 | 653 | 870 | 551 |
| Bhat | 909 | 1,016 | 1,049 | 1,124 | 767 | 829 | 861 |
| Gujar | 755 | 814 | 907 | 766 | 620 | 709 | 767 |
| Dhangar | 853 | 685 | 769 | 517 | 1,339 | 1,094 | 857 |
| Sondhia | 1,160 | 862 | 961 | 1,900 | 1,516 | 1,008 | 1,372 |
| Bania | 1,032 | 1,163 | 1,065 | 1,197 | 1,089 | 894 | 1,048 |
| „ Agarwal | 1,108 | 1,283 | 1,297 | 1,335 | 1,003 | 960 | 1,057 |
| „ Mahesri | 1,139 | 1,307 | 1,279 | 1,931 | 1,246 | 775 | 1,189 |
| „ Oswal | 1,067 | 1,387 | 1,121 | 1,226 | 1,479 | 842 | 985 |
| „ Porwal | 950 | 1,076 | 961 | 1,013 | 990 | 877 | 938 |
| „ Gahohi | 837 | 786 | 776 | 751 | 693 | 810 | 1,072 |
| Khangar | 906 | 690 | 925 | 1,088 | 1,242 | 891 | 860 |
| Kachera | 1,000 | 956 | 870 | 847 | 672 | 943 | 1,663 |
| Bhilala | 1,017 | 1,079 | 961 | 923 | 1,146 | 1,014 | 954 |
| Saharia | 950 | 1,029 | 932 | 911 | 1,192 | 997 | 659 |
| Bhil | 1,002 | 1,037 | 1,030 | 627 | 969 | 942 | 1,291 |
| Gond | 1,107 | 1,131 | 1,066 | 874 | 1,045 | 1,104 | 1,276 |
| Kol | 1,080 | 1,011 | 1,032 | 980 | 1,131 | 1,168 | 1,077 |
| Musalman | 906 | 1,014 | 924 | 986 | 904 | 869 | 869 |
| „ Shaikh | 937 | 982 | 913 | 1,115 | 982 | 911 | 903 |
| „ Sayad | 844 | 972 | 980 | 803 | 903 | 737 | 817 |
| „ Pathan | 885 | 1,070 | 928 | 902 | 820 | 849 | 838 |

# CHAPTER VII.

## Civil Condition.

59. In the East where living is comparatively cheap marriage, by adding a helpmate to the household, and later, workers to a family, has always been a much desired end. The mixture of religion with custom gave the habit a great impulse until marriage in the eyes of a Hindu became the most important event in life, a sacrament never to be omitted. Finally religion intervened to ordain that a son, real or adopted, is required to perform the last funeral rites and is the only means of saving the souls of those Hindus who have departed from the torments of disgusting hells. As a natural corollary, a daughter must never reach puberty unmarried. **Introductory.**

The preponderance of Hindus in Central India has resulted in the adoption to a greater or lesser degree of these ideas by Animists and even Musalmans.

This universality of marriage is in strong contrast with Western conditions as the inset shows. Child marriage is prevalent and the rules governing marriage, exogamy, endogamy and the restrictions imposed by prohibitive degrees in relationship and the concomitant difficulty of finding husbands all tend to encourage it. These are dealt with under "Marriage and Caste."

| Locality. | Number of married females per mille at 15—45. |
|---|---|
| Central India | 803 |
| England | 149 |
| France | 228 |
| Germany | 226 |

It should be remarked that while the practice of early marriage is very general, cohabitation is not contemporaneous with marriage but ordinarily takes place after the girl has had her first menses, which in this country often occurs before 14 years of age, the age at which it is popularly considered that a husband and wife should live together. In many cases a second ceremony takes place before cohabitation commences, while the girl lives with her parents until this period arrives.

While child marriage is less common among Musalmans it is nevertheless very general, due to the influence of Hindu surroundings which are especially strong in States where the ruling family is itself Hindu. The Animists, wherever they come into touch with more civilised communities, gradually adopt this custom regarded by them as a sign of superior rank and status.

Widow marriage is another touchstone of social status and apparently a more delicate test than the adoption of child marriage even.

Another cause of child marriage is expense. Throughout this Agency among the better classes of every community bridegrooms have to be paid for, and a considerable *dot* is expected. The older a girl is the higher the price that can be demanded, hence the eagerness to settle everything as soon as possible. The "Central India Rajput Hitkarni Sabha" has laid down certain rules, advocating indeed at its last meeting 16 as the minimum age for the marriage of girls and 20 for boys, but it is practically impossible to enforce these rules in most cases, public opinion is not strong enough, while the influence of the zenana, always thrown into the scale of high expenditure and early marriage, is in almost every case the determining factor.

In the Musalman community the restrictions as to marriage are strongest among occupational groups such as Rangrez, Pinjara, etc., whose communities are very similar to real castes.

60. Tables VII and XIV and the Subsidiary Tables at the end of this Chapter contain the figures discussed. These figures show that although 45 out of every 100 men are unmarried, 90 per cent. are under 15 years of age. At 15-20, 44 per cent. are married while at 20-40 the figure rises to above 76 per cent. At the age of 20 and over some 84 girls in every 100 are married while 13 are already widows before they are 40. Those girls who are not married by 20 are either physically defective or prostitutes. Exceptions do, however, occur especially in the higher sections of the Rajput caste owing to the difficulty of finding a suitable husband. In one instance in Central India the daughter of **General statistics.**

a chief was not married till she was over 40, and cases of girls being over 20 and still unmarried are known. It may thus be said without exaggeration that ordinarily a genuine "old maid" is unknown in the Agency except among Christians or Others.

### *Marriage and Religion.*

**Hindus.**

61. The predominance of Hindus make their returns very similar to those for the Agency as a whole. The absolute necessity for marriage has been already referred to. Hindus show 2 per cent. more married than Musalmans among both males and females; however at 40-60 the Musalman figures are higher, but as would be expected their return for widows is lower. The fall in the figures for unmarried females after 15 is very marked, being 37 per cent. lower than that for 10-15.

*Diagram showing the number per 1000 aged 0-10 who are married (by religion.)*

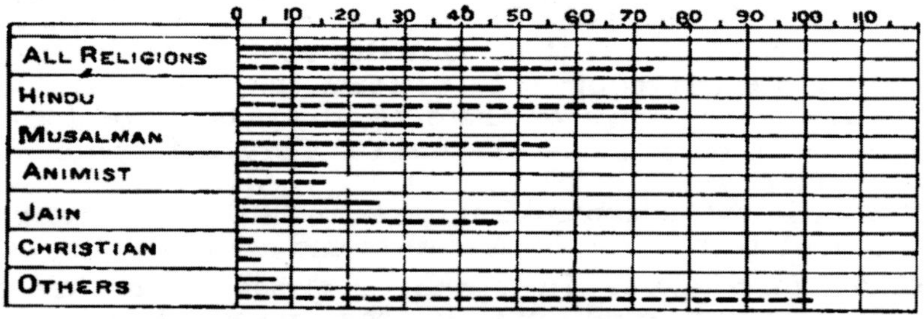


As regards widowhood Hindu females stand second, 8 per cent. behind Jains, while their males are less numerous in this condition than either Jains or Musalmans. The inclusion of so many Animists on this occasion has, no doubt, tended to lower the figure for widows.

*Diagram showing the number per 1000 aged 15-40 who are widowed (by religions)*

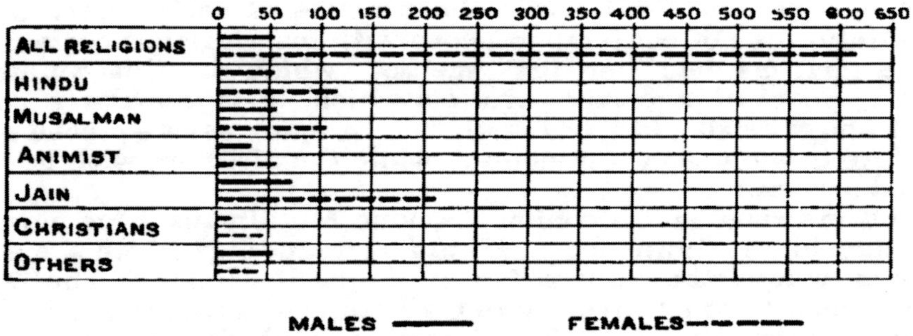


**Jains.**

Jains show 7 per cent. fewer married males and 5 per cent. fewer females than Hindus. The age returns also show that 5 per cent. fewer girls are wives at 10-15 while the number of unmarried after 15 is 42 per cent. lower than at 10-15.

Widow marriage is less common than among Hindus, 67 per cent. at 40 and over being widows, 5 per cent. more than among Hindus.

**Animists.**

The Animists show the most unmarried males, 7 per cent. more than Hindus and 6 per cent. more than Musalmans; among females they show 11 per cent. more spinsters than Hindus and 9 per cent. more than Musalmans. Among the widowed, Animist males are 3 per cent. less numerous than either Hindus or Musalmans and their females 7 per cent. less.

Marriage is clearly later, only 10 boys and 26 girls in every hundred at 10-15 being married, to 25 boys and 58 girls among Hindus and 11 boys and 39 girls among Musalmans. Widows of 20-40 number only 7 per cent. and of 40-60 only 47 per cent. as compared with 13 and 55 per cent. among Hindus and 12 and 51 per cent. among Musalmans showing the general practice of remarriage.

**Christians and others.**

These figures it would be unprofitable to examine in detail. The population in the first case is artificial, depending mainly on the garrisons in the British Cantonments, and in the latter case consists chiefly of immigrants, Parsis, Sikhs, etc. Briefly, child marriage is not prevalent and unmarried men predominate.

### *Religion and Locality.*

62. Locality has a distinct effect on marriage. The Plateau and Hilly tracts show most bachelors, the Low-lying tract being some 2 per cent. behind; among females the same tract also possesses the smallest number of spinsters, 2 per cent. less than the Plateau, and 7 per cent. less than the Hilly tract. On the other hand boys marry soon in the Low-lying tract, while girls marry to the same extent as on the Plateau. Among the widowed, both as to males and females, the Plateau and Low-lying figures are not far apart while the Hilly tract, as would be expected, favours remarriage most.

Taking the main religions, Hindu males marry younger in the Low-lying and Hilly than in the Plateau tract, the Low-lying figure showing 9 males in every 100 married at 5-10 to 5 on the Plateau and 8 in the Hills. Among females, however, the Plateau stands first with 15 girls at 5-10 married in every 100 to 14 in the Low-lying and 13 in the Hilly tract.

Musalmans show no material variation as regards males of 5-10, but females of this period marry more freely in the Low-lying tract, some 2 per cent. more being wives.

*Diagram showing the proportion of the married per 1000 of each age period by natural divisions.*

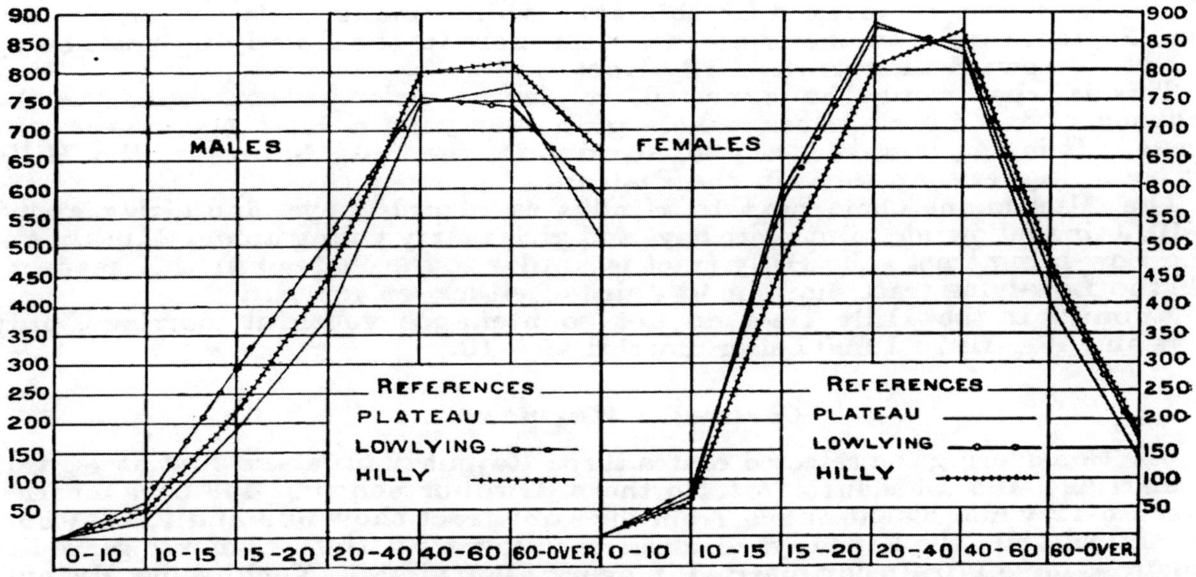


Among Animists the difference is very marked. Boys of 5-10 who are married fall below 1 per cent. in the Hilly tract and girls show only just 2 per cent., while the more Hinduised jungle tribes of the Plateau and Low-lying sections show between 4 and 5 per cent.

Jains in the Low-lying tract are most prone to early marriage, showing at 5-10, 7 boys in every 100 married to about 3 elsewhere, and 14 girls to 6 elsewhere.

Widowhood among Hindus is least common in the Hilly tract; among Musalmans males show the lowest figure in the Hills, females in the Low-lying tract.

Polygamy in Central India is broadly speaking a matter of income. **Polygamy.** Among Hindus and Musalmans well-to-do men of position often have more than one wife as do also the Animists. In all there are 991 married females to 1,000 males while Hindus show the same figure. Musalmans show 39 less. The Animists alone show more wives than husbands. The Natural Divisions hence show most wives in the Animistic Hilly tracts.

Jains curiously show an equal number of wives and husbands in the Plateau, while in the Low-lying tract they show fewer wives.

Polygamy is thus undoubtedly not common excepting among jungle tribes. Polyandry is quite unknown.

### *Child Marriage.*

63. In considering this question it should be recollected that marriage and cohabitation are not contemporaneous. No point is so noticeable in examining the civil condition and age figures as the return of married children. Among classes of high caste or good social standing the custom has been in vogue from very early days. Among those in the lower grades of society child marriage is mainly due to aping the customs of superiors. The real origin of this custom among the higher castes is problematical, but the pressure due to the difficulty in marrying off daughters seems the most likely cause. Once introduced it became a cachet of rank and was followed for the distinction which it conferred by those in the lower strata of society. Daughters are throughout Central India, except among the jungle tribes, expensive luxuries and the necessity for marrying them entails in all the better castes great hardships on fathers, the expenses often impoverishing a much-daughtered family for generations. While the physiological side is undoubtedly one for consideration, in Central India among the rural classes cohabitation is not ordinarily allowed until the girl is of suitable age, as can be seen in the sturdy peasants who could never have sprung from immature mothers. On the other hand in the higher castes and in towns there is a tendency to allow cohabitation too soon with all its attendant evils. It is not, however, as yet an evil which affects the population as a whole.

The figures for Hindus show 72 boys and 85 girls in every 1,000 married between 5-10 years of age. But 39 more boys in the Low-lying and 28 more in the Hilly tract are married at this age, while among girls the figures are closer, 20 more girls on the Plateau and 11 more in the Low-lying tract being wives at this period than in the Hilly tract.

This is what would be expected, so far as girls are concerned, as the prevalence of the jungle tribes, whose girls marry at a later age, lowers the average. It is not, however, easy to account for the male figures in the Hilly tract being higher than those in the Plateau.

The Musalmans come next to Hindus as regards boys and girls married at 5-10, Jains following. But more boys and girls marry young among Musalmans in the Low-lying tract ; the Hilly tract is similar to the Plateau in this respect ; while the Low-lying tract shows most Jains of either sex married.

Animists in the Hilly tract do not countenance youthful marriage, only 9 boys and 17 girls in 1,000 being married at 5-10.

### *Caste and Marriage.*

64. Considering the selected castes three Rajput clans stand first as regards boy marriage, the Bhadaurias of Northern Gwalior showing 453 boys married between 5-12 while Kachhwahas from the same tract show 302 and the Rathors from Malwa 189 ; the Sanadhya Brahmans follow with 159. Among girls the Bhadaurias have 170 already married in every 1,000 at 0-5, Kachhwaha Rajputs with 148 standing next, followed by Shrimali (102) and Sarwaria Brahmans (82) ; at 5-12, Ajnas a cultivating class in Malwa (399) take first place ; among Rajputs Rathors lead (254). The contrast on examining the jungle tribes is most marked, Bhil and Bhilala showing under 1 per cent. married of both sexes at 0-5 and very low figures at 5-12 while the more Hinduised Gond shows a much higher ratio.

The Shrimali Brahman figure is curiously low at 0-5 for boys and must be due to some error. The influence of locality on caste is shown in the inset. Those living on the more Hinduised Plateau or Low-lying tracts show the highest figures at the earliest years.

| Caste. | Females per 1,000 by Natural Division who are married at | | | | | |
|---|---|---|---|---|---|---|
| | Plateau. | | Low-lying. | | Hilly. | |
| | 0-5 | 5-12 | 0-5 | 5-12 | 0-5 | 5-12 |
| Agarwal | 91 | 157 | 58 | 329 | ... | ... |
| Chauhan | 71 | 255 | 94 | 122 | 16 | 197 |
| Bhil (Hindu) | 14 | 184 | ... | ... | 3 | 28 |
| Bhil (Animist) | 29 | 113 | ... | ... | 4 | 52 |

The tendency is for child marriage to increase. While those who have always followed it adhere to it, the jungle tribes, which are every year coming more and more under Hindu influence as States develop their territories, adopt the system. Public opinion is not against the custom and the voice of the more enlightened is too weak to have much effect, and even to these the reply is often given that it is early cohabitation, not early marriage, that matters.

As regards widow marriage, the Brahmans show the least prevalence of this custom, the Sanadhyas of Northern Gwalior (662), Bhagors of the same tract (659) and the Sarwarias (625) from the east stand first; next follow the Agarwals (622), Jijhotia Brahmans (608), Oswal Banias (606), Marathas (596), Porwals (551) and Gahohis (553). Widowhood.

It is difficult to explain how Bhadaurias and Kachhwahas who marry young also have fewest widows since widow marriage is not practised.

The more modern views held by the better classes on widow marriage, especially of virgin widows, have not become general. A few isolated instances of such marriages among the more enlightened have occurred, but generally speaking, the country is conservative in this respect.

### *Birth Customs.*

65. As soon as pregnancy is known sweet balls of sugar and *gur* are distributed. Six, seven or eight months previous to delivery ceremonies commence with singing, caste dinners, and other entertainments to keep the woman cheerful. She is also given savoury food, while any articles craved for by her are provided. Neighbours and relatives often bring delicate and nutritious food for her and offer clothes (*Lugra* and *Choli* or simply a *Choli*). Dakshani people call this *Dohalejewana*, other Hindus *Agarni*, and the Boharas *Sātwāsā*. Singing is always loudly carried on to ensure a hearing.

It is customary in some parts to celebrate the 7th or 8th month of pregnancy by inviting a number of women to the house to sing songs appropriate to the occasion. These women are then given some *Batāshās* or sweets and the pregnant woman has her lap filled with sweets and dry fruit. After delivery some sweets are sent to her parents by her father-in-law, and the parents in return send *Hansli* (necklace) *Karā* (bracelets) for the child and clothes for the son-in-law, daughters and other members of the family according to their means.

In some Mahājan families this ceremony of sending ornaments and clothes for the baby and others is performed by the parents of the pregnant woman even before the child is born.

No general practice of causing abortion exists in these parts even when the diviner declares that the child in the womb is a female, and no traces of couvade are met with.

If a Hindu woman dies in childbirth (*i.e.*, before delivery has taken place) the child is taken out by cutting open the woman's womb, and the bodies of both the mother and child are then burnt together. Should the woman die after the child is born her body is burnt, the child being taken care of by the father or other relations. When the body of the dead mother is carried away for cremation mustard is sprinkled upon it on the way. During cremation every care is taken to see that no part of the body is left unburnt, as there is in such cases great danger of her spirit becoming the familiar of a *Dakanī* (witch) and doing evil, as witches are believed to be able to compel the souls of such dead persons to do their bidding. The body of a woman who dies after delivery is very carefully removed. Nails are driven in at every threshold the body will pass on its way to cremation and are also driven into the ground at the spot where she died so that she may not return and plague the second wife.

If the child has teeth when it dies it is burnt, otherwise buried. Some marks are usually made on its body so that when it comes back to the same house it will be recognised.

The birth of a child in a family is, in parts of Malwa, announced by the woman beating a platter or a *Sūp* (winnowing basket) according as the child born is male or female. The following ceremony, known as the "*chauk,*" is usually performed in Malwa after the 10th day of the birth. The mother and the child are bathed and clothed in new garments and the mother, placing the child in a *Sūp* (winnowing basket), takes it to the centre of the courtyard of the house which has been plastered with cowdung and where a *chauk* (a small square) has been made of wheat flour over which a seat for her and the child has been placed. There the mother sits with the child in her arms and has her nails pared. The ceremony then concludes with her worshipping the sun god and the local well. The day is one of rejoicing for the family and relations.

Should, however, the birth take place in the *Mūl Nakshatra* the father is not allowed to see the face of the child till the 27th day (there are 27 Nakshatras) when special ceremonies have to be gone through and the father is allowed to see the face of the child as reflected in a cup of oil. The ceremonies consist in giving the father, mother and child a bath from an earthen jar having 27 holes and containing water drawn from 27 different wells, while the leaves of 27 different trees are put into the water. The bath being over, the father sees the face of the child as reflected in a cup of oil. Then 7 different kinds of grain (or gold or silver) are used to make an effigy of the *Mūl Nakshatra* and a piece of iron and cup of oil are given away to a Garoria Brahman.

As soon as a woman delivers a child she is kept aloof for 10 days in a closed room and is made to lie down, being nursed by a *Dai*.

No food is given to her for three days, after which a little light food is allowed. For five days no sweets or anything that is supposed to have heat-producing properties is given. After 10 days liquid tonic food is given. After seclusion extending up to three months the woman is allowed to walk about freely as usual.

In parts of Malwa, however, acting on the advice of the family Pandit, the mother and child are given their first bath three, four or five days after delivery. All old earthen pots are changed on that day, the *liping* of the house with cowdung is done and all the dirty clothes belonging to the mother are washed. Still the woman is not considered clean till one month is over.

It is usual to summon a Jyotishi who fixes an auspicious moment and assigns a name for special use (*Janmarashi nām*) while the name for everyday use (*Bolta nām*) is given by the parents, and is usually that of some ancestor. This takes place generally on the 12th day. Relatives are invited and make presents. If the child behaves abnormally, will not cry, cries excessively, or will not suck for 11 days, ancestors are invoked, and the name of the ancestor whose name causes normal behaviour to be assumed, is given to the child. In the Nimar district of Indore children are often named by woman. A woman is called in and proposes a name, at the same time tying a white *couri* and glass beads round the child's wrist.

Muhammadans often simply turn over the leaves of the Kuran at random and begin the names of their children with the first letter of the first word on the page that turns up.

The rite of feeding a child for the first time consists in putting a little *Khīr* (rice boiled in milk and sweetened) on a rupee by the child's aunt (father's sister) or sister and letting it touch the child's lips seven times. This ceremony is generally performed when the child is six months old. The rupee on which the *Khīr* is placed is given to caste fellows and the day is observed as one of rejoicing by the family.

Sneezing by the children during illness is taken as an indication that they will recover. Grinding of teeth by children when ill is regarded as a sign that they are under the influence of some god who must be appeased and pacified to allow the children to recover.

The boring of ear, nose, etc., is done on any auspicious day after a child is three or four months old. Sometimes the child is three or four years old when this ceremony takes place.

Among the Bohoras the boring is done by a thorn and not an instrument.

There are no puberty ceremonies which have for their object the impregnation of women. There is, however, a ceremony known as the ceremony of *Phūl chauk*, which is performed when the woman has her first monthly course. The ceremony consists in filling the lap or loose fold of her dress with cocoanut and sweets the day she is free from her first menses and takes her bath. She puts on new and good clothes that day, and singing, music and rejoicing take place in the family.

### *Terms of Relationship.*

66. No local customs appear to prevail in Central India by which the maternal uncle arranges marriages or takes a prominent part in the marriage ceremony.

In Bundelkhand, however, there are two ceremonies in a marriage, "Chikat" and "Kannar," in which the maternal uncle takes a part.

The maternal aunt does not usually here, as in many parts of India, name the child, this being generally done by the father or an elderly member of the family after consultation with a Jyotishi. Among the Bhils, however, the paternal aunt names the child. The Jyotishi is often consulted and the first letter of the name which he gives is fixed by the Rashi, Nakshatra, etc., on which the horoscope is based and the child's future is ascertained.

The sister's son can only officiate at funerals in the absence of male issue in the father's line. These rites are performed by the son, grandson, brother, father, or any other male member related.

Among higher castes where widow marriage exists, a widow cannot, as a rule, marry any member of the deceased husband's family.

Widows among the aboriginal tribes generally and low castes such as Dhimars, Kachhis, Nais, Ahirs, Basors, Chamars, Bhangis, etc., accept a second husband but not necessarily the first husband's younger brother or any other male relative. It is optional with the widows to choose from among the members of the first husband's family or from some other family of their own caste. Among the Baghelkhand aboriginals, except Panika, the deceased husband's younger brother can take his widow to wife. In Malwa only the Bargundas appear to generally follow the custom of the younger brother's taking the widow of the elder brother to wife by the Nātra ceremony. But even they do not recognise this as the younger brother's in-alienable right.

"Sālā" and "Susara" or "Sasur" are only considered abusive when applied to those who do not bear these relationships.

A list of terms of relationship has been given at the end of this Chapter. The more important dialects spoken in the Agency by different communities have been taken. Of these the languages used by the Bargundas and the aboriginal tribes in Baghelkhand (Gonds, Kols, etc.) are the most unusual and seem to show traces of words of non-Sanskritic origin.

In giving these terms of relationship the original order has been slightly altered, so that when a male and female use the same word in speaking these terms can be placed in one group.

It will be evident that there are various relationships which are distinguished in the local nomenclature but which are not so distinguished in English.

For instance the term "uncle" includes both father's and mother's brothers and may even refer to the husband of a father's or mother's sister. All these have separate terms appropriated to them in the local speech (Kākā, Chāchā, Bābā; Māmā, Māmū; Phupha, Phua; Mausa, Masa;), being respectively used for them. Other instances are "Nephew" and "Niece" "Brother-in-law" and "Sister-in-law," "Grand-father" and "Grand-mother," "Grand-son" and "Grand-daughter," also "sister (elder or younger)" and "Brother (elder or younger)" and so on. No particular reason can be adduced for the differentiation except possibly that owing to the joint family system the ties of relationship are in India stronger and more persistent than where no such system exists.

On the other hand there are a few relationships which are differentiated in English but not in the vernacular, *e.g.*, "Cousin" (Bhāi, Bhain being equally used for a cousin as for a brother and sister).

As noted above *Bhāi* and *Bhain* are used for cousins (sons and daughters of father's brother or sister, and of mother's brother or sister) as also for brothers or sisters. The term *Kākā* is used for father, paternal uncle; *Dādā* for elder brother, grand-father and sometimes for uncle; *Bāi* is used for elder sister, mother and sometimes for husband's elder brother's wife or his sister. Terms in this category, *i.e.*, Bhāi and Bhain, Kākā and Kākī, Māmā and Māmī, Sālā and Sālī, Sasur and Sās, etc., are also commonly applied to any kinsmen whose connection approaches such relationships.

It would be out of place for one who is not an expert to attempt to guide through the maze which has sprung up from this investigation into terms of relationship. The origin of the family is still undetermined, the evidence collected being very conflicting, while the theories of McLennan, Morgan, and others are by no means convincing. Terms of relationship are studied in this connection with a view to obtaining a clue to the constitution of the family in early days, but observers often give contradictory reports of the same customs and hold diametrically opposed views. McLennan, for instance, considers that the classificatory system of relationship is based on a previous polyandrous state of society and was devised purely for the purpose of salutation while Morgan has devised a complicated and not at all convincing system by which he groups the world's system of relationship into five classes. It may be stated as a fact, however, that in very early times the only relationships distinguished by names were those of father, mother, son, daughter, brother and sister. Later on the father's brother, mother' brother and grandfather received separate appellations, and later still, daughter-in-law, etc. ; only very much later, however, were any terms devised to distinguish the members of the family of a man's wife. Her relations were not considered because she was held to have passed as any other "possession" absolutely into the family of the husband—at most they were addressed as "friend." Even in Greek "in-laws" were addressed merely as *Kedestes* (Κηδεστης) *i.e.*, those concerned with funeral obsequies (Κηδος). In early days therefore, this non-recognition of agnates as distinct from cognates resulted in children recognising their father's but not their mother's brothers. No known early language indeed has any words for agnates. The wife and her children belonged to the husband and the wife's relatives were of no account.

The list here given, however, shows a very different state of affairs, as words exist for both cognates and agnates, while minute distinctions are often made even between elder and younger.

The reader who desires to study this subject further should consult the works of McLennan, Lang, Morgan, Lord Avebury, Westermarck, Starcke, Hartland, Durkheim, Spencer and Gillen and others. A very useful book giving references to all authorities on this subject is the admirable *Real-lexicon Der Indogermanisch Altertums-kunde* of Schrader.

## List of terms of relationship —*contd.*

| | English. | Mālwī. | Bhīlī or Bhilālī. | Nimādī. |
|---|---|---|---|---|
| 1 | 2 | 3 | 4 | 5 |
| 1 | Father | Bāp, Bā, Bābā, Kākā, Dādā | Bā. | Bāp, Bāpū, Dādā. |
| 2 | Mother | Mā, Bāi, Jiji, Bhābī | Mai, Ai. | Mā, Awi Bau. |
| 3 | Son | Betā, Nānā, Bāpū | Pūria, Nānā. } Unloved child is called by name. | Betā, Nānā. |
| 4 | Daughter | Betī, Nānī, Bāī | Purī, Nānī. | Betī. |
| 5 | Elder brother (M. S. & W. S.) | Dādā, Bade Bhāi | Motlā Bhāi or Dādā. | Dādā. |
| 6 | Younger brother (M. S. & W. S.) | Bhaiya, Chhote Bhāi, Kūkā Nānā. | Nānlā, Bhāi. | Bhāi. |
| 7 | Elder sister (M. S. & W. S.) | Badī Ben, Jiji, Bāi, Bdī Bhain. | Motlī Jījī. | Jījī. |
| 8 | Younger sister (M. S. & W. S.) | Chhoti Ben, Ben, Bai. | Nānī, Nāndī. | Ben. |
| 9 | Father's brother { Elder | Bā, Barā Bā, Bābā, Bājī. | Bābā. | Kākā. |
| | { Younger | Kākā. Bābā, Chāchā. | Kākā. | Kākā. |
| 10 | Brother's child (M. S. & W. S.) | Bhatījā, Nānā, Bhatījī. | Bhatarjā or Nānā. (No special word). | Nānā or Nānī, Bhatījā or Bhatījī. |
| 11 | Father's brother's wife. { Elder | Badī Mā, Motī Jījī, Dādī. | Bābī. | Badī Mā. |
| | { Younger. | Kākī, Chāchī. | Kākī. | Kākī. |
| 12 | Husband's brother's child | Bhatījā, Bhatījī. | No distinctive word. Puriā, Betā, Puri are used. | Nānā. |
| 13 | Father's brother's child | Kākā Bābā Ke Bhāi or Ben. | Kāke Bhāi, Kāke Bahīn. | Bhāi, Ben. |
| 14 | Father's sister | Phuphī, Bhua. | Phūpī. | Phuī. |
| 15 | Father's sister's husband | Phuphā, Phuā. | Phuphā. | Phuwājī. |
| 16 | Wife's brother's child | No special name. Generally called Bhatījā, Bhatījī. | Called by name. | Bhatijā. |
| 17 | Father's sister's child | Phuphera Bhāi or Ben, Bhuā Bhai or Ben. | Bhuā Bhāi, Bhuā Bahin. | Phuwā Bhāi. |
| 18 | Mother's brother | Māmā. | Māmā. | Māmū. |
| 19 | Sister's child (M. S. & W. S.) | Bhānej, Bhānjī. | Bhānej. Bhanjī or called by name. | Bhanej. |
| 20 | Mother's brother's wife | Māmī. | Māmī. | Māmī. |
| 21 | Husband's sister's child | No words, generally called Bhānja, Bhānej. | No word. Bhānej, Bhānjī. | Bhānej, Bhānjī. |
| 22 | Mother's brother's child | Mamera Bhāi or Ben. | Māme Bhāi, Māme Bahīn, | Māmā Bhāi, Māmā Bahen. |
| 23 | Mother's sister | Māsī, Mausī. | Māsī. | Māsī. |
| 24 | Mother's sister's husband | Māsā, Mausā, Kākā. | Māsā. | Mausā, Kākā. |
| 25 | Wife's sister's child | No word, Bhatījā, Bhatījī. | Bhānej, Bhānajī. | Bhatījā, Bhatījī. |
| 26 | Mother's sister's child | Mausera Bhāi or Ben. | Māse Bhāi, Māse Bhain. | Mauserā Bhāi or Bahin. |
| 27 | Father's father | Dādā, Bājī, Barābā. | Motā bā, Nānā. | Dādājī Dājī. |
| 28 | Son's son (M. S. & W. S.) | Potā, Natī. | Puriā, Betā, Potā. | Nānā, Potā. |
| 29 | Father's mother | Dādī, Motī Mā. | Dāhli Mai, Nānī. | Dādī. |
| 30 | Mother's father | Nānā, Bā. | Dahlā Bā, Motā Bā, Nānā. | Bhotā, Bā. |
| 31 | Daughter's son (M. S. & W. S.) | Nātī. | Nānin Puriā, Puriā, Doyatā. | Nānā. |
| 32 | Mother's mother | Nānī. | Dahli Mai, Dādī Mā, Nānī Mā. | ...... |
| 33 | Husband | Dhanī, Gharwālā, Admī. | Nānan bāhas. | Dhanī. |
| 34 | Wife | Gharwālī, Aurat, Lugāi. | Nānanāis, Naninais or Purināis. | Lugāi. |
| 35 | Wife's father | Susra. | Dahlā, Sasrā. | Susro. |
| 36 | Wife's mother | Sās. | Dāhdabābē, Sās. | Sās. |
| 37 | Husband's father | Susrā. | Sasrā. | Susro. |
| 38 | Husband's mother | Sās. Sāsujī | Sāsu. | Sāsujī. |
| 39 | Daughter's husband (M. S. & W. S.). | Jawāin, Jamāi. | Jamai. | Jamāi. |
| 40 | Son's wife (M. S. & W. S.) | Bahū, Lādī. | Auhari, Bahū. | Bahū, Beta bahū. |
| 41 | Wife's brother | Sālā. | Sālā. | Sālā. |
| 42 | Sister's husband (M. S. & W. S.) | Jījā, Banej. Bahnoi. | Pāhna, Bainoī. | Jiajī. |
| 43 | Wife's sister | Sālī. | Sālī. | Sālī. |
| 44 | Husband's brother. { Elder | Jeth. | Jeth. | Jeth. |
| | { Younger | Dewar. | Deora. | Dewar. |
| 45 | Brother's wife (M. S. & W. S.). | Bhāwaj, Bhojāī, Bhābhī. | Bhābhī. | Bhābhī, Bhābījī Rāj Lādī bahū. |
| 46 | Husband's sister, her husband | Nanand, Nanadoi. | Deoranī. | Nanand. |
| 47 | Wife's sister's husband | Sādhū, Sādū. | Bahinwe, Sādū. | Sādū, Sādū Bhāi. |
| 48 | Husband's brother's wife. { Elder | Jethānī. | Jethānī. | Jithānī. |
| | { Younger | Dorānī, Deorānī. | Dehrānī. | Dorānī. |
| 49 | Son's wife's parents | Samadhī, Samadhan. | No distinctive name. Bewai, Bewān or Dādā, Jījī are used. | Samdhī, Samadhan. |
| 50 | Daughter's husband's parents | Do. | | Do. |

## List of terms of relationship.—*concld.*

| | Bargundī. | Gondī and aboriginal tribes of Baghelkhand. | Baghelkhandī. | Bundelkhandī. |
|---|---|---|---|---|
| 1 | 6 | 7 | 8 | 9 |
| 1 | Kakājī. | Daddā, Dāu. | Bāp, Dāu, Daddā. Bābū Bape. | Daddā, Bāpū, Bāp. |
| 2 | Gam. | Dāi. | Mātā, Mā, Ammā Dīdī. | Bau, Matārī, Wanwājū, Auri, Ammā. |
| 3 | Ghot. | Bābū, Larikā, Bitawā. | Betau, Dādū, Betā, Hīra. | Betā, Bhaiyā or called by name. |
| 4 | Pāl. | Baiya, Larikī. | Butū, Betī. | Bāi, Binnū, Bitiā or called by name. |
| 5 | Bhadtam, Lem. | Tikāit Bhāi. | Dādā Bhai, Dādā, Jethā Bhai. | Daddā, Dāwajū, Bhaiyā, Bade Bhaiyā. |
| 6 | Sirtam, Lem. | Chhotkā Bābū. | Dādū, Chhutkau, Ladura Bhāi. | Bhaiyā or called by name. |
| 7 | Angash. | Bāiji, Dīdī, Jeth Bahin. | Dīdī, Diddā, Jethī Bahin. | Jījī, Jijji or Jījī Bāi. |
| 8 | Sitangash. | Bhanto, Chhotkī Bahin. | Baiya, Būtū, Butuwā, Lahurī Bahin. | Bāi, Binnū or called by name. |
| 9 | Kakājī. | Kākū. | Kakkā, Kākū, Kakā. | Kakkā, Chachehā. |
| | Bayā, Kakā. | Kakā. | Kākā, Kākū, Kakā. | ...... |
| 10 | Bhathijā, Bhatijī. | Patia Bhāi, or Bahin. | Dādābhai, Dādā or Dīdī, Diddā. | Bhaiya or called by name. |
| | | Patia Bhai or Bahin. | Kakia Bhāi or Bahin. | ...... |
| 11 | Mā. | Badī Kākī. | Kākī. | Kakko, Kakī, Chāchī. |
| | Kākī. | Kākī. | Kaki. | ...... |
| 12 | ...... | ...... | Bhatīj. | Bhatījā, Bhatījī. |
| 13 | ...... | Patiā Bhāi or Bhain. | Dādā Bhai, Dādā, Dīdī, Didā, Kakiyawat or Pitiawat Bhāi or Bahin. | Bhaiya or called by name. |
| 14 | Phuī. | Phuwā. | Phuwā, Phuphū. | Phuwā, Phuwānu, Bawā. |
| 15 | Māmā. | Phuphā. | Phuphā. | Phuphā. |
| 16 | ...... | ...... | Sārpūt, Sārputī. | Sārekā Larkā or Larkī. |
| 17 | ...... | Dudh Bhāi or Bahin. | Phuphuāwat Bhāi or Bahin. | Called by name. |
| 18 | Māmā. | Māmā. | Māmā. | Māmmā, Māmā, Māmū. |
| 19 | Bhānej, Bhānjī. | Bhaine, Bhaini. | Bhaine. Bhainī, Bhanej. | Bhaiya, Binnū or by name. |
| 20 | Māmī. | Māmī. | Mānī, Māin. | Māin. |
| 21 | Bhānej, or called by name. | ...... | ...... | Bhaiya, Binnū, Bhānjā or Bhānjī. |
| 22 | Tendko. | Mamia Bhāi or Bahin. | Mamiyāwat Bhāi or Bahin. | Bhāi or Behen. |
| 23 | Māsī. | Mausī. | Mausī. | Mosī. |
| 24 | Māsā. | Mosā. | Mausiā. | Mosiā. |
| 25 | Bhānjā, Bhānjī. Called by name. | ...... | ...... | Sadu kā larka or by name. |
| 26 | Called by name. | Mausiāwat, Bhāi or Bahin. | Mausiyāwat Bhāi or Bahin. | Mausiyāpata Bhāi or by name. |
| 27 | Gaphān, Dājī. | Babā, Ājā, Dādī. | Bābā, Ājā. | Babbā, Bābā, Dādā. |
| 28 | Potā or Betā, Natyā. | Nātī. | Bachchā, Nātī. | Called by name, Nātī, Potā. |
| 29 | Dādī Mā, Aī. | Badkādāi, Aī | Buā Dāi, Ājī. | Ājī Dādī, Bau. |
| 30 | Gaphān. | Nānā. | Nānā. | Nānā. Babbā. |
| 31 | Betā. | Bitia, Nātī. | Nātī. | Called by name. Nawāsā, Nātī. |
| 32 | Nānī Mā. | Nānī. | Nānī. | Nānī, Bau. |
| 33 | Bharthār or Khāwind. | Manserū, Mansedhū | Manus, Bhatār. | Khasam, Mūnsa, Madai, Gharwāla. |
| 34 | Kundash (not called by name) | Parānī. | Mehrī, Mehrārū, Dulahī. | Lugāi. Gharwālī, Maharaiyā. |
| 35 | Susrājī, Gamān. | Sasur, Babā. | Bāwujū, Dādājū. | Sahujū, Sasur. |
| 36 | Phuijī. | Māp, Maiya, Māi. | Sās, Bhaujijū. | Sāwanjū, Sās. |
| 37 | Amān, Gamān. | ...... | Sasur, Wawujū, Dādājū. | Sasur or whatever the husband calls it. |
| 38 | Sasujī, Gal. | Sās, Māyā, Maiyā. | Sās. | Sās or whatever her husband calls her. |
| 39 | Jamai. | Dāmād, Pahunā. | Damāt, Pahunā. | Lallā, Lālā, Dāmād. |
| 40 | Wad. | Dulahiyā, Bahū Putau. | Putau, Dulahī. | Bahū, Bahuria or by name. |
| 41 | Sālā. | Sarwā. | Sār. | Sālā, Bhaiya or by name. |
| 42 | Mechyān. | Bhānto. | Jījā, Bahnoī. | Jījā. Bahanoī. |
| 43 | Sālī. | Sārī. | Sārī. | Sālī. Sārī, Dīdī, Jījī, Jiyā. |
| 44 | Jeth. | Jeth-ut, Bhasur. | Dādājū. | Jeth. |
| | Dewar. | Dewā. | Dādū, Lallā, Dewar, Lālā. | Dewar. |
| 45 | Bhābhī, Bhojāi. | Tikāit Bhaujī. | Bhaujāi, Bhaujī, Dulahī. | Bhauj, Bhojāī, Bhauji, Bhābi, Bahū. |
| 46 | ...... | Nanand, Nandoi. | Diddā, Nanan, Dīdī, Baiyā, Būtū, Nanadoi. | Nand, Jījī, Bāi, or by name. |
| 47 | Sādū. | Sādhū. | Sādhū. | Sādū, Bhai if elder, by name if younger. |
| 48 | Jethānī. | Badī Maiji, Jethānī. | Jethānī, Didijū. | Jethānī or Jījī. |
| | Derānī. | Lādī. | Deorānī, Dalahī. | Called by name. |
| 49 | Samdaī, Samdin, Wevāi, Wewan. | Samdhījī, Samdhanjī. | Samadhī and Samadhan. | Different castes call differently general terms are Samadhī and Samadhin. |
| 50 | Do. | Do. | Do. | Do. |

SUBSIDIARY TABLE I.—**Distribution by Civil Condition of 1,000 of each Sex, Religion and main Age Period at each of the last two Censuses.**

| Religion and Age. | Unmarried. | | | | Married. | | | | Widowed. | | | |
|---|---|---|---|---|---|---|---|---|---|---|---|---|
| | Males. | | Females. | | Males. | | Females. | | Males. | | Females. | |
| | 1911. | 1901. | 1911. | 1901. | 1911. | 1901. | 1911. | 1901. | 1911. | 1901. | 1911. | 1901. |
| 1 | 2 | 3 | 4 | 5 | 6 | 7 | 8 | 9 | 10 | 11 | 12 | 13 |
| **All Religions** | **455** | **443** | **316** | **307** | **483** | **470** | **505** | **492** | **62** | **87** | **179** | **201** |
| 0-5 | 975 | 980 | 974 | 967 | 24 | 18 | 23 | 29 | 1 | 2 | 3 | 4 |
| 5-10 | 930 | 922 | 859 | 862 | 67 | 73 | 135 | 130 | 3 | 5 | 6 | 8 |
| 10-15 | 756 | 760 | 431 | 502 | 236 | 223 | 553 | 465 | 8 | 17 | 16 | 33 |
| 15-20 | 538 | 522 | 97 | 179 | 442 | 407 | 865 | 752 | 20 | 41 | 38 | 69 |
| 20-40 | 177 | 191 | 27 | 95 | 762 | 714 | 841 | 722 | 61 | 95 | 132 | 183 |
| 40-60 | 67 | 75 | 16 | 23 | 773 | 712 | 436 | 482 | 160 | 218 | 548 | 495 |
| 60 and over | 63 | 90 | 12 | 17 | 598 | 567 | 153 | 246 | 339 | 343 | 835 | 737 |
| **Hindu** | **451** | **437** | **309** | **295** | **486** | **474** | **509** | **501** | **63** | **89** | **182** | **204** |
| 0-5 | 974 | 979 | 973 | 966 | 25 | 19 | 24 | 30 | 1 | 2 | 3 | 4 |
| 5-10 | 925 | 918 | 848 | 846 | 72 | 77 | 145 | 146 | 3 | 5 | 7 | 8 |
| 10-15 | 740 | 745 | 403 | 436 | 252 | 238 | 580 | 511 | 8 | 17 | 17 | 33 |
| 15-20 | 523 | 504 | 84 | 158 | 457 | 455 | 877 | 773 | 20 | 41 | 39 | 69 |
| 20-40 | 175 | 190 | 25 | 103 | 762 | 715 | 840 | 714 | 63 | 95 | 135 | 183 |
| 40-60 | 68 | 76 | 14 | 21 | 769 | 709 | 433 | 488 | 163 | 215 | 553 | 491 |
| 60 and over | 65 | 97 | 11 | 15 | 592 | 551 | 150 | 250 | 343 | 352 | 889 | 735 |
| **Musalman** | **462** | **442** | **334** | **329** | **472** | **476** | **490** | **480** | **66** | **82** | **176** | **191** |
| 0-5 | 978 | 988 | 964 | 962 | 21 | 10 | 31 | 31 | 1 | 2 | 5 | 7 |
| 5-10 | 951 | 954 | 906 | 918 | 46 | 39 | 86 | 71 | 2 | 7 | 8 | 11 |
| 10-15 | 877 | 830 | 597 | 655 | 115 | 155 | 387 | 317 | 8 | 15 | 16 | 28 |
| 15-20 | 676 | 627 | 139 | 209 | [illegible] | 337 | 826 | 730 | 24 | 36 | 35 | 61 |
| 20-40 | 203 | 196 | 45 | 55 | 733 | 716 | 837 | 788 | 64 | 88 | 118 | 157 |
| 40-60 | 51 | 78 | 28 | 31 | 803 | 742 | 457 | 468 | 146 | 180 | 515 | 501 |
| 60 and over | 48 | 46 | 22 | 29 | 645 | 687 | 168 | 190 | 307 | 267 | 810 | 781 |
| **Animist** | **516** | **483** | **420** | **384** | **453** | **438** | **470** | **437** | **31** | **79** | **110** | **179** |
| 0-5 | 986 | 980 | 989 | 971 | 13 | 18 | 8 | 26 | 1 | 2 | 3 | 3 |
| 5-10 | 979 | 931 | 970 | 917 | 20 | 65 | 27 | 74 | 1 | 4 | 3 | 9 |
| 10-15 | 900 | 817 | 733 | 698 | 98 | 167 | 262 | 269 | 2 | 16 | 5 | 33 |
| 15-20 | 670 | 589 | 251 | 299 | 320 | 369 | 733 | 627 | 10 | 42 | 16 | 74 |
| 20-40 | 139 | 175 | 40 | 74 | 829 | 721 | 893 | 730 | 32 | 104 | 67 | 196 |
| 40-60 | 48 | 57 | 26 | 33 | 860 | 736 | 506 | 463 | 92 | 207 | 468 | 504 |
| 60 and over | 40 | 50 | 18 | 23 | 714 | 644 | 194 | 280 | 246 | 306 | 788 | 697 |
| **Jain** | **475** | **447** | **281** | **257** | **424** | **449** | **456** | **482** | **101** | **104** | **263** | **261** |
| 0-5 | 985 | 985 | 980 | 979 | 14 | 11 | 16 | 13 | 1 | 4 | 4 | 8 |
| 5-10 | 930 | 955 | 913 | 901 | 37 | 37 | 78 | 91 | 3 | 8 | 9 | 8 |
| 10-15 | 872 | 835 | 447 | 442 | 122 | 150 | 528 | 531 | 6 | 15 | 25 | 27 |
| 15-20 | 610 | 599 | 65 | 76 | 372 | 372 | 853 | 849 | 18 | 29 | 82 | 75 |
| 20-40 | 264 | 250 | 31 | 22 | 652 | 661 | 727 | 750 | 84 | 89 | 242 | 228 |
| 40-60 | 122 | 118 | 18 | 12 | 631 | 639 | 367 | 365 | 247 | 243 | 615 | 623 |
| 60 and over | 94 | 80 | 9 | 6 | 457 | 504 | 123 | 104 | 449 | 416 | 868 | 890 |
| **Christian** | **764** | **772** | **517** | **574** | **221** | **199** | **413** | **360** | **15** | **29** | **70** | **66** |
| 0-5 | 996 | 994 | 996 | 989 | 4 | 3 | 4 | 11 | ... | 3 | ... | .. |
| 5-10 | 1,000 | 983 | 994 | 876 | ... | 17 | 3 | 122 | ... | ... | 3 | 2 |
| 10-15 | 990 | 949 | 926 | 930 | 5 | 51 | 74 | 62 | 5 | ... | ... | 8 |
| 15-20 | 922 | 839 | 652 | 541 | 75 | 158 | 338 | 408 | 3 | 3 | 10 | 51 |
| 20-40 | 766 | 776 | 172 | 270 | 226 | 205 | 774 | 660 | 8 | 19 | 54 | 70 |
| 40-60 | 209 | 528 | 113 | 242 | 709 | 385 | 549 | 572 | 82 | 87 | 338 | 186 |
| 60 and over | 193 | 312 | 77 | 170 | 554 | 488 | 185 | 305 | 253 | 200 | 738 | 525 |
| **Others** | **472** | **407** | **403** | **417** | **475** | **538** | **505** | **488** | **53** | **55** | **92** | **95** |
| 0-5 | 1,000 | 995 | 876 | 983 | .. | 5 | 118 | 17 | ... | . | 6 | .. |
| 5-10 | 986 | 975 | 917 | 945 | 14 | 17 | 83 | 55 | ... | 8 | ... | ... |
| 10-15 | 950 | 795 | 793 | 811 | 50 | 168 | 207 | 168 | .. | 37 | ... | 21 |
| 15-20 | 743 | 689 | 528 | 488 | 244 | 283 | 454 | 512 | 13 | 28 | 18 | ... |
| 20-40 | 322 | 254 | 168 | 144 | 619 | 692 | 790 | 806 | 59 | 54 | 42 | 50 |
| 40-60 | 73 | 84 | 44 | 26 | 827 | 821 | 708 | 645 | 100 | 95 | 253 | 329 |
| 60 and over | 18 | 111 | 33 | 77 | 727 | 762 | 246 | 282 | 255 | 127 | 721 | 641 |

SUBSIDIARY TABLE II.—**Distribution by Civil Condition of 1,000**

| Religion and Natural Division. | MALES. | | | | | | | | | | | | | | | | | |
|---|---|---|---|---|---|---|---|---|---|---|---|---|---|---|---|---|---|---|
| | All ages. | | | 0—5. | | | 5—10. | | | 10—15. | | | 15—40. | | | 40 and over. | | |
| | Unmarried. | Married. | Widowed. | Unmarried. | Married. | Widowed. | Unmarried. | Married. | Widowed. | Unmarried. | Married. | Widowed. | Unmarried. | Married. | Widowed. | Unmarried. | Married. | Widowed. |
| 1 | 2 | 3 | 4 | 5 | 6 | 7 | 8 | 9 | 10 | 11 | 12 | 13 | 14 | 15 | 16 | 17 | 18 | 19 |
| **Central India.** | | | | | | | | | | | | | | | | | | |
| All Religions | 455 | 483 | 62 | 975 | 24 | 1 | 930 | 67 | 3 | 756 | 236 | 8 | 247 | 700 | 53 | 66 | 741 | 193 |
| Hindu | 451 | 486 | 63 | 974 | 25 | 1 | 925 | 72 | 3 | 740 | 252 | 8 | 243 | 703 | 54 | 67 | 737 | 196 |
| Musalman | 462 | 472 | 66 | 978 | 21 | 1 | 951 | 46 | 3 | 877 | 115 | 8 | 291 | 652 | 57 | 50 | 769 | 181 |
| Animist | 516 | 453 | 31 | 986 | 13 | 1 | 979 | 20 | 1 | 900 | 98 | 2 | 231 | 741 | 28 | 46 | 836 | 118 |
| Jain | 475 | 424 | 101 | 985 | 14 | 1 | 960 | 37 | 3 | 872 | 122 | 6 | 333 | 596 | 71 | 116 | 596 | 288 |
| Christian | 764 | 221 | 15 | 996 | 4 | ... | 1,000 | ... | ... | 990 | 5 | 5 | 778 | 214 | 8 | 207 | 686 | 107 |
| Others | 472 | 475 | 53 | 1,000 | ... | ... | 986 | 14 | ... | 950 | 50 | ... | 386 | 562 | 52 | 64 | 809 | 127 |
| *Plateau.* All Religions | 463 | 472 | 65 | 986 | 13 | 1 | 950 | 48 | 2 | 801 | 192 | 7 | 265 | 680 | 55 | 61 | 741 | 198 |
| *Plateau.* Hindu | 461 | 474 | 65 | 987 | 12 | 1 | 948 | 50 | 2 | 788 | 204 | 8 | 259 | 685 | 56 | 62 | 740 | 198 |
| *Plateau.* Musalman | 466 | 467 | 67 | 990 | 9 | 1 | 958 | 40 | 2 | 896 | 100 | 4 | 300 | 644 | 56 | 45 | 769 | 186 |
| *Plateau.* Animist | 490 | 476 | 34 | 959 | 39 | 2 | 952 | 45 | 3 | 858 | 138 | 4 | 228 | 739 | 33 | 57 | 826 | 116 |
| *Plateau.* Jain | 481 | 412 | 107 | 986 | 13 | 1 | 973 | 25 | 2 | 900 | 95 | 5 | 341 | 583 | 76 | 118 | 582 | 300 |
| *Plateau.* Christian | 782 | 205 | 13 | 995 | 5 | ... | 1,000 | ... | ... | 994 | ... | 6 | 797 | 198 | 5 | 225 | 676 | 99 |
| *Plateau.* Others | 475 | 470 | 55 | 1,000 | ... | ... | 991 | 9 | ... | 990 | 10 | ... | 398 | 545 | 57 | 60 | 820 | 120 |
| *Low-lying.* All Religions | 437 | 495 | 68 | 969 | 30 | 1 | 910 | 87 | 3 | 703 | 288 | 9 | 243 | 700 | 57 | 78 | 714 | 208 |
| *Low-lying.* Hindu | 436 | 496 | 68 | 968 | 31 | 1 | 909 | 89 | 2 | 697 | 294 | 9 | 241 | 702 | 57 | 79 | 712 | 209 |
| *Low-lying.* Musalman | 451 | 479 | 70 | 979 | 19 | 2 | 942 | 53 | 5 | 845 | 140 | 15 | 288 | 651 | 61 | 59 | 757 | 184 |
| *Low-lying.* Animist | 454 | 509 | 37 | 990 | 10 | ... | 953 | 44 | 3 | 823 | 172 | 5 | 176 | 795 | 29 | 32 | 839 | 129 |
| *Low-lying.* Jain | 455 | 449 | 96 | 977 | 22 | 1 | 924 | 71 | 5 | 801 | 189 | 10 | 308 | 622 | 70 | 117 | 620 | 263 |
| *Low-lying.* Christian | 787 | 184 | 29 | 1,000 | ... | ... | 1,000 | ... | ... | 1,000 | ... | ... | 847 | 138 | 15 | 187 | 667 | 146 |
| *Low-lying.* Others | 430 | 530 | 40 | 1,000 | ... | ... | 941 | 59 | ... | 929 | 71 | ... | 315 | 629 | 56 | 80 | 880 | 40 |
| *Hilly.* All Religions | 468 | 483 | 49 | 966 | 32 | 2 | 930 | 67 | 3 | 776 | 216 | 8 | 224 | 733 | 43 | 55 | 784 | 161 |
| *Hilly.* Hindu | 458 | 491 | 51 | 960 | 37 | 3 | 918 | 78 | 4 | 747 | 244 | 9 | 218 | 736 | 46 | 56 | 778 | 166 |
| *Hilly.* Musalman | 462 | 480 | 58 | 940 | 59 | 1 | 942 | 54 | 4 | 877 | 114 | 9 | 266 | 680 | 54 | 56 | 787 | 157 |
| *Hilly.* Animist | 530 | 441 | 29 | 994 | 6 | ... | 990 | 9 | 1 | 918 | 81 | 1 | 237 | 737 | 26 | 44 | 839 | 117 |
| *Hilly.* Jain | 482 | 430 | 88 | 993 | 6 | 1 | 963 | 34 | 3 | 892 | 104 | 4 | 338 | 609 | 53 | 105 | 613 | 282 |
| *Hilly.* Christian | 523 | 453 | 24 | 1,000 | ... | ... | 1,000 | ... | ... | 968 | 32 | ... | 277 | 701 | 22 | 115 | 787 | 98 |
| *Hilly.* Others | 480 | 470 | 50 | 1,000 | ... | ... | 1,000 | ... | ... | 800 | 200 | ... | 347 | 642 | 11 | 75 | 700 | 225 |

**of each Sex at certain Ages in each Religion and Natural Division.**

| Females. | | | | | | | | | | | | | | | | | |
|---|---|---|---|---|---|---|---|---|---|---|---|---|---|---|---|---|---|
| All ages. | | | 0—5. | | | 5—10. | | | 10—15. | | | 15—40. | | | 40 and over. | | |
| Unmarried. | Married. | Widowed. | Unmarried. | Married. | Widowed. | Unmarried. | Married. | Widowed. | Unmarried. | Married. | Widowed. | Unmarried. | Married. | Widowed. | Unmarried. | Married. | Widowed. |
| 20 | 21 | 22 | 23 | 24 | 25 | 26 | 27 | 28 | 29 | 30 | 31 | 32 | 33 | 34 | 35 | 36 | 37 |
| 316 | 505 | 179 | 974 | 23 | 3 | 859 | 135 | 6 | 431 | 553 | 16 | 15 | 373 | 612 | 309 | 508 | 183 |
| 309 | 509 | 182 | 973 | 24 | 3 | 848 | 145 | 7 | 403 | 580 | 17 | 35 | 846 | 119 | 14 | 370 | 616 |
| 334 | 490 | 176 | 964 | 31 | 5 | 906 | 86 | 8 | 597 | 387 | 16 | 61 | 835 | 104 | 26 | 386 | 588 |
| 420 | 470 | 110 | 989 | 8 | 3 | 970 | 27 | 3 | 733 | 262 | 5 | 76 | 866 | 58 | 24 | 443 | 533 |
| 281 | 456 | 263 | 980 | 16 | 4 | 913 | 78 | 9 | 447 | 528 | 25 | 37 | 751 | 212 | 16 | 311 | 673 |
| 517 | 413 | 70 | 996 | 4 | ... | 994 | 3 | 3 | 926 | 74 | ... | 306 | 652 | 42 | 107 | 485 | 408 |
| 403 | 505 | 92 | 876 | 118 | 6 | 917 | 83 | ... | 793 | 207 | ... | 237 | 725 | 38 | 41 | 575 | 384 |
| | | | | | | | | | | | | | | | | | |
| 307 | 504 | 189 | 972 | 26 | 2 | 851 | 143 | 6 | 394 | 590 | 16 | 38 | 838 | 124 | 19 | 343 | 638 |
| 302 | 507 | 191 | 973 | 25 | 2 | 840 | 154 | 6 | 362 | 621 | 17 | 35 | 839 | 126 | 17 | 340 | 643 |
| 335 | 485 | 180 | 962 | 36 | 2 | 913 | 80 | 7 | 608 | 376 | 16 | 64 | 827 | 109 | 26 | 373 | 601 |
| 376 | 498 | 126 | 987 | 10 | 3 | 935 | 57 | 8 | 590 | 400 | 10 | 49 | 878 | 73 | 26 | 406 | 568 |
| 280 | 451 | 269 | 983 | 13 | 4 | 933 | 58 | 9 | 473 | 508 | 19 | 39 | 745 | 216 | 12 | 299 | 689 |
| 528 | 402 | 70 | 997 | 3 | ... | 996 | 4 | ... | 937 | 63 | ... | 331 | 626 | 43 | 126 | 457 | 417 |
| 387 | 518 | 95 | 829 | 162 | 9 | 884 | 116 | ... | 788 | 212 | ... | 262 | 705 | 33 | 47 | 576 | 377 |
| | | | | | | | | | | | | | | | | | |
| 295 | 513 | 192 | 978 | 20 | 2 | 851 | 142 | 7 | 401 | 580 | 19 | 32 | 843 | 125 | 11 | 378 | 611 |
| 293 | 514 | 193 | 979 | 19 | 2 | 848 | 145 | 7 | 394 | 587 | 19 | 30 | 844 | 126 | 10 | 376 | 614 |
| 320 | 500 | 180 | 961 | 26 | 13 | 884 | 102 | 14 | 540 | 440 | 20 | 66 | 837 | 97 | 32 | 407 | 561 |
| 398 | 493 | 109 | 988 | 12 | ... | 952 | 45 | 3 | 644 | 349 | 7 | 53 | 880 | 67 | 48 | 521 | 431 |
| 279 | 475 | 246 | 973 | 24 | 3 | 851 | 137 | 12 | 380 | 581 | 39 | 38 | 754 | 208 | 23 | 367 | 610 |
| 481 | 429 | 90 | 1,000 | ... | ... | 974 | ... | 26 | 923 | 77 | ... | 318 | 642 | 40 | 51 | 559 | 390 |
| 539 | 427 | 34 | 1,000 | ... | ... | 1,000 | ... | ... | 833 | 167 | ... | 189 | 784 | 27 | ... | 800 | 200 |
| | | | | | | | | | | | | | | | | | |
| 359 | 494 | 147 | 972 | 23 | 5 | 879 | 115 | 6 | 520 | 467 | 13 | 50 | 860 | 90 | 16 | 415 | 569 |
| 346 | 501 | 153 | 968 | 26 | 6 | 859 | 134 | 7 | 471 | 514 | 15 | 45 | 859 | 96 | 14 | 413 | 573 |
| 348 | 491 | 161 | 977 | 21 | 2 | 912 | 82 | 6 | 635 | 352 | 13 | 45 | 860 | 95 | 19 | 399 | 582 |
| 435 | 460 | 105 | 989 | 7 | 4 | 981 | 17 | 2 | 777 | 219 | 4 | 87 | 861 | 52 | 21 | 447 | 532 |
| 286 | 449 | 265 | 979 | 17 | 4 | 939 | 56 | 5 | 480 | 500 | 20 | 29 | 769 | 202 | 17 | 272 | 711 |
| 475 | 467 | 58 | 989 | 11 | ... | 1,000 | ... | ... | 846 | 154 | ... | 109 | 853 | 38 | 70 | 558 | 372 |
| 428 | 459 | 113 | 1,000 | ... | ... | 1,000 | ... | ... | 800 | 200 | ... | 82 | 836 | 82 | ... | 444 | 556 |

SUBSIDIARY TABLE III.—**Distribution by main Age Periods and Civil Conditions of 10,000 of each Sex and Religion.**

| Religion and Age. | Males. | | | Females. | | |
|---|---|---|---|---|---|---|
| | Unmarried | Married. | Widowed. | Unmarried. | Married. | Widowed. |
| 1 | 2 | 3 | 4 | 5 | 6 | 7 |
| **All Religions** | **4,552** | **4,828** | **620** | **3,162** | **5,046** | **1,792** |
| 0-10 | 9,543 | 438 | 19 | 9,236 | 717 | 47 |
| 10-15 | 7,555 | 2,363 | 82 | 4,306 | 5,528 | 166 |
| 15-04 | 2,474 | 6,904 | 532 | 393 | 8,453 | 1,154 |
| 40 and over | 660 | 7,413 | 1,927 | 150 | 3,732 | 6,118 |
| **Hindu** | **4,508** | **4,861** | **631** | **3,090** | **5,081** | **1,829** |
| 0-10 | 9,514 | 466 | 20 | 9,183 | 770 | 47 |
| 10-15 | 7,396 | 2,519 | 85 | 4,025 | 5,803 | 172 |
| 15-40 | 2,432 | 7,025 | 543 | 354 | 8,459 | 1,187 |
| 40 and over | 673 | 7,369 | 1,958 | 138 | 3,699 | 6,163 |
| **Musalman** | **4,616** | **4,723** | **661** | **3,339** | **4,897** | **1,764** |
| 0-10 | 9,657 | 323 | 20 | 9,386 | 554 | 60 |
| 10-15 | 8,768 | 1,153 | 79 | 5,964 | 3,874 | 162 |
| 15-40 | 2,910 | 6.521 | 569 | 610 | 8,350 | 1,040 |
| 40 and over | 504 | 7,690 | 1,806 | 263 | 3,861 | 5,876 |
| **Animist** | **5,158** | **4,534** | **308** | **4,196** | **4,705** | **1,099** |
| 0-10 | 9,829 | 161 | 10 | 9,814 | 153 | 33 |
| 10-15 | 8,996 | 985 | 19 | 7,326 | 2,620 | 54 |
| 15-40 | 2,307 | 7,411 | 282 | 762 | 8,658 | 580 |
| 40 and over | 462 | 8.359 | 1,179 | 244 | 4,431 | 5,325 |
| **Jain** | **4,745** | **4,240** | **1,015** | **2,807** | **4,565** | **2,628** |
| 0-10 | 9,734 | 249 | 17 | 9,482 | 456 | 62 |
| 10-15 | 8,720 | 1,219 | 61 | 4.474 | 5,277 | 249 |
| 15-40 | 3,329 | 5,964 | 707 | 371 | 7,509 | 2,120 |
| 40 and over | 1,161 | 5,956 | 2.883 | 155 | 3,113 | 6,732 |
| **Christian** | **7,639** | **2,207** | **154** | **5,166** | **4,128** | **706** |
| 0-10 | 9,977 | 23 | ... | 9,953 | 35 | 12 |
| 10-15 | 9,906 | 47 | 47 | 9,261 | 739 | ... |
| 15-40 | 7.780 | 2,145 | 75 | 3,058 | 6,520 | 422 |
| 40 and over | 2,068 | 6,863 | 1,069 | 1,072 | 4,853 | 4,075 |
| **Others** | **4,718** | **4,752** | **530** | **4,037** | **5,039** | **924** |
| 0-10 | 9.931 | 69 | ... | 8,951 | 1,014 | 35 |
| 10-15 | 9,496 | 504 | ... | 7,927 | 2,073 | ... |
| 15-40 | 3,858 | 5,617 | 525 | 2,375 | 7,250 | 375 |
| 40 and over | 635 | 8,095 | 1,270 | 411 | 5,753 | 3,836 |

SUBSIDIARY TABLE IV.—**Proportion of the Sexes by Civil Condition at certain Ages for Religious and Natural Divisions.**

| Natural Division and Religion. | Number of Females per 1,000 Males. | | | | | | | | | | | | | | |
|---|---|---|---|---|---|---|---|---|---|---|---|---|---|---|---|
| | All ages. | | | 0—10. | | | 10—15. | | | 15—40. | | | 40 and over. | | |
| | Unmarried. | Married. | Widowed. | Unmarried. | Married. | Widowed. | Unmarried. | Married. | Widowed. | Unmarried. | Married. | Widowed. | Unmarried. | Married. | Widowed. |
| 1 | 2 | 3 | 4 | 5 | 6 | 7 | 8 | 9 | 10 | 11 | 12 | 13 | 14 | 15 | 16 |
| **Central India** | | | | | | | | | | | | | | | |
| All Religions | 659 | 991 | 2,745 | 953 | 1,610 | 2,832 | 448 | 1,839 | 1,595 | 149 | 1,131 | 2,029 | 230 | 510 | 3,213 |
| Hindu | 650 | 991 | 2,748 | 958 | 1,618 | 2,362 | 425 | 1,797 | 1,570 | 135 | 1,123 | 2,040 | 210 | 513 | 3,215 |
| Musalman | 664 | 952 | 2,450 | 962 | 1,699 | 2,992 | 551 | 2,721 | 1,654 | 191 | 1,699 | 1,662 | 471 | 453 | 2,938 |
| Animist | 828 | 1,056 | 3,627 | 999 | 955 | 3,253 | 715 | 2,337 | 2,512 | 352 | 1,245 | 2,191 | 531 | 534 | 4,545 |
| Jain | 540 | 984 | 2,365 | 958 | 1,799 | 3,588 | 397 | 3,354 | 3,143 | 100 | 1,123 | 2,674 | 127 | 495 | 2,213 |
| Christian | 339 | 966 | 2,368 | 994 | 1,500 | ... | 1,123 | 19,000 | ... | 148 | 1,943 | 2,118 | 345 | 470 | 2,533 |
| Others | 554 | 686 | 1,128 | 892 | 1,450 | ... | 492 | 2,429 | ... | 335 | 702 | 389 | 450 | 494 | 2,100 |
| Plateau. All Religions | 620 | 998 | 2,747 | 918 | 2,468 | 2,808 | 376 | 2,355 | 1,744 | 184 | 1,145 | 2,068 | 299 | 457 | 3,194 |
| Plateau. Hindu | 614 | 1,001 | 2,772 | 912 | 2,588 | 2,806 | 349 | 2,305 | 1,664 | 125 | 1,139 | 2,076 | 287 | 460 | 8,237 |
| Plateau. Musalman | 660 | 939 | 2,465 | 949 | 2,332 | 3,523 | 554 | 3,079 | 2,831 | 198 | 1,187 | 1,811 | 499 | 424 | 2,825 |
| Plateau. Animist | 764 | 1,043 | 3,686 | 982 | 654 | 1,783 | 683 | 2,424 | 2,000 | 227 | 1,234 | 2,256 | 469 | 500 | 4,901 |
| Plateau. Jain | 533 | 1,000 | 2,267 | 952 | 1,784 | 5,143 | 390 | 1,816 | 3,167 | 104 | 1,167 | 2,602 | 97 | 479 | 2,143 |
| Plateau. Christian | 335 | 972 | 2,503 | 979 | 1,000 | ... | 1,193 | ... | ... | 150 | 1,147 | 2,900 | 374 | 454 | 2,825 |
| Plateau. Others | 530 | 717 | 1,128 | 782 | 29,000 | ... | 525 | 14,000 | ... | 360 | 707 | 312 | 600 | 536 | 2,400 |
| Low-lying. All Religions | 629 | 967 | 2,620 | 952 | 1,305 | 2,370 | 437 | 1,544 | 1,576 | 119 | 1,088 | 1,966 | 146 | 547 | 3,035 |
| Low-lying. Hindu | 627 | 968 | 2,635 | 950 | 1,292 | 2,304 | 432 | 1,525 | 1,597 | 114 | 1,089 | 1,989 | 129 | 547 | 3,045 |
| Low-lying. Musalman | 633 | 932 | 2,285 | 941 | 1,714 | 3,386 | 505 | 2,488 | 1,061 | 190 | 1,074 | 1,321 | 529 | 522 | 2,954 |
| Low-lying. Animist | 904 | 997 | 3,029 | 1,092 | 1,158 | 1,167 | 704 | 1,819 | 1,286 | 308 | 1,124 | 2,850 | 1,527 | 636 | 3,424 |
| Low-lying. Jain | 548 | 946 | 2,285 | 954 | 1,787 | 2,571 | 385 | 2,496 | 3,000 | 104 | 1,016 | 2,490 | 182 | 555 | 2,173 |
| Low-lying. Christian | 266 | 1,288 | 1,348 | 1,038 | ... | ... | 1,143 | ... | ... | 111 | 1,378 | 778 | 167 | 516 | 1,643 |
| Low-lying. Others | 738 | 475 | 500 | 1,636 | ... | ... | 385 | 1,000 | ... | 250 | 518 | 200 | ... | 364 | 2,000 |
| Hilly. All Religions | 762 | 1,019 | 2,993 | 105 | 1,326 | 2,228 | 568 | 1,825 | 1,438 | 220 | 1,169 | 2,068 | 287 | 542 | 3,627 |
| Hilly. Hindu | 750 | 1,014 | 2,946 | 1,006 | 1,342 | 2,126 | 530 | 1,773 | 1,402 | 201 | 1151 | 2,069 | 266 | 548 | 3,564 |
| Hilly. Musalman | 718 | 975 | 2,663 | 1,029 | 885 | 1,516 | 608 | 2,564 | 1,214 | 164 | 1,215 | 1,699 | 308 | 463 | 3,379 |
| Hilly. Animist | 841 | 1,067 | 3,672 | 997 | 1,432 | 5,839 | 753 | 2,399 | 3,625 | 397 | 1,260 | 2,146 | 478 | 534 | 4,554 |
| Hilly. Jain | 559 | 984 | 2,823 | 984 | 1,900 | 2,333 | 449 | 4,015 | 3,667 | 76 | 1,126 | 4,931 | 168 | 455 | 2,589 |
| Hilly. Christian | 794 | 903 | 2,091 | 1,036 | ... | ... | 733 | 4,000 | ... | 323 | 1,000 | 1,400 | 429 | 500 | 2,667 |
| Hilly. Others | 594 | 649 | 1,500 | 1,100 | ... | ... | 400 | 400 | ... | 152 | 836 | 5,000 | ... | 286 | 1,111 |

SUBSIDIARY TABLE V.—**Distribution by Civil Condition of**

| Caste. | Distribution of 1,000 Males of each age by Civil Condition. | | | | | | | | | | | | | | | | | |
|---|---|---|---|---|---|---|---|---|---|---|---|---|---|---|---|---|---|---|
| | All ages. | | | 0—5. | | | 5—12. | | | 12—20. | | | 20—40. | | | 40 and over. | | |
| | Unmarried. | Married. | Widowed. | Unmarried. | Married. | Widowed. | Unmarried. | Married. | Widowed. | Unmarried. | Married. | Widowed. | Unmarried. | Married. | Widowed. | Unmarried. | Married. | Widowed. |
| 1 | 2 | 3 | 4 | 5 | 6 | 7 | 8 | 9 | 10 | 11 | 12 | 13 | 14 | 15 | 16 | 17 | 18 | 19 |
| Brahman | 440 | 448 | 112 | 926 | 70 | 4 | 850 | 144 | 6 | 494 | 454 | 52 | 244 | 659 | 97 | 124 | 566 | 310 |
| " Shrigaud | 433 | 456 | 111 | 965 | 19 | 16 | 882 | 88 | 30 | 638 | 290 | 72 | 228 | 665 | 107 | 112 | 657 | 231 |
| " Shrimali | 316 | 507 | 177 | 993 | 7 | ... | 863 | 128 | 9 | 308 | 534 | 158 | 141 | 680 | 179 | 48 | 610 | 342 |
| " Sarwaria | 452 | 464 | 84 | 942 | 53 | 5 | 836 | 159 | 5 | 495 | 478 | 27 | 216 | 706 | 78 | 112 | 624 | 264 |
| " Sanadhya | 389 | 438 | 173 | 844 | 154 | 2 | 839 | 159 | 2 | 459 | 452 | 89 | 265 | 604 | 131 | 122 | 477 | 401 |
| " Jijhotia | 491 | 414 | 95 | 979 | 20 | 1 | 896 | 90 | 14 | 526 | 431 | 43 | 288 | 614 | 98 | 171 | 581 | 248 |
| " Bhagor | 491 | 405 | 104 | 982 | 17 | 1 | 937 | 59 | 4 | 550 | 361 | 89 | 311 | 604 | 85 | 160 | 573 | 267 |
| Rajput | 456 | 435 | 109 | 908 | 85 | 7 | 846 | 142 | 12 | 539 | 411 | 50 | 264 | 612 | 124 | 130 | 605 | 265 |
| " Chauhan | 457 | 433 | 110 | 946 | 47 | 7 | 865 | 99 | 36 | 530 | 400 | 70 | 218 | 678 | 104 | 132 | 602 | 266 |
| " Tonwar | 476 | 423 | 101 | 954 | 39 | 7 | 889 | 103 | 8 | 531 | 433 | 36 | 272 | 605 | 123 | 134 | 595 | 271 |
| " Ponwar | 438 | 418 | 144 | 952 | 44 | 4 | 832 | 109 | 9 | 549 | 405 | 46 | 198 | 606 | 196 | 166 | 541 | 293 |
| " Kachhwaha | 515 | 292 | 193 | 838 | 143 | 19 | 638 | 302 | 60 | 650 | 250 | 100 | 523 | 302 | 175 | 68 | 413 | 519 |
| " Rathod | 437 | 466 | 97 | 923 | 68 | 9 | 799 | 189 | 12 | 512 | 439 | 49 | 234 | 660 | 106 | 142 | 624 | 234 |
| " Gahalot | 391 | 486 | 123 | 994 | 6 | ... | 949 | 51 | ... | 478 | 486 | 36 | 118 | 722 | 160 | 46 | 693 | 261 |
| " Bhadauria | 473 | 466 | 61 | 355 | 636 | 9 | 545 | 453 | 2 | 509 | 457 | 34 | 562 | 343 | 95 | 130 | 535 | 335 |
| " Bundela | 433 | 454 | 83 | 971 | 19 | 10 | 841 | 131 | 28 | 445 | 527 | 28 | 258 | 667 | 75 | 239 | 523 | 238 |
| " Baghel | 455 | 439 | 76 | 954 | 28 | 18 | 920 | 74 | 6 | 579 | 398 | 23 | 233 | 677 | 90 | 54 | 761 | 185 |
| Maratha | 367 | 449 | 184 | 930 | 19 | 1 | 908 | 76 | 16 | 448 | 493 | 54 | 174 | 630 | 193 | 57 | 519 | 424 |
| Ajna | 414 | 432 | 154 | 952 | 40 | 8 | 804 | 176 | 20 | 397 | 445 | 158 | 281 | 620 | 99 | 198 | 470 | 332 |
| Bhat | 436 | 413 | 151 | 956 | 34 | 10 | 870 | 113 | 17 | 559 | 407 | 34 | 202 | 610 | 188 | 82 | 555 | 363 |
| Gujar | 437 | 452 | 111 | 893 | 100 | 7 | 824 | 165 | 11 | 515 | 454 | 31 | 284 | 603 | 110 | 112 | 589 | 299 |
| Dhangar | 546 | 353 | 101 | 900 | 57 | 43 | 885 | 93 | 22 | 642 | 310 | 48 | 204 | 670 | 126 | 136 | 584 | 280 |
| Sondhia | 451 | 436 | 113 | 937 | 31 | 2 | 882 | 115 | 3 | 569 | 391 | 40 | 250 | 615 | 135 | 92 | 639 | 269 |
| Bania | 428 | 446 | 126 | 934 | 59 | 7 | 860 | 131 | 9 | 502 | 462 | 36 | 210 | 637 | 153 | 117 | 575 | 308 |
| " Agarwal | 426 | 457 | 117 | 947 | 35 | 18 | 884 | 111 | 5 | 493 | 472 | 32 | 215 | 656 | 129 | 125 | 588 | 287 |
| " Mahesri | 408 | 432 | 160 | 941 | 58 | 1 | 883 | 107 | 10 | 455 | 507 | 38 | 237 | 521 | 242 | 151 | 558 | 291 |
| " Oswal | 445 | 402 | 153 | 977 | 20 | 3 | 925 | 69 | 6 | 611 | 358 | 31 | 209 | 603 | 188 | 122 | 525 | 353 |
| " Porwal | 430 | 432 | 138 | 972 | 24 | 4 | 905 | 82 | 13 | 535 | 432 | 33 | 201 | 635 | 164 | 83 | 574 | 343 |
| " Gahohi | 453 | 448 | 99 | 964 | 36 | ... | 844 | 138 | 18 | 474 | 484 | 42 | 257 | 655 | 88 | 122 | 583 | 295 |
| Khangar | 448 | 468 | 84 | 814 | 156 | 30 | 844 | 120 | 36 | 599 | 334 | 67 | 148 | 759 | 93 | 160 | 679 | 161 |
| Kachera | 432 | 464 | 104 | 984 | 9 | 7 | 798 | 197 | 5 | 467 | 496 | 37 | 98 | 815 | 87 | 58 | 525 | 417 |
| Bhilala | 550 | 420 | 30 | 996 | 4 | ... | 987 | 13 | ... | 718 | 279 | 3 | 168 | 800 | 32 | 39 | 832 | 129 |
| Saharia | 487 | 450 | 63 | 987 | 13 | ... | 958 | 30 | 12 | 528 | 418 | 54 | 147 | 819 | 34 | 69 | 681 | 250 |
| Bhil | 511 | 463 | 26 | 991 | 9 | ... | 979 | 20 | 1 | 832 | 163 | 5 | 124 | 845 | 31 | 30 | 877 | 93 |
| Gond | 464 | 465 | 71 | 894 | 104 | 2 | 780 | 211 | 9 | 557 | 406 | 37 | 161 | 761 | 78 | 124 | 664 | 212 |
| Kol | 434 | 479 | 87 | 933 | 64 | 3 | 830 | 156 | 14 | 495 | 453 | 52 | 97 | 819 | 84 | 95 | 651 | 254 |
| Musalman | 435 | 483 | 82 | 981 | 18 | 1 | 925 | 70 | 5 | 642 | 338 | 20 | 178 | 736 | 86 | 54 | 738 | 208 |
| " Shaikh | 433 | 486 | 81 | 982 | 17 | 1 | 914 | 80 | 6 | 665 | 310 | 25 | 169 | 741 | 90 | 48 | 760 | 192 |
| " Sayad | 452 | 464 | 84 | 989 | 10 | 1 | 920 | 77 | 3 | 589 | 389 | 22 | 211 | 698 | 91 | 65 | 712 | 223 |
| " Pathan | 434 | 483 | 83 | 977 | 22 | 1 | 939 | 55 | 6 | 633 | 352 | 15 | 180 | 738 | 82 | 61 | 715 | 224 |

## 1,000 of each Sex at certain Ages for Selected Castes :

| Distribution of 1,000 Females of each age by Civil Condition. | | | | | | | | | | | | | | | | | | | |
|---|---|---|---|---|---|---|---|---|---|---|---|---|---|---|---|---|---|---|---|
| All ages. | | | 0—5. | | | 5—12 | | | 12—20. | | | 20—40. | | | 40 and over. | | | | Locality. |
| Unmarried. | Married. | Widowed. | Unmarried. | Married. | Widowed. | Unmarried. | Married. | Widowed. | Unmarried. | Married. | Widowed. | Unmarried. | Married. | Widowed. | Unmarried. | Married. | Widowed. | | |
| 20 | 21 | 22 | 23 | 24 | 25 | 26 | 27 | 28 | 29 | 30 | 31 | 32 | 33 | 34 | 35 | 36 | 37 | | 38 |
| 306 | 449 | 245 | 917 | 60 | 23 | 760 | 215 | 25 | 219 | 699 | 82 | 39 | 708 | 253 | 30 | 340 | 630 | | |
| 386 | 443 | 171 | 950 | 43 | 7 | 853 | 128 | 19 | 341 | 599 | 60 | 82 | 673 | 245 | 72 | 500 | 428 | | Malwa. |
| 460 | 391 | 149 | 898 | 102 | ... | 803 | 194 | 3 | 313 | 629 | 58 | 208 | 535 | 257 | 223 | 398 | 379 | | Malwa. |
| 313 | 460 | 227 | 879 | 82 | 39 | 745 | 225 | 30 | 220 | 702 | 78 | 41 | 739 | 220 | 36 | 339 | 625 | | Baghelkhand and Bundelkhand. |
| 286 | 423 | 291 | 966 | 28 | 6 | 772 | 204 | 24 | 212 | 689 | 99 | 33 | 644 | 323 | 16 | 322 | 662 | | Northern Gwalior. |
| 288 | 473 | 239 | 965 | 34 | 1 | 798 | 195 | 7 | 172 | 755 | 73 | 20 | 741 | 239 | 19 | 373 | 608 | | Bundelkhand. |
| 307 | 442 | 251 | 957 | 41 | 2 | 772 | 213 | 15 | 237 | 696 | 67 | 49 | 693 | 258 | 41 | 300 | 659 | | Northern Gwalior and Bundelkhand. |
| 367 | 447 | 186 | 942 | 51 | 7 | 830 | 154 | 16 | 349 | 560 | 91 | 71 | 732 | 197 | 85 | 437 | 478 | | |
| 388 | 409 | 203 | 930 | 59 | 11 | 829 | 152 | 19 | 434 | 493 | 73 | 89 | 700 | 211 | 103 | 386 | 511 | | Northern Gwalior and Malwa. |
| 398 | 451 | 151 | 979 | 19 | 2 | 897 | 94 | 9 | 228 | 724 | 48 | 54 | 760 | 186 | 20 | 451 | 529 | | Northern Gwalior. |
| 311 | 473 | 216 | 982 | 14 | 4 | 863 | 126 | 11 | 323 | 578 | 99 | 37 | 760 | 203 | 25 | 451 | 524 | | Malwa. |
| 423 | 451 | 126 | 847 | 148 | 5 | 765 | 231 | 4 | 414 | 483 | 103 | 184 | 684 | 132 | 236 | 451 | 313 | | Northern Gwalior. |
| 327 | 467 | 206 | 953 | 39 | 8 | 734 | 254 | 12 | 258 | 643 | 99 | 79 | 687 | 234 | 42 | 449 | 509 | | Malwa. |
| 347 | 461 | 192 | 995 | 4 | 1 | 897 | 98 | 5 | 197 | 729 | 74 | 44 | 589 | 367 | 35 | 583 | 382 | | Malwa and Baghelkhand. |
| 527 | 366 | 107 | 803 | 170 | 27 | 768 | 184 | 48 | 591 | 348 | 61 | 110 | 759 | 131 | 465 | 300 | 235 | | Northern Gwalior. |
| 323 | 487 | 190 | 973 | 23 | 4 | 840 | 146 | 14 | 317 | 604 | 79 | 36 | 793 | 168 | 19 | 422 | 559 | | Bundelkhand. |
| 351 | 445 | 204 | 954 | 34 | 12 | 877 | 106 | 17 | 327 | 474 | 199 | 49 | 793 | 158 | 48 | 405 | 547 | | Baghelkhand. |
| 287 | 440 | 273 | 952 | 43 | 5 | 801 | 171 | 28 | 307 | 615 | 78 | 62 | 629 | 309 | 27 | 377 | 596 | | Gwalior, Indore, Dhar, Dewas. |
| 387 | 470 | 143 | 920 | 79 | 1 | 588 | 399 | 13 | 389 | 523 | 88 | 244 | 598 | 158 | 215 | 466 | 319 | | Malwa. |
| 376 | 426 | 198 | 959 | 35 | 6 | 806 | 191 | 3 | 418 | 525 | 57 | 67 | 687 | 246 | 31 | 437 | 532 | | Malwa and Baghelkhand. |
| 352 | 500 | 148 | 953 | 44 | 3 | 809 | 183 | 8 | 341 | 609 | 50 | 92 | 777 | 131 | 43 | 532 | 425 | | Northern Gwalior. |
| 408 | 426 | 166 | 984 | 16 | ... | 815 | 178 | 7 | 524 | 351 | 125 | 28 | 754 | 218 | 8 | 584 | 408 | | Malwa. |
| 274 | 520 | 206 | 952 | 35 | 13 | 753 | 209 | 38 | 243 | 611 | 146 | 67 | 694 | 239 | 57 | 575 | 368 | | Malwa. |
| 325 | 454 | 221 | 954 | 37 | 9 | 759 | 224 | 17 | 291 | 636 | 73 | 51 | 688 | 261 | 30 | 579 | 391 | | |
| 319 | 437 | 244 | 927 | 49 | 24 | 687 | 283 | 20 | 289 | 621 | 90 | 55 | 660 | 285 | 45 | 333 | 622 | | General. |
| 309 | 494 | 197 | 978 | 22 | ... | 806 | 183 | 11 | 282 | 654 | 64 | 43 | 654 | 303 | 8 | 545 | 447 | | Malwa. |
| 370 | 405 | 225 | 979 | 18 | 3 | 883 | 109 | 8 | 374 | 573 | 53 | 34 | 664 | 302 | 24 | 370 | 606 | | Malwa. |
| 334 | 461 | 205 | 961 | 34 | 5 | 806 | 183 | 11 | 288 | 644 | 68 | 69 | 705 | 226 | 45 | 404 | 551 | | Malwa. |
| 286 | 485 | 229 | 985 | 12 | 3 | 802 | 185 | 13 | 230 | 717 | 53 | 43 | 720 | 237 | 11 | 436 | 553 | | Bundelkhand and Baghelkhand. |
| 302 | 513 | 185 | 974 | 20 | 6 | 735 | 237 | 28 | 241 | 665 | 94 | 22 | 811 | 167 | 12 | 459 | 529 | | Northern Gwalior and Bundelkhand. |
| 360 | 461 | 179 | 962 | 31 | 7 | 876 | 108 | 16 | 432 | 468 | 100 | 24 | 780 | 196 | 35 | 574 | 391 | | Malwa and Bundelkhand. |
| 501 | 424 | 75 | 995 | 5 | ... | 960 | 39 | 1 | 581 | 406 | 13 | 79 | 864 | 57 | 26 | 590 | 384 | | Hilly Tract. |
| 404 | 514 | 82 | 990 | 9 | 1 | 902 | 91 | 7 | 265 | 680 | 55 | 21 | 869 | 110 | 11 | 690 | 299 | | Do. |
| 405 | 482 | 113 | 992 | 7 | 1 | 939 | 58 | 3 | 413 | 568 | 19 | 28 | 906 | 66 | 7 | 522 | 471 | | Do. |
| 405 | 453 | 142 | 968 | 30 | 2 | 838 | 152 | 10 | 381 | 575 | 44 | 68 | 783 | 149 | 56 | 519 | 425 | | Baghelkhand and Bhopal. |
| 366 | 494 | 140 | 913 | 80 | 7 | 757 | 219 | 24 | 392 | 562 | 46 | 54 | 833 | 113 | 64 | 478 | 458 | | Hilly Tract. |
| 341 | 490 | 169 | 977 | 20 | 3 | 858 | 129 | 13 | 305 | 668 | 27 | 42 | 821 | 137 | 31 | 446 | 523 | | |
| 328 | 492 | 180 | 976 | 20 | 4 | 839 | 147 | 14 | 287 | 683 | 30 | 42 | 808 | 150 | 32 | 438 | 530 | | General. |
| 377 | 477 | 146 | 973 | 24 | 3 | 879 | 100 | 21 | 349 | 620 | 31 | 46 | 835 | 119 | 23 | 508 | 469 | | Do. |
| 349 | 491 | 160 | 978 | 20 | 2 | 877 | 114 | 9 | 317 | 660 | 23 | 43 | 834 | 123 | 32 | 443 | 525 | | Do. |

# CHAPTER VIII.

## Education.

**Scope of Return.**

67. The Tables dealt with in this Chapter are VIII and IX, the former showing literacy as distributed by age, sex, and religion, and the latter, the literates among certain selected castes.

The test applied on this occasion was similar to that of 1901, and, as no literacy was recorded previous to that enumeration, it has not been necessary to adjust figures with regard to the different standard applied in 1891. On this occasion, to make the definition more certain, it was laid down that a "literate" person was one who could both write a letter and read the answer to it. This has made the test more accurate, and, as the results prove, has excluded a large class consisting of those who, while knowing their letters only, were, on the last occasion, returned as literate.

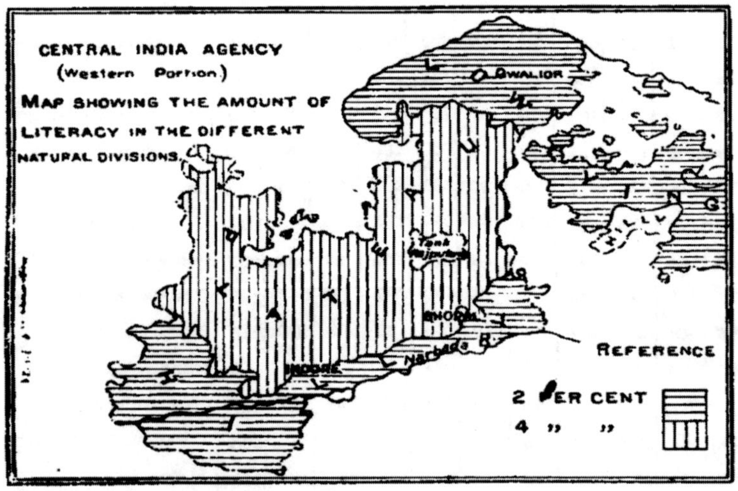


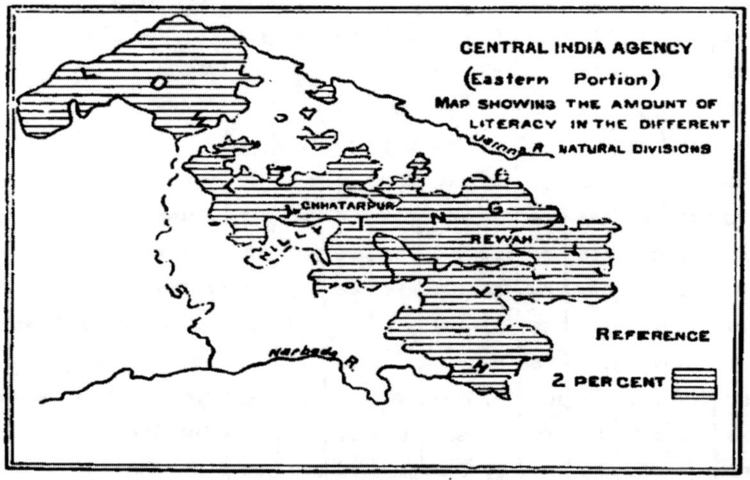


The figures give us 26 per thousand literate in all religions for both sexes, of all ages, showing that 1 male in every 20 and 1 female in every 330 was able to satisfy the test. Of literate males 7 per cent. are over 20 years of age and 6 per cent. of school-going age (15-20). Under 10 there are 5 males per thousand. Females can only produce 3 literates per thousand of over 29, 5 of school-going age, and 1 under 10.

**English.**

68. Of those knowing English 4 males per thousand and less than 1 per thousand among females were returned.

On this occasion no return of languages was made, but no change in the relative positions of the main written languages Hindi, Urdu, and Marathi, can have taken place, their importance in daily use being indicated by this order.

**Religious Distribution.**

69. Comparing the religions Christians, as might be expected, stand first with 67 per cent. literate, males 78 per cent. and females 47. Of the three classes of this community Europeans show 90 per cent. (males 96 and females

66), while the age return shows that after 10-15 all are literate; the Anglo-Indian figures show the same percentage (78) due to the fact that the population is

*Diagram showing the number of persons per 1000 in each Natural Division who are literate*

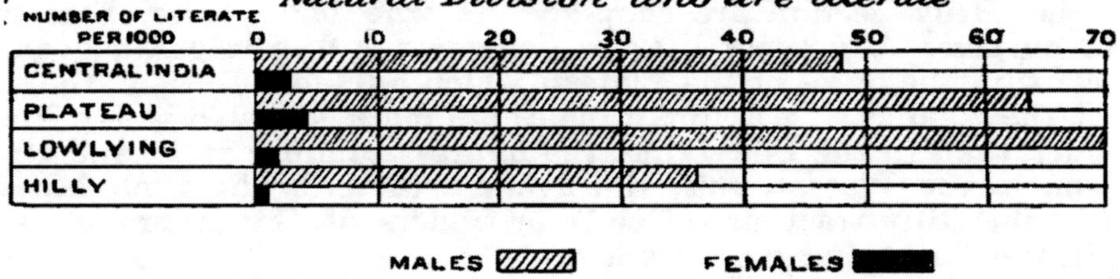


indigenous and not fortuitous, as in the case of Europeans who are mainly civil and military officials of mature age.

Indian Christians show 46 per cent. males and 34 females. In this case the females at 10-15 exceed the males, a fact due to the female education carried on by the missions, who, in 1900, obtained a large number of recruits from those left orphans in the great famine of that year. English education also necessarily predominates in this class.

Turning to the Indian religions the Jains stand out with 21 per cent. literate, 15 per cent. more than the next highest, this figure being made up of 39 per cent males but only 2 per cent. females. Regular instruction is shown by the rising figures for age periods.

Musalmans follow with 6 per cent., 11 males and 1 female. The return for the school-going age (15-20) shows that 13 per cent. are literate.

Third on the list comes the Hindu community with 2 per cent. literate, 4 males in every hundred, and 1 female in every thousand. In English knowledge they show 2 per thousand less than Jains or Musalmans.

**Locality.**

70. Of the Natural Divisions the Plateau stands first with 3 per cent.,

*Diagram showing the number per 1000 of each main religion who are literate.*

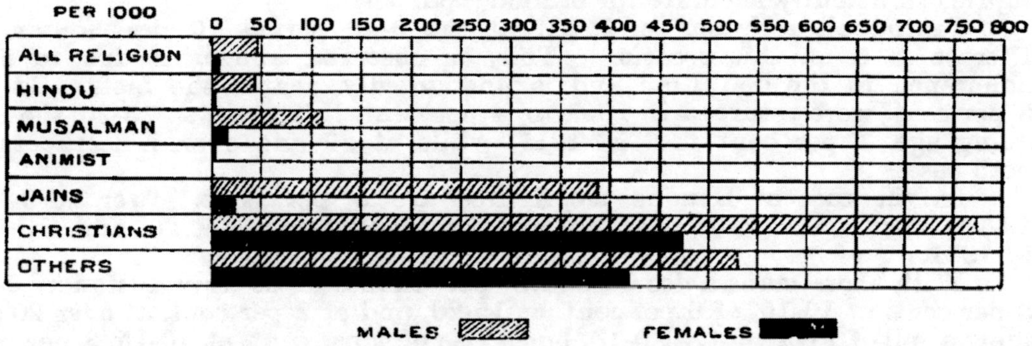


63 males and 4 females per thousand being literate; the figures for the two remaining tracts are nearly the same. The predominance of the Plateau is due to its towns, 41 of the 77 towns in the Agency falling in this area. The little difference noticeable between the Low-lying and the Hilly tract is due to the impossibility of excluding a certain amount of the other tracts from the Hilly section.

The variation between urban and rural figures is well illustrated by the returns for Lashkar, Rewah, Indore, Bhopal and Ratlam treated locally as "cities," of which the first two stand in the Low-lying and the last three in the Plateau area. In spite of the effects of plague and the closing of the schools in all these places, except Rewah, the literacy rises to 13 and 14 per cent., males showing 26 per cent. in the Low-lying area and females nearly 3 in the Plateau. These figures show clearly the concentration of literacy in towns.

The figures for the school-going age are very high, reaching 28 per cent. among males in the Low-lying tract and 5 per cent. among females in the Plateau.

The presence of the trading classes, head-quarters of administrations and big scholastic institutions is responsible for the high figures.

The religions also show local variations. Jain males are more educated in the Hilly tract than elsewhere, being, as regards males, 2 per cent. in advance of those on the Plateau. This is due to the fact that such Jains as live in the Hilly section are shop-keepers who have come there purely for business purposes. In cities literate Jains reach 64 per cent., even touching 66 per cent. in the cities of the Plateau which includes Ratlam, the great Jain centre of the Agency. Musalman males are more educated in the Plateau and Hilly tract than in the Low-lying, the figures standing at 11 and 10 per cent. The towns in the Plateau raise the average there, while such Musalmans as inhabit in the Hilly tract are officials or traders of the Bohra class. Female figures in the Low-lying tract are low.

Hindu males in the Plateau show 2 per cent. more literate than elsewhere, due to the greater number of towns in this tract.

The Animist figures are higher in the Plateau owing to the Bhils in this tract being more civilised while the Malwa Bhil Corps, formerly situated at Sardarpur in the Hilly Natural Division, is now at Indore on the Plateau.

Christian figures need no comment.

Among those classed as "Others" the literacy is high owing to the number of Parsis in this group, who, however, reside mainly in the west of the Agency, few living in Northern Gwalior or the Eastern Political Charges, a fact which accounts for the fall in the standard in the cities of the Low-lying tract.

### *Comparative.*

71. No material alteration has taken place in the general percentage of literates since 1901. This in itself points to some rise, as on the last occasion very many who had no right to be classed as literate were so treated, especially in the Rewah State.

Females show a fall of 1 per thousand. Turning to the age figures it has not been possible to adjust these for the territorial changes which have taken place, but the nature of the return makes comparison with the unadjusted figures sufficiently accurate for ordinary purposes.

**Males.** Taking all religions in 1901, at the 0-10 period 10 per thousand were literate to 5 on this occasion. This, as observed above, is due to stricter adherence to the definition and is undoubtedly nearer the facts. At 10-15, 5 per cent. were returned in 1901 to 4 per cent. this year; at 15-20, the school-going age, 7 per cent. to 6 in 1911, while at 20 and over, it is the same in both cases.

In the case of Hindus the figures are 5 per cent. lower at 0-10 and 10-15, 8 per cent. lower at 15-20, and 3 per cent. lower at 20 and over than in 1901.

With Musalmans a decrease of 8 per thousand is found under 0-10, of 3 per cent. at 10-15, of 6 per cent. at 15-20, and of 2 per cent. at over 20; Jains show a fall of 2 per cent. at 0-10, but a rise of 4 per cent. at 10-15, 3 per cent. at 15-20, and 6 per cent. at over 20.

Christian figures are mainly artificial and vary with the cantonment population. There is a large fall in the 0-10 period of 15 per cent., elsewhere there is a fall of about 10 per cent.

Local variations are also noticeable. A fall of 1 per cent. in the Plateau and Hilly tracts is recorded since 1901. At the same time the figures for the 10-15 period show a rise of 1 per cent. on the Plateau but a fall of 2 per cent. in the Low-lying tract. A fall is noticeable in all tracts at 15-20 and over 20, except in the Low-lying tract at over 20 where there is a rise of 1 per cent.

**Females.** The female figures show no marked variation except a rise of 3 per thousand in the Plateau at 10-15 and a fall of 8 per thousand in the Hilly tract at 15-20.

**English.** No general variation is perceptible in the knowledge of English among either males or females since 1901, but a fall among males of 3 per thousand on the Plateau is balanced by arise of 8 per thousand among Hindus in the Low-lying and 6 per thousand in the Hilly tract.

### *Education by Caste.*

72. If the castes are grouped into Brahmans, Traders, and Rajputs we get the figures in the marginal inset; the result is what would be expected. On examining the figures of each group striking differences are met with. Among Brahmans (only the local sections are dealt with) the Shrigaud stand first with 17 per cent. literate of both sexes and 32 per cent. males, the Shrimali following with 12 per cent. of both sexes and 28 per cent. males. The rest fall much below this level. Jijhotias from the east of the Agency show 6 per cent. of both sexes and 12 per cent. males, Sanadhya 5 per cent. of both sexes and 10 per cent. males, and Sarwarias 4 per cent. of both sexes and 7 per cent. males.

| Caste. | Percentage of literate. | |
|---|---|---|
| | On Total. | Males. |
| Brahmans . . . . | 5 | 10 |
| Traders . . . . | 14 | 29 |
| Rajputs . . . . | 3 | 6 |

In the trading group, the Oswals head the list with 21 per cent., 42 per cent. of their males being literate, Mahesris with 17 per cent. and 34 per cent. males, Porwals with 15 per cent. and 27 per cent. males, Agarwals with 13 per cent. and 27 per cent. males, following. Mahesri females show 3 per cent. literate.

Among the Rajputs the average is much the same for all classes, 3 per cent. for both sexes and 6 per cent. for males. The Marathas stand out from among the others of the fighting class with 18 per cent. literate, 32 per cent. literate males; being followed by the Maratha Ponwars with 13 per cent. literate in each case. The Marathas are found chiefly among the families and entourage of the big Jagirdars in Gwalior State and are a well-to-do and educated community.

Of the rest none shows double figures except the Musalman Sayads with 12 per cent. literate of both sexes and 20 per cent. males. Shaikhs with 6 per cent. of both sexes and 11 per cent. males, and the Gahohis with 11 per cent. of both sexes and 19 per cent. males. The Dhangar community which is locally important at Indore shows 3 per cent. literate and 5 per cent. males.

In English Marathas, owing to the high figure from Gwalior where much is being done to educate this class, stand first with 5 per cent. of both sexes and 9 per cent. males literate, Shrimali Brahmans 2 per cent. and 5 per cent., Shrigaud 2 per cent. and 3 per cent. English.

The trading classes fall behind, the Mahesris showing 2 per cent. of males and the Oswals 1 per cent. literate in English. The fact is that English is not used by the majority of this class in their business transactions.

### *Comparative.*

73. Compared with the figures for 1901 the Shrigaud Brahmans show a fall of 4 per cent., male literacy having fallen by 10 per cent., while the female figures show nearly 1 per cent. rise. Shrimalis show a fall of 10 per cent. also. Marathas show a rise of 6 per cent., the male figures being 9 per cent. higher than in 1901.

No other comparative figures are available.

Of the trading classes, Oswals alone show a higher percentage than in 1901, 6 per cent. higher for both sexes and 14 per cent. higher for males and 2 per cent. higher for females.

The Musalman figures likewise show a rise among Sayads and Pathans of 3 per cent. among male literates. The Shaikhs show a fall of 5 per cent. among males.

Subsidiary Table VII gives such statistics as are available regarding scholastic institutions. Educational Department Statistics.

Educational institutions have doubled since 1901 while scholars have increased by 82 per cent. Comparison is made in the inset with those of school-going age returned.

| | Number per 10,000 of population. | |
|---|---|---|
| | Literate at 15-20. | Scholars on registers. |
| Males . . . . | 51 | 122 |
| Females . . . . | 4 | 11 |
| Total . | 28 | 68 |

Education is spreading steadily and in all States is receiving very particular attention.

It is not possible to compare the statistics for castes on the school registers and at 15-20 except in the case of Marathas and Dhangars as the Rajput clans were not recorded in 1901.

**Local publications.**

Subsidiary Table VII-A is printed to allow of comparison in 1921.

Subsidiary Tables IX and X deal with local publications. These appear to have decreased during the decade. The figures are in no case important.

SUBSIDIARY TABLE I.—**Education by Age, Sex and Religion.**

| Religion. | NUMBER PER MILLE WHO ARE LITERATE. | | | | | | | | | | | NUMBER PER MILLE WHO ARE ILLITERATE. | | | NUMBER PER MILLE WHO ARE LITERATE IN ENGLISH. | | |
|---|---|---|---|---|---|---|---|---|---|---|---|---|---|---|---|---|---|
| | All ages. | | | 0—10. | | 10—15. | | 15—20. | | 20 and over. | | | | | | | |
| | Total. | Male. | Female. | Male. | Female. | Male. | Female. | Male. | Female. | Male. | Female. | Total. | Male. | Female. | Total. | Male. | Female. |
| 1 | 2 | 3 | 4 | 5 | 6 | 7 | 8 | 9 | 10 | 11 | 12 | 13 | 14 | 15 | 16 | 17 | 18 |
| **ALL RELIGIONS** | **26** | **48** | **3** | **5** | **1** | **45** | **4** | **61** | **5** | **69** | **3** | **974** | **952** | **997** | **2** | ... | ... |
| Hindu | 22 | 43 | 1 | 4 | ... | 40 | 2 | 53 | 3 | 60 | 2 | 978 | 958 | 999 | 1 | 2 | .. |
| Musalman | 61 | 107 | 12 | 10 | 3 | 93 | 18 | 133 | 20 | 147 | 14 | 939 | 893 | 988 | 3 | 7 | .. |
| Animist | 1 | 1 | ... | ... | ... | 1 | ... | 2 | ... | 2 | ... | 999 | 999 | 1,000 | ... | ... | ... |
| Jain | 212 | 388 | 20 | 56 | 6 | 375 | 28 | 483 | 30 | 498 | 23 | 788 | 612 | 980 | 3 | 5 | ... |
| Christian | 670 | 776 | 466 | 152 | 122 | 636 | 669 | 736 | 688 | 897 | 550 | 330 | 224 | 534 | 535 | 675 | 264 |
| Europeans | 900 | 957 | 656 | 248 | 142 | 1,000 | 1,000 | 1,000 | 1,000 | 1,000 | 1,000 | 100 | 43 | 344 | 900 | 957 | 656 |
| Anglo-Indians | 784 | 787 | 781 | 300 | 262 | 1,000 | 1,000 | 1,000 | 1,000 | 1,000 | 1,000 | 216 | 213 | 219 | 784 | 787 | 781 |
| Indian Christians | 406 | 463 | 345 | 91 | 78 | 480 | 587 | 627 | 614 | 597 | 306 | 594 | 537 | 655 | 105 | 170 | 32 |
| Others | 482 | 526 | 415 | 204 | 119 | 511 | 610 | 420 | 523 | 631 | 500 | 518 | 474 | 585 | 215 | 221 | 204 |

SUBSIDIARY TABLE II.—**Education by Age, Sex and Locality.**

| Natural Division. | NUMBER PER MILLE WHO ARE LITERATE. | | | | | | | | | | |
|---|---|---|---|---|---|---|---|---|---|---|---|
| | All ages. | | | 0—10. | | 10—15. | | 15—20. | | 20 and over. | |
| | Total. | Male. | Female. | Male. | Female. | Male. | Female. | Male. | Female. | Male. | Female. |
| 1 | 2 | 3 | 4 | 5 | 6 | 7 | 8 | 9 | 10 | 11 | 12 |
| **Central India** | **26** | **48** | **3** | **5** | **1** | **45** | **4** | **61** | **5** | **69** | **3** |
| Plateau | 35 | 63 | 4 | 7 | 1 | 60 | 7 | 77 | 8 | 89 | 5 |
| Low-lying Tract | 21 | 40 | 2 | 4 | ... | 35 | 2 | 47 | 3 | 57 | 2 |
| Hilly Tract | 19 | 36 | 1 | 3 | ... | 38 | 2 | 55 | 3 | 52 | 2 |
| **Cities** | **136** | **240** | **20** | **33** | **6** | **254** | **38** | **266** | **42** | **299** | **20** |
| Plateau | 132 | 228 | 24 | 33 | 7 | 206 | 49 | 254 | 54 | 292 | 24 |
| Low-lying Tract | 142 | 262 | 12 | 32 | 4 | 332 | 19 | 285 | 17 | 311 | 13 |

## SUBSIDIARY TABLE III.—Education by Religion, Sex and Locality.

| Natural Division. | NUMBER PER MILLE WHO ARE LITERATE. | | | | | | | | | | | |
|---|---|---|---|---|---|---|---|---|---|---|---|---|
| | HINDU. | | MUSALMAN. | | ANIMIST. | | JAIN. | | CHRISTIAN. | | OTHERS. | |
| | Male. | Female. | Male. | Female. | Male. | Female. | Male. | Female. | Male. | Female. | Male. | Female. |
| 1 | 2 | 3 | 4 | 5 | 6 | 7 | 8 | 9 | 10 | 11 | 12 | 13 |
| **Central India** | **42** | **1** | **107** | **12** | **1** | . | **388** | **20** | **776** | **466** | **526** | **415** |
| Plateau | 52 | 2 | 111 | 15 | 2 | ... | 438 | 26 | 803 | 490 | 540 | 449 |
| Low-lying Tract | 36 | 1 | 95 | 7 | 3 | .. | 221 | 6 | 871 | 568 | 497 | 247 |
| Hilly Tract | 35 | 1 | 108 | 8 | 1 | ... | 457 | 21 | 319 | 231 | 450 | 293 |
| **Cities** | **266** | **13** | **153** | **20** | **28** | ... | **643** | **85** | **628** | **468** | **348** | **178** |
| Plateau | 247 | 14 | 153 | 23 | 9 | | 662 | 86 | 593 | 504 | 320 | 175 |
| Low-lying Tract | 290 | 12 | 152 | 9 | 81 | ... | 384 | 77 | 813 | 284 | 538 | 195 |

## SUBSIDIARY TABLE IV.—English Education by Age, Sex and Locality.

| Natural Division. | LITERATE IN ENGLISH PER 10,000. | | | | | | | | | | | |
|---|---|---|---|---|---|---|---|---|---|---|---|---|
| | 1911. | | | | | | | | | | 1901. | |
| | 0—10. | | 10—15. | | 15—20. | | 20 and over. | | All Ages. | | All Ages. | |
| | Male. | Female. | Male. | Female. | Male. | Female. | Male. | Female. | Male. | Female. | Male. | Female. |
| 1 | 2 | 3 | 4 | 5 | 6 | 7 | 8 | 9 | 10 | 11 | 12 | |
| **Central India** | **1** | **1** | **20** | **3** | **54** | **6** | **52** | **3** | **35** | **3** | **35** | **3** |
| Plateau | 3 | 2 | 39 | 7 | 88 | 12 | 87 | 6 | 60 | 6 | 63 | 7 |
| Low-lying Tract | 1 | ... | 18 | 2 | 36 | 2 | 34 | 2 | 24 | 1 | 16 | 1 |
| Hilly Tract | ... | ... | 7 | 1 | 25 | 2 | 18 | 1 | 12 | 1 | 6 | ... |

## SUBSIDIARY TABLE V.—Progress of Education since 1901.

| Natural Division. | NUMBER OF LITERATE PER MILLE. | | | | | | | | | | | | | | | |
|---|---|---|---|---|---|---|---|---|---|---|---|---|---|---|---|---|
| | All Ages. | | | | 10—15. | | | | 15—20. | | | | 20 and over. | | | |
| | Male. | | Female. | | Male. | | Female. | | Male. | | Female. | | Male. | | Female. | |
| | 1911. | 1901. | 1911. | 1901. | 1911. | 1901 | 1911. | 1901. | 1911. | 1901. | 1911. | 1901. | 1911. | 1901. | 1911. | 1901. |
| 1 | 2 | 3 | 4 | 5 | 6 | 7 | 8 | 9 | 10 | 11 | 12 | 13 | 14 | 15 | 16 | 17 |
| **Central India** | **48** | **55** | **3** | **4** | **45** | **49** | **4** | **4** | **61** | **76** | **5** | **8** | **69** | **72** | **3** | **3** |
| Plateau | 63 | 71 | 4 | 4 | 60 | 52 | 7 | 4 | 77 | 84 | 8 | 8 | 89 | 95 | 5 | 5 |
| Low-lying Tract | 40 | 43 | 2 | 3 | 35 | 52 | 2 | 3 | 47 | 69 | 3 | 4 | 57 | 52 | 2 | 2 |
| Hilly Tract | 36 | 47 | 1 | 4 | 38 | 37 | 2 | 5 | 65 | 72 | 3 | 12 | 52 | 62 | 2 | 3 |

## SUBSIDIARY TABLE VI.—Education by Caste.

| Caste. | NUMBER PER 1,000 WHO ARE | | | | | | NUMBER PER 10,000 | | |
|---|---|---|---|---|---|---|---|---|---|
| | LITERATE. | | | ILLITERATE. | | | LITERATE IN ENGLISH. | | |
| | Total. | Male. | Female. | Total. | Male. | Female. | Total. | Male. | Female. |
| 1 | 2 | 3 | 4 | 5 | 6 | 7 | 8 | 9 | 10 |
| Ajna | 8 | 14 | ... | 992 | 986 | 1,000 | ... | ... | ... |
| | *4* | *6* | ... | *996* | *994* | *1,000* | *4* | *5* | ... |
| Bania | 143 | 278 | 13 | 857 | 722 | 987 | 49 | 92 | 4 |
| | *170* | *309* | *5* | *830* | *691* | *995* | *29* | *53* | ... |
| „ Agarwal | 133 | 271 | 8 | 867 | 729 | 992 | 86 | 167 | 13 |
| | *152* | *270* | *5* | *848* | *730* | *995* | *39* | *71* | ... |
| „ Gahohi | 107 | 194 | 3 | 893 | 806 | 997 | 6 | 10 | ... |
| „ Kasaundhan | 41 | 84 | 2 | 959 | 916 | 998 | 1 | 2 | ... |
| „ Kesar | 6 | 11 | ... | 994 | 989 | 1,000 | 1 | 2 | ... |
| „ Kharia | 35 | 87 | ... | 965 | 913 | 1,000 | ... | ... | ... |
| „ Mahesri | 172 | 338 | 27 | 828 | 662 | 983 | 86 | 183 | 2 |
| | *229* | *388* | *3* | *771* | *612* | *997* | *30* | *52* | ... |
| „ Oswal | 214 | 423 | 18 | 786 | 577 | 982 | 60 | 123 | 1 |
| | *146* | *278* | *4* | *854* | *722* | *996* | *18* | *35* | ... |
| „ Porwal | 147 | 274 | 14 | 853 | 726 | 986 | 19 | 37 | ... |
| Bhat | 36 | 65 | 5 | 964 | 935 | 995 | 21 | 39 | 2 |
| | *36* | *67* | *1* | *964* | *933* | *999* | ... | ... | ... |
| Bhil | 1 | 1 | ... | 999 | 999 | 1,000 | ... | ... | ... |
| Bhilala | ... | 1 | ... | 1,000 | 999 | 1,000 | ... | ... | ... |
| Brahman | 51 | 99 | 3 | 949 | 901 | 997 | 19 | 37 | 1 |
| | *97* | *183* | *3* | *903* | *817* | *997* | *13* | *26* | ... |
| „ Bhagor | 69 | 129 | 3 | 931 | 871 | 997 | 14 | 25 | 1 |
| „ Jijhotia | 65 | 121 | 2 | 935 | 879 | 998 | 16 | 30 | ... |
| | *66* | *123* | *3* | *934* | *877* | *997* | *4* | *7* | ... |
| „ Sanadhya | 55 | 104 | 2 | 945 | 896 | 998 | 23 | 43 | 1 |
| „ Sarwaria | 38 | 75 | 2 | 962 | 925 | 998 | 9 | 18 | [illegible] |
| „ Shrigaud | 169 | 319 | 9 | 831 | 681 | 991 | 159 | 307 | ... |
| | *208* | *414* | *1* | *792* | *586* | *999* | *51* | *102* | ... |
| „ Shrimali | 125 | 277 | 12 | 875 | 723 | 988 | 203 | 470 | 4 |
| | *217* | *373* | *10* | *783* | *627* | *990* | *31* | *55* | ... |
| Dhangar | 26 | 49 | 4 | 974 | 951 | 996 | 25 | 50 | 2 |
| | *64* | *110* | *6* | *936* | *890* | *994* | *50* | *86* | *4* |
| Gond | ... | 1 | ... | 1,000 | 999 | 1,000 | ... | ... | ... |
| Gujar | 11 | 19 | 1 | 989 | 981 | 999 | 5 | 9 | ... |
| | *8* | *14* | ... | *992* | *986* | *1,000* | *1* | *2* | ... |
| Khangar | 6 | 11 | ... | 994 | 989 | 1,000 | 1 | 2 | ... |
| | *8* | *16* | ... | *992* | *984* | *1,000* | *1* | *2* | ... |
| Maratha | 178 | 325 | 13 | 822 | 675 | 987 | 481 | 902 | 7 |
| | *120* | *231* | *10* | *880* | *769* | *990* | *117* | *222* | *12* |
| Panika | 2 | 5 | ... | 998 | 995 | 1,000 | ... | ... | ... |
| Rajput | 35 | 59 | 5 | 965 | 941 | 995 | 19 | 33 | 1 |
| | *22* | *41* | *2* | *978* | *959* | *998* | *6* | *11* | ... |
| „ Bhadauria | 27 | 45 | 1 | 973 | 955 | 999 | 42 | 71 | 2 |
| „ Baghela | 60 | 103 | 15 | 940 | 897 | 985 | 10 | 19 | ... |
| „ Bundela | 49 | 89 | 8 | 951 | 911 | 992 | 22 | 43 | 1 |
| „ Bundela Ponwar | ... | ... | ... | 1,000 | 1,000 | 1,000 | ... | ... | ... |
| „ Chauhan | 42 | 84 | 3 | 958 | 916 | 997 | 38 | 78 | 2 |
| „ Dhandera | 32 | 60 | 4 | 968 | 940 | 996 | 8 | 16 | ... |
| „ Dikhit | 26 | 45 | ... | 974 | 955 | 1,000 | 8 | 13 | ... |
| „ Gahalot | 7 | 11 | 1 | 993 | 989 | 999 | ... | ... | ... |
| | ... | ... | ... | *1,000* | *1,000* | *1,000* | ... | ... | ... |
| „ Gaharwar | 49 | 70 | 25 | 951 | 930 | 975 | 4 | 8 | ... |
| „ Gaud | 51 | 93 | 2 | 949 | 907 | 998 | 1 | 2 | ... |
| „ Kachhwaha | 27 | 50 | 2 | 973 | 950 | 998 | 26 | 50 | 1 |
| „ Khichi | 42 | 71 | 7 | 958 | 929 | 993 | 8 | 14 | ... |
| „ Parihar | 38 | 67 | 4 | 962 | 933 | 996 | 21 | 39 | ... |
| „ Ponwar | 30 | 52 | 2 | 970 | 948 | 998 | 13 | 24 | ... |
| „ „ Maratha | 130 | 129 | 132 | 870 | 871 | 868 | 17 | 32 | ... |
| „ Rathod | 45 | 72 | 11 | 955 | 928 | 987 | 31 | 54 | 4 |
| „ Sengar | 29 | 64 | 2 | 971 | 936 | 998 | 10 | 28 | ... |
| „ Sisodia | 32 | 45 | 19 | 966 | 955 | 981 | 13 | 25 | ... |
| „ Solanki | 25 | 42 | 3 | 975 | 958 | 997 | 6 | 11 | ... |
| „ Tonwar | 29 | 41 | 2 | 971 | 959 | 998 | 4 | 4 | 2 |
| Sondhia | 5 | 10 | 1 | 995 | 990 | 999 | 1 | 1 | ... |
| | *1* | *3* | ... | *999* | *997* | *1,000* | ... | ... | ... |
| Musalman | 65 | 115 | 10 | 935 | 885 | 990 | 47 | 88 | 1 |
| | *77* | *133* | *17* | *923* | *867* | *983* | *48* | *83* | *11* |
| „ Pathan | 64 | 112 | 11 | 936 | 888 | 989 | 33 | 61 | 1 |
| | *46* | *88* | *3* | *954* | *912* | *997* | *10* | *46* | ... |
| „ Sayad | 121 | 204 | 22 | 879 | 796 | 978 | 140 | 256 | 2 |
| | *106* | *168* | *34* | *894* | *832* | *966* | *143* | *246* | *28* |
| „ Shaikh | 62 | 111 | 8 | 938 | 889 | 992 | 47 | 89 | 1 |
| | *95* | *160* | *26* | *905* | *840* | *974* | *49* | *78* | *17* |
| „ Shaikh Behena | 14 | 27 | 1 | 986 | 973 | 999 | 2 | 4 | ... |

*Note.*—The figures in italics relate to 1901.

SUBSIDIARY TABLE VII.—**Number of Institutions and Pupils according to the Returns of State Educational Departments.**

| Class of Institutions. | 1911. Number of Institutions. | 1911. Number of Scholars. | 1901. Number of Institutions. | 1901. Number of Scholars. | 1891. Number of Institutions. | 1891. Number of Scholars. |
|---|---|---|---|---|---|---|
| 1 | 2 | 3 | 4 | 5 | 6 | 7 |
| **All Kinds** | **1,135** | **63,659** | **570** | **34,987** | **299** | **15,241** |
| For males and females. Arts College | 1 | 106 | 1 | 30 | 1 | 25 |
| High School | 1 | 62 | 1 | 113 | ... | ... |
| Primary Schools | 22 | 646 | 4 | 292 | 5 | 319 |
| Secondary Schools | 3 | 103 | ... | ... | ... | ... |
| Special School | 1 | 172 | 1 | 48 | ... | ... |
| **Total** | **28** | **1,089** | **7** | **483** | **6** | **344** |
| For males. Arts Colleges | 2 | 221 | 2 | 191 | ... | ... |
| High Schools | 25 | 6,720 | 20 | 4,038 | 15 | 2,530 |
| Primary Schools | 921 | 41,877 | 455 | 24,498 | 231 | 10,292 |
| Secondary Schools | 50 | 7,896 | 21 | 3,519 | 11 | 724 |
| Training School | 1 | 24 | ... | ... | ... | ... |
| Special Schools | 12 | 475 | 3 | 119 | ... | ... |
| Vedic Schools | 31 | 736 | 29 | 533 | 15 | 286 |
| **Total** | **1,042** | **57,949** | **530** | **32,898** | **272** | **13,832** |
| For females. High School | 1 | 130 | 1 | 50 | 1 | 10 |
| Primary Schools | 56 | 3,948 | 29 | 1,343 | 18 | 1,001 |
| Secondary Schools | 6 | 425 | 2 | 142 | 2 | 54 |
| Special Schools | 2 | 118 | 1 | 71 | ... | ... |
| **Total** | **65** | **4,621** | **33** | **1,606** | **21** | **1,065** |

SUBSIDIARY TABLE VII-A.—**Number of Scholars showing Caste as recorded in School Registers.**

| Caste, Tribe or Race. | Number. | Caste, Tribe or Race | Number. | Caste, Tribe or Race. | Number. |
|---|---|---|---|---|---|
| 1 | 2 | 1 | 2 | 1 | 2 |
| Abir | 122 | Halwai | 640 | Sonar | 246 |
| Bairagi | 36 | Jat | 47 | Sutar | 136 |
| Bania | 6,545 | Kahar | 39 | Tamboli | 76 |
| „ Asada | 12 | Kalal | 69 | Teli | 220 |
| Beldar | 17 | Kasera | 30 | Vidur | 5 |
| Bhambhai | 1 | Kayasth | 1,794 | Sikh | 17 |
| Bharbhunja | 14 | Khangar | 36 | Porwal | 71 |
| Bhat | 14 | Khati | 23 | Bhil | 51 |
| Bhoi | 8 | Khatri | 22 | Mina | 9 |
| Brahman | 16,647 | Koli | 52 | Bohra | 123 |
| Charan | 1 | Kulmi | 98 | Musalman | 9,587 |
| Chhipa | 27 | Kumbhar | 82 | Naita | 1 |
| Dangi | 25 | Lakhera | 15 | Anglo-Indian | 21 |
| Darzi | 89 | Lohar | 118 | Christian | 832 |
| Deswali | 10 | Mali | 103 | European | 47 |
| Dhangar | 345 | Mallah | 1 | German | 3 |
| Dhimar | 61 | Maratha | 971 | Goanese | 26 |
| Dhobi | 24 | Mirdha | 5 | Parsee | 145 |
| Dhoi | 16 | Nai | 168 | Jew | 4 |
| Gadaria | 12 | Pasi | 3 | Unspecified | 19,688 |
| Gaoli | 5 | Rajput | 4,091 | | |
| Gujar | 29 | „ Raghubansi | 19 | | |
| Gusain | 12 | Sikligar | 3 | TOTAL | 63,659 |

SUBSIDIARY TABLE VIII.—**Main Results of University Examinations.**

| Examination. | 1911. | | 1901. | | 1891. | | Remarks. |
|---|---|---|---|---|---|---|---|
| | Candidates. | Passed. | Candidates. | Passed. | Candidates. | Passed. | |
| 1 | 2 | 3 | 4 | 5 | 6 | 7 | 8 |
| Matriculation (Entrance) | 246 | 104 | 171 | 83 | 50 | 28 | In 1911 four females appeared, out of whom one passed. |
| F. A. or Intermediate Examination | 92 | 36 | 66 | 29 | 4 | 2 | In 1911 one female appeared but failed. |
| B. A. Examination | 43 | 19 | 19 | 5 | ... | ... | |
| B. Sc. Examination | 9 | 4 | ... | ... | ... | ... | |
| **Total** | **390** | **163** | **256** | **117** | **54** | **30** | |

SUBSIDIARY TABLE IX.—**Number and Circulation of Newspapers, etc.**

| Language. | Class of Newspapers (daily, weekly, etc.) | 1911 | | 1901. | | 1891. | |
|---|---|---|---|---|---|---|---|
| | | No. | Circulation. | No. | Circulation. | No. | Circulation. |
| 1 | 2 | 3 | 4 | 5 | 6 | 7 | 8 |
| **Total** | | **8** | **1,492** | **5** | **2,101** | **4** | **2,180** |
| English | Weekly | 1 | 21 | ... | ... | ... | ... |
| English and Hindi | do. | 2 | 828 | 3 | 1,217 | 2 | 800 |
| Hindi | do. | 1 | 150 | 1 | 500 | ... | ... |
| Urdu | do. | 1 | 100 | ... | ... | ... | ... |
| Hindi and Urdu | do. | ... | ... | ... | .. | 1 | 1,000 |
| **Total, Weekly** | | **5** | **1,099** | **4** | **1,717** | **3** | **1,800** |
| English | Fortnightly | ... | ... | 1 | 384 | 1 | 380 |
| Hindi | do. | 1 | 200 | ... | ... | ... | ... |
| **Total, Fortnightly** | | **1** | **200** | **1** | **384** | **1** | **380** |
| English and Hindi | Monthly | 1 | 133 | ... | .. | ... | ... |
| Hindi and Urdu | do. | 1 | 60 | ... | ... | ... | ... |
| **Total, Monthly** | | **2** | **193** | ... | ... | ... | ... |

SUBSIDIARY TABLE X.—**Number of Books published in each Language.**

| Language in which issued. | NUMBER OF BOOKS PUBLISHED IN EACH LANGUAGE. | | | | | | | | | | Total of Decade. | | |
|---|---|---|---|---|---|---|---|---|---|---|---|---|---|
| | 1901. | 1902. | 1903. | 1904. | 1905. | 1906. | 1907. | 1908. | 1909. | 1910. | 1901 to 1910. | 1891 to 1900. | 1881 to 1891. |
| 1 | 2 | 3 | 4 | 5 | 6 | 7 | 8 | 9 | 10 | 11 | 12 | 13 | 14 |
| **Total** | **5** | **6** | **10** | **13** | **39** | **37** | **51** | **45** | **43** | **29** | **278** | **417** | **20** |
| **English** | 1 | 1 | ... | 8 | 2 | 5 | 8 | 3 | 5 | 8 | 41 | 29 | ... |
| **Hindi** | ... | 2 | 5 | 3 | 8 | 7 | 8 | 9 | 25 | 12 | 79 | 271 | 2 |
| **Marathi** | 2 | 2 | ... | 1 | 1 | ... | ... | ... | ... | ... | 6 | 36 | ... |
| **Urdu** | 2 | 1 | 4 | 1 | 28 | 23 | 31 | 27 | 5 | 8 | 130 | 45 | 18 |
| **Sanskrit** | ... | ... | ... | ... | ... | ... | 1 | ... | 2 | ... | 3 | 30 | ... |
| **Arabic** | ... | ... | ... | ... | ... | ... | ... | ... | ... | ... | ... | 6 | ... |
| **English and Hindi** | ... | ... | ... | ... | ... | 1 | ... | ... | ... | ... | 1 | ... | ... |
| **English, Hindi and Urdu** | ... | ... | ... | ... | ... | ... | ... | 1 | ... | ... | 1 | ... | ... |
| **Sanskrit and Hindi** | ... | ... | 1 | ... | ... | 1 | 2 | ... | ... | ... | 4 | ... | ... |
| **Prakrat** | ... | ... | ... | ... | ... | ... | 1 | 2 | 2 | ... | 5 | ... | ... |
| **Gujarati** | ... | ... | ... | ... | ... | ... | ... | 3 | 4 | 1 | 8 | ... | ... |

# CHAPTER IX.

## Language.

74. The Table dealt with in this Chapter is Table X.

75. Dr. Grierson's Linguistic Survey has made any detailed discussion of the dialects of Central India unnecessary.

The survey divides the Indo-aryan vernacular into three bands :—

I. Language of the Midland or Inner Band, ***Western Hindi*** (Urdu, etc.)

II. Intermediate Languages, borrowed from both Inner and Outer Bands.

(*a*) More nearly allied to the Midland Languages, ***Rajasthani.***

(*b*) More allied to the Outer Languages, ***Eastern Hindi*** (Bagheli).

III. Outer Languages.

***Marathi, Bengali, Kashmiri, etc.***

The dialects proper to Central India all fall within the first two bands as the Gondi and Korku of this tract are only bastard forms of Malwi, etc.

The Indo-Aryan tribes penetrating through the Punjab into the Madhyadesh or Middle-land (the tract lying between the Himalayas and Vindhyas and Sirhind and Allahabad) imported their own speech which, passing through Sanskrit, the Prakrits and the Apabhramsas, gave rise to what is loosely termed Hindi. This language is easily divisible into three—Bihari, Eastern Hindi (Bagheli) and Western Hindi (Urdu, etc.).

Eastern Hindi, represented in Central India mainly by Bagheli, is in part influenced by its neighbours of the Outer Band. Eastern Hindi as the language of the Jain teacher Mahavira, in one of its Prakrit forms and of Tulsi Das in the 17th century, has an extensive literature, especially in the Awadhi form. Bagheli literature is a modern growth fostered by the Rewah Chiefs.

Western Hindi, the language par excellence of the Middle-land, was first the vernacular of the Gangetic-duab. From Delhi a Persianised form spread later on with the extension of the Muhammadan dominion, and thus Urdu became the *lingua franca* of Northern India. In the Intermediate group of tongues, the influence of the Middle-land language is predominant. Rajasthani is its most important form in this Agency, the Malwi dialect being its standard local variety.

As education spreads these tongues gradually approximate to a common form. But education has still much to do before it can have any appreciable effect on the local vernaculars of Central India, with their rough intonation and fine vigorous expressions. The Musalman rulers of Central India left but few traces of their speech, except in revenue and technical terms, the Rajput ruling element serving to preserve the indigenous forms, while the Maratha influx of the 17th and 18th century assisted in further weakening the influence of Persian. Outside the cities the absence of Persian words is very noticeable, especially in localities remote from towns and in the language of ordinary cultivators. The headmen, who come into contact with officials, are more sophisticated and use mutilated Persian words more freely. Even the educated speak the local dialects almost exclusively in their own homes, where their womenfolk would not, as a rule, comprehend the language which their husbands employ in public or when speaking in the presence of strangers.

Among students, clerks *et hoc genus omne* a new *lingua franca* has arisen consisting of Urdu, Hindi, or Marathi as the case may be freely interlarded with English words and modes of construction, which is employed even when the speaker is not really capable of conversing in English.

Thus the mass of the people, educated and uneducated, Hindu and Musalman, speak a local dialect with the members of their families. Away from home Urdu, leaning more or less to Hindi, as the speaker is more or less educated, is spoken, this tongue being also used in talk with strangers and when it is considered desirable to impress inferiors, as when an official is addressing villagers. In Central India Hindi is the official language except in Musalman States where Urdu is employed save in village revenue papers such as those kept by the Patwaris. Marathi was till lately the language in Maratha States, but the inconvenience of an official tongue only known to officials, and not even to all of them, has resulted in its replacement by Hindi. There is not at present any very strong racial feeling on the subject of the official use of Hindi and Urdu, or between these tongues and Marathi, although instances have occurred in the last case, in which attempts were made by the Marathi-speaking bureaucracies to strengthen their hold over the administration by insisting on the use of this language in all official communications.

On this occasion particular attention was paid to the instructions for recording language. It was laid down that the language a man spoke every day in the bosom of his family (*bhasha, madri-zaban*) and not any school-acquired tongue or the speech used by him only in polite society or the bazars was wanted. On the whole these instructions were carefully adhered to, the only cases in which the entries *Hindi* and *Urdu* were used indiscriminately being met with in the schedules of some Gwalior districts where the remaining entries showed that the work was characterised by general carelessness and disregard of orders.

In Bhopal, however, there was a strong feeling that not only all Musalmans but even Hindus as subjects of a Muhammadan State should be returned as speaking Urdu. The Census Officer, by assiduous attention, overcame this. An attempt was then made by a pseudonymous writer in Bhopal city to the *Paisa Akhbar* at Lahore to make political capital out of these instructions and rouse antipathetic feeling between the Musalman and Hindu officials of the State, while he at the same time condemned the action of the Census Officer in carrying out the orders of the Census Superintendent.

It must be recollected that a record of local dialects is always difficult as philological distinctions are not, in many cases, recognised by separate names in the locality in which they are spoken, though these names are familiar to grammarians, while on the other hand variants are recognized locally which are not sufficiently distinct to be considered as separate dialects. A few dialects such as Malwi, Rangri, Bundelkhandi, and Bagheli are more or less generally recognised and are easily recorded while the rest are apt to become merged in the general classification of Hindi.

**Distribution.**

76. The maps show clearly how the main groups fall, all the important dialects met with belonging to the Indo-European family, and the Western and Mediate Groups, the Western group tongues pervading the whole Agency except Baghelkhand, where the Mediate group holds sway. Gondi and Korku as spoken in Central India do not deserve to be classed as Munda and Dravidian languages. As spoken locally they are to all intents and purposes merely corrupt forms of Malwi or Baghelkhandi.

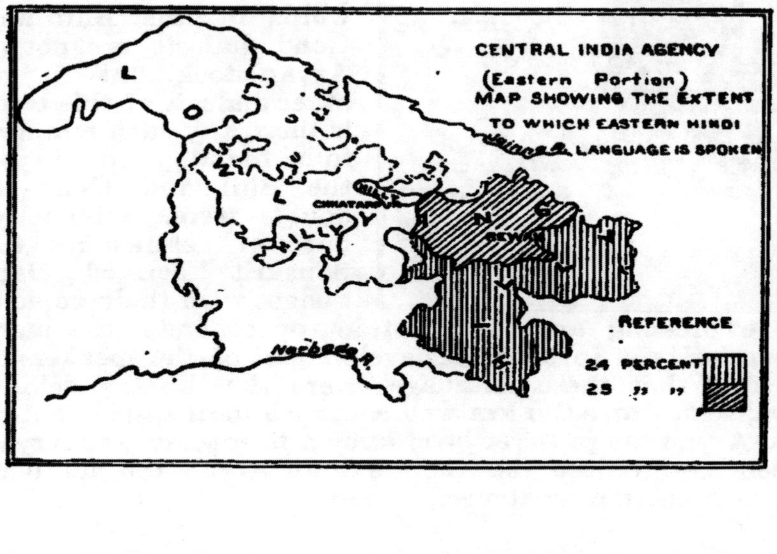

The tongues most favoured by immigrants are Marwari, Marathi and Purbi, the two former in the West and the latter in Northern Gwalior and the East of the Agency. The speakers of Marwari form the merchant community of Western Central India, while Marathi is spoken in towns in Maratha States. These communities have to a great extent become localised, although still maintaining their connections with Marwar and the Dekkhan.

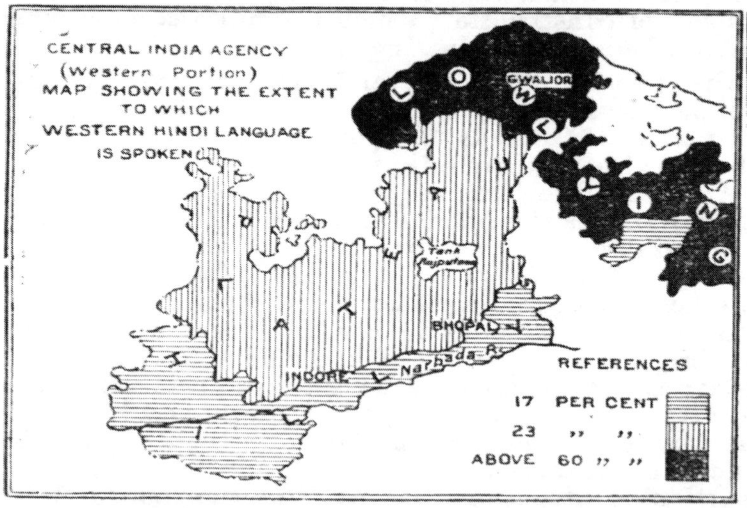


**Classification.**

77. The only alteration from the scheme of 1901 is inclusion of Korku under the Austro-Asiatic instead of the Dravidian family, but as noted above Korkus in Central India speak only a bastard form of Malwi and should not be separately classed.

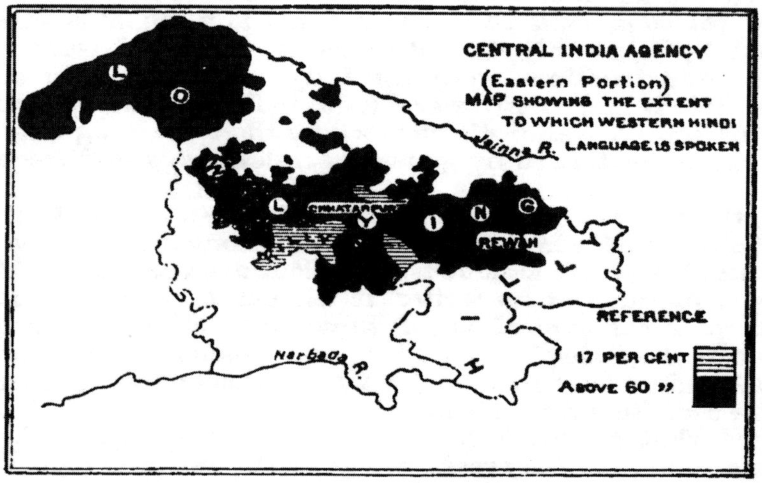


The Aryan sub-family includes 97 per cent. of the languages spoken, and of these languages 81 per cent. fall in the Western group. Western Hindi (40 per cent.) with Bundelkhandi (20 per cent.) and Hindi (11 per cent.) stand first; and next Rajasthani (37) with Malwi (28) per cent.

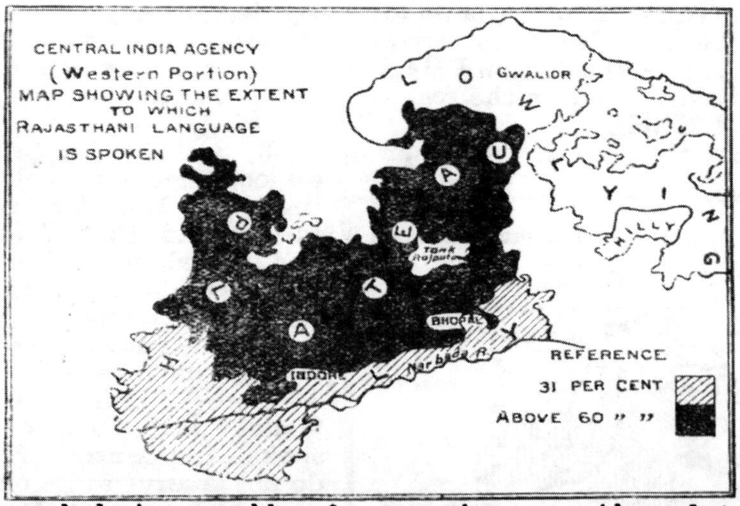


**Province of Aryan tongues.**

78. In Central India practically no traces, or only uncertain indications, remain of non-Aryan tongues. It is possible that a few words in the Bhil and Gond dialects are not of Aryan stock, but in no other dialects of this tract is there any such remnant to be found. Non-Aryan the Bhil and Gond no doubt were, ethnically, but as elsewhere the Sanskrit derived languages with their copious vocabularies capable of expressing any idea abstract or concrete, the more advanced civilisation, superiority of intellectual development of the speakers of those tongues, and the fact that these languages were the literary vehicle of an established religion, soon drove the less well-equipped local speech out of use. In no case has a non-Aryan tongue ever been known to supersede an Aryan form of speech. Between Aryan blood and the use of an Aryan tongue there is, of course, no necessary connection whatever.

The only local speech with a literature is Bagheli, and literature is of modern origin, being due to the encouragement given by the Chiefs of Rewah State.

Malwi and its cognate dialects are used for songs and poems, but these are not written down.

79. Various small but sufficiently well-defined local variations are met with in the speech of persons belonging either to certain communities in the same locality or to the same community in different localities. These differences are too slight even to warrant classification as separate dialects, though sufficiently noticeable to the trained ear. Thus, the Audich, Nagar, and Shrimali Brahmans when speaking what is undoubtedly Malwi use certain forms not usual in Malwi. The Audich and Nagars came originally from Gujarat but the Audich have been longest settled in Malwa. A Nagar Brahman in speaking retains the Gujarati तमें (you) क्यारे (when) सवार (morning) विवा (marriage) भात (rice), etc., while the Audich uses तम, कदे, सवेर, ब्याव and चोखा. The men do not, in either caste, now use the Gujarati future or शे, शूं, शो for है, हूं, हो but Nagar womenfolk do so. Both castes also retain the Gujarati genitive in नो and नी and the ablative थी where Malwi has को, कोऊं respectively. The Shrimalis use in their own houses a corrupt Malwi and are inclined to use Rangri genitive in रो or री instead of the Malwi को or की while there is a tendency to turn स into ह as in Rangri हवारे for सवारे. Local Shibboleths.

The Harina-goth and Bagada Brahmans originally from Jaipur speak a mixed Malwi and Jaipuri dialect retaining छे, छूं or छा and छो using synonyms for various common words not usual in Malwa, *e.g.*, दिनुग्या (दिन+उग्या) for सवेरे, डावडा for लडका, जाण for घास, कोडेक for किनो, etc. In the future also the form is different, *e.g.*, for Malwi जावेगा they use जावेला.

The method of speaking and especially intonation is a great indicator of locality or community. The Gonds even when using ordinary Hindi speak it with a peculiar spasmodic jerking emphasis particularly on the final syllables of long words and they are apt to add aspirates giving a harsher form to consonants, *e.g.*, they say झन for जन (man).

In Bagheli, besides the sibilant past tense in *is* मारीस which forces itself on even an untrained ear, other minor differences discover a man's habitat, and locally five dialects are distinguished, roughly those of North, South, East, West and the portion round the chief town, but men can often be at once assigned even to a certain Tahsil by the use of certain expressions. In Southern portions of Rewah रहो है and हुओ है are used where in the North of Rewah a man would say रहा and हुआ and in the Eastern part only are the particles बाटो and हो ever heard. A man from Singroli in Bardi Tahsil of Rewah would say मोरे के and तोरे के for the मोहो and तोहो of ordinary Bagheli.

As regards mutual comprehension of each other's speech no difficulty is experienced by persons living in Malwa in understanding the speech of any Rajasthani dialect. Bundelkhandi and Baghelkhandi, however, appear not to be readily understood by people from Malwa. Generally also women are more unintelligible than men, especially in the less developed parts where they use dialect forms more freely.

There do not appear to be any social linguistic differences, such caste variations as are met with being due to the retention of forms of speech belonging to the country of origin of the caste as noticed in the case of Audich and Nagar Brahmans.

All school books are written in Hindi, Urdu or Marathi and are usually those which have been adopted in the United Provinces and Bombay. Practically no languages now remain in Central India except those of Sanskritic origin, but many generations will pass before the dialects disappear, as wives and daughters will use the local forms even after education has banished them from the tongues of their menfolk.

SUBSIDIARY TABLE I.—**Distribution of Total Population by Languages.**

## (a) *According to Census.*

| Language. | Total number of speakers. 1911. | 1901. | Number per mille of population of province. | Name of State or locality where chiefly spoken. |
|---|---|---|---|---|
| 1 | 2 | 3 | 4 | 5 |
| ***Total*** | ***9,356,980*** | ***8,628,781*** | ***1,000*** | |
| **Austro-Asiatic Family** | **89** | **42** | ... | |
| Korku | 89 | 42 | ... | Bhopal. |
| **Tibeto-Chinese Family** | **1** | ... | ... | |
| Burmese | 1 | ... | ... | |
| **Dravidian Family** | **216,761** | **23,344** | **23·2** | |
| Gondi | 214,276 | 21,183 | 22·9 | Bhopal and Rewah. |
| Others | 2,485 | 2,161 | 0·3 | |
| **Indo-European Family** | **9,114,492** | **8,590,776** | **974·1** | |
| Malwi | 2,633,790 | 1,497,264 | 281·5 | Malwa States. |
| Bundelkhandi | 1,877,883 | 1,828,592 | 200·7 | Bundelkhand States. |
| Baghelkhandi | 1,372,663 | 1,396,538 | 146·7 | Baghelkhand States. |
| Hindi | 1,060,582 | 1,445,525 | 113·3 | Gwalior and Indore. |
| Nimadi | 379,695 | 177,945 | 40·6 | Nimar districts of Indore, and Dhar. |
| Bhadaori | 276,047 | 377,866 | 29·5 | Northern Gwalior. |
| Urdu | 256,771 | 672,682 | 27·4 | Bhopal and generally throughout Central India. |
| Bhili | 205,635 | 27,580 | 22·9 | Bhopawar Agency States. |
| Bhilali | 105,385 | 137,798 | 11·3 | Ditto. |
| Khichiwadi | 104,123 | 32,826 | 11·1 | Country round Guna. |
| Umatwadi | 90,748 | 24,304 | 9·7 | Rajgarh and Narsinghgarh. |
| Kachhawahi | 90,002 | ... | 9·6 | Northern Gwalior. |
| Marwadi | 85,607 | 93,986 | 9·2 | Wherever Marwadi Banias are settled. |
| Hindostani | 82,541 | 98,978 | 8·8 | General. |
| Purbi | 78,381 | 191,135 | 8·4 | Gwalior, Indore and Rewah. |
| Mewadi | 73,289 | 31,185 | 7·8 | Gwalior and Indore. |
| Marathi | 65.738 | 110,603 | 7·0 | Gwalior, Indore, Dhar, Dewas, Barwani and Ali-Rajpur. |
| Gujarati | 61,253 | 57,423 | 6·6 | Gwalior, Indore, Dhar, Barwani and Ali-Rajpur. |
| Brijabhasha | 41,389 | 245,064 | 4·4 | Narsinghgarh and Northern Gwalior. |
| Sondhia | 37,018 | 27,033 | 4·0 | Malwa districts of Gwalior and Indore, Rewah, and Narsinghgarh. |
| Rathawi | 36,691 | 53,831 | 3·9 | Barwani and generally in Bhil tract. |
| Jatwari | 22,810 | ... | 2·4 | Northern Gwalior. |
| Mewati | 10,458 | 3,147 | 1·1 | Gwalior, Indore and Jaora. |
| Others | 66,493 | 59,471 | 7·1 | |
| **Unclassed Languages** | **18,350** | **9,578** | **1·9** | |
| Banjari | 17,126 | 8,004 | 1·8 | Rajgarh, Gwalior, Indore and Barwani. |
| Others | 1,224 | 1,574 | 0·1 | |
| **Asiatic Languages** | **1,405** | **800** | **0·2** | |
| **Indo-European Family** | **787** | **262** | **0·1** | |
| Persian | 787 | 262 | 0·1 | Gwalior and Bhopal. |
| **Semitic Family** | **618** | **538** | **0·1** | |
| Arabic | 618 | 538 | 0·1 | Gwalior and Bhopal. |
| **European Languages** | **5,882** | **4,241** | **0·6** | |
| **Indo-European Family** | **5,882** | **4,241** | **0·6** | |
| English | 5,850 | 4,119 | 0·6 | Mhow, Nimach, Nowgong, and Indore Camp. |
| Others | 32 | 122 | | |

SUBSIDIARY TABLE I.—**Distribution of Total Population by Languages**—contd.

## (*b*) *According to Linguistic Survey*.

| Language. | Total number of speakers. | Number per mille of population of province. | Name of State or locality where chiefly spoken. |
|---|---|---|---|
| 1 | 2 | 3 | 4 |
| ***Total*** | ***9,356,980*** | ***1,000*** | |
| **Austro-Asiatic Family** | **89** | ... | |
| **Munda Sub-Family** | **89** | ... | |
| Korku | 89 | ... | Bhopal. |
| **Tibeto-Chinese Family** | **1** | ... | |
| **Tibeto-Burman Sub-Family** | **1** | ... | |
| **Assam-Burmese Branch** | **1** | ... | |
| Burmese | 1 | ... | |
| **Dravidian Family** | **216,761** | **23·2** | |
| **Dravida Group** | **1,215** | **0·1** | |
| Tamil | 933 | 0·1 | Mhow. |
| Malayalam | 1 | ... | |
| Canarese | 281 | ... | |
| **Intermediate Language** | **214,276** | **22·9** | |
| Gondi | 214,276 | 22·9 | Bhopal and Rewah. |
| **Andhra Group** | **1,270** | **0·2** | |
| Telugu | 1,270 | 0·2 | Mhow. |
| **Indo-European Family** | **9,114,492** | **974·1** | |
| **Aryan Sub-Family** | **1,754** | **0·2** | |
| **Eranian Branch** | **1,754** | **0·2** | |
| **Eastern Group** | **1,754** | **0·2** | |
| Balochi | 95 | ... | |
| Pashto | 1,659 | 0·2 | Gwalior, Bhopal and Mhow. |
| **Indian Branch** | **67** | ... | |
| **Non-Sanskritic Sub-Branch** | **67** | ... | |
| **Shina Khowar Group** | **67** | ... | |
| Kashmiri | 67 | ... | |
| **Sanskritic Sub-Branch** | **9,112,671** | **973·9** | |
| **Sanskrit Group** | **3** | ... | |
| Sanskrit | 3 | ... | |
| **North-western Group** | **521** | **0·1** | |
| Lahnda | 59 | ... | |
| Sindhi | 462 | 0·1 | Dhar. |
| **Southern Group** | **65,913** | **7·0** | |
| **Marathi** | **65,913** | **7·0** | |
| Marathi | 65,738 | 7·0 | Gwalior, Indore, Dhar, Dewas, Barwani and Ali Rajpur. |
| Others | 175 | ... | |
| **Eastern Group** | **79,302** | **8·5** | |
| **Bihari** | **78,398** | **8·4** | |
| Purbi | 78,381 | 8·4 | Gwalior, Indore and Rewah. |
| Others | 17 | ... | |
| **Oriya** | **9** | ... | |
| **Bengali** | **894** | **0·1** | Gwalior and Rewah. |
| **Assamese** | **1** | ... | |
| **Mediate Group** | **1,376,523** | **147·1** | |
| **Eastern Hindi** | **1,376,523** | **147·1** | |
| Baghelkhandi | 1,372,663 | 146·7 | Baghelkhand States. |
| Others | 3,860 | 0·4 | |

SUBSIDIARY TABLE I.—**Distribution of Total Population by Languages**—concld.

## (*b*) *According to Linguistic Survey.*

| Language. | Total number of speakers. | Number per mille of population of province. | Name of States or localities where chiefly spoken. |
|---|---|---|---|
| 1 | 2 | 3 | 4 |
| **Western Group** | **7,590,344** | **811·2** | |
| **Western Hindi** | **3,718,944** | **397·5** | |
| Brijabhasha | 41,389 | 4·4 | Narsinghgarh and Northern Gwalior. |
| Bundelkhandi | 1,877,883 | 200·7 | Bundelkhand States. |
| Bhadaori | 276,047 | 29·5 | Northern Gwalior. |
| Kachhawahi | 90,002 | 9·6 | Do. |
| Hindostani | 82,541 | 8·8 | General. |
| Hindi | 1,060,582 | 113·3 | Gwalior and Indore. |
| Urdu | 256,711 | 27·4 | Bhopal and generally throughout Central India. |
| Jatwari | 22,310 | 2·4 | Northern Gwalior. |
| Others | 11,419 | 1·4 | |
| **Rajasthani** | **3,427,442** | **366·3** | |
| Khichiwadi | 104,123 | 11·1 | Country round Guna. |
| Malwi | 2,633,790 | 281·5 | Malwa States. |
| Marwadi | 85,607 | 9·2 | Wherever Marwadi Banias are settled. |
| Mewadi | 73,289 | 7·8 | Gwalior and Indore. |
| Mewati | 10,458 | 1·1 | Gwalior, Indore and Jaora. |
| Nimadi | 379,695 | 40·6 | Nimar districts of Indore and Dhar. |
| Sondhi | 37,018 | 4·0 | Malwa districts of Gwalior and Indore, Rewah and Narsinghgarh. |
| Umatwadi | 90,748 | 9·7 | Rajgarh and Narsinghgarh. |
| Others | 12,714 | 1·3 | |
| **Gujarati** | **421,726** | **45·1** | |
| **Gujarati** | **61,253** | **6·6** | |
| **Bhil dialects** | **349,805** | **37·4** | |
| Bhili | 205,635 | 22·0 | Bhopawar Agency States. |
| Bhilali | 105,385 | 11·3 | Ditto. |
| Rathawi | 36,691 | 3·9 | Barwani and generally in Bhil tract. |
| Others | 2,094 | 0·2 | |
| **Khandeshi** | **8,272** | **0·9** | Barwani. |
| **Kathiawadi** | **2,396** | **0·2** | Gwalior, Jhabua and Barwani. |
| **Punjabi** | **19,092** | **2·0** | Gwalior, Indore, Guna, Bhopawar Minor Estates, Gwalior, Minor Estates and Indore Camp. |
| **Western Pahadi** | **3,140** | **0·3** | Gwalior and Rajgarh. |
| **Northern Group** | **65** | ... | |
| Central Pahadi | 5 | ... | |
| Nepali | 60 | ... | |
| **Unclassed languages** | **18,350** | **1·9** | |
| Banjari | 17,126 | 1·8 | Rajgarh, Gwalior, Indore and Barwani. |
| Others | 1,224 | 0·1 | |
| **Asiatic Languages** | **1,405** | **0·2** | |
| **Indo-European Family** | **787** | **0·1** | |
| **Eranian group** | **787** | **0·1** | |
| Persian | 787 | 0·1 | Gwalior and Bhopal. |
| **Semitic Family** | **618** | **0·1** | |
| **Southern Group** | **618** | **0·1** | |
| Arabic | 618 | 0·1 | Gwalior and Bhopal. |
| **Indo-European Family** | **5,882** | **0·6** | |
| **Greek Group** | **2** | ... | |
| Greek | 2 | ... | |
| **Romance Group** | **29** | ... | |
| French | 16 | ... | |
| Portuguese | 13 | ... | |
| **Teutonic Group** | **5,851** | **0·6** | |
| **English** | 5,850 | 0·6 | Indore, Nimach, Nowgong, and Indore Camp. |
| **German** | 1 | ... | |

## SUBSIDIARY TABLE II.—Distribution by Language of the Population of each Natural Division.

| Natural Division. | Number per 10,000 of population speaking | | | | | | |
|---|---|---|---|---|---|---|---|
| | Malwi. | Bundel-khandi. | Baghel-khandi. | Hindi. | Nimadi. | Bhil dialect. | Other languages. |
| 1 | 2 | 3 | 4 | 5 | 6 | 7 | 8 |
| **Central India.** | **2,814·8** | **2,006·9** | **1,467·0** | **1,133·5** | **405·8** | **373·8** | **1,798·2** |
| Plateau . . . | 6,175·9 | 907·1 | 2·2 | 830·5 | 23·3 | 113·0 | 1,948·0 |
| Lowlying Tract . | 25·2 | 3,950·1 | 2,458·5 | 2,101·7 | 0·9 | 0·2 | 1,463·4 |
| Hilly Tract . . | 1,483·6 | 998·8 | 2,361·2 | 249·2 | 1,569·5 | 1,304·0 | 2,033·7 |

## SUBSIDIARY TABLE III.—Comparison of Caste and Language Tables.

| Tribe. | | Strength of Tribe (Table XIII). | | Number speaking Tribal Language (Table X). | |
|---|---|---|---|---|---|
| 1 | | 2 | | 3 | |
| Bhil . . | Hindu . . | 25,831 | 295,741 | | |
| | Animist . | 269,910 | | | |
| Bhilala . | Hindu . . | 33,764 | 123,376 | | |
| | Animist . | 89,612 | | | |
| | | | 419,117 | 349,805 | |
| Gond . | Hindu . . | | 163,285 | | |
| | Animist . | | 71,387 | | |
| | | | 234,672 | 214,276 | |

# CHAPTER X.

## Infirmities.

80. This Chapter deals with the information recorded in column 16 of the Schedule, and collected in Tables XII and XII-A and the Subsidiary Tables at the end of the text.

**Accuracy of Return.**

81. On this occasiou, in order to minimise the danger of missing the entries in this column, which are few and far between, the figures were separately abstracted on special slips.

**Classes of Infirmities.**

82. The same four infirmities are dealt with as in 1901, *viz.*, Insanity, Deaf-mutism, Blindness and Leprosy. This is only the second occasion in which infirmities have been recorded. In 1901 enumerators received very little instruction and the record was very indifferent.

| Province. | Persons afflicted per 100,000 of the population. | | | | | | | |
|---|---|---|---|---|---|---|---|---|
| | Insane. | | Deaf-mutes. | | Blind. | | Lepers. | |
| | M. | F. | M. | F. | M. | F. | M. | F. |
| Central India 1901 . . | 5 | 2 | 19 | 13 | 41 | 35 | 7 | 4 |
| Central India 1911 . . | 10 | 6 | 27 | 19 | 109 | 136 | 19 | 9 |
| India . . | 28 | 17 | 62 | 42 | 121 | 120 | 46 | 17 |
| United Provinces | 19 | 10 | 46 | 28 | 168 | 178 | 36 | 11 |

Not much faith can, however, be placed in these returns and it would be idle to theorise on them, although the higher figures show that the instructions have been far more carefully carried out than in 1901. This is clear from the comparative figures in the inset table.

It should be added, however, that it has been impossible to adjust the figures of 1901 to those for 1911 for infirmities, and that comparison is therefore only approximate. The real increase is in fact somewhat, though not very much, larger than that shown.

Actual figures for 1911 and 1901 :—

| Name. | 1911. | | | 1901. | | |
|---|---|---|---|---|---|---|
| | Total. | Male. | Female. | Total. | Male. | Female. |
| Insane . . . . . | 751 | 485 | 266 | 331 | 230 | 101 |
| Deaf-mutes . . . . . | 2,159 | 1,302 | 857 | 1,392 | 859 | 533 |
| Blind . . . . . | 11,058 | 5,253 | 5,805 | 3,303 | 1,819 | 1,484 |
| Lepers . . . . . | 1,288 | 894 | 394 | 426 | 272 | 154 |
| Total . | 15,256 | 7,934 | 7,322 | 5,452 | 3,180 | 2,272 |

In addition to the natural tendency to minimise these defects in the very young and in marriageable girls, especially among the higher classes, there is the difficulty of diagnosis.

Among the insane many who are only weak-minded are sure to be included. Deaf-mutism is particularly difficult to distinguish, although great stress was laid on the fact that those recorded must have been deaf and dumb from birth, and the returns prove that some persons suffering from senile deafness have been entered. Total blindness is easier to diagnose, as blindness of one eye is distinguished by a special vernacular term (*kana*). Real leprosy is often confounded with leucoderma, syphilitic diseases, etc., and moreover is apt to be concealed except among the lower classes. Of the diseases dealt with, insanity is far more common in Western countries than in the East, the ratio being about 12 to 1, due largely, no doubt, to the strain of modern conditions of life. Deaf-mutism on the other hand is more common in India, where about 6 males and 4 females per 10,000 of the population are afflicted. Blindness is also an eastern affliction, 12 persons in every 10,000 in India being blind to about 8 in England. Leprosy is little met with in the West.

## *Insanity.*

83. The figures this time are double those of 1901 but they are probably still too low, as the figures for the contiguous tracts of the United Provinces and Rajputana in 1901 were higher. **Comparative.**

| Province. | Number per 100,000. | |
|---|---|---|
| | Males. | Females. |
| Central India . . . . | 10 | 6 |
| India . . . . | 28 | 17 |
| United Provinces . . . . | 19 | 10 |
| Rajputana . . . . | 12 | 8 |
| Central Provinces . . . | 18 | 9 |

In the Natural Divisions the increase is highest in the Hilly tract, where the greatest advance was made in carrying out the enumeration. The figures in the Plateau area are largest, but greater facilities in enumerating and the prevalence of towns would account for this. The local distribution is given in the maps below. **Local distribution.**

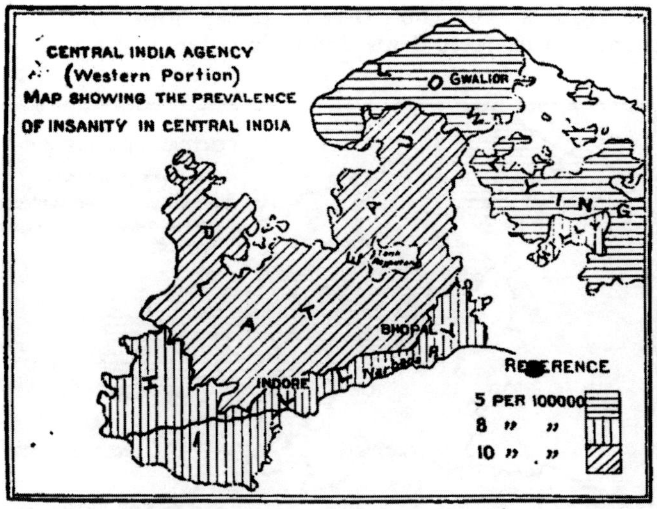


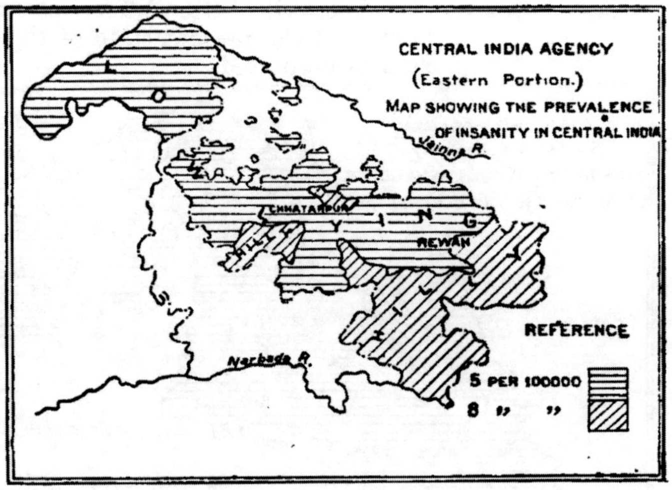


The sex and age figures are dealt with in Subsidiary Tables II and III which show the afflicted in 10,000 of each sex and per 100,000 of each period, as well as the proportion of afflicted females to 1,000 males. **Age, Sex, and Insanity.**

The number of insane is greatest at 20-30 in both sexes. At 5-10, 20-25, 40-45 and 60 and over, females exceed males.

As usual the number of insane males exceeds that of females, the ratio being 5 females to every 10 men. The ratios in the natural divisions are Plateau and Hilly 6 females to 10 males, Lowlying 4 to 10.

The diagram shows that in youth and old age the sex figures approach equality. The curves for males and females on this occasion show a curious similarity. In each case the maximum is reached at 40-50 and the minimum at 30-40. Among females there is practically no variation between 20 and 30. The males show a rise, but it is slight while it does not continue up to 30-40 as might have been expected, this being the period in which virility is most active. The maximum at 40-50 among females coincides with the period of change of life in that sex.

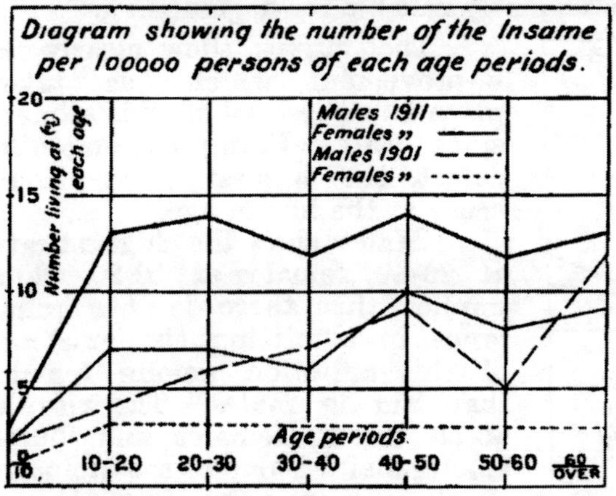


The rise at 60 and over must be due to the inclusion of persons suffering from senile decay.

## *Deaf-Mutism.*

**84.** The returns for deaf mutes show an increase of 55 per cent. This is certainly not due to an increase in deaf-mutes but to better enumeration. The figure is still, however, in all probability too low.

| Province. | Deaf-Mutes. | |
|---|---|---|
| | Males. | Females. |
| Central India, 1911 . . . . . . . | 27 | 19 |
| India . . . . . . . . . | 62 | 42 |
| United Provinces . . . . . . . | 46 | 28 |
| Rajputana . . . . . . . | 22 | 15 |
| Central Provinces . . . . . . . | 54 | 39 |

Local distribution.

There is little difference in the figures for the three tracts, and it would, in the present state of the return, be unsafe to draw deductions from the results tabulated.

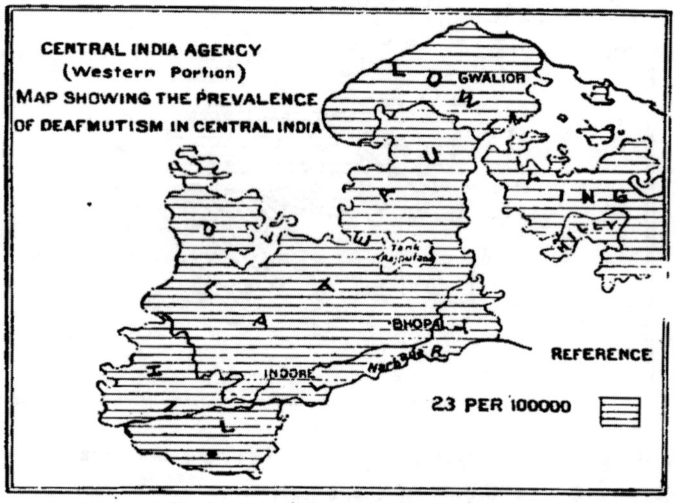


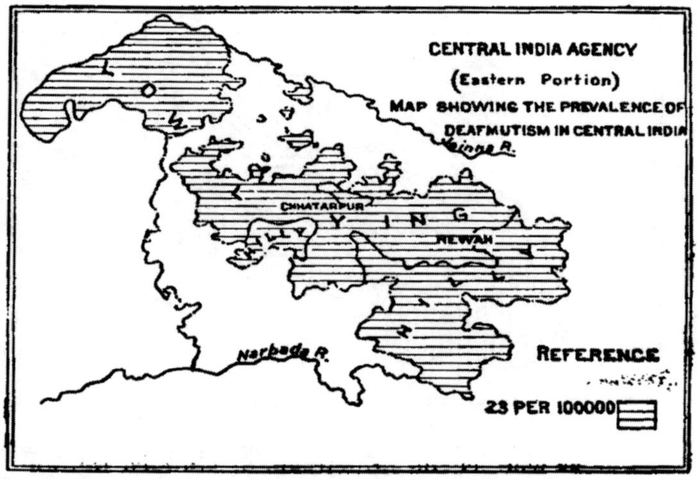


Age, Sex and Deaf-mutism.

Deaf-mutism is a congenital defect and those who suffer from it are weaklings soon left behind in the race of life. An examination of the age returns, however, shows a rise up to the 30-35 age-period among males and the 25-30 among females. The largest returns should, if the record was correct, fall at the earliest periods.

The figures for sex show an excess proportion of males up to 30-35 (except at 0-5); after this period there is little difference till 60 and over where females preponderate, but the figures are not sufficiently reliable for dogmatising.

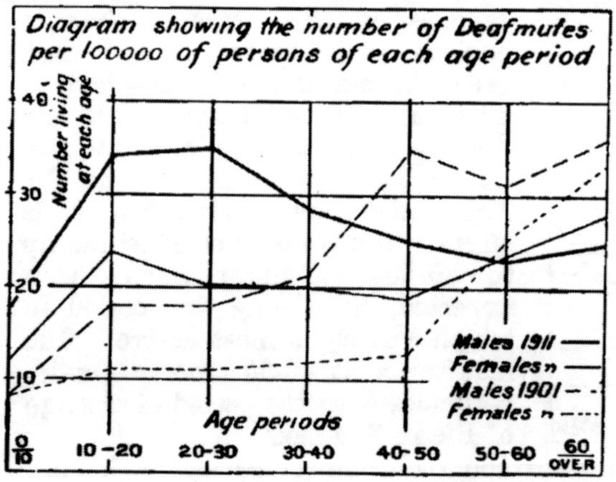


The curves show clearly the improvement which has taken place in the record of this ailment since 1901. Being a congenital defect, the highest point should occur at the lowest age.

Males show the highest ratio at 20-30, females at 10-20, which implies that there is less reluctance in admitting the existence of this affliction among females than among males. The rise at 40-50 among females and 50-60 among males is due to the inclusion of those who have become deaf through old age, and indicates that females suffer earlier than males from this defect.

| Provinces. | Males. | Females. |
|---|---|---|
| Central India, 1901 . | 41 | 35 |
| Central India, 1911 . | 109 | 128 |
| United Provinces . | 168 | 178 |

### *Blindness.*

85. The blind have increased by 235 per cent. on the 1901 figures—due to improved enumeration, as a comparison with other parts of India shows. **Comparative.**

The statement below gives operations for cataract in 1901 and 1911 :—

OPERATIONS FOR CATARACT.

| Natural Division. | 1911. | 1901. |
|---|---|---|
| | Successful. | Successful. |
| **Central India.** | 3,348 | 1,351 |
| Plateau . . . . . . . . . | 2,675 | 1,024 |
| Lowlying . . . . . . . . | 464 | 137 |
| Hilly . . . . . . . . | 209 | 190 |

Of the Natural Divisions the Plateau shows the highest number, a fact due to the greater number of towns and also to the better enumeration in that tract. **Local distribution**

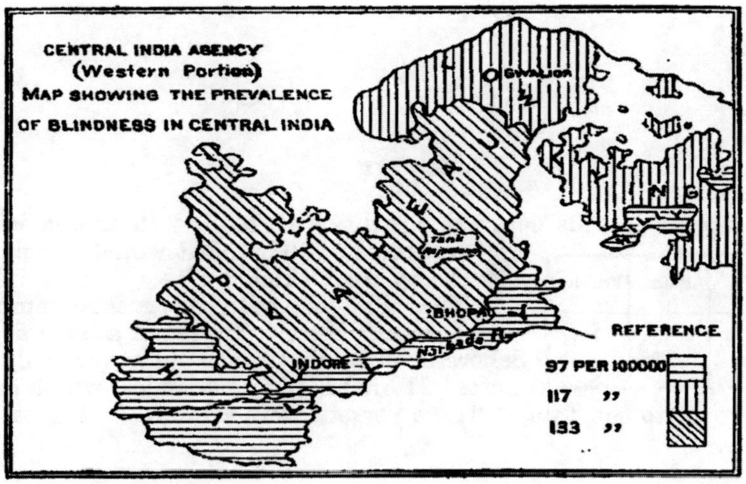


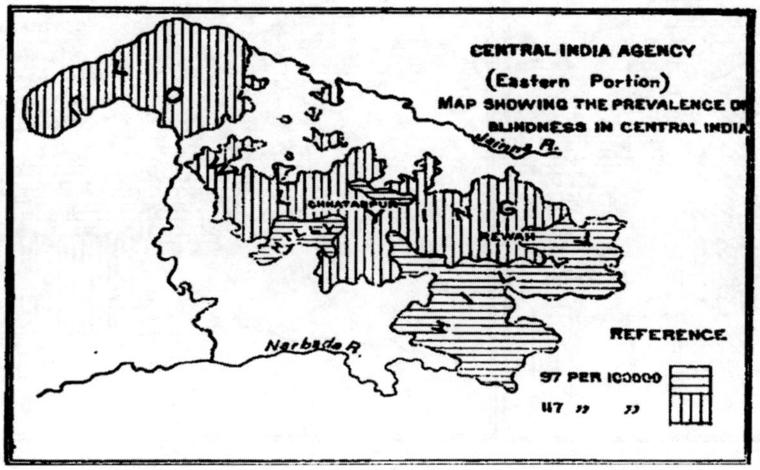

**Age, Sex, and Blindness.**

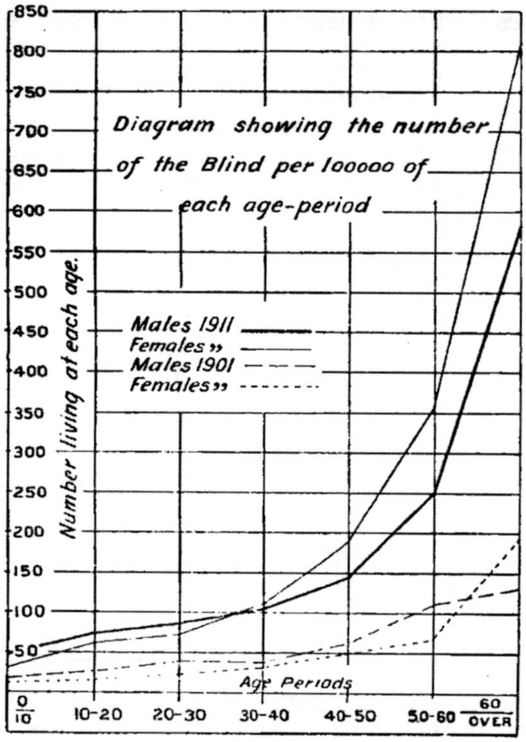


Females in this case exceed males. Under five years of age the balance is in favour of the males but after that the female figures rise rapidly. Congenital eye diseases are said to be more prevalent among males, which would in part account for the difference. Cooking over smoky fires in a small space and the general neglect of disease among females is responsible for much blindness among old women.

The curves show the great improvement made since 1901 in recording this defect. Essentially a defect of old age, the curve should rise rapidly at the later periods. This it does, the female curve commencing a decided upward tendency at 20-30 and the male at 30-40.

The rise among females is rapid and agrees with the known prevalence of blindness in this sex at old age.

## *Leprosy.*

**Local distribution.**

86. The figures in this case are clearly still too low though considerably higher than in 1901, and it would be idle to base any theory upon them.

| Province. | Males. | Females. |
|---|---|---|
| India . . . | 48 | 17 |
| United Provinces . | 36 | 11 |

The Plateau with its greater number of towns stands first. There is a leper asylum at Sehore in this tract, with, however, only 32 inmates, 21 males and 11 females, which makes no material difference to the total. These persons were all born in Bhopal State.

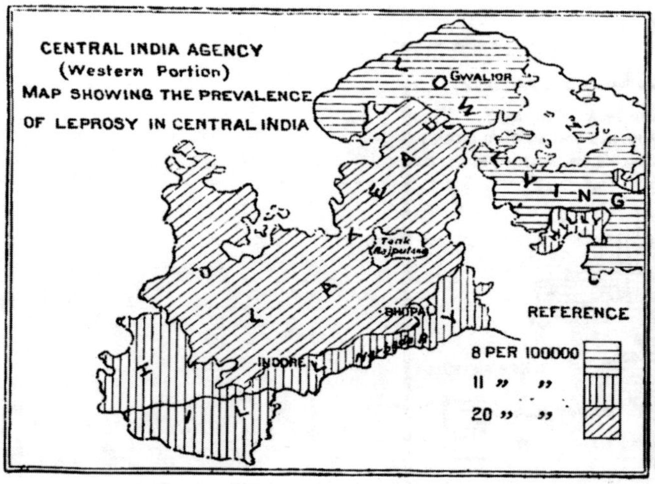


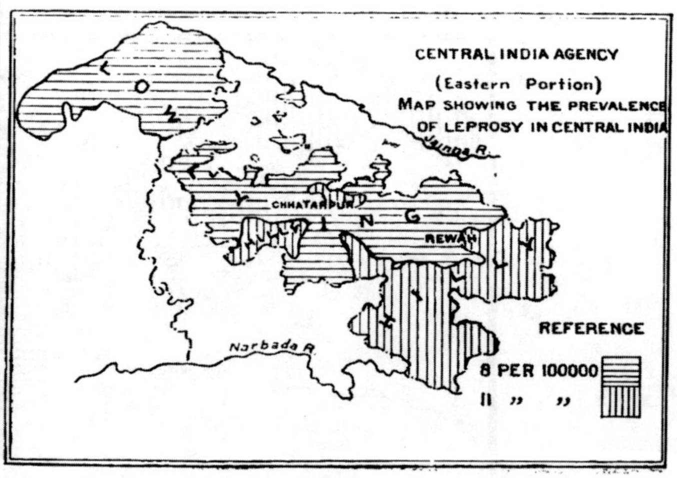

**Age, Sex and Leprosy.**

Male lepers exceed female. This is a feature noticed wherever leprosy prevails, and though it may be due in part to concealment of female lepers it cannot be entirely due to this cause, but to men being more liable to the disease. The age figures show a great excess of females at 0-5.

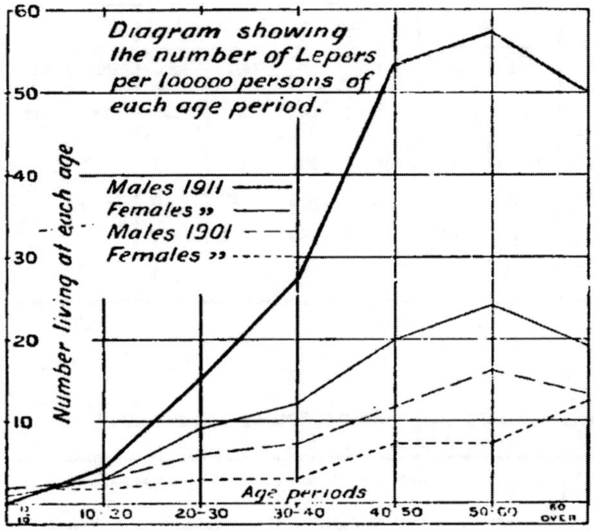


| Age period. | Variation in number of lepers. |
|---|---|
| 0-10 | − 22 |
| 10-20 | + 12 |
| 20-30 | + 152 |
| 30-40 | + 215 |
| 40-50 | + 264 |
| 50-60 | + 154 |
| 60 and over | + 87 |

The male curve shows a rapid rise from the 10-20 period while the decline after 50-60 is also sharp showing that lepers are not long lived. The female curve shows similar conditions, the decline setting in at the same age.

The greatest increase among lepers is found at 40-50, the period from 30 to 50 being apparently that at which the disease usually attacks people.

The Census Report for India in 1891 and the Leprosy Commission put the age of greatest susceptibility at 25 to 30.

It is questionable whether the figures in this case are of any value at all for statistical purposes.

**Caste and Infirmity.**

87. Taking male figures the highest ratio is given by Gahohi Banias, 39 men in every 10,000 being afflicted. Next come Shaikhs 31, Bhadauria Rajputs 27, and Jijhotia, Sanadhya, and Shrigaud Brahmans 28 each, in every 10,000. In other cases the ratios are below. It would be rash to base any particular deductions on these results.

Among the Insane the Shrigaud Brahmans stand first with 51 afflicted in every 100,000, Shaikhs 37, Bundelas 34, and Bhadaurias 30, stand next. Among Deaf-mutes the order is Shaikhs 58, Shrimalis 56, Gahohis 51, Kachhwahas 48, Ponwars 46, Sanadhyas and Bhats 45, while Gahohis 300, Jijhotias 202, Sanadhyas 190, Shaikhs 189, Bhadaurias 178, Oswals 175, Shrigauds 167, and Ponwars 160, show most blind. The female figures are also high in this case, Gahalots 512, Gahohis 324, Jijhotias 242, and Bundelas 222. Among Lepers Bundelas 57, Bhilalas 51, Shrigauds 39, Sondhias 34, Bhils 33, Rathods 32, stand first.

It will also be noticed that while a considerable number of castes show no females afflicted, due no doubt to concealment, only a few, in the case of Insane and Lepers, give a blank return for males.

## SUBSIDIARY TABLE I.—Number afflicted per 100,000 of the Population at each of the last two Censuses.

| Natural Division. | Insane. | | | | Deaf-Mute. | | | | Blind. | | | | Lepers. | | | |
|---|---|---|---|---|---|---|---|---|---|---|---|---|---|---|---|---|
| | Male. | | Female. | | Male. | | Female. | | Male. | | Female. | | Male. | | Female. | |
| | 1911 | 1901 | 1911 | 1901 | 1911 | 1901 | 1911 | 1901 | 1911 | 1901 | 1911 | 1901 | 1911 | 1901 | 1911 | 1901 |
| 1 | 2 | 3 | 4 | 5 | 6 | 7 | 8 | 9 | 10 | 11 | 12 | 13 | 14 | 15 | 16 | 17 |
| **Central India** | **10** | **5** | **6** | **2** | **27** | **19** | **19** | **13** | **109** | **41** | **128** | **35** | **19** | **7** | **9** | **4** |
| Plateau . . | 13 | 6 | 8 | 3 | 26 | 25 | 19 | 14 | 120 | 56 | 147 | 36 | 27 | 8 | 13 | 6 |
| Lowlying tract . | 7 | 6 | 3 | 3 | 29 | 23 | 17 | 18 | 110 | 39 | 124 | 50 | 11 | 7 | 5 | 3 |
| Hilly tract . . | 10 | 2 | 6 | 1 | 27 | 3 | 19 | 2 | 11 | 17 | 104 | 10 | 15 | 1 | 7 | ... |

## SUBSIDIARY TABLE II.—Distribution of the infirmities by age per 10,000 of each sex.

| Age. | Insane. | | | | Deaf-Mute. | | | | Blind. | | | | Lepers. | | | |
|---|---|---|---|---|---|---|---|---|---|---|---|---|---|---|---|---|
| | Male. | | Female. | | Male. | | Female. | | Male. | | Female. | | Male. | | Female. | |
| | 1911 | 1901 | 1911 | 1901 | 1911 | 1901 | 1911 | 1901 | 1911 | 1901 | 1911 | 1901 | 1911 | 1901 | 1911 | 1901 |
| 1 | 2 | 3 | 4 | 5 | 6 | 7 | 8 | 9 | 10 | 11 | 12 | 13 | 14 | 15 | 16 | 17 |
| **Total** . | **10,000** | **10,000** | **10,000** | **10,000** | **10,000** | **10,000** | **10,000** | **10,000** | **10,000** | **10,000** | **10,000** | **10,000** | **10,000** | **10,000** | **10,000** | **10,000** |
| 0—5 . . | 300 | 174 | 113 | 207 | 390 | 373 | 513 | 432 | 516 | 357 | 307 | 411 | 34 | 441 | 152 | ... |
| 5—10 . . | 392 | 632 | 940 | 495 | 1,421 | 512 | 1,284 | 919 | 703 | 605 | 422 | 438 | 34 | 368 | 76 | 974 |
| 10—15 . . | 1,093 | 1,044 | 1,052 | 1,188 | 1,290 | 1,118 | 992 | 844 | 605 | 665 | 372 | 435 | 168 | 257 | 203 | 455 |
| 15—20 . . | 1,196 | 565 | 835 | 891 | 1,021 | 1,048 | 1,004 | 888 | 621 | 808 | 377 | 411 | 257 | 919 | 381 | 649 |
| 20—25 . . | 1,010 | 1,087 | 1,128 | 990 | 1,183 | 803 | 1,038 | 888 | 779 | 808 | 500 | 654 | 637 | 404 | 863 | 649 |
| 25—30 . . | 1,526 | 1,087 | 1,203 | 1,585 | 1,229 | 908 | 1,085 | 888 | 725 | 937 | 639 | 728 | 928 | 1,360 | 1,244 | 779 |
| 30—35 . . | 948 | 1,304 | 940 | 594 | 1,183 | 803 | 934 | 760 | 860 | 830 | 781 | 977 | 1,275 | 1,140 | 1,193 | 649 |
| 35—40 . . | 928 | 826 | 480 | 1,089 | 530 | 885 | 712 | 633 | 643 | 681 | 501 | 600 | 1,051 | 772 | 863 | 779 |
| 40—45 . . | 866 | 957 | 1,203 | 990 | 614 | 1,176 | 735 | 604 | 885 | 889 | 958 | 1,031 | 2,093 | 1,250 | 1,370 | 1,104 |
| 45—50 . . | 577 | 913 | 451 | 594 | 323 | 745 | 280 | 469 | 463 | 618 | 527 | 579 | 839 | 735 | 989 | 1,169 |
| 50—55 . . | 557 | 348 | 714 | 495 | 369 | 780 | 525 | 1,013 | 895 | 913 | 1,280 | 937 | 1,398 | 1,080 | 1,447 | 1,104 |
| 55—60 . . | 124 | 304 | 150 | 207 | 108 | 244 | 210 | 375 | 394 | 819 | 420 | 418 | 324 | 635 | 254 | 335 |
| 60 and over . | 474 | 739 | 752 | 495 | 330 | 605 | 688 | 1,197 | 1,008 | 1,050 | 2,916 | 2,351 | 973 | 699 | 1,015 | 1,364 |

## SUBSIDIARY TABLE III.—Number afflicted per 100,000 persons of each age period and number of females afflicted per 1,000 males.

| Age. | Number afflicted per 100,000. | | | | | | | | | | Number of Females afflicted per 1,000 Males. | | | | |
|---|---|---|---|---|---|---|---|---|---|---|---|---|---|---|---|
| | Total afflicted. | | Insane. | | Deaf-Mute. | | Blind. | | Lepers. | | Total afflicted. | Insane. | Deaf-mute. | Blind. | Lepers. |
| | Male. | Female. | Male. | Female. | Male. | Female. | Male. | Female. | Male. | Female. | | | | | |
| 1 | 2 | 3 | 4 | 5 | 6 | 7 | 8 | 9 | 10 | 11 | 12 | 13 | 14 | 15 | 16 |
| **Total** . | **165** | **162** | **10** | **6** | **27** | **19** | **109** | **128** | **19** | **9** | **923** | **548** | **658** | **1,105** | **441** |
| 0—5 . . . | 48 | 31 | 2 | ... | 7 | 6 | 39 | 24 | ... | 1 | 677 | 200 | 846 | 657 | 2,000 |
| 5—10 . . . | 96 | 70 | 3 | 5 | 31 | 20 | 61 | 44 | 1 | 1 | 663 | 1,316 | 595 | 60 | 1,000 |
| 10—15 . . . | 115 | 88 | 11 | 7 | 35 | 22 | 66 | 57 | 3 | 2 | 608 | 528 | 506 | 679 | 533 |
| 15—20 . . . | 134 | 104 | 14 | 7 | 33 | 26 | 81 | 66 | 6 | 5 | 636 | 397 | 647 | 672 | 652 |
| 20—25 . . . | 154 | 96 | 11 | 7 | 36 | 19 | 94 | 63 | 13 | 7 | 663 | 612 | 578 | 709 | 607 |
| 25—30 . . . | 159 | 119 | 16 | 7 | 34 | 20 | 82 | 81 | 18 | 11 | 781 | 432 | 581 | 974 | 590 |
| 30—35 . . . | 161 | 139 | 10 | 6 | 32 | 18 | 95 | 104 | 24 | 11 | 790 | 544 | 507 | 1,002 | 412 |
| 35—40 . . . | 184 | 155 | 15 | 5 | 23 | 24 | 114 | 113 | 32 | 13 | 731 | 288 | 884 | 861 | 388 |
| 40—45 . . . | 235 | 223 | 13 | 10 | 24 | 20 | 141 | 176 | 57 | 17 | 911 | 762 | 788 | 1,196 | 289 |
| 45—50 . . . | 239 | 264 | 17 | 8 | 26 | 17 | 150 | 213 | 46 | 26 | 977 | 429 | 571 | 1,259 | 493 |
| 50—55 . . . | 328 | 398 | 13 | 9 | 24 | 21 | 230 | 342 | 61 | 26 | 1,290 | 704 | 938 | 1,581 | 456 |
| 55—60 . . . | 381 | 457 | 9 | 7 | 21 | 30 | 308 | 403 | 43 | 17 | 1,078 | 667 | 1,286 | 1,179 | 345 |
| 60 and over . . | 673 | 859 | 13 | 10 | 25 | 28 | 584 | 802 | 51 | 19 | 1,569 | 868 | 1,872 | 1,690 | 460 |

SUBSIDIARY TABLE IV.—**Number afflicted per 100,000 persons of each Caste and number of females afflicted per 1,000 males.**

| Caste, Tribe or Race. | Number afflicted per 100,000. | | | | | | | | | | Number of females afflicted per 1,000 males. | | | | |
|---|---|---|---|---|---|---|---|---|---|---|---|---|---|---|---|
| | Total afflicted. | | Insane. | | Deaf-mute. | | Blind. | | Lepers. | | Total afflicted. | Insane. | Deaf-mute. | Blind. | Lepers. |
| | Male. | Female. | Male. | Female. | Male. | Female. | Male. | Female. | Male. | Female. | | | | | |
| 1 | 2 | 3 | 4 | 5 | 6 | 7 | 8 | 9 | 10 | 11 | 12 | 13 | 14 | 15 | 16 |
| **Total** | **66** | **61** | **5** | **3** | **11** | **8** | **43** | **47** | **7** | **3** | **872** | **545** | **678** | **1,027** | **431** |
| Ajna | 92 | 89 | 13 | ... | 7 | 9 | 46 | 62 | 26 | 18 | 714 | ... | 1,000 | 1,000 | 500 |
| Bania | 172 | 132 | 12 | 4 | 27 | 26 | 125 | 97 | 8 | 3 | 805 | 353 | 1,105 | 811 | 364 |
| „ Agarwal | 198 | 201 | 7 | 3 | 41 | 68 | 140 | 127 | 10 | 3 | 1,121 | 500 | 1,833 | 1,000 | 333 |
| „ Gahohi | 388 | 377 | 22 | 9 | 51 | 35 | 300 | 324 | 15 | 9 | 811 | 333 | 571 | 992 | 500 |
| „ Mahesri | 200 | 88 | 10 | ... | 30 | 9 | 160 | 79 | ... | ... | 500 | ... | 333 | 563 | ... |
| „ Oswal | 227 | 151 | 26 | 12 | 22 | 41 | 175 | 90 | 4 | 8 | 712 | 500 | 2,000 | 550 | 2,000 |
| „ Porwal | 245 | 168 | 25 | ... | 40 | 26 | 160 | 142 | 20 | ... | 653 | ... | 625 | 844 | ... |
| Bhat | 239 | 238 | 15 | 16 | 45 | 25 | 157 | 181 | 22 | 16 | 906 | 1,000 | 500 | 1,048 | 667 |
| Bhil | 102 | 85 | 8 | 4 | 24 | 19 | 37 | 49 | 33 | 13 | 840 | 545 | 806 | 1,333 | 388 |
| Bhilala | 211 | 167 | 18 | 11 | 39 | 50 | 103 | 92 | 51 | 14 | 806 | 636 | 1,292 | 905 | 290 |
| Brahman | 111 | 97 | 10 | 3 | 23 | 13 | 71 | 75 | 7 | 6 | 785 | 275 | 516 | 948 | 757 |
| „ Bhagor | 182 | 201 | 12 | 7 | 41 | 7 | 117 | 168 | 12 | 19 | 1,000 | 500 | 143 | 1,300 | 1,500 |
| „ Jijhotia | 276 | 324 | 12 | 13 | 38 | 49 | 202 | 242 | 24 | 20 | 1,054 | 1,000 | 1,154 | 1,073 | 750 |
| „ Sanadhya | 275 | 203 | 20 | 7 | 45 | 18 | 190 | 173 | 20 | 5 | 701 | 313 | 378 | 865 | 250 |
| „ Sarwaria | 138 | 98 | 17 | 3 | 42 | 21 | 74 | 66 | 5 | 8 | 746 | 160 | 532 | 936 | 1,625 |
| „ Shrigaud | 283 | 193 | 51 | ... | 26 | ... | 167 | 165 | 39 | 28 | 636 | ... | ... | 923 | 667 |
| „ Shrimali | 168 | 42 | ... | ... | 56 | ... | 112 | 42 | ... | ... | 333 | ... | ... | 500 | ... |
| Chamar | 158 | 171 | 5 | 6 | 21 | 15 | 115 | 141 | 17 | 9 | 1,052 | 1,130 | 692 | 1,193 | 500 |
| Dhangar | 132 | 116 | 33 | ... | ... | 39 | 99 | 77 | ... | ... | 750 | ... | ... | 667 | ... |
| Gond | 92 | 84 | 5 | 3 | 15 | 8 | 67 | 73 | 5 | ... | 1,020 | 800 | 588 | 1,200 | ... |
| Gujar | 157 | 162 | 7 | 4 | 20 | 21 | 118 | 132 | 12 | 5 | 777 | 429 | 810 | 840 | 308 |
| Kachera | 125 | 31 | ... | ... | 31 | ... | 94 | 31 | ... | ... | 250 | ... | ... | 333 | ... |
| Khangar | 149 | 109 | 10 | 5 | 20 | 38 | 104 | 66 | 15 | ... | 667 | 500 | 1,750 | 571 | ... |
| Kol | 84 | 72 | 7 | 4 | 23 | 15 | 49 | 52 | 5 | 1 | 923 | 571 | 714 | 1,156 | 200 |
| Mina | 146 | 145 | 18 | 8 | 21 | 11 | 89 | 115 | 18 | 11 | 946 | 429 | 500 | 1,235 | 571 |
| Pathan | 197 | 140 | 20 | 9 | 25 | 23 | 136 | 105 | 16 | 3 | 628 | 400 | 833 | 680 | 167 |
| Rajput | 68 | 60 | 5 | 3 | 13 | 4 | 42 | 49 | 8 | 4 | 746 | 500 | 279 | 988 | 412 |
| „ Baghel | 47 | 25 | ... | ... | 16 | 17 | 31 | 8 | ... | ... | 500 | ... | 1,000 | 250 | ... |
| „ Bhadauria | 267 | 61 | 30 | ... | 37 | 10 | 178 | 51 | 22 | ... | 167 | ... | 200 | 208 | ... |
| „ Bundela | 205 | 280 | 34 | 35 | 23 | 23 | 91 | 222 | 57 | ... | 1,333 | 1,000 | 1,000 | 2,375 | ... |
| „ Chauhan | 147 | 91 | 16 | 5 | 32 | 14 | 94 | 62 | 5 | 10 | 679 | 333 | 500 | 722 | 2,000 |
| „ Gahlot | 133 | 555 | ... | 11 | 28 | ... | 77 | 512 | 28 | 32 | 2,737 | ... | ... | 4,364 | 750 |
| „ Kachhwaha | 159 | 101 | ... | 9 | 48 | 9 | 87 | 66 | 24 | 17 | 600 | ... | 167 | 727 | 667 |
| „ Ponwar | 167 | 230 | 13 | 5 | 46 | 11 | 100 | 203 | 8 | 11 | 1,075 | 333 | 182 | 1,683 | 1,000 |
| „ Rathod | 140 | 47 | 11 | ... | 27 | ... | 70 | 47 | 32 | ... | 269 | ... | ... | 538 | ... |
| „ Tonwar | 133 | 97 | 8 | 8 | 20 | 16 | 89 | 49 | 16 | 24 | 364 | 500 | 400 | 273 | 750 |
| Saharia | 65 | 74 | 5 | 3 | 7 | 8 | 41 | 58 | 12 | 5 | 1,074 | 500 | 1,000 | 1,353 | 400 |
| Sayad | 155 | 162 | 17 | 27 | 35 | 33 | 86 | 95 | 17 | 7 | 889 | 1,333 | 833 | 933 | 333 |
| Shaikh | 307 | 268 | 37 | 17 | 58 | 40 | 189 | 200 | 23 | 11 | 812 | 429 | 686 | 986 | 444 |
| Sondhia | 147 | 119 | 6 | 8 | 18 | 5 | 89 | 106 | 34 | ... | 938 | 1,500 | 333 | 1,379 | ... |
| Teli | 138 | 159 | 3 | 8 | 24 | 16 | 104 | 128 | 7 | 8 | 1,067 | 2,333 | 609 | 1,130 | 1,000 |

# CHAPTER XI.

## Caste, Tribe or Race.

88. This Chapter deals with the statistics collected in column 8 of the schedule. It has been usual in this Chapter to deal with the composition of local castes and peculiar customs, but the delay in receiving information has necessitated the relegation of the information on local castes to a separate note.

**Accuracy of return.**

89. The return on this occasion is noticeably more accurate. A caste index was compiled on the results of the last census and this together with the very complete instruction given in the census schools has undoubtedly improved the return. There were far fewer doubtful entries and these were, in practically every case, adjusted on reference.

In all 105 names of castes were recorded which comprise 1,000 or more individuals each. The classification adopted on this occasion in Subsidiary Table I is that of *traditional* occupation, that is to say, a Bhil will be classed under Forest, Hill Tribes, etc., even if he is actually a Subadhar in the Malwa Bhil Corps and has never been a professional hunter or fowler. In 1891 this classification was partially adopted, while in 1901 classification by social precedence was introduced, an unsatisfactory method, and one, moreover, which roused a good deal of antagonism between certain classes of the community.

**Caste.**

90. It is not proposed to enter into the growth of the caste system as the various theories put forward can be studied in the works devoted to that subject. Having thus decided to avoid theoretical discussion and to relegate the caste list to a separate note, all that can be done is to deal with the distribution of the principal castes and their connection with the old traditional occupations. A caste for the purpose of this Chapter may be defined in the words of the census report for 1901 as "An endogamous group or a collection of several groups bearing a common name who, by reason of similarity of traditional occupation and reputed origin, are generally regarded by those of their castemen who are competent to give an opinion, as forming a single homogeneous community, the constituent parts of which are more nearly related to each other than they are to any other section of the society." It may be noted that endogamy, traditional occupation and a common origin are the three principles on which caste is based.

**Distribution.**

91. The total number of castes or sections of the community recorded are given in the inset. The reduction in the number is solely due to better classification.

| Religion. | 1911. | 1901. |
|---|---|---|
| Hindu . . . | 145 | 238 |
| Jain . . . | 24 | 27 |
| Animist . . | 11 | 12 |
| Musalman . . | 48 | 47 |
| Total | 228 | 324 |

Brahmans of all clans number 986,050, forming 12 per cent. of the Hindu population and 11 per cent. of the total population. The Sarvarias, found mostly in Baghelkhand, are by far the most numerous in this portion of the community. Rajputs of all clans number 755,819 or 9 per cent. of the Hindu and 8 per cent. of the total population, the Parmar being the most numerous. The Bania community, Jain and Hindu, numbers 373,917 and forms 4 per cent. of the total population, the Agarwals being the most numerous. Of remaining castes the Chamars (859,000) far exceed all others forming 9 per cent. of the whole population, Kachhi (372,000), Ahir (281,000) and Lodhi (228,000) following.

**Hindu Castes.**

92. The relative strength of Hindu castes containing 50,000 or more individuals is given in the diagram attached. The first point that is brought out is the enormous excess of Chamars over all other castes. They exceed the Kachhis, who come next, by about 490,000 and form 10 per cent. of the Hindu

population. This caste is met with chiefly in Northern Gwalior, Baghelkhand and Bundelkhand where 56 per cent. are found.

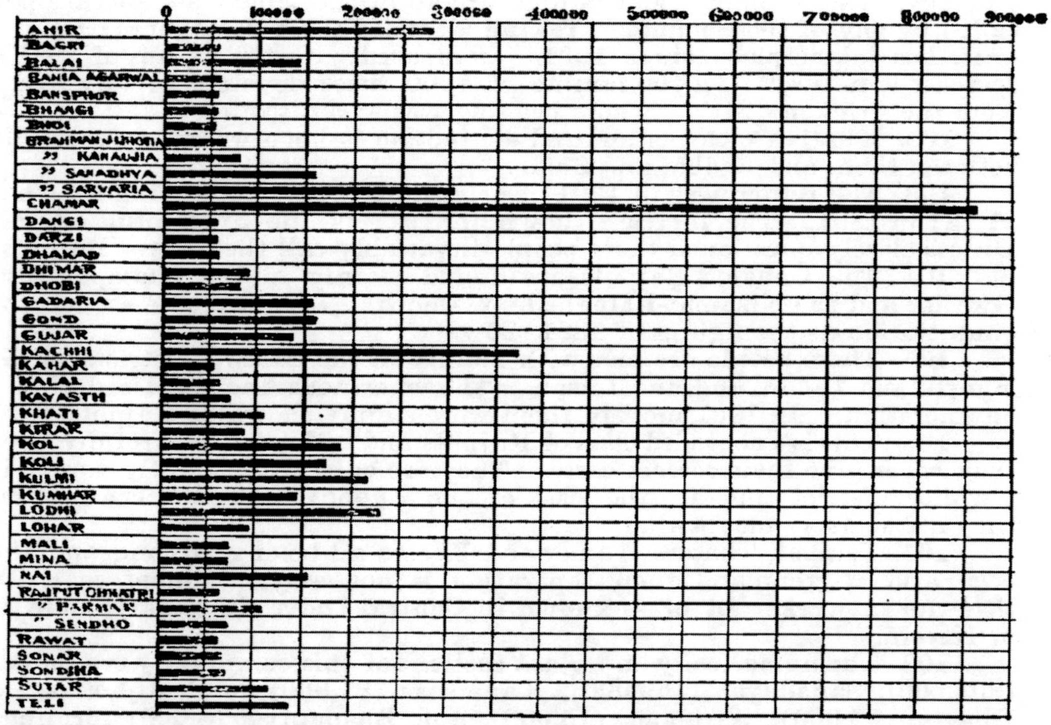


93. The Kachhis, a cultivating class, forming 4 per cent. of the population, is met with throughout the Agency, though more numerous in Orchha, Datia, and Northern Gwalior. The Sarvaria Brahmans who are third in order of numerical importance are chiefly found in Baghelkhand. **Kachhi.**

94. Ahirs follow being chiefly met with in Northern Gwalior, Baghelkhand and Bundelkhand where about 70 per cent. reside. A decrease of 12 per cent. has occurred among Ahirs as compared with the figure of 1901. This is due mainly to the fact that the Bharuds, who follow the same profession in the Bhil country, were included among Ahirs in 1901. **Ahir.**

95. This caste has risen by 165 per cent. since 1901. This increase is found chiefly in the Malwa tract. The largest increase is reported from the Malwa districts of Gwalior (Ujjain, Shajapur, Mandsaur), the Bhopal district round Ashta, Dewas, Rajgarh and Narsinghgarh. **Bagri.**

The number in 1911 compares favourably with that of 1891. The famine of 1900 severely affected this wandering tribe while by constantly changing their place of residence they pass from one part of the country to another.

96. This caste is found exclusively in Rewah. The increase of 120 per cent. is entirely due to more careful enumeration. Bemariha, previously shown as a separate caste, was, on investigation, found to be a sub-division of Baiga. The number returned in 1891 compares favourably with the figures of 1911. **Baiga.**

97. This class shows a decrease of 31 per cent. The principal decrease is found in the Malwa districts of Gwalior. Latterly this class has taken to cultivation and working in factories and they are extensively concealing their real caste as they rise. The Balais also being more or less allied with Balahars, Kotwars, Basors, etc., who are all classed together in ordinary parlance, were probably shown under the common term of Balai in 1901. **Balai.**

98. A large increase is perceptible among Bansphors due to reasons noted above. **Bansphor.**

99. This is a very doubtful caste entry at any time as many persons are apt to be classed as Beldars because they work as coolies. The increase is chiefly in the Indore State and is caused apparently by the large public works in progress of which there were none in 1901. **Beldar.**

The explanation against *Ahir* will explain the increase. **Bharna.**

**Deswali.** 100. The rise of 291 per cent. is found chiefly in the Nimar district of Indore, the Bhopal districts bordering on the Narbada, Dhar, Dewas and Narsinghgarh, and is due to more accurate enumeration.

**Gusain.** 101. Gusain, Babaji, and Bairagi are all of the same class and are popularly called by any of these names. Taking all these three together a rise of 53 per cent. has taken place since 1901. Compared with the figures of 1891 a small decrease is noticed. In the famine of 1900 these devotees rapidly disappeared from the stricken districts where begging was at a discount.

**Khati.** 102. Khatis are carpenters and distinction is not always very carefully made between them and Badhai and Sutar.

**Korku.** 103. The return was in 1901 clearly faulty, only 9,667 being shewn against 21,131 in 1891. The increase shown in 1911 is due to careful enumeration. Unless closely questioned these people invariably call themselves Rajputs.

**Gahalot.** 104. The Gahalot Rajputs are found mainly in the Shajapur district of Gwalior and the Nizamat-i-Maghrib of Bhopal. The increase is due to better enumeration as the figures of 1891 show.

**Raghubansi.** 105. These people are met with mainly in the Malwa districts of Gwalior, Bhopal and Indore and in Rewah. The enormous increase is due to better enumeration. In 1901 most of them were simply shown as Rajputs.

**Rawat.** 106. This is a degraded class of Rajputs and unless very carefully questioned they never give their correct caste. They are cultivators mostly found in Gird Gwalior district and in the east of the Agency. In Western Central India they are sparsely met with.

**Tambat.** 107. Tambat, Thatera, Tamer and Kasera all belong to one and the same occupational group and their separation is not easy. Tambat is a Dekkani title for a worker in brass known in Central India either as Thatera, Tamera or Kasera.

**Brahman.** 108. The numerically important sections of this community are the Sarvarias (303,000), Sanadhyas (159,000), Kanaujias (81,000), and Jijhotias (64,000), Bhagor (32,000), Shrigaud (15,000), and Bhadaurias (8,000) forming 29 per cent. of the local Brahman community. All these groups belong to Northern Gwalior and Bundelkhand, the Jijhotias being peculiar to that region, while the Shrigauds are chiefly met with in the Gwalior districts in Malwa and in the Indore district of Nimar.

**Rajput.** 109. Among the Rajputs, the Parmars stand first forming 14 per cent. of the whole Rajput community being found almost wholly in Malwa. It is not possible to show variations as in 1901 these clans were not shown separately, except Gahalot and Raghubansi and in their case the return was very imperfect.

**Bania.** 110. Here we have both Jain and Hindu members of the community who in many cases intermarry freely and may, therefore, be taken as homogeneous groups.

The Agarwals (61,000) are the most numerous section of the community. They are chiefly found in Northern Gwalior and Rewah. The Gahohis (25,000) are confined to the East of the Agency, while the Kesar (14,000) are peculiar to the Rewah State.

Mahesri (23,000) are met with in appreciable number in the Malwa districts of Gwalior and other States. Only Agarwals, Oswals and Porwals were recorded in 1901. The Agarwals show a rise of 47 per cent., the Porwals of 99 per cent. due to the separate record of all castes. In 1901 they came under Bani.

**Other Castes.** 111. Of the 105 castes in Subsidiary Table II, 59 show a rise since 1901. Among these, as already noted, a very large difference is to be seen in some cases. In one case only, Chhatri, is there any considerable fall. This is due to the separate record of all Rajput clans on this occasion.

**Animist.** 112. Among the Animistic Tribes the Bhils, who number 270,000 or 56 per

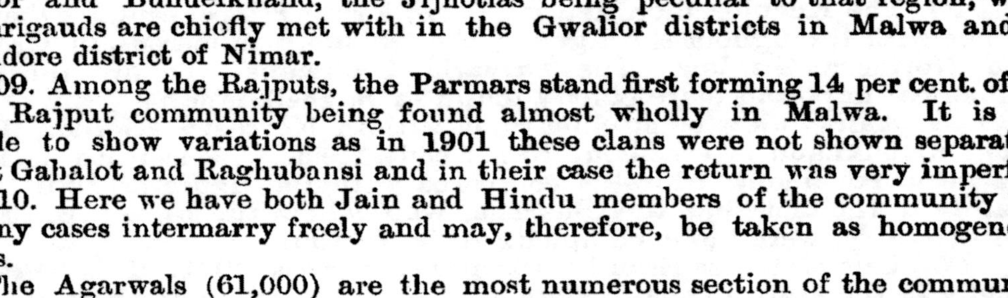

cent. are the strongest; after them come the Bhilala, Gond and Saharia, who form respectively 19, 15 and 7 per cent.

**Musalman.**

113. Among Muhammadans the Shaikhs are numerically the strongest.

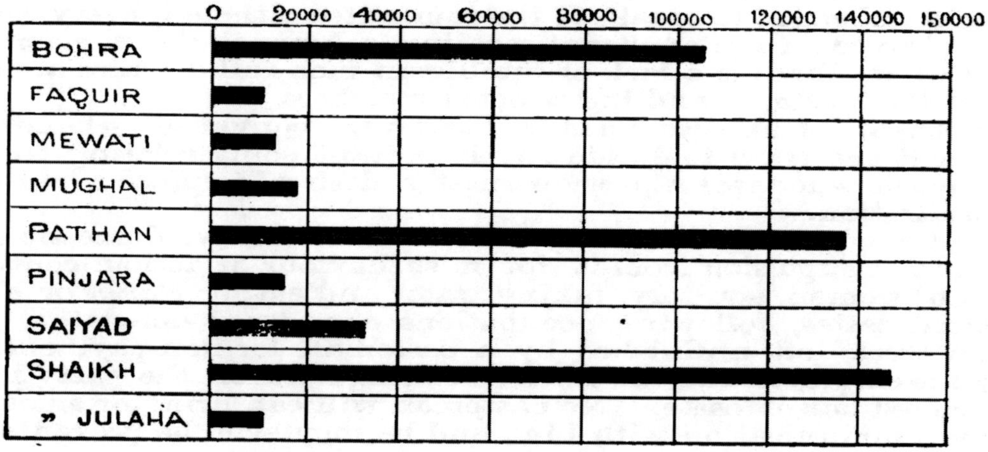


Next come the Pathans, Bohras, Saiyad, Mughals. The Mughals show a rise of 22 per cent. chiefly in the States of Baghelkhand, Jaora, and Chhatarpur.

**Caste and traditional Occupation.**

114. Subsidiary Table I gives caste and traditional occupations. The cultivating class stands first with about 18 per cent. following their traditional occupation; Forest and Hill Tribes give 12 per cent.; Priests following with 11 per cent.; leather workers 9 per cent.; and land holders with 8 and Graziers with 5 per cent.; the rest all fall below 5 per cent. only one in every thousand among Bards and Astrologers and confectioners following their real trade.

**New castes.**

115. New castes are most often formed by new settlements. Being disconnected from their parent stock they form new habits and customs which alienate them. The parent stock, moreover, is apt to suspect their strict adherence to caste rules especially in marriage and refuse to recognise the connection. A few instances are given below :—

The "Dhusar" Banias now claim descent from the Brahman Rishi Bhargava and a Bania woman. They persist in being called Brahmans. They are, however, really Banias and have been treated as such in the United Provinces where they predominate. The real Brahman descendants of Bhargava Rishi are the Bhagor or Bhargava Brahmans found in Orchha and Northern Gwalior. They have no connection with the Dhusar.

The "Lodas" were originally Tonwar Rajputs of Delhi. They assert that at the bidding of the Emperor they subdued Nawagarh but were subsequently expelled and called "Loda." Gradually they increased in number and spread over the Umatwara tract forming a separate caste 13,943, being returned in the census of 1911 They appear to have been included among Lodhas or Lodhis in the previous census.

The Ruwalas were originally inhabitants of Mewar where they were known as Muwala Rajputs. Migrating to Umatwara they abandoned the *parda* system, lost status and were called "Ruwala" and became a separate caste. The number of persons returned in 1911 was 3,377. They appear to have been included among Rajputs previously.

The Chamars of the Jathua sub-caste have begun to form themselves into a separate caste. These people came originally from Bharatpur and having taken to carpentry and manual work renounced all connection with their original caste. In the present census these persons, who were found in Indore and Mhow, have been included under Chamars.

### *Caste Government.*

116. All the functional groups and a majority of the inferior castes, such as Kachchis, Gaolis, Dhobis, Chamars, etc., with the exception of a few tribes, as well as Brahmans and Rajputs are governed by Panchayats or standing caste committees which deal with breaches of caste rules and religious matters.

The chief object of a Panchayat is to regulate matters relating to the calling followed by the caste. It usually consists of a headman, called Chaudhari or Mahton with the leading members of the community, not less than four, selected by him. Other castemen attend but not usually many. These men are the working members, so to speak, of the committee although every caste fellow has a right of voice in a Panchayat meeting. Among the inferior or less educated classes where there is a lack of intelligent men all disputes are settled on the opinion of the headman and the selected members.

A full Panchayat of all castemen is, however, convened whenever the members consider it necessary to decide any important point relating to social or moral questions or whenever a party earnestly desires to place a matter before them for arbitration.

The subjects brought before this body concern matrimony, domestic affairs, restoration to caste or expulsion from it for misbehaviour or action contrary to rules, abduction of women, adultery, taking water and eating *Pakki* or *Kachchi roti* of prohibited castes, following occupations considered derogatory to the caste, taking up work left unfinished by a casteman for non-payment of his just demand by his employer and the like. Pending decision the party in fault is temporarily placed out of caste. No casteman will eat, drink or smoke with him or have any communication with him, and he may even be prevented from following his calling.

The members of the committee hear the complainant and the accused, examine witnesses, hold open discussion and finally decide by majority. The proceedings are generally oral.

The punishment usually awarded is either penance (*Prayaschit*) entailing a visit to the Ganges or some shrine, for the purpose of bathing and washing away the sin, ex-communication, the giving of a caste feast, or a fine, the last being utilized in charitable gifts. For trifling matters an apology with folded hands and bended head is considered sufficient.

In these days the influence of the Panchayats is decreasing, except among the inferior castes such as Gaolis, Dhobis, Bhangis, etc., there being an increasing tendency for each man to judge for himself. The younger and educated generation especially, imbued with western ideas, has commenced to marry more freely beyond the old caste restrictions and to take food and drink anywhere, to visit Europe or America and on their return to quietly rejoin their caste brethren without any Prayaschit. A recent notable instance of marriage outside the old endogamous group is that of the Bundela Chief of Panna with the daughter of the Bhavnagar Chief, who is a Gohil Rajput.

### *Caste Control by Hindu Rajas.*

**117.** In former days the Hindu Rajas exercised a considerable control over caste matters and up to quite recent date there were religious councils at Gwalior and Indore appointed by the Chief, composed of learned *Shastris* to whom important matters on caste questions were submitted. The decision of these committees was nominally final but their decisions were often overruled by the Maharajas wherever an aggrieved party could obtain the ear of the Chief. His orders were absolutely final. The Chief of Barwani till quite recently had control over the decision of certain caste Panchayats. This control is now no longer exercised.

### *Caste Restrictions.*

**118.** A number of restrictions have been imposed by Hindu laws with respect to the life of a man. Although nowadays many of these are not very strictly observed, the following may be mentioned as nominally binding on every person in the caste.

(1) That he should not intermarry with his own sub-caste.

(2) That no girl should attain puberty before marriage, that is, she should be married before she passes the age of 12 years.

(3) That a widow of a Brahman, Rajput or Bania should not remarry. Those who practise this were formerly considered degraded and no strict persons in the caste would hold communication with them, intermarry, eat or drink with them.

(4) That a man should not take food or drink from the hands of prohibited castes and castes lower than himself

(5) That he should not follow an occupation derogatory to his caste. The prohibition is never regarded as binding in these days as Brahmans and Banias now freely trade in wines and leather articles. The business, however, is supposed not to pollute them, as they do not themselves make the articles. In eastern Central India Brahmans and Banias, though cultivators, are prohibited from actually holding the plough. In other parts of the Agency they personally plough the land. Castes such as Ahirs and Kumbis are prohibited from begging, others from scavenging, stable service, shoe-making, etc.

(6) The Malwi Brahmans and all Banias are prohibited from eating flesh and fish or drinking wine, fermented liquors and distilled water.

(7) That they should not touch Mochis, Chamars, Dhobis, Domars, Bhangis or Basors. If they do so, they must purify themselves by bathing and washing their clothes.

(8) That they should not draw water from a well used by the above classes or allow them to draw water from their own wells.

Within the last twenty years conditions have materially changed and though to a great extent easy communication has increased the cohesion between different sections of the same community, at the same time caste restrictions are not so strictly adhered to. The first distinction to go was dress. Distinctive caste dress has almost wholly disappeared among educated classes of the younger generation. The *Pagri* has been replaced by a felt cap, *Sapha*, and even sola hats, the *Angrakha* by coats of European cut, the *Kurta* and *Bandi* by shirts, *Paijamas* and *Dhotis* by trousers, native *Juta* by English shoes and boots, and so on. Added to these is the practice of shaving after the western fashion which gives no indication as to whether the person is a Hindu, Musalman, Anglo-Indian or Parsi still less whether he is a Brahman, Rajput, Nai, Teli, etc. Formerly a man's caste could be distinguished at a glance by his peculiar dress. Travelling by rail and education in schools and colleges, where all castes sit on one bench, has done away with pollution by touch or proximity, while public institutions such as hospitals, jails and boarding houses do not respect caste restrictions. Coming in contact with western education and ideas restrictions of food and drink have gone out of fashion and now high and low castes dine freely in public refreshment rooms served by Christians, Musalmans and even low caste Hindus, while articles of food made in Europe and imported are generally eaten.

**Caste and Occupation.**

119. Agriculture is the principal occupation followed in Central India and Brahmans, Banias, Rajputs and Chamars and even the Bhils all alike pursue it. The true agricultural castes form 26 per cent. of the Hindu population, the most important are shewn below. These eight castes form 18 per cent. of the total population and 14 per cent. of the Hindu population of the Agency :—

| Name. | Total. | Malwa. | Northern Gwalior and Bundelkhand. | Baghelkhand. |
|---|---|---|---|---|
| Dangi | 62,000 | 52,200 | 9,200 | 600 |
| Gujar | 185,000 | 107,700 | 77,100 | 200 |
| Jat | 46,000 | 35,100 | 9,800 | 1,100 |
| Kachhi | 371,000 | 125,600 | 186,300 | 59 100 |
| Kumawat | 5,000 | 4,990 | 10 | ... |
| Kunbi | 215,000 | 108,300 | 42,400 | 64,300 |
| Lodhi | 228,000 | 122,100 | 92,500 | 13,400 |
| Mali | 72,000 | 57,600 | 10,500 | 3,900 |
| TOTAL | 1,184,000 | 613,590 | 427,810 | 142,600 |

**Herdsmen.**

120. The real herdsmen are confined practically to three castes Ahirs, Gadarias and Gaolis which are not very carefully distinguished in ordinary parlance. They form 5 per cent. of the total and 6 per cent. of the Hindu population :—

| Name. | Total. | Malwa. | Northern Gwalior and Bundelkhand. | Baghelkhand. |
|---|---|---|---|---|
| Ahir | 281,000 | 124,500 | 82,700 | 78,800 |
| Gadaria | 159,000 | 64,900 | 74,300 | 19,300 |
| Gaoli | 44,000 | 22,000 | 21,200 | 800 |
| TOTAL | 484,000 | 211,400 | 178,200 | 94,400 |

**Craftsmen.**

121. Genuine craftsmen are included in the castes given below. They form 8 per cent. of the total population and 9 per cent. of the Hindu population :—

| Name. | Total. | Malwa. | Northern Gwalior and Bundelkhand. | Baghelkhand. |
|---|---|---|---|---|
| Darzi | 58,000 | 33,800 | 13,500 | 10,700 |
| Kasera | 3,000 | 1,900 | 300 | 800 |
| Kumhar | 143,000 | 72,200 | 49,700 | 21,100 |
| Lohar | 95,000 | 46,000 | 26,000 | 23,000 |
| Mochi | 6,000 | 3,700 | 1,400 | 900 |
| Salvi | 2,000 | 1,980 | 20 | ... |
| Sonar | 66,000 | 33,700 | 20,000 | 12,300 |
| Sutar | 115,000 | 75,700 | 30,100 | 9,200 |
| Jingar | 800 | 740 | 60 | ... |
| Kachera | 6,000 | 2,100 | 1,300 | 2,600 |
| Kanghigar | 500 | ... | 500 | ... |
| Kandera | 19,000 | 4,300 | 12,400 | 2,300 |
| Koli | 173,000 | 59,300 | 88,700 | 25,000 |
| Komti | 1,000 | 1,000 | ... | ... |
| Koshti | 2,000 | 1,500 | 500 | ... |
| Lakhera | 8,000 | 4,200 | 2,600 | 1,200 |
| Maru | 3,000 | 2,980 | 20 | ... |
| Tambat | 5,000 | 3,600 | 1,100 | 300 |
| Patwa | 3,000 | 1,400 | 1,300 | 300 |
| TOTAL | 709,300 | 350,100 | 249,500 | 109,700 |

**Traders.**

122. Traders have few castes but are a most important body of men. They form 4 per cent. of the total population and 4 per cent. of the Hindu and Jain population :—

| Name. | Total. | Malwa. | Northern Gwalior and Bundelkhand. | Baghelkhand. |
|---|---|---|---|---|
| Agarwal | 61,000 | 29,200 | 25,400 | 6,400 |
| Gahohi | 25,000 | 5,800 | 18,800 | 400 |
| Kasaundhan | 8,700 | ... | 1,200 | 7,500 |
| Kesar | 14,200 | ... | 200 | 14,000 |
| Khariaj | 4,400 | ... | ... | 4,400 |
| Mahesri | 23,000 | 21,840 | 660 | 500 |
| Oswal | 47,000 | 43,500 | 3,000 | 500 |
| Porwal | 39,000 | 27,300 | 11,000 | 700 |
| Others | 150,700 | 97,260 | 40,840 | 12,600 |
| TOTAL | 373,000 | 224,900 | 101,100 | 47,000 |

**Warrior classes.**

123. The principal warrior classes are given below. They form 10 per cent. of the total population and 11 per cent. of Hindus and Musalmans :—

| Name. | Total. | Malwa. | Northern Gwalior and Bundelkhand. | Baghelkhand. |
|---|---|---|---|---|
| Rajputs | 755,000 | 424,800 | 190,800 | 139,400 |
| Dhangar | 5,000 | 4,000 | 700 | 300 |
| Maratha | 28,000 | 18,650 | 9,300 | 50 |
| Pathan | 138,000 | 92,700 | 33,600 | 11,700 |
| TOTAL | 926,000 | 540,150 | 234,400 | 151,450 |

**Priests and Devotees.**

124. The most important priestly classes are those shown here who form 3 per cent. of the Hindu population :—

| Name. | Total. | Malwa. | Northern Gwalior and Bundelkhand. | Baghelkhand. |
|---|---|---|---|---|
| Brahman Bhargava | 32,000 | 16,800 | 15,000 | 200 |
| " Jijhotia | 63,000 | 8,400 | 53,800 | 800 |
| " Sanadhya | 159,000 | 41,800 | 115,500 | 1,700 |
| " Shrigaud | 15,000 | 13,800 | 900 | 300 |
| TOTAL | 269,000 | 80,800 | 185,200 | 3,000 |

125. Bards, astrologers, actors and mimes are given below :— **Bards and Astrologers.**

| Name. | Total. | Malwa. | Northern Gwalior and Bundelkhand. | Baghelkhand. |
|---|---|---|---|---|
| Bhat | 25,000 | 13,600 | 7,300 | 4,100 |
| Charan | 3,000 | 2,990 | 10 | ... |
| Bhand | 2,000 | 900 | 1,100 | ... |
| Gondhali | 80 | 80 | ... | ... |
| Nat | 8,000 | 4,900 | 1,700 | 1,400 |
| TOTAL | 38,080 | 22,470 | 10,110 | 5,500 |

126. The most numerous of the depressed classes are entered below. They form 11 per cent. of the total population :— **Depressed classes.**

| Name. | Total. | Malwa. | Northern Gwalior and Bundelkhand. | Baghelkhand. |
|---|---|---|---|---|
| Bhangi (M) | 3,000 | 2,700 | 300 | ... |
| „ (H) | 52,300 | 27,800 | 19,300 | 5,200 |
| Chamar | 859,000 | 389,300 | 351,700 | 118,000 |
| Dhobi (M) | 600 | 270 | 200 | 130 |
| „ (H) | 81,000 | 46,470 | 34,500 | 30 |
| Dom | 300 | 150 | 50 | 100 |
| Kanjar | 1,000 | 200 | 200 | 600 |
| Mahar | 6,000 | 5,700 | 300 | ... |
| Mang | 500 | 500 | ... | ... |
| Sor | 13,000 | ... | 13,000 | ... |
| TOTAL | 1,016,700 | 473,090 | 419,550 | 124,060 |

SUBSIDIARY TABLE I.—**Castes classified according to their Traditional Occupations.**

| Group and caste. | Strength 000's omitted. |
|---|---|
| **Land Holders** | **756**<br>**81** |
| Rajput | 756 |
| **Cultivators** | **1,673**<br>**179** |
| Ajana | 26 |
| Bharud | 49 |
| Dangi | 63 |
| Dhakad | 62 |
| Gujar | 186 |
| Jat | 47 |
| Kachhi | 372 |
| Kalota | 22 |
| Kirar | 90 |
| Kulmi | 215 |
| Lodhi | 228 |
| Mali | 72 |
| Mina | 75 |
| Sondhia | 71 |
| Others | 95 |
| **Labourers** | **8**<br>**1** |
| Kir | 6 |
| Lunia | 2 |
| **Forest and Hill Tribes, Hunters and Fowlers.** | **1,164**<br>**124** |
| Bagri | 53 |
| Bhil | 296 |
| Bhilala | 123 |
| Gond | 235 |
| Kol | 193 |
| Korku | 25 |
| Kotwal | 28 |
| Maji | 21 |
| Pardhi | 25 |
| Patlia | 22 |
| Saharia | 81 |
| Others | 62 |
| **Graziers and dairy-men** | **485**<br>**52** |
| Ahir | 281 |
| Gadaria | 160 |
| Goali | 44 |
| **Fishermen, boatmen, and palki-bearers.** | **236**<br>**25** |
| Bhoi | 52 |
| Dhimar | 89 |
| Kahar | 57 |
| Kewat | 29 |
| Others | 9 |
| **Priests and devotees** | **1,073**<br>**115** |
| Bairagi | 49 |
| Baiga | 23 |
| Brahman | 986 |
| Others | 15 |
| **Temple servants** (Dhami 634, Gurao 257-891) | **1**<br>**0** |

| Group and caste. | Strength 000's omitted. |
|---|---|
| **Genealogists** | **30**<br>**3** |
| Bhat | 26 |
| Others | 4 |
| **Bards and astrologers** | **10**<br>**1** |
| Joshi | 10 |
| **Writers** | **74**<br>**8** |
| Kayasth | 71 |
| Others | 3 |
| **Musicians, singers, dancers, mimes and jugglers.** | **62**<br>**7** |
| Dholi | 15 |
| Others | 47 |
| **Traders and pedlars** | **404**<br>**43** |
| Bania | 374 |
| Bohra | 16 |
| Others | 14 |
| **Carriers by pack animals** | **36**<br>**4** |
| Banjara | 32 |
| Others | 4 |
| **Barbers** | **156**<br>**17** |
| Nai | 156 |
| **Washermen** | **82**<br>**9** |
| Dhobi | 82 |
| **Weavers** | **262**<br>**28** |
| Chhipa | 18 |
| Koli | 174 |
| Panika | 27 |
| Others | 43 |
| **Tailors** | **59**<br>**6** |
| Darzi | 59 |
| **Carpenters** | **224**<br>**24** |
| Khati | 107 |
| Sutars | 115 |
| Others | 2 |
| **Masons** | **6**<br>**1** |
| Silawat | 6 |

NOTE.—The number below the total strength of each group indicates the proportion per mille to the total population.

SUBSIDIARY TABLE I.—**Castes classified according to their Traditional Occupations**—*continued.*

| Group and caste. | Strength 000's omitted. |
|---|---|
| **Potters** | **145** / **16** |
| Kumhar | 145 |
| **Glass and lac workers** | **22** / **2** |
| Kachera | 6 |
| Kasera | 4 |
| Lakhera | 10 |
| Manihar | 2 |
| **Black-smiths** | **97** / **10** |
| Lohar | 97 |
| **Gold and silver-smiths** | **67** / **7** |
| Sonar | 67 |
| **Brass and copper-smiths** | **29** / **3** |
| Bharewa | 23 |
| Others | 6 |
| **Confectioners and grain parchers** | **9** / **1** |
| Bharbunja | 6 |
| Halwai | 3 |
| **Oil-pressers** | **187** / **20** |
| Teli | 187 |
| **Toddy drawers and distillers** | **70** / **7** |
| Kalal | 64 |
| Others | 6 |
| **Butchers** | **25** / **3** |
| Khatik | 21 |
| Others | 4 |
| **Leather-workers** | **874** / **93** |
| Chamar | 859 |
| Others | 15 |
| **Basket workers and mat makers** | **59** / **6** |
| Bansphor | 52 |
| Bargunda | 7 |
| **Earth, salt, etc., workers and quarriers.** | **32** / **3** |
| Beldar | 26 |
| Others | 6 |
| **Domestic servants** | ... |
| **Village watchmen and menials** | **163** / **18** |
| Balai | 140 |
| Mirdha | 17 |
| Others | 6 |
| **Sweepers** | **57** / **6** |
| Bhangi | 57 |
| **Others** | **720** / **77** |
| Christians | 9 |
| Deswali | 34 |
| Gusain | 21 |
| Jogi | 15 |
| Kandera | 20 |
| Khangar | 38 |
| Maratha | 28 |
| Mughal | 18 |
| Pathan | 139 |
| Pinjara | 19 |
| Rawat | 64 |
| Saiyad | 32 |
| Shaikh | 147 |
| Shaikh Behna | 24 |
| Tamboli | 15 |
| Others | 97 |

NOTE.—The number below the total strength of each group indicate the proportion per mille to the total population.

SUBSIDIARY TABLE II.—**Variation in Caste, tribe, race, etc., since 1881.**

| | Caste, tribe or race. | Persons 000's omitted. | | | | Percentage of variation Increase (+) Decrease (—). | | | Net variation. | |
|---|---|---|---|---|---|---|---|---|---|---|
| | | 1911. | 1901. | 1891. | 1881. | 1901 to 1911. | 1891 to 1901. | 1881 to 1891. | 1891 to 1911. | 1881 to 1911. |
| | 1 | 2 | 3 | 4 | 5 | 6 | 7 | 8 | 9 | 10 |
| 1 | Ahir | 281 | 321 | 374 | 246 | —12·3 | —14·1 | +51·6 | —24·7 | +14·2 |
| 2 | Ajana | 26 | 23 | 19 | ... | +13·3 | +24·9 | ... | +41·6 | ... |
| 3 | Bagri | 53 | 20 | 57 | | +165·1 | —65·2 | ... | —7·8 | ... |
| 4 | Baiga | 23 | 9 | 16 | | +152·6 | —42·6 | ... | +45·0 | ... |
| 5 | Bairagi | 49 | 34 | 59 | ... | +44·2 | —42·3 | ... | —16·7 | ... |
| 6 | Balai | 140 | 203 | 347 | 170 | —31·0 | —41·5 | +103·3 | —59·6 | —17·9 |
| | **Bania** | **374** | **359** | **265** | **287** | **+4·1** | **+35·6** | **—7·6** | **+41·1** | **+30·4** |
| 7 | Bania Agarwal | 61 | 42 | ... | ... | +47·3 | ... | ... | ... | ... |
| 8 | ,, Gahohi | 25 | ... | ... | ... | ... | ... | ... | ... | ... |
| 9 | ,, Kesar | 14 | ... | ... | ... | ... | ... | ... | ... | ... |
| 10 | ,, Mahesri | 23 | 20 | ... | ... | +14·8 | ... | ... | ... | ... |
| 11 | ,, Oswal | 47 | 54 | 36 | ... | —12·2 | +50·2 | ... | +31·8 | ... |
| 12 | ,, Porwal | 39 | 20 | ... | ... | +99·7 | ... | ... | ... | ... |
| 13 | Banjara | 32 | 26 | 39 | ... | +20·3 | —32·1 | ... | —18·4 | ... |
| 14 | Banshpor | 52 | 39 | 44 | ... | +34·8 | —11·4 | ... | +19·5 | ... |
| 15 | Beldar | 26 | 8 | 8 | ... | +250·1 | —6·6 | ... | +227·0 | ... |
| 16 | Bhangi | 57 | 54 | 38 | ... | +4·7 | +42·7 | ... | +49·4 | ... |
| 17 | Bharewa | 23 | ... | ... | ... | ... | ... | ... | ... | ... |
| 18 | Bharud | 49 | 9 | 11 | ... | +421·6 | —18·2 | ... | +327·7 | ... |
| 19 | Bhat | 26 | 31 | 39 | | —18·6 | —18·8 | ... | —33·1 | ... |
| 20 | Bhil | 296 | 206 | 354 | 217 | +43·6 | —41·8 | +63·2 | —16·5 | +36·3 |
| 21 | Bhilala | 123 | 131 | 159 | ... | —6·9 | —17·6 | ... | —22·6 | ... |
| 22 | Bhoi | 52 | 59 | 17 | ... | —11·8 | +250·1 | ... | +208·8 | ... |
| | **Brahman** | **986** | **878** | **955** | **962** | **+11·0** | **—8·2** | **—0·7** | **+3·2** | **+2·5** |
| 23 | Brahman Bhagor | 32 | ... | ... | ... | ... | ... | ... | ... | |
| 24 | ,, Lakshani | 34 | ... | ... | ... | ... | ... | ... | ... | ... |
| 25 | ,, Gujargaud | 19 | ... | ... | ... | ... | ... | ... | . | ... |
| 26 | ,, Gujarati | 40 | ... | ... | ... | ... | ... | ... | | ... |
| 27 | ,, Jijhotia | 64 | 54 | ... | ... | +18·9 | ... | ... | ... | ... |
| 28 | ,, Kanojia | 81 | ... | | ... | ... | ... | ... | ... | ... |
| 29 | ,, Sanadhya | 159 | ... | ... | ... | ... | | ... | ... | ... |
| 30 | ,, Sarvaria | 303 | ... | ... | ... | ... | ... | | ... | |
| 31 | ,, Shrigaud | 15 | 13 | ... | ... | +19·5 | ... | ... | ... | ... |
| 32 | Chamar | 859 | 717 | 888 | 1,077 | +19·8 | —19·1 | +17·6 | —3·2 | —20·2 |
| 33 | Chhipa | 18 | 17 | 21 | ... | +6·6 | —20·8 | ... | —14·1 | ... |
| 34 | Dangi | 63 | 38 | 59 | ... | +66·2 | —35·6 | ... | +7·0 | ... |
| 35 | Darzi | 59 | 56 | 66 | ... | +5·0 | —15·0 | ... | —10·5 | ... |
| 36 | Deswali | 34 | 9 | 38 | 15 | +291·2 | —77·1 | +157·5 | —10·5 | +130·4 |
| 37 | Dhakad | 63 | 41 | 52 | ... | +53·0 | —20·8 | | +21·5 | |
| 38 | Dhimar | 89 | 66 | 69 | ... | +34·1 | —4·6 | ... | +27·9 | ... |
| 39 | Dhobi | 82 | 79 | 97 | ... | +3·7 | —17·7 | ... | —15·4 | ... |
| 40 | Dholi | 15 | 9 | 17 | ... | +68·0 | —45·1 | ... | —14·7 | ... |
| 41 | Gadaria | 160 | 148 | 171 | ... | +7·6 | —13·3 | ... | —6·8 | ... |
| 42 | Gaoli | 44 | 36 | 10 | | +24·1 | +255·4 | ... | +342·2 | ... |
| 43 | Gond | 235 | 195 | 254 | 414 | +20·3 | —23·3 | —38·5 | —7·8 | —43·3 |
| 44 | Gusain | 21 | 45 | 36 | ... | —52·9 | —29·1 | ... | —40·4 | ... |
| 45 | Gujar | 186 | 161 | 205 | 337 | +16·6 | —21·5 | —39·4 | —9·2 | —45·0 |
| 46 | Jat | 47 | 53 | 57 | ... | —12·7 | —5·5 | ... | —17·3 | ... |
| 47 | Jogi | 15 | ... | 10 | ... | ... | ... | ... | +47·0 | ... |
| 48 | Kachhi | 372 | 347 | 472 | 183 | +10·0 | —26·5 | +157·9 | —21·3 | +103·1 |
| 49 | Kahar | 57 | 29 | 81 | ... | +94·4 | —64·0 | ... | —30·1 | ... |
| 50 | Kalal | 64 | 62 | 12 | ... | +3·2 | +410·0 | ... | +426·2 | ... |
| 51 | Kalota | 27 | 27 | 21 | ... | +2·7 | +28·2 | ... | +31·6 | ... |
| 52 | Kandera | 20 | 17 | 22 | ... | +13·6 | —20·9 | ... | —10·2 | ... |
| 53 | Kayasth | 71 | 79 | 74 | ... | —9·2 | +5·5 | ... | —4·1 | ... |
| 54 | Kewat | 29 | 28 | 32 | ... | +4·1 | —12·0 | ... | —8·4 | ... |
| 55 | Khangar | 48 | 34 | 38 | ... | +41·8 | —10·6 | ... | +26·8 | ... |
| 56 | Khati | 107 | 57 | 85 | ... | +89·0 | —33·5 | ... | +25·8 | ... |
| 57 | Khatik | 21 | 21 | 18 | ... | —0·3 | +13·0 | ... | +12·7 | ... |
| 58 | Kirar | 90 | 94 | 114 | ... | —4·6 | —17·2 | ... | —21·0 | ... |
| 59 | Kol | 193 | 156 | 217 | 187 | +23·2 | —27·8 | +15·1 | —11·3 | +2·8 |
| 60 | Koli | 174 | 170 | 123 | ... | +1·9 | +38·0 | ... | +40·6 | ... |
| 61 | Korku | 25 | 10 | 21 | ... | +162·4 | —58·3 | ... | +13·6 | ... |
| 62 | Kotwal | 28 | 32 | 28 | ... | —13·7 | +14·2 | ... | —2·3 | ... |
| 63 | Kulmi | 215 | 229 | 222 | 168 | —5·8 | +3·0 | +32·1 | —3·2 | +28·1 |
| 64 | Kumhar | 144 | 136 | 157 | ... | +5·8 | —18·4 | ... | —13·7 | ... |
| 65 | Lodhi | 228 | 216 | 253 | ... | +5·0 | —14·3 | ... | —9·7 | ... |
| 66 | Lohar | 97 | 93 | 107 | ... | +3·6 | —13·0 | ... | —9·8 | ... |
| 67 | Maji | 31 | 26 | ... | ... | —19·4 | ... | ... | ... | ... |
| 68 | Mali | 72 | 72 | 91 | ... | +0·6 | —21·1 | ... | —20·7 | ... |

SUBSIDIARY TABLE II.—**Variation in Caste, tribe, race, etc., since 1881**—contd.

| | Caste, tribe or race. | Persons 000's omitted. | | | | Percentage of variation Increase (+) Decrease (−). | | | Net variation. | |
|---|---|---|---|---|---|---|---|---|---|---|
| | | 1911. | 1901. | 1891. | 1881. | 1901 to 1911. | 1891 to 1901. | 1881 to 1891. | 1891 to 1911. | 1881 to 1911. |
| | 1 | 2 | 3 | 4 | 5 | 6 | 7 | 8 | 9 | 10 |
| 69 | Maratha | 28 | 34 | 36 | ... | −18·3 | −3·7 | ... | −21·3 | ... |
| 70 | Mina | 75 | 98 | 119 | 50 | −24·0 | −17·0 | +137·8 | −37·0 | +49·8 |
| 71 | Mirdha | 17 | 10 | 16 | ... | +68·2 | −35·9 | ... | +7·6 | ... |
| 72 | Nai (barb-r) | 156 | 152 | 171 | ... | +2·7 | −10·7 | ... | −8·4 | ... |
| 73 | Panika | 27 | 24 | 34 | ... | +9·8 | −27·6 | ... | −20.5 | ... |
| 74 | Pardhi | 25 | 6 | 6 | ... | +302·9 | −2·9 | ... | +290·9 | ... |
| 75 | Patlia | 22 | 14 | 12 | ... | +53·2 | +16·7 | ... | +78·9 | ... |
| | **Rajput** | **756** | **654** | **602** | **803** | **+15·6** | **+8·6** | **−25·1** | **+26·6** | **−5·9** |
| 76 | Rajput Badgujar | 16 | ... | ... | ... | ... | ... | ... | ... | ... |
| 77 | " Baghela | 25 | ... | ... | ... | ... | ... | ... | ... | ... |
| 78 | " Bhadauria | 23 | ... | ... | ... | ... | ... | ... | ... | ... |
| 79 | " Bundela | 17 | ... | ... | ... | ... | ... | ... | ... | ... |
| 80 | " Chhatri | 62 | 488 | ... | ... | −87·3 | ... | ... | ... | ... |
| 81 | Chohan | 40 | ... | ... | ... | ... | ... | ... | ... | ... |
| 82 | Gahalot | 24 | 11 | 21 | ... | +122·7 | −49·1 | ... | +13·3 | .. |
| 83 | Kachhwaha | 24 | ... | .. | ... | ... | ... | ... | ... | ... |
| 84 | Parihar | 18 | ... | ... | ... | ... | ... | ... | ... | ... |
| 85 | Ponwar | 43 | ... | ... | ... | ... | ... | .. | ... | ... |
| 86 | Parmar | 109 | ... | ... | ... | ... | ... | ... | ... | ... |
| 87 | Raghubansi | 40 | 6 | 14 | ... | +516·6 | −55·2 | ... | +175·7 | ... |
| 88 | Rathor | 33 | ... | ... | ... | ... | .. | ... | ... | ... |
| 89 | Sendho | 71 | ... | ... | ... | ... | .. | ... | ... | ... |
| 90 | Solanki | 16 | ... | .. | ... | .. | ... | ... | ... | ... |
| 91 | Tonwar | 37 | ... | ... | ... | ... | ... | ... | ... | ... |
| 92 | Rawat | 64 | 32 | 24 | ... | +97·5 | +36·9 | ... | +162·4 | ... |
| 93 | Saharia | 81 | 44 | 70 | ... | +83·5 | −36·9 | ... | +15·8 | ... |
| 94 | Sonar | 67 | 75 | 74 | ... | −10·9 | +1·2 | ... | −11·2 | ... |
| 95 | Sondhia | 71 | 75 | 8 | ... | −5·4 | +827·4 | ... | +777·0 | ... |
| 96 | Sor | 14 | 15 | ... | .. | −6·1 | ... | ... | ... | ... |
| 97 | Sutar | 115 | 120 | 128 | ... | −3·8 | −6·3 | ... | −9·9 | .. |
| 98 | Tamboli | 15 | 17 | 24 | ... | −10·1 | −39·9 | ... | −37·9 | ... |
| 99 | Teli | 187 | 160 | 211 | 250 | +16·2 | −24·3 | −15·6 | −11·6 | −25·3 |
| | **Musalman** | **511** | **514** | **569** | **511** | **−0·6** | **−9·6** | **+11·3** | **−10·1** | **+0·1** |
| 100 | Musalman Bohra | 16 | 16 | 15 | ... | +1·5 | +5·1 | ... | +6·6 | ... |
| 101 | " Mughal | 18 | 15 | 10 | ... | +24·9 | +46·0 | ... | +82·4 | ... |
| 102 | " Pathan | 139 | 144 | 170 | ... | −3·8 | −15·3 | ... | −18·5 | ... |
| 103 | " Pinjara | 19 | 18 | 22 | ... | +6 8 | −19·2 | ... | −13·3 | ... |
| 104 | " Saiyad | 32 | 37 | 35 | ... | −13·7 | +7·0 | ... | −7·7 | ... |
| 105 | " Shaikh | 184 | 199 | 235 | ... | −7·5 | −15·4 | ... | −21·7 | ... |

## CHAPTER XII.

# Occupation or Means of Livelihood.

127. The statistics dealt with in this Chapter are given in Imperial Tables XV and XVI and the Subsidiary Tables at the end of the Chapter. Table XV is divided into five parts. The general principles underlying the arrangement adopted in the different parts of Table XV are these. In Table XV-A a man is classified according to his principal occupation, while except partial dependency on agriculture no subsidiary occupations are concerned in this part. In parts B and C subsidiary occupations are dealt with. XV-B gives the subsidiary occupations of agriculturists who are actual workers, these being classed as :—

1. Rent receivers (Landlords).
2. Rent payers (Actual Cultivators).
3. Farm Servants and Field Labourers.

XV-C gives returns for certain common fixed occupations, showing principal and subsidiary means of livelihood.

XV-D shows distribution of occupations by religions.

XV-E gives statistics relating to industrial undertakings employing 20 or more persons at the date of the census.

**Scheme of Classification.**

128. The scheme of classification adopted on this occasion was entirely different from that employed in 1891 and 1901. The system followed on those occasions was based on Indian conditions only, while that employed in 1911 aims at making the results comparable with those of other countries. The system followed was adapted from that put forward by M. Bertillon, the French statistician, at Paris in 1881 and at Vienna in 1893, before the International Institute of Statistics. This system attempts to secure uniformity in the record of occupational statistics throughout the world, so that results may be comparable. To enable this to be carried out some elasticity is necessary and hence three forms of classification are employed. The first is very condensed and contains only 61 heads, the second reproduces some of the general headings and subdivides them, and a third form makes a still more minute sub-division. While there are strong objections to changing a scheme of classification once adopted there can be no two opinions on the advantages which the present has over that hitherto pursued. Statistics which are comparable only with similar statistics for previous years collected in the same region are far less valuable than those which are recorded on such lines as to make general comparison possible with statistics of the same class of occupation collected in other lands. Another advantage of the present system is its far greater simplicity. This the table below brings out :—

| System of 1891 and 1901. | | | | System of 1911. | | | |
|---|---|---|---|---|---|---|---|
| Class. | Orders. | Sub-orders. | Groups. | Class. | Sub-classes. | Orders. | Groups. |
| A.—Government | 3 | 7 | 24 | A.—Production of raw materials | 2 | 5 | 20 |
| B.—Pasture and Agriculture | 2 | 6 | 35 | B.—Preparation and supply of material substances. | 3 | 36 | 118 |
| C.—Personal service | 1 | 3 | 16 | C.—Public administration and liberal arts. | 4 | 10 | 23 |
| D.—Preparation and supply of material substances. | 11 | 37 | 316 | D.—Miscellaneous | 3 | 4 | 8 |
| E.—Commerce, transport and storage. | 2 | 9 | 52 | | | | |
| F.—Professions | 2 | 11 | 56 | | | | |
| G.—Unskilled labour, not agriculture. | 2 | 4 | 10 | | | | |
| H.—Means of subsistence, independent of occupation. | 1 | 2 | 11 | | | | |
| TOTAL | 24 | 79 | 520 | TOTAL | 12 | 55 | 169 |

That the scheme followed in the previous enumerations was far too elaborate had been recognised and it was, therefore, wise to seize the opportunity of making the Indian returns simpler and at the same time comparable with those of other countries.

129. The essence of M. Bertillon's scheme is that the main divisions of classes and sub-classes should be retained in order that the statistics may be comparable with those of other communities, while the minor sub-divisions can be adapted to local circumstances. M. Bertillon in his scheme has four Classes, 12 Sub-classes, 61 Orders and 499 Groups. Mr. Gait has retained the Classes and Sub-classes but has reduced the Orders from 61 to 55 by omitting 5 Orders not needed in India and combining Maritime and Fresh water transport under one head, "Transport by water." Sub-orders are only used under Order No. 1, Pasture and Agriculture, which has 5 Sub-orders. The Groups have been reduced from 499 to 169. This gives:— **M. Bertillon's Scheme.**

| M. Bertillon. | India scheme. |
|---|---|
| 4 Classes.<br>12 Sub-classes.<br>61 Orders.<br><br>499 Groups. | 4 Classes.<br>12 Sub-classes.<br>55 Orders.<br>5 Sub-orders (to Order No. 1 only).<br>169 Groups. |

130. No class of entries in a census record give such opportunities for error as that of occupation. Very particular attention was paid to the directions issued and the instructions given to the enumerators in the schools on the recording of this information. Three columns had to be filled in: **Accuracy of Record.**

Column 9. Principal occupation of Actual workers.
" 10. Subsidiary occupation of Actual workers.
" 11. Means of subsistence of dependants on workers.

By means of detailed instruction and much training before the census all that was possible was done to ensure accuracy and the return shows an enormous advance on that of 1901, which was the first occasion in which such a record had been attempted.

131. The Census Report of 1901 notes seven limitations in this record:— **Limitations of the Return.**

(i) It must be borne in mind that these returns refer to the state of affairs on a single day in a certain month, industries which are seasonable, therefore, may possibly not be recorded at all. As regards the month in which this census was taken, *viz.*, March, the following occupations are in abeyance, agricultural operations generally, grass cutting, ginning of cotton, and transport by carts.

(ii) Another cause is the difficulty of deciding what is actually a principal occupation in many cases. Numbers of people follow more than one pursuit as a means of livelihood; thus fishermen are always boatmen; Chaukidars are generally cultivators; landlords often money-lenders. The caprice of the person enumerated, or the views of census officials may affect the result in such instances.

(iii) Mixed occupations again cause confusion, and in the case of agricultural peasants this is particularly so, a rent-payer may also receive rents from others, a man may own a field but also work for another.

(iv) Vague entries are also a source of trouble; but these were comparatively few on this occasion, great stress being laid on the necessity of specification and the uselessness of entries such as "clerk," "shop-keeper," "railway employé," and the like.

(v) Errors in the entries are likely owing to the confusion between a man's actual and traditional occupation, which he may not be actually following at all, or may only follow as a subsidiary calling. Another fruitful source of mistake was the entry as a dependant of a man who was working as the servant of some other person, while the entries in the case of the members of a man's household, who actually assisted him in his occupation, often gave rise to difficulty.

(vi) Makers and sellers are often indistinguishable and in most cases are one and the same person; thus a fisherman catches and sells fish, a butcher kills animals and sells their flesh.

(vii) Errors in compilation were minimised by the fact that all the tabulation was done under the supervision of the Census Superintendent and any errors of classification made were at any rate constant. Moreover no abbreviations were allowed which obviated the error so often caused by the use of abbreviated entries in cases where an occupation lengthily described really approximated only in class to one of those indicated by an abbreviation.

Careful re-examination brought a few discrepancies to light which were adjusted by referring back.

**General Conclusion.**

132. On the whole the return is probably as accurate as any such return can well be, the taking of a census being obviously not suited to a really accurate record of so complicated a nature. The Classes and Sub-classes, and indeed almost all the Orders may be accepted with confidence, but it is not possible to give equal credence to the Groups.

**General discussion of the Result.**

133. The diagram below gives at a glance the relative population engaged in the various occupations shown by Sub-classes. As would be expected Agriculture leads, being 52 per cent. ahead of any other pursuit, Industry

*Diagram showing the general distribution of the population by occupation (Sub-classes)*

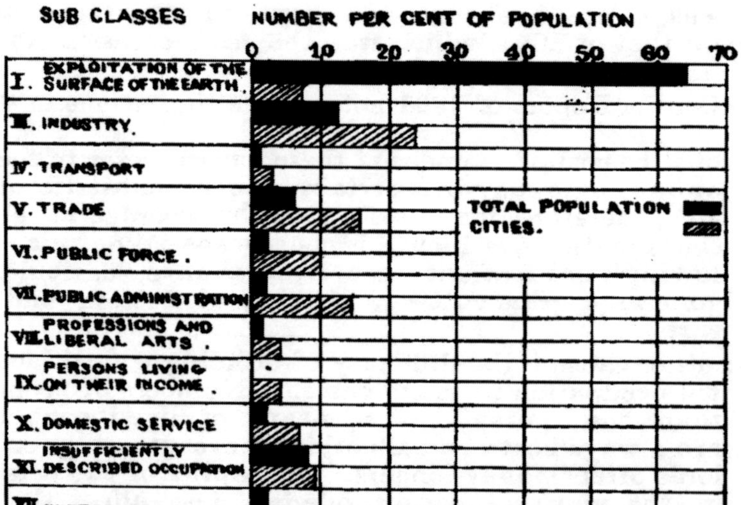


coming next with only 12 per cent. In cities Industry and Trade take the leading places with 24 and 15 per cent. The artificial occupations of Public Administration and Public forces come next. No other Sub-class can show double figures.

**Natural Divisions and Occupations.**

134. Turning to the Natural Divisions the Hilly tract shows the highest figure for Agriculture, 66 per cent., the Lowlying 61 and the Plateau 57. As might be expected the more civilised Plateau and Lowlying tracts return the highest percentage for Industry, Commerce and the Professions.

**135.** When a comparison is made between the occupations in villages and those in Lashkar, Indore, Bhopal and Ratlam, treated locally as cities for the purpose, it appears that the occupations in the latter have distinctly urban **Comparison between the Occupations of Cities and Villages.**

*Diagram showing the distribution of the population by occupation (classes) in each Natural Division.*

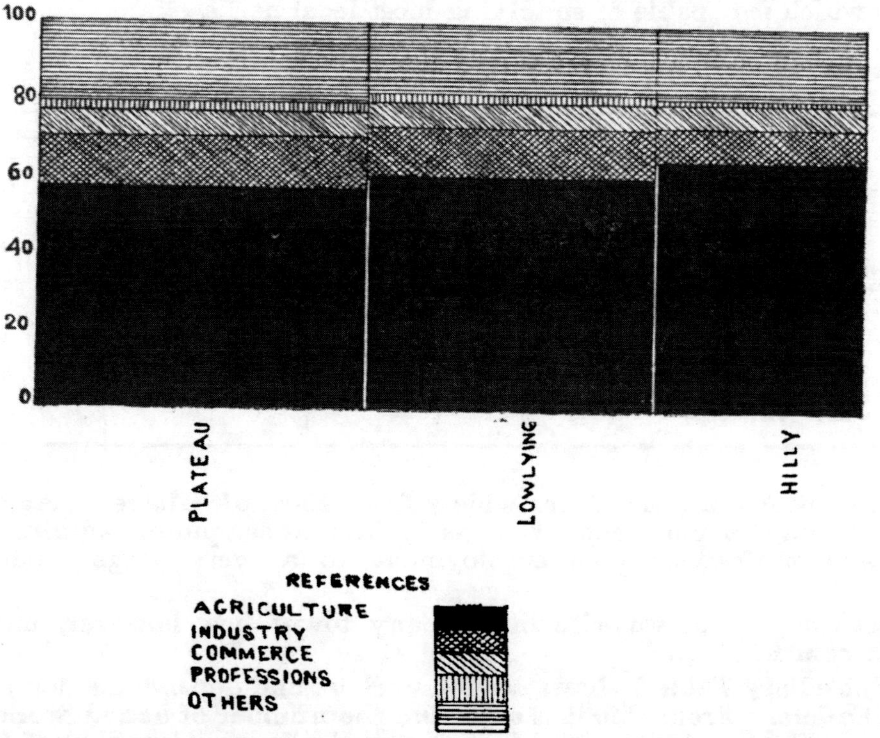


characteristics while those in villages and the other so-called towns, which are merely overgrown villages, are practically rural. As a rule agriculture is the prevailing occupation in all villages, while the industries, service in the public administration, domestic service, arts and professions predominate in cities.

The statistics of occupations usually followed in rural areas will be found in the subjoined table :—

| Occupation. | Groups included. | Number per 10,000 of total population. |
|---|---|---|
| 1. Landlords and tenants | 1,2,6 | 4,463 |
| 2. Labourers | 4,98,104,168 | 1,603 |
| (a) Agricultural labourers | 4 | 1,591 |
| (b) General labourers | 98, 104, 168 | 12 |
| 3. Stock-owners, milkmen and herdsmen | 9, 10, 12, 61 | 225 |
| 4. Cotton workers (not in mills) | 21, 22 | 142 |
| 5. Goldsmiths and blacksmiths | 41, 89 | 105 |
| 6. Brass, Copper and bell metal workers | 42 | 13 |
| 7. Carpenters | 8, 36 | 108 |
| 8. Fishermen and boatmen | 14, 60, 97, 116 | 14 |
| 9. Oil-pressers | 58, 118 | 102 |
| 10. Barbers | 72 | 90 |
| 11. Washermen | 71 | 59 |
| 12. Toddy-drawers and sellers | 65, 114 | 24 |
| 13. Grain-parchers | 58 | 8 |
| 14. Leather-workers | 32, 108, 109 | 43 |
| 15. Basket-makers, scavengers and drummers | 37, 93, 160 | 139 |
| 16. Priests | 137, 148, 151 | 32 |
| 17. Potters | 47, 48, 112 | 97 |
| 18. Mendicants | 149, 169 | 279 |
| 19. Village quacks and midwives | 155 | 4 |
| 20. Grocers and confectioners | 65, 117, 119 | 96 |
| 21. Graindealers and money-lenders | 106, 121 | 178 |
| 22. Tailors | 68 | 63 |
| 23. Vegetable and fruit sellers | 90, 120 | 41 |
| 24. Other shop-keepers | 135 | 67 |
| 25. Makers and sellers of bangles. | 45,90, 132 | 30 |
| 26. Silk-worm rearers and silk weavers | 13, 27 | 1 |
| TOTAL | ... | 8,026 |

Out of every 100 persons 80 per cent. are supported by the village occupations shown above. In villages, moreover, occupations are largely hereditary, a Kunbi will cultivate, a tailor will sew clothes, a barber will shave, a potter will make earthen vessels and the like and receive in return their recognised share of grain when the crop is reaped. At marriages and similar ceremonies and dinner parties they also receive food, money, presents and clothes. Thus the inhabitants of villages still to a great extent form within themselves an organised community which is capable of supplying most local needs.

The urban occupations are chiefly those given below :—

| Occupation. | Number supported per 1,000 in | |
|---|---|---|
| | Central India. | Cities. |
| Public force | 19 | 95 |
| Public administration | 15 | 145 |
| Domestic service | 25 | 66 |
| Agriculture | 607 | 40 |
| Pasture | 24 | 13 |
| Textile industry | 18 | 34 |
| Food industries | 7 | 39 |
| Industries of dress and the toilet | 42 | 56 |
| Professions and liberal arts | 15 | 41 |
| Persons living on their own income | 13 | 44 |

The occupations in cities differ widely from those of villages. Agriculture here supports only 4 per cent. whereas public force, public administration, industries and professions give employment to a very large number of persons.

The fact that plague was rife in so many towns has, however, materially affected this return.

**Workers and Dependants.**

136. Subsidiary Table I shows actual workers and dependants for all Sub-classes and Orders. From this it is seen that the number of actual workers and dependants for Central India as a whole is practically equal to that of Class A, *viz.*, 57 workers and 43 dependants in every 100 of the population. The largest number of dependants is found under Sub-class II Order 4 Quarries of hard rocks and 5 Salt, but the total figures under these heads are so very small that a slight variation causes a large difference. As a rule dependants are in a minority, but under Banks and Brokerage (V-24-25 ) the reverse is the case as also in the Professions (VIII) and Persons living on their incomes (IX). The lowest return occurs in the case of workers in refuse matters (V-40) and inmates of jails and asylums (XII-54).

**Agricultural Occupation.**

137. The first Order "Pasture and Agriculture" supports 5,900,000 persons or 63 per cent. of the population and gives occupation to 36 per cent. of the actual workers of the community. The importance of this Order has necessitated its being sub-divided into 5 Sub-orders, though none of the remaining 54 Orders is so treated. It is still further divided into 13 Groups.

Subsidiary Table VII gives comparative figures for 1901 and 1911. The figure under Pastoral and Agricultural pursuits has risen from 4,570,000 in 1901 to 5,936,000 in 1911, an increase of just under 30 per cent. This is easily accounted for by the general progress which has taken place since 1901 and the unfavourable conditions obtaining in 1899-1900 just before the census was taken.

**Landlords**

138. It will be noticed that the general classification of Rent-receivers and Rent-payers used in 1901 has been wisely dropped as it was impossible to separate these two classes effectually. The result has been a considerable fall in the numbers of those who live on the rent of agricultural land. The return in 1901 included many who were merely cultivators or even labourers, and owned a small field insufficient for their support, which they let out to another.

| Landlords. | | Percentage of variation. |
|---|---|---|
| 1911. | 1901. | |
| 123,000 | 234,000 | – 47·4 |

139. The term "Ordinary cultivators" refers to those who grow the field crops and staple products of the season as distinct from gardeners, tea planters, etc. It would have been better, probably, to have used some term such as "Growers of staple products and ordinary crops" as the Sub-order "Ordinary cultivator" which includes landlords, managers and cultivators of ordinary crops and also of special products is apt to be confused with it. There has been a rise of 28 per cent. in this Group in part due to the inclusion of persons of the Landlord class and in part to the improved agricultural conditions obtaining during the years preceding the census. **Cultivators.**

| Cultivators. | | Percentage of variation. |
|---|---|---|
| 1911. | 1901. | |
| 4,038,000 | 3,154,000 | + 28·0 |

Subsidiary Table IV gives occupations with which agriculture is combined as a subsidiary means of livelihood.

The inset gives the six principal Sub-classes. Examination of these figures in detail shows that "Industries of dress and the toilet (166)" "Metal industries (127)" "Hotels, cafés, etc. (109)" "Fishing and hunting (107)" "Trade in food stuffs (100)" are the most important. This is accounted for largely in the case of the first two by the grants of land made to barbers, blacksmiths and other village servants; those engaged in "Fishing and hunting" all cultivate; while "Trade in food stuffs" includes "Sellers of milk and butter" "dealers in sheep and goats" who invariably own land.

| Sub-class. | Number of mille. |
|---|---|
| VIII. Professions and liberal arts. | 166 |
| III. Industry | 117 |
| V. Trade | 98 |
| VI. Public force | 75 |
| IV. Transport | 72 |
| X. Domestic service | 47 |

The Natural Division figures are also interesting. They show that those who belong to Professions, Industry, Trade and Transport in the Lowlying tract engage more in agriculture than elsewhere owing to the small development of industrial concerns. In the case of "Public force" and "Domestic service" the Hilly tract has the highest figures.

Table XV-B shows persons following agriculture as the principal means of livelihood while the details are brought out in Subsidiary Table V where these categories are used. Rent-receivers (Landlords), Rent-payers (Tenants) and Farm-servants and Field Labourers. Of Landlords 2,300 in every 10,000 of the population are also payers of rent, while 699 are labourers and 337 money-lenders and grain dealers. The remaining figures are insignificant. It shows how the land lies almost entirely in the hands of the agricultural classes. Of the Rent-payers (Cultivators) practically none follows any other occupation, though a few also receive rent and some are petty shop-keepers or breeders of cattle. Among Farm-servants none follows any occupation save general labour.

There is, therefore, no danger at present of the land passing out of the hands of the agricultural classes in the Agency.

140. The total number engaged in raising animals is 221,000 or 26 per cent. of the total population. In 1901 stock breeding and dealing were not separated and the comparative figures are very approximate therefore. **Pasture.**

| Pastoral. | | Percentage of variation. |
|---|---|---|
| 1911. | 1901. | |
| 221,000 | 176,000 | + 25·6 |

141. This form of occupation supports 12,000 persons or below 1 per cent. and shows a rise of 86 per cent. since 1901. This rise is due to the abandonment in 1901 of the jungle tracts where the Bhils could no longer support themselves. This reduced the population in those areas, the great increase which has actually taken place among the jungle tribes being another cause. **Fishing and Hunting.**

142. The extraction of minerals supports only some 4,000 persons of whom 2,000 are found in the Rewah State coal mine at Umaria. **Mining.**

The mining industry is still in its infancy and until a complete scientific economic survey of the mineral deposits in Central India has been made, real development is impossible; that such industries will some day arise seems certain, at any rate in parts of the Agency which is free from Trap rock. The Gwalior and Indore Darbars are taking steps in this direction.

**Industry.**

143. This is the most important Sub-class next to Agriculture. Over 1,145,000 persons are supported by the groups which fall under this Order or 122 per 1,000 of the population. The most important industries are noted in the inset. Industries of dress and the toilet thus support nearly one-third of the total industrial population.

| Order. | Number supported per 1,000. |
|---|---|
| 13. Industries of dress and the toilet. | 42 |
| 6. Textile . . . | 18 |
| 8. Wood . . . | 14 |
| 10. Ceramics . . | 11 |
| 9. Metals . . . | 8 |
| 11. Chemical products . | 8 |
| 18. Industries of luxury . | 6 |

**Textiles.**

144. Among the textile industries cotton spinning-and-weaving takes the first place with 106,000 persons or 63 per cent. of those supported by this Order. Of these most are workers at hand looms, weavers of fine muslin (*saris*, etc.) for which Chanderi, Maheshwar and other places are still noted. Mills only employ in all 2,800 persons out of the 106,000 returned. Cotton ginning, cleaning and pressing come next with 26,000. The remaining groups are all under 20,000, dyeing and bleaching (17,000) and wool-workers (11,000) being next in importance.

**Hides, Skins, etc.**

145. Industries connected with hides, skins and hard animal substances support 23,000 persons or 2 per mille of the population, all of whom are either tanners (11,000) or leather workers (12,000), exclusive of shoe-makers who are shown under Order 13. The work they do is of a primitive kind there being no scientifically managed tannery in the Agency, skins being tanned in the usual way with babul bark solution.

**Bone.**

146. The bone industry is quite in its infancy and only supports 4 persons.

**Wood.**

147. This is the most important occupation next to textiles, giving support to 133,000 persons, or 14 per 1,000 of the population. It includes sawyers, carpenters, turners, joiners, etc. (64,000) and basket makers, etc. (69,000).

Carpenter is a general term for the man who does all village work such as mending wooden agricultural implements, assisting to build houses, etc., while the turners make *charpoy* legs, swings, cradles, etc. Wood carving is also a part of this industry. Basket makers and leaf plate makers are met with chiefly in Gwalior, Rewah, Indore, Bhopal, Orchha and other States in Bundelkhand.

**Metal.**

148. Metal workers number 70,000 and form 8 per cent. of the population. The most numerous group is that of "Other workers in iron, etc. (51,800)" workers in brass and copper being next in numerical strength (12,000). The most numerous class includes the Lohars or village blacksmiths who make and repair the iron implements used by the agriculturist, while the brass and copper workers manufacture and mend the necessary household pots and pans.

**Ceramics.**

149. Ceramics support 100,000 persons or 11 per cent. of the population, 86,000 of whom are potters. They are met with chiefly in Northern Gwalior, Rewah and Bhopal.

**Chemical Products.**

150. Of the 71,000 persons supported, 66,000 are engaged in refining vegetable oils, the Teli class falling under this head.

**Food Industries.**

151. Food industries number 65,000 persons of whom most fall under flour-grinders (18,000) and sweetmeat makers (17,000). Rice is little grown in the Agency and those returned in group 56 are all flour-grinders.

**Industries of Dress and the Toilet.**

152. This is the most important of all the industries supporting 391,000 or 42 per cent. of the population. Far the most numerous class is that of the shoe-makers (189,000); barbers (84,000), tailors (59,000) and dyers and cleaners (55,000) stand next in importance.

**Furniture Industries.**

153. This only returns 300 persons, and probably they are only domestic, retained to look after palace furniture and the like.

**Building.**

154. The building industry supports 28,000 persons, of whom 17,000 are bricklayers and masons.

**Construction of Means of Transport.**

155. This is also a small Order, 1,300 out of the total of 1,400 being saddlers and harness makers.

**Production and Transmission of Physical Forces.**

156. The State electric works in the cities of Lashkar, Indore and Bhopal provide most of the employment under this head.

**Industries of Luxuries.**

157. The 52,000 supported are mostly jewellers (46,000).

158. These are the contractors for conservancy and sweepers and scavengers (38,000). Industries concerned with Refuse Matter.

159. Of the 52,000 persons supported by transport 37,800 carry on transport by land and of these 22,800 are carters, drivers, etc. Transport by water occupies 1,300, almost all of whom are boatmen plying on the rivers. Of the rest 10,000 are met with on railways and 2,000 in the post and telegraph service. Transport.

160. The 513,900 persons supported by trade are mainly traders in textiles (27,000) and shop-keepers (62,000). Trade.

161. Public administration in its various branches accounts for 490,900 persons. Of these 89,000 are in military service, 8,000 being in the Imperial Service troops; police employ 92,000 and the various branches of the Public Administration 139,000, of whom 69,000 are officials of the various Darbars. Public Administration.

162. The professions employ 138,000, religion claiming the greatest number 94,000. Among these priests, etc., number 54,000, mendicants 32,000, and catechists, etc., about 500. Professions.

163. Those with private incomes number 31,000. They are practically all land owners though a few may have invested funds. A certain number are pensioners. Persons with Private Incomes.

164. This form of occupation supports 214,000 persons and of these 204,800 are indoor servants. Domestic Service.

165. The occupations of 754,000 persons were too insufficiently described to allow of their being classed. Of these 741,000 were workmen and labourers. Insufficiently described Occupations.

166. Jails, asylums and the like accounted for 4,000 out of the 230,000 whose occupations were unproductive; beggars complete the tale. Unproductive.

### *Factory Statistics.*

167. So far no distinction has been made between factories and home industries. The information for factories has been collected in Table XV-E which gives a return for all factories, mills, etc., which were employing 20 or more people on March 10th 1911.

This Table, while it supplies very little material in itself, only 16,000 persons being supported by work in factories, shows to what a small extent industrial enterprise has spread in Central India. Only 144 institutions were working and of these 86 lay in the Gwalior and Indore Residency Political Charges which supported 9,000 persons between them. The weaving mills at Indore employed the largest individual number of hands (2,234). The east of the Agency only shows 19 such institutions of which 17 lie in Baghelkhand and 2 in Bundelkhand.

The factories classified are shown in the inset. The various processes of dealing with cotton claim 105 of these factories; 112 employ steam wholly or in part. Of those employed 12,000 are males and 3,900 are females. The supervision is in the hands of 37 Europeans and Anglo-Indians and 759 Indians while 34 skilled workmen are Europeans or Anglo-Indians and 6,000 are Indians. Of the unskilled labourers who number 5,894 males and 3,233 females, 8,300 are over and 750 are under 14 years of age.

| The classification of factories. | Number. |
|---|---|
| Mines | 4 |
| Ginning factories | 81 |
| Cotton presses | 10 |
| Other factories connected with cotton | 14 |
| Food industries | 12 |
| Other industries | 23 |
| TOTAL | 144 |

Table XV-E. Parts III and IV deal with the owners and managers respectively. The Agarwal Banias head the list, Mahesri Banias and Bohras (Musalman) following, while all classes manage cotton mills or presses.

168. Table XV-D. Subsidiary Table IX and the attached diagram show occupations by religions for the twelve Sub-classes. Occupation and Religion.

The diagram deals with all who are supported by the religion and not with actual workers only.

*Diagram showing the main distribution by occupation (Subclass) for religion.*

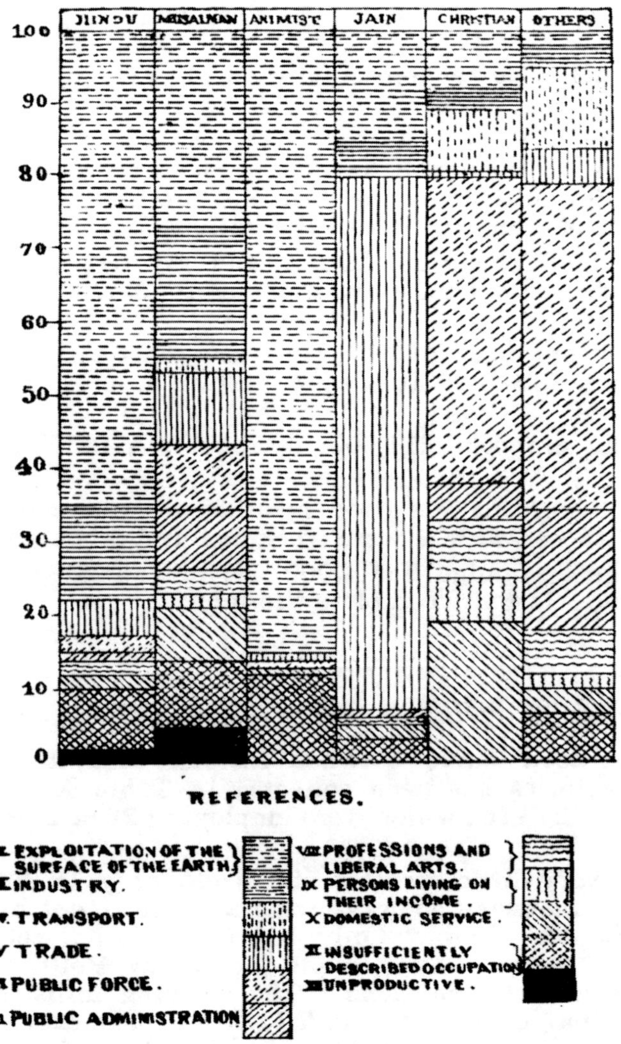


Hindus preponderate showing much the same ratios as the whole population; of this religion, 65 per cent. follow agricultural and pastoral pursuits and 13 per cent. transport (Sub-class IV).

The Muhammadans are also mainly found engaged in agriculture, but 18 per cent. follow trade and 10 per cent. are employed in the army and police as against the 5 per cent. of Hindus.

Animists are almost all engaged in agriculture and pastoral pursuits, 85 per cent. falling under Sub-class I.

Jains, as would be expected, follow trade chiefly, 73 per cent. falling under Sub-class V, while 15 per cent. follow agriculture.

Christians are practically all engaged in the Public force being mainly British soldiers, while 19 per cent. are in domestic service, the latter being Indian-Christians.

"Others" are mainly Sikhs, etc., serving in the army and police.

**Caste and Occupation.**

169. Imperial Table XVI and Subsidiary Table VIII deal with occupation and caste. This shows that now-a-days no caste adheres strictly to its traditional occupation, if indeed it ever did do so.

Thus of Banias 65 per cent. follow trade and 14 per cent. agriculture. Among the various castes of Bania while all follow trade to about this extent, the Agarwals are the most addicted to cultivation, nearly 19 per cent. following this occupation.

Of Bhats 20 per cent. follow the traditional occupation while some 40 per cent. follow various kinds of agricultural labour and 12 per cent. are beggars and criminals, etc.

Of Brahmans only 9 per cent. follow the traditional occupation, 60 per cent. being cultivators. Of the different castes the Shrimalis (27) and the Shrigaud (24) show the highest percentages following the traditional occupation, while the Sarvarias show only 6 per cent.

Rajputs show 13 per cent. following their traditional occupation, about 60 per cent. being agriculturists. The Baghelas stand first with 24 per cent., the Tonwar last with 7 per cent.

Of Musalmans 20 per cent. follow their traditional occupation and serve in the army or police, while about 30 per cent. live on the land. The occupations followed in this case are very varied.

### *Decaying Industries.*

170. Modern conditions have resulted in the decay of many industries once in a flourishing state.

The oil pressing industry has decayed largely owing to the export of the seed and the impossibility of competing with modern machines. Kerosine oil, moreover, has ousted country oil to a great extent as an illuminant. Country oil was formerly used universally by classes who now buy imported oils. The Telis are taking to agriculture, merchandise, preparation of foodstuffs, etc. **Teli.**

The country potter finds that cheap china, empty Kerosine oil tins and enamelled ware are taking the place of earthen vessels. Agriculture, water-carrying and mercantile business are now followed freely by Kumhars. **Kumhar.**

The maker of arms has been almost wholly ousted under modern conditions. They now enter the public service or become carpenters and blacksmiths. **Arms.**

The Patwas find cheap imported ornaments are interfering seriously with this trade. **Patwas.**

Iron articles are replacing stone cut grills, balconies and the like. **Stone workers.**

The old form of transport in *Palkis, palanquins,* and the picturesque and often highly ornamented bullock *rath* used by the rich, has been superseded by motors and modern carriages; hence the manufacture of these means of conveyance is yearly diminishing. **Badhais.**

Fine weaving, for which Malwa was famous, the cloth of Chanderi, Sironj, Sehore and other places being sold all over India, has almost wholly died out in competition with imported cloth. Imported thread has also affected thread makers. **Weaving.**

The lac industry as followed in Central India, where the primitive methods are still largely used, has suffered in competition with the more advanced system introduced in Burma. **Lac.**

The importation of European goods has seriously injured the stamped cloth industry. **Chhipa.**

Powder except for fireworks is now scarcely made anywhere, and even fireworks are to some extent imported. **Barudgar.**

### *Female Occupations.*

171. The actual workers number 3,288,000 males and 2,900,000 females in the Agency as a whole, therefore in every 1,000 actual workers 618 are females.

The maps below give proportions in the Natural Divisions. This shows

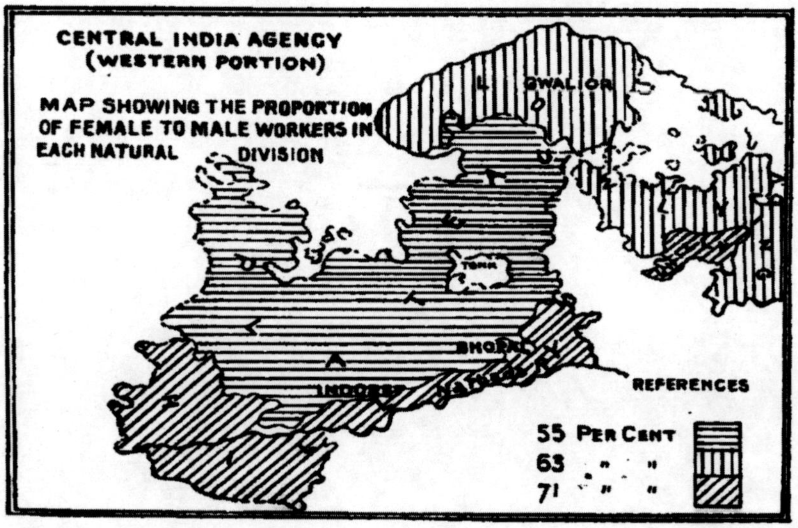


that women work most in the Hilly tract, and least in the Plateau. Towns predominate on the Plateau and with towns the proportions of artisans and traders increases. Women work most where the country is agricultural and pastoral and hence the predominance in the Hilly tract. Looking at the Sub-classes and Groups this soon becomes clear.

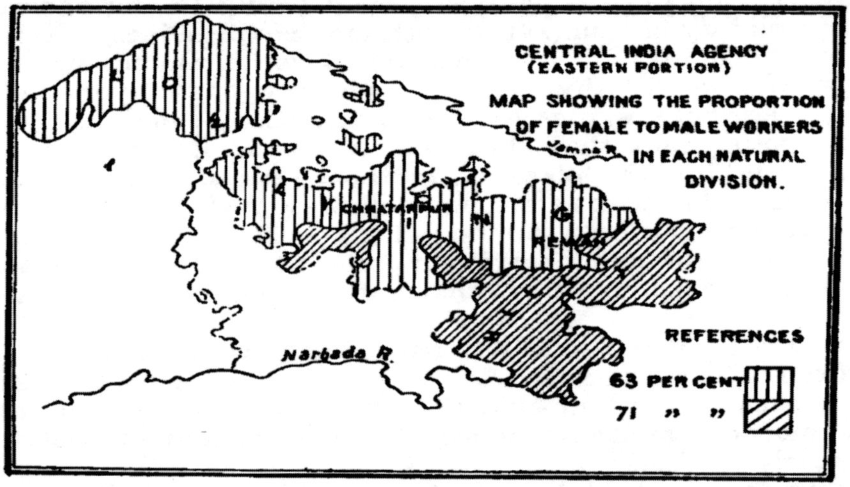


The Orders in which occupations are chiefly feminine are given in the inset.

| Order, group and occupation. | | | Number of females per 1,000 males. |
|---|---|---|---|
| 12 | 56 | Flour-grinders . | 5,200 |
| 28 | 110 | Trade in wood . | 2,500 |
| 48 | 155B | Midwives . | 2,300 |
| 12 | 62 | Sugar-making . | 2,100 |
| 13 | 73 | Toilet industries. | 1,900 |

Certain occupations are almost monopolised by females; these are flour-grinding, midwifery, sugar-making, toilet industries, toymaking and the wood trade. In no case, however, is the total population engaged large. Among occupations in which women take a large share are basket-making in which there are 90 women to 100 men, potters (57), sweepers (71), sellers of grocery and oil, etc. (68), sellers of milk (86), sellers of betel nut, etc. (102), dealers in grass (130), cooks, etc. (55).

SUBSIDIARY TABLE I.—**General Distribution by Occupation.**

| Class, Sub-class and order. | Number per 10,000 of total population. | | Percentage in each class, sub-class and order of | | Percentage of actual workers employed. | | Percentage of dependants to actual worker. | |
|---|---|---|---|---|---|---|---|---|
| | Persons supported. | Actual workers. | Actual workers. | Dependants. | In cities. | In rural areas. | In cities. | In rural areas. |
| 1 | 2 | 3 | 4 | 5 | 6 | 7 | 8 | 9 |
| **CENTRAL INDIA** | **10,000** | **5,686** | **56.9** | **43.1** | **1.8** | **98.2** | **85.6** | **75.7** |
| ***A.—Production of raw materials*** | ***6,362*** | ***3,659*** | ***57.5*** | ***42.5*** | ***0.2*** | ***99.8*** | ***70.4*** | ***73.9*** |
| **I.—Exploitation of surface of the earth** | **6,358** | **3,657** | **57.5** | **42.5** | **0.2** | **99.8** | **71.5** | **73.9** |
| 1. Pasture and agriculture | 6,345 | 3,650 | 57.5 | 42.5 | 0.2 | 99.8 | 72.7 | 73.8 |
| 2. Fishing and hunting | 13 | 7 | 55.5 | 44.5 | 8.5 | 91.5 | 57.4 | 82.2 |
| **II.—Extraction of minerals** | **4** | **2** | **45.2** | **54.8** | **12.2** | **87.8** | **37.1** | **132.9** |
| 3. Mines | 3 | 2 | 48.7 | 51.3 | 15.1 | 84.9 | 37.1 | 117.7 |
| 4. Quarries of hard rock | ... | ... | 28.6 | 76.4 | ... | 100.0 | ... | 323.1 |
| 5. Salt, etc. | 1 | ... | 36.3 | 63.7 | ... | 100.0 | ... | 175.7 |
| ***B.—Preparation and supply of material substances*** | ***1,829*** | ***950*** | ***51.9*** | ***48.1*** | ***4.3*** | ***95.7*** | ***92.8*** | ***91.4*** |
| **III.—Industry** | **1,224** | **645** | **52.1** | **47.3** | **3.8** | **96.2** | **82.0** | **90.1** |
| 6. Textiles | 180 | 103 | 57.4 | 42.6 | 3.5 | 96.5 | 78.5 | 74.1 |
| 7. Hides, skins and hard materials from the animal kingdom | 25 | 13 | 53.0 | 47.0 | 1.7 | 98.3 | 89.2 | 88.7 |
| 8. Wood | 142 | 77 | 53.8 | 46.2 | 2.8 | 97.2 | 75.7 | 86.0 |
| 9. Metals | 76 | 35 | 45.7 | 54.8 | 5.0 | 95.0 | 122.5 | 118.4 |
| 10. Ceramics | 107 | 63 | 58.5 | 41.5 | 2.2 | 97.8 | 70.0 | 71.9 |
| 11. Chemical products properly so called and analogous | 76 | 40 | 53.0 | 47.0 | 1.5 | 98.5 | 84.6 | 88.6 |
| 12. Food industries | 70 | 38 | 55.1 | 44.9 | 11.3 | 88.7 | 68.9 | 83.2 |
| 13. Industries of dress and the toilet | 418 | 209 | 50.0 | 50.0 | 2.9 | 97.1 | 77.1 | 100.9 |
| 14. Furniture industries | ... | ... | 58.4 | 41.6 | 12.7 | 87.3 | 137.2 | 61.6 |
| 15. Building industries | 31 | 15 | 49.7 | 50.3 | 11.7 | 88.3 | 99.4 | 101.5 |
| 16. Construction of means of transport | 2 | 1 | 53.6 | 46.4 | 17.2 | 82.8 | 81.3 | 87.5 |
| 17. Production and transmission of physical forces | ... | ... | 62.1 | 37.9 | 57.6 | 42.4 | 52.9 | 72.0 |
| 18. Industries of luxury and those pertaining to literature and the arts and sciences | 56 | 25 | 43.9 | 56.1 | 5.4 | 94.6 | 113.9 | 128.6 |
| 19. Industries connected with refuse matter | 41 | 26 | 62.6 | 37.4 | 5.1 | 94.9 | 68.5 | 59.2 |
| **IV.—Transport** | **56** | **29** | **51.0** | **49.0** | **10.3** | **89.7** | **96.6** | **95.9** |
| 20. Transport by water | 2 | 1 | 57.4 | 42.6 | 0.8 | 99.2 | 50.0 | 74.3 |
| 21. Transport by road | 40 | 22 | 53.3 | 46.7 | 7.9 | 92.1 | 69.7 | 89.1 |
| 22. Transport by rail | 12 | 5 | 44.0 | 56.0 | 22.8 | 77.2 | 127.6 | 127.5 |
| 23. Post Office, Telegraph and Telephone services | 2 | 1 | 43.1 | 56.9 | 8.3 | 91.7 | 207.3 | 125.4 |
| **V.—Trade** | **549** | **276** | **50.3** | **49.7** | **4.9** | **95.1** | **112.4** | **97.9** |
| 24. Banks, establishments of credit, exchange and insurance | 39 | 16 | 40.7 | 59.3 | 6.7 | 93.3 | 136.2 | 146.1 |
| 25. Brokerage, commission and export | 6 | 2 | 36.8 | 63.2 | 16.1 | 83.9 | 177.6 | 170.4 |
| 26. Trade in textiles | 29 | 14 | 47.8 | 52.2 | 7.2 | 92.8 | 143.5 | 106.4 |
| 27. Trade in skins, leather and furs | 2 | 1 | 43.7 | 56.3 | 2.4 | 97.6 | 131.8 | 128.6 |
| 28. Trade in wood | 2 | 1 | 69.8 | 30.2 | 7.8 | 92.2 | 125.3 | 36.3 |
| 29. Trade in metals | 3 | 1 | 38.3 | 61.7 | 5.8 | 94.2 | 252.9 | 155.7 |
| 30. Trade in pottery | ... | ... | 55.6 | 44.4 | ... | 100.0 | ... | 80.0 |
| 31. Trade in chemical products | 7 | 4 | 53.4 | 46.6 | 2.7 | 97.3 | 100.0 | 87.1 |
| 32. Hotels, cafes, restaurants, etc. | 26 | 12 | 46.5 | 53.5 | 6.1 | 93.9 | 95.7 | 116.7 |
| 33. Other trade in food stuffs | 314 | 164 | 52.2 | 47.8 | 4.4 | 95.6 | 98.0 | 98.2 |
| 34. Trade in clothing and toilet articles | 10 | 7 | 68.0 | 32.0 | 8.2 | 91.8 | 64.5 | 45.5 |
| 35. Trade in furniture | 1 | ... | 50.8 | 49.2 | 6.3 | 93.7 | 170.0 | 91.9 |
| 36. Trade in building materials | ... | ... | 48.3 | 51.7 | 9.4 | 90.6 | 122.7 | 105.7 |
| 37. Trade in means of transport | 5 | 2 | 46.0 | 54.0 | 0.5 | 99.5 | 70.0 | 117.4 |
| 38. Trade in fuel | 14 | 8 | 55.8 | 44.2 | 6.3 | 93.7 | 125.8 | 76.0 |
| 39. Trade in articles of luxury and those pertaining to letters and the arts and sciences | 19 | 10 | 52.4 | 47.6 | 8.2 | 91.8 | 111.6 | 88.9 |
| 40. Trade in refuse matters | ... | ... | 75.0 | 25.0 | ... | 100.0 | ... | 33.9 |
| 41. Trade of other sorts | 72 | 34 | 47.0 | 53.0 | 2.7 | 97.3 | 168.7 | 111.1 |

SUBSIDIARY TABLE I.—**General Distribution by Occupation**—*contd.*

| Class, Sub-class and order. | Number per 10,000 of total population. | | Percentage in each class, sub-class and order of | | Percentage of actual workers employed. | | Percentage of dependants to actual worker. | |
|---|---|---|---|---|---|---|---|---|
| | Persons supported. | Actual workers. | Actual workers. | Dependants. | In cities. | In rural areas. | In cities. | In rural areas. |
| 1 | 2 | 3 | 4 | 5 | 6 | 7 | 8 | 9 |
| ***C.—Public administration and liberal arts*** | *525* | *235* | *44·8* | *55·2* | *13·0* | *87·0* | *99·0* | *126·5* |
| **VI.—Public force** | **195** | **99** | **50·8** | **49·2** | **9·5** | **90·5** | **89·3** | **97·5** |
| 42. Army | 96 | 52 | 54·5 | 45·5 | 13·5 | 86·5 | 96·5 | 81·4 |
| 43. Navy | ... | ... | ... | ... | ... | ... | ... | ... |
| 44. Police | 99 | 47 | 47·3 | 52·7 | 5·2 | 94·8 | 68·5 | 113·8 |
| **VII.—Public administration** | **149** | **60** | **40·4** | **59·6** | **20·9** | **79·1** | **113·2** | **156·7** |
| 45. Public administration | 149 | 60 | 40·4 | 59·6 | 20·9 | 79·1 | 113·2 | 156·7 |
| **VIII.—Professions and liberal arts** | **148** | **62** | **42·1** | **57·9** | **6·3** | **93·7** | **94·4** | **140·3** |
| 46. Religion | 101 | 39 | 38·3 | 61·7 | 4·1 | 95·9 | 96·1 | 163·8 |
| 47. Law | 4 | 1 | 36·4 | 63·6 | 17·1 | 82·3 | 181·8 | 172·8 |
| 48. Medicine | 6 | 3 | 47·4 | 52·6 | 15·8 | 84·2 | 91·5 | 114·5 |
| 49. Instruction | 8 | 3 | 47·1 | 52·9 | 12·9 | 87·1 | 70·3 | 118·4 |
| 50. Letters and arts and sciences | 29 | 16 | 53·7 | 46·3 | 7·3 | 92·7 | 83·4 | 86·5 |
| **IX.—Persons living on their income** | **33** | **14** | **40·7** | **59·3** | **33·6** | **66·4** | **83·8** | **177·3** |
| 51. Persons living principally on their income | 33 | 14 | 40·7 | 59·3 | 33·6 | 66·4 | 83·8 | 177·3 |
| ***D.—Miscellaneous*** | *1,224* | *842* | *65·6* | *34·4* | *2·6* | *97·4* | *58·0* | *52·3* |
| **X.—Domestic service** | **229** | **134** | **58·4** | **41·6** | **5·5** | **94·5** | **69·4** | **71·3** |
| 52. Domestic service | 229 | 134 | 58·4 | 41·6 | 5·5 | 94·5 | 69·4 | 71·3 |
| **XI.—Insufficiently described occupation** | **806** | **533** | **66·1** | **33·9** | **2·0** | **98·0** | **57·4** | **51·8** |
| 53. General terms which do not indicate a definite occupation | 806 | 533 | 66·1 | 33·9 | 2·0 | 98·0 | 57·4 | 51·8 |
| **XII.—Unproductive** | **249** | **175** | **70·5** | **29·5** | **2·2** | **97·8** | **38·4** | **42·0** |
| 54. Inmates of jails and asylums and hospitals | 5 | 4 | 84·5 | 15·5 | 21·9 | 78·1 | 8·2 | 21·2 |
| 55. Beggars, vagrants, prostitutes | 244 | 171 | 70·2 | 29·8 | 1·8 | 98·2 | 46·1 | 42·4 |

SUBSIDIARY TABLE II.—**Distribution by Occupation in Natural Division.**

| Occupation. | Number per mille of total population supported in | | | |
|---|---|---|---|---|
| | Central India. | Plateau. | Lowlying. | Hilly. |
| 1 | 2 | 3 | 4 | 5 |
| *Total* | *1,000* | *1,000* | *1,000* | *1,000* |
| **I.—Exploitation of the surface of the earth** | **636** | **600** | **634** | **695** |
| 1.—(a) **Agriculture** | **607** | **573** | **606** | **660** |
| (1) Income from rent of agricultural land | 13 | 9 | 20 | 10 |
| (2) Ordinary cultivators | 432 | 391 | 443 | 480 |
| (3) Agents, managers of landed estates (not planters), clerks, rent collectors, etc. | 1 | 2 | 1 | 1 |
| (4) Farm servants and field labourers | 159 | 170 | 140 | 168 |
| (5) Tea, coffee, cinchona and indigo plantation | ... | ... | ... | ... |
| (6) Fruit, flower, vegetable, betel, vine, areca nut, etc., growers | 2 | 1 | 2 | 1 |
| (b) **Pasture** | **24** | **21** | **23** | **28** |
| (9) Cattle and buffalo breeders and keepers | 2 | 3 | 1 | 2 |
| (10) Sheep, goat and pig breeders | ... | ... | ... | 1 |
| (11) Breeders of other animals (horses, mules, camels, asses, etc.) | 2 | ... | 3 | 3 |
| (12) Herdsmen, shepherds, goatherds, etc. | 20 | 18 | 19 | 22 |
| (13) Birds, bees, silk worms, etc. | ... | ... | ... | ... |
| 2.—**Fishing and hunting** | **1** | **1** | **1** | **2** |
| *Others (7—8)* | *4* | *5* | *4* | *5* |
| **II.—Extraction of minerals** | ... | ... | **1** | **1** |
| **III.—Industry** | **122** | **132** | **133** | **91** |
| 6. Textile industries | 18 | 17 | 23 | 11 |
| 8. Wood industries | 14 | 14 | 16 | 12 |
| 9. Metal industries | 7 | 7 | 8 | 7 |
| 12. Food industries | 7 | 8 | 7 | 6 |
| 13. Industries of dress and the toilet | 42 | 50 | 43 | 28 |
| Other industries | 34 | 36 | 36 | 27 |
| **IV.—Transport** | **6** | **8** | **3** | **6** |
| **V.—Trade** | **55** | **63** | **53** | **44** |
| 26. Trade in textiles | 3 | 3 | 2 | 3 |
| 32. Hotels, cafes, restaurants, etc. | 3 | 3 | 2 | 3 |
| 33. Other trade in food stuffs | 31 | 32 | 33 | 27 |
| Other trade | 18 | 25 | 16 | 11 |
| **VI.—Public force** | **19** | **22** | **22** | **12** |
| **VII.—Public administration** | **15** | **20** | **15** | **8** |
| **VIII.—Professions and liberal arts** | **15** | **14** | **20** | **8** |
| **IX.—Persons living on their income** | **3** | **5** | **1** | **3** |
| **X.—Domestic service** | **23** | **29** | **21** | **16** |
| **XI.—Insufficiently described occupation** | **81** | **73** | **83** | **90** |
| **XII.—Unproductive** | **25** | **34** | **14** | **26** |

SUBSIDIARY TABLE III.—**Distribution of the agricultural, industrial, commercial and professional population in Natural Division.**

| Natural Division. | Agriculture. | | | | Industry (including mines). | | | |
|---|---|---|---|---|---|---|---|---|
| | Population supported by agriculture. | Proportion of agricultural population per 1,000 of Natural Division population. | Percentage on agricultural population. | | Population supported by industry. | Proportion of industrial population per 1,000 of Natural Division population. | Percentage on industrial population. | |
| | | | Actual workers. | Dependants. | | | Actual workers. | Dependants. |
| 1 | 2 | 3 | 4 | 5 | 6 | 7 | 8 | 9 |
| **CENTRAL INDIA** | **5,675,281** | **607** | **57·1** | **42·9** | **1,149,140** | **123** | **52·6** | **47·4** |
| Plateau | 2,108,441 | 572 | 54·6 | 45·4 | 488,301 | 133 | 48·1 | 51·9 |
| Lowlying | 2,007,526 | 606 | 58·5 | 41·5 | 443,690 | 134 | 55·7 | 44·3 |
| Hilly | 1,559,314 | 660 | 58·6 | 41·4 | 217,149 | 92 | 56·6 | 43·4 |
| **Cities** | **7,060** | **40** | **56·9** | **43·1** | **42,323** | **240** | **55·1** | **44·9** |

SUBSIDIARY TABLE III.—**Distribution of the agricultural, industrial, commercial and professional population in Natural Division.**

| Natural Division. | Commerce. | | | | Professions. | | | | Other occupations. | | | |
|---|---|---|---|---|---|---|---|---|---|---|---|---|
| | Population supported by commerce. | Proportion of commercial population per 1,000 of Natural Division population. | Percentage on commercial population. | | Population supported by profession. | Proportion of professional population per 1,000 of Natural Division population. | Percentage on professional population. | | Population supported by other occupations. | Proportion of other occupation followers per 1,000 of Natural Division population. | Percentage on other occupation followers of | |
| | | | Actual workers. | Dependants. | | | Actual workers. | Dependants. | | | Actual workers. | Dependants. |
| 1 | 10 | 11 | 12 | 13 | 14 | 15 | 16 | 17 | 18 | 19 | 20 | 21 |
| **CENTRAL INDIA** | **566,344** | **60** | **50·4** | **49·6** | **138,390** | **15** | **42·1** | **57·9** | **1,827,825** | **195** | **61·8** | **38·2** |
| Plateau | 263,304 | 71 | 44·6 | 55·4 | 51,372 | 14 | 48·0 | 52·0 | 772,073 | 210 | 57·1 | 42·9 |
| Lowlying | 185,779 | 56 | 55·0 | 45·0 | 66,566 | 20 | 36·2 | 63·8 | 607,142 | 184 | 63·8 | 36·2 |
| Hilly | 117,261 | 49 | 56·1 | 43·9 | 20,452 | 9 | 46·6 | 53·4 | 448,610 | 190 | 67·3 | 32·7 |
| **Cities** | **32,419** | **184** | **47·7** | **52·3** | **7,148** | **41** | **51·4** | **48·6** | **87,110** | **495** | **55·5** | **44·5** |

SUBSIDIARY TABLE IV.—**Occupations combined with agriculture (where agriculture is the subsidiary occupation).**

| OCCUPATION. | NUMBER PER MILLE WHO ARE PARTIALLY AGRICULTURISTS. | | | |
|---|---|---|---|---|
| | Central India. | Plateau. | Lowlying. | Hilly. |
| 1 | 2 | 3 | 4 | 5 |
| ***Total*** | *32* | *24* | *46* | *23* |
| **I.—Exploitation of the Surface of the Earth** | **11** | **6** | **18** | **9** |
| 1.—(*a*). **Agriculture** | **9** | **4** | **16** | **5** |
| (1). Income from rent of agricultural land | ... | .. | ... | ... |
| (2). Ordinary cultivators | ... | ... | ... | ... |
| (3). Agents, managers of landed estates (not planters), clerks, rent collectors, etc. | 70 | 78 | 71 | 41 |
| (4). Farm servants and field labourers | 26 | 9 | 58 | 15 |
| (5). Tea, coffee, cinchona and indigo plantations | ... | ... | ... | ... |
| (6). Fruit, flower, vegetable, betel, vine, areca nut, etc., growers | 100 | 47 | 129 | 60 |
| (*b*). **Pasture** | **64** | **62** | **52** | **77** |
| (9). Cattle and buffalo breeders and keepers | 24 | 21 | 13 | 60 |
| (10). Sheep, goat and pig breeders | 36 | 30 | ... | 17 |
| (11). Breeders of other animals, (horses, mules, camels, asses, etc.) | 25 | 8 | 42 | 9 |
| (12). Herdsmen, shepherds, goatherds, etc. | 72 | 69 | 58 | 86 |
| (13). Birds, bees, silkworms, etc. | 45 | ... | ... | 400 |
| 2.—**Fishing and Hunting** | **107** | **50** | **186** | **108** |
| *Others. (7-8)* | *20* | *18* | *38* | *5* |
| **II.—Extraction of Minerals** | **29** | **8** | **49** | **6** |
| **III.—Industry** | **117** | **85** | **159** | **96** |
| 6. Textile Industries | 80 | 59 | 116 | 38 |
| 8. Wood Industries | 95 | 88 | 116 | 72 |
| 9. Metal Industries | 127 | 87 | 160 | 126 |
| 12. Food Industries | 41 | 11 | 93 | 17 |
| 13. Industries of dress and the toilet | 166 | 119 | 24 | 130 |
| Other Industries | 106 | 67 | 134 | 159 |
| **IV.—Transport** | **72** | **23** | **111** | **141** |
| **V.—Trade** | **98** | **68** | **133** | **92** |
| 26. Trade in textiles | 42 | 21 | 83 | 36 |
| 32. Hotels, cafes, restaurants, etc. | 109 | 84 | 168 | 104 |
| 33. Trade in food stuffs | 100 | 67 | 130 | 96 |
| Other trades | 98 | 75 | 140 | 91 |
| **VI.—Public Force** | **75** | **75** | **71** | **96** |
| **VII.—Public Administration** | **7** | **72** | **75** | **105** |
| **VIII.—Professions and Liberal Arts** | **166** | **59** | **284** | **94** |
| **IX.—Persons Living on their Income** | **26** | **79** | **23** | **50** |
| **X.—Domestic Service** | **47** | **19** | **27** | **37** |
| **XI.—Insufficiently Described Occupations** | **7** | **68** | **9** | **7** |
| **XII.—Unproductive** | **12** | **3** | **14** | **9** |

SUBSIDIARY TABLE V.—**Occupations combined with agriculture (where agriculture is the principal occupation).**

| LANDLORDS (Rent Receivers). Subsidiary Occupation. | Number per 10,000 who follow it. |
|---|---|
| 1 | 2 |
| *Total* | *4,726* |
| (a) **Agricultural** | **3,012** |
| Rent payers | 2,313 |
| Agricultural labourers | 699 |
| (b) **Non-Agricultural** | **1,714** |
| Government employés of all kinds | 88 |
| Money lenders and grain dealers | 337 |
| Other traders of all kinds | 146 |
| Priests | 238 |
| Clerks of all kinds (not Government) | 77 |
| School masters | 25 |
| Lawyers | 5 |
| Estate Agents and Managers | 11 |
| Medical practitioners | 12 |
| Artisans | 50 |
| Others | 725 |

| CULTIVATORS (Rent Payers). Subsidiary Occupation. | Number per 10,000 who follow it. |
|---|---|
| 3 | 4 |
| *Total* | *647* |
| (a) **Agricultural** | **173** |
| Rent receivers | 79 |
| Agricultural labourers | 94 |
| (b) **Non-Agricultural** | **474** |
| General labourers | 93 |
| Government employés of all kinds | ... |
| Money lenders and grain dealers | 33 |
| Other traders of all kinds | 34 |
| Fishermen and boatmen | 10 |
| Cattle breeders and milkmen | 34 |
| Village watchmen | 13 |
| Weavers | 7 |
| Barbers | 14 |
| Oil-pressers | 22 |
| Washermen | 12 |
| Potters | 11 |
| Blacksmiths and carpenters | 17 |
| Others | 174 |

| FARM SERVANTS AND FIELD LABOURERS. Subsidiary Occupation. | Number per 10,000 who follow it. |
|---|---|
| 5 | 6 |
| *Total* | *588* |
| (a) **Agricultural** | **91** |
| Rent receivers | 29 |
| Rent payers | 62 |
| (b) **Non-Agricultural** | **497** |
| General labourers | 166 |
| Village watchmen | 12 |
| Cattle breeders and milkmen | 35 |
| Mill hands | 16 |
| Fishermen and boatmen | 8 |
| Rice pounders | 2 |
| Traders of all kinds | 16 |
| Oil-pressers | 8 |
| Weavers | 18 |
| Potters | 10 |
| Leather workers | 45 |
| Blacksmiths and carpenters | 12 |
| Washermen | 22 |
| Others | 127 |

SUBSIDIARY TABLE VI.—**Occupations of females by subclasses, and selected orders and groups.**

| Group No. | Occupation. | Number of actual workers. Males. | Number of actual workers. Females. | Number of females per 1,000 males. |
|---|---|---|---|---|
| 1 | 2 | 3 | 4 | 5 |
| | **CENTRAL INDIA** | **3,288,363** | **2,032,029** | **618** |
| | **I.—Exploitation of the surface of the earth** | **2,065,646** | **1,356,540** | **657** |
| | 1. Pasture and Agriculture | 2,059,905 | 1,355,300 | 658 |
| 1 | Income from rent of agricultural land | 43,762 | 10,279 | 235 |
| 2 | Ordinary cultivators | 1,425,548 | 711,868 | 499 |
| 4 | Farm servants and field labourers | 452,295 | 584,219 | 1,292 |
| 8 | Wood cutters, firewood, lac, catechu, rubber, etc., collectors and charcoal burners. | 14,367 | 10,781 | 750 |
| 9 | Cattle and buffalo breeders and keepers | 8,617 | 2,296 | 266 |
| 11 | Breeders of other animals (horses, camels, mules, asses, etc.) | 10,113 | 1,568 | 155 |
| 12 | Herdsmen, shepherds, goatherds, etc. | 93,160 | 29,708 | 319 |
| | **II.—Extraction of minerals** | **1,384** | **454** | **328** |
| | **III.—Industry** | **416,117** | **187,117** | **450** |
| | 6. Textiles | 56,373 | 40,065 | 711 |
| 21 | Cotton ginning, cleaning and pressing, | 9,817 | 3,769 | 384 |
| 22 | Cotton spinning, pressing and weaving | 34,117 | 29,922 | 677 |
| 30 | Dyeing, bleaching, printing, preparation and sponging of textiles. | 5,794 | 3,358 | 580 |
| | 7. Hides, skins and hard materials from the animal kingdom | 11,171 | 1,369 | 123 |
| | 8. Wood | 49,369 | 22,303 | 452 |
| 36 | Sawyers, carpenters, turners, and joiners | 26,391 | 1,693 | 64 |
| 37 | Basket makers and other industries of woody material including leaves. | 22,978 | 20,610 | 897 |
| | 9. Metals | 25,595 | 6,794 | 265 |
| 41 | Other workers in iron and makers of implements and tools principally or exclusively of iron | 19,073 | 4,948 | 259 |
| | 10. Ceramics | 36,587 | 21,925 | 599 |
| 47 | Potters and earthen pipe and bowl makers | 32,052 | 18,122 | 569 |
| | 11. Chemical products properly so called and analogous | 21,581 | 16,334 | 758 |
| 53 | Manufacture and refining of vegetable and mineral oils | 19,649 | 15,237 | 775 |
| | 12. Food industries | 19,506 | 16,307 | 836 |
| 56 | Rice pounders and huskers and flour grinders | 1,853 | 9,751 | 5,262 |
| 62 | Makers of sugar, molasses and gur | 41 | 90 | 2,195 |
| | 13. Industries of dress and toilet | 149,756 | 45,736 | 305 |
| 68 | Tailors, milliners, dressmakers and darners, embroiderers on linen | 21,927 | 9,624 | 439 |
| 69 | Shoe, boot, and sandal makers | 72,071 | 20,299 | 282 |
| 71 | Washing, cleaning and dyeing | 19,413 | 14,055 | 724 |
| 72 | Barbers, hairdressers and wig makers | 35,513 | 1,214 | 34 |
| 73 | Other industries connected with the toilet (tattooers, shampooers, bath houses, etc.) | 17 | 33 | 1,941 |
| | 15. Building industries | 11,412 | 2,780 | 244 |
| | 18. Industry of luxury and those pertaining to literature and the arts and sciences | 19,702 | 3,318 | 168 |
| 89 | Workers in precious stones and metals, enamellers, imitation of jewellery makers and gilders, etc. | 17,598 | 2,295 | 130 |
| 91 | Toy, kite, cage, fishing tackle, etc., makers, taxidermists, etc. | 85 | 144 | 1,694 |
| | 19. Industries connected with refuse matter | 14,136 | 10,050 | 711 |
| 93 | Sweepers, scavengers, dust and sweeping contractor | 14,136 | 10,050 | 711 |
| | **IV.—Transport** | **23,611** | **3,130** | **133** |
| | 21. Transport by road | 17,371 | 2,780 | 160 |
| 99 | Cart owners and drivers, coachmen, stable boys, tramway, mail carriage, etc., managers and employés (including private servants) | 10,971 | 1,024 | 93 |
| | **V.—Trade** | **177,151** | **81,540** | **460** |
| | 24. Banks, establishments of credit exchange and insurance | 12,065 | 2,642 | 219 |
| 106 | Bank managers, money lenders, exchange and insurance agents, money changers and brokers and their employés. | 12,065 | 2,642 | 219 |
| | 26. Trade in textile | 11,161 | 1,810 | 162 |
| 108 | Trade in textile piece goods, wool, cotton, silk, hair and other textiles. | 11,161 | 1,810 | 162 |
| | 28. Trade in wood | 343 | 879 | 2,563 |
| 110 | Trade in wood (not firewood, cork, bark, etc.) | 343 | 879 | 2,563 |
| | 32. Hotels, cafes, restaurants, etc. | 8,504 | 2,725 | 320 |

SUBSIDIARY TABLE VI.—**Occupations of females by subclasses, and selected orders and groups.**—*contd.*

| Group No. | Occupation. | Number of actual workers. Males. | Females. | Number of females per 1,000 males. |
|---|---|---|---|---|
| 1 | 2 | 3 | 4 | 5 |
| | **V.—Trade**—*contd.* | | | |
| 114 | Vendors of wine, liquors and aerated waters | 7,941 | 2,159 | 272 |
| | 33. Other trade in food stuffs | 96,745 | 56,789 | 587 |
| 117 | Grocers and sellers of vegetable oil, salt and other condiments | 19,106 | 13,016 | 681 |
| 118 | Sellers of milk, butter, ghee, poultry, eggs | 9,115 | 7,852 | 861 |
| 120 | Cardamom, betel-leaf, vegetables, fruit and arecanut sellers | 11,120 | 11,439 | 1,029 |
| 121 | Grain, pulse dealers | 45,718 | 17,107 | 374 |
| 124 | Dealers in hay, grass and fodder | 3,577 | 4,661 | 1,303 |
| | 41. Trade in other sorts | 23,735 | 7,923 | 330 |
| 135 | Shopkeepers otherwise unspecified | 21,824 | 7,427 | 340 |
| | **VI.—Public Force** | **90,182** | **2,321** | **26** |
| | 44. Police | 41,367 | 2,321 | 56 |
| 143 | Village watchmen | 22,589 | 2,321 | 103 |
| | **VII.—Public Administration** | **54,282** | **2,056** | **38** |
| | 45. Public administration | 54,282 | 2,056 | 38 |
| 145c | Menials | 14,411 | 2,037 | 141 |
| | **VIII.—Profession and liberal arts** | **49,162** | **9,121** | **186** |
| | 46. Religion | 33,161 | 3,087 | 93 |
| 148 | Priests, ministers, etc. | 19,677 | 875 | 44 |
| 19 | Religious mendicants, inmates of monasteries, etc. | 9,886 | 1,990 | 201 |
| 155B | Midwives, vaccinators, compounders, nurses, masseurs, etc. (Native States). | 521 | 1,209 | 2,321 |
| | 50. Letters and arts and sciences | 10,362 | 4,238 | 409 |
| 160 | Music composers and masters, players on all kinds of musical instruments (not military), singers, actors and dancers. | 8,317 | 4,155 | 500 |
| | **IX.—Persons living on their income** | **8,313** | **4,362** | **525** |
| | 51. Persons living on their income | 8,313 | 4,362 | 525 |
| 161 | Proprietors (other than of agricultural land), fund and scholarship holders and pensioners. | 8,313 | 4,362 | 525 |
| | **X.—Domestic service** | **81,543** | **43,565** | **534** |
| | 52. Domestic service | 81,543 | 43,565 | 534 |
| 162 | Cooks, water carriers, door keepers, watchmen and other indoor servants. | 77,503 | 43,032 | 555 |
| | **XI.—Insufficiently described occupations** | **223,103** | **275,887** | **1,237** |
| | 53. General terms which do not indicate a definite occupation | 223,103 | 275,887 | 1,237 |
| 167 | Labourers and workmen otherwise unspecified | 218,249 | 275,641 | 1,263 |
| | **XII.—Unproductive** | **97,869** | **65,936** | **674** |
| | 55. Beggars, vagrants, prostitutes | 94,865 | 65,435 | 690 |
| 169 | Beggars, vagrants, procurers, prostitutes, receivers of stolen goods, cattle poisoners | 64,865 | 65,435 | 690 |

SUBSIDIARY TABLES VII.—**Selected Occupations, 1911 and 1901.**

| Group No. | Occupation. | Population supported in 1911. | Population supported in 1901. | Percentage of variation. |
|---|---|---|---|---|
| 1 | 2 | 3 | 4 | 5 |
| | **I.—Exploitation of the surface of the earth** | **5,949,356** | **4,579,754** | **+29·9** |
| | 1. Pasture and Agriculture | 5,936,785 | 4,573,008 | +29·8 |
| 1 | Income from rent of agricultural land | 123,516 | 234,188 | —47·3 |
| 2 | Ordinary cultivators | 4,038,048 | 3,154,343 | +28·0 |
| 3 | Agents, managers of landed estates (not planters), clerks, rent collectors, etc. | 11,024 | 4,959 | +122·3 |
| 4 | Farm servants and field labourers | 1,488,403 | 924,975 | +60·9 |
| 6 | Fruits, flowers, vegetable, betel, vine, arecanut, etc., growers | 14,140 | 22,184 | —36·3 |
| 8 | Wood cutters, firewood, lac, catechu, rubber, etc., collectors, and charcoal burners. | 37,288 | 43,006 | —13·3 |
| 9 | Cattle and buffalo breeders and keepers | 17,745 | 20,543 | —13·6 |
| 11 | Breeders of other animals (horses, camels, mules, asses, etc.) | 17,402 | 7,839 | +122·0 |
| 12 | Herdsmen, shepherds, goatherds, etc | 182,763 | 148,421 | +23·1 |
| | 2. Fishing and hunting | 12,571 | 6,746 | +86·3 |
| 14 | Fishing | 10,687 | 4,846 | +120·6 |
| | **II.—Extraction of minerals** | **4,067** | **4,600** | **—11·6** |
| | 3. Mines | 3,039 | 2,514 | +20·9 |
| | 4. Quarries of hard rock | 110 | 569 | —80·7 |
| | 5. Salt, etc. | 918 | 1,517 | —39·5 |
| | **III.—Industry** | **1,145,073** | **1,117,644** | **+2·5** |
| | 6. Textiles | 168,021 | 217,665 | —22·8 |
| 21 | Cotton ginning, cleaning and pressing | 26,587 | 25,453 | +4·5 |
| 22 | Cotton spinning, pressing and weaving | 106,726 | 158,335 | —32·6 |
| 26 | Wool carders and spinners, weavers of woollen blankets, carpets, etc. | 11,198 | 9,665 | +15·9 |
| 30 | Dyeing, bleaching, printing, preparation and sponging of textiles. | 17,746 | 18,742 | —5·3 |
| | 7. Hides, skins and hard materials from the animal kingdom | 23,570 | 55,746 | —57·7 |
| 32 | Tanners, curiers, leather dressers and dyers, etc. | 11,036 | 44,925 | —75·3 |
| 33 | Makers of leather articles, such as trunks, water bags, etc. | 12,630 | 10,822 | +16·7 |
| | 8. Wood | 133,102 | 103,592 | +28·5 |
| 36 | Sawyers, carpenters, turners and joiners, etc. | 64,075 | 62,730 | +2·1 |
| 37 | Basket makers and other industries of woody material including leaves. | 69,027 | 40,862 | +68·9 |
| | 9. Metals | 70,801 | 59,152 | +19·7 |
| 41 | Other workers in iron and makers of implements and tools principally or exclusively of iron. | 51,851 | 45,417 | +14·2 |
| 42 | Workers in brass, copper and bell metal | 12·036 | 4,544 | +164·8 |
| | 10. Ceramics | 100·011 | 76,754 | +30·3 |
| 47 | Potters and earthen pipe and bowl makers | 86,035 | 61,551 | +39·8 |
| | 11. Chemical products properly so called and analogous | 71,493 | 56,117 | +27·4 |
| 53 | Manufacture and refining of vegetable and mineral oils | 66,063 | 38,325 | +72·4 |
| | 12. Food industries | 65,028 | 63,708 | +2·1 |
| 56 | Rice pounders and huskers and flour grinders | 18,470 | 21,534 | —14·2 |
| 59 | Butchers | 14,179 | 14,273 | —0·7 |
| 63 | Sweetmeat makers, preparers of jam and condiments | 17,599 | 9,011 | +95·3 |
| | 13. Industries of dress and the toilet | 391,413 | 352,704 | +11·0 |
| 68 | Tailors, milliners, dressmakers and darners, embroiderers on linen. | 59,027 | 48,849 | +20·8 |
| 69 | Shoe, boot, and sandal makers | 189,695 | 160,147 | +18·5 |
| 71 | Washing, cleaning and dyeing | 55,605 | 52,339 | +6·2 |
| 72 | Barbers, hairdressers and wig makers | 84,441 | 81,321 | +3·8 |
| | 14. Furniture industries | 363 | 382 | —5·0 |
| | 15. Building industries | 28,566 | 33,242 | —14·1 |
| 78 | Stone and marble workers, masons and bricklayers | 17,683 | 23,114 | —23·5 |
| | 16. Construction of means of transport | 1,443 | 2,333 | —38·1 |
| | 17. Production and transmission of physical forces | 95 | ... | +100·0 |
| | 18. Industries of luxury and those pertaining to literature and the arts and sciences. | 52,450 | 54,138 | —3·1 |
| 89 | Workers in precious stones and metals, enamellers, imitation jewellery makers and gilders, etc. | 46,592 | 45,297 | +2·9 |
| | 19. Industries concerned with refuse matter | 38,614 | 42,110 | —7·3 |
| 93 | Sweepers, scavengers, dust and sweeping contractors | 38,614 | 42,110 | —7·3 |
| | **IV.—Transport** | **52,412** | **36,420** | **+44·0** |
| | 20. Transport by water | 1,393 | 1,282 | +8·7 |
| | 21. Transport by road | 37,800 | 27,194 | +39·2 |
| 99 | Cart owners, and drivers, coachmen, stable boys, tramway, mail carriage, etc., managers and employés (including private servants.) | 22,858 | 5,739 | +298·3 |
| | 22. Transport by rail | 10,923 | 6,092 | +79·3 |
| 103 | Railway employés of all kinds other than construction coolies | 10,194 | 6,092 | +79·3 |
| | 23. Post Office, Telegraph and Telephone services | 2,296 | 1,852 | +24·0 |

SUBSIDIARY TABLES VII.—**Selected Occupations, 1911 and 1901**—*contd.*

| Group No. | Occupation. | Population supported in 1911. | Population supported in 1901. | Percentage of variation. |
|---|---|---|---|---|
| 1 | 2 | 3 | 4 | 5 |
| | **V.—Trade** | **513,932** | **657,264** | **—21·8** |
| | 24. Banks, establishments of credit, exchange and insurance | 36,093 | 46,414 | —22·6 |
| | 25. Brokerage, commission and export | 5,195 | 9,690 | —46·4 |
| | 26. Trade in textile | 27,121 | 27,095 | +0·1 |
| | 27. Trade in skins, leather and furs | 2,095 | 2,691 | —22·1 |
| | 28. Trade in wood | 1,750 | 29,979 | —94·2 |
| | 29. Trade in metals | 3,159 | 518 | +509·8 |
| | 30. Trade in pottery | 18 | 19,436 | +99 9 |
| | 31. Trade in chemical products | 6,945 | 9,313 | —25·4 |
| | 32. Hotels, cafes, restaurants, etc. | 24,152 | 23,179 | +4·2 |
| 114 | Vendors of wine, liquors and aerated waters | 22,330 | 22,843 | —2·2 |
| | 33. Other trade in food stuff | 294,305 | 324,106 | —9·2 |
| 117 | Grocers and sellers of vegetable oil, salt and their condiments | 62,100 | 59,159 | +5·0 |
| 118 | Sellers of milk, butter, ghee, poultry, eggs, etc. | 29,194 | 28,123 | +3·8 |
| 119 | Sellers of sweetmeats, sugar, gur and molasses | 10,488 | 5,087 | +106·2 |
| 120 | Cardamom, betel-leaf, vegetables, fruit and arecanut sellers | 38,752 | 65,744 | —41·1 |
| 121 | Grain pulse dealers | 130,110 | 93,133 | +39·7 |
| 124 | Dealers in hay, grass and fodder | 13,152 | 52,685 | —75·0 |
| | 34. Trade in clothing and toilet articles | 9,614 | 9,414 | +2·1 |
| | 35. Trade in furniture | 626 | 11,924 | —94·8 |
| | 36. Trade in building materials | 485 | 956 | —49·2 |
| | 37. Trade in means of transport | 4,296 | 3,766 | +14·1 |
| | 38. Trade in fuel | 12,797 | 13,812 | —7·3 |
| | 39. Trade in articles of luxury and those pertaining to letters and arts and sciences. | 17,938 | 16,998 | +5·5 |
| 132 | Dealers in common bangles, bead, necklaces, fans, small articles, toys, hunting and fishing tackle, flowers, etc. | 14,021 | 10,997 | +27·5 |
| | 40. Trade in refuse matters | 4 | ... | +100 |
| | 41. Trade in other sorts | 67,339 | 107,773 | —37·8 |
| 135 | Shopkeepers otherwise unspecified | 62,447 | 99,724 | —37 4 |
| | **VI.—Public Force** | **181,938** | **104,752** | **+73·7** |
| | 42. Army | 89,551 | 83,839 | +6·8 |
| 139 | Army (Government) | 11,474 | 12,454 | —8·0 |
| 140 | Army (Imperial and Native States) | 78,077 | 71,384 | +9·4 |
| | 43. Navy | ... | ... | ... |
| | 44. Police | 92,387 | 20,913 | +341·8 |
| 142 | Police (Government and Native States) | 40,707 | 4,630 | +779·2 |
| 143 | Village watchmen | 51,680 | 16,283 | +217·4 |
| | **VII.—Public administration** | **139,485** | **262,508** | **—46·9** |
| 145 | Service of Native and Foreign States | 108,143 | 251,044 | —56·9 |
| 147 | Village officials and servants other than watchmen | 24,095 | 5,038 | +378·3 |
| | **VIII.—Professions and liberal arts** | **138,390** | **103,099** | **+34·2** |
| | 46. Religion | 94,629 | 63,799 | +48·3 |
| 148 | Priests, ministers, etc. | 54,227 | 37,148 | +46·0 |
| 149 | Religious mendicants, inmates of monasteries, etc. | 32,327 | 9,611 | +236·4 |
| | 47. Law | 3,663 | 3,241 | +13·0 |
| | 48. Medicine | 5,954 | 7,708 | —22·8 |
| | 49. Instruction | 6,951 | 6,588 | +5·5 |
| | 50. Letters and arts and sciences | 27,193 | 21,763 | +24·9 |
| 160 | Music composers and masters, players on all kinds of musical instruments (not military), singers, actors and dancers. | 22,706 | 17,593 | +29·1 |
| | **IX.—Persons living on their income** | **31,173** | **38,817** | **—19·8** |
| | **X.—Domestic service** | **214,177** | **293,583** | **—27·0** |
| 162 | Cooks, water carriers, door keepers, watchmen and other indoor servants. | 204,889 | 279,272 | —26·6 |
| | **XI.—Insufficiently described occupations** | **754,480** | **1,149,240** | **—34·3** |
| 167 | Labourers and workmen otherwise unspecified | 741,728 | 1,109,608 | —33·2 |
| | **XII.—Unproductive** | **232,497** | **281,100** | **—17·3** |
| | 54. Inmates of jails and asylums and hospitals | 4,148 | 5,154 | —19·5 |
| | 55. Beggars, vagrants, procurers, prostitutes | 228,349 | 275,946 | —17·2 |

SUBSIDIARY TABLE VIII.—**Occupation of Selected Castes.**

| Caste and occupation. | Number per 1,000 workers engaged on each occupation | Number of female workers per 100 males. |
|---|---|---|
| 1 | 2 | 3 |
| **Ajana.—Agriculture** | **725** | **44** |
| Field labourers, wood cutters, etc. | 74 | 141 |
| Labourers, unspecified | 152 | 175 |
| Others | 49 | 23 |
| **Bania.—Trade** | **653** | **36** |
| Income from rent of land | 20 | 322 |
| Cultivators of all kinds | 145 | 33 |
| Artisans and other workmen | 9 | 95 |
| Public administration | 5 | ... |
| Arts and professions | 8 | 15 |
| Persons living on their income | 24 | 58 |
| Domestic service | 46 | 20 |
| Labourers, unspecified | 76 | 170 |
| Beggars, prostitutes, criminals and inmates of jails and asylums | 6 | 171 |
| Others | 8 | 29 |
| **Bania Agarwal.—Trade** | **659** | **32** |
| Income from rent of land | 31 | 617 |
| Cultivators of all kinds | 132 | 24 |
| Persons living on their income | 25 | 176 |
| Domestic service | 41 | 19 |
| Labourers, unspecified | 82 | 187 |
| Others | 30 | 21 |
| **Bania Gahohi.—Trade** | **685** | **40** |
| Income from rent of land | 186 | 53 |
| Cultivators of all kinds | 24 | 32 |
| Labourers, unspecified | 71 | 94 |
| Others | 34 | 44 |
| **Bania Mahesri.—Trade** | **598** | **46** |
| Cultivators of all kinds | 90 | 47 |
| Persons living on their income | 54 | 18 |
| Domestic service | 99 | 16 |
| Labourers, unspecified | 87 | 250 |
| Others | 72 | 46 |
| **Bania Oswal.—Trade** | **695** | **27** |
| Cultivators of all kinds | 100 | 53 |
| Artisans and other workmen | 24 | 141 |
| Domestic service | 60 | 15 |
| Labourers, unspecified | 58 | 315 |
| Others | 63 | 67 |
| **Bania Porwal.—Trade** | **650** | **26** |
| Cultivators of all kinds | 123 | 39 |
| Persons living on their income | 29 | 33 |
| Domestic service | 45 | 29 |
| Labourers, unspecified | 105 | 170 |
| Others | 48 | 63 |
| **Bhat.—Legend Singer** | **198** | **38** |
| Income from rent of land | 33 | 17 |
| Cultivators of all kinds | 290 | 51 |
| Field labourers, wood cutters, etc. | 132 | 116 |
| Labourers, unspecified | 120 | 199 |
| Beggars, prostitutes, criminals and inmates of jails and asylums | 118 | 91 |
| Others | 109 | 31 |

SUBSIDIARY TABLE VIII.—**Occupation of Selected Castes**—*contd.*

| Caste and occupation. | Number per 1,000 workers engaged on each occupation. | Number of female workers per 100 males. |
|---|---|---|
| 1 | 2 | 3 |
| **Bhil.—Agriculture** | **537** | **54** |
| Field labourers, wood cutters, etc. | 261 | 156 |
| Raisers of livestock, milkmen and herdsmen | 29 | 35 |
| Artisans and other workmen | 4 | 37 |
| Public force | 5 | ... |
| Public administration | 4 | ... |
| Domestic service | 8 | 41 |
| Labourers, unspecified | 143 | 105 |
| Beggars, prostitutes, criminals and inmates of jails and asylums | 3 | 40 |
| Others | 6 | 39 |
| **Bhilala.—Agriculture** | **864** | **100** |
| Field labourers, wood cutters, etc. | 72 | 103 |
| Raisers of livestock, milkmen and herdsmen | 16 | 37 |
| Domestic service | 7 | 40 |
| Labourers, unspecified | 33 | 62 |
| Others | 8 | 31 |
| **Brahman.—Priest** | **89** | **36** |
| Income from rent of land | 34 | 28 |
| Cultivators of all kinds | 596 | 42 |
| Agents and Managers of landed estates, planters, forest officers and their clerks, rent collectors, etc. | 4 | ... |
| Field labourers, wood cutters, etc. | 60 | 87 |
| Raisers of livestock, milkmen and herdsmen | 8 | 18 |
| Artisans and other workmen | 8 | 33 |
| Labourers, boatmen, carters, palki bearers | 8 | 22 |
| Trade | 13 | 77 |
| Public force | 13 | ... |
| Public administration | 15 | ... |
| Arts and professions | 3 | 9 |
| Persons living on their income | 7 | 48 |
| Domestic service | 24 | 24 |
| Labourers, unspecified | 67 | 131 |
| Beggars, prostitutes, criminals and inmates of jails and asylums | 59 | 69 |
| Others | 2 | 19 |
| **Brahman Bhagor.—Priest** | **148** | **38** |
| Income from rent of land | 52 | 176 |
| Cultivators of all kinds | 489 | 54 |
| Field labourers, wood cutters, etc. | 80 | 220 |
| Labourers, unspecified | 41 | 74 |
| Beggars, prostitutes, criminals and inmates of jails and asylums | 79 | 24 |
| Others | 111 | 15 |
| **Brahman Jijhotia.—Priest** | **157** | **20** |
| Income from rent of land | 87 | 10 |
| Cultivators of all kinds | 393 | 39 |
| Field labourers, wood cutters, etc. | 91 | 133 |
| Public force | 16 | ... |
| Public administration | 21 | ... |
| Domestic service | 32 | 44 |
| Labourers, unspecified | 91 | 127 |
| Beggars, prostitutes, criminals and inmates of jails and asylums | 69 | 81 |
| Others | 43 | 23 |
| **Brahman Sanadhya.—Priest** | **88** | **13** |
| Income from rent of land | 29 | 21 |
| Cultivators of all kinds | 568 | 48 |
| Field labourers, wood cutters, etc. | 54 | 51 |
| Raisers of livestock, milkmen and herdsmen | 7 | 11 |
| Trade | 16 | 28 |
| Public force | 22 | ... |
| Public administration | 17 | ... |
| Persons living on their income | 11 | 20 |
| Domestic service | 28 | 14 |
| Labourers, unspecified | 102 | 151 |
| Beggars, prostitutes, criminals and inmates of jails and asylums | 46 | 29 |
| Others | 12 | 13 |

SUBSIDIARY TABLE VIII.—**Occupation of Selected Castes**—*contd.*

| Caste and occupation. | Number per 1,000 workers engaged on each occupation. | Number of female workers per 100 males. |
|---|---|---|
| 1 | 2 | 3 |
| **Brahman Sarwaria.—Priest** | **59** | **54** |
| Income from rent of land | 23 | 27 |
| Cultivators of all kinds | 687 | 40 |
| Agents and Managers of landed estates, planters, forest officers and their clerks, rent collectors, etc. | 6 | ... |
| Field labourers, wood cutters, etc. | 54 | 82 |
| Raisers of livestock, milkmen and herdsmen | 9 | 25 |
| Labourers, boatmen, carters, palki bearers | 3 | 31 |
| Trade | 11 | 5 |
| Public force | 5 | ... |
| Public administration | 10 | ... |
| Persons living on their income | 4 | 67 |
| Domestic service | 17 | 22 |
| Labourers, unspecified | 47 | 128 |
| Beggars, prostitutes, criminals and inmates of jails and asylums | 61 | 105 |
| Others | 4 | 23 |
| **Brahman Shrigaud.—Priest** | **249** | **99** |
| Cultivators of all kinds | 222 | 25 |
| Field labourers, wood cutters, etc. | 70 | 132 |
| Domestic service | 92 | 37 |
| Labourers, unspecified | 71 | 74 |
| Beggars, prostitutes, criminals and inmates of jails and asylums | 60 | 13 |
| Others | 236 | 14 |
| **Brahman Shrimali.—Priest** | **275** | **217** |
| Cultivators of all kinds | 218 | 56 |
| Public administration | 71 | ... |
| Labourers, unspecified | 90 | 43 |
| Others | 316 | 26 |
| **Dhangar.—Military and Dominant** | **256** | **10** |
| Cultivators of all kinds | 128 | 33 |
| Field labourers, wood cutters, etc. | 103 | 153 |
| Domestic service | 130 | 71 |
| Labourers, unspecified | 216 | 123 |
| Others | 167 | 87 |
| **Gond.—Agriculture and Hunting** | **598** | **84** |
| Field labourers, wood cutters, etc. | 197 | 112 |
| Raisers of livestock, milkmen and herdsmen | 17 | 23 |
| Trade | 5 | 62 |
| Domestic service | 4 | 30 |
| Labourers, unspecified | 165 | 126 |
| Beggars, prostitutes, criminals and inmates of jails and asylums | 6 | 9[illegible] |
| Others | 8 | [illegible]6 |
| **Gujar.—Agriculture** | **660** | **32** |
| Field labourers, wood cutters, etc. | 96 | 58 |
| Raisers of livestock, milkmen and heardsmen | 67 | 9 |
| Artisans and other workmen | 5 | 9 |
| Trade | 6 | 6 |
| Public force | 8 | ... |
| Domestic service | 13 | 16 |
| Labourers, unspecified | 129 | 100 |
| Others | 16 | 35 |
| **Kachera.—Glass and Lac Workers** | **590** | **67** |
| Cultivators of all kinds | 120 | 63 |
| Field labourers, wood cutters, etc. | 112 | 41 |
| Others | 178 | 84 |
| **Khangar.—Watchmen** | **166** | **2** |
| Cultivators of all kinds | 334 | 65 |
| Field labourers, wood cutters, etc. | 159 | 195 |
| Public administration | 23 | ... |
| Domestic service | 45 | 119 |
| Labourers, unspecified | 190 | 103 |
| Others | 84 | 44 |

T

SUBSIDIARY TABLE VIII.—**Occupations of Selected Castes**—*contd.*

| Caste and occupation. | Number per 1,000 workers engaged on each occupation. | Number of female workers per 100 males. |
|---|---|---|
| 1 | 2 | 3 |
| **Kol.—Hunting and collecting Jungle produce** | **277** | **104** |
| Cultivators of all kinds | 89 | 41 |
| Field labourers, wood cutters, etc. | 806 | 110 |
| Raisers of livestock, milkmen and herdsmen | 23 | 34 |
| Persons living on their income | 8 | 7 |
| Domestic service | 18 | 29 |
| Labourers, unspecified | 262 | 163 |
| Beggars, prostitutes, criminals and inmates of jails and asylums | 13 | 31 |
| Others | 9 | 37 |
| **Maratha.—Military and Dominant** | **405** | **7** |
| Cultivators of all kinds | 170 | 75 |
| Field labourers, wood cutters, etc. | 76 | 144 |
| Artisans and other workmen | 66 | 428 |
| Public administration | 23 | ... |
| Domestic service | 78 | 117 |
| Labourers, unspecified | 78 | 181 |
| Others | 104 | 50 |
| **Rajput.—Military and Dominant** | **132** | ... |
| Income from rent of land | 68 | 33 |
| Cultivators of all kinds | 525 | 34 |
| Field labourers, wood cutters, etc. | 113 | 75 |
| Raisers of livestock, milkmen and herdsmen | 15 | 9 |
| Artisans and other workmen | 17 | 43 |
| Trade | 9 | 38 |
| Public administration | 4 | ... |
| Arts and professions | 3 | 21 |
| Persons living on their income | 7 | 101 |
| Domestic service | 27 | 51 |
| Labourers, unspecified | 66 | 115 |
| Beggars, prostitutes, criminals and inmates of jails and asylums | 7 | 50 |
| Others | 7 | 21 |
| **Rajput Baghela.—Military and Dominant** | **239** | ... |
| Income from rent of land | 151 | 24 |
| Cultivators of all kinds | 414 | 44 |
| Field labourers, wood cutters, etc. | 46 | 38 |
| Domestic service | 52 | 46 |
| Labourers, unspecified | 51 | 103 |
| Others | 47 | 30 |
| **Rajput Bhadauria.—Military and Dominant** | **48** | ... |
| Income from rent of land | 170 | 197 |
| Cultivators of all kinds | 614 | 23 |
| Field labourers, wood cutters, etc. | 64 | 144 |
| Labourers, unspecified | 67 | 28 |
| Others | 87 | 92 |
| **Rajput Bundela.—Military and Dominant** | **174** | ... |
| Income from rent of land | 126 | 31 |
| Cultivators of all kinds | 475 | 35 |
| Field labourers, wood cutters, etc. | 118 | 102 |
| Others | 107 | 41 |
| **Rajput Chauhan.—Military and Dominant** | **160** | ... |
| Income from rent of land | 42 | 52 |
| Cultivators of all kinds | 432 | 52 |
| Field labourers, wood cutters, etc. | 151 | 88 |
| Domestic service | 40 | 23 |
| Labourers, unspecified | 90 | 182 |
| Others | 85 | 36 |
| **Rajput Gahalot.—Military and Dominant** | **136** | ... |
| Cultivators of all kinds | 577 | 35 |
| Field labourers, wood cutters, etc. | 133 | 87 |
| Labourers, unspecified | 80 | 107 |
| Others | 74 | 35 |

SUBSIDIARY TABLE VIII.—**Occupations of Selected Castes**—*contd.*

| Caste and occupation. | Number per 1,000 workers engaged on each occupation. | Number of female workers per 100 males. |
|---|---|---|
| 1 | 2 | 3 |
| **Rajput Kachhwaha.—Military and Dominant** | **144** | ... |
| Cultivators of all kinds | 604 | 28 |
| Field labourers, wood cutters, etc. | 68 | 37 |
| Labourers, unspecified | 45 | 122 |
| Others | 139 | 96 |
| **Rajput Ponwar.—Military and Dominant** | **146** | ... |
| Income from rent of land | 46 | 11 |
| Cultivators of all kinds | 484 | 28 |
| Field labourers, wood cutters, etc. | 124 | 48 |
| Artisans and other workmen | 40 | 85 |
| Domestic service | 23 | 26 |
| Labourers, unspecified | 83 | 12 |
| Others | 54 | 12 |
| **Rajput Rathod.—Military and Dominant** | **125** | ... |
| Income from rent of land | 58 | 114 |
| Cultivators of all kinds | 493 | 57 |
| Field labourers, wood cutters, etc. | 119 | 66 |
| Artisans and other workmen | 29 | 12 |
| Domestic service | 34 | 63 |
| Labourers, unspecified | 71 | 104 |
| Others | 71 | 39 |
| **Rajput Tonwar.—Military and Dominant** | **72** | ... |
| Income from rent of land | 62 | 38 |
| Cultivators of all kinds | 696 | 20 |
| Field labourers, wood cutters, etc. | 83 | 29 |
| Labourers, unspecified | 46 | 55 |
| Others | 41 | 24 |
| **Saharia.—Hunting and collecting Jungle produce** | **138** | **15** |
| Cultivators of all kinds | 287 | 55 |
| Field labourers, wood cutters, etc. | 200 | 11 |
| Public force | 28 | ... |
| Domestic service | 14 | 136 |
| Labourers, unspecified | 302 | 134 |
| Beggars, prostitutes, criminals and inmates of jails and asylums | 11 | 107 |
| Others | 20 | 18 |
| **Sondhia.—Agriculture and Dacoity** | **684** | **33** |
| Field labourers, wood cutters, etc. | 200 | 154 |
| Raisers of livestock, milkmen and herdsmen | 36 | 16 |
| Labourers, unspecified | 40 | 79 |
| Others | 40 | 17 |
| **Musalman.—Military and Dominant** | **205** | **2** |
| Income from rent of land | 9 | 39 |
| Cultivators of all kinds | 216 | 42 |
| Agents and managers of landed estates, planters, forest officers and their clerks, rent collectors, etc. | 3 | 34 |
| Field labourers, wood cutters, etc. | 106 | 83 |
| Raisers of livestock, milkmen and herdsmen | 11 | 17 |
| Fishing and hunting | 3 | 51 |
| Artisans and other workmen | 76 | 85 |
| Labourers, boatmen, carters, palki bearers | 11 | 14 |
| Trade | 72 | 42 |
| Public administration | 24 | ... |
| Arts and professions | 23 | 24 |
| Persons living on their income | 20 | 45 |
| Domestic service | 81 | 19 |
| Labourers, unspecified | 95 | 126 |
| Beggars, prostitutes, criminals and inmates of jails and asylums | 47 | 53 |
| Others | 4 | 4 |

SUBSIDIARY TABLE VIII.—**Occupations of Selected Castes**—*concld*

| Caste and occupation. | Number per 1,000 workers engaged on each occupation. | Number of female workers per 100 males. |
|---|---|---|
| 1 | 2 | 3 |
| **Musalman Pathan.—Military and Dominant** | **234** | ... |
| Income from rent of land | 10 | 36 |
| Cultivators of all kinds | 229 | 42 |
| Field labourers, wood cutters etc. | 17 | 87 |
| Raisers of livestock, milkmen and herdsmen | 10 | 21 |
| Artisans and other workmen | 72 | 97 |
| Labourers, boatmen, carters, palki bearers | 12 | 19 |
| Trade | 55 | 44 |
| Public administration | 27 | ... |
| Arts and professions | 21 | 28 |
| Persons living on their income | 21 | 46 |
| Domestic service | 74 | 24 |
| Labourers, unspecified | 88 | 97 |
| Beggars, prostitutes, criminals and inmates of jails and asylums | 42 | 37 |
| Others | 8 | 23 |
| **Musalman Sayad.—Military and Dominant** | **265** | ... |
| Income from rent of land | 200 | 29 |
| Field labourers, wood cutters, etc. | 87 | 138 |
| Artisans and other workmen | 55 | 108 |
| Trade | 52 | 35 |
| Public administration | 25 | ... |
| Persons living on their income | 31 | 45 |
| Domestic service | 64 | 34 |
| Labourers, unspecified | 41 | 73 |
| Beggars, prostitutes, criminals and inmates of jails and asylums | 109 | 80 |
| Others | 68 | 21 |
| **Musalman Shaikh.—Military and Dominant** | **171** | **5** |
| Income from rent of land | 7 | 35 |
| Cultivators of all kinds | 197 | 46 |
| Field labourers, wood cutters, etc. | 116 | 75 |
| Raisers of livestock, milkmen and herdsmen | 13 | 16 |
| Artisans and other workmen | 84 | 76 |
| Labourers, boatmen, carters, palki bearers | 9 | 10 |
| Trade | 89 | 42 |
| Public administration | 22 | 20 |
| Arts and professions | 24 | ... |
| Persons living on their income | 16 | 44 |
| Domestic service | 90 | 16 |
| Labourers, unspecified | 111 | 155 |
| Beggars, prostitutes, criminals and inmates of jails and asylums | 40 | 56 |
| Others | 11 | 29 |
| **Christians** (excluding Indian Christians) | ... | ... |
| Owners, managers, ships' officers, etc. | 65 | ... |
| Public force | 846 | ... |
| Arts and professions | 55 | 48 |
| Others | 34 | 40 |
| **Anglo-Indians** | ... | ... |
| | | ... |
| Owners, managers, ships' officers, etc. | 446 | ... |
| Arts and professions | 315 | 56 |
| Others | 239 | 42 |
| **Europeans** | ... | ... |
| Owners, managers, ships' officers, etc. | 42 | ... |
| Public force | 895 | ... |
| Arts and professions | 39 | 44 |
| Others | 24 | 22 |

SUBSIDIARY TABLE IX.—**Occupations by Religion for Orders and selected Groups.**

| Orders and selected groups. | Distribution by religion of 10,000 persons following each occupation. | | | | | | Distribution by occupation of 10,000 persons of each religion. | | | | | |
|---|---|---|---|---|---|---|---|---|---|---|---|---|
| | Hindu. | Musalman. | Animist. | Jain. | Christian. | Others. | Hindu. | Musalman. | Animist. | Jain. | Christian. | Others. |
| 1 | 2 | 3 | 4 | 5 | 6 | 7 | 8 | 9 | 10 | 11 | 12 | 13 |
| **CENTRAL INDIA** | **8,830** | **546** | **517** | **94** | **10** | **3** | **10,000** | **10,000** | **10,000** | **10,000** | **10,000** | **10,000** |
| **1.—Pasture and Agriculture** | **9,057** | **232** | **688** | **22** | **1** | .. | **6,507** | **2,699** | **8,445** | **1,422** | **827** | **164** |
| 1. Income from rent of agricultural land | 9,399 | 447 | 97 | 56 | 1 | .. | 141 | 108 | 25 | 80 | 7 | 17 |
| 2. Ordinary cultivators | 9,031 | 220 | 719 | 28 | 2 | .. | 4,414 | 1,741 | 6,001 | 1,305 | 738 | 123 |
| 3. Agents, managers of landed estates (not planters), clerks, rent collectors, etc. | 6,081 | 3,848 | 21 | 49 | .. | 1 | 8 | 83 | .. | 6 | .. | 3 |
| 4. Farm servants and field labourers | 9,108 | 213 | 675 | 4 | .. | .. | 1,641 | 619 | 2,080 | 73 | 19 | 3 |
| 6. Fruit, flowers, vegetable, betel vine, arecanut, etc., growers | 9,484 | 439 | 40 | 11 | 26 | .. | 16 | 12 | 1 | 2 | 40 | .. |
| 8. Wood cutters, firewood, lac, catechu, rubber, etc., collectors and charcoal burners | 8,057 | 221 | 1,722 | .. | .. | .. | 36 | 16 | 141 | .. | .. | .. |
| 9. Cattle and buffalo breeders and keepers | 9,526 | 434 | 29 | 11 | .. | .. | 20 | 15 | 1 | 2 | .. | .. |
| 11. Breeders of other animals (horses, camels, mules, asses, etc.) | 9,106 | 154 | 734 | 6 | .. | .. | 19 | 5 | 26 | 1 | .. | .. |
| 12. Herdsmen, shepherds, goatherds, etc. | 9,356 | 174 | 468 | 1 | 1 | .. | 207 | 62 | 18 | 2 | 11 | .. |
| **2.—Fishing and Hunting** | **8,904** | **904** | **192** | .. | .. | .. | **14** | **22** | **5** | .. | .. | .. |
| 14. Fishing | 9,006 | 972 | 22 | .. | .. | .. | 12 | 20 | .. | .. | .. | .. |
| **3.—Mines** | **8,045** | **1,869** | **30** | **39** | **10** | **7** | **3** | **11** | .. | **1** | **3** | **7** |
| **4.—Quarries of hard rocks** | **9,727** | **273** | .. | .. | .. | .. | .. | .. | .. | .. | .. | .. |
| **5.—Salt, etc.** | **6,253** | **3,671** | .. | **76** | .. | .. | **1** | **7** | .. | **1** | .. | .. |
| **6.—Textiles** | **8,020** | **1,900** | **53** | **25** | **1** | **1** | **163** | **625** | **19** | **48** | **11** | **45** |
| 21. Cotton ginning, cleaning and pressing | 5,772 | 4,206 | .. | 18 | .. | 4 | 19 | 210 | .. | 5 | .. | 24 |
| 22. Cotton spinning, pressing and weaving | 8,957 | 938 | 77 | 27 | 1 | .. | 116 | 196 | 17 | 33 | 11 | .. |
| 26. Wool carders and spinners, weavers of woollen blankets, carpets, etc. | 9,706 | 289 | 5 | .. | .. | .. | 13 | 6 | .. | .. | .. | .. |
| 30. Dyeing, bleaching, printing, preparation and sponging of textiles | 4,293 | 5,691 | 2 | 12 | .. | 2 | 9 | 198 | .. | 3 | .. | 10 |
| **7.—Hides, skins and hard materials from the animal kingdom** | **9,817** | **179** | **4** | .. | .. | .. | **28** | **8** | .. | .. | .. | .. |
| 32. Tanners, curriers, leather dressers and dyers, etc. | 9,797 | 202 | .. | .. | .. | .. | 13 | 4 | .. | .. | .. | .. |
| 33. Makers of leather articles, such as trunks, water bags, etc. | 9,836 | 160 | 4 | .. | .. | .. | 15 | 4 | .. | .. | .. | .. |
| **8.—Wood** | **9,870** | **90** | **36** | **3** | **1** | .. | **159** | **23** | **10** | **4** | **6** | **10** |
| 36. Sawyers, carpenters, and joiners, etc. | 9,833 | 142 | 19 | 5 | 1 | .. | 76 | 18 | 3 | 3 | 6 | .. |
| 37. Basket makers and other industries of woody material including leaves | 9,904 | 42 | 52 | .. | 1 | 1 | 83 | 5 | 7 | 1 | .. | 10 |
| **9.—Metals** | **8,717** | **1,252** | **13** | **18** | .. | .. | **75** | **173** | **2** | **14** | .. | **10** |
| 41. Other workers in iron and makers of implements and tools principally or exclusively of iron | 8,774 | 1,206 | 17 | 3 | .. | .. | 55 | 122 | 2 | 2 | .. | 7 |
| 42. Workers in brass, copper and bell metal | 9,349 | 580 | 1 | 69 | .. | 1 | 14 | 14 | .. | 10 | .. | 8 |
| **10.—Ceramics** | **9,691** | **301** | **7** | **1** | .. | .. | **117** | **59** | **1** | **1** | .. | .. |
| 47. Potters and earthen pipe and bowl makers | 9,966 | 29 | 5 | .. | .. | .. | 104 | 5 | 1 | .. | .. | .. |
| **11.—Chemical products properly so called and analogous** | **9,709** | **279** | **11** | **1** | .. | .. | **84** | **39** | **2** | **1** | .. | .. |
| 53. Manufacture and refining of vegetable and mineral oils | 9,925 | 69 | 5 | 1 | .. | .. | 70 | 9 | 1 | 1 | .. | .. |
| **12.—Food industries** | **7,878** | **1,808** | **57** | **251** | **3** | **3** | **60** | **230** | **8** | **387** | **16** | **68** |
| 56. Rice pounders and huskers and flour grinders | 7,967 | 1,627 | 155 | 250 | 1 | .. | 18 | 59 | 6 | 53 | 1 | .. |
| 59. Butchers | 5,387 | 4,608 | 5 | .. | .. | .. | 9 | 128 | .. | .. | .. | .. |
| 63. Sweetmeat makers, preparers of jam and condiments, etc. | 8,338 | 186 | 22 | 1,454 | .. | .. | 18 | 6 | 1 | 202 | .. | .. |
| **13.—Industries of dress and the toilet** | **9,665** | **323** | **3** | **5** | **2** | **2** | **159** | **247** | **2** | **21** | **92** | **182** |
| 68. Tailors, milliners, dressmakers and darners, embroiderers on linen | 9,172 | 771 | 14 | 30 | 12 | 1 | 66 | 80 | 2 | 20 | 77 | 17 |
| 69. Shoe, boot and sandal makers | 9,878 | 119 | .. | .. | .. | 3 | 227 | 44 | .. | .. | 6 | 161 |
| 71. Washing, cleaning and dyeing | 9,312 | 886 | .. | .. | 2 | .. | 63 | 75 | .. | .. | 9 | .. |
| 72. Barbers, hairdressers and wig makers | 9,824 | 175 | 1 | .. | .. | .. | 100 | 29 | .. | .. | .. | .. |

SUBSIDIARY TABLE IX.—**Occupation by Religion for Orders and selected Groups**—*contd.*

| Orders and selected groups. | Distribution by religion of 10,000 persons following each occupation. | | | | | | Distribution by occupation of 10,000 persons of each religion. | | | | | |
|---|---|---|---|---|---|---|---|---|---|---|---|---|
| | Hindu. | Musalman. | Animist. | Jain. | Christian. | Others. | Hindu. | Musalman. | Animist. | Jain. | Christian. | Others. |
| 1 | 2 | 3 | 4 | 5 | 6 | 7 | 8 | 9 | 10 | 11 | 12 | 13 |
| **14.—Furniture industries** | **3,774** | **6,226** | .. | .. | .. | .. | .. | **4** | .. | .. | .. | .. |
| **15.—Building industries** | **7,902** | **2,056** | **28** | **14** | .. | .. | **27** | **115** | **2** | **5** | **1** | .. |
| 78. Stone and marble workers, masons and bricklayers | 7,791 | 2,183 | 25 | 1 | .. | .. | 17 | 76 | 1 | .. | .. | .. |
| **16.—Construction of means of transport** | **9,723** | **201** | **48** | **21** | **7** | .. | **2** | **1** | .. | .. | **1** | .. |
| **17.—Production and transmission of physical forces** | **5,789** | **3,474** | .. | .. | **737** | .. | .. | **2** | .. | .. | **8** | .. |
| **18.—Industries of luxury and those pertaining to literature and the arts and sciences** | **8,414** | **1,543** | .. | **33** | **9** | **1** | **53** | **158** | .. | **20** | **48** | **17** |
| 89. Workers in precious stones and metals, enamellers, imitation jewellery makers and gilders | 8,653 | 1,312 | .. | 35 | .. | .. | 49 | 120 | .. | 19 | .. | .. |
| **19.—Industries concerned with refuse matter** | **8,690** | **1,286** | **10** | **1** | **11** | **2** | **41** | **97** | **1** | .. | **46** | **24** |
| 93. Sweepers, scavengers, dust and sweeping contractors | 8,690 | 1,286 | 10 | 1 | 11 | 2 | 41 | 97 | 1 | .. | 46 | 24 |
| **20.—Transport by water** | **9,382** | **553** | **36** | **29** | .. | .. | **2** | **1** | .. | .. | .. | .. |
| **21.—Transport by road** | **7,510** | **2,304** | **139** | **35** | **4** | **8** | **34** | **170** | **11** | **15** | **16** | **110** |
| 99. Cart owners, and drivers, coachmen, stable boys, tramway, mail carriage, etc., managers and employés (including private servants) | 6,753 | 2,996 | 189 | 47 | 7 | 8 | 19 | 134 | 9 | 12 | 16 | 65 |
| **22.—Transport by rail** | **6,613** | **2,252** | **176** | **39** | **660** | **260** | **9** | **48** | **4** | **5** | **771** | **973** |
| 103. Railway employés of all kinds other than construction coolies | 6,515 | 2,388 | 79 | 42 | 704 | 272 | 8 | 48 | 2 | 5 | 767 | 95 |
| **23.—Post Office, Telegraph and Telephone services** | **7,400** | **1,912** | **505** | **9** | **139** | **35** | **2** | **9** | **2** | .. | **34** | **27** |
| **24.—Banks, establishments of credit, exchange and insurance** | **6,648** | **354** | **4** | **2,990** | .. | **4** | **29** | **25** | .. | **1,234** | .. | **55** |
| 106. Bank managers, money lenders, exchange and insurance agents, money changers and brokers and their employés. | 6,648 | 354 | 4 | 2,990 | .. | 4 | 29 | 25 | .. | 1,234 | .. | 55 |
| **25.—Brokerage, commission and export** | **7,111** | **776** | **13** | **2,089** | **12** | .. | **4** | **8** | .. | **124** | **6** | .. |
| 107. Brokers, commission agents, commercial travellers, warehouse owners and employés | 7,111 | 776 | 13 | 2,089 | 12 | .. | 4 | 8 | .. | 124 | 6 | .. |
| **26.—Trade in textiles** | **6,538** | **1,313** | **2** | **2,134** | **12** | **1** | **21** | **70** | .. | **662** | **35** | **7** |
| 108. Trade in textile piece-goods, wool, cotton, silk, hair and other textiles | 6,583 | 1,313 | 2 | 2,134 | 12 | 1 | 21 | 70 | .. | 662 | 35 | 7 |
| **27.—Trade in skins, leather and furs** | **7,207** | **1,356** | **14** | **1,418** | **5** | .. | **2** | **5** | .. | **34** | **1** | .. |
| **28.—Trade in wood** | **7,497** | **1,394** | **772** | **337** | .. | .. | **2** | **5** | **3** | **7** | .. | .. |
| **29.—Trade in metals** | **6,895** | **2,976** | **81** | **48** | .. | .. | **3** | **13** | **1** | **2** | .. | .. |
| **30.—Trade in pottery** | **5,000** | **2,222** | .. | **2,778** | .. | .. | .. | .. | .. | **1** | .. | .. |
| **31.—Trade in chemical products** | **6,554** | **3,374** | **29** | **30** | **4** | **9** | **6** | **46** | .. | **2** | **3** | **20** |
| **32.—Hotels, cafes, restaurants, etc.** | **9,263** | **590** | **43** | **68** | **9** | **22** | **27** | **28** | **2** | **19** | **24** | **125** |
| 114. Vendors of wine, liquors and aerated waters | 9,433 | 420 | 46 | 74 | 3 | 24 | 25 | 18 | 2 | 10 | 7 | 116 |
| **33.—Other trade in food stuffs.** | **7,974** | **822** | **102** | **1,162** | .. | .. | **284** | **473** | **62** | **3,706** | **11** | **41** |
| 117. Grocers and sellers of vegetable oil, salt and their condiments. | 7,833 | 1,121 | 29 | 1,016 | 1 | .. | 59 | 195 | 4 | 722 | 6 | .. |
| 118. Sellers of milk, butter, ghee, poultry, eggs | 9,583 | 315 | 3 | 98 | 1 | .. | 34 | 18 | .. | 33 | 3 | .. |
| 119. Sellers of sweetmeats, sugar, gur and molasses | 9,298 | 172 | 2 | 528 | .. | .. | 12 | 4 | .. | 63 | .. | .. |
| 120. Caradmom, betel-leaf, vegetables, fruit and arecanut sellers | 8,757 | 1,175 | 54 | 14 | .. | .. | 41 | 89 | 4 | 6 | .. | .. |
| 121. Grain and pulse dealers | 7,491 | 623 | 5 | 1,881 | .. | .. | 118 | 150 | 1 | 2,797 | 1 | 21 |
| 124. Dealers in hay, grass and fodder | 6,571 | 1,511 | 1,918 | .. | .. | .. | 10 | 39 | 52 | .. | .. | .. |

SUBSIDIARY TABLE IX.—**Occupation by Religion for Orders and selected Groups**—*concld.*

| Orders and selected groups. | Distribution by religion of 10,000 persons following each occupation. | | | | | | Distribution by occupation of 10,000 persons of each religion. | | | | | |
|---|---|---|---|---|---|---|---|---|---|---|---|---|
| | Hindu. | Musalman. | Animist. | Jain. | Christian. | Others. | Hindu. | Musalman. | Animist. | Jain. | Christian. | Others. |
| 1 | 2 | 3 | 4 | 5 | 6 | 7 | 8 | 9 | 10 | 11 | 12 | 13 |
| **34.—Trade in clothing and toilet articles** | **4,842** | **4,760** | .. | **398** | .. | .. | **6** | **89** | .. | **44** | .. | .. |
| **35.—Trade in furniture** | **8,418** | **1,358** | .. | **224** | .. | .. | **1** | **2** | .. | **2** | .. | .. |
| **36.—Trade in building materials** | **7,981** | **2,011** | .. | .. | .. | .. | .. | **2** | .. | .. | .. | .. |
| **37.—Trade in means of transport** | **8,121** | **1,578** | **203** | **98** | .. | .. | **4** | **13** | **2** | **5** | .. | .. |
| **38.—Trade in fuel** | **7,731** | **1,068** | **1,168** | **31** | .. | **2** | **12** | **27** | **31** | **5** | .. | **10** |
| 130. Dealers in firewood, charcoal, coal, cowdung, etc. | 7,731 | 1,068 | 1,168 | 31 | .. | 2 | 12 | 27 | 31 | 4 | .. | 10 |
| **39.—Trade in articles of luxury and those pertaining to letters and arts and sciences** | **7,269** | **2,215** | .. | **513** | .. | **3** | **16** | **78** | .. | **105** | .. | **14** |
| 132. Dealers in common bangles, bead, necklaces, fans, small articles, toys, hunting and fishing tackle, flowers | 7,308 | 2,678 | .. | 14 | .. | .. | 12 | 73 | .. | 2 | .. | .. |
| **40.—Trade in refuse matters.** | **10,000** | .. | .. | .. | .. | .. | .. | .. | .. | .. | .. | .. |
| **41.—Trade in other sorts** | **7,145** | **1,160** | **4** | **1,682** | **2** | **5** | **58** | **153** | **1** | **1,295** | **15** | **123** |
| 135. Shop-keepers otherwise unspecified | 7,152 | 1,031 | 4 | 1,805 | 2 | 6 | 54 | 126 | 1 | 1,288 | 15 | 120 |
| **42.—Army** | **6,742** | **2,618** | **68** | **3** | **434** | **135** | **73** | **459** | **13** | **3** | **4,158** | **4,128** |
| 139. Army (Government) | 3,345 | 2,500 | 138 | .. | 3,328 | 689 | 5 | 156 | 3 | .. | 4,080 | 2,710 |
| 140. Army (Native States and Imperial Service) | 7,281 | 2,635 | 58 | 3 | 10 | 53 | 68 | 403 | 10 | 3 | 78 | 1,418 |
| **43.—Navy** | .. | .. | .. | .. | .. | .. | .. | .. | .. | .. | .. | .. |
| **44.—Police** | **7,379** | **2,190** | **406** | **7** | **5** | **13** | **83** | **396** | **78** | **8** | **50** | **418** |
| 142. Police (Native States and Government) | 5,325 | 4,275 | 355 | 3 | 12 | 30 | 26 | 341 | 30 | 1 | 50 | 418 |
| 143. Village watchmen | 8,996 | 547 | 446 | 11 | .. | .. | 57 | 55 | 48 | 7 | .. | .. |
| **45.—Public administration** | **6,979** | **2,7** | **104** | **64** | **35** | **33** | **118** | **760** | **30** | **103** | **516** | **1,572** |
| 145B. Durbar officials | 7,124 | 2,713 | .. | 108 | 35 | 20 | 60 | 348 | .. | 86 | 254 | 480 |
| 145C. Menials | 5,506 | 4,417 | 13 | 19 | 4 | 41 | 26 | 333 | 1 | 8 | 18 | 534 |
| 147. Village officials and servants other than watchmen | 9,046 | 342 | 581 | 31 | .. | .. | 26 | 16 | 27 | 9 | .. | .. |
| **46.—Religion** | **9,636** | **250** | **18** | **46** | **42** | **8** | **110** | **46** | **3** | **50** | **427** | **240** |
| 148. Priests, ministers, etc. | 9,764 | 167 | 6 | 41 | 11 | 11 | 64 | 19 | 1 | 25 | 62 | 212 |
| 149. Religious mendicants, inmates of monasteries, etc. | 9,643 | 247 | 40 | 64 | 5 | 1 | 38 | 16 | 3 | 24 | 18 | 7 |
| **47.—Law** | **7,144** | **2,697** | .. | **115** | .. | **44** | **3** | **19** | .. | **5** | .. | **55** |
| **48.—Medicine** | **7,366** | **2,410** | **29** | **54** | **176** | **25** | **5** | **28** | .. | **4** | **112** | **51** |
| **49.—Instruction** | **7,941** | **1,790** | **12** | **63** | **131** | **63** | **7** | **24** | .. | **5** | **97** | **151** |
| **50.—Letters and arts and sciences** | **7,322** | **2,584** | **45** | **6** | **35** | **8** | **24** | **137** | **3** | **2** | **103** | **79** |
| 160. Music composers and masters, players on all kinds of musical instruments (not military), singers, actors, and dancers | 7,135 | 2 800 | 51 | 7 | 7 | .. | 20 | 163 | 2 | 2 | 16 | .. |
| **51.—Persons living principally on their income.** | **6,326** | **3,362** | **24** | **102** | **165** | **21** | **24** | **205** | **2** | **36** | **550** | **223** |
| 161. Proprietors (other than of agricultural land) fund and scholarship and pensioners | 6,326 | 3,362 | 24 | 102 | 165 | 21 | 24 | 205 | 2 | 36 | 550 | 223 |
| **52.—Domestic service** | **7,969** | **1,722** | **143** | **84** | **84** | **4** | **206** | **722** | **68** | **212** | **1,925** | **301** |
| 162. Cooks, water carriers, door keepers, watchmen and other indoor servants | 8,001 | 1,694 | 140 | 90 | 72 | 3 | 198 | 679 | 59 | 211 | 1,571 | 202 |
| **53.—General terms which do not indicate a definite occupation** | **8,619** | **596** | **745** | **34** | **1** | **3** | **787** | **883** | **1,163** | **296** | **43** | **[illegible]** |
| 167. Labourers and workmen otherwise unspecified | 8,634 | 582 | 754 | 29 | 1 | .. | 775 | 845 | 1,158 | 244 | 38 | 69 |
| **54.—Inmates of jails and asylums and hospitals** | **8,194** | **1,005** | **702** | **10** | **89** | .. | **4** | **8** | **6** | .. | **40** | .. |
| **55.—Beggars, vagrants, prostitutes** | **8,769** | **17 0** | **49** | **12** | .. | .. | **242** | **523** | **23** | **32** | **4** | .. |
| 169. Beggars, vagrants, procurers, prostitutes, receivers of stolen goods, cattle poisoners | 8,769 | 1,170 | 49 | 12 | .. | .. | 242 | 523 | 23 | 32 | 4 | .. |

SUBSIDIARY TABLE X.—**Number of persons employed on the 10th March 1911 on Railways and in the Irrigation, Post Office and Telegraph Departments.**

| Class of persons employed. | Europeans and Anglo-Indians. | Indians. |
|---|---|---|
| 1 | 2 | 3 |
| **RAILWAYS.** | | |
| *Total Persons Employed* | *188* | *8,641* |
| **Persons directly employed** | **186** | **6,737** |
| Officers | 15 | ... |
| Subordinates drawing more than Rs. 75 per mensem | 134 | 46 |
| Subordinates drawing from Rs. 20 to Rs. 75 per mensem | 37 | 885 |
| Subordinates drawing under Rs. 20 per mensem | ... | 5,806 |
| **Persons indirectly employed** | **2** | **1,904** |
| Contractors | 2 | 107 |
| Contractor's regular employés | ... | 164 |
| Coolies | ... | 1,633 |
| **IRRIGATION DEPARTMENT.** | | |
| *Total Persons Employed* | *28* | *29,010* |
| **Persons directly employed** | **4** | **791** |
| Officers | 4 | 34 |
| Upper subordinates | ... | 99 |
| Lower subordinates | ... | 290 |
| Peons and other servants | ... | 339 |
| Coolies | ... | 29 |
| **Persons indirectly employed** | **24** | **28,219** |
| Contractors | 2 | 310 |
| Contractor's regular employés | 22 | 1,295 |
| Mistri | ... | 46 |
| Dâk Runners | ... | 8 |
| Coolies | ... | 26.560 |
| **POSTAL DEPARTMENT.** | | |
| *Total Persons Employed* | ... | *1,157* |
| Officers (including probationery Superintendents and Inspectors, and all officers of higher rank than these) | ... | 18 |
| Postmasters (including Deputy, Assistant, Sub and Branch Postmasters) | ... | 161 |
| Miscellaneous Agents, School Masters, Station Masters, etc. | ... | 114 |
| Clerks (English and Vernacular) | ... | 72 |
| Postmen and other servants | ... | 413 |
| Road Establishments, consisting of Overseers, Runners, Clerks and Booking Agents, Boatmen, Syces, Coachmen, Bearers and others | ... | 336 |
| Sorters | ... | 17 |
| Mail Guards and Agents | ... | 1 |
| **Combined Officers** | ... | **30** |
| Signallers | ... | 13 |
| Messengers and other servants | ... | 17 |
| **TELEGRAPH DEPARTMENT.** | | |
| *Total Persons Employed* | *28* | *107* |
| Administrative Establishment | ... | ... |
| Signalling Establishment | 27 | 10 |
| Clerks | 1 | 4 |
| Skilled labour | ... | 39 |
| Unskilled labour | ... | 1 |
| Messengers and other servants | ... | 53 |

**Appendix showing the Classes, Sub-classes and Orders of the M. Bertillon's new classification of occupations adopted in 1911 and the total number of persons in the Census as supported by each division given after it in brackets.**

| Class. | Sub-class. | Orders. |
|---|---|---|
| 1 | 2 | 3 |
| A.—Production of raw materials. (5,953,423.) | I.—Exploitation of the surface of the earth. (5,949,356.) | 1. Pasture and Agriculture. (5,936,785.) |
| | | (*a*) Ordinary cultivation. (5,660,991.) |
| | | (*b*) Growers of special products and market gardening. (14,290.) |
| | | (*c*) Forestry. (40,139.) |
| | | (*d*) Raising of farm stock. (221,276.) |
| | | (*e*) Raising of small animals. (89.) |
| | | 2. Fishing and hunting. (12,571.) |
| | II.—Extraction of minerals. (4,067.) | 3. Mines. (3,039.) |
| | | 4. Quarries of hard rocks. (110.) |
| | | 5. Salt, etc. (918.) |
| B.—Preparation and supply of material substances. (1,711,417.) | III.—Industry. (1,145,073.) | 6. Textiles. (168,024.) |
| | | 7. Hides, skins and hard materials from the animal kingdom. (23,670.) |
| | | 8. Wood. (133,102.) |
| | | 9. Metals. (70,801.) |
| | | 10. Ceramics. (100,011.) |
| | | 11. Chemical products properly so called, and analogous. (71,493.) |
| | | 12. Food industries. (65,028.) |
| | | 13. Industries of dress and the toilet. (391,413.) |
| | | 14. Furniture industries. (363.) |
| | | 15. Building industries. (28,566.) |
| | | 16. Construction of means of transport. (1,448.) |
| | | 17. Production and transmission of physical forces (heat, light, electricity, motive power, etc.) (95.) |
| | | 18. Industries of luxury and those pertaining to literature and the arts and sciences. (52,450.) |
| | | 19. Industries concerned with refuse matter. (38,614.) |
| | IV.—Transport. (52,412.) | 20. Transport by water. (1,393.) |
| | | 21. Transport by road. (37,800.) |
| | | 22. Transport by rail. (10,923.) |
| | | 23. Post Office, Telegraph and Telephone services. (2,296.) |
| | V.—Trade. (513,932.) | 24. Banks, establishments of credit, exchange and insurance. (36,093.) |
| | | 25. Brokerage, commission and export. (5,195.) |
| | | 26. Trade in textiles. (27,121.) |
| | | 27. Trade in skins, leather and furs. (2,095.) |
| | | 28. Trade in wood. (1,750.) |
| | | 29. Trade in metals. (3,159.) |
| | | 30. Trade in pottery. (18.) |
| | | 31. Trade in chemical products. (6,945.) |
| | | 32. Hotels, cafes, restaurants, etc. (24,152.) |
| | | 33. Other trade in food stuffs. (294,305.) |
| | | 34. Trade in clothing and toilet articles. (9,614.) |
| | | 35. Trade in furniture. (626.) |
| | | 36. Trade in building materials. (485.) |
| | | 37. Trade in means of transport. (4,296.) |
| | | 38. Trade in fuel. (12,797.) |
| | | 39. Trade in articles of luxury and those pertaining to letters and the arts and sciences. (17,938.) |
| | | 40. Trade in refuse matter. (4.) |
| | | 41. Trade of other sorts. (67,339.) |
| C.—Public administration and liberal arts. (490,986.) | VI.—Public force. (181,938.) | 42. Army. (89,551.) |
| | | 43. Navy. ( 00 .) |
| | | 44. Police. (92,387.) |
| | VII.—Public administration. (139,485.) | 45. Public Administration. (139,485.) |
| | VIII.—Professions and liberal arts. (138,390.) | 46. Religion. (94,629.) |
| | | 47. Law. (3,663.) |
| | | 48. Medicine. (5,954.) |
| | | 49. Instruction. (6,951.) |
| | | 50. Letters and arts and sciences. (27,193.) |
| | IX.—Persons living on their income. (31,173.) | 51. Persons living principally on their income. (31,173.) |
| D.—Miscellaneous. (1,201,154.) | X.—Domestic service. (214,177.) | 52. Domestic service. (214,177.) |
| | XI.—Insufficiently described occupations. (754,480.) | 53. General terms which do not indicate a definite occupation. (754,480.) |
| | XII.—Unproductive. (232,497.) | 54. Inmates of jails, asylums and hospitals. (4,148.) |
| | | 55. Beggars, vagrants, prostitutes. (228,349.) |

# Part II.—TABLES.

# TABLE OF CONTENTS

## Part II.—IMPERIAL AND PROVINCIAL TABLES.


| | | | Page |
|---|---|---|---|
| Imperial Table | I. | Area, Houses and Population | 1 |
| „ „ | II. | Variation in Population since 1881 | 3 |
| „ „ | III. | Towns and Villages Classified by Population | 5 |
| „ „ | IV. | Towns Classified by Population with Variation since 1881 | 7 |
| „ „ | V. | Towns arranged Territorially with Population by Religion | 11 |
| „ „ | VI. | Religion | 15 |
| „ „ | VII. | Part A—Age, Sex and Civil Condition (Agency Summary) | 17 |
| | | „ B— „ „ „ „ (Details by Natural Divisions) | 21 |
| „ „ | VIII. | Part A—Education by Religion and Age (Agency Summary). | 33 |
| | | „ B— „ „ „ „ „ (Details by Natural Divisions) | 35 |
| „ „ | IX. | Education by Selected Caste, Tribe or Race | 41 |
| „ „ | X. | Language | 43 |
| | | Appendix to (Details of Minor Languages) | 45 |
| „ „ | XI. | Birthplace | 49 |
| | | Appendix to—(showing the Birthplaces of Persons enumerated in the main States) | 52 |
| „ „ | XII. | Infirmities | 55 |
| | | Part I (Distribution by Age) | 56 |
| „ „ | XIIA. | Infirmities by Selected Caste, Tribe or Race | 57 |
| „ „ | XIII. | Caste, Tribe or Race | 59 |
| „ „ | XIV. | Civil Condition by Age for Selected Castes, etc. | 63 |
| „ „ | XVA. | Occupation or Means of Livelihood | 67 |
| „ „ | XVB :— | | |
| | | (1) Subsidiary Occupations of Agriculturist Rent Receivers | 74 |
| | | (2) „ „ „ „ Payers | *ib.* |
| | | (3) „ „ „ Farm Servants and Field Labourers | 75 |
| „ „ | XVC. | Showing for certain mixed occupations the number of persons who returned each as their (*a*) Principal and (*b*) Subsidiary Means of Livelihood | 76 |
| „ „ | XVD. | Occupation or Means of Livelihood (Distribution by Religion) | 77 |
| „ „ | XVE. | Statistics of Industries | 83 |
| | | Part I. Agency Summary | 84 |
| | | „ II. Distribution by Political Charges | 86 |
| | | „ III. Particulars as to Ownership of Factories, etc. | 88 |
| | | „ IV. Caste or Race of Managers of Factories, etc. | *ib.* |
| „ „ | XVI. | Occupation by Selected Caste, Tribe or Race | 91 |
| „ „ | XVII. | Territorial Distribution of the Christian Population by Sect and Race | 101 |
| „ „ | XVIII. | Europeans, Armenians, and Anglo-Indians by Race and Age | 103 |
| Special Table. | | Showing the adjusted figures for different Political Charges for 1901 and 1891 | 105 |
| Provincial Table | I. | Area and Population of States | i |
| | | Appendix A—Area and Population of minor States, Estates, British Cantonments and Civil Stations | iv |
| „ „ | II. | Population of States by Religion and Education | ix |
| | | Appendix B—Population of minor States, Estates, British Cantonments and Civil Stations by Religion and Education | xii |
| „ „ | III. | Railway Stations in Central India Agency by States, Political Charges and Railway Lines | xvii |

# TABLE I.

## *AREA, HOUSES AND POPULATION.*

This table gives figures for each Political Charge. The area of the agencies has been reduced by the transfer of the three Tonk State districts of Chhabra, Pirawa and Sironj to the Rajputana Agency, while various internal adjustments have also taken place in Political Charges.

Provincial Tables I and II giving leading statistics for States of any size have been printed at the end of this Volume.

| | |
|---|---|
| Area of Central India Agency, 1901 . . . . . . . . | 78,772 |
| *Deduct*—Three Tonk Parganas . . . . . . . . | 1,439 |
| | 77,333 |
| *Add*—Certain outlying areas . . . . . . . | 34 |
| Present area . . . . . . . . . . | 77,367 |

*Details of areas under British Administration.*

| Cantonments, Stations, etc. | Area in square miles. | Population. | | |
|---|---|---|---|---|
| | | Persons. | Males. | Females. |
| 1 | 2 | 3 | 4 | 5 |
| **Total** | **31·84** | **86,712** | **49,400** | **37,312** |
| CANTONMENTS AND MILITARY STATIONS. | ***22·50*** | ***67,886*** | ***38,823*** | ***29,063*** |
| Mhow Cantonment | 6·00 | 29,820 | 17,723 | 12,097 |
| Nimach Cantonment | 4·00 | 12,318 | 6,741 | 5,577 |
| Nowgong Cantonment | 7·50 | 9,421 | 5,454 | 3,967 |
| Agar Station | 1·00 | 3,487 | 1,981 | 1,506 |
| Guna Station | 2·00 | 5,099 | 2,768 | 2,331 |
| Sehore Station | 2·00 | 7,741 | 4,156 | 3,585 |
| CIVIL STATIONS | ***9·34*** | ***18,826*** | ***10,577*** | ***8,249*** |
| Gwalior Residency Head-quarters | 0·50 | 304 | 223 | 81 |
| Indore Residency Head-quarters | 1·00 | 9,195 | 5,362 | 3,833 |
| Nowgong (Bundelkhand Agency Head-quarters) | Included in Nowgong | 674 | 439 | 235 |
| *Sardarpur (Bhopawar Agency Head-quarters) | 1·00 | 1,650 | 851 | 799 |
| Satna (Baghelkhand Agency Head-quarters) | 0·14 | 394 | 257 | 137 |
| Manpur (British Pargana) | 6·70 | 6,609 | 3,445 | 3,164 |

* This place has since been made over to the Gwalior State, the head-quarters being transferred to Manpur.

# TABLE I.—Area, Houses and Population.

| Serial No. | Political Charge. | Area in square miles. | Towns. | Villages. | Occupied Houses. Total. | Occupied Houses. In Towns. | Occupied Houses. In Villages. | Population. Persons. Total. | Persons. Urban. | Persons. Rural. | Males. Total. | Males. Urban. | Males. Rural. | Females. Total. | Females. Urban. | Females. Rural. |
|---|---|---|---|---|---|---|---|---|---|---|---|---|---|---|---|---|
| 1 | 2 | 3 | 4 | 5 | 6 | 7 | 8 | 9 | 10 | 11 | 12 | 13 | 14 | 15 | 16 | 17 |
| | **Central India** | 77,367 | 77 | 33,028 | 2,039,955 | 210,991 | 1,828,964 | 9,356,980 | 786,114 | 8,570,866 | 4,801,459 | 412,859 | 4,388,600 | 4,555,521 | 373,255 | 4,182,266 |
| 1 | Gwalior Residency | 24,384 | 28 | 10,306 | *661,424* | 75,341 | 586,083 | *3,090,798* | 277,789 | 2,813,009 | *1,627,581* | 147,812 | 1,479,769 | *1,463,217* | 129,977 | 1,333,240 |
| 2 | Indore Residency | 9,004 | 11 | 3,439 | *232,732* | 39,888 | 192,844 | *979,360* | 138,415 | 840,945 | *506,659* | 75,287 | 431,372 | *472,701* | 63,128 | 409,573 |
| 3 | Baghelkhand Agency | 14,706 | 7 | 6,412 | *362,533* | 15,799 | 346,734 | *1,772,574* | 59,995 | 1,712,579 | *879,090* | 31,373 | 847,717 | *893,484* | 28,622 | 864,862 |
| 4 | Bhopal Agency | 9,154 | 11 | 4,579 | *241,190* | 29,027 | 212,163 | *1,050,735* | 111,363 | 939,372 | *536,458* | 57,483 | 478,975 | *514,277* | 53,880 | 460,397 |
| 5 | Bhopawar Agency | 7,274 | 3 | 3,207 | *145,550* | 5,523 | 140,027 | *698,455* | 20,999 | 677,456 | *349,553* | 10,488 | 339,065 | *348,902* | 10,511 | 338,391 |
| 6 | Bundelkhand Agency | 10,118 | 11 | 3,768 | *302,487* | 25,037 | 277,450 | *1,375,817* | 98,824 | 1,276,493 | *703,042* | 50,308 | 652,734 | *672,775* | 48,516 | 623,759 |
| 7 | Malwa Agency | 2,727 | 6 | 1,310 | *94,039* | 20,376 | 73,663 | *389,741* | 78,729 | 311,012 | *199,076* | 40,108 | 158,968 | *190,665* | 38,621 | 152,044 |

# TABLE II.

## *VARIATION IN POPULATION SINCE 1881.*

Various adjustments have been necessary owing to the transfer of certain units to Rajputana and the inclusion of island tracts formerly excluded. These are given below. Numerous minor internal transfers between Political Charges have also taken place. A special table is being given showing all details. This will come in the Report. (See Table at page 105).

| Adjustment of Areas. | 1901. | | | 1891. | | | 1881. | | |
|---|---|---|---|---|---|---|---|---|---|
| | Total. | Males. | Females. | Total. | Males. | Females. | Total. | Males. | Females. |
| 1 | 2 | 3 | 4 | 5 | 6 | 7 | 8 | 9 | 10 |
| Population of Central India Agency as shown in Central India Imperial Table II. | 8,628,781 | 4,428,790 | 4,199,991 | 10,318,812 | 5,395,536 | 4,923,276 | 9,261,907 | 4,882,823 | 4,379,084 |
| | | | | | | | *Tonk Parganas were not included in Central India totals which dealt with states only and not agencies.* | | |
| ***DEDUCT—*** | | | | | | | | | |
| *To Rajputana, 3 Parganas of Tonk.* | *—129,871* | *67,155* | *62,716* | *181,135* | *96,345* | *84,790* | | | |
| | 8,498,910 | 4,361,635 | 4,137,275 | 10,137,677 | 5,299,191 | 4,838,486 | | | |
| *To Rajputana, Chhabra Railway Station (in Tonk State).* | *—66* | *40* | *26* | *No* | *Railway* | *existed.* | | | |
| | 8,498,844 | 4,361,595 | 4,137,249 | 10,137,677 | 5,299,191 | 4,838,486 | | | |
| *To United Provinces, population of Allahabad villages in Rewah State.* | *—2,079* | *1,016* | *1,063* | *2,498* | *1,208* | *1,290* | | | |
| | 8,496,765 | 4,360,579 | 4,136,186 | 10,135,179 | 5,297,983 | 4,837,196 | | | |
| **ADD—** | | | | | | | | | |
| **From United Provinces, population of Rewah villages in Allahabad district.** | **+ 1,040** | **557** | **483** | **1,224** | **619** | **605** | | | |
| | **8,497,805** | **4,361,136** | **4,136,669** | **10,136,403** | **5,298,602** | **4,837,801** | **9,261,907** | **4,882,823** | **4,379,084** |
| **DISTRIBUTED BY POLITICAL CHARGES—** | | | | | | | | | |
| **Gwalior Residency . .** | **2,952,000** | **1,551,250** | **1,400,750** | **3,377,922** | **1,807,308** | **1,570,614** | | | |
| **Indore Residency . .** | **842,107** | **436,680** | **405,427** | **1,060,794** | **561,959** | **498,835** | | | |
| **Baghelkhand Agency .** | **1,553,985** | **770,842** | **783,143** | **1,787,058** | **897,651** | **889,407** | | | |
| **Bhopal Agency . .** | **926,619** | **468,550** | **458,069** | **1,284,369** | **669,722** | **614,647** | | | |
| **Bhopawar Agency . .** | **548,694** | **276,606** | **272,088** | **713,595** | **365,325** | **348,270** | | | |
| **Bundelkhand Agency .** | **1,308,326** | **671,285** | **637,041** | **1,457,327** | **758,888** | **698,439** | | | |
| **Malwa Agency . .** | **366,074** | **185,923** | **180,151** | **455,338** | **237,749** | **217,589** | | | |

# TABLE II.—VARIATION IN POPULATION SINCE 1881.

| Serial No. | Political Charge. | Persons. | | | | Males. | | | | Females. | | | | Variation, Increase + Decrease —. | | | Net Variation in Period 1881 to 1911. Increase + Decrease —. |
|---|---|---|---|---|---|---|---|---|---|---|---|---|---|---|---|---|---|
| | | 1911. | 1901. | 1891. | 1881. | 1911. | 1901. | 1891. | 1881. | 1911. | 1901. | 1891. | 1881. | 1901 to 1911. | 1891 to 1901. | 1881 to 1891. | |
| 1 | 2 | 3 | 4 | 5 | 6 | 7 | 8 | 9 | 10 | 11 | 12 | 13 | 14 | 15 | 16 | 17 | 18 |
| | **Central India** | **9,356,980** | **8,497,805** | **10,136,403** | **9,261,907** | **4,801,459** | **4,361,136** | **5,298,602** | **4,882,823** | **4,555,521** | **4,136,669** | **4,837,801** | **4,379,084** | **+859,175** | **—1,638,598** | **+874,496** | **+95,073** |
| 1 | Gwalior Residency | 3,090,798 | 2,952,000 | 3,377,922 | Not available. | 1,627,581 | 1,551,250 | 1,807,308 | Not available. | 1,463,217 | 1,400,750 | 1,570,614 | Not available. | +138,798 | —425 922 | | |
| 2 | Indore Residency | 979,360 | 842,107 | 1,060,794 | | 506,659 | 436,680 | 561,959 | | 472,701 | 405,427 | 498,835 | | +137,253 | —218,687 | | |
| 3 | Baghelkhand Agency | 1,772,574 | 1,553,985 | 1,787,058 | | 879,090 | 770,842 | 897,651 | | 893,484 | 783,143 | 889,407 | | +218,589 | —233,073 | | |
| 4 | Bhopal Agency | 1,050,735 | 926,619 | 1,284,369 | | 536,458 | 468,550 | 669,722 | | 514,277 | 458,069 | 614,647 | | +124,116 | —357,750 | | |
| 5 | Bhopawar Agency | 698,455 | 548,694 | 713,595 | | 349,553 | 276,606 | 365,325 | | 348,902 | 272,088 | 348,270 | | +149,761 | —164,901 | | |
| 6 | Bundelkhand Agency | 1,375,317 | 1,308,326 | 1,457,327 | | 703,042 | 671,285 | 758,888 | | 672,275 | 637,041 | 698,439 | | +66,991 | —149,001 | | |
| 7 | Malwa Agency | 389,741 | 366,074 | 455,338 | | 199,076 | 185,923 | 237,749 | | 190,665 | 180,151 | 217,589 | | +23,667 | —89,264 | | |

## TABLE III.

### *TOWNS AND VILLAGES CLASSIFIED BY POPULATION.*

The Native States in the Central India Agency have not been all cadastrally surveyed and the Mauza or revenue village has, as far as possible, been taken as a village. Every pos sible care has been taken to include all outlying hamlets in parent villages to which they appertain.

# TABLE III.—TOWNS AND VILLAGES CLASSIFIED BY POPULATION.

| Serial No. | Political Charge. | Total number of inhabited Towns and Villages. | Population. | Under 500. | | 500—1,000. | | 1,000—2,000. | | 2,000—5,000. | | 5,000—10,000. | | 10,000—20,000. | | 20,000—50,000. | | 50,000—100,000. | | Encampment, Boat and Railway Population unclassed. |
|---|---|---|---|---|---|---|---|---|---|---|---|---|---|---|---|---|---|---|---|---|
| | | | | Number. | Population. | Number. | Population. | Number. | Population. | Number. | Population. | Number. | Population. | Number. | Population. | Number. | Population. | Number. | Population. | |
| 1 | 2 | 3 | 4 | 5 | 6 | 7 | 8 | 9 | 10 | 11 | 12 | 13 | 14 | 15 | 16 | 17 | 18 | 19 | 20 | 21 |
| | **Central India** . | **33,100** | **9,356,980** | **29,007** | **4,778,466** | **2,895** | **2,001,070** | **907** | **1,221,362** | **234** | **647,299** | **39** | **277,542** | **11** | **155,334** | **6** | **215,125** | **1** | **55,953** | **4,334** |
| 1 | Gwalior Residency . | 10,336 | 3,090,798 | 8,988 | 1,503,995 | 969 | 688,110 | 318 | 440,016 | 74 | 202,212 | 15 | 101,599 | 5 | 68,002 | 2 | 86,247 | .. | .. | 617 |
| 2 | Indore Residency . | 3,450 | 979,360 | 3,087 | 515,443 | 262 | 171,018 | 71 | 96,645 | 20 | 61,345 | 8 | 60,142 | .. | .. | 2 | 74,767 | .. | .. | .. |
| 3 | Baghelkhand Agency . | 6,419 | 1,772,574 | 5,525 | 955,671 | 669 | 445,301 | 195 | 251,260 | 26 | 73,801 | 3 | 20,294 | .. | .. | 1 | 26,247 | .. | .. | .. |
| 4 | Bhopal Agency . | 4,590 | 1,050,735 | 4,234 | 634,280 | 259 | 177,947 | 71 | 92,404 | 20 | 54,062 | 5 | 35,825 | .. | .. | .. | .. | 1 | 55,953 | 264 |
| 5 | Bhopawar Agency . | 3,210 | 698,455 | 2,995 | 461,173 | 157 | 109,244 | 38 | 44,113 | 22 | 62,926 | 3 | 20,999 | .. | .. | .. | .. | .. | .. | .. |
| 6 | Bundelkhand Agency . | 3,779 | 1,375,817 | 3,001 | 518,384 | 510 | 342,680 | 199 | 268,260 | 61 | 155,386 | 4 | 32,759 | 4 | 53,998 | .. | .. | .. | .. | 3,355 |
| 7 | Malwa Agency . | 1,316 | 389,741 | 1,182 | 189,520 | 90 | 66,770 | 20 | 28,664 | 11 | 37,567 | 1 | 5,924 | 2 | 33,334 | 1 | 27,864 | .. | .. | 98 |

## TABLE IV.

### *TOWNS CLASSIFIED BY POPULATION WITH VARIATION SINCE 1881.*

The population of certain towns fell below the normal figures owing to the prevalence of plague at the time of the actual census (10th March 1911). These localities were accordingly recounted on convenient dates in July 1911 after the normal condition was re-established. The figures for both enumerations are given below :—

| Localities. | Date of re-counting. | Total on 10th March 1911, excluding railway population. | | | Recount total in July 1911, exclusive of railway population. | | | Difference. |
|---|---|---|---|---|---|---|---|---|
| | | Persons. | Males. | Females. | Persons. | Males. | Females. | |
| 1 | 2 | 3 | 4 | 5 | 6 | 7 | 8 | 9 |
| Lashkar City . . | 8th July 1911 | 46,952 | 24,245 | 22,707 | 60,921 | 32,241 | 28,680 | +13,969 |
| Indore City . . | 20th do. | 44,385 | 24,424 | 19,961 | 68,733 | 37,910 | 30,823 | +24,348 |
| Morar . . . | 8th do. | 13,533 | 8,579 | 4,954 | 16,251 | 10,213 | 6,038 | +2,718 |
| Lashkar Brigade . | Do. | 9,235 | 6,288 | 2,947 | 11,488 | 7,704 | 3,784 | +2,253 |
| Dhar . . . | 2nd do. | 7,472 | 3,850 | 3,622 | 17,016 | 8,821 | 8,195 | +9,544 |
| Sanawad . . | 20th do. | 3,426 | 1,818 | 1,608 | 5,595 | 2,886 | 2,709 | +2,169 |

Note—The Bhopal City, also affected with plague, was recounted on 10th July 1911 but practically shewed no difference, hence it has not been included in the above table.

Ten towns, *viz.*, Karahia, MungaoliTal, Manasa, Sunel, Gautampura, Nadigaon, Sironj, Chhabra, and Pirawa treated as towns in the previous Census, have been omitted from this table on the present occasion, the first seven having lost their importance and the last three belonging to the Tonk State, having been transferred with their districts to the Rajputana Agency. Seven new places, on the other hand, *viz.*, Sipri, Morena, Sanawad, Maharajpur, Rajnagar, Nagod and Raisen, have been included in the towns owing to their growing importance in urban characteristics or as trade centres or as being places of historic fame.

# TABLE IV.—Towns classified by Population with Variation since 1881.

| Serial No. | Towns. | States. | Municipality suburbs, cantonments, etc. | Population. 1911. | Population. 1901. | Population. 1891. | Population. 1881. | Variation. Increase (+) Decrease (—). 1901 to 1911. | Variation. 1891 to 1901. | Variation. 1881 to 1891. | Variation in period 1881 to 1911. Increase (+) Decrease (—). | Males. 1911. | Males. 1901. | Males. 1891. | Females. 1911. | Females. 1901. | Females. 1891. | Serial No. |
|---|---|---|---|---|---|---|---|---|---|---|---|---|---|---|---|---|---|---|
| 1 | 2 | 3 | 4 | 5 | 6 | 7 | 8 | 9 | 10 | 11. | 12 | 13 | 14 | 15 | 16 | 17 | 18 | 19 |
| | **Central India** | | | **786,114** | **959,942** | **997,006** | .. | **—173,828** | **—37,064** | .. | .. | **412,859** | **499,846** | **530,874** | **373,255** | **460,096** | **466,132** | |
| 1 | Bhopal | Bhopal | | 56,204 | 77,023 | 70,338 | 55,402 | —20,819 | +6,685 | +14,936 | +802 | 29,043 | 39,177 | 36,891 | 27,161 | 37,846 | 33,447 | 1 |
| 2 | Lashkar | Gwalior | | 46,952 | 89,154 | 104,083 | 88,066 | —42,202 | —14,929 | +16,017 | —41,114 | 24,245 | 45,886 | 54,553 | 22,707 | 43,268 | 49,530 | 2 |
| 3 | Indore | Indore | | 44,947 | 86,686 | 82,984 | 75,401 | —41,739 | +3,702 | +7,583 | —30,454 | 24,792 | 46,164 | 46,328 | 20,155 | 40,522 | 36,656 | 3 |
| 4 | Ujjain | Gwalior | | 39,295 | 39,892 | 34,691 | 32,932 | —597 | +5,201 | +1,759 | +6,363 | 20,864 | 20,829 | 18,292 | 18,431 | 19,063 | 16,399 | 4 |
| 5 | Mhow (Cantonment) | Indore | Cantonment | 29,820 | 36,039 | 31,773 | 27,227 | —6,219 | +4,266 | +4,546 | +2,593 | 17,723 | 20,788 | 18,300 | 12,097 | 15,251 | 13,473 | 5 |
| 6 | Ratlam | Ratlam | | 27,957 | 36,321 | 29,822 | 31,066 | —8,364 | +6,499 | —1,244 | —3,109 | 14,340 | 18,519 | 15,322 | 13,617 | 17,802 | 14,500 | 6 |
| 7 | Rewah. | Rewah | | 26,247 | 24,608 | 23,626 | 22,016 | +1,639 | +982 | +1,610 | +4,231 | 14,248 | 12,202 | 12,155 | 11,999 | 12,406 | 11,471 | 7 |
| 8 | Jaora | Jaora | | 18,054 | 23,854 | 21,844 | 19,902 | —5,800 | +2,010 | +1,942 | —1,848 | 9,146 | 11,805 | 11,010 | 8,908 | 12,049 | 10,834 | 8 |
| 9 | Datia | Datia | | 17,329 | 24,071 | 27,566 | 28,346 | —6,742 | —3,495 | —780 | —11,017 | 8,766 | 12,283 | 14,213 | 8,563 | 11,788 | 13,353 | 9 |
| 10 | Mandasor | Gwalior | | 16,785 | 20,936 | 25,785 | 22,596 | —4,151 | —4,849 | +3,189 | —5,811 | 8,602 | 10,812 | 13,164 | 8,183 | 10,124 | 12,621 | 10 |
| 11 | Tikamgarh | Orchha | | 15,495 | 14,050 | 17,610 | 18,344 | +1,445 | —3,560 | —734 | —2,849 | 8,013 | 7,105 | 9,200 | 7,482 | 6,945 | 8,410 | 11 |
| 12 | Dewas | Dewas | | 15,285 | 15,403 | 15,068 | 11,921 | —118 | +335 | +3,147 | +3,364 | 7,858 | 7,914 | 8,051 | 7,427 | 7,489 | 7,017 | 12 |
| 13 | Gwalior | Gwalior | | 14,694 | 16,807 | 15,750 | .. | —2,113 | +1,057 | .. | .. | 7,458 | 8,580 | 8,023 | 7,236 | 8,218 | 7,727 | 13 |
| 14 | Morar | Do. | | 13,577 | 19,179 | 24,518 | 24,022 | —5,602 | —5,339 | +496 | —10,445 | 8,610 | 11,450 | 15,375 | 4,967 | 7,729 | 9,143 | 14 |
| 15 | Nimach (Cantonment) | Do. | Cantonment | 12,318 | 15,398 | 15,291 | 13,069 | —3,080 | +107 | +2,222 | —751 | 6,741 | 8,632 | 8,763 | 5,577 | 6,766 | 6,528 | 15 |
| 16 | Panna | Panna | | 10,756 | 11,846 | 14,705 | 14,676 | —590 | —3,359 | +29 | —3,920 | 5,361 | 5,702 | 7,766 | 5,395 | 6,644 | 6,939 | 16 |
| 17 | Sipri | Gwalior | | 10,628 | 5,592 | 8,110 | .. | +5,036 | —2,518 | .. | .. | 5,603 | 2,855 | 4,229 | 5,025 | 2,737 | 3,881 | 17 |
| 18 | Chhatarpur | Chhatarpur. | | 10,413 | 10,029 | 12,957 | 13,474 | +384 | —2,928 | —517 | —3,061 | 5,055 | 4,634 | 6,604 | 5,358 | 5,395 | 6,353 | 18 |
| 19 | Maharajnagar | Charkhari | | 9,879 | 11,718 | 13,068 | 13,196 | —1,839 | —1,350 | —128 | —3,317 | 4,840 | 5,767 | 6,668 | 5,039 | 5,951 | 6,400 | 19 |
| 20 | Maheshwar | Indore | | 9,599 | 7,042 | 9,230 | .. | +2,557 | —2,188 | .. | .. | 4,708 | 3,544 | 4,670 | 4,891 | 3,498 | 4,560 | 20 |
| 21 | Khargon | Do. | | 9,423 | 7,624 | 9,147 | .. | +1,799 | —1,523 | .. | .. | 4,603 | 3,644 | 4,388 | 4,820 | 3,980 | 4,759 | 21 |
| 22 | Nowgong (Cantonment) | Chhatarpur. | Cantonment | 9,421 | 11,507 | 10,902 | 7,492 | —2,086 | +605 | +3,410 | +1,929 | 5,454 | 6,773 | 6,946 | 3,967 | 4,734 | 3,956 | 22 |
| 23 | Lashkar (Brigade | Gwalior | | 9,235 | 18,472 | 11,353 | .. | —4,237 | +2,119 | .. | .. | 6,288 | 8,226 | 7,257 | 2,947 | 5,246 | 4,096 | 23 |
| 24 | Indore Residency | Indore | | 9,195 | 11,118 | 9,345 | 7,690 | —1,923 | +1,773 | +1,655 | +1,505 | 5,362 | 6,768 | 6,099 | 3,833 | 4,350 | 3,246 | 24 |
| 25 | Narsinghgarh | Narsinghgarh | | 9,164 | 8,778 | 8,561 | 11,400 | +386 | +217 | —2,839 | —2,236 | 4,779 | 4,627 | 4,548 | 4,385 | 4,151 | 4,013 | 25 |
| 26 | Bhind | Gwalior | | 9,133 | 8,032 | 9,188 | 7,412 | +1,101 | —1,156 | +1,776 | —1,721 | 5,081 | 4,338 | 5,576 | 4,052 | 3,694 | 3,612 | 26 |
| 27 | Shajapur | Do. | | 8,876 | 9,953 | 11,043 | 9,247 | —1,077 | —1,090 | +1,796 | —371 | 4,410 | 5,053 | 5,592 | 4,466 | 4,900 | 5,451 | 27 |
| 28 | Barnagar | Do. | | 8,634 | 10,856 | 10,261 | 7,908 | —2,222 | +595 | +2,353 | +726 | 4,434 | 5,583 | 5,334 | 4,200 | 5,273 | 4,927 | 28 |
| 29 | Bhilsa | Do. | | 8,427 | 7,481 | 9,670 | 7,070 | +946 | —2,189 | +2,600 | +1,357 | 4,428 | 3,731 | 5,284 | 3,999 | 3,750 | 4,386 | 29 |
| 30 | Rampura | Indore | | 7,799 | 8,273 | 11,935 | .. | —474 | —3,662 | .. | .. | 3,815 | 4,229 | 6,133 | 3,984 | 4,044 | 5,802 | 30 |
| 31 | Sehore (Station) | Bhopal | | 7,741 | 11,755 | 11,124 | 10,389 | —4,014 | +631 | +735 | —2,648 | 4,156 | 6,244 | 6,084 | 3,585 | 5,511 | 5,040 | 31 |
| 32 | Dhar | Dhar | | 7,472 | 17,792 | 18,430 | 15,224 | —10,320 | —638 | +3,206 | —7,752 | 3,850 | 9,063 | 9,701 | 3,622 | 8,729 | 8,729 | 32 |
| 33 | Samthar | Samthar | | 7,441 | 8,286 | 7,865 | 7,891 | —845 | +421 | —26 | —450 | 3,799 | 4,504 | 4,192 | 3,642 | 3,782 | 3,673 | 33 |
| 34 | Barwani | Barwani | | 7,279 | 6,277 | 6,054 | 5,581 | +1,002 | +223 | +473 | +1,698 | 3,540 | 3,030 | 2,930 | 3,739 | 3,247 | 3,124 | 34 |
| 35 | Sarangpur | Dewas | | 7,198 | 6,339 | 5,486 | 7,104 | +859 | +853 | —1,618 | +94 | 3,561 | 3,026 | 2,876 | 3,637 | 3,318 | 2,610 | 35 |
| 36 | Satna (Raghurajnagar) | Rewah | | 7,192 | 7,471 | 6,771 | 5,385 | —279 | +700 | +1,386 | +1,807 | 3,829 | 3,929 | 3,802 | 3,363 | 3,542 | 2,969 | 36 |
| 37 | Barwaha | Indore | | 7,184 | 6,094 | 6,639 | .. | +1,090 | —545 | .. | .. | 3,866 | 3,434 | 3,650 | 3,318 | 2,660 | 2,989 | 37 |
| 38 | Maihar | Maihar | | 7,094 | 6,884 | 6,457 | 6,487 | +210 | +427 | —30 | +607 | 3,390 | 3,391 | 3,179 | 3,704 | 3,493 | 3,278 | 38 |
| 39 | Biaora | Rajgarh | | 6,663 | 5,607 | 6,476 | .. | +1,056 | —869 | .. | .. | 3,408 | 2,917 | 3,339 | 3,255 | 2,690 | 3,137 | 39 |
| 40 | Guna (Town) | Gwalior | | 6,586 | 5,415 | 6,000 | .. | +1,171 | —585 | .. | .. | 3,514 | 2,789 | 3,151 | 3,072 | 2,626 | 2,849 | 40 |

| | | | | | | | | | | | | | | | | |
|---|---|---|---|---|---|---|---|---|---|---|---|---|---|---|---|---|
| 41 | Jawad | Gwalior | 6,505 | 8,005 | 8,920 | .. | −1,500 | −915 | .. | .. | 3,239 | 4,007 | 4,555 | 3,266 | 3,998 | 4,365 | 41 |
| 42 | Khachraud | Do. | 6,496 | 9,186 | 9,034 | 9,489 | −2,690 | +152 | −455 | −2,993 | 3,415 | 4,539 | 4,504 | 3,081 | 4,647 | 4,530 | 42 |
| 43 | Rajgarh | Rajgarh | 6,389 | 5,399 | 5,894 | 6,881 | +990 | −495 | .. | .. | 3,268 | 2,795 | 3,032 | 3,121 | 2,604 | 2,862 | 43 |
| 44 | Kukshi | Dhar | 6,248 | 5,402 | 6,346 | 6,212 | +846 | −944 | +134 | +36 | 3,098 | 2,686 | 3,188 | 3,150 | 2,716 | 3,158 | 44 |
| 45 | Bijawar | Bijawar | 6,018 | 5,220 | 7,543 | 7,192 | +798 | −2,323 | +351 | −1,174 | 3,042 | 2,679 | 4,114 | 2,976 | 2,541 | 3,429 | 45 |
| 46 | Umaria | Rewah | 6,008 | 5,381 | 5,694 | .. | +627 | −313 | .. | .. | 3,140 | 2,925 | 3,032 | 2,868 | 2,456 | 2,662 | 46 |
| 47 | Shujalpur | Gwalior | 5,938 | 5,731 | 6,669 | 7,136 | +207 | −938 | −467 | −1,198 | 3,028 | 2,822 | 3,351 | 2,910 | 2,909 | 3,318 | 47 |
| 48 | Sitamau | Sitamau | 5,924 | 5,877 | 5,861 | 5,764 | +47 | +16 | +97 | +160 | 3,020 | 2,925 | 3,017 | 2,904 | 2,952 | 2,844 | 48 |
| 49 | Khilchipur | Khilchipur | 5,868 | 5,121 | 5,494 | .. | +747 | −373 | .. | .. | 2,964 | 2,569 | 2,766 | 2,004 | 2,552 | 2,728 | 49 |
| 50 | Bhanpura | Indore | 5,859 | 4,639 | 6,626 | .. | +1,220 | −1,987 | .. | .. | 2,920 | 2,257 | 3,290 | 2,939 | 2,382 | 3,336 | 50 |
| 51 | Agar (Town) | Gwalior | 5,734 | 6,452 | 7,692 | 6,193 | −718 | −1,240 | +1,499 | −459 | 2,928 | 3,257 | 4,137 | 2,806 | 3,195 | 3,555 | 51 |
| 52 | Mehidpur | Indore | 5,620 | 6,681 | 8,263 | 8,906 | −1,061 | −1,582 | −645 | −3,288 | 2,826 | 3,303 | 4,017 | 2,794 | 3,378 | 4,246 | 52 |
| 53 | Sheopur | Gwalior | 5,531 | 6,712 | 7,600 | 8,403 | −1,181 | −888 | −803 | −2,872 | 2,753 | 3,305 | 3,894 | 2,778 | 3,407 | 3,706 | 53 |
| 54 | Tarana | Indore | 5,463 | 4,490 | 5,840 | .. | +973 | −1,350 | .. | .. | 2,801 | 2,317 | 2,973 | 2,662 | 2,173 | 2,867 | 54 |
| 55 | Gohad | Gwalior | 5,139 | 5,343 | 5,378 | .. | −204 | −35 | .. | .. | 2,659 | 2,807 | 2,778 | 2,480 | 2,536 | 2,600 | 55 |
| 56 | Guna (Station) | Do. | 5,099 | 6,037 | 4,693 | .. | −938 | +1,344 | .. | .. | 2,768 | 3,376 | 2,729 | 2,331 | 2,661 | 1,964 | 56 |
| 57 | Baroda (Sheopur) | Do. | 5,073 | 6,381 | 6,780 | 6,787 | −1,308 | −399 | −7 | −1,714 | 2,592 | 3,146 | 3,380 | 2,481 | 3,235 | 3,400 | 57 |
| 58 | Nimach (Town) | Do. | 4,989 | 6,190 | 6,309 | 5,161 | −1,201 | −119 | +1,148 | −172 | 2,565 | 3,222 | 3,337 | 2,424 | 2,968 | 2,972 | 58 |
| 59 | Sabalgarh | Do. | 4,985 | 6,039 | 6,111 | .. | −1,054 | −72 | .. | .. | 2,605 | 3,080 | 3,213 | 2,380 | 2,959 | 2,898 | 59 |
| 60 | Govindgarh | Rewah | 4,919 | 5,022 | 4,970 | .. | −103 | +52 | .. | .. | 2,466 | 2,867 | 2,666 | 2,453 | 2,155 | 2,304 | 60 |
| 61 | Ashta | Bhopal | 4,855 | 5,534 | 6,280 | 5,793 | −679 | −746 | +487 | −938 | 2,451 | 2,785 | 3,215 | 2,404 | 2,749 | 3,065 | 61 |
| 62 | Maharajpur | Chhatarpur | 4,783 | 4,055 | 4,419 | .. | +728 | −364 | .. | .. | 2,398 | 2,031 | 2,215 | 2,385 | 2,024 | 2,204 | 62 |
| 63 | Unchahra | Nagod | 4,507 | 3,785 | 5,442 | .. | +722 | −1,657 | .. | .. | 2,225 | 1,768 | 2,714 | 2,282 | 2,017 | 2,728 | 63 |
| 64 | Sehore (Town) | Bhopal | 4,364 | 5,109 | 5,108 | 5,206 | −745 | +1 | −98 | −842 | 2,225 | 2,036 | 2,563 | 2,139 | 2,473 | 2,545 | 64 |
| 65 | Bhander | Gwalior | 4,317 | 5,133 | 5,967 | .. | −816 | −834 | .. | .. | 2,150 | 2,617 | 3,065 | 2,167 | 2,516 | 2,902 | 65 |
| 66 | Sailana | Sailana | 4,311 | 4,255 | 5,113 | 4,659 | +56 | −858 | +454 | −348 | 2,183 | 2,103 | 2,626 | 2,128 | 2,152 | 2,487 | 66 |
| 67 | Nagod | Nagod | 4,028 | 3,887 | 3,957 | .. | +141 | −70 | .. | .. | 2,075 | 1,934 | 2,004 | 1,953 | 1,953 | 1,953 | 67 |
| 68 | Seondha | Datia | 3,954 | 5,542 | 6,409 | 7,988 | −1,588 | −867 | −1,579 | −4,034 | 2,019 | 2,767 | 3,244 | 1,935 | 2,775 | 3,165 | 68 |
| 69 | Ichhawar | Bhopal | 3,914 | 4,352 | 5,018 | .. | −438 | −666 | .. | .. | 2,059 | 2,152 | 2,653 | 1,855 | 2,200 | 2,365 | 69 |
| 70 | Narwar | Gwalior | 3,913 | 4,929 | 6,190 | .. | −1,016 | −1,261 | .. | .. | 1,976 | 2,453 | 3,174 | 1,937 | 2,476 | 3,016 | 70 |
| 71 | Raisen | Bhopal | 3,577 | 3,495 | 3,536 | .. | +82 | −41 | .. | .. | 1,793 | 1,728 | 1,761 | 1,784 | 1,767 | 1,775 | 71 |
| 72 | Sanawad | Indore | 3,506 | 7,880 | 5,693 | .. | −4,374 | +2,187 | .. | .. | 1,871 | 4,140 | 3,006 | 1,635 | 3,740 | 2,687 | 72 |
| 73 | Agar (Station) | Gwalior | 3,487 | 3,990 | 4,031 | .. | −503 | −41 | .. | .. | 1,981 | 2,401 | 2,532 | 1,506 | 1,589 | 1,499 | 73 |
| 74 | Rajnagar | Chhatarpur | 3,335 | 4,058 | 3,696 | .. | −723 | +362 | .. | .. | 1,561 | 2,188 | 1,849 | 1,774 | 1,920 | 1,847 | 74 |
| 75 | Chanderi | Gwalior | 2,753 | 4,093 | 5,073 | .. | −1,340 | −980 | .. | .. | 1,414 | 2,095 | 2,553 | 1,339 | 1,996 | 2,520 | 75 |
| 76 | Morena | Do. | 2,690 | 2,099 | 2,394 | .. | +591 | −295 | .. | .. | 1,461 | 1,053 | 1,257 | 1,229 | 1,046 | 1,137 | 76 |
| 77 | Berasia | Bhopal | 2,624 | 4,276 | 5,437 | .. | −1,652 | −1,161 | .. | .. | 1,337 | 2,205 | 2,832 | 1,287 | 2,071 | 2,605 | 77 |

## TABLE V.

### *TOWNS ARRANGED TERRITORIALLY WITH POPULATION BY RELIGION.*

**This table gives the religious distribution of the population of each town. The number of towns treated is the same as that in Table IV. The animistic population shews a considerable reduction owing to most of this class having returned themselves as Hindus instead of Animists on the present occasion.**

# TABLE V.—Towns arranged territorially

| Serial No. | District or State. | Town, Municipality, suburbs, cantonments, etc. | POPULATION. Persons. | Males. | Females. | INDO (a) Hindu Brahamanic. Persons. | Males. | Females. | (b) Hindu Arya. Persons. | Males. | Females. | (c) Hindu Brahmos. Persons. | Males. | Females. | (d) Sikh. Persons. | Males. | Females. |
|---|---|---|---|---|---|---|---|---|---|---|---|---|---|---|---|---|---|
| 1 | 2 | 3 | 4 | 5 | 6 | 7 | 8 | 9 | 10 | 11 | 12 | 13 | 14 | 15 | 16 | 17 | 18 |
| | **Central India** | | **786,114** | **412,859** | **373,255** | **546,013** | **286,940** | **259,073** | **77** | **50** | **27** | **9** | **6** | **3** | **1,076** | **759** | **317** |
| 1 | Gwalior | Lashkar | 46,952 | 24,245 | 22,707 | 35,432 | 18,263 | 17,169 | 7 | 2 | 5 | .. | .. | .. | 15 | 8 | 7 |
| 2 | ,, | Ujjain | 39,295 | 20,864 | 18,431 | 27,024 | 14,425 | 12,599 | .. | .. | .. | .. | .. | .. | .. | .. | .. |
| 3 | ,, | Mandasor | 16,785 | 8,602 | 8,183 | 10,889 | 5,580 | 5,309 | .. | .. | .. | .. | .. | .. | .. | .. | .. |
| 4 | ,, | Gwalior | 14,694 | 7,458 | 7,236 | 10,653 | 5,453 | 5,200 | .. | .. | .. | .. | .. | .. | .. | .. | .. |
| 5 | ,, | Morar | 13,577 | 8,610 | 4,967 | 9,470 | 6,092 | 3,378 | .. | .. | .. | .. | .. | .. | .. | .. | .. |
| 6 | ,, | Nimach (Cantonment) | 12,318 | 6,741 | 5,577 | 7,474 | 3,972 | 3,502 | 8 | 5 | 3 | .. | .. | .. | 3 | 2 | 1 |
| 7 | ,, | Sipri | 10,628 | 5,603 | 5,025 | 8,360 | 4,393 | 3,967 | .. | .. | .. | .. | .. | .. | .. | .. | .. |
| 8 | ,, | Lashkar (Brigade) | 9,235 | 6,288 | 2,947 | 6,489 | 4,444 | 2,045 | .. | .. | .. | .. | .. | .. | .. | .. | .. |
| 9 | ,, | Bhind | 9,133 | 5,081 | 4,052 | 6,970 | 3,883 | 3,087 | .. | .. | .. | .. | .. | .. | .. | .. | .. |
| 10 | ,, | Shajapur | 8,876 | 4,410 | 4,466 | 6,026 | 2,993 | 3,033 | .. | .. | .. | .. | .. | .. | .. | .. | .. |
| 11 | ,, | Barnagar | 8,634 | 4,434 | 4,200 | 5,743 | 2,934 | 2,809 | .. | .. | .. | .. | .. | .. | .. | .. | .. |
| 12 | ,, | Bhilsa | 8,427 | 4,428 | 3,999 | 6,652 | 3,497 | 3,155 | .. | .. | .. | .. | .. | .. | .. | .. | .. |
| 13 | ,, | Guna (Town) | 6,586 | 3,514 | 3,072 | 5,217 | 2,763 | 2,454 | .. | .. | .. | .. | .. | .. | .. | .. | .. |
| 14 | ,, | Jawad | 6,505 | 3,239 | 3,266 | 4,352 | 2,178 | 2,174 | .. | .. | .. | .. | .. | .. | .. | .. | .. |
| 15 | ,, | Khachraud | 6,496 | 3,415 | 3,081 | 4,647 | 2,421 | 2,226 | .. | .. | .. | .. | .. | .. | .. | .. | .. |
| 16 | ,, | Shujalpur | 5,938 | 3,028 | 2,910 | 4,132 | 2,104 | 2,028 | .. | .. | .. | .. | .. | .. | .. | .. | .. |
| 17 | ,, | Agar (Town) | 5,734 | 2,928 | 2,806 | 3,691 | 1,886 | 1,805 | .. | .. | .. | .. | .. | .. | .. | .. | .. |
| 18 | ,, | Sheopur | 5,531 | 2,753 | 2,778 | 3,743 | 1,866 | 1,877 | .. | .. | .. | .. | .. | .. | .. | .. | .. |
| 19 | ,, | Gohad | 5,139 | 2,659 | 2,480 | 4,515 | 2,361 | 2,154 | .. | .. | .. | .. | .. | .. | .. | .. | .. |
| 20 | ,, | Guna (Station) | 5,099 | 2,768 | 2,331 | 3,516 | 1,820 | 1,687 | .. | .. | .. | .. | .. | .. | 271 | 199 | 72 |
| 21 | ,, | Baroda (Sheopur) | 5,073 | 2,592 | 2,481 | 4,715 | 2,357 | 2,358 | .. | .. | .. | .. | .. | .. | .. | .. | .. |
| 22 | ,, | Nimach (Town) | 4,989 | 2,565 | 2,424 | 3,521 | 1,834 | 1,687 | .. | .. | .. | .. | .. | .. | .. | .. | .. |
| 23 | ,, | Sabalgarh | 4,985 | 2,605 | 2,380 | 4,242 | 2,216 | 2,026 | .. | .. | .. | .. | .. | .. | .. | .. | .. |
| 24 | ,, | Bhander | 4,317 | 2,150 | 2,167 | 3,710 | 1,877 | 1,833 | .. | .. | .. | .. | .. | .. | .. | .. | .. |
| 25 | ,, | Narwar | 3,913 | 1,976 | 1,937 | 3,185 | 1,627 | 1,558 | .. | .. | .. | .. | .. | .. | .. | .. | .. |
| 26 | ,, | Agar (Station) | 3,487 | 1,981 | 1,506 | 2,219 | 1,156 | 1,063 | .. | .. | .. | .. | .. | .. | 215 | 185 | 30 |
| 27 | ,, | Chanderi | 2,753 | 1,414 | 1,339 | 1,798 | 929 | 869 | .. | .. | .. | .. | .. | .. | .. | .. | .. |
| 28 | ,, | Morena | 2,690 | 1,461 | 1,229 | 2,657 | 1,441 | 1,216 | .. | .. | .. | .. | .. | .. | .. | .. | .. |
| 29 | Indore | Indore | 44,947 | 24,792 | 20,155 | 31,663 | 17,536 | 14,127 | .. | .. | .. | .. | .. | .. | 211 | 134 | 77 |
| 30 | ,, | Mhow (Cantonment). | 29,820 | 17,723 | 12,097 | 17,379 | 10,087 | 7,292 | 8 | 4 | 4 | .. | .. | .. | 3 | 1 | 2 |
| 31 | ,, | Maheshwar | 9,599 | 4,708 | 4,891 | 8,265 | 4,064 | 4,201 | .. | .. | .. | .. | .. | .. | 3 | 2 | 1 |
| 32 | ,, | Khargon | 9,423 | 4,603 | 4,820 | 6,570 | 3,231 | 3,339 | .. | .. | .. | .. | .. | .. | .. | .. | .. |
| 33 | ,, | Indore Residency | 9,195 | 5,362 | 3,833 | 5,575 | 3,374 | 2,201 | 17 | 14 | 3 | .. | .. | .. | 12 | 11 | 1 |
| 34 | ,, | Rampura | 7,799 | 3,815 | 3,984 | 4,855 | 2,441 | 2,414 | .. | .. | .. | .. | .. | .. | .. | .. | .. |
| 35 | ,, | Barwaha | 7,184 | 3,866 | 3,318 | 5,724 | 3,095 | 2,629 | .. | .. | .. | .. | .. | .. | 3 | 1 | 2 |
| 36 | ,, | Bhanpura | 5,859 | 2,920 | 2,939 | 3,634 | 1,798 | 1,836 | .. | .. | .. | .. | .. | .. | .. | .. | .. |
| 37 | ,, | Mehidpur | 5,620 | 2,826 | 2,794 | 3,087 | 1,586 | 1,501 | .. | .. | .. | .. | .. | .. | .. | .. | .. |
| 38 | ,, | Tarana | 5,463 | 2,801 | 2,662 | 4,548 | 2,345 | 2,203 | .. | .. | .. | .. | .. | .. | .. | .. | .. |
| 39 | ,, | Sanawad | 3,506 | 1,871 | 1,635 | 2,719 | 1,445 | 1,274 | .. | .. | .. | .. | .. | .. | .. | .. | .. |
| 40 | Bhopal | Bhopal | 56,204 | 29,043 | 27,161 | 22,025 | 11,566 | 10,459 | .. | .. | .. | .. | .. | .. | 221 | 125 | 96 |
| 41 | ,, | Sehore (Station) | 7,741 | 4,156 | 3,585 | 5,821 | 3,133 | 2,688 | 3 | 3 | .. | .. | .. | .. | 8 | 5 | 3 |
| 42 | ,, | Ashta | 4,855 | 2,451 | 2,404 | 2,876 | 1,458 | 1,418 | .. | .. | .. | .. | .. | .. | .. | .. | .. |
| 43 | ,, | Sehore (Town) | 4,364 | 2,225 | 2,139 | 2,463 | 1,249 | 1,214 | .. | .. | .. | .. | .. | .. | 1 | 1 | .. |
| 44 | ,, | Ichhawar | 3,914 | 2,059 | 1,855 | 2,735 | 1,421 | 1,314 | .. | .. | .. | .. | .. | .. | .. | .. | .. |
| 45 | ,, | Raisen | 3,577 | 1,793 | 1,784 | 2,258 | 1,156 | 1,102 | .. | .. | .. | .. | .. | .. | .. | .. | .. |
| 46 | ,, | Berasia | 2,624 | 1,337 | 1,287 | 1,804 | 922 | 882 | .. | .. | .. | .. | .. | .. | .. | .. | .. |
| 47 | Rewah | Rewah | 26,247 | 14,248 | 11,999 | 20,914 | 11,709 | 9,205 | .. | .. | .. | .. | .. | .. | 9 | 7 | 2 |
| 48 | ,, | Satna (Raghurajnagar) | 7,192 | 3,829 | 3,363 | 6,043 | 3,226 | 2,817 | .. | .. | .. | .. | .. | .. | .. | .. | .. |
| 49 | ,, | Umaria | 6,008 | 3,140 | 2,868 | 4,985 | 2,627 | 2,358 | .. | .. | .. | .. | .. | .. | .. | .. | .. |
| 50 | ,, | Govindgarh | 4,919 | 2,466 | 2,453 | 4,445 | 2,203 | 2,242 | .. | .. | .. | .. | .. | .. | .. | .. | .. |
| 51 | Orchha | Tikamgarh | 15,495 | 8,013 | 7,482 | 11,363 | 5,903 | 5,460 | .. | .. | .. | .. | .. | .. | .. | .. | .. |
| 52 | Datia | Datia | 17,329 | 8,766 | 8,563 | 14,435 | 7,303 | 7,132 | .. | .. | .. | .. | .. | .. | .. | .. | .. |
| 53 | ,, | Seondha | 3,954 | 2,019 | 1,935 | 3,609 | 1,858 | 1,751 | .. | .. | .. | .. | .. | .. | .. | .. | .. |
| 54 | Dhar | Dhar | 7,472 | 3,850 | 3,622 | 5,476 | 2,827 | 2,649 | 15 | 10 | 5 | .. | .. | .. | .. | .. | .. |
| 55 | ,, | Kukshi | 6,248 | 3,098 | 3,150 | 3,951 | 1,994 | 1,957 | 2 | 2 | .. | .. | .. | .. | .. | .. | .. |
| 56 | Dewas, Senior Branch and Junior Branch | Dewas | 15,285 | 7,858 | 7,427 | 10,801 | 5,534 | 5,267 | .. | .. | .. | .. | .. | .. | .. | .. | .. |
| 57 | ,, | Sarangpur | 7,198 | 3,561 | 3,637 | 4,465 | 2,230 | 2,235 | .. | .. | .. | .. | .. | .. | .. | .. | .. |
| 58 | Samthar | Samthar | 7,441 | 3,799 | 3,642 | 6,341 | 3,273 | 3,068 | .. | .. | .. | .. | .. | .. | .. | .. | .. |
| 59 | Jaora | Jaora | 18,054 | 9,146 | 8,908 | 7,415 | 3,780 | 3,635 | .. | .. | .. | .. | .. | .. | 15 | 12 | 3 |
| 60 | Ratlam | Ratlam | 27,957 | 14,340 | 13,617 | 16,189 | 8,285 | 7,904 | 5 | 1 | 4 | .. | .. | .. | .. | .. | .. |
| 61 | Panna | Panna | 10,756 | 5,361 | 5,395 | 8,741 | 4,352 | 4,389 | .. | .. | .. | .. | .. | .. | 21 | 18 | 3 |
| 62 | Charkhari | Maharajnagar | 9,879 | 4,840 | 5,039 | 7,412 | 3,711 | 3,701 | .. | .. | .. | .. | .. | .. | .. | .. | .. |
| 63 | Bijawar | Bijawar | 6,018 | 3,042 | 2,976 | 4,809 | 2,445 | 2,364 | .. | .. | .. | .. | .. | .. | .. | .. | .. |
| 64 | Chhatarpur | Chhatarpur | 10,413 | 5,055 | 5,358 | 8,655 | 4,267 | 4,388 | .. | .. | .. | .. | .. | .. | .. | .. | .. |
| 65 | ,, | Nowgong (Cantonment) | 9,421 | 5,454 | 3,967 | 5,461 | 2,906 | 2,555 | .. | .. | .. | .. | .. | .. | 49 | 39 | 10 |
| 66 | ,, | Maharajpur | 4,783 | 2,398 | 2,385 | 4,668 | 2,327 | 2,341 | .. | .. | .. | .. | .. | .. | .. | .. | .. |
| 67 | ,, | Rajnagar | 3,335 | 1,561 | 1,774 | 2,876 | 1,370 | 1,506 | .. | .. | .. | .. | .. | .. | .. | .. | .. |
| 68 | Sitamau | Sitamau | 5,924 | 3,020 | 2,904 | 4,449 | 2,258 | 2,191 | .. | .. | .. | .. | .. | .. | .. | .. | .. |
| 69 | Sailana | Sailana | 4,311 | 2,183 | 2,128 | 3,329 | 1,651 | 1,678 | .. | .. | .. | .. | .. | .. | .. | .. | .. |
| 70 | Rajgarh | Rajgarh | 6,389 | 3,268 | 3,121 | 4,898 | 2,512 | 2,386 | .. | .. | .. | .. | .. | .. | .. | .. | .. |
| 71 | ,, | Biaora | 6,668 | 3,408 | 3,255 | 5,409 | 2,771 | 2,638 | .. | .. | .. | .. | .. | .. | 1 | 1 | .. |
| 72 | Narsinghgarh | Narsinghgarh | 9,164 | 4,779 | 4,385 | 7,738 | 4,026 | 3,712 | .. | .. | .. | .. | .. | .. | 9 | 4 | 5 |
| 73 | Nagod | Nagod | 4,028 | 2,075 | 1,953 | 3,171 | 1,633 | 1,538 | .. | .. | .. | .. | .. | .. | 2 | 2 | .. |
| 74 | ,, | Unchahra | 4,507 | 2,225 | 2,282 | 3,796 | 1,869 | 1,927 | .. | .. | .. | .. | .. | .. | .. | .. | .. |
| 75 | Maihar | Maihar | 7,094 | 3,390 | 3,704 | 5,668 | 2,684 | 2,984 | .. | .. | .. | .. | .. | .. | .. | .. | .. |
| 76 | Barwani | Barwani | 7,279 | 3,540 | 3,739 | 4,521 | 2,240 | 2,281 | 12 | 9 | 3 | 9 | 6 | 3 | 4 | 2 | 2 |
| 77 | Khilchipur | Khilchipur | 5,868 | 2,964 | 2,904 | 4,937 | 2,485 | 2,452 | .. | .. | .. | .. | .. | .. | .. | .. | .. |

WITH POPULATION BY RELIGION.

| ARYANS. (c) Jains. | | | Animists. | | | Musalmans. | | | Christians. | | | Parsis. | | | Jews. | | | Serial No. |
|---|---|---|---|---|---|---|---|---|---|---|---|---|---|---|---|---|---|---|
| Persons. | Males. | Females. | Persons. | Males. | Females. | Persons. | Males. | Females. | Persons. | Males. | Females. | Persons. | Males. | Females. | Persons. | Males. | Females. | |
| 19 | 20 | 21 | 22 | 23 | 24 | 25 | 26 | 27 | 28 | 29 | 30 | 31 | 32 | 33 | 34 | 35 | 36 | 37 |
| **20,956** | **10,949** | **10,007** | **3,608** | **1,952** | **1,656** | **205,493** | **106,384** | **99,109** | **7,689** | **5,210** | **2,479** | **1,142** | **581** | **561** | **51** | **28** | **23** | |
| 307 | 169 | 138 | 70 | 37 | 33 | 10,923 | 5,659 | 5,264 | 136 | 72 | 64 | 62 | 35 | 27 | .. | .. | .. | 1 |
| 727 | 392 | 335 | 10 | 7 | 3 | 11,404 | 5,961 | 5,443 | 114 | 66 | 48 | 16 | 13 | 3 | .. | .. | .. | 2 |
| 968 | 519 | 449 | 9 | 5 | 4 | 4,899 | 2,491 | 2,408 | 9 | 3 | 6 | 11 | 4 | 7 | .. | .. | .. | 3 |
| 44 | 19 | 25 | .. | .. | .. | 3,991 | 1,982 | 2,009 | 6 | 4 | 2 | .. | .. | .. | .. | .. | .. | 4 |
| 57 | 38 | 19 | 11 | 6 | 5 | 3,980 | 2,442 | 1,538 | 58 | 31 | 27 | 1 | 1 | .. | .. | .. | .. | 5 |
| 158 | 82 | 76 | 9 | 5 | 4 | 3,530 | 1,898 | 1,632 | 989 | 711 | 278 | 147 | 66 | 81 | .. | .. | .. | 6 |
| 143 | 76 | 67 | 32 | 31 | 1 | 2,088 | 1,099 | 989 | .. | .. | .. | 5 | 4 | 1 | .. | .. | .. | 7 |
| 2 | .. | 2 | 56 | 34 | 22 | 2,646 | 1,801 | 845 | 29 | 6 | 23 | 13 | 3 | 10 | .. | .. | .. | 8 |
| 730 | 431 | 299 | 2 | .. | 2 | 1,420 | 762 | 658 | 11 | 5 | 6 | .. | .. | .. | .. | .. | .. | 9 |
| 361 | 194 | 167 | 4 | 2 | 2 | 2,485 | 1,221 | 1,264 | .. | .. | .. | .. | .. | .. | .. | .. | .. | 10 |
| 755 | 387 | 368 | 1 | 1 | .. | 2,131 | 1,109 | 1,022 | 1 | 1 | .. | 3 | 2 | 1 | .. | .. | .. | 11 |
| 512 | 249 | 263 | .. | .. | .. | 1,255 | 678 | 577 | 8 | 4 | 4 | .. | .. | .. | .. | .. | .. | 12 |
| 205 | 106 | 99 | 2 | 2 | .. | 1,134 | 627 | 507 | 28 | 16 | 12 | .. | .. | .. | .. | .. | .. | 13 |
| 696 | 337 | 359 | 59 | 27 | 32 | 1,397 | 697 | 700 | 1 | .. | 1 | .. | .. | .. | .. | .. | .. | 14 |
| 450 | 243 | 207 | .. | .. | .. | 1,398 | 750 | 648 | .. | .. | .. | 1 | 1 | .. | .. | .. | .. | 15 |
| 359 | 186 | 173 | .. | .. | .. | 1,446 | 737 | 709 | 1 | 1 | .. | .. | .. | .. | .. | .. | .. | 16 |
| 603 | 315 | 288 | 83 | 43 | 40 | 1,357 | 684 | 673 | .. | .. | .. | .. | .. | .. | .. | .. | .. | 17 |
| 99 | 53 | 46 | 12 | 7 | 5 | 1,677 | 827 | 850 | .. | .. | .. | .. | .. | .. | .. | .. | .. | 18 |
| 17 | 6 | 11 | .. | .. | .. | 607 | 292 | 315 | .. | .. | .. | .. | .. | .. | .. | .. | .. | 19 |
| 100 | 54 | 46 | 75 | 35 | 40 | 1,095 | 632 | 463 | 42 | 19 | 23 | .. | .. | .. | .. | .. | .. | 20 |
| 19 | 15 | 4 | .. | .. | .. | 339 | 220 | 119 | .. | .. | .. | .. | .. | .. | .. | .. | .. | 21 |
| 217 | 100 | 117 | 18 | 10 | 8 | 1,135 | 571 | 564 | 84 | 41 | 43 | 14 | 9 | 5 | .. | .. | .. | 22 |
| .. | .. | .. | .. | .. | .. | 743 | 389 | 354 | .. | .. | .. | .. | .. | .. | .. | .. | .. | 23 |
| .. | .. | .. | .. | .. | .. | 607 | 273 | 334 | .. | .. | .. | .. | .. | .. | .. | .. | .. | 24 |
| 177 | 91 | 86 | .. | .. | .. | 551 | 258 | 293 | .. | .. | .. | .. | .. | .. | .. | .. | .. | 25 |
| 78 | 51 | 27 | 15 | 6 | 9 | 928 | 560 | 368 | 32 | 23 | 9 | .. | .. | .. | .. | .. | .. | 26 |
| 203 | 93 | 110 | .. | .. | .. | 752 | 392 | 360 | .. | .. | .. | .. | .. | .. | .. | .. | .. | 27 |
| 6 | 4 | 2 | .. | .. | .. | 26 | 15 | 11 | 1 | 1 | .. | .. | .. | .. | .. | .. | .. | 28 |
| 915 | 515 | 400 | 27 | 23 | 4 | 11,953 | 6,484 | 5,469 | 157 | 86 | 71 | 21 | 14 | 7 | .. | .. | .. | 29 |
| 305 | 155 | 150 | 17 | 10 | 7 | 8,120 | 4,533 | 3,587 | 3,532 | 2,707 | 825 | 427 | 209 | 218 | 29 | 17 | 12 | 30 |
| 109 | 55 | 54 | 86 | 33 | 53 | 1,136 | 554 | 582 | .. | .. | .. | .. | .. | .. | .. | .. | .. | 31 |
| 6 | 4 | 2 | .. | .. | .. | 2,839 | 1,364 | 1,475 | 5 | 1 | 4 | 3 | 3 | .. | .. | .. | .. | 32 |
| 25 | 20 | 5 | 817 | 465 | 352 | 1,727 | 1,011 | 716 | 801 | 367 | 434 | 219 | 99 | 120 | 2 | 1 | 1 | 33 |
| 556 | 272 | 284 | .. | .. | .. | 2,388 | 1,102 | 1,286 | .. | .. | .. | .. | .. | .. | .. | .. | .. | 34 |
| 206 | 103 | 103 | .. | .. | .. | 1,247 | 663 | 584 | 1 | 1 | .. | 3 | 3 | .. | .. | .. | .. | 35 |
| 719 | 385 | 334 | .. | .. | .. | 1,502 | 736 | 766 | 4 | 1 | 3 | .. | .. | .. | .. | .. | .. | 36 |
| 579 | 277 | 302 | 89 | 55 | 34 | 1,865 | 908 | 957 | .. | .. | .. | .. | .. | .. | .. | .. | .. | 37 |
| 6 | 4 | 2 | 1 | .. | 1 | 906 | 451 | 455 | 2 | 1 | 1 | .. | .. | .. | .. | .. | .. | 38 |
| 165 | 91 | 74 | 2 | 1 | 1 | 609 | 326 | 283 | 8 | 5 | 3 | 3 | 3 | .. | .. | .. | .. | 39 |
| 644 | 314 | 330 | 21 | 13 | 8 | 33,005 | 16,859 | 16,146 | 218 | 127 | 91 | 64 | 36 | 28 | 6 | 3 | 3 | 40 |
| 85 | 41 | 44 | .. | .. | .. | 1,722 | 915 | 807 | 97 | 55 | 42 | 5 | 4 | 1 | .. | .. | .. | 41 |
| 251 | 128 | 123 | 11 | 11 | .. | 1,716 | 853 | 863 | 1 | 1 | .. | .. | .. | .. | .. | .. | .. | 42 |
| 62 | 27 | 35 | .. | .. | .. | 1,836 | 946 | 890 | 2 | 2 | .. | .. | .. | .. | .. | .. | .. | 43 |
| 78 | 40 | 38 | 3 | 2 | 1 | 1,096 | 594 | 502 | 1 | 1 | .. | 1 | 1 | .. | .. | .. | .. | 44 |
| 60 | 32 | 28 | 14 | 9 | 5 | 1,245 | 596 | 649 | .. | .. | .. | .. | .. | .. | .. | .. | .. | 45 |
| 58 | 24 | 34 | 3 | 3 | .. | 759 | 388 | 371 | .. | .. | .. | .. | .. | .. | .. | .. | .. | 46 |
| 65 | 34 | 31 | .. | .. | .. | 5,253 | 2,495 | 2,758 | 6 | 3 | 3 | .. | .. | .. | .. | .. | .. | 47 |
| 96 | 58 | 38 | .. | .. | .. | 1,031 | 533 | 498 | 22 | 12 | 10 | .. | .. | .. | .. | .. | .. | 48 |
| 20 | 6 | 14 | .. | .. | .. | 947 | 479 | 468 | 56 | 28 | 28 | .. | .. | .. | .. | .. | .. | 49 |
| .. | .. | .. | .. | .. | .. | 474 | 263 | 211 | .. | .. | .. | .. | .. | .. | .. | .. | .. | 50 |
| 625 | 316 | 309 | 188 | 87 | 101 | 3,317 | 1,706 | 1,611 | 2 | 1 | 1 | .. | .. | .. | .. | .. | .. | 51 |
| 3 | 2 | 1 | .. | .. | .. | 2,886 | 1,458 | 1,428 | 5 | 3 | 2 | .. | .. | .. | .. | .. | .. | 52 |
| 6 | 4 | 2 | .. | .. | .. | 339 | 157 | 182 | .. | .. | .. | .. | .. | .. | .. | .. | .. | 53 |
| 74 | 43 | 31 | 185 | 109 | 76 | 1,551 | 798 | 753 | 165 | 59 | 106 | 6 | 4 | 2 | .. | .. | .. | 54 |
| 290 | 148 | 142 | 588 | 296 | 202 | 1,417 | 658 | 759 | .. | .. | .. | .. | .. | .. | .. | .. | .. | 55 |
| 474 | 260 | 214 | .. | .. | .. | 4,003 | 2,060 | 1,943 | 5 | 2 | 3 | 2 | 2 | .. | .. | .. | .. | 56 |
| 182 | 66 | 66 | .. | .. | .. | 2,601 | 1,265 | 1,336 | .. | .. | .. | .. | .. | .. | .. | .. | .. | 57 |
| .. | .. | .. | .. | .. | .. | 1,100 | 526 | 574 | .. | .. | .. | .. | .. | .. | .. | .. | .. | 58 |
| 1,273 | 702 | 571 | 127 | 73 | 54 | 9,176 | 4,556 | 4,620 | 18 | 7 | 11 | 24 | 13 | 11 | 6 | 3 | 3 | 59 |
| 3,715 | 1,915 | 1,800 | 130 | 68 | 62 | 7,475 | 3,844 | 3,631 | 377 | 192 | 185 | 59 | 32 | 27 | 7 | 3 | 4 | 60 |
| 123 | 66 | 57 | 267 | 139 | 128 | 1,581 | 771 | 810 | 23 | 15 | 8 | .. | .. | .. | .. | .. | .. | 61 |
| .. | .. | .. | .. | .. | .. | 2,467 | 1,129 | 1,338 | .. | .. | .. | .. | .. | .. | .. | .. | .. | 62 |
| 33 | 17 | 16 | .. | .. | .. | 1,175 | 579 | 596 | 1 | 1 | .. | .. | .. | .. | .. | .. | .. | 63 |
| 84 | 33 | 51 | .. | .. | .. | 1,674 | 755 | 919 | .. | .. | .. | .. | .. | .. | .. | .. | .. | 64 |
| 38 | 22 | 16 | 1 | 1 | .. | 3,240 | 1,956 | 1,284 | 619 | 522 | 97 | 12 | 7 | 5 | 1 | 1 | .. | 65 |
| .. | .. | .. | .. | .. | .. | 115 | 71 | 44 | .. | .. | .. | .. | .. | .. | .. | .. | .. | 66 |
| 60 | 25 | 35 | .. | .. | .. | 399 | 166 | 233 | .. | .. | .. | .. | .. | .. | .. | .. | .. | 67 |
| 395 | 210 | 185 | .. | .. | .. | 1,069 | 546 | 523 | 8 | 4 | 4 | 3 | 2 | 1 | .. | .. | .. | 68 |
| 266 | 144 | 122 | 68 | 42 | 26 | 647 | 345 | 302 | .. | .. | .. | 1 | 1 | .. | .. | .. | .. | 69 |
| 2 | 1 | 1 | .. | .. | .. | 1,489 | 755 | 734 | .. | .. | .. | .. | .. | .. | .. | .. | .. | 70 |
| 106 | 49 | 57 | .. | .. | .. | 1,142 | 584 | 558 | .. | .. | .. | 5 | 3 | 2 | .. | .. | .. | 71 |
| 63 | 31 | 32 | .. | .. | .. | 1,354 | 718 | 636 | .. | .. | .. | .. | .. | .. | .. | .. | .. | 72 |
| 34 | 16 | 18 | .. | .. | .. | 821 | 424 | 397 | .. | .. | .. | .. | .. | .. | .. | .. | .. | 73 |
| .. | .. | .. | .. | .. | .. | 711 | 356 | 355 | .. | .. | .. | .. | .. | .. | .. | .. | .. | 74 |
| 30 | 14 | 16 | .. | .. | .. | 1,394 | 691 | 703 | 2 | 1 | 1 | .. | .. | .. | .. | .. | .. | 75 |
| 115 | 61 | 54 | 495 | 254 | 241 | 2,111 | 960 | 1,151 | 1 | 1 | .. | 11 | 7 | 4 | .. | .. | .. | 76 |
| 12 | 9 | 3 | .. | .. | .. | 919 | 470 | 449 | .. | .. | .. | .. | .. | .. | .. | .. | .. | 77 |

# TABLE VI.

## *RELIGION.*

The animistic population shows a considerable decrease on the present occasion owing to the reluctance of the majority of these tribes to return themselves as animistic. Most of the persons of this class have on this occasion returned their religion as Hindu. The figures for the main tribes are given below :—

| Tribes. | Persons. | Males. | Females. |
|---|---|---|---|
| 1 | 2 | 3 | 4 |
| Bhil | H. 25,831<br>A. 269,910 | 13,693<br>134,045 | 12,138<br>135,865 |
| Bhilala | H. 33,764<br>A. 89,612 | 16,351<br>44,821 | 17,413<br>44,791 |
| Gond | H. 163,285<br>A. 71,387 | 76,753<br>34,611 | 86,532<br>36,776 |
| Kirar | H. 86,885<br>A. 3,037 | 45,547<br>1,541 | 41,338<br>1,496 |
| Kotwal | H. 27,086<br>A. 523 | 14,537<br>254 | 12,549<br>269 |
| Patlia | H. 21,616<br>A. 9 | 13,568<br>5 | 8,048<br>4 |
| Seheria | H. 49,244<br>A. 31,798 | 25,373<br>16,187 | 23,871<br>15,611 |

### TERRITORIAL DISTRIBUTION OF CHRISTIAN POPULATION.

| Political Charge. | Population. | | | European and Allied Races. | | | Anglo-Indians. | | | Indian Christians. | | |
|---|---|---|---|---|---|---|---|---|---|---|---|---|
| | Persons. | Males. | Females. | Persons. | Males. | Females. | Persons. | Males. | Females. | Persons. | Males. | Females. |
| 1 | 2 | 3 | 4 | 5 | 6 | 7 | 8 | 9 | 10 | 11 | 12 | 13 |
| **Central India** | **9,358** | **6,170** | **3,188** | **4,582** | **3,716** | **866** | **565** | **296** | **269** | **4,211** | **2,158** | **2,053** |
| 1 Gwalior Residency | 1,670 | 1,079 | 591 | 839 | 698 | 141 | 135 | 60 | 75 | 696 | 321 | 375 |
| 2 Indore Residency | 4,824 | 3,412 | 1,412 | 2,768 | 2,284 | 484 | 259 | 138 | 121 | 1,797 | 990 | 807 |
| 3 Baghelkhand Agency | 163 | 85 | 78 | 101 | 51 | 50 | 9 | 4 | 5 | 53 | 30 | 23 |
| 4 Bhopal Agency | 331 | 194 | 137 | 190 | 116 | 74 | 23 | 21 | 2 | 118 | 57 | 61 |
| 5 Bhopawar Agency | 1,084 | 533 | 551 | 19 | 13 | 6 | 8 | 3 | 5 | 1,057 | 517 | 540 |
| 6 Bundelkhand Agency | 812 | 626 | 186 | 607 | 522 | 85 | 22 | 11 | 11 | 183 | 93 | 90 |
| 7 Malwa Agency | 474 | 241 | 233 | 58 | 32 | 26 | 109 | 59 | 50 | 307 | 150 | 157 |

# TABLE VI.—Religion.

| Serial No. | Political Charge. | Population. Persons. | Population. Males. | Population. Females. | Indo-Aryans. (a) Hindu Brahamanic. Persons. | (a) Hindu Brahamanic. Males. | (a) Hindu Brahamanic. Females. | (b) Hindu Arya. Persons. | (b) Hindu Arya. Males. | (b) Hindu Arya. Females. | (c) Hindu Brahmos. Persons. | (c) Hindu Brahmos. Males. | (c) Hindu Brahmos. Females. | (d) Sikh. Persons. | (d) Sikh. Males. | (d) Sikh. Females. | (e) Jains. Persons. | (e) Jains. Males. | (e) Jains. Females. |
|---|---|---|---|---|---|---|---|---|---|---|---|---|---|---|---|---|---|---|---|
| 1 | 2 | 3 | 4 | 5 | 6 | 7 | 8 | 9 | 10 | 11 | 12 | 13 | 14 | 15 | 16 | 17 | 18 | 19 | 20 |
| | **Central India** . | **9,356,980** | **4,801,459** | **4,555,521** | **8,262,638** | **4,241,694** | **4,020,944** | **139** | **90** | **49** | **9** | **6** | **3** | **1,384** | **953** | **431** | **87,471** | **45,711** | **41,760** |
| 1 | Gwalior Residency . | 3,090,798 | 1,627,581 | 1,463,217 | 2,839,443 | 1,494,919 | 1,344,524 | 35 | 20 | 15 | .. | .. | .. | 554 | 430 | 124 | 37,488 | 19,829 | 17,659 |
| 2 | Indore Residency . | 979,360 | 506,659 | 472,701 | 848,014 | 437,860 | 410,154 | 29 | 20 | 9 | .. | .. | .. | 438 | 272 | 166 | 10,397 | 5,418 | 4,979 |
| 3 | Baghelkhand Agency | 1,772,574 | 879,090 | 893,484 | 1,727,163 | 856,192 | 870,971 | .. | .. | .. | .. | .. | .. | 29 | 27 | 2 | 700 | 346 | 354 |
| 4 | Bhopal Agency . | 1,050,735 | 536,458 | 514,277 | 884,144 | 452,547 | 431,597 | 8 | 6 | 2 | .. | .. | .. | 242 | 137 | 105 | 6,425 | 3,241 | 3,184 |
| 5 | Bhopawar Agency . | 698,455 | 349,553 | 348,902 | 369,897 | 185,572 | 184,325 | 61 | 42 | 19 | 9 | 6 | 3 | 16 | 10 | 6 | 8,682 | 4,526 | 4,156 |
| 6 | Bundelkhand Agency | 1,375,317 | 703,042 | 672,275 | 1,286,654 | 657,683 | 628,971 | .. | .. | .. | .. | .. | .. | 89 | 64 | 25 | 12,886 | 6,605 | 6,281 |
| 7 | Malwa Agency . | 389,741 | 199,076 | 190,665 | 307,323 | 156,921 | 150,402 | 6 | 2 | 4 | .. | .. | .. | 16 | 13 | 3 | 10,893 | 5,746 | 5,147 |

| Serial No. | Political Charge. | Animists. Persons. | Animists. Males. | Animists. Females. | Musalmans. Persons. | Musalmans. Males. | Musalmans. Females. | Christians. Persons. | Christians. Males. | Christians. Females. | Parsis. Persons. | Parsis. Males. | Parsis. Females. | Jews. Persons. | Jews. Males. | Jews. Females. |
|---|---|---|---|---|---|---|---|---|---|---|---|---|---|---|---|---|
| 1 | 2 | 21 | 22 | 23 | 24 | 25 | 26 | 27 | 28 | 29 | 30 | 31 | 32 | 33 | 34 | 35 |
| | **Central India** . | **483,394** | **239,618** | **243,776** | **511,200** | **266,494** | **244,706** | **9,358** | **6,170** | **3,188** | **1,330** | **689** | **641** | **57** | **34** | **23** |
| 1 | Gwalior Residency . | 42,523 | 21,539 | 20,984 | 168,786 | 89,615 | 79,171 | 1,670 | 1,079 | 591 | 299 | 150 | 149 | .. | .. | .. |
| 2 | Indore Residency . | 36,092 | 18,053 | 18,039 | 78,839 | 41,258 | 37,581 | 4,824 | 3,412 | 1,412 | 690 | 342 | 348 | 37 | 24 | 13 |
| 3 | Baghelkhand Agency | 3,915 | 1,932 | 1,983 | 40,596 | 20,504 | 20,092 | 163 | 85 | 78 | 8 | 4 | 4 | .. | .. | .. |
| 4 | Bhopal Agency . | 58,775 | 28,118 | 30,657 | 100,674 | 52,134 | 48,540 | 331 | 194 | 137 | 130 | 78 | 52 | 6 | 3 | 3 |
| 5 | Bhopawar Agency . | 285,941 | 142,088 | 143,853 | 32,674 | 16,723 | 15,951 | 1,084 | 533 | 551 | 91 | 53 | 38 | .. | .. | .. |
| 6 | Bundelkhand Agency | 27,859 | 13,742 | 14,117 | 46,997 | 24,313 | 22,684 | 812 | 626 | 186 | 19 | 8 | 11 | 1 | 1 | .. |
| 7 | Malwa Agency . | 28,289 | 14,146 | 14,143 | 42,634 | 21,947 | 20,687 | 474 | 241 | 233 | 93 | 54 | 39 | 13 | 6 | 7 |

## TABLE VII.

### *AGE, SEX AND CIVIL CONDITION.*

This table is divided into two parts. *Part A* shows the distribution for the Agency as a whole of the total population and of each religion by age, sex and civil condition. *Part B* shows the distribution for the three Natural Divisions of the total population and of each religion by age, sex and civil condition.

The distribution by Political Charges from this table onwards has been omitted, as these statistics are not of any value.

# TABLE VII.—Age, Sex and Civil Condition. Part A.—Agency Summary.

| Age. | Population. | | | Unmarried. | | | Married. | | | Widowed. | | |
|---|---|---|---|---|---|---|---|---|---|---|---|---|
| | Persons. | Males. | Females. | Persons. | Males. | Females. | Persons. | Males. | Females. | Persons. | Males. | Females. |
| 1 | 2 | 3 | 4 | 5 | 6 | 7 | 8 | 9 | 10 | 11 | 12 | 13 |
| **Central India.** | | | | | | | | | | | | |
| **ALL RELIGIONS** | **9,356,980** | **4,801,459** | **4,555,521** | **3,626,128** | **2,185,834** | **1,440,294** | **4,616,823** | **2,318,145** | **2,298,678** | **1,114,029** | **297,480** | **816,549** |
| 0—1 | 329,210 | 165,912 | 163,298 | 326,177 | 164,137 | 162,040 | 2,866 | 1,688 | 1,178 | 167 | 87 | 80 |
| 1—2 | 215,313 | 105,795 | 109,518 | 212,287 | 104,330 | 107,957 | 2,790 | 1,356 | 1,434 | 236 | 109 | 127 |
| 2—3 | 280,580 | 134,639 | 145,941 | 273,490 | 130,940 | 142,550 | 6,713 | 3,548 | 3,165 | 377 | 151 | 226 |
| 3—4 | 315,091 | 150,352 | 164,739 | 305,806 | 146,648 | 159,158 | 7,976 | 3,485 | 4,491 | 1,309 | 219 | 1,090 |
| 4—5 | 282,497 | 143,768 | 138,729 | 268,636 | 136,932 | 131,704 | 12,649 | 6,498 | 6,151 | 1,212 | 338 | 874 |
| *Total 0—5* | *1,422,691* | *700,466* | *722,225* | *1,386,396* | *682,987* | *703,409* | *32,994* | *16,575* | *16,419* | *3,301* | *904* | *2,397* |
| 5—10 | 1,165,603 | 603,859 | 561,744 | 1,044,162 | 561,699 | 482,463 | 116,194 | 40,575 | 75,619 | 5,247 | 1,585 | 3,662 |
| 10—15 | 864,283 | 483,893 | 380,390 | 529,397 | 365,586 | 163,811 | 324,622 | 114,351 | 210,271 | 10,264 | 3,956 | 6,308 |
| 15—20 | 737,911 | 403,981 | 333,930 | 249,997 | 217,555 | 32,442 | 467,403 | 178,465 | 288,938 | 20,511 | 7,961 | 12,550 |
| 20—25 | 890,806 | 433,021 | 457,785 | 156,719 | 138,251 | 18,468 | 687,763 | 277,981 | 409,782 | 46,324 | 16,789 | 29,535 |
| 25—30 | 927,638 | 467,654 | 459,984 | 96,302 | 84,143 | 12,159 | 761,780 | 357,941 | 403,848 | 69,547 | 25,570 | 43,977 |
| 30—35 | 909,684 | 474,650 | 435,034 | 59,350 | 50,635 | 8,715 | 741,425 | 389,922 | 351,503 | 108,909 | 34,093 | 74,816 |
| 35—40 | 553,979 | 297,470 | 256,509 | 27,771 | 23,162 | 4,609 | 436,659 | 248,159 | 188,500 | 89,549 | 26,149 | 63,400 |
| 40—45 | 646,273 | 331,091 | 315,182 | 28,810 | 23,187 | 5,623 | 438,060 | 267,490 | 170,570 | 179,403 | 40,414 | 138,989 |
| 45—50 | 305,452 | 161,548 | 143,904 | 12,826 | 10,646 | 2,180 | 195,264 | 126,976 | 68,288 | 97,362 | 23,926 | 73,436 |
| 50—55 | 421,274 | 204,029 | 217,245 | 15,509 | 12,586 | 2,923 | 212,808 | 149,948 | 62,860 | 192,957 | 41,495 | 151,462 |
| 55—60 | 127,594 | 67,128 | 60,466 | 5,433 | 4,473 | 960 | 66,263 | 46,456 | 19,807 | 55,898 | 16,199 | 39,699 |
| 60—65 | 246,017 | 106,253 | 139,764 | 7,900 | 6,354 | 1,546 | 86,522 | 65,750 | 20,772 | 151,595 | 34,149 | 117,446 |
| 65—70 | 52,776 | 26,910 | 25,866 | 2,075 | 1,701 | 374 | 21,359 | 16,250 | 5,109 | 29,342 | 8,959 | 20,383 |
| 70 and over | 84,999 | 39,506 | 45,493 | 3,481 | 2,869 | 612 | 27,698 | 21,306 | 6,392 | 53,820 | 15,331 | 38,489 |
| **HINDU** | **8,262,638** | **4,241,694** | **4,020,944** | **3,154,459** | **1,911,990** | **1,242,469** | **4,105,234** | **2,062,058** | **2,043,176** | **1,002,945** | **267,646** | **735,299** |
| 0—1 | 288,721 | 145,736 | 142,985 | 286,094 | 144,156 | 141,938 | 2,474 | 1,502 | 972 | 153 | 78 | 75 |
| 1—2 | 188,385 | 92,610 | 95,775 | 185,796 | 91,382 | 94,414 | 2,588 | 1,132 | 1,256 | 201 | 96 | 105 |
| 2—3 | 245,201 | 117,637 | 127,564 | 238,641 | 114,157 | 124,484 | 6,224 | 3,347 | 2,877 | 336 | 133 | 203 |
| 3—4 | 274,839 | 131,004 | 143,835 | 266,656 | 127,771 | 138,885 | 7,112 | 3,033 | 4,079 | 1,071 | 200 | 871 |
| 4—5 | 246,913 | 125,962 | 120,951 | 234,066 | 119,519 | 114,547 | 11,750 | 6,135 | 5,615 | 1,097 | 308 | 789 |
| *Total 0—5* | *1,244,059* | *612,949* | *631,110* | *1,211,253* | *596,985* | *614,268* | *29,948* | *15,149* | *14,799* | *2,858* | *815* | *2,043* |
| 5—10 | 1,029,043 | 533,377 | 495,666 | 914,091 | 493,614 | 420,477 | 110,222 | 38,321 | 71,901 | 4,730 | 1,442 | 3,288 |
| 10—15 | 767,773 | 431,335 | 336,438 | 454,422 | 318,996 | 135,426 | 303,892 | 108,658 | 195,234 | 9,459 | 3,681 | 5,778 |
| 15—20 | 654,645 | 360,849 | 293,796 | 213,469 | 188,659 | 24,810 | 422,621 | 164,976 | 257,645 | 18,555 | 7,214 | 11,341 |
| 20—25 | 784,659 | 383,001 | 401,658 | 133,270 | 118,389 | 14,881 | 609,555 | 249,476 | 360,079 | 41,834 | 15,136 | 26,698 |
| 25—30 | 817,023 | 412,250 | 404,773 | 83,580 | 73,478 | 10,102 | 670,604 | 315,774 | 354,830 | 62,839 | 22,998 | 39,841 |
| 30—35 | 803,041 | 418,642 | 384,399 | 52,447 | 45,342 | 7,105 | 652,165 | 342,619 | 309,546 | 98,429 | 30,681 | 67,748 |
| 35—40 | 489,935 | 261,977 | 227,958 | 24,595 | 20,864 | 3,731 | 383,933 | 217,438 | 166,495 | 81,407 | 23,675 | 57,732 |
| 40—45 | 572,133 | 292,199 | 279,934 | 25,414 | 20,814 | 4,600 | 385,115 | 234,890 | 150,225 | 161,604 | 36,495 | 125,109 |
| 45—50 | 272,313 | 143,276 | 129,037 | 11,441 | 9,675 | 1,766 | 172,834 | 112,004 | 60,830 | 88,038 | 21,597 | 66,441 |
| 50—55 | 374,890 | 180,792 | 194,098 | 13,781 | 11,363 | 2,418 | 187,810 | 132,133 | 55,677 | 173,299 | 37,296 | 136,003 |
| 55—60 | 114,343 | 59,937 | 54,406 | 4,790 | 3,986 | 804 | 58,919 | 41,232 | 17,687 | 50,634 | 14,719 | 35,915 |
| 60—65 | 218,231 | 93,348 | 124,883 | 7,009 | 5,731 | 1,278 | 75,204 | 56,981 | 18,223 | 136,018 | 30,636 | 105,382 |
| 65—70 | 46,289 | 23,357 | 22,932 | 1,765 | 1,464 | 301 | 18,468 | 14,033 | 4,435 | 26,056 | 7,860 | 18,196 |
| 70 and over | 74,261 | 34,405 | 39,856 | 3,132 | 2,630 | 502 | 23,944 | 18,374 | 5,570 | 47,185 | 13,401 | 33,784 |
| **ARYA** | **139** | **90** | **49** | **54** | **41** | **13** | **77** | **45** | **32** | **8** | **4** | **4** |
| 0—1 | 4 | 1 | 3 | 4 | 1 | 3 | .. | .. | .. | .. | .. | .. |
| 1—2 | 1 | 1 | .. | 1 | 1 | .. | .. | .. | .. | .. | .. | .. |
| 2—3 | 2 | 2 | .. | 2 | 2 | .. | .. | .. | .. | .. | .. | .. |
| 3—4 | 2 | 1 | 1 | 2 | 1 | 1 | .. | .. | .. | .. | .. | .. |
| 4—5 | 3 | 1 | 2 | 3 | 1 | 2 | .. | .. | .. | .. | .. | .. |
| *Total 0—5* | *12* | *6* | *6* | *12* | *6* | *6* | .. | .. | .. | .. | .. | .. |
| 5—10 | 13 | 8 | 5 | 11 | 7 | 4 | 2 | 1 | 1 | .. | .. | .. |
| 10—15 | 8 | 5 | 3 | 5 | 4 | 1 | 3 | 1 | 2 | .. | .. | .. |
| 15—20 | 16 | 11 | 5 | 8 | 8 | .. | 8 | 3 | 5 | .. | .. | .. |
| 20—25 | 29 | 21 | 8 | 12 | 11 | 1 | 17 | 10 | 7 | .. | .. | .. |
| 25—30 | 31 | 20 | 11 | 5 | 4 | 1 | 24 | 15 | 9 | 2 | 1 | 1 |
| 30—35 | 8 | 8 | .. | 1 | 1 | .. | 7 | 7 | .. | .. | .. | .. |
| 35—40 | 6 | 3 | 3 | .. | .. | .. | 4 | 2 | 2 | 2 | 1 | 1 |
| 40—45 | 7 | 3 | 4 | .. | .. | .. | 7 | 3 | 4 | .. | .. | .. |
| 45—50 | 4 | 3 | 1 | .. | .. | .. | 3 | 2 | 1 | 1 | 1 | .. |
| 50—55 | 4 | 2 | 2 | .. | .. | .. | 2 | 1 | 1 | 2 | 1 | 1 |
| 55—60 | 1 | .. | 1 | .. | .. | .. | .. | .. | .. | 1 | .. | 1 |
| 60—65 | .. | .. | .. | .. | .. | .. | .. | .. | .. | .. | .. | .. |
| 65—70 | .. | .. | .. | .. | .. | .. | .. | .. | .. | .. | .. | .. |
| 70 and over | .. | .. | .. | .. | .. | .. | .. | .. | .. | .. | .. | .. |
| **BRAHMO** | **9** | **6** | **3** | **5** | **4** | **1** | **4** | **2** | **2** | .. | .. | .. |
| 0—1 | .. | .. | .. | .. | .. | .. | .. | .. | .. | .. | .. | .. |
| 1—2 | 1 | 1 | .. | 1 | 1 | .. | .. | .. | .. | .. | .. | .. |
| 2—3 | .. | .. | .. | .. | .. | .. | .. | .. | .. | .. | .. | .. |
| 3—4 | .. | .. | .. | .. | .. | .. | .. | .. | .. | .. | .. | .. |
| 4—5 | .. | .. | .. | .. | .. | .. | .. | .. | .. | .. | .. | .. |
| *Total 0—5* | *1* | *1* | .. | *1* | *1* | .. | .. | .. | .. | .. | .. | .. |
| 5—10 | 2 | 2 | .. | 2 | 2 | .. | .. | .. | .. | .. | .. | .. |
| 10—15 | 2 | 1 | 1 | 2 | 1 | 1 | .. | .. | .. | .. | .. | .. |
| 15—20 | .. | .. | .. | .. | .. | .. | .. | .. | .. | .. | .. | .. |
| 20—25 | 1 | .. | 1 | .. | .. | .. | 1 | .. | 1 | .. | .. | .. |
| 25—30 | .. | .. | .. | .. | .. | .. | .. | .. | .. | .. | .. | .. |
| 30—35 | .. | .. | .. | .. | .. | .. | .. | .. | .. | .. | .. | .. |
| 35—40 | 1 | 1 | .. | .. | .. | .. | 1 | 1 | .. | .. | .. | .. |
| 40—45 | 1 | .. | 1 | .. | .. | .. | 1 | .. | 1 | .. | .. | .. |
| 45—50 | .. | .. | .. | .. | .. | .. | .. | .. | .. | .. | .. | .. |
| 50—55 | .. | .. | .. | .. | .. | .. | .. | .. | .. | .. | .. | .. |
| 55—60 | 1 | 1 | .. | .. | .. | .. | 1 | 1 | .. | .. | .. | .. |
| 60—65 | .. | .. | .. | .. | .. | .. | .. | .. | .. | .. | .. | .. |
| 65—70 | .. | .. | .. | .. | .. | .. | .. | .. | .. | .. | .. | .. |
| 70 and over | .. | .. | .. | .. | .. | .. | .. | .. | .. | .. | .. | .. |

## TABLE VII.—Age, Sex and Civil Condition. Part A.—Agency Summary.

| Age. | Population. | | | Unmarried. | | | Married. | | | Widowed. | | |
|---|---|---|---|---|---|---|---|---|---|---|---|---|
| | Persons. | Males. | Females. | Persons. | Males. | Females. | Persons. | Males. | Females. | Persons. | Males. | Females. |
| 1 | 2 | 3 | 4 | 5 | 6 | 7 | 8 | 9 | 10 | 11 | 12 | 13 |
| **SIKH** | **1,384** | **853** | **431** | **520** | **387** | **133** | **755** | **508** | **247** | **109** | **58** | **51** |
| 0—1 | 31 | 16 | 15 | 31 | 16 | 15 | .. | .. | .. | .. | .. | .. |
| 1—2 | 19 | 11 | 8 | 19 | 11 | 8 | .. | .. | .. | .. | .. | .. |
| 2—3 | 31 | 21 | 10 | 31 | 21 | 10 | .. | .. | .. | .. | .. | .. |
| 3—4 | 28 | 13 | 15 | 28 | 13 | 15 | .. | .. | .. | .. | .. | .. |
| 4—5 | 34 | 16 | 18 | 34 | 16 | 18 | .. | .. | .. | .. | .. | .. |
| *Total 0—5* | *143* | *77* | *66* | *143* | *77* | *66* | .. | .. | .. | .. | .. | .. |
| 5—10 | 95 | 48 | 47 | 94 | 48 | 46 | 1 | .. | 1 | .. | .. | .. |
| 10—15 | 81 | 64 | 17 | 67 | 58 | 9 | 14 | 6 | 8 | .. | .. | .. |
| 15—20 | 139 | 99 | 40 | 73 | 63 | 10 | 64 | 34 | 30 | 2 | 2 | .. |
| 20—25 | 223 | 180 | 43 | 83 | 81 | 2 | 134 | 93 | 41 | 6 | 6 | .. |
| 25—30 | 225 | 158 | 67 | 35 | 35 | .. | 172 | 107 | 65 | 18 | 16 | 2 |
| 30—35 | 180 | 124 | 56 | 13 | 13 | .. | 153 | 100 | 53 | 14 | 11 | 3 |
| 35—40 | 94 | 71 | 23 | 3 | 3 | .. | 79 | 61 | 18 | 12 | 7 | 5 |
| 40—45 | 56 | 42 | 14 | 4 | 4 | .. | 47 | 38 | 9 | 5 | .. | 5 |
| 45—50 | 44 | 34 | 10 | 2 | 2 | .. | 33 | 28 | 5 | 9 | 4 | 5 |
| 50—55 | 38 | 22 | 16 | 2 | 2 | .. | 22 | 16 | 6 | 14 | 4 | 10 |
| 55—60 | 10 | 7 | 3 | 1 | 1 | .. | 8 | 5 | 3 | 1 | 1 | .. |
| 60—65 | 28 | 13 | 15 | .. | .. | .. | 16 | 10 | 6 | 12 | 3 | 9 |
| 65—70 | 5 | 2 | 3 | .. | .. | .. | 2 | 2 | .. | 8 | .. | 3 |
| 70 and over | 23 | 12 | 11 | .. | .. | .. | 10 | 8 | 2 | 13 | 4 | 9 |
| **JAIN** | **87,471** | **45,711** | **41,760** | **33,414** | **21,691** | **11,723** | **38,440** | **19,379** | **19,061** | **15,617** | **4,641** | **10,976** |
| 0—1 | 2,540 | 1,342 | 1,198 | 2,519 | 1,332 | 1,187 | 19 | 10 | 9 | 2 | .. | 2 |
| 1—2 | 1,513 | 718 | 795 | 1,492 | 711 | 781 | 20 | 7 | 13 | 1 | .. | 1 |
| 2—3 | 2,166 | 1,073 | 1,093 | 2,127 | 1,058 | 1,069 | 32 | 15 | 17 | 7 | .. | 7 |
| 3—4 | 2,142 | 1,064 | 1,078 | 2,101 | 1,045 | 1,056 | 36 | 16 | 20 | 5 | 3 | 2 |
| 4—5 | 2,071 | 1,074 | 997 | 2,012 | 1,047 | 965 | 50 | 25 | 25 | 9 | 2 | 7 |
| *Total 0—5* | *10,432* | *5,271* | *5,161* | *10,251* | *5,193* | *5,058* | *157* | *73* | *84* | *24* | *5* | *19* |
| 5—10 | 9,379 | 4,719 | 4,660 | 8,785 | 4,531 | 4,254 | 540 | 176 | 364 | 54 | 12 | 42 |
| 10—15 | 8,097 | 4,563 | 3,534 | 5,560 | 3,979 | 1,581 | 2,421 | 556 | 1,865 | 116 | 28 | 88 |
| 15—20 | 7,347 | 3,993 | 3,354 | 2,653 | 2,436 | 217 | 4,348 | 1,485 | 2,863 | 346 | 72 | 274 |
| 20—25 | 8,651 | 4,409 | 4,242 | 2,006 | 1,831 | 175 | 5,879 | 2,421 | 3,458 | 766 | 157 | 609 |
| 25—30 | 8,196 | 4,308 | 3,888 | 1,253 | 1,122 | 131 | 5,843 | 2,888 | 2,955 | 1,100 | 298 | 802 |
| 30—35 | 8,279 | 4,385 | 3,894 | 970 | 883 | 87 | 5,712 | 3,046 | 2,666 | 1,597 | 456 | 1,141 |
| 35—40 | 5,675 | 3,067 | 2,608 | 497 | 439 | 58 | 3,748 | 2,185 | 1,563 | 1,430 | 443 | 987 |
| 40—45 | 6,411 | 3,242 | 3,169 | 521 | 446 | 75 | 3,622 | 2,199 | 1,423 | 2,268 | 597 | 1,671 |
| 45—50 | 3,718 | 2,075 | 1,643 | 248 | 226 | 22 | 2,053 | 1,358 | 695 | 1,417 | 491 | 926 |
| 50—55 | 4,756 | 2,395 | 2,361 | 315 | 290 | 25 | 1,967 | 1,380 | 587 | 2,474 | 725 | 1,749 |
| 55—60 | 1,881 | 1,029 | 852 | 122 | 103 | 19 | 823 | 581 | 242 | 936 | 345 | 591 |
| 60—65 | 2,809 | 1,303 | 1,506 | 137 | 128 | 9 | 798 | 606 | 187 | 1,879 | 569 | 1,310 |
| 65—70 | 807 | 435 | 372 | 48 | 41 | 7 | 247 | 196 | 51 | 512 | 198 | 314 |
| 70 and over | 1,033 | 517 | 516 | 48 | 43 | 5 | 287 | 229 | 58 | 698 | 245 | 453 |
| **ANIMIST** | **483,394** | **239,618** | **243,776** | **225,896** | **123,603** | **102,293** | **223,340** | **108,632** | **114,708** | **34,158** | **7,383** | **26,775** |
| 0—1 | 20,313 | 10,008 | 10,305 | 20,144 | 9,888 | 10,256 | 164 | 115 | 49 | 5 | 5 | .. |
| 1—2 | 14,661 | 7,069 | 7,592 | 14,556 | 6,992 | 7,564 | 88 | 68 | 20 | 17 | 9 | 8 |
| 2—3 | 18,580 | 8,806 | 9,774 | 18,411 | 8,699 | 9,712 | 154 | 95 | 59 | 15 | 12 | 3 |
| 3—4 | 21,910 | 10,527 | 11,383 | 21,519 | 10,356 | 11,163 | 264 | 166 | 98 | 127 | 5 | 122 |
| 4—5 | 19,595 | 9,855 | 9,740 | 19,215 | 9,665 | 9,550 | 333 | 183 | 150 | 47 | 7 | 40 |
| *Total 0—5* | *95,059* | *46,265* | *48,794* | *93,845* | *45,600* | *48,245* | *1,003* | *627* | *376* | *211* | *38* | *173* |
| 5—10 | 66,584 | 34,538 | 32,046 | 64,911 | 33,824 | 31,087 | 1,531 | 669 | 862 | 142 | 45 | 97 |
| 10—15 | 40,778 | 21,709 | 19,069 | 33,500 | 19,530 | 13,970 | 7,134 | 2,138 | 4,996 | 144 | 41 | 103 |
| 15—20 | 35,318 | 17,227 | 18,091 | 16,079 | 11,540 | 4,539 | 18,788 | 5,522 | 13,266 | 451 | 165 | 286 |
| 20—25 | 44,623 | 18,827 | 25,796 | 7,827 | 6,156 | 1,671 | 35,693 | 12,243 | 23,450 | 1,103 | 428 | 675 |
| 25—30 | 49,415 | 23,160 | 26,255 | 3,952 | 3,008 | 944 | 43,566 | 19,477 | 24,089 | 1,897 | 675 | 1,222 |
| 30—35 | 47,909 | 24,937 | 22,972 | 2,118 | 1,514 | 604 | 42,681 | 22,537 | 20,144 | 3,110 | 886 | 2,224 |
| 35—40 | 27,837 | 15,145 | 12,692 | 992 | 686 | 306 | 24,472 | 13,813 | 10,659 | 2,373 | 646 | 1,727 |
| 40—45 | 29,485 | 15,505 | 13,980 | 1,129 | 704 | 425 | 22,285 | 13,702 | 8,583 | 6,071 | 1,099 | 4,972 |
| 45—50 | 12,340 | 6,481 | 5,859 | 541 | 364 | 177 | 8,871 | 5,651 | 3,220 | 2,928 | 466 | 2,462 |
| 50—55 | 15,898 | 7,563 | 8,335 | 450 | 302 | 148 | 8,861 | 6,198 | 2,663 | 6,587 | 1,063 | 5,524 |
| 55—60 | 4,156 | 1,986 | 2,170 | 168 | 127 | 41 | 2,476 | 1,573 | 903 | 1,512 | 286 | 1,226 |
| 60—65 | 9,236 | 4,038 | 5,198 | 212 | 128 | 84 | 3,913 | 2,985 | 928 | 5,111 | 925 | 4,186 |
| 65—70 | 1,922 | 891 | 1,031 | 80 | 59 | 21 | 894 | 620 | 274 | 948 | 212 | 736 |
| 70 and over | 2,834 | 1,346 | 1,488 | 92 | 61 | 31 | 1,172 | 877 | 295 | 1,570 | 408 | 1,162 |
| **MUSALMAN** | **511,200** | **266,494** | **244,706** | **204,700** | **123,001** | **81,699** | **245,711** | **125,872** | **119,839** | **60,789** | **17,621** | **43,168** |
| 0—1 | 17,308 | 8,656 | 8,652 | 17,092 | 8,591 | 8,501 | 209 | 61 | 148 | 7 | 4 | 3 |
| 1—2 | 10,536 | 5,288 | 5,248 | 10,227 | 5,135 | 5,092 | 292 | 149 | 143 | 17 | 4 | 13 |
| 2—3 | 14,360 | 6,987 | 7,373 | 14,045 | 6,890 | 7,155 | 296 | 91 | 205 | 19 | 6 | 13 |
| 3—4 | 15,903 | 7,617 | 8,286 | 15,241 | 7,337 | 7,904 | 557 | 269 | 288 | 105 | 11 | 94 |
| 4—5 | 13,681 | 6,755 | 6,926 | 13,112 | 6,580 | 6,532 | 510 | 154 | 356 | 59 | 21 | 38 |
| *Total 0—5* | *71,788* | *35,303* | *36,485* | *69,717* | *34,533* | *35,184* | *1,864* | *724* | *1,140* | *207* | *46* | *161* |
| 5—10 | 59,670 | 30,760 | 28,910 | 55,463 | 29,267 | 26,196 | 3,887 | 1,407 | 2,480 | 320 | 86 | 234 |
| 10—15 | 46,943 | 25,933 | 21,010 | 35,268 | 22,737 | 12,531 | 11,131 | 2,991 | 8,140 | 544 | 205 | 339 |
| 15—20 | 39,503 | 21,402 | 18,101 | 16,986 | 14,478 | 2,508 | 21,368 | 6,417 | 14,951 | 1,149 | 507 | 642 |
| 20—25 | 50,033 | 24,500 | 25,533 | 11,502 | 9,901 | 1,601 | 35,926 | 13,544 | 22,382 | 2,605 | 1,055 | 1,550 |
| 25—30 | 50,862 | 26,339 | 24,523 | 6,334 | 5,421 | 913 | 40,868 | 19,348 | 21,520 | 3,660 | 1,570 | 2,090 |
| 30—35 | 49,400 | 25,973 | 23,427 | 3,511 | 2,625 | 886 | 40,166 | 21,300 | 18,866 | 5,723 | 2,048 | 3,675 |
| 35—40 | 29,830 | 16,815 | 13,015 | 1,513 | 1,044 | 469 | 24,032 | 14,407 | 9,625 | 4,285 | 1,364 | 2,921 |
| 40—45 | 37,761 | 19,836 | 17,925 | 1,663 | 1,154 | 509 | 26,690 | 16,473 | 10,217 | 9,408 | 2,209 | 7,199 |
| 45—50 | 16,756 | 9,508 | 7,248 | 559 | 357 | 202 | 11,275 | 7,802 | 3,473 | 4,922 | 1,349 | 3,573 |
| 50—55 | 25,444 | 13,125 | 12,319 | 934 | 611 | 323 | 13,989 | 10,123 | 3,866 | 10,521 | 2,391 | 8,130 |
| 55—60 | 7,104 | 4,109 | 2,995 | 341 | 251 | 90 | 3,971 | 3,017 | 954 | 2,792 | 841 | 1,951 |
| 60—65 | 15,599 | 7,485 | 8,114 | 532 | 359 | 173 | 6,544 | 5,126 | 1,418 | 8,523 | 2,000 | 6,523 |
| 65—70 | 3,716 | 2,206 | 1,510 | 175 | 133 | 42 | 1,731 | 1,387 | 344 | 1,810 | 686 | 1,124 |
| 70 and over | 6,791 | 3,200 | 3,591 | 202 | 180 | 72 | 2,269 | 1,806 | 463 | 4,320 | 1,264 | 3,056 |

# TABLE VII.—Age, Sex and Civil Condition. Part A.—Agency Summary.

| Age. | Population. | | | Unmarried. | | | Married. | | | Widowed. | | |
|---|---|---|---|---|---|---|---|---|---|---|---|---|
| | Persons. | Males. | Females. | Persons. | Males. | Females. | Persons. | Males. | Females. | Persons. | Males. | Females. |
| 1 | 2 | 3 | 4 | 5 | 6 | 7 | 8 | 9 | 10 | 11 | 12 | 13 |
| **CHRISTIAN** | **9,358** | **6,170** | **3,188** | **6,360** | **4,713** | **1,647** | **2,678** | **1,362** | **1,316** | **320** | **95** | **225** |
| 0—1 | 266 | 138 | 128 | 266 | 138 | 128 | .. | .. | .. | .. | .. | .. |
| 1—2 | 177 | 38 | 89 | 177 | 88 | 89 | .. | .. | .. | .. | .. | .. |
| 2—3 | 207 | 101 | 106 | 205 | 101 | 104 | 2 | .. | 2 | .. | .. | .. |
| 3—4 | 237 | 114 | 123 | 236 | 113 | 123 | 1 | 1 | .. | .. | .. | .. |
| 4—5 | 171 | 95 | 76 | 170 | 94 | 76 | 1 | 1 | .. | .. | .. | .. |
| *Total 0—5* | *1,058* | *536* | *522* | *1,054* | *534* | *520* | *4* | *2* | *2* | .. | .. | .. |
| 5—10 | 647 | 318 | 329 | 645 | 318 | 327 | 1 | .. | 1 | 1 | .. | 1 |
| 10—15 | 471 | 214 | 257 | 450 | 212 | 238 | 20 | 1 | 19 | 1 | 1 | .. |
| 15—20 | 825 | 348 | 477 | 632 | 321 | 311 | 187 | 26 | 161 | 6 | 1 | 5 |
| 20—25 | 2,461 | 2,032 | 429 | 1,944 | 1,844 | 100 | 508 | 182 | 326 | 9 | 6 | 3 |
| 25—30 | 1,725 | 1,336 | 389 | 1,074 | 1,032 | 42 | 624 | 295 | 329 | 27 | 9 | 18 |
| 30—35 | 739 | 501 | 238 | 260 | 229 | 31 | 450 | 265 | 185 | 29 | 7 | [illegible] |
| 35—40 | 498 | 324 | 174 | 145 | 107 | 38 | 318 | 206 | 112 | 35 | 11 | [illegible] |
| 40—45 | 330 | 208 | 122 | 71 | 61 | 10 | 220 | 137 | 83 | 39 | 10 | [illegible] |
| 45—50 | 207 | 136 | 71 | 34 | 22 | 12 | 136 | 99 | 37 | 37 | 15 | [illegible] |
| 50—55 | 179 | 94 | 85 | 20 | 12 | 8 | 109 | 72 | 37 | 50 | 10 | [illegible] |
| 55—60 | 70 | 40 | 30 | 10 | 5 | 5 | 43 | 31 | 12 | 17 | 4 | 13 |
| 60—65 | 85 | 51 | 34 | 10 | 8 | 2 | 40 | 32 | 8 | 35 | 11 | 24 |
| 65—70 | 22 | 12 | 10 | 4 | 3 | 1 | 8 | 6 | 2 | 10 | 3 | 7 |
| 70 and over | 41 | 20 | 21 | 7 | 5 | 2 | 10 | 8 | 2 | 24 | 7 | 17 |
| **PARSI** | **1,330** | **689** | **641** | **688** | **381** | **307** | **564** | **280** | **284** | **78** | **28** | **50** |
| 0—1 | 26 | 15 | 11 | 26 | 15 | 11 | .. | .. | .. | .. | .. | .. |
| 1—2 | 19 | 8 | 11 | 17 | 8 | 9 | 2 | .. | 2 | .. | .. | .. |
| 2—3 | 32 | 11 | 21 | 27 | 11 | 16 | 5 | .. | 5 | .. | .. | .. |
| 3—4 | 29 | 12 | 17 | 23 | 12 | 11 | 5 | .. | 5 | 1 | .. | 1 |
| 4—5 | 28 | 10 | 18 | 24 | 10 | 14 | 4 | .. | 4 | .. | .. | .. |
| *Total 0—5* | *134* | *56* | *78* | *117* | *56* | *61* | *16* | .. | *16* | *1* | .. | *1* |
| 5—10 | 163 | 86 | 77 | 154 | 85 | 69 | 9 | 1 | 8 | .. | .. | .. |
| 10—15 | 122 | 63 | 59 | 115 | 63 | 52 | 7 | .. | 7 | .. | .. | .. |
| 15—20 | 109 | 48 | 61 | 92 | 47 | 45 | 15 | 1 | 14 | 2 | .. | 2 |
| 20—25 | 121 | 48 | 73 | 72 | 36 | 36 | 48 | 11 | 37 | 1 | 1 | .. |
| 25—30 | 161 | 83 | 78 | 69 | 43 | 26 | 88 | 37 | 51 | 4 | 3 | 1 |
| 30—35 | 124 | 79 | 45 | 30 | 28 | 2 | 88 | 48 | 40 | 6 | 3 | 3 |
| 35—40 | 96 | 61 | 35 | 20 | 13 | 7 | 71 | 46 | 25 | 5 | 2 | 3 |
| 40—45 | 83 | 50 | 33 | 7 | 3 | 4 | 69 | 44 | 25 | 7 | 3 | 4 |
| 45—50 | 68 | 35 | 33 | 1 | .. | 1 | 57 | 32 | 25 | 10 | 3 | 7 |
| 50—55 | 63 | 34 | 29 | 7 | 6 | 1 | 47 | 24 | 23 | 9 | 4 | 5 |
| 55—60 | 28 | 19 | 9 | 1 | .. | 1 | 22 | 16 | 6 | 5 | 3 | 2 |
| 60—65 | 28 | 14 | 14 | .. | .. | .. | 12 | 10 | 2 | 16 | 4 | 12 |
| 65—70 | 15 | 7 | 8 | 3 | 1 | 2 | 9 | 6 | 3 | 3 | .. | 3 |
| 70 and over | 15 | 6 | 9 | .. | .. | .. | 6 | 4 | 2 | 9 | 2 | 7 |
| **JEW** | **57** | **34** | **23** | **32** | **23** | **9** | **20** | **7** | **13** | **5** | **4** | **1** |
| 0—1 | 1 | .. | 1 | 1 | .. | 1 | .. | .. | .. | .. | .. | .. |
| 1—2 | 1 | 1 | .. | 1 | 1 | .. | .. | .. | .. | .. | .. | .. |
| 2—3 | 1 | 1 | .. | 1 | 1 | .. | .. | .. | .. | .. | .. | .. |
| 3—4 | 1 | .. | 1 | .. | .. | .. | 1 | .. | 1 | .. | .. | .. |
| 4—5 | 1 | .. | 1 | .. | .. | .. | 1 | .. | 1 | .. | .. | .. |
| *Total 0—5* | *5* | *2* | *3* | *3* | *2* | *1* | *2* | .. | *2* | .. | .. | .. |
| 5—10 | 7 | 3 | 4 | 6 | 3 | 3 | 1 | .. | 1 | .. | .. | .. |
| 10—15 | 8 | 6 | 2 | 8 | 6 | 2 | .. | .. | .. | .. | .. | .. |
| 15—20 | 9 | 4 | 5 | 5 | 3 | 2 | 4 | 1 | 3 | .. | .. | .. |
| 20—25 | 5 | 3 | 2 | 3 | 2 | 1 | 2 | 1 | 1 | .. | .. | .. |
| 25—30 | .. | .. | .. | .. | .. | .. | .. | .. | .. | .. | .. | .. |
| 30—35 | 4 | 1 | 3 | .. | .. | .. | 3 | .. | 3 | 1 | 1 | .. |
| 35—40 | 7 | 6 | 1 | 6 | 6 | .. | 1 | .. | 1 | .. | .. | .. |
| 40—45 | 6 | 6 | .. | 1 | 1 | .. | 4 | 4 | .. | 1 | 1 | .. |
| 45—50 | 2 | .. | 2 | .. | .. | .. | 2 | .. | 2 | .. | .. | .. |
| 50—55 | 2 | 2 | .. | .. | .. | .. | 1 | 1 | .. | 1 | 1 | .. |
| 55—60 | .. | .. | .. | .. | .. | .. | .. | .. | .. | .. | .. | .. |
| 60—65 | 1 | 1 | .. | .. | .. | .. | .. | .. | .. | 1 | 1 | .. |
| 65—70 | .. | .. | .. | .. | .. | .. | .. | .. | .. | .. | .. | .. |
| 70 and over | 1 | .. | 1 | .. | .. | .. | .. | .. | .. | 1 | .. | 1 |

## TABLE VII.

### Part B.—PLATEAU.

# TABLE VII.—Age, Sex and Civil Condition.

| Division. | Age. | Population. | | | Unmarried. | | | Married. | | | Widowed. | | |
|---|---|---|---|---|---|---|---|---|---|---|---|---|---|
| | | Persons. | Males. | Females. | Persons. | Males. | Females. | Persons. | Males. | Females. | Persons. | Males. | Females. |
| | 1 | 2 | 3 | 4 | 5 | 6 | 7 | 8 | 9 | 10 | 11 | 12 | 13 |
| PLATEAU | **ALL RELIGIONS** | **3,683,491** | **1,963,120** | **1,780,371** | **1,428,221** | **881,728** | **546,493** | **1,795,496** | **898,698** | **896,798** | **459,774** | **122,694** | **337,080** |
| | 0—1 | 138,331 | 69,443 | 68,888 | 137,350 | 69,097 | 68,253 | 934 | 331 | 603 | 47 | 15 | 32 |
| | 1—2 | 90,860 | 44,759 | 46,101 | 80,667 | 44,428 | 45,239 | 1,100 | 305 | 795 | 93 | 26 | 67 |
| | 2—3 | 118,196 | 57,327 | 60,869 | 115,818 | 56,514 | 59,304 | 2,234 | 777 | 1,457 | 144 | 36 | 108 |
| | 3—4 | 125,666 | 60,937 | 64,729 | 122,329 | 59,864 | 62,465 | 3,153 | 1,026 | 2,127 | 184 | 47 | 137 |
| | 4—5 | 115,068 | 59,611 | 55,457 | 110,676 | 58,043 | 52,633 | 4,047 | 1,489 | 2,558 | 345 | 79 | 266 |
| | *Total 0—5* | *588,121* | *292,077* | *296,044* | *575,840* | *287,946* | *287,894* | *11,468* | *3,928* | *7,540* | *813* | *203* | *610* |
| | 5—10 | 423,398 | 222,774 | 200,624 | 382,170 | 211,544 | 170,626 | 39,478 | 10,760 | 28,718 | 1,750 | 470 | 1,280 |
| | 10—15 | 299,097 | 169,382 | 129,715 | 186,724 | 135,665 | 51,059 | 109,009 | 32,491 | 76,518 | 3,364 | 1,226 | 2,138 |
| | 15—20 | 288,640 | 155,263 | 133,377 | 103,353 | 92,923 | 10,430 | 177,186 | 59,267 | 117,919 | 8,101 | 3,073 | 5,028 |
| | 20—25 | 369,954 | 180,964 | 188,980 | 72,416 | 64,781 | 7,635 | 278,344 | 109,124 | 169,220 | 19,194 | 7,059 | 12,135 |
| | 25—30 | 367,116 | 186,764 | 180,352 | 41,453 | 36,244 | 5,209 | 296,683 | 139,422 | 157,261 | 28,980 | 11,098 | 17,882 |
| | 30—35 | 367,288 | 193,053 | 174,235 | 25,038 | 20,754 | 4,284 | 295,981 | 158,159 | 137,822 | 46,269 | 14,140 | 32,129 |
| | 35—40 | 234,446 | 127,811 | 106,635 | 11,448 | 8,955 | 2,493 | 182,002 | 107,426 | 745,726 | 40,996 | 11,430 | 29,566 |
| | 40—45 | 263,415 | 136,185 | 127,230 | 11,000 | 8,203 | 2,797 | 175,176 | 111,061 | 64,115 | 77,239 | 16,921 | 60,318 |
| | 45—50 | 123,091 | 65,933 | 57,158 | 5,258 | 4,182 | 1,076 | 76,391 | 52,154 | 24,237 | 41,442 | 9,597 | 31,845 |
| | 50—55 | 168,125 | 82,500 | 85,625 | 6,217 | 4,675 | 1,542 | 82,143 | 60,206 | 21,937 | 79,765 | 17,619 | 62,146 |
| | 55—60 | 45,908 | 24,088 | 21,820 | 2,002 | 1,522 | 480 | 23,022 | 16,708 | 6,314 | 20,884 | 5,858 | 15,026 |
| | 60—65 | 91,942 | 40,007 | 51,935 | 3,046 | 2,490 | 556 | 30,478 | 23,727 | 6,751 | 58,418 | 13,790 | 44,628 |
| | 65—70 | 19,734 | 10,264 | 9,470 | 817 | 663 | 154 | 7,696 | 5,927 | 1,769 | 11,221 | 3,674 | 7,547 |
| | 70—and over | 33,216 | 16,055 | 17,161 | 1,439 | 1,181 | 258 | 10,439 | 8,338 | 2,101 | 21,338 | 6,536 | 14,802 |
| | **HINDU** | **3,213,388** | **1,658,967** | **1,554,421** | **1,234,085** | **764,673** | **469,412** | **1,574,522** | **786,971** | **787,551** | **404,781** | **107,323** | **297,458** |
| | 0—1 | 121,260 | 60,800 | 60,460 | 120,536 | 60,578 | 59,958 | 683 | 210 | 473 | 41 | 12 | 29 |
| | 1—2 | 80,328 | 39,633 | 40,695 | 79,350 | 39,382 | 39,968 | 908 | 233 | 675 | 70 | 18 | 52 |
| | 2—3 | 103,564 | 50,172 | 53,392 | 101,508 | 49,482 | 52,026 | 1,942 | 668 | 1,274 | 114 | 22 | 92 |
| | 3—4 | 109,766 | 53,328 | 56,438 | 106,888 | 52,439 | 54,449 | 2,724 | 847 | 1,877 | 154 | 42 | 112 |
| | 4—5 | 101,185 | 52,619 | 48,566 | 97,293 | 51,238 | 46,055 | 3,592 | 1,316 | 2,276 | 300 | 65 | 235 |
| | *Total 0—5* | *516,103* | *256,552* | *259,551* | *505,575* | *253,119* | *252,456* | *9,849* | *3,274* | *6,575* | *679* | *159* | *520* |
| | 5—10 | 369,442 | 194,641 | 174,801 | 331,407 | 184,574 | 146,833 | 36,522 | 9,650 | 26,872 | 1,513 | 417 | 1,096 |
| | 10—15 | 259,625 | 147,612 | 112,013 | 156,841 | 116,290 | 40,551 | 99,774 | 30,192 | 69,582 | 3,010 | 1,130 | 1,880 |
| | 15—20 | 251,890 | 136,168 | 115,722 | 87,748 | 79,799 | 7,949 | 157,051 | 53,573 | 103,478 | 7,091 | 2,796 | 4,295 |
| | 20—25 | 321,643 | 157,296 | 164,347 | 60,429 | 54,377 | 6,052 | 244,315 | 96,659 | 147,656 | 16,899 | 6,260 | 10,639 |
| | 25—30 | 319,360 | 162,207 | 157,153 | 35,014 | 30,733 | 4,281 | 258,822 | 121,728 | 137,094 | 25,524 | 9,746 | 15,778 |
| | 30—35 | 321,821 | 169,102 | 152,719 | 21,597 | 18,083 | 3,514 | 259,367 | 138,629 | 120,738 | 40,857 | 12,390 | 28,467 |
| | 35—40 | 205,816 | 111,700 | 94,116 | 9,842 | 7,777 | 2,065 | 159,353 | 93,832 | 65,521 | 36,621 | 10,091 | 26,530 |
| | 40—45 | 230,057 | 118,553 | 111,504 | 9,394 | 7,001 | 2,393 | 152,057 | 96,654 | 55,403 | 68,606 | 14,898 | 53,708 |
| | 45—50 | 107,694 | 57,320 | 50,374 | 4,620 | 3,732 | 888 | 66,404 | 45,222 | 21,182 | 36,670 | 8,366 | 28,304 |
| | 50—55 | 146,238 | 71,305 | 74,933 | 5,331 | 4,057 | 1,274 | 70,723 | 51,838 | 18,885 | 70,184 | 15,410 | 54,774 |
| | 55—60 | 39,870 | 20,675 | 19,195 | 1,705 | 1,312 | 393 | 19,781 | 14,268 | 5,513 | 18,384 | 5,095 | 13,289 |
| | 60—65 | 78,946 | 33,679 | 45,267 | 2,645 | 2,202 | 443 | 25,273 | 19,549 | 5,724 | 51,028 | 11,928 | 39,100 |
| | 65—70 | 16,886 | 8,617 | 8,269 | 684 | 560 | 124 | 6,500 | 4,941 | 1,559 | 9,702 | 3,116 | 6,586 |
| | 70—and over | 27,997 | 13,540 | 14,457 | 1,253 | 1,057 | 196 | 8,731 | 6,962 | 1,769 | 18,013 | 5,521 | 12,492 |
| | **ARYA** | **87** | **57** | **30** | **36** | **28** | **8** | **45** | **26** | **19** | **6** | **3** | **3** |
| | 0—1 | 4 | 1 | 3 | 4 | 1 | 3 | .. | .. | .. | .. | .. | .. |
| | 1—2 | .. | .. | .. | .. | .. | .. | .. | .. | .. | .. | .. | .. |
| | 2—3 | 1 | 1 | .. | 1 | 1 | .. | .. | .. | .. | .. | .. | .. |
| | 3—4 | 2 | 1 | 1 | 2 | 1 | 1 | .. | .. | .. | .. | .. | .. |
| | 4—5 | 1 | .. | 1 | 1 | .. | 1 | .. | .. | .. | .. | .. | .. |
| | *Total 0—5* | *8* | *3* | *5* | *8* | *3* | *5* | .. | .. | .. | .. | .. | .. |
| | 5—10 | 9 | 5 | 4 | 8 | 5 | 3 | 1 | .. | 1 | .. | .. | .. |
| | 10—15 | 6 | 4 | 2 | 4 | 4 | .. | 2 | .. | 2 | .. | .. | .. |
| | 15—20 | 9 | 6 | 3 | 5 | 5 | .. | 4 | 1 | 3 | .. | .. | .. |
| | 20—25 | 17 | 13 | 4 | 9 | 9 | .. | 8 | 4 | 4 | .. | .. | .. |
| | 25—30 | 18 | 12 | 6 | 1 | 1 | .. | 16 | 11 | 5 | 1 | .. | 1 |
| | 30—35 | 7 | 7 | .. | 1 | 1 | .. | 6 | 6 | .. | .. | .. | .. |
| | 35—40 | 4 | 3 | 1 | .. | .. | .. | 2 | 2 | .. | 2 | 1 | 1 |
| | 40—45 | 2 | .. | 2 | .. | .. | .. | 2 | .. | 2 | .. | .. | .. |
| | 45—50 | 3 | 2 | 1 | .. | .. | .. | 2 | 1 | 1 | 1 | 1 | .. |
| | 50—55 | 4 | 2 | 2 | .. | .. | .. | 2 | 1 | 1 | 2 | 1 | 1 |
| | 55—60 | .. | .. | .. | .. | .. | .. | .. | .. | .. | .. | .. | .. |
| | 60—65 | .. | .. | .. | .. | .. | .. | .. | .. | .. | .. | .. | .. |
| | 65—70 | .. | .. | .. | .. | .. | .. | .. | .. | .. | .. | .. | .. |
| | 70—and over | .. | .. | .. | .. | .. | .. | .. | .. | .. | .. | .. | .. |
| | **SIKH** | **1,091** | **763** | **328** | **393** | **299** | **94** | **613** | **417** | **196** | **85** | **47** | **38** |
| | 0—1 | 19 | 11 | 8 | 19 | 11 | 8 | .. | .. | .. | .. | .. | .. |
| | 1—2 | 14 | 9 | 5 | 14 | 9 | 5 | .. | .. | .. | .. | .. | .. |
| | 2—3 | 18 | 12 | 6 | 18 | 12 | 6 | .. | .. | .. | .. | .. | .. |
| | 3—4 | 21 | 12 | 9 | 21 | 12 | 9 | .. | .. | .. | .. | .. | .. |
| | 4—5 | 25 | 13 | 12 | 25 | 13 | 12 | .. | .. | .. | .. | .. | .. |
| | *Total 0—5* | *97* | *57* | *40* | *97* | *57* | *40* | .. | .. | .. | .. | .. | .. |
| | 5—10 | 77 | 41 | 36 | 76 | 41 | 35 | 1 | .. | 1 | .. | .. | .. |
| | 10—15 | 53 | 39 | 14 | 46 | 38 | 8 | 7 | 1 | 6 | .. | .. | .. |
| | 15—20 | 114 | 80 | 34 | 63 | 53 | 10 | 49 | 25 | 24 | 2 | 2 | .. |
| | 20—25 | 173 | 141 | 32 | 69 | 68 | 1 | 98 | 67 | 31 | 6 | 6 | .. |
| | 25—30 | 187 | 133 | 54 | 26 | 26 | .. | 144 | 92 | 52 | 17 | 15 | 2 |
| | 30—35 | 150 | 106 | 44 | 9 | 9 | .. | 129 | 88 | 41 | 12 | 9 | 3 |
| | 35—40 | 81 | 63 | 18 | 3 | 3 | .. | 70 | 55 | 15 | 8 | 5 | 3 |
| | 40—45 | 49 | 36 | 13 | 4 | 4 | .. | 40 | 22 | 8 | 5 | .. | 5 |
| | 45—50 | 37 | 28 | 9 | .. | .. | .. | 30 | 25 | 5 | 7 | 3 | 4 |
| | 50—55 | 25 | 15 | 10 | .. | .. | .. | 16 | 12 | 4 | 9 | 3 | 6 |
| | 55—60 | 8 | 5 | 3 | .. | .. | .. | 8 | 5 | 3 | .. | .. | .. |
| | 60—65 | 19 | 9 | 10 | .. | .. | .. | 10 | 6 | 4 | 9 | 3 | 6 |
| | 65—70 | 4 | 2 | 2 | .. | .. | .. | 2 | 2 | .. | 2 | .. | 2 |
| | 70—and over | 17 | 8 | 9 | .. | .. | .. | 9 | 7 | 2 | 8 | 1 | 7 |

## Part B.—Details for Natural Divisions.

| Division. | Age. | Population. | | | Unmarried. | | | Married. | | | Widowed. | | |
|---|---|---|---|---|---|---|---|---|---|---|---|---|---|
| | | Persons. | Males. | Females. | Persons. | Males. | Females. | Persons. | Males. | Females. | Persons. | Males. | Females. |
| | 1 | 2 | 3 | 4 | 5 | 6 | 7 | 8 | 9 | 10 | 11 | 12 | 13 |
| PLATEAU | **JAIN** | **52,839** | **27,600** | **25,239** | **20,332** | **13,264** | **7,068** | **22,767** | **11,383** | **11,384** | **9,740** | **2,953** | **6,787** |
| | 0—1 | 1,526 | 801 | 725 | 1,517 | 794 | 723 | 8 | 7 | 1 | 1 | .. | 1 |
| | 1—2 | 957 | 458 | 499 | 952 | 458 | 494 | 5 | .. | 5 | .. | .. | .. |
| | 2—3 | 1,330 | 656 | 674 | 1,303 | 644 | 659 | 22 | 12 | 10 | 5 | .. | 5 |
| | 3—4 | 1,245 | 601 | 644 | 1,224 | 591 | 633 | 20 | 9 | 11 | 1 | 1 | .. |
| | 4—5 | 1,253 | 632 | 621 | 1,219 | 619 | 600 | 27 | 12 | 15 | 7 | 1 | 6 |
| | *Total 0—5* | *6,311* | *3,148* | *3,163* | *6,215* | *3,106* | *3,109* | *83* | *40* | *43* | *14* | *2* | *12* |
| | 5—10 | 5,571 | 2,876 | 2,695 | 5,315 | 2,800 | 2,515 | 227 | 71 | 156 | 29 | 5 | 24 |
| | 10—15 | 4,633 | 2,658 | 1,975 | 3,326 | 2,393 | 933 | 1,257 | 253 | 1,004 | 50 | 12 | 38 |
| | 15—20 | 4,495 | 2,374 | 2,121 | 1,661 | 1,523 | 138 | 2,614 | 819 | 1,795 | 220 | 32 | 188 |
| | 20—25 | 5,385 | 2,721 | 2,664 | 1,281 | 1,161 | 120 | 3,618 | 1,462 | 2,156 | 486 | 98 | 388 |
| | 25—30 | 4,956 | 2,602 | 2,354 | 760 | 678 | 82 | 3,484 | 1,723 | 1,761 | 712 | 201 | 511 |
| | 30—35 | 4,977 | 2,566 | 2,411 | 588 | 530 | 58 | 3,392 | 1,750 | 1,642 | 997 | 286 | 711 |
| | 35—40 | 3,569 | 1,962 | 1,607 | 317 | 281 | 36 | 2,335 | 1,373 | 962 | 917 | 308 | 609 |
| | 40—45 | 3,945 | 2,017 | 1,928 | 307 | 271 | 36 | 2,211 | 1,372 | 839 | 1,427 | 374 | 1,053 |
| | 45—50 | 2,266 | 1,272 | 994 | 144 | 137 | 7 | 1,219 | 810 | 409 | 903 | 325 | 578 |
| | 50—55 | 2,939 | 1,480 | 1,459 | 202 | 194 | 8 | 1,162 | 819 | 343 | 1,575 | 467 | 1,108 |
| | 55—60 | 1,070 | 600 | 470 | 73 | 61 | 12 | 453 | 341 | 112 | 544 | 198 | 346 |
| | 60—65 | 1,684 | 794 | 890 | 81 | 76 | 5 | 450 | 355 | 95 | 1,153 | 363 | 790 |
| | 65—70 | 483 | 266 | 217 | 36 | 32 | 4 | 134 | 104 | 30 | 313 | 130 | 183 |
| | 70—and over | 555 | 264 | 291 | 26 | 21 | 5 | 129 | 91 | 38 | 400 | 152 | 248 |
| | **ANIMIST** | **110,312** | **55,248** | **55,064** | **47,757** | **27,070** | **20,687** | **53,693** | **26,287** | **27,406** | **8,862** | **1,891** | **6,971** |
| | 0—1 | 4,720 | 2,408 | 2,312 | 4,619 | 2,313 | 2,306 | 99 | 93 | 6 | 2 | 2 | .. |
| | 1—2 | 3,225 | 1,542 | 1,683 | 3,150 | 1,482 | 1,668 | 59 | 52 | 7 | 16 | 8 | 8 |
| | 2—3 | 4,272 | 2,044 | 2,228 | 4,180 | 1,978 | 2,202 | 80 | 55 | 25 | 12 | 11 | 1 |
| | 3—4 | 5,101 | 2,465 | 2,636 | 4,932 | 2,346 | 2,586 | 153 | 118 | 35 | 16 | 1 | 15 |
| | 4—5 | 4,416 | 2,248 | 2,168 | 4,273 | 2,150 | 2,123 | 136 | 96 | 90 | 7 | 2 | 5 |
| | *Total 0—5* | *21,734* | *10,707* | *11,027* | *21,154* | *10,269* | *10,885* | *527* | *414* | *113* | *53* | *24* | *29* |
| | 5—10 | 14,124 | 7,489 | 6,635 | 13,329 | 7,127 | 6,202 | 720 | 340 | 380 | 75 | 22 | 53 |
| | 10—15 | 7,946 | 4,333 | 3,613 | 5,848 | 3,718 | 2,130 | 2,044 | 597 | 1,447 | 54 | 18 | 36 |
| | 15—20 | 7,971 | 3,894 | 4,077 | 2,980 | 2,464 | 516 | 4,827 | 1,384 | 3,443 | 164 | 46 | 118 |
| | 20—25 | 11,121 | 4,830 | 6,291 | 1,803 | 1,476 | 327 | 9,009 | 3,228 | 5,781 | 309 | 126 | 183 |
| | 25—30 | 12,004 | 5,751 | 6,253 | 1,024 | 814 | 210 | 10,448 | 4,732 | 5,716 | 532 | 205 | 327 |
| | 30—35 | 11,212 | 5,915 | 5,297 | 568 | 457 | 111 | 9,739 | 5,208 | 4,531 | 905 | 250 | 655 |
| | 35—40 | 6,580 | 3,591 | 2,989 | 318 | 246 | 72 | 5,561 | 3,170 | 2,391 | 701 | 175 | 526 |
| | 40—45 | 6,826 | 3,619 | 3,207 | 285 | 216 | 69 | 5,021 | 3,140 | 1,881 | 1,520 | 263 | 1,257 |
| | 45—50 | 3,022 | 1,573 | 1,449 | 161 | 112 | 49 | 2,037 | 1,338 | 699 | 824 | 123 | 701 |
| | 50—55 | 3,824 | 1,774 | 2,050 | 142 | 73 | 69 | 2,020 | 1,468 | 552 | 1,662 | 233 | 1,429 |
| | 55—60 | 994 | 452 | 542 | 41 | 24 | 17 | 543 | 348 | 195 | 410 | 80 | 330 |
| | 60—65 | 2,084 | 898 | 1,186 | 53 | 36 | 17 | 826 | 654 | 172 | 1,155 | 208 | 947 |
| | 65—70 | 376 | 173 | 203 | 21 | 15 | 6 | 151 | 110 | 41 | 204 | 48 | 156 |
| | 70—and over | 544 | 249 | 295 | 30 | 23 | 7 | 220 | 156 | 64 | 294 | 70 | 224 |
| | **MUSALMAN** | **297,238** | **154,961** | **142,277** | **119,870** | **72,194** | **47,676** | **141,375** | **72,379** | **68,996** | **35,993** | **10,388** | **25,605** |
| | 0—1 | 10,554 | 5,295 | 5,259 | 10,407 | 5,273 | 5,134 | 144 | 21 | 123 | 3 | 1 | 2 |
| | 1—2 | 6,197 | 3,050 | 3,147 | 6,064 | 3,030 | 3,034 | 126 | 20 | 106 | 7 | .. | 7 |
| | 2—3 | 8,833 | 4,354 | 4,479 | 8,636 | 4,309 | 4,327 | 184 | 42 | 142 | 13 | 3 | 10 |
| | 3—4 | 9,329 | 4,434 | 4,895 | 9,068 | 4,380 | 4,688 | 249 | 51 | 198 | 12 | 3 | 9 |
| | 4—5 | 8,050 | 4,024 | 4,026 | 7,733 | 3,949 | 3,784 | 286 | 64 | 222 | 31 | 11 | 20 |
| | *Total 0—5* | *42,963* | *21,157* | *21,806* | *41,908* | *20,941* | *20,967* | *989* | *198* | *791* | *66* | *18* | *48* |
| | 5—10 | 28,582 | 17,420 | 16,162 | 31,453 | 16,696 | 14,757 | 1,996 | 698 | 1,298 | 133 | 26 | 107 |
| | 10—15 | 26,360 | 14,517 | 11,843 | 20,205 | 13,004 | 7,201 | 5,906 | 1,448 | 4,458 | 249 | 65 | 184 |
| | 15—20 | 23,364 | 12,410 | 10,954 | 10,269 | 8,766 | 1,503 | 12,475 | 3,447 | 9,028 | 620 | 197 | 423 |
| | 20—25 | 29,387 | 14,129 | 15,258 | 7,013 | 5,999 | 1,014 | 20,886 | 7,565 | 13,321 | 1,488 | 565 | 923 |
| | 25—30 | 29,123 | 14,956 | 14,167 | 3,731 | 3,151 | 580 | 23,223 | 10,882 | 12,341 | 2,169 | 923 | 1,246 |
| | 30—35 | 28,457 | 14,914 | 13,543 | 2,058 | 1,483 | 575 | 22,928 | 12,236 | 10,692 | 3,471 | 1,195 | 2,276 |
| | 35—40 | 17,937 | 10,200 | 7,737 | 837 | 556 | 281 | 14,384 | 8,802 | 5,582 | 2,716 | 842 | 1,874 |
| | 40—45 | 22,216 | 11,764 | 10,452 | 945 | 658 | 287 | 15,629 | 9,728 | 5,901 | 5,642 | 1,378 | 4,264 |
| | 45—50 | 9,852 | 5,611 | 4,241 | 306 | 185 | 121 | 6,552 | 4,661 | 1,891 | 2,994 | 765 | 2,229 |
| | 50—55 | 14,910 | 7,822 | 7,088 | 518 | 335 | 183 | 8,101 | 5,994 | 2,107 | 6,291 | 1,493 | 4,798 |
| | 55—60 | 3,895 | 2,316 | 1,579 | 174 | 121 | 53 | 2,189 | 1,714 | 475 | 1,532 | 481 | 1,051 |
| | 60—65 | 9,180 | 4,580 | 4,600 | 260 | 171 | 89 | 3,884 | 3,134 | 750 | 5,036 | 1,275 | 3,761 |
| | 65—70 | 1,954 | 1,190 | 764 | 70 | 53 | 17 | 894 | 759 | 135 | 990 | 378 | 612 |
| | 70—and over | 4,058 | 1,975 | 2,083 | 123 | 75 | 48 | 1,339 | 1,113 | 226 | 2,596 | 787 | 1,809 |
| | **CHRISTIAN** | **7,368** | **4,923** | **2,445** | **5,144** | **3,852** | **1,292** | **1,992** | **1,010** | **982** | **232** | **61** | **171** |
| | 0—1 | 223 | 113 | 110 | 223 | 113 | 110 | .. | .. | .. | .. | .. | .. |
| | 1—2 | 124 | 61 | 63 | 124 | 61 | 63 | .. | .. | .. | .. | .. | .. |
| | 2—3 | 150 | 77 | 73 | 149 | 77 | 72 | 1 | .. | 1 | .. | .. | .. |
| | 3—4 | 178 | 86 | 92 | 177 | 85 | 92 | 1 | 1 | .. | .. | .. | .. |
| | 4—5 | 115 | 67 | 48 | 114 | 66 | 48 | 1 | 1 | .. | .. | .. | .. |
| | *Total 0—5* | *790* | *404* | *386* | *787* | *402* | *385* | *3* | *2* | *1* | .. | .. | .. |
| | 5—10 | 467 | 231 | 236 | 466 | 231 | 235 | 1 | .. | 1 | .. | .. | .. |
| | 10—15 | 367 | 162 | 205 | 353 | 161 | 192 | 13 | .. | 13 | 1 | 1 | .. |
| | 15—20 | 689 | 281 | 408 | 538 | 265 | 273 | 148 | 16 | 132 | 3 | .. | 3 |
| | 20—25 | 2,117 | 1,789 | 328 | 1,740 | 1,655 | 85 | 372 | 131 | 241 | 5 | 3 | 2 |
| | 25—30 | 1,330 | 1,031 | 299 | 833 | 802 | 31 | 475 | 224 | 251 | 22 | 5 | 17 |
| | 30—35 | 564 | 386 | 178 | 195 | 171 | 24 | 347 | 209 | 138 | 22 | 6 | 16 |
| | 35—40 | 369 | 235 | 134 | 107 | 74 | 33 | 236 | 155 | 81 | 26 | 6 | 20 |
| | 40—45 | 247 | 153 | 94 | 57 | 49 | 8 | 157 | 98 | 59 | 33 | 6 | 27 |
| | 45—50 | 151 | 95 | 56 | 26 | 16 | 10 | 92 | 68 | 24 | 33 | 11 | 22 |
| | 50—55 | 129 | 73 | 56 | 17 | 10 | 7 | 79 | 55 | 24 | 33 | 8 | 25 |
| | 55—60 | 48 | 25 | 23 | 8 | 4 | 4 | 30 | 19 | 11 | 10 | 2 | 8 |
| | 60—65 | 54 | 35 | 19 | 7 | 5 | 2 | 27 | 22 | 5 | 20 | 8 | 12 |
| | 65—70 | 16 | 9 | 7 | 3 | 2 | 1 | 6 | 5 | 1 | 7 | 2 | 5 |
| | 70—and over | 30 | 14 | 16 | 7 | 5 | 2 | 6 | 6 | .. | 17 | 3 | 14 |

# TABLE VII.—Age, Sex and Civil Condition. Part B.—Details for Natural Divisions.

| Division. | Age. | Population. | | | Unmarried. | | | Married. | | | Widowed. | | |
|---|---|---|---|---|---|---|---|---|---|---|---|---|---|
| | | Persons. | Males. | Females. | Persons. | Males. | Females. | Persons. | Males. | Females. | Persons. | Males. | Females. |
| | 1 | 2 | 3 | 4 | 5 | 6 | 7 | 8 | 9 | 10 | 11 | 12 | 13 |
| PLATEAU. | **PARSI** | **1,112** | **568** | **544** | **572** | **325** | **247** | **470** | **219** | **251** | **70** | **24** | **46** |
| | 0—1 | 24 | 14 | 10 | 24 | 14 | 10 | .. | .. | .. | .. | .. | .. |
| | 1—2 | 14 | 5 | 9 | 12 | 5 | 7 | 2 | .. | 2 | .. | .. | .. |
| | 2—3 | 27 | 10 | 17 | 22 | 10 | 12 | 5 | .. | 5 | .. | .. | .. |
| | 3—4 | 23 | 10 | 13 | 17 | 10 | 7 | 5 | .. | 5 | 1 | .. | 1 |
| | 4—5 | 22 | 8 | 14 | 18 | 8 | 10 | 4 | .. | 4 | .. | .. | .. |
| | *Total 0—5* | *110* | *47* | *63* | *93* | *47* | *46* | *16* | .. | *16* | *1* | .. | *1* |
| | 5—10 | 119 | 68 | 51 | 110 | 67 | 43 | 9 | 1 | 8 | .. | .. | .. |
| | 10—15 | 99 | 51 | 48 | 93 | 51 | 42 | 6 | .. | 6 | .. | .. | .. |
| | 15—20 | 99 | 46 | 53 | 84 | 45 | 39 | 14 | 1 | 13 | 1 | .. | 1 |
| | 20—25 | 106 | 42 | 64 | 60 | 34 | 35 | 36 | 7 | 29 | 1 | 1 | .. |
| | 25—30 | 138 | 72 | 66 | 64 | 39 | 25 | 71 | 30 | 41 | 3 | 3 | .. |
| | 30—35 | 96 | 56 | 40 | 22 | 20 | 2 | 70 | 33 | 37 | 4 | 3 | 1 |
| | 35—40 | 83 | 51 | 32 | 18 | 12 | 6 | 60 | 37 | 23 | 5 | 2 | 3 |
| | 40—45 | 68 | 38 | 30 | 7 | 3 | 4 | 56 | 34 | 22 | 5 | 1 | 4 |
| | 45—50 | 64 | 32 | 32 | 1 | .. | 1 | 53 | 29 | 24 | 10 | 3 | 7 |
| | 50—55 | 54 | 27 | 27 | 7 | 6 | 1 | 39 | 18 | 21 | 8 | 3 | 5 |
| | 55—60 | 23 | 15 | 8 | 1 | .. | 1 | 18 | 13 | 5 | 4 | 2 | 2 |
| | 60—65 | 24 | 11 | 13 | .. | .. | .. | 8 | 7 | 1 | 16 | 4 | 12 |
| | 65—70 | 15 | 7 | 8 | 3 | 1 | 2 | 9 | 6 | 3 | 3 | .. | 3 |
| | 70—and over | 14 | 5 | 9 | .. | .. | .. | 5 | 3 | 2 | 9 | 2 | 7 |
| | **JEW** | **56** | **33** | **23** | **32** | **23** | **9** | **19** | **6** | **13** | **5** | **4** | **1** |
| | 0—1 | 1 | .. | 1 | 1 | .. | 1 | .. | .. | .. | .. | .. | .. |
| | 1—2 | 1 | 1 | .. | 1 | 1 | .. | .. | .. | .. | .. | .. | .. |
| | 2—3 | 1 | 1 | .. | 1 | 1 | .. | .. | .. | .. | .. | .. | .. |
| | 3—4 | 1 | .. | 1 | .. | .. | .. | 1 | .. | 1 | .. | .. | .. |
| | 4—5 | 1 | .. | 1 | .. | .. | .. | 1 | .. | 1 | .. | .. | .. |
| | *Total 0—5* | *5* | *2* | *3* | *3* | *2* | *1* | *2* | .. | *2* | .. | .. | .. |
| | 5—10 | 7 | 3 | 4 | 6 | 3 | 3 | 1 | .. | 1 | .. | .. | .. |
| | 10—15 | 8 | 6 | 2 | 8 | 6 | 2 | .. | .. | .. | .. | .. | .. |
| | 15—20 | 9 | 4 | 5 | 5 | 3 | 2 | 4 | 1 | 3 | .. | .. | .. |
| | 20—25 | 5 | 3 | 2 | 3 | 2 | 1 | 2 | 1 | 1 | .. | .. | .. |
| | 25—30 | .. | .. | .. | .. | .. | .. | .. | .. | .. | .. | .. | .. |
| | 30—35 | 4 | 1 | 3 | .. | .. | .. | 3 | .. | 3 | 1 | 1 | .. |
| | 35—40 | 7 | 6 | 1 | 6 | 6 | .. | 1 | .. | 1 | .. | .. | .. |
| | 40—45 | 5 | 5 | .. | 1 | 1 | .. | 3 | 3 | .. | 1 | 1 | .. |
| | 45—50 | 2 | .. | 2 | .. | .. | .. | 2 | .. | 2 | .. | .. | .. |
| | 50—55 | 2 | 2 | .. | .. | .. | .. | 1 | 1 | .. | 1 | 1 | .. |
| | 55—60 | .. | .. | .. | .. | .. | .. | .. | .. | .. | .. | .. | .. |
| | 60—65 | 1 | 1 | .. | .. | .. | .. | .. | .. | .. | 1 | 1 | .. |
| | 65—70 | .. | .. | .. | .. | .. | .. | .. | .. | .. | .. | .. | .. |
| | 70—and over | 1 | .. | 1 | .. | .. | .. | .. | .. | .. | 1 | .. | 1 |

## TABLE VII.

### PART B.—LOW-LYING.

## TABLE VII.—Age, Sex and Civil Condition.

| Division. | Age. | Population. | | | Unmarried. | | | Married. | | | Widowed. | | |
|---|---|---|---|---|---|---|---|---|---|---|---|---|---|
| | | Persons. | Males. | Females. | Persons. | Males. | Females. | Persons. | Males. | Females. | Persons. | Males. | Females. |
| | 1 | 2 | 3 | 4 | 5 | 6 | 7 | 8 | 9 | 10 | 11 | 12 | 13 |
| LOW-LYING. | **ALL RELIGIONS** | **3,310,703** | **1,713,851** | **1,596,852** | **1,229,067** | **749,189** | **479,878** | **1,666,963** | **847,627** | **819,336** | **423,873** | **117,235** | **306,638** |
| | 0—1 | 100,553 | 51,707 | 48,846 | 99,899 | 51,327 | 48,572 | 626 | 367 | 259 | 28 | 13 | 15 |
| | 1—2 | 64,041 | 31,221 | 32,820 | 63,333 | 30,848 | 32,485 | 665 | 358 | 307 | 43 | 15 | 28 |
| | 2—3 | 85,838 | 41,128 | 44,710 | 83,356 | 39,418 | 43,938 | 2,377 | 1,663 | 714 | 105 | 47 | 58 |
| | 3—4 | 99,617 | 48,306 | 51,311 | 97,388 | 47,363 | 50,025 | 2,007 | 873 | 1,134 | 222 | 70 | 152 |
| | 4—5 | 88,098 | 45,690 | 42,408 | 82,536 | 42,292 | 40,244 | 5,020 | 3,230 | 1,790 | 542 | 168 | 374 |
| | *Total 0—5* | *438,147* | *218,052* | *220,095* | *426,512* | *211,248* | *215,264* | *10,695* | *6,491* | *4,204* | *940* | *313* | *627* |
| | 5—10 | 414,262 | 213,572 | 200,690 | 365,225 | 194,452 | 170,773 | 47,065 | 18,569 | 28,496 | 1,972 | 551 | 1,421 |
| | 10—15 | 341,667 | 193,493 | 148,174 | 195,505 | 136,052 | 59,453 | 141,605 | 55,672 | 85,933 | 4,557 | 1,769 | 2,788 |
| | 15—20 | 277,047 | 157,835 | 119,212 | 84,739 | 75,660 | 9,079 | 183,867 | 78,974 | 104,893 | 8,441 | 3,201 | 5,240 |
| | 20—25 | 309,780 | 155,570 | 154,210 | 49,661 | 44,343 | 5,318 | 242,629 | 104,691 | 137,938 | 17,490 | 6,536 | 10,954 |
| | 25—30 | 326,399 | 167,169 | 159,230 | 35,174 | 31,211 | 3,963 | 264,281 | 126,534 | 137,747 | 26,944 | 9,424 | 17,520 |
| | 30—35 | 310,592 | 162,062 | 148,530 | 21,389 | 19,293 | 2,096 | 248,414 | 129,454 | 118,960 | 40,789 | 13,315 | 27,474 |
| | 35—40 | 189,083 | 99,774 | 89,309 | 10,807 | 9,840 | 967 | 145,945 | 79,935 | 66,010 | 32,331 | 9,999 | 22,332 |
| | 40—45 | 230,041 | 115,707 | 114,334 | 11,534 | 9,993 | 1,541 | 152,786 | 90,038 | 62,748 | 65,721 | 15,676 | 50,045 |
| | 45—50 | 114,833 | 60,205 | 54,628 | 5,383 | 4,769 | 614 | 72,020 | 45,397 | 26,623 | 37,430 | 10,039 | 27,391 |
| | 50—55 | 159,024 | 77,055 | 81,969 | 6,469 | 5,752 | 717 | 79,381 | 54,925 | 24,456 | 73,174 | 16,378 | 56,796 |
| | 55—60 | 53,963 | 29,159 | 24,804 | 2,297 | 2,088 | 209 | 27,844 | 19,530 | 8,314 | 23,822 | 7,541 | 16,281 |
| | 60—65 | 94,276 | 39,866 | 54,410 | 3,265 | 2,683 | 582 | 31,757 | 23,516 | 8,241 | 59,254 | 13,667 | 45,587 |
| | 65—70 | 20,984 | 10,479 | 10,505 | 787 | 669 | 118 | 8,527 | 6,362 | 2,165 | 11,670 | 3,448 | 8,222 |
| | 70—and over | 30,605 | 13,853 | 16,752 | 1,320 | 1,136 | 184 | 10,147 | 7,539 | 2,608 | 19,188 | 5,178 | 13,960 |
| | **HINDU** | **3,136,307** | **1,622,581** | **1,513,726** | **1,151,093** | **707,695** | **443,398** | **1,582,133** | **804,003** | **778,130** | **403,081** | **110,883** | **292,198** |
| | 0—1 | 95,190 | 48,936 | 46,254 | 94,583 | 48,575 | 46,008 | 583 | 351 | 232 | 24 | 10 | 14 |
| | 1—2 | 60,569 | 29,498 | 31,071 | 59,929 | 29,154 | 30,775 | 604 | 331 | 273 | 36 | 13 | 23 |
| | 2—3 | 81,476 | 39,027 | 42,449 | 79,081 | 37,359 | 41,722 | 2,296 | 1,623 | 673 | 99 | 45 | 54 |
| | 3—4 | 94,238 | 45,767 | 48,466 | 92,210 | 44,876 | 47,334 | 1,892 | 829 | 1,063 | 131 | 62 | 69 |
| | 4—5 | 83,317 | 43,292 | 40,025 | 77,932 | 39,969 | 37,963 | 4,861 | 3,162 | 1,699 | 524 | 161 | 363 |
| | *Total 0—5* | *414,785* | *206,520* | *208,265* | *403,735* | *199,933* | *203,802* | *10,236* | *6,296* | *3,940* | *814* | *291* | *523* |
| | 5—10 | 393,434 | 203,058 | 190,376 | 346,082 | 184,542 | 161,540 | 45,543 | 18,013 | 27,530 | 1,809 | 503 | 1,306 |
| | 10—15 | 324,836 | 184,165 | 140,671 | 183,736 | 128,321 | 55,415 | 136,813 | 54,193 | 82,620 | 4,287 | 1,651 | 2,636 |
| | 15—20 | 263,462 | 150,206 | 113,256 | 79,342 | 71,119 | 8,223 | 176,090 | 76,087 | 100,003 | 8,030 | 3,000 | 5,030 |
| | 20—25 | 292,960 | 146,902 | 146,058 | 46,027 | 41,213 | 4,814 | 230,388 | 99,569 | 130,819 | 16,545 | 6,120 | 10,425 |
| | 25—30 | 308,870 | 157,648 | 151,222 | 32,740 | 29,089 | 3,651 | 250,505 | 119,676 | 130,829 | 25,625 | 8,883 | 16,742 |
| | 30—35 | 294,176 | 153,259 | 140,917 | 20,133 | 18,292 | 1,841 | 235,025 | 122,299 | 112,726 | 39,018 | 12,668 | 26,350 |
| | 35—40 | 179,060 | 94,291 | 84,769 | 10,141 | 9,354 | 787 | 137,982 | 75,405 | 62,577 | 30,937 | 9,532 | 21,405 |
| | 40—45 | 217,349 | 109,216 | 108,133 | 10,792 | 9,535 | 1,257 | 143,998 | 84,755 | 59,243 | 62,559 | 14,926 | 47,633 |
| | 45—50 | 108,868 | 56,873 | 51,995 | 5,107 | 4,568 | 539 | 67,914 | 42,743 | 25,171 | 35,847 | 9,562 | 26,285 |
| | 50—55 | 150,132 | 72,526 | 77,606 | 6,060 | 5,474 | 586 | 74,436 | 51,490 | 22,946 | 69,636 | 15,562 | 54,074 |
| | 55—60 | 51,106 | 27,660 | 23,446 | 2,177 | 1,994 | 183 | 26,242 | 18,485 | 7,757 | 22,687 | 7,181 | 15,506 |
| | 60—65 | 89,209 | 37,529 | 51,680 | 3,052 | 2,550 | 502 | 29,680 | 21,996 | 7,684 | 56,477 | 12,983 | 43,494 |
| | 65—70 | 19,590 | 9,782 | 9,808 | 731 | 637 | 94 | 7,842 | 5,919 | 1,923 | 11,017 | 3,226 | 7,791 |
| | 70—and over | 28,470 | 12,946 | 15,524 | 1,238 | 1,074 | 164 | 9,439 | 7,077 | 2,362 | 17,793 | 4,795 | 12,998 |
| | **ARYA** | **24** | **12** | **12** | **9** | **5** | **4** | **14** | **7** | **7** | **1** | .. | **1** |
| | 0—1 | .. | .. | .. | .. | .. | .. | .. | .. | .. | .. | .. | .. |
| | 1—2 | .. | .. | .. | .. | .. | .. | .. | .. | .. | .. | .. | .. |
| | 2—3 | .. | .. | .. | .. | .. | .. | .. | .. | .. | .. | .. | .. |
| | 3—4 | .. | .. | .. | .. | .. | .. | .. | .. | .. | .. | .. | .. |
| | 4—5 | 1 | .. | 1 | 1 | .. | 1 | .. | .. | .. | .. | .. | .. |
| | *Total 0—5* | *1* | .. | *1* | *1* | .. | *1* | .. | .. | .. | .. | .. | .. |
| | 5—10 | 4 | 3 | 1 | 3 | 2 | 1 | 1 | 1 | .. | .. | .. | .. |
| | 10—15 | 1 | 1 | .. | .. | .. | .. | 1 | 1 | .. | .. | .. | .. |
| | 15—20 | 5 | 4 | 1 | 2 | 2 | .. | 3 | 2 | 1 | .. | .. | .. |
| | 20—25 | 4 | 2 | 2 | 1 | .. | 1 | 3 | 2 | 1 | .. | .. | .. |
| | 25—30 | 4 | 1 | 3 | 2 | 1 | 1 | 2 | .. | 2 | .. | .. | .. |
| | 30—35 | .. | .. | .. | .. | .. | .. | .. | .. | .. | .. | .. | .. |
| | 35—40 | 1 | .. | 1 | .. | .. | .. | 1 | .. | 1 | .. | .. | .. |
| | 40—45 | 3 | 1 | 2 | .. | .. | .. | 3 | 1 | 2 | .. | .. | .. |
| | 45—50 | .. | .. | .. | .. | .. | .. | .. | .. | .. | .. | .. | .. |
| | 50—55 | .. | .. | .. | .. | .. | .. | .. | .. | .. | .. | .. | .. |
| | 55—60 | 1 | .. | 1 | .. | .. | .. | .. | .. | .. | 1 | .. | 1 |
| | 60—65 | .. | .. | .. | .. | .. | .. | .. | .. | .. | .. | .. | .. |
| | 65—70 | .. | .. | .. | .. | .. | .. | .. | .. | .. | .. | .. | .. |
| | 70—and over | .. | .. | .. | .. | .. | .. | .. | .. | .. | .. | .. | .. |
| | **SIKH** | **118** | **90** | **28** | **39** | **29** | **10** | **72** | **55** | **17** | **7** | **6** | **1** |
| | 0—1 | 2 | 1 | 1 | 2 | 1 | 1 | .. | .. | .. | .. | .. | .. |
| | 1—2 | .. | .. | .. | .. | .. | .. | .. | .. | .. | .. | .. | .. |
| | 2—3 | 2 | 1 | 1 | 2 | 1 | 1 | .. | .. | .. | .. | .. | .. |
| | 3—4 | 3 | .. | 3 | 3 | .. | 3 | .. | .. | .. | .. | .. | .. |
| | 4—5 | 2 | 1 | 1 | 2 | 1 | 1 | .. | .. | .. | .. | .. | .. |
| | *Total 0—5* | *9* | *3* | *6* | *9* | *3* | *6* | .. | .. | .. | .. | .. | .. |
| | 5—10 | 4 | 1 | 3 | 4 | 1 | 3 | .. | .. | .. | .. | .. | .. |
| | 10—15 | 5 | 3 | 2 | 4 | 3 | 1 | 1 | .. | 1 | .. | .. | .. |
| | 15—20 | 8 | 7 | 1 | 5 | 5 | .. | 3 | 2 | 1 | .. | .. | .. |
| | 20—25 | 27 | 26 | 1 | 8 | 8 | .. | 19 | 18 | 1 | .. | .. | .. |
| | 25—30 | 20 | 15 | 5 | 6 | 6 | .. | 13 | 8 | 5 | 1 | 1 | .. |
| | 30—35 | 20 | 15 | 5 | 1 | 1 | .. | 17 | 12 | 5 | 2 | 2 | .. |
| | 35—40 | 8 | 7 | 1 | .. | .. | .. | 6 | 5 | 1 | 2 | 2 | .. |
| | 40—45 | 5 | 4 | 1 | .. | .. | .. | 5 | 4 | 1 | .. | .. | .. |
| | 45—50 | 4 | 4 | .. | 1 | 1 | .. | 2 | 2 | .. | 1 | 1 | .. |
| | 50—55 | 4 | 2 | 2 | .. | .. | .. | 3 | 2 | 1 | 1 | .. | 1 |
| | 55—60 | 1 | 1 | .. | 1 | 1 | .. | .. | .. | .. | .. | .. | .. |
| | 60—65 | 2 | 1 | 1 | .. | .. | .. | 2 | 1 | 1 | .. | .. | .. |
| | 65—70 | .. | .. | .. | .. | .. | .. | .. | .. | .. | .. | .. | .. |
| | 70—and over | 1 | 1 | .. | .. | .. | .. | 1 | 1 | .. | .. | .. | .. |

## PART B.—DETAILS FOR NATURAL DIVISIONS.

| Division. | Age. | POPULATION. | | | UNMARRIED. | | | MARRIED. | | | WIDOWED. | | |
|---|---|---|---|---|---|---|---|---|---|---|---|---|---|
| | | Persons. | Males | Females. | Persons. | Males. | Females. | Persons. | Males. | Females. | Persons. | Males. | Females. |
| | 1 | 2 | 3 | 4 | 5 | 6 | 7 | 8 | 9 | 10 | 11 | 12 | 13 |
| LOW-LYING. | **JAIN** | **21,085** | **11,135** | **9,950** | **7,843** | **5,067** | **2,776** | **9,724** | **4,997** | **4,727** | **3,518** | **1,071** | **2,447** |
| | 0—1 | 611 | 317 | 294 | 604 | 317 | 287 | 7 | .. | 7 | .. | .. | .. |
| | 1—2 | 338 | 154 | 184 | 323 | 147 | 176 | 14 | 7 | 7 | 1 | .. | 1 |
| | 2—3 | 466 | 244 | 222 | 455 | 241 | 214 | 9 | 3 | 6 | 2 | .. | 2 |
| | 3—4 | 537 | 277 | 260 | 525 | 269 | 256 | 10 | 7 | 3 | 2 | 1 | 1 |
| | 4—5 | 526 | 292 | 234 | 509 | 280 | 229 | 16 | 11 | 5 | 1 | 1 | .. |
| | *Total 0—5* | *2,478* | *1,284* | *1,194* | *2,416* | *1,254* | *1,162* | *56* | *28* | *28* | *6* | *2* | *4* |
| | 5—10 | 2,820 | 1,120 | 1,200 | 2,056 | 1,035 | 1,021 | 245 | 80 | 165 | 19 | 5 | 14 |
| | 10—15 | 2,245 | 1,240 | 1,005 | 1,375 | 993 | 382 | 818 | 234 | 584 | 52 | 13 | 39 |
| | 15—20 | 1,712 | 998 | 714 | 569 | 520 | 49 | 1,067 | 446 | 621 | 76 | 32 | 44 |
| | 20—25 | 1,942 | 976 | 966 | 396 | 359 | 37 | 1,376 | 581 | 795 | 170 | 36 | 134 |
| | 25—30 | 1,902 | 1,037 | 865 | 290 | 253 | 37 | 1,361 | 720 | 641 | 251 | 64 | 187 |
| | 30—35 | 1,954 | 1,108 | 846 | 245 | 230 | 15 | 1,357 | 765 | 592 | 352 | 113 | 239 |
| | 35—40 | 1,259 | 649 | 610 | 119 | 104 | 15 | 820 | 455 | 365 | 320 | 90 | 230 |
| | 40—45 | 1,539 | 756 | 783 | 133 | 105 | 28 | 890 | 510 | 380 | 516 | 141 | 375 |
| | 45—50 | 936 | 523 | 413 | 74 | 62 | 12 | 563 | 359 | 204 | 299 | 102 | 197 |
| | 50—55 | 1,120 | 598 | 522 | 75 | 70 | 5 | 526 | 371 | 155 | 519 | 157 | 362 |
| | 55—60 | 523 | 270 | 253 | 30 | 24 | 6 | 262 | 157 | 105 | 231 | 89 | 142 |
| | 60—65 | 664 | 317 | 347 | 41 | 37 | 4 | 207 | 150 | 57 | 416 | 130 | 286 |
| | 65—70 | 209 | 113 | 96 | 10 | 7 | 3 | 81 | 63 | 18 | 118 | 43 | 75 |
| | 70—and over | 282 | 146 | 136 | 14 | 14 | .. | 95 | 78 | 17 | 173 | 54 | 119 |
| | **ANIMIST** | **30,857** | **15,203** | **15,654** | **13,132** | **6,897** | **6,235** | **15,465** | **7,745** | **7,720** | **2,260** | **561** | **1,699** |
| | 0—1 | 1,268 | 633 | 635 | 1,261 | 631 | 630 | 7 | 2 | 5 | .. | .. | .. |
| | 1—2 | 811 | 362 | 449 | 806 | 359 | 447 | 5 | 3 | 2 | .. | .. | .. |
| | 2—3 | 975 | 453 | 522 | 968 | 449 | 519 | 7 | 4 | 3 | .. | .. | .. |
| | 3—4 | 1,260 | 598 | 662 | 1,242 | 592 | 650 | 18 | 6 | 12 | .. | .. | .. |
| | 4—5 | 1,222 | 591 | 631 | 1,195 | 578 | 617 | 26 | 12 | 14 | 1 | 1 | .. |
| | *Total 0—5* | *5,536* | *2,637* | *2,899* | *5,472* | *2,609* | *2,863* | *63* | *27* | *36* | *1* | *1* | .. |
| | 5—10 | 4,112 | 1,972 | 2,140 | 3,917 | 1,880 | 2,037 | 183 | 87 | 96 | 12 | 5 | 7 |
| | 10—15 | 2,799 | 1,474 | 1,325 | 2,067 | 1,213 | 854 | 716 | 254 | 462 | 16 | 7 | 9 |
| | 15—20 | 2,220 | 1,163 | 1,057 | 766 | 578 | 188 | 1,413 | 568 | 845 | 41 | 17 | 24 |
| | 20—25 | 2,731 | 1,192 | 1,539 | 293 | 214 | 79 | 2,346 | 949 | 1,397 | 92 | 29 | 63 |
| | 25—30 | 3,117 | 1,484 | 1,633 | 241 | 203 | 38 | 2,739 | 1,239 | 1,500 | 137 | 42 | 95 |
| | 30—35 | 2,869 | 1,557 | 1,312 | 88 | 69 | 19 | 2,579 | 1,431 | 1,148 | 202 | 57 | 145 |
| | 35—40 | 1,691 | 868 | 823 | 53 | 38 | 15 | 1,507 | 795 | 712 | 131 | 35 | 96 |
| | 40—45 | 2,007 | 983 | 1,024 | 138 | 26 | 112 | 1,468 | 880 | 588 | 401 | 77 | 324 |
| | 45—50 | 935 | 485 | 450 | 26 | 26 | .. | 709 | 417 | 292 | 200 | 42 | 158 |
| | 50—55 | 1,264 | 629 | 635 | 29 | 19 | 10 | 817 | 532 | 285 | 418 | 78 | 340 |
| | 55—60 | 359 | 151 | 208 | 10 | 6 | 4 | 265 | 128 | 137 | 84 | 17 | 67 |
| | 60—65 | 740 | 379 | 361 | 20 | 9 | 11 | 370 | 267 | 103 | 350 | 103 | 247 |
| | 65—70 | 222 | 120 | 102 | 1 | .. | 1 | 166 | 109 | 57 | 55 | 11 | 44 |
| | 70—and over | 255 | 109 | 146 | 11 | 7 | 4 | 124 | 62 | 62 | 120 | 40 | 80 |
| | **MUSALMAN** | **121,077** | **63,989** | **57,088** | **47,097** | **28,842** | **18,255** | **59,229** | **30,656** | **28,573** | **14,751** | **4,491** | **10,260** |
| | 0—1 | 3,465 | 1,809 | 1,656 | 3,432 | 1,792 | 1,640 | 29 | 14 | 15 | 4 | 3 | 1 |
| | 1—2 | 2,302 | 1,195 | 1,107 | 2,254 | 1,176 | 1,078 | 42 | 17 | 25 | 6 | 2 | 4 |
| | 2—3 | 2,897 | 1,397 | 1,500 | 2,828 | 1,362 | 1,466 | 65 | 33 | 32 | 4 | 2 | 2 |
| | 3—4 | 3,563 | 1,653 | 1,910 | 3,387 | 1,615 | 1,772 | 87 | 31 | 56 | 89 | 7 | 82 |
| | 4—5 | 3,007 | 1,504 | 1,503 | 2,874 | 1,454 | 1,420 | 117 | 45 | 72 | 16 | 5 | 11 |
| | *Total 0—5* | *15,234* | *7,558* | *7,676* | *14,775* | *7,399* | *7,376* | *340* | *140* | *200* | *119* | *19* | *100* |
| | 5—10 | 14,287 | 7,372 | 6,915 | 13,063 | 6,946 | 6,117 | 1,093 | 388 | 705 | 131 | 38 | 93 |
| | 10—15 | 11,720 | 6,579 | 5,141 | 8,264 | 5,491 | 2,773 | 3,254 | 990 | 2,264 | 202 | 98 | 104 |
| | 15—20 | 9,565 | 5,427 | 4,138 | 4,000 | 3,413 | 587 | 5,273 | 1,863 | 3,410 | 292 | 151 | 141 |
| | 20—25 | 11,877 | 6,279 | 5,598 | 2,750 | 2,373 | 377 | 8,447 | 3,557 | 4,890 | 680 | 349 | 331 |
| | 25—30 | 12,204 | 6,744 | 5,460 | 1,664 | 1,436 | 228 | 9,611 | 4,875 | 4,736 | 929 | 433 | 496 |
| | 30—35 | 11,454 | 6,041 | 5,413 | 859 | 644 | 215 | 9,385 | 4,923 | 4,462 | 1,210 | 474 | 736 |
| | 35—40 | 6,979 | 3,897 | 3,082 | 459 | 314 | 145 | 5,585 | 3,247 | 2,338 | 935 | 336 | 599 |
| | 40—45 | 9,089 | 4,715 | 4,374 | 463 | 320 | 143 | 6,382 | 3,864 | 2,518 | 2,244 | 531 | 1,713 |
| | 45—50 | 4,053 | 2,291 | 1,762 | 169 | 107 | 62 | 2,805 | 1,856 | 949 | 1,079 | 328 | 751 |
| | 50—55 | 6,474 | 3,284 | 3,190 | 302 | 187 | 115 | 3,580 | 2,518 | 1,062 | 2,592 | 579 | 2,013 |
| | 55—60 | 1,958 | 1,066 | 892 | 79 | 63 | 16 | 1,065 | 751 | 314 | 814 | 252 | 562 |
| | 60—65 | 3,634 | 1,627 | 2,007 | 149 | 84 | 65 | 1,486 | 1,094 | 392 | 1,999 | 449 | 1,550 |
| | 65—70 | 960 | 462 | 498 | 44 | 24 | 20 | 438 | 271 | 167 | 478 | 167 | 311 |
| | 70—and over | 1,589 | 647 | 942 | 57 | 41 | 16 | 485 | 319 | 166 | 1,047 | 287 | 760 |
| | **CHRISTIAN** | **1,137** | **792** | **345** | **789** | **623** | **166** | **294** | **148** | **146** | **54** | **23** | **31** |
| | 0—1 | 15 | 10 | 5 | 15 | 10 | 5 | .. | .. | .. | .. | .. | .. |
| | 1—2 | 19 | 11 | 8 | 19 | 11 | 8 | .. | .. | .. | .. | .. | .. |
| | 2—3 | 20 | 6 | 14 | 20 | 6 | 14 | .. | .. | .. | .. | .. | .. |
| | 3—4 | 18 | 10 | 8 | 18 | 10 | 8 | .. | .. | .. | .. | .. | .. |
| | 4—5 | 20 | 10 | 10 | 20 | 10 | 10 | .. | .. | .. | .. | .. | .. |
| | *Total 0—5* | *92* | *47* | *45* | *92* | *47* | *45* | .. | .. | .. | .. | .. | .. |
| | 5—10 | 72 | 33 | 39 | 71 | 33 | 38 | .. | .. | .. | 1 | .. | .. |
| | 10—15 | 47 | 21 | 26 | 45 | 21 | 24 | 2 | .. | 2 | .. | .. | .. |
| | 15—20 | 72 | 29 | 43 | 52 | 22 | 30 | 18 | 6 | 12 | 2 | 1 | 1 |
| | 20—25 | 232 | 192 | 40 | 185 | 176 | 9 | 44 | 14 | 30 | 3 | 2 | 1 |
| | 25—30 | 274 | 238 | 36 | 229 | 222 | 7 | 44 | 15 | 29 | 1 | 1 | .. |
| | 30—35 | 111 | 76 | 35 | 60 | 54 | 6 | 47 | 21 | 26 | 4 | 1 | 3 |
| | 35—40 | 82 | 60 | 22 | 34 | 30 | 4 | 42 | 26 | 16 | 6 | 4 | 2 |
| | 40—45 | 42 | 26 | 16 | 8 | 7 | 1 | 33 | 18 | 15 | 1 | 1 | .. |
| | 45—50 | 36 | 29 | 7 | 6 | 5 | 1 | 26 | 20 | 6 | 4 | 4 | .. |
| | 50—55 | 26 | 12 | 14 | 3 | 2 | 1 | 15 | 8 | 7 | 8 | 2 | 6 |
| | 55—60 | 15 | 11 | 4 | .. | .. | .. | 10 | 9 | 1 | 5 | 2 | 3 |
| | 60—65 | 25 | 12 | 13 | 3 | 3 | .. | 10 | 7 | 3 | 12 | 2 | 10 |
| | 65—70 | 3 | 2 | 1 | 1 | 1 | .. | .. | .. | .. | 2 | 1 | 1 |
| | 70—and over | 8 | 4 | 4 | .. | .. | .. | 3 | 2 | 1 | 5 | 2 | 3 |

# TABLE VII.—Age, Sex and Civil Condition. Part B.—Details for Natural Divisions.

| Division. | Age. | Population. | | | Unmarried. | | | Married. | | | Widowed. | | |
|---|---|---|---|---|---|---|---|---|---|---|---|---|---|
| | | Persons. | Males. | Females. | Persons. | Males. | Females. | Persons. | Males. | Females. | Persons. | Males. | Females. |
| | 1 | 2 | 3 | 4 | 5 | 6 | 7 | 8 | 9 | 10 | 11 | 12 | 13 |
| *LOW-LYING.* | **Parsi** | **97** | **48** | **49** | **65** | **31** | **34** | **31** | **17** | **14** | **1** | .. | **1** |
| | 0—1 | 2 | 1 | 1 | 2 | 1 | 1 | .. | .. | .. | .. | .. | .. |
| | 1—2 | 2 | 1 | 1 | 2 | 1 | 1 | .. | .. | .. | .. | .. | .. |
| | 2—3 | 2 | .. | 2 | 2 | .. | 2 | .. | .. | .. | .. | .. | .. |
| | 3—4 | 3 | 1 | 2 | 3 | 1 | 2 | .. | .. | .. | .. | .. | .. |
| | 4—5 | 3 | .. | 3 | 3 | .. | 3 | .. | .. | .. | .. | .. | .. |
| | *Total 0—5* | *12* | *3* | *9* | *12* | *3* | *9* | .. | .. | .. | .. | .. | .. |
| | 5—10 | 29 | 13 | 16 | 29 | 13 | 16 | .. | .. | .. | .. | .. | .. |
| | 10—15 | 14 | 10 | 4 | 14 | 10 | 4 | .. | .. | .. | .. | .. | .. |
| | 15—20 | 3 | 1 | 2 | 3 | 1 | 2 | .. | .. | .. | .. | .. | .. |
| | 20—25 | 7 | 1 | 6 | 1 | .. | 1 | 6 | 1 | 5 | .. | .. | .. |
| | 25—30 | 8 | 2 | 6 | 2 | 1 | 1 | 6 | 1 | 5 | .. | .. | .. |
| | 30—35 | 8 | 6 | 2 | 3 | 3 | .. | 4 | 3 | 1 | 1 | .. | 1 |
| | 35—40 | 3 | 2 | 1 | 1 | .. | 1 | 2 | 2 | .. | .. | .. | .. |
| | 40—45 | 6 | 5 | 1 | .. | .. | .. | 6 | 5 | 1 | .. | .. | .. |
| | 45—50 | 1 | .. | 1 | .. | .. | .. | 1 | .. | 1 | .. | .. | .. |
| | 50—55 | 4 | 4 | .. | .. | .. | .. | 4 | 4 | .. | .. | .. | .. |
| | 55—60 | .. | .. | .. | .. | .. | .. | .. | .. | .. | .. | .. | .. |
| | 60—65 | 2 | 1 | 1 | .. | .. | .. | 2 | 1 | 1 | .. | .. | .. |
| | 65—70 | .. | .. | .. | .. | .. | .. | .. | .. | .. | .. | .. | .. |
| | 70—and over | .. | .. | .. | .. | .. | .. | .. | .. | .. | .. | .. | .. |
| | **Jew** | **1** | **1** | .. | .. | .. | .. | **1** | **1** | .. | .. | .. | .. |
| | 0—1 | .. | .. | .. | .. | .. | .. | .. | .. | .. | .. | .. | .. |
| | 1—2 | .. | .. | .. | .. | .. | .. | .. | .. | .. | .. | .. | .. |
| | 2—3 | .. | .. | .. | .. | .. | .. | .. | .. | .. | .. | .. | .. |
| | 3—4 | .. | .. | .. | .. | .. | .. | .. | .. | .. | .. | .. | .. |
| | 4—5 | .. | .. | .. | .. | .. | .. | .. | .. | .. | .. | .. | .. |
| | *Total 0-5* | .. | .. | .. | .. | .. | .. | .. | .. | .. | .. | .. | .. |
| | 5—10 | .. | .. | .. | .. | .. | .. | .. | .. | .. | .. | .. | .. |
| | 10—15 | .. | .. | .. | .. | .. | .. | .. | .. | .. | .. | .. | .. |
| | 15—20 | .. | .. | .. | .. | .. | .. | .. | .. | .. | .. | .. | .. |
| | 20—25 | .. | .. | .. | .. | .. | .. | .. | .. | .. | .. | .. | .. |
| | 25—30 | .. | .. | .. | .. | .. | .. | .. | .. | .. | .. | .. | .. |
| | 30—35 | .. | .. | .. | .. | .. | .. | .. | .. | .. | .. | .. | .. |
| | 35—40 | .. | .. | .. | .. | .. | .. | .. | .. | .. | .. | .. | .. |
| | 40—45 | 1 | 1 | .. | .. | .. | .. | 1 | 1 | .. | .. | .. | .. |
| | 45—50 | .. | .. | .. | .. | .. | .. | .. | .. | .. | .. | .. | .. |
| | 50—55 | .. | .. | .. | .. | .. | .. | .. | .. | .. | .. | .. | .. |
| | 55—60 | .. | .. | .. | .. | .. | .. | .. | .. | .. | .. | .. | .. |
| | 60—65 | .. | .. | .. | .. | .. | .. | .. | .. | .. | .. | .. | .. |
| | 65—70 | .. | .. | .. | .. | .. | .. | .. | .. | .. | .. | .. | .. |
| | 70—and over | .. | .. | .. | .. | .. | .. | .. | .. | .. | .. | .. | .. |

## TABLE VII.

### PART B.—HILLY.

# TABLE VII.—Age, Sex and Civil Condition.

| Division. | Age. | Population. | | | Unmarried. | | | Married. | | | Widowed. | | |
|---|---|---|---|---|---|---|---|---|---|---|---|---|---|
| | | Persons. | Males. | Females. | Persons. | Males. | Females. | Persons. | Males. | Females. | Persons. | Males. | Females. |
| | 1 | 2 | 3 | 4 | 5 | 6 | 7 | 8 | 9 | 10 | 11 | 12 | 13 |
| HILLY. | **ALL RELIGIONS** | **2,362,784** | **1,184,488** | **1,178,296** | **977,840** | **554,917** | **422,923** | **1,154,364** | **571,820** | **582,544** | **230,580** | **57,751** | **172,8[illegible]** |
| | 0—1 | 90,326 | 44,762 | 45,564 | 88,928 | 43,713 | 45,215 | 1,306 | 990 | 316 | 92 | 59 | [illegible] |
| | 1—2 | 60,412 | 29,815 | 30,597 | 59,287 | 29,054 | 30,233 | 1,025 | 693 | 332 | 100 | 68 | [illegible] |
| | 2—3 | 76,546 | 36,184 | 40,362 | 74,316 | 35,008 | 39,308 | 2,102 | 1,108 | 994 | 128 | 68 | [illegible] |
| | 3—4 | 89,808 | 41,109 | 48,699 | 86,109 | 39,421 | 46,668 | 2,816 | 1,586 | 1,230 | 903 | 102 | [illegible] |
| | 4—5 | 79,331 | 38,467 | 40,864 | 75,424 | 36,597 | 38,827 | 3,582 | 1,779 | 1,803 | 325 | 91 | [illegible] |
| | *Total 0—5* | *396,493* | *190,337* | *206,086* | *384,044* | *183,793* | *200,251* | *10,831* | *6,156* | *4,675* | *1,548* | *388* | *1,16[illegible]* |
| | 5—10 | 327,943 | 167,513 | 160,430 | 296,767 | 155,703 | 141,064 | 29,651 | 11,246 | 18,405 | 1,525 | 564 | 961 |
| | 10—15 | 223,519 | 121,018 | 102,501 | 147,168 | 93,869 | 53,299 | 74,008 | 26,188 | 47,820 | 2,343 | 961 | 1,382 |
| | 15—20 | 172,224 | 90,883 | 81,341 | 61,905 | 48,972 | 12,933 | 106,350 | 40,224 | 66,126 | 3,969 | 1,687 | 2,282 |
| | 20—25 | 211,072 | 96,487 | 114,585 | 34,642 | 29,127 | 5,515 | 166,790 | 64,166 | 102,624 | 9,640 | 3,194 | 6,446 |
| | 25—30 | 234,123 | 113,721 | 120,402 | 19,675 | 16,688 | 2,987 | 200,825 | 91,985 | 108,840 | 13,623 | 5,048 | 8,575 |
| | 30—35 | 231,804 | 119,535 | 112,269 | 12,923 | 10,588 | 2,335 | 197,030 | 102,309 | 94,721 | 21,851 | 6,638 | 15,213 |
| | 35—40 | 130,450 | 69,885 | 60,565 | 5,516 | 4,367 | 1,149 | 108,712 | 60,798 | 47,914 | 16,222 | 4,720 | 11,502 |
| | 40—45 | 152,817 | 79,199 | 73,618 | 6,276 | 4,991 | 1,285 | 110,098 | 66,391 | 43,707 | 36,443 | 7,817 | 28,626 |
| | 45—50 | 67,528 | 35,410 | 32,118 | 2,185 | 1,695 | 490 | 46,853 | 29,425 | 17,428 | 18,490 | 4,290 | 14,200 |
| | 50—55 | 94,125 | 44,474 | 49,651 | 2,823 | 2,159 | 664 | 51,284 | 34,817 | 16,467 | 40,018 | 7,498 | 32,520 |
| | 55—60 | 27,723 | 13,881 | 13,842 | 1,134 | 863 | 271 | 15,397 | 10,218 | 5,179 | 11,192 | 2,800 | 8,392 |
| | 60—65 | 59,799 | 26,380 | 33,419 | 1,589 | 1,181 | 408 | 24,287 | 18,507 | 5,780 | 33,923 | 6,692 | 27,231 |
| | 65—70 | 12,058 | 6,167 | 5,891 | 471 | 369 | 102 | 5,136 | 3,961 | 1,175 | 6,451 | 1,837 | 4,614 |
| | 70— and over | 21,178 | 9,598 | 11,580 | 722 | 552 | 170 | 7,112 | 5,429 | 1,683 | 13,344 | 3,617 | 9,727 |
| | **HINDU** | **1,912,943** | **960,146** | **952,797** | **769,281** | **439,622** | **329,659** | **948,579** | **471,084** | **477,495** | **195,083** | **49,440** | **145,643** |
| | 0—1 | 72,271 | 36,000 | 36,271 | 70,975 | 35,003 | 35,972 | 1,208 | 941 | 267 | 88 | 56 | 32 |
| | 1—2 | 47,488 | 23,479 | 24,009 | 46,517 | 22,846 | 23,671 | 876 | 568 | 308 | 95 | 65 | 30 |
| | 2—3 | 60,161 | 28,438 | 31,723 | 58,052 | 27,316 | 30,736 | 1,986 | 1,056 | 930 | 123 | 66 | 57 |
| | 3—4 | 70,840 | 31,909 | 38,931 | 67,558 | 30,456 | 37,102 | 2,496 | 1,357 | 1,139 | 786 | 96 | 690 |
| | 4—5 | 62,411 | 30,051 | 32,360 | 58,841 | 28,312 | 30,529 | 3,297 | 1,657 | 1,640 | 273 | 82 | 191 |
| | *Total 0—5* | *313,171* | *149,877* | *163,294* | *301,943* | *143,933* | *158,010* | *9,863* | *5,579* | *4,284* | *1,365* | *365* | *1,000* |
| | 5—10 | 266,167 | 135,678 | 130,489 | 236,602 | 124,498 | 112,104 | 28,157 | 10,658 | 17,499 | 1,408 | 522 | 886 |
| | 10—15 | 183,312 | 99,558 | 83,754 | 113,845 | 74,385 | 39,460 | 67,305 | 24,273 | 43,032 | 2,162 | 900 | 1,262 |
| | 15—20 | 139,293 | 74,475 | 64,818 | 46,379 | 37,741 | 8,638 | 89,480 | 35,316 | 54,164 | 3,434 | 1,418 | 2,016 |
| | 20—25 | 170,056 | 78,803 | 91,253 | 26,814 | 22,799 | 4,015 | 134,852 | 53,248 | 81,604 | 8,390 | 2,756 | 5,634 |
| | 25—30 | 188,793 | 92,395 | 96,398 | 15,826 | 13,656 | 2,170 | 161,277 | 74,370 | 86,907 | 11,690 | 4,369 | 7,321 |
| | 30—35 | 187,044 | 96,281 | 90,763 | 10,717 | 8,967 | 1,750 | 157,773 | 81,691 | 76,082 | 18,554 | 5,623 | 12,931 |
| | 35—40 | 105,059 | 55,986 | 49,073 | 4,612 | 3,733 | 879 | 86,598 | 48,201 | 38,397 | 13,849 | 4,052 | 9,797 |
| | 40—45 | 124,727 | 64,430 | 60,297 | 5,228 | 4,278 | 950 | 89,060 | 53,481 | 35,579 | 30,439 | 6,671 | 23,768 |
| | 45—50 | 55,751 | 29,083 | 26,668 | 1,714 | 1,375 | 339 | 38,516 | 24,039 | 14,477 | 15,521 | 3,669 | 11,852 |
| | 50—55 | 78,520 | 36,961 | 41,559 | 2,390 | 1,832 | 558 | 42,651 | 28,805 | 13,846 | 33,479 | 6,324 | 27,155 |
| | 55—60 | 23,367 | 11,602 | 11,765 | 908 | 680 | 228 | 12,896 | 8,479 | 4,417 | 9,563 | 2,443 | 7,120 |
| | 60—65 | 50,076 | 22,140 | 27,936 | 1,312 | 979 | 333 | 20,251 | 15,436 | 4,815 | 28,513 | 5,725 | 22,788 |
| | 65—70 | 19,813 | 4,958 | 4,855 | 350 | 267 | 83 | 4,126 | 3,173 | 953 | 5,337 | 1,518 | 3,819 |
| | 70— and over | 17,794 | 7,919 | 9,875 | 641 | 499 | 142 | 5,774 | 4,335 | 1,439 | 11,379 | 3,085 | 8,294 |
| | **ARYA** | **28** | **21** | **7** | **9** | **8** | **1** | **18** | **12** | **6** | **1** | **1** | |
| | 0—1 | .. | .. | .. | .. | .. | .. | .. | .. | .. | .. | .. | .. |
| | 1—2 | 1 | 1 | .. | 1 | 1 | .. | .. | .. | .. | .. | .. | .. |
| | 2—3 | 1 | 1 | .. | 1 | 1 | .. | .. | .. | .. | .. | .. | .. |
| | 3—4 | .. | .. | .. | .. | .. | .. | .. | .. | .. | .. | .. | .. |
| | 4—5 | 1 | 1 | .. | 1 | 1 | .. | .. | .. | .. | .. | .. | .. |
| | *Total 0—5* | *3* | *3* | .. | *3* | *3* | .. | .. | .. | .. | .. | .. | .. |
| | 5—10 | .. | .. | .. | .. | .. | .. | .. | .. | .. | .. | .. | .. |
| | 10—15 | 1 | .. | 1 | 1 | .. | 1 | .. | .. | .. | .. | .. | .. |
| | 15—20 | 2 | 1 | 1 | 1 | 1 | .. | 1 | .. | 1 | .. | .. | .. |
| | 20—25 | 8 | 6 | 2 | 2 | 2 | .. | 6 | 4 | 2 | .. | .. | .. |
| | 25—30 | 9 | 7 | 2 | 2 | 2 | .. | 6 | 4 | 2 | 1 | 1 | .. |
| | 30—35 | 1 | 1 | .. | .. | .. | .. | 1 | 1 | .. | .. | .. | .. |
| | 35—40 | 1 | .. | 1 | .. | .. | .. | 1 | .. | 1 | .. | .. | .. |
| | 40—45 | 2 | 2 | .. | .. | .. | .. | 2 | 2 | .. | .. | .. | .. |
| | 45—50 | 1 | 1 | .. | .. | .. | .. | 1 | 1 | .. | .. | .. | .. |
| | 50—55 | .. | .. | .. | .. | .. | .. | .. | .. | .. | .. | .. | .. |
| | 55—60 | .. | .. | .. | .. | .. | .. | .. | .. | .. | .. | .. | .. |
| | 60—65 | .. | .. | .. | .. | .. | .. | .. | .. | .. | .. | .. | .. |
| | 65—70 | .. | .. | .. | .. | .. | .. | .. | .. | .. | .. | .. | .. |
| | 70— and over | .. | .. | .. | .. | .. | .. | .. | .. | .. | .. | .. | .. |
| | **BRAHMO** | **9** | **6** | **3** | **5** | **4** | **1** | **4** | **2** | **2** | .. | .. | .. |
| | 0—1 | .. | .. | .. | .. | .. | .. | .. | .. | .. | .. | .. | .. |
| | 1—2 | 1 | 1 | .. | 1 | 1 | .. | .. | .. | .. | .. | .. | .. |
| | 2—3 | .. | .. | .. | .. | .. | .. | .. | .. | .. | .. | .. | .. |
| | 3—4 | .. | .. | .. | .. | .. | .. | .. | .. | .. | .. | .. | .. |
| | 4—5 | .. | .. | .. | .. | .. | .. | .. | .. | .. | .. | .. | .. |
| | *Total 0—5* | *1* | *1* | .. | *1* | *1* | .. | .. | .. | .. | .. | .. | .. |
| | 5—10 | 2 | 2 | .. | 2 | 2 | .. | .. | .. | .. | .. | .. | .. |
| | 10—15 | 2 | 1 | 1 | 2 | 1 | 1 | .. | .. | .. | .. | .. | .. |
| | 15—20 | .. | .. | .. | .. | .. | .. | .. | .. | .. | .. | .. | .. |
| | 20—25 | 1 | .. | 1 | .. | .. | .. | 1 | .. | 1 | .. | .. | .. |
| | 25—30 | .. | .. | .. | .. | .. | .. | .. | .. | .. | .. | .. | .. |
| | 30—35 | .. | .. | .. | .. | .. | .. | .. | .. | .. | .. | .. | .. |
| | 35—40 | 1 | 1 | .. | .. | .. | .. | 1 | 1 | .. | .. | .. | .. |
| | 40—45 | 1 | .. | 1 | .. | .. | .. | 1 | .. | 1 | .. | .. | .. |
| | 45—50 | .. | .. | .. | .. | .. | .. | .. | .. | .. | .. | .. | .. |
| | 50—55 | .. | .. | .. | .. | .. | .. | .. | .. | .. | .. | .. | .. |
| | 55—60 | 1 | 1 | .. | .. | .. | .. | 1 | 1 | .. | .. | .. | .. |
| | 60—65 | .. | .. | .. | .. | .. | .. | .. | .. | .. | .. | .. | .. |
| | 65—70 | .. | .. | .. | .. | .. | .. | .. | .. | .. | .. | .. | .. |
| | 70— and over | .. | .. | .. | .. | .. | .. | .. | .. | .. | .. | .. | .. |

## Part B.—Details for Natural Divisions.

| Division. | Age. | Population. | | | Unmarried. | | | Married. | | | Widowed. | | |
|---|---|---|---|---|---|---|---|---|---|---|---|---|---|
| | | Persons. | Males. | Females. | Persons. | Males. | Females. | Persons. | Males. | Females. | Persons. | Males. | Females. |
| | 1 | 2 | 3 | 4 | 5 | 6 | 7 | 8 | 9 | 10 | 11 | 12 | 13 |
| HILLY. | **SIKH** | **175** | **100** | **75** | **88** | **59** | **29** | **70** | **36** | **34** | **17** | **5** | **12** |
| | 0—1 | 10 | 4 | 6 | 10 | 4 | 6 | .. | .. | .. | .. | .. | .. |
| | 1—2 | 5 | 2 | 3 | 5 | 2 | 3 | .. | .. | .. | .. | .. | .. |
| | 2—3 | 11 | 8 | 3 | 11 | 8 | 3 | .. | .. | .. | .. | .. | .. |
| | 3—4 | 4 | 1 | 3 | 4 | 1 | 3 | .. | .. | .. | .. | .. | .. |
| | 4—5 | 7 | 2 | 5 | 7 | 2 | 5 | .. | .. | .. | .. | .. | .. |
| | *Total 0—5* | *37* | *17* | *20* | *37* | *17* | *20* | .. | .. | .. | .. | .. | .. |
| | 5—10 | 14 | 6 | 8 | 14 | 6 | 8 | .. | .. | .. | .. | .. | .. |
| | 10—15 | 23 | 22 | 1 | 17 | 17 | .. | 6 | 5 | 1 | .. | .. | .. |
| | 15—20 | 17 | 12 | 5 | 5 | 5 | .. | 12 | 7 | 5 | .. | .. | .. |
| | 20—25 | 23 | 13 | 10 | 6 | 5 | 1 | 17 | 8 | 9 | .. | .. | .. |
| | 25—30 | 18 | 10 | 8 | 3 | 3 | .. | 15 | 7 | 8 | | .. | .. |
| | 30—35 | 10 | 3 | 7 | 3 | 3 | .. | 7 | .. | 7 | .. | .. | .. |
| | 35—40 | 5 | 1 | 4 | .. | .. | .. | 3 | 1 | 2 | 2 | .. | 2 |
| | 40—45 | 2 | 2 | .. | .. | .. | .. | 2 | 2 | .. | .. | .. | .. |
| | 45—50 | 3 | 2 | 1 | 1 | 1 | .. | 1 | 1 | .. | 1 | .. | 1 |
| | 50—55 | 9 | 5 | 4 | 2 | 2 | .. | 3 | 2 | 1 | 4 | 1 | 3 |
| | 55—60 | 1 | 1 | .. | .. | .. | .. | .. | .. | .. | 1 | 1 | .. |
| | 60—65 | 7 | 3 | 4 | .. | .. | .. | 4 | 3 | 1 | 3 | .. | 3 |
| | 65—70 | 1 | .. | 1 | .. | .. | .. | .. | .. | .. | 1 | .. | 1 |
| | 70—and over | 5 | 3 | 2 | .. | .. | .. | .. | .. | .. | 5 | 3 | 2 |
| | **JAIN** | **13,547** | **6,976** | **6,571** | **5,239** | **3,360** | **1,879** | **5,949** | **2,999** | **2,950** | **2,359** | **617** | **1,742** |
| | 0—1 | 403 | 224 | 179 | 398 | 221 | 177 | 4 | 3 | 1 | 1 | .. | 1 |
| | 1—2 | 218 | 106 | 112 | 217 | 106 | 111 | 1 | .. | 1 | .. | .. | .. |
| | 2—3 | 370 | 173 | 197 | 369 | 173 | 196 | 1 | .. | 1 | .. | .. | .. |
| | 3—4 | 360 | 186 | 174 | 352 | 185 | 167 | 6 | .. | 6 | 2 | 1 | 1 |
| | 4—5 | 292 | 150 | 142 | 284 | 148 | 136 | 7 | 2 | 5 | 1 | .. | 1 |
| | *Total 0—5* | *1,643* | *839* | *804* | *1,690* | *833* | *787* | *19* | *5* | *14* | *4* | *1* | *3* |
| | 5—10 | 1,488 | 723 | 765 | 1,414 | 696 | 718 | 68 | 25 | 43 | 6 | 2 | 4 |
| | 10—15 | 1,219 | 665 | 554 | 859 | 593 | 266 | 346 | 69 | 277 | 14 | 3 | 11 |
| | 15—20 | 1,140 | 621 | 519 | 423 | 393 | 30 | 667 | 220 | 447 | 50 | 8 | 42 |
| | 20—25 | 1,324 | 712 | 612 | 329 | 311 | 18 | 885 | 378 | 507 | 110 | 23 | 87 |
| | 25—30 | 1,338 | 669 | 669 | 203 | 191 | 12 | 998 | 445 | 553 | 137 | 33 | 104 |
| | 30—35 | 1,348 | 711 | 637 | 137 | 123 | 14 | 963 | 531 | 432 | 248 | 57 | 191 |
| | 35—40 | 847 | 456 | 391 | 61 | 54 | 7 | 593 | 357 | 236 | 193 | 45 | 148 |
| | 40—45 | 927 | 469 | 458 | 81 | 70 | 11 | 521 | 317 | 204 | 325 | 82 | 243 |
| | 45—50 | 516 | 280 | 236 | 30 | 27 | 3 | 271 | 189 | 82 | 215 | 64 | 151 |
| | 50—55 | 697 | 317 | 380 | 38 | 26 | 12 | 279 | 190 | 89 | 380 | 101 | 279 |
| | 55—60 | 288 | 159 | 129 | 19 | 18 | 1 | 108 | 83 | 25 | 161 | 58 | 103 |
| | 60—65 | 461 | 192 | 269 | 15 | 15 | .. | 136 | 101 | 35 | 310 | 76 | 234 |
| | 65—70 | 115 | 56 | 59 | 2 | 2 | .. | 32 | 29 | 3 | 81 | 25 | 56 |
| | 70—and over | 196 | 107 | 89 | 8 | 8 | .. | 63 | 60 | 3 | 125 | 39 | 86 |
| | **ANIMIST** | **342,225** | **169,167** | **173,058** | **165,007** | **89,636** | **75,371** | **154,182** | **74,600** | **79,582** | **23,036** | **4,931** | **18,105** |
| | 0—1 | 14,325 | 6,967 | 7,358 | 14,264 | 6,944 | 7,320 | 58 | 20 | 38 | 3 | 3 | .. |
| | 1—2 | 10,625 | 5,165 | 5,460 | 10,600 | 5,151 | 5,449 | 24 | 13 | 11 | 1 | 1 | .. |
| | 2—3 | 13,333 | 6,309 | 7,024 | 13,263 | 6,272 | 6,991 | 67 | 36 | 31 | 3 | 1 | 2 |
| | 3—4 | 15,549 | 7,464 | 8,085 | 15,345 | 7,418 | 7,927 | 93 | 42 | 51 | 111 | 4 | 107 |
| | 4—5 | 13,957 | 7,016 | 6,941 | 13,747 | 6,937 | 6,810 | 171 | 75 | 96 | 39 | 4 | 35 |
| | *Total 0—5* | *67,789* | *32,921* | *34,868* | *67,219* | *32,722* | *34,497* | *413* | *186* | *227* | *157* | *13* | *144* |
| | 5—10 | 48,348 | 25,077 | 23,271 | 47,665 | 24,817 | 22,848 | 628 | 242 | 386 | 55 | 18 | 37 |
| | 10—15 | 30,033 | 15,902 | 14,131 | 25,585 | 14,599 | 10,986 | 4,374 | 1,287 | 3,087 | 74 | 16 | 58 |
| | 15—20 | 25,127 | 12,170 | 12,957 | 12,333 | 8,498 | 3,835 | 12,548 | 3,570 | 8,978 | 246 | 102 | 144 |
| | 20—25 | 30,771 | 12,805 | 17,966 | 5,731 | 4,466 | 1,265 | 24,338 | 8,066 | 16,272 | 702 | 273 | 429 |
| | 25—30 | 34,294 | 15,925 | 18,369 | 2,687 | 1,991 | 696 | 30,379 | 13,506 | 16,873 | 1,228 | 428 | 800 |
| | 30—35 | 33,828 | 17,465 | 16,363 | 1,462 | 988 | 474 | 30,363 | 15,898 | 14,465 | 2,003 | 579 | 1,424 |
| | 35—40 | 19,566 | 10,686 | 8,880 | 621 | 402 | 219 | 17,404 | 9,848 | 7,556 | 1,541 | 436 | 1,105 |
| | 40—45 | 20,652 | 10,903 | 9,749 | 706 | 462 | 244 | 15,796 | 9,682 | 6,114 | 4,150 | 759 | 3,391 |
| | 45—50 | 8,383 | 4,423 | 3,960 | 354 | 226 | 128 | 6,125 | 3,896 | 2,229 | 1,904 | 301 | 1,603 |
| | 50—55 | 10,810 | 5,160 | 5,650 | 279 | 210 | 69 | 6,024 | 4,198 | 1,826 | 4,507 | 752 | 3,755 |
| | 55—60 | 2,803 | 1,383 | 1,420 | 117 | 97 | 20 | 1,668 | 1,097 | 571 | 1,018 | 189 | 829 |
| | 60—65 | 6,462 | 2,761 | 3,701 | 139 | 83 | 56 | 2,717 | 2,064 | 653 | 3,606 | 614 | 2,992 |
| | 65—70 | 1,324 | 598 | 726 | 58 | 44 | 14 | 577 | 401 | 176 | 689 | 153 | 536 |
| | 70—and over | 2,035 | 988 | 1,047 | 51 | 31 | 20 | 828 | 659 | 169 | 1,156 | 298 | 858 |
| | **MUSALMAN** | **92,885** | **47,544** | **45,341** | **37,733** | **21,965** | **15,768** | **45,107** | **22,837** | **22,270** | **10,045** | **2,742** | **7,303** |
| | 0—1 | 3,289 | 1,552 | 1,737 | 3,253 | 1,526 | 1,727 | 36 | 26 | 10 | .. | .. | .. |
| | 1—2 | 2,037 | 1,043 | 994 | 1,909 | 929 | 980 | 124 | 112 | 12 | 4 | 2 | 2 |
| | 2—3 | 2,630 | 1,236 | 1,394 | 2,581 | 1,219 | 1,362 | 47 | 16 | 31 | 2 | 1 | 1 |
| | 3—4 | 3,011 | 1,530 | 1,481 | 2,786 | 1,342 | 1,444 | 221 | 187 | 34 | 4 | 1 | 3 |
| | 4—5 | 2,624 | 1,227 | 1,397 | 2,505 | 1,177 | 1,328 | 107 | 45 | 62 | 12 | 5 | 7 |
| | *Total 0—5* | *13,591* | *6,588* | *7,003* | *13,034* | *6,193* | *6,841* | *535* | *386* | *149* | *22* | *9* | *13* |
| | 5—10 | 11,901 | 5,968 | 5,833 | 10,947 | 5,625 | 5,322 | 798 | 321 | 477 | 56 | 22 | 34 |
| | 10—15 | 8,863 | 4,837 | 4,026 | 6,799 | 4,242 | 2,557 | 1,971 | 553 | 1,418 | 93 | 42 | 51 |
| | 15—20 | 6,574 | 3,565 | 3,009 | 2,717 | 2,299 | 418 | 3,620 | 1,107 | 2,513 | 237 | 159 | 78 |
| | 20—25 | 8,769 | 4,092 | 4,677 | 1,739 | 1,529 | 210 | 6,593 | 2,422 | 4,171 | 437 | 141 | 296 |
| | 25—30 | 9,535 | 4,639 | 4,896 | 939 | 834 | 105 | 8,034 | 3,591 | 4,443 | 562 | 214 | 348 |
| | 30—35 | 9,489 | 5,018 | 4,471 | 594 | 498 | 96 | 7,853 | 4,141 | 3,712 | 1,042 | 379 | 663 |
| | 35—40 | 4,914 | 2,718 | 2,196 | 217 | 174 | 43 | 4,063 | 2,358 | 1,705 | 634 | 186 | 448 |
| | 40—45 | 6,456 | 3,357 | 3,099 | 255 | 176 | 79 | 4,679 | 2,881 | 1,798 | 1,522 | 300 | 1,222 |
| | 45—50 | 2,851 | 1,606 | 1,245 | 84 | 65 | 19 | 1,918 | 1,285 | 633 | 849 | 256 | 593 |
| | 50—55 | 4,060 | 2,019 | 2,041 | 114 | 89 | 25 | 2,308 | 1,611 | 697 | 1,638 | 319 | 1,319 |
| | 55—60 | 1,251 | 727 | 524 | 88 | 67 | 21 | 717 | 552 | 165 | 446 | 108 | 338 |
| | 60—65 | 2,785 | 1,278 | 1,507 | 123 | 104 | 19 | 1,174 | 898 | 276 | 1,488 | 276 | 1,212 |
| | 65—70 | 802 | 554 | 248 | 61 | 56 | 5 | 399 | 357 | 42 | 342 | 141 | 201 |
| | 70—and over | 1,144 | 578 | 566 | 22 | 14 | 8 | 445 | 374 | 71 | 677 | 190 | 487 |

# TABLE VII.—Age, Sex and Civil Condition. Part B.—Details for Natural Divisions.

| Division. | Age. | Population. | | | Unmarried. | | | Married. | | | Widowed. | | |
|---|---|---|---|---|---|---|---|---|---|---|---|---|---|
| | | Persons. | Males. | Females. | Persons. | Males. | Females. | Persons. | Males. | Females. | Persons. | Males. | Females. |
| | 1 | 2 | 3 | 4 | 5 | 6 | 7 | 8 | 9 | 10 | 11 | 12 | 13 |
| HILLY. | **CHRISTIAN** | **853** | **455** | **398** | **427** | **238** | **189** | **392** | **206** | **186** | **34** | **11** | **23** |
| | 0—1 | 28 | 15 | 13 | 28 | 15 | 13 | .. | .. | .. | .. | .. | .. |
| | 1—2 | 34 | 16 | 18 | 34 | 16 | 18 | .. | .. | .. | .. | .. | .. |
| | 2—3 | 37 | 18 | 19 | 36 | 18 | 18 | 1 | .. | 1 | .. | .. | .. |
| | 3—4 | 41 | 18 | 23 | 41 | 18 | 23 | .. | .. | .. | .. | .. | .. |
| | 4—5 | 36 | 18 | 18 | 36 | 18 | 18 | .. | .. | .. | .. | .. | .. |
| | *Total 0—5* | *176* | *85* | *91* | *175* | *85* | *90* | *1* | .. | *1* | .. | .. | .. |
| | 5—10 | 108 | 54 | 54 | 108 | 54 | 54 | .. | .. | .. | .. | .. | .. |
| | 10—15 | 57 | 31 | 26 | 52 | 30 | 22 | 5 | 1 | 4 | .. | .. | .. |
| | 15—20 | 64 | 38 | 26 | 42 | 34 | 8 | 21 | 4 | 17 | 1 | .. | 1 |
| | 20—25 | 112 | 51 | 61 | 19 | 13 | 6 | 92 | 37 | 55 | 1 | 1 | .. |
| | 25—30 | 121 | 67 | 54 | 12 | 8 | 4 | 105 | 56 | 49 | 4 | 3 | 1 |
| | 30—35 | 64 | 39 | 25 | 5 | 4 | 1 | 56 | 35 | 21 | 3 | .. | 3 |
| | 35—40 | 47 | 29 | 18 | 4 | 3 | 1 | 40 | 25 | 15 | 3 | 1 | 2 |
| | 40—45 | 41 | 29 | 12 | 6 | 5 | 1 | 30 | 21 | 9 | 5 | 3 | 2 |
| | 45—50 | 20 | 12 | 8 | 2 | 1 | 1 | 18 | 11 | 7 | .. | .. | .. |
| | 50—55 | 24 | 9 | 15 | .. | .. | .. | 15 | 9 | 6 | 9 | .. | 9 |
| | 55—60 | 7 | 4 | 3 | 2 | 1 | 1 | 3 | 3 | .. | 2 | .. | 2 |
| | 60—65 | 6 | 4 | 2 | .. | .. | .. | 3 | 3 | .. | 3 | 1 | 2 |
| | 65—70 | 3 | 1 | 2 | .. | .. | .. | 2 | 1 | 1 | 1 | .. | 1 |
| | 70—and over | 3 | 2 | 1 | .. | .. | .. | 1 | .. | 1 | 2 | 2 | .. |
| | **PARSI** | **121** | **73** | **48** | **51** | **25** | **26** | **63** | **44** | **19** | **7** | **4** | **3** |
| | 0—1 | .. | .. | .. | .. | .. | .. | .. | .. | .. | .. | .. | .. |
| | 1—2 | 3 | 2 | 1 | 3 | 2 | 1 | .. | .. | .. | .. | .. | .. |
| | 2—3 | 3 | 1 | 2 | 3 | 1 | 2 | .. | .. | .. | .. | .. | .. |
| | 3—4 | 3 | 1 | 2 | 3 | 1 | 2 | .. | .. | .. | .. | .. | .. |
| | 4—5 | 3 | 2 | 1 | 3 | 2 | 1 | .. | .. | .. | .. | .. | .. |
| | *Total 0—5* | *12* | *6* | *6* | *12* | *6* | *6* | .. | .. | .. | .. | .. | .. |
| | 5—10 | 15 | 5 | 10 | 15 | 5 | 10 | .. | .. | .. | .. | .. | .. |
| | 10—15 | 9 | 2 | 7 | 8 | 2 | 6 | 1 | .. | 1 | .. | .. | .. |
| | 15—20 | 7 | 1 | 6 | 5 | 1 | 4 | 1 | .. | 1 | 1 | .. | 1 |
| | 20—25 | 8 | 5 | 3 | 2 | 2 | .. | 6 | 3 | 3 | .. | .. | .. |
| | 25—30 | 15 | 9 | 6 | 3 | 3 | .. | 11 | 6 | 5 | 1 | .. | 1 |
| | 30—35 | 20 | 17 | 3 | 5 | 5 | .. | 14 | 12 | 2 | 1 | .. | 1 |
| | 35—40 | 10 | 8 | 2 | 1 | 1 | .. | 9 | 7 | 2 | .. | .. | .. |
| | 40—45 | 9 | 7 | 2 | .. | .. | .. | 7 | 5 | 2 | 2 | 2 | .. |
| | 45—50 | 3 | 3 | .. | .. | .. | .. | 3 | 3 | .. | .. | .. | .. |
| | 50—55 | 5 | 3 | 2 | .. | .. | .. | 4 | 2 | 2 | 1 | 1 | .. |
| | 55—60 | 5 | 4 | 1 | .. | .. | .. | 4 | 3 | 1 | 1 | 1 | .. |
| | 60—65 | 2 | 2 | .. | .. | .. | .. | 2 | 2 | .. | .. | .. | .. |
| | 65—70 | .. | .. | .. | .. | .. | .. | .. | .. | .. | .. | .. | .. |
| | 70—and over | 1 | 1 | .. | .. | .. | .. | 1 | 1 | .. | .. | .. | .. |

# TABLE VIII.

## *EDUCATION BY RELIGION AND AGE.*

This table like Table VII is divided into two parts. *Part A* shows the extent of literacy in the Agency as a whole amongst the total population for each religion returned; *Part B* gives details for the three Natural Divisions, for the total population and for each religion.

The number of persons literate in English has also been shown. The number of such persons appear both in the column "Literate" and in the column "Literate in English." The latter must, therefore, be left out of account in calculating the literate number of persons.

The number of Christian population literate in English include :—

| Age periods. | Europeans and Allied Races and Anglo-Indians. | | | Indians. | | |
|---|---|---|---|---|---|---|
| | Persons. | Males. | Females. | Persons. | Males. | Females. |
| 1 | 2 | 3 | 4 | 5 | 6 | 7 |
| *Total* . . . . . | *4,567* | *3,788* | *779* | *440* | *376* | *64* |
| 0—10 . . . . . | 154 | 81 | 73 | 6 | .. | 6 |
| 10—15 . . . . . | 115 | 64 | 51 | 30 | 9 | 21 |
| 15—20 . . . . . | 192 | 101 | 91 | 118 | 81 | 37 |
| 20 and over . . . | 4,106 | 3,542 | 564 | 286 | 286 | .. |

# TABLE VIII.—EDUCATION BY RELIGION AND AGE. PART A.—AGENCY SUMMARY.

| AGE, ETC. | POPULATION. | | | | | | | | | LITERATE IN ENGLISH. | | |
|---|---|---|---|---|---|---|---|---|---|---|---|---|
| | TOTAL. | | | LITERATE. | | | ILLITERATE. | | | | | |
| | Persons. | Males. | Females. | Persons. | Males. | Females. | Persons. | Males. | Females. | Persons. | Males. | Females. |
| 1 | 2 | 3 | 4 | 5 | 6 | 7 | 8 | 9 | 10 | 11 | 12 | 13 |
| **Central India** | | | | | | | | | | | | |
| ALL RELIGIONS | 9,356,980 | 4,801,459 | 4,555,521 | 242,820 | 231,203 | 11,617 | 9,114,160 | 4,570,256 | 4,543,904 | 18,144 | 16,868 | 1,276 |
| 1—10 | 2,588,294 | 1,304,325 | 1,283,969 | 7,060 | 6,257 | 803 | 2,581,234 | 1,298,068 | 1,283,166 | 292 | 194 | 98 |
| 10—15 | 864,283 | 483,893 | 380,390 | 23,031 | 21,600 | 1,431 | 841,252 | 462,293 | 378,959 | 1,109 | 985 | 124 |
| 15—20 | 737,911 | 403,981 | 333,930 | 26,117 | 24,448 | 1,669 | 711,794 | 379,533 | 332,261 | 2,362 | 2,167 | 195 |
| 20 and over | 5,166,492 | 2,609,260 | 2,557,232 | 186,612 | 178,898 | 7,714 | 4,979,880 | 2,430,362 | 2,549,518 | 14,381 | 13,522 | 859 |
| HINDU | 8,262,638 | 4,241,694 | 4,020,944 | 184,966 | 179,002 | 5,964 | 8,077,672 | 4,062,692 | 4,014,980 | 16,476 | 16,315 | 161 |
| 1—10 | 2,273,102 | 1,146,326 | 1,126,776 | 5,220 | 4,814 | 406 | 2,267,882 | 1,141,512 | 1,126,370 | 84 | 76 | 8 |
| 10—15 | 767,773 | 431,335 | 336,438 | 17,965 | 17,244 | 721 | 749,808 | 414,091 | 335,717 | 733 | 715 | 18 |
| 15—20 | 654,645 | 360,849 | 293,796 | 20,118 | 19,302 | 816 | 634,527 | 341,547 | 292,980 | 1,663 | 1,632 | 31 |
| 20 and over | 4,567,118 | 2,303,184 | 2,263,934 | 141,663 | 137,642 | 4,021 | 4,425,455 | 2,165,542 | 2,259,913 | 7,996 | 7,892 | 104 |
| ARYA | 139 | 90 | 49 | 74 | 63 | 11 | 65 | 27 | 38 | 28 | 26 | 2 |
| 1—10 | 25 | 14 | 11 | 1 | 1 | .. | 24 | 13 | 11 | .. | .. | .. |
| 10—15 | 8 | 5 | 3 | 4 | 3 | 1 | 4 | 2 | 2 | .. | .. | .. |
| 15—20 | 16 | 11 | 5 | 10 | 8 | 2 | 6 | 3 | 3 | 3 | 3 | .. |
| 20 and over | 90 | 60 | 30 | 59 | 51 | 8 | 31 | 9 | 22 | 25 | 23 | 2 |
| BRAHMO | 9 | 6 | 3 | 6 | 4 | 2 | 3 | 2 | 1 | 3 | 1 | 2 |
| 1—10 | 3 | 3 | .. | 1 | 1 | .. | 2 | 2 | .. | .. | .. | .. |
| 10—15 | 2 | 1 | 1 | 1 | 1 | .. | 1 | .. | 1 | .. | .. | .. |
| 15—20 | .. | .. | .. | .. | .. | .. | .. | .. | .. | .. | .. | .. |
| 20 and over | 4 | 2 | 2 | 4 | 2 | 2 | .. | .. | .. | 3 | 1 | 2 |
| SIKH | 1,384 | 953 | 431 | 366 | 353 | 13 | 1,018 | 600 | 418 | 25 | 25 | .. |
| 1—10 | 238 | 125 | 113 | 8 | 8 | .. | 230 | 117 | 113 | .. | .. | .. |
| 10—15 | 81 | 64 | 17 | 13 | 12 | 1 | 68 | 52 | 16 | 1 | 1 | .. |
| 15—20 | 139 | 99 | 40 | 28 | 27 | 1 | 111 | 72 | 39 | 2 | 2 | .. |
| 20 and over | 926 | 665 | 261 | 317 | 306 | 11 | 609 | 359 | 250 | 22 | 22 | .. |
| JAIN | 87,471 | 45,711 | 41,760 | 18,586 | 17,750 | 836 | 68,885 | 27,961 | 40,924 | 255 | 249 | 6 |
| 1—10 | 19,811 | 9,990 | 9,821 | 625 | 562 | 63 | 19,186 | 9,428 | 9,758 | 3 | 3 | .. |
| 10—15 | 8,097 | 4,563 | 3,534 | 1,809 | 1,710 | 99 | 6,288 | 2,853 | 3,435 | 34 | 34 | .. |
| 15—20 | 7,347 | 3,993 | 3,354 | 2,032 | 1,930 | 102 | 5,315 | 2,063 | 3,252 | 74 | 73 | 1 |
| 20 and over | 52,216 | 27,165 | 25,051 | 14,120 | 13,548 | 572 | 38,096 | 13,617 | 24,479 | 144 | 139 | 5 |
| ANIMIST | 483,394 | 239,618 | 243,776 | 303 | 295 | 8 | 483,091 | 239,323 | 243,768 | 3 | 3 | .. |
| 1—10 | 161,643 | 80,803 | 80,840 | 6 | 6 | .. | 161,637 | 80,797 | 80,840 | .. | .. | .. |
| 10—15 | 40,778 | 21,709 | 19,069 | 22 | 21 | 1 | 40,756 | 21,688 | 19,068 | .. | .. | .. |
| 15—20 | 35,318 | 17,227 | 18,091 | 41 | 39 | 2 | 35,277 | 17,188 | 18,089 | .. | .. | .. |
| 20 and over | 245,655 | 119,879 | 125,776 | 234 | 229 | 5 | 245,421 | 119,650 | 125,771 | 3 | 3 | .. |
| MUSALMAN | 511,200 | 266,494 | 244,706 | 31,284 | 28,437 | 2,847 | 479,916 | 238,057 | 241,859 | 1,776 | 1,745 | 31 |
| 1—10 | 131,458 | 66,063 | 65,395 | 882 | 686 | 196 | 130,576 | 65,377 | 65,199 | 20 | 19 | 1 |
| 10—15 | 46,943 | 25,933 | 21,010 | 2,806 | 2,418 | 388 | 44,137 | 23,515 | 20,622 | 139 | 134 | 5 |
| 15—20 | 39,503 | 21,402 | 18,101 | 3,216 | 2,853 | 363 | 36,287 | 18,549 | 17,738 | 260 | 254 | 6 |
| 20 and over | 293,296 | 153,096 | 140,200 | 24,380 | 22,480 | 1,900 | 268,916 | 130,616 | 138,300 | 1,357 | 1,338 | 19 |
| CHRISTIAN | 9,358 | 6,170 | 3,188 | 6,273 | 4,787 | 1,486 | 3,085 | 1,383 | 1,702 | 5,007 | 4,164 | 843 |
| 1—10 | 1,705 | 854 | 851 | 234 | 130 | 104 | 1,471 | 724 | 747 | 160 | 81 | 79 |
| 10—15 | 471 | 214 | 257 | 308 | 136 | 172 | 163 | 78 | 85 | 145 | 73 | 72 |
| 15—20 | 825 | 348 | 477 | 584 | 256 | 328 | 241 | 92 | 149 | 310 | 182 | 128 |
| 20 and over | 6,357 | 4,754 | 1,603 | 5,147 | 4,265 | 882 | 1,210 | 489 | 721 | 4,392 | 3,828 | 564 |
| PARSI | 1,330 | 689 | 641 | 928 | 490 | 438 | 402 | 199 | 203 | 547 | 322 | 225 |
| 1—10 | 297 | 142 | 155 | 82 | 48 | 34 | 215 | 94 | 121 | 24 | 14 | 10 |
| 10—15 | 122 | 63 | 59 | 101 | 54 | 47 | 21 | 9 | 12 | 57 | 28 | 29 |
| 15—20 | 109 | 48 | 61 | 84 | 32 | 52 | 25 | 16 | 9 | 49 | 21 | 28 |
| 20 and over | 802 | 436 | 366 | 661 | 356 | 305 | 141 | 80 | 61 | 417 | 259 | 158 |
| JEW | 57 | 34 | 23 | 34 | 22 | 12 | 23 | 12 | 11 | 24 | 18 | 6 |
| 1—10 | 12 | 5 | 7 | 1 | 1 | .. | 11 | 4 | 7 | 1 | 1 | .. |
| 10—15 | 8 | 6 | 2 | 2 | 1 | 1 | 6 | 5 | 1 | .. | .. | .. |
| 15—20 | 9 | 4 | 5 | 4 | 1 | 3 | 5 | 3 | 2 | 1 | .. | 1 |
| 20 and over | 28 | 19 | 9 | 27 | 19 | 8 | 1 | .. | 1 | 22 | 17 | 5 |

## TABLE VIII.

### Part B.—PLATEAU.

# TABLE VIII.—Education by Religion and Age. Part B.—Details for Natural Divisions.

| Division. | Age, etc. | Population. Total. Persons. | Total. Males. | Total. Females. | Literate. Persons. | Literate. Males. | Literate. Females. | Illiterate. Persons. | Illiterate. Males. | Illiterate. Females | Literate in English. Persons. | Literate in English. Males. | Literate in English. Females. |
|---|---|---|---|---|---|---|---|---|---|---|---|---|---|
| | 1 | 2 | 3 | 4 | 5 | 6 | 7 | 8 | 9 | 10 | 11 | 12 | 13 |
| PLATEAU. | **ALL RELIGIONS** | **3,683,491** | **1,903,120** | **1,780,371** | **127,622** | **120,218** | **7,404** | **3,555,869** | **1,782,902** | **1,772,967** | **12,374** | **11,391** | **983** |
| | 1—10 | 1,011,519 | 514,851 | 496,668 | 4,001 | 3,470 | 531 | 1,007,518 | 511,381 | 496,137 | 208 | 130 | 78 |
| | 10—15 | 299,097 | 169,382 | 129,715 | 11,053 | 10,146 | 907 | 288,044 | 159,236 | 128,808 | 747 | 654 | 93 |
| | 15—20 | 288,640 | 155,263 | 133,377 | 13,092 | 12,019 | 1,073 | 275,548 | 143,244 | 132,304 | 1,525 | 1,369 | 156 |
| | 20 and over | 2,084,235 | 1,063,624 | 1,020,611 | 99,476 | 94,583 | 4,893 | 1,984,759 | 969,041 | 1,015,718 | 9,894 | 9,238 | 656 |
| | **HINDU** | **3,213,388** | **1,658,967** | **1,554,421** | **89,091** | **86,053** | **3,038** | **3,124,297** | **1,572,914** | **1,551,383** | **6,393** | **6,290** | **103** |
| | 1—10 | 885,545 | 451,193 | 434,352 | 2,707 | 2,473 | 234 | 882,838 | 448,720 | 434,118 | 44 | 39 | 5 |
| | 10—15 | 259,625 | 147,612 | 112,013 | 7,778 | 7,415 | 363 | 251,847 | 140,197 | 111,650 | 457 | 448 | 9 |
| | 15—20 | 251,890 | 136,168 | 115,722 | 9,059 | 8,656 | 403 | 242,831 | 127,512 | 115,319 | 970 | 952 | 18 |
| | 20 and over | 1,816,328 | 923,994 | 892,334 | 69,547 | 67,509 | 2,038 | 1,746,781 | 856,485 | 890,296 | 4,922 | 4,851 | 71 |
| | **ARYA** | **87** | **57** | **30** | **53** | **45** | **8** | **34** | **12** | **22** | **23** | **21** | **2** |
| | 1—10 | 17 | 8 | 9 | 1 | 1 | .. | 16 | 7 | 9 | .. | .. | .. |
| | 10—15 | 6 | 4 | 2 | 4 | 3 | 1 | 2 | 1 | 1 | .. | .. | .. |
| | 15—20 | 9 | 6 | 3 | 7 | 6 | 1 | 2 | .. | 2 | 2 | 2 | .. |
| | 20 and over | 55 | 39 | 16 | 41 | 35 | 6 | 14 | 4 | 10 | 21 | 19 | 2 |
| | **SIKH** | **1,091** | **763** | **328** | **299** | **294** | **5** | **792** | **469** | **323** | **17** | **17** | .. |
| | 1—10 | 174 | 98 | 76 | 7 | 7 | .. | 167 | 91 | 76 | .. | .. | .. |
| | 10—15 | 53 | 39 | 14 | 8 | 8 | .. | 45 | 31 | 14 | 1 | 1 | .. |
| | 15—20 | 114 | 80 | 34 | 25 | 24 | 1 | 89 | 56 | 33 | 2 | 2 | .. |
| | 20 and over | 750 | 546 | 204 | 259 | 255 | 4 | 491 | 291 | 200 | 14 | 14 | .. |
| | **JAIN** | **52,839** | **27,600** | **25,239** | **12,748** | **12,102** | **646** | **40,091** | **15,498** | **24,593** | **223** | **217** | **6** |
| | 1—10 | 11,882 | 6,024 | 5,858 | 451 | 411 | 40 | 11,431 | 5,613 | 5,818 | 2 | 2 | .. |
| | 10—15 | 4,633 | 2,658 | 1,975 | 1,196 | 1,121 | 75 | 3,437 | 1,537 | 1,900 | 31 | 31 | .. |
| | 15—20 | 4,495 | 2,374 | 2,121 | 1,395 | 1,316 | 79 | 3,100 | 1,058 | 2,042 | 67 | 66 | 1 |
| | 20 and over | 31,829 | 16,544 | 15,285 | 9,706 | 9,254 | 452 | 22,123 | 7,290 | 14,833 | 123 | 118 | 5 |
| | **ANIMIST** | **110,312** | **55,248** | **55,064** | **136** | **136** | .. | **110,176** | **55,112** | **55,064** | **2** | **2** | .. |
| | 1—10 | 35,858 | 18,196 | 17,662 | 1 | 1 | .. | 35,857 | 18,195 | 17,662 | .. | .. | .. |
| | 10—15 | 7,946 | 4,333 | 3,613 | 6 | 6 | .. | 7,940 | 4,327 | 3,613 | .. | .. | .. |
| | 15—20 | 7,971 | 3,894 | 4,077 | 17 | 17 | .. | 7,954 | 3,877 | 4,077 | .. | .. | .. |
| | 20 and over | 58,537 | 28,825 | 29,712 | 112 | 112 | .. | 58,425 | 28,713 | 29,712 | 2 | 2 | .. |
| | **MUSALMAN** | **297,238** | **154,961** | **142,277** | **19,315** | **17,208** | **2,107** | **277,923** | **137,753** | **140,170** | **1,151** | **1,125** | **26** |
| | 1—10 | 76,545 | 38,577 | 37,968 | 579 | 427 | 152 | 75,966 | 38,150 | 37,816 | 13 | 12 | 1 |
| | 10—15 | 26,360 | 14,517 | 11,843 | 1,718 | 1,438 | 280 | 24,642 | 13,079 | 11,563 | 90 | 86 | 4 |
| | 15—20 | 23,364 | 12,410 | 10,954 | 1,995 | 1,748 | 247 | 21,369 | 10,662 | 10,707 | 176 | 171 | 5 |
| | 20 and over | 170,969 | 89,457 | 81,512 | 15,023 | 13,595 | 1,428 | 155,946 | 75,862 | 80,084 | 872 | 856 | 16 |
| | **CHRISTIAN** | **7,368** | **4,923** | **2,445** | **5,150** | **3,952** | **1,198** | **2,218** | **971** | **1,247** | **4,071** | **3,438** | **633** |
| | 1—10 | 1,257 | 635 | 622 | 186 | 106 | 80 | 1,071 | 529 | 542 | 125 | 63 | 62 |
| | 10—15 | 367 | 162 | 205 | 255 | 109 | 146 | 112 | 53 | 59 | 116 | 61 | 55 |
| | 15—20 | 689 | 281 | 408 | 516 | 221 | 295 | 173 | 60 | 113 | 264 | 157 | 107 |
| | 20 and over | 5,055 | 3,845 | 1,210 | 4,193 | 3,516 | 677 | 862 | 329 | 533 | 3,566 | 3,157 | 409 |
| | **PARSI** | **1,112** | **568** | **544** | **797** | **407** | **390** | **315** | **161** | **154** | **471** | **264** | **207** |
| | 1—10 | 229 | 115 | 114 | 68 | 43 | 25 | 161 | 72 | 89 | 23 | 13 | 10 |
| | 10—15 | 99 | 51 | 48 | 86 | 45 | 41 | 13 | 6 | 7 | 52 | 27 | 25 |
| | 15—20 | 99 | 46 | 53 | 74 | 30 | 44 | 25 | 16 | 9 | 43 | 19 | 24 |
| | 20 and over | 685 | 356 | 329 | 569 | 289 | 280 | 116 | 67 | 49 | 358 | 205 | 148 |
| | **JEW** | **56** | **33** | **23** | **33** | **21** | **12** | **23** | **12** | **11** | **23** | **17** | **6** |
| | 1—10 | 12 | 5 | 7 | 1 | 1 | .. | 11 | 4 | 7 | 1 | 1 | .. |
| | 10—15 | 8 | 6 | 2 | 2 | 1 | 1 | 6 | 5 | 1 | .. | .. | .. |
| | 15—20 | 9 | 4 | 5 | 4 | 1 | 3 | 5 | 3 | 2 | 1 | .. | 1 |
| | 20 and over | 27 | 18 | 9 | 26 | 18 | 8 | 1 | .. | 1 | 21 | 16 | 5 |

## TABLE VIII.

### PART B.—LOW-LYING.

## TABLE VIII.—Education by Religion and Age. Part B.—Details for Natural Divisions.

| Division. | Age, etc. | Population. Total. Persons. | Males. | Females. | Literate. Persons. | Males. | Females. | Illiterate. Persons. | Males. | Females. | Literate in English. Persons. | Males. | Females. |
|---|---|---|---|---|---|---|---|---|---|---|---|---|---|
| | 1 | 2 | 3 | 4 | 5 | 6 | 7 | 8 | 9 | 10 | 11 | 12 | 13 |
| LOW-LYING. | **ALL RELIGIONS** | **3,310,703** | **1,713,851** | **1,596,852** | **70,935** | **68,424** | **2,511** | **3,239,768** | **1,645,427** | **1,594,341** | **4,272** | **4,059** | **213** |
| | 1—10 | 852,409 | 431,624 | 420,785 | 1,729 | 1,578 | 151 | 850,680 | 430,046 | 420,634 | 67 | 50 | 17 |
| | 10—15 | 341,667 | 193,493 | 148,174 | 7,168 | 6,845 | 323 | 334,499 | 186,648 | 147,851 | 271 | 249 | 22 |
| | 15—20 | 277,047 | 157,835 | 119,212 | 7,771 | 7,395 | 376 | 269,276 | 150,440 | 118,836 | 599 | 573 | 26 |
| | 20 and over | 1,839,580 | 930,899 | 908,681 | 54,267 | 52,606 | 1,661 | 1,785,313 | 878,293 | 907,020 | 3,335 | 3,187 | 148 |
| | **HINDU** | **3,136,307** | **1,622,581** | **1,513,726** | **60,938** | **59,082** | **1,856** | **3,075,369** | **1,563,499** | **1,511,870** | **2,925** | **2,885** | **40** |
| | 1—10 | 808,219 | 409,578 | 398,641 | 1,451 | 1,351 | 100 | 806,768 | 408,227 | 398,541 | 34 | 31 | 3 |
| | 10—15 | 324,836 | 184,165 | 140,671 | 6,270 | 6,039 | 231 | 318,566 | 178,126 | 140,440 | 202 | 194 | 8 |
| | 15—20 | 263,462 | 150,206 | 113,256 | 6,801 | 6,514 | 287 | 256,661 | 143,692 | 112,969 | 495 | 487 | 8 |
| | 20 and over | 1,739,790 | 878,632 | 861,158 | 46,416 | 45,178 | 1,238 | 1,693,374 | 833,454 | 859,920 | 2,194 | 2,173 | 21 |
| | **ARYA** | **24** | **12** | **12** | **3** | **3** | .. | **21** | **9** | **12** | .. | .. | .. |
| | 1—10 | 5 | 3 | 2 | .. | .. | .. | 5 | 3 | 2 | .. | .. | .. |
| | 10—15 | 1 | 1 | .. | .. | .. | .. | 1 | 1 | .. | .. | .. | .. |
| | 15—20 | 5 | 4 | 1 | 1 | 1 | .. | 4 | 3 | 1 | .. | .. | .. |
| | 20 and over | 13 | 4 | 9 | 2 | 2 | .. | 11 | 2 | 9 | .. | .. | .. |
| | **SIKH** | **118** | **90** | **28** | **48** | **41** | **7** | **70** | **49** | **21** | **5** | **5** | .. |
| | 1—10 | 13 | 4 | 9 | 1 | 1 | .. | 12 | 3 | 9 | .. | .. | .. |
| | 10—15 | 5 | 3 | 2 | 1 | .. | 1 | 4 | 3 | 1 | .. | .. | .. |
| | 15—20 | 8 | 7 | 1 | 3 | 3 | .. | 5 | 4 | 1 | .. | .. | .. |
| | 20 and over | 92 | 76 | 16 | 43 | 37 | 6 | 49 | 39 | 10 | 5 | 5 | .. |
| | **JAIN** | **21,085** | **11,135** | **9,950** | **2,515** | **2,460** | **55** | **18,570** | **8,675** | **9,895** | **19** | **19** | .. |
| | 1—10 | 4,798 | 2,404 | 2,394 | 73 | 65 | 8 | 4,725 | 2,339 | 2,386 | 1 | 1 | .. |
| | 10—15 | 2,245 | 1,240 | 1,005 | 268 | 259 | 9 | 1,977 | 981 | 996 | 1 | 1 | .. |
| | 15—20 | 1,712 | 998 | 714 | 277 | 273 | 4 | 1,435 | 725 | 710 | 2 | 2 | .. |
| | 20 and over | 12,330 | 6,493 | 5,837 | 1,897 | 1,863 | 34 | 10,433 | 4,630 | 5,808 | 15 | 15 | .. |
| | **ANIMIST** | **30,857** | **15,203** | **15,654** | **42** | **41** | **1** | **30,815** | **15,162** | **15,653** | .. | .. | .. |
| | 1—10 | 9,648 | 4,609 | 5,039 | 1 | 1 | .. | 9,647 | 4,608 | 5,039 | .. | .. | .. |
| | 10—15 | 2,799 | 1,474 | 1,325 | 3 | 3 | .. | 2,796 | 1,471 | 1,325 | .. | .. | .. |
| | 15—20 | 2,220 | 1,163 | 1,057 | 7 | 7 | .. | 2,213 | 1,156 | 1,057 | .. | .. | .. |
| | 20 and over | 16,190 | 7,957 | 8,233 | 31 | 30 | 1 | 16,159 | 7,927 | 8,232 | .. | .. | .. |
| | **MUSALMAN** | **121,077** | **63,989** | **57,088** | **6,457** | **6,076** | **381** | **114,620** | **57,913** | **56,707** | **474** | **470** | **4** |
| | 1—10 | 29,521 | 14,930 | 14,591 | 161 | 139 | 22 | 29,360 | 14,791 | 14,569 | 3 | 3 | .. |
| | 10—15 | 11,720 | 6,579 | 5,141 | 589 | 524 | 65 | 11,131 | 6,055 | 5,076 | 44 | 43 | 1 |
| | 15—20 | 9,565 | 5,427 | 4,138 | 632 | 573 | 59 | 8,933 | 4,854 | 4,079 | 62 | 61 | 1 |
| | 20 and over | 70,271 | 37,053 | 33,218 | 5,075 | 4,840 | 235 | 65,196 | 32,213 | 32,983 | 365 | 363 | 2 |
| | **CHRISTIAN** | **1,137** | **792** | **345** | **886** | **690** | **196** | **251** | **102** | **149** | **824** | **661** | **163** |
| | 1—10 | 164 | 80 | 84 | 36 | 18 | 18 | 128 | 62 | 66 | 29 | 15 | 14 |
| | 10—15 | 47 | 21 | 26 | 29 | 13 | 16 | 18 | 8 | 10 | 22 | 10 | 12 |
| | 15—20 | 72 | 29 | 43 | 47 | 23 | 24 | 25 | 6 | 19 | 38 | 22 | 16 |
| | 20 and over | 854 | 662 | 192 | 774 | 636 | 138 | 80 | 26 | 54 | 785 | 614 | 121 |
| | **PARSI** | **97** | **48** | **49** | **45** | **30** | **15** | **52** | **18** | **34** | **24** | **18** | **6** |
| | 1—10 | 41 | 16 | 25 | 6 | 3 | 3 | 35 | 13 | 22 | .. | .. | .. |
| | 10—15 | 14 | 10 | 4 | 8 | 7 | 1 | 6 | 3 | 3 | 2 | 1 | 1 |
| | 15—20 | 3 | 1 | 2 | 3 | 1 | 2 | .. | .. | .. | 2 | 1 | 1 |
| | 20 and over | 39 | 21 | 18 | 28 | 19 | 9 | 11 | 2 | 9 | 20 | 16 | 4 |
| | **JEW** | **1** | **1** | .. | **1** | **1** | .. | .. | .. | .. | **1** | **1** | .. |
| | 1—10 | .. | .. | .. | .. | .. | .. | .. | .. | .. | .. | .. | .. |
| | 10—15 | .. | .. | .. | .. | .. | .. | .. | .. | .. | .. | .. | .. |
| | 15—20 | .. | .. | .. | .. | .. | .. | .. | .. | .. | .. | .. | .. |
| | 20 and over | 1 | 1 | .. | 1 | 1 | .. | .. | .. | .. | 1 | 1 | .. |

# TABLE VIII.

## PART B.—HILLY.

# TABLE VIII.—Education by Religion and Age. Part B.—Details for Natural Divisions.

| Division. | Age, etc. | Population. Total. Persons. | Total. Males. | Total. Females. | Literate. Persons. | Literate. Males. | Literate. Females. | Illiterate. Persons. | Illiterate. Males. | Illiterate. Females. | Literate in English. Persons. | Literate in English. Males. | Literate in English. Females. |
|---|---|---|---|---|---|---|---|---|---|---|---|---|---|
| | 1 | 2 | 3 | 4 | 5 | 6 | 7 | 8 | 9 | 10 | 11 | 12 | 13 |
| HILLY. | **ALL RELIGIONS** | **2,362,786** | **1,184,488** | **1,178,298** | **44,263** | **42,561** | **1,702** | **2,318,523** | **1,141,927** | **1,176,596** | **1,498** | **1,418** | **80** |
| | 1—10 | 724,366 | 357,850 | 366,516 | 1,330 | 1,209 | 121 | 723,036 | 356,641 | 366,395 | 17 | 14 | 3 |
| | 10—15 | 223,519 | 121,018 | 102,501 | 4,810 | 4,609 | 201 | 218,709 | 116,409 | 102,300 | 91 | 82 | 9 |
| | 15—20 | 172,224 | 90,883 | 81,341 | 5,254 | 5,034 | 220 | 166,970 | 85,849 | 81,121 | 238 | 225 | 13 |
| | 20 and over | 1,242,677 | 614,737 | 627,940 | 32,869 | 31,709 | 1,160 | 1,209,808 | 583,028 | 626,780 | 1,152 | 1,097 | 55 |
| | **HINDU** | **1,912,943** | **960,146** | **952,797** | **34,937** | **33,867** | **1,070** | **1,878,006** | **926,279** | **951,727** | **1,158** | **1,140** | **18** |
| | 1—10 | 579,338 | 285,555 | 293,783 | 1,062 | 990 | 72 | 578,276 | 284,565 | 293,711 | 6 | 6 | .. |
| | 10—15 | 183,312 | 99,558 | 83,754 | 3,917 | 3,790 | 127 | 179,395 | 95,768 | 83,627 | 74 | 73 | 1 |
| | 15—20 | 139,293 | 74,475 | 64,818 | 4,258 | 4,132 | 126 | 135,035 | 70,343 | 64,692 | 198 | 193 | 5 |
| | 20 and over | 1,011,000 | 500,558 | 510,442 | 25,700 | 24,955 | 745 | 986,300 | 475,603 | 509,697 | 880 | 868 | 12 |
| | **ARYA** | **28** | **21** | **7** | **18** | **15** | **3** | **10** | **6** | **4** | **5** | **5** | .. |
| | 1—10 | 3 | 3 | .. | .. | .. | .. | 3 | 3 | .. | .. | .. | .. |
| | 10—15 | 1 | .. | 1 | .. | .. | .. | 1 | .. | 1 | .. | .. | .. |
| | 15—20 | 2 | 1 | 1 | 2 | 1 | 1 | .. | .. | .. | 1 | 1 | .. |
| | 20 and over | 22 | 17 | 5 | 16 | 14 | 2 | 6 | 3 | 3 | 4 | 4 | .. |
| | **BRAHMO** | **9** | **6** | **3** | **6** | **4** | **2** | **3** | **2** | **1** | **3** | **1** | **2** |
| | 1—10 | 3 | 3 | .. | 1 | 1 | .. | 2 | 2 | .. | .. | .. | .. |
| | 10—15 | 2 | 1 | 1 | 1 | 1 | .. | 1 | .. | 1 | .. | .. | .. |
| | 15—20 | .. | .. | .. | .. | .. | .. | .. | .. | .. | .. | .. | .. |
| | 20 and over | 4 | 2 | 2 | 4 | 2 | 2 | .. | .. | .. | 3 | 1 | 2 |
| | **SIKH** | **175** | **100** | **75** | **19** | **18** | **1** | **156** | **82** | **74** | **3** | **3** | .. |
| | 1—10 | 51 | 23 | 28 | .. | .. | .. | 51 | 23 | 28 | .. | .. | .. |
| | 10—15 | 23 | 22 | 1 | 4 | 4 | .. | 19 | 18 | 1 | .. | .. | .. |
| | 15—20 | 17 | 12 | 5 | .. | .. | .. | 17 | 12 | 5 | .. | .. | .. |
| | 20 and over | 84 | 43 | 41 | 15 | 14 | 1 | 69 | 29 | 40 | 3 | 3 | .. |
| | **JAIN** | **13,547** | **6,976** | **6,571** | **3,323** | **3,188** | **135** | **10,224** | **3,788** | **6,436** | **13** | **13** | .. |
| | 1—10 | 3,131 | 1,562 | 1,569 | 101 | 86 | 15 | 3,030 | 1,476 | 1,554 | .. | .. | .. |
| | 10—15 | 1,219 | 665 | 554 | 345 | 330 | 15 | 874 | 335 | 539 | 2 | 2 | .. |
| | 15—20 | 1,140 | 621 | 519 | 360 | 341 | 19 | 780 | 280 | 500 | 5 | 5 | .. |
| | 20 and over | 8,057 | 4,128 | 3,929 | 2,517 | 2,431 | 86 | 5,540 | 1,697 | 3,843 | 6 | 6 | .. |
| | **ANIMIST** | **342,225** | **169,167** | **173,058** | **125** | **118** | **7** | **342,100** | **169,049** | **173,051** | **1** | **1** | .. |
| | 1—10 | 116,137 | 57,998 | 58,139 | 4 | 4 | .. | 116,133 | 57,994 | 58,139 | .. | .. | .. |
| | 10—15 | 30,033 | 15,902 | 14,131 | 13 | 12 | 1 | 30,020 | 15,890 | 14,130 | .. | .. | .. |
| | 15—20 | 25,127 | 12,170 | 12,957 | 17 | 15 | 2 | 25,110 | 12,155 | 12,955 | .. | .. | .. |
| | 20 and over | 170,928 | 83,097 | 87,831 | 91 | 87 | 4 | 170,837 | 83,010 | 87,827 | 1 | 1 | .. |
| | **MUSALMAN** | **92,885** | **47,544** | **45,341** | **5,512** | **5,153** | **359** | **87,373** | **42,391** | **44,982** | **151** | **150** | **1** |
| | 1—10 | 25,392 | 12,556 | 12,836 | 142 | 120 | 22 | 25,250 | 12,436 | 12,814 | 4 | 4 | .. |
| | 10—15 | 8,863 | 4,837 | 4,026 | 499 | 456 | 43 | 8,364 | 4,381 | 3,983 | 5 | 5 | .. |
| | 15—20 | 6,574 | 3,565 | 3,009 | 589 | 532 | 57 | 5,985 | 3,033 | 2,952 | 22 | 22 | .. |
| | 20 and over | 52,056 | 26,586 | 25,470 | 4,282 | 4,045 | 237 | 47,774 | 22,541 | 25,233 | 120 | 119 | 1 |
| | **CHRISTIAN** | **853** | **455** | **398** | **237** | **145** | **92** | **616** | **310** | **306** | **112** | **65** | **47** |
| | 1—10 | 284 | 139 | 145 | 12 | 6 | 6 | 272 | 133 | 139 | 6 | 3 | 3 |
| | 10—15 | 57 | 31 | 26 | 24 | 14 | 10 | 33 | 17 | 16 | 7 | 2 | 5 |
| | 15—20 | 64 | 38 | 26 | 21 | 12 | 9 | 43 | 26 | 17 | 8 | 3 | 5 |
| | 20 and over | 448 | 247 | 201 | 180 | 113 | 67 | 268 | 134 | 134 | 91 | 57 | 34 |
| | **PARSI** | **121** | **73** | **48** | **86** | **53** | **33** | **35** | **20** | **15** | **52** | **40** | **12** |
| | 1—10 | 27 | 11 | 16 | 8 | 2 | 6 | 19 | 9 | 10 | 1 | 1 | .. |
| | 10—15 | 9 | 2 | 7 | 7 | 2 | 5 | 2 | .. | 2 | 3 | .. | 3 |
| | 15—20 | 7 | 1 | 6 | 7 | 1 | 6 | .. | .. | .. | 4 | 1 | 3 |
| | 20 and over | 78 | 59 | 19 | 64 | 48 | 16 | 14 | 11 | 3 | 44 | 38 | 6 |

# TABLE IX.

## *EDUCATION BY SELECTED CASTE, TRIBE OR RACE.*

This table repeats the information given in Table VIII in respect of Education, with this difference, that, whereas in that table the population is distributed by age and religion, it is here arranged according to the caste or tribe. Moreover in Table VIII the whole population is dealt with, while this table refers only to selected castes and tribes. The minor castes and tribes have been left out of account altogether.

# TABLE IX.—EDUCATION BY SELECTED CASTE, TRIBE OR RACE.

| Serial Number. | Caste, Tribe or Race. | POPULATION. TOTAL. Persons. | Males. | Females. | LITERATE. Persons. | Males. | Females. | ILLITERATE. Persons. | Males. | Females. | LITERATE IN ENGLISH. Persons. | Males. | Females. | Locality. |
|---|---|---|---|---|---|---|---|---|---|---|---|---|---|---|
| 1 | 2 | 3 | 4 | 5 | 6 | 7 | 8 | 9 | 10 | 11 | 12 | 13 | 14 | 15 |
| | **Central India** | **2,537,990** | **1,301,624** | **1,236,366** | **104,157** | **99,279** | **4,878** | **2,433,833** | **1,202,345** | **1,231,488** | **5,934** | **5,818** | **116** | |
| | ***Hindu*** | ***1,709,119*** | ***880,449*** | ***828,670*** | ***69,920*** | ***67,222*** | ***2,698*** | ***1,639,199*** | ***813,227*** | ***825,972*** | ***4,138*** | ***4,041*** | ***97*** | |
| 1 | Ajna | 26,465 | 15,172 | 11,293 | 208 | 208 | .. | 26,257 | 14,964 | 11,293 | .. | .. | .. | Malwa. |
| 2 | Bania | 163,200 | 79,509 | 83,691 | 19,445 | 18,629 | 816 | 143,755 | 60,880 | 82,875 | 868 | 826 | 42 | |
| | *(1) Agarwal* | *58,288* | *27,710* | *30,578* | *7,762* | *7,519* | *243* | *50,526* | *20,191* | *30,335* | *504* | *464* | *40* | General. |
| | *(2) Gahohi* | *25,082* | *13,657* | *11,425* | *2,679* | *2,646* | *33* | *22,403* | *11,011* | *11,392* | *14* | *14* | .. | Bundelkhand. |
| | *(3) Kasaundhan* | *8,787* | *4,213* | *4,574* | *359* | *352* | *7* | *8,428* | *3,861* | *4,567* | *1* | *1* | .. | Baghelkhand. |
| | *(4) Kesar* | *14,469* | *7,433* | *7,036* | *792* | *684* | *108* | *13,677* | *6,749* | *6,928* | *3* | *3* | .. | Ditto. |
| | *(5) Kharia* | *4,497* | *1,800* | *2,697* | *157* | *157* | .. | *4,340* | *1,643* | *2,697* | .. | .. | .. | Ditto. |
| | *(6) Mahesri* | *21,412* | *10,008* | *11,404* | *3,685* | *3,378* | *307* | *17,727* | *6,630* | *11,097* | *185* | *183* | *2* | Malwa. |
| | *(7) Oswal* | *14,309* | *6,072* | *8,237* | *1,773* | *1,701* | *72* | *12,536* | *4,371* | *8,165* | *122* | *122* | .. | Ditto. |
| | *(8) Porwal* | *16,356* | *8,616* | *7,740* | *2,238* | *2,192* | *46* | *14,118* | *6,424* | *7,694* | *39* | *39* | .. | Ditto. |
| 3 | Bhat | 25,161 | 13,181 | 11,980 | 915 | 851 | 64 | 24,246 | 12,330 | 11,916 | 54 | 52 | 2 | Malwa, Baghelkhand. |
| 4 | Bhil | 25,831 | 13,693 | 12,138 | 15 | 15 | .. | 25,816 | 13,678 | 12,138 | .. | .. | .. | Hilly tracts. |
| 5 | Bhilala | 33,764 | 16,351 | 17,413 | 13 | 12 | 1 | 33,751 | 16,339 | 17,412 | .. | .. | .. | Ditto. |
| 6 | Brahman | 577,968 | 289,803 | 288,165 | 29,529 | 28,803 | 726 | 548,439 | 261,000 | 287,439 | 1,104 | 1,078 | 26 | |
| | *(1) Bhagor, Bhargava* | *32,480* | *17,035* | *15,445* | *2,250* | *2,205* | *45* | *30,230* | *14,830* | *15,400* | *44* | *43* | *1* | Northern Gwalior, Bundelkhand. |
| | *(2) Jijhotia* | *63,932* | *33,696* | *30,236* | *4,130* | *4,064* | *66* | *59,802* | *29,632* | *30,170* | *100* | *100* | .. | Bundelkhand. |
| | *(3) Sanadhya* | *159,124* | *81,579* | *77,545* | *8,685* | *8,497* | *138* | *150,439* | *73,082* | *77,357* | *360* | *353* | *7* | Northern Gwalior, Baghelkhand. |
| | *(4) Sarwaria* | *303,206* | *147,925* | *155,281* | *11,395* | *11,060* | *335* | *291,811* | *136,865* | *154,946* | *276* | *259* | *17* | |
| | *(5) Shrigaud* | *15,031* | *7,780* | *7,251* | *2,[illegible]44* | *2,482* | *62* | *12,487* | *5,298* | *7,189* | *239* | *239* | .. | Malwa. |
| | *(6) Shrimali* | *4,195* | *1,788* | *2,407* | *[illegible]25* | *495* | *30* | *3,670* | *1,293* | *2,377* | *85* | *84* | *1* | Ditto. |
| 7 | Dhangar | 5,608 | 3,027 | 2,581 | 292 | 268 | 24 | 5,316 | 2,759 | 2,557 | 28 | 27 | 1 | Ditto. |
| 8 | Gond | 163,285 | 76,753 | 86,532 | 80 | 78 | 2 | 163,205 | 76,675 | 86,530 | .. | .. | .. | Baghelkhand. |
| 9 | Gujar | 185,728 | 105,834 | 79,894 | 2,020 | 1,966 | 54 | 183,708 | 103,868 | 79,840 | 97 | 97 | .. | Northern Gwalior. |
| 10 | Khangar | 38,448 | 20,178 | 18,270 | 220 | 212 | 8 | 38,228 | 19,961 | 18,262 | 5 | 5 | .. | Northern Gwalior and Bundelkhand. |
| 11 | Maratha | 28,008 | 14,821 | 13,187 | 4,984 | 4,817 | 167 | 23,024 | 10,004 | 13,020 | 1,346 | 1,337 | 9 | Northern Gwalior and Malwa. |
| 12 | Panika | 26,656 | 13,732 | 12,924 | 65 | 64 | 1 | 26,591 | 13,668 | 12,923 | .. | .. | .. | Baghelkhand. |
| 13 | Rajput | 338,456 | 185,738 | 152,718 | 11,775 | 10,959 | 816 | 326,681 | 174,779 | 151,902 | 632 | 616 | 16 | |
| | *(1) Bhadauria* | *23,343* | *13,501* | *9,842* | *624* | *610* | *14* | *22,719* | *12,891* | *9,828* | *98* | *96* | *2* | Northern Gwalior. |
| | *(2) Baghela* | *24,852* | *12,708* | *12,144* | *1,490* | *1,305* | *185* | *23,362* | *11,403* | *11,959* | *24* | *24* | .. | Baghelkhand. |
| | *(3) Bundela* | *17,362* | *8,785* | *8,577* | *850* | *780* | *70* | *16,512* | *8,005* | *8,507* | *39* | *38* | *1* | Bundelkhand. |
| | *(4) Bundela Ponwar* | *301* | *266* | *35* | .. | .. | .. | *301* | *266* | *35* | .. | .. | .. | Ditto. |
| | *(5) Chauhan* | *39,978* | *19,056* | *20,922* | *1,679* | *1,610* | *69* | *38,299* | *17,446* | *20,853* | *153* | *149* | *4* | Northern Gwalior, Malwa. |
| | *(6) Dhandera* | *3,759* | *1,929* | *1,830* | *122* | *115* | *7* | *3,637* | *1,814* | *1,823* | *3* | *3* | .. | Bundelkhand. |
| | *(7) Dikhit* | *1,330* | *784* | *546* | *35* | *35* | .. | *1,295* | *749* | *546* | *1* | *1* | .. | Baghelkhand and Bundelkhand. |
| | *(8) Gaharwar* | *2,344* | *1,231* | *1,113* | *114* | *86* | *28* | *2,230* | *1,145* | *1,085* | *1* | *1* | .. | Baghelkhand. |
| | *(9) Gahalot* | *23,653* | *14,288* | *9,365* | *161* | *156* | *5* | *23,492* | *14,132* | *9,360* | .. | .. | .. | Malwa, Baghelkhand. |
| | *(10) Gaur* | *7,293* | *3,968* | *3,325* | *375* | *370* | *5* | *6,918* | *3,598* | *3,320* | *1* | *1* | .. | Bhopal. |
| | *(11) Kachhwaha* | *24,420* | *12,550* | *11,870* | *651* | *633* | *18* | *23,769* | *11,917* | *11,852* | *64* | *63* | *1* | Northern Gwalior. |
| | *(12) Khichi* | *2,519* | *1,386* | *1,133* | *106* | *98* | *8* | *2,413* | *1,288* | *1,125* | *2* | *2* | .. | Ditto. |
| | *(13) Parihar* | *18,208* | *9,796* | *8,412* | *691* | *657* | *34* | *17,517* | *9,139* | *8,378* | *38* | *38* | .. | Baghelkhand and Bundelkhand. |
| | *(14) Ponwar* | *42,696* | *24,021* | *18,675* | *1,291* | *1,254* | *37* | *41,405* | *22,767* | *18,638* | *57* | *57* | .. | Malwa. |
| | *(15) Maratha Ponwar* | *606* | *311* | *295* | *79* | *40* | *39* | *527* | *271* | *256* | *1* | *1* | .. | Ditto. |
| | *(16) Rathod, Rathor* | *33,395* | *18,479* | *14,916* | *1,491* | *1,330* | *161* | *31,904* | *17,149* | *14,755* | *105* | *99* | *6* | Ditto. |
| | *(17) Sengar* | *10,819* | *4,817* | *6,002* | *318* | *307* | *11* | *10,501* | *4,510* | *5,991* | *11* | *11* | .. | Malwa and Northern Gwalior. |
| | *(18) Sisodia, Sesodia* | *8,575* | *4,321* | *4,254* | *275* | *196* | *79* | *8,300* | *4,125* | *4,175* | *11* | *11* | .. | Baghelkhand. |
| | *(19) Solanki* | *15,901* | *8,771* | *7,130* | *392* | *370* | *22* | *15,509* | *8,401* | *7,108* | *10* | *10* | .. | Malwa. |
| | *(20) Tonwar* | *37,102* | *24,770* | *12,332* | *1,031* | *1,007* | *24* | *36,071* | *23,763* | *12,308* | *13* | *11* | *2* | Northern Gwalior. |
| 14 | Sondhia | 70,546 | 32,662 | 37,884 | 359 | 340 | 19 | 70,187 | 32,322 | 37,865 | 4 | 3 | 1 | Malwa. |
| | ***Jain*** | ***55,659*** | ***28,181*** | ***27,478*** | ***11,850*** | ***11,256*** | ***594*** | ***43,809*** | ***16,925*** | ***26,884*** | ***198*** | ***195*** | ***3*** | |
| 1 | Oswal | 32,956 | 16,764 | 16,192 | 8,331 | 7,960 | 371 | 24,625 | 8,804 | 15,821 | 162 | 159 | 3 | Malwa. |
| 2 | Porwal | 22,703 | 11,417 | 11,286 | 3,519 | 3,296 | 223 | 19,184 | 8,121 | 11,063 | 36 | 36 | .. | Northern Gwalior and Bundelkhand. |
| | ***Animist*** | ***430,909*** | ***213,477*** | ***217,432*** | ***213*** | ***209*** | ***4*** | ***430,696*** | ***213,268*** | ***217,428*** | ***3*** | ***3*** | .. | |
| 1 | Bhil | 269,910 | 134,045 | 135,865 | 144 | 142 | 2 | 269,766 | 133,903 | 135,863 | 2 | 2 | .. | Hilly tracts. |
| 2 | Bhilala | 89,612 | 44,821 | 44,791 | 33 | 32 | 1 | 89,579 | 44,789 | 44,790 | 1 | 1 | .. | Ditto. |
| 3 | Gond | 71,387 | 34,611 | 36,776 | 36 | 35 | 1 | 71,351 | 34,576 | 36,775 | .. | .. | .. | Ditto. |
| | ***Musalman*** | ***349,303*** | ***179,517*** | ***169,786*** | ***22,174*** | ***20,592*** | ***1,582*** | ***320,129*** | ***158,925*** | ***161,204*** | ***1,595*** | ***1,579*** | ***16*** | |
| 1 | Pathan | 138,522 | 73,476 | 65,046 | 8,890 | 8,203 | 687 | 129,632 | 65,273 | 64,359 | 452 | 446 | 6 | Northern Gwalior, Indore and Bhopal. |
| 2 | Sayad | 32,197 | 17,459 | 14,738 | 3,881 | 3,561 | 320 | 28,316 | 13,898 | 14,418 | 450 | 447 | 3 | Ditto. |
| 3 | Shaikh | 171,584 | 88,582 | 83,002 | 9,403 | 8,828 | 575 | 162,181 | 79,754 | 82,427 | 693 | 686 | 7 | |
| | *(1) Behena* | *24,368* | *12,323* | *12,045* | *344* | *327* | *17* | *24,024* | *11,996* | *12,028* | *6* | *6* | .. | Bhopal and Baghelkhand. |
| | *(2) Shaikh* | *147,216* | *76,259* | *70,957* | *9,059* | *8,501* | *558* | *138,157* | *67,758* | *70,399* | *687* | *680* | *7* | Northern Gwalior, Indore, Bhopal and Ratlam. |

## TABLE X.

### *LANGUAGE.*

This table shows the number of persons speaking the dialects of the Agency as a whole and also gives the details for each Natural Division.

This table is somewhat defective as the majority of persons speaking dialects current round Gwalior returned their language as Hindi and only a few named the actual dialects spoken by them. Similarly a number of persons returned Bundelkhandi and Malwi as their dialects and a few the other forms of Bundelkhandi and Malwi, such as Khatola, Banaphari and Rangari.

The number of persons speaking Hindi, Bundelkhandi and Malwi is, therefore, necessarily high as compared with that returned in 1901.

# TABLE X—LANGUAGES.

| Languages. | Population. | | | Plateau. | | | Low-lying. | | | Hilly. | | |
|---|---|---|---|---|---|---|---|---|---|---|---|---|
| | Persons. | Males. | Females. | Persons. | Males. | Females. | Persons. | Males. | Females. | Persons. | Males. | Females. |
| 1 | 2 | 3 | 4 | 5 | 6 | 7 | 8 | 9 | 10 | 11 | 12 | 13 |
| **Central India** | **9,356,980** | **4,801,459** | **4,555,521** | **3,683,491** | **1,903,120** | **1,780,371** | **3,310,763** | **1,713,851** | **1,596,852** | **2,362,786** | **1,184,488** | **1,178,298** |
| *Languages Proper to Central India* | *8,866,681* | *4,550,252* | *4,316,429* | *3,403,443* | *1,759,125* | *1,644,318* | *3,254,459* | *1,685,664* | *1,568,795* | *2,208,779* | *1,105,463* | *1,103,316* |
| Indo-European Family | 8,634,138 | 4,456,593 | 4,177,545 | 3,387,043 | 1,750,766 | 1,636,277 | 3,252,361 | 1,684,751 | 1,567,610 | 1,994,734 | 1,021,076 | 973,658 |
| EASTERN HINDI | *1,372,823* | *698,011* | *674,812* | *813* | *311* | *502* | *814,102* | *399,294* | *414,808* | *557,908* | *298,406* | *259,502* |
| Baghelkhandi | 1,372,663 | 697,937 | 674,726 | 813 | 311 | 502 | 813,942 | 399,220 | 414,722 | 557,908 | 298,406 | 259,502 |
| Barme | 160 | 74 | 86 | .. | .. | .. | 160 | 74 | 86 | .. | .. | .. |
| GUJARATI | *349,805* | *174,789* | *175,016* | *41,640* | *20,877* | *20,763* | *58* | *30* | *28* | *308,107* | *153,882* | *154,225* |
| BHIL DIALECTS | **349,805** | **174,789** | **175,016** | **41,640** | **20,877** | **20,763** | **58** | **30** | **28** | **308,107** | **153,882** | **154,225** |
| Bhagori | 74 | 25 | 49 | 19 | .. | 19 | .. | .. | .. | 55 | 25 | 30 |
| Bhili | 205,635 | 102,906 | 102,729 | 39,889 | 19,997 | 19,892 | 58 | 30 | 28 | 165,688 | 82,879 | 82,809 |
| Bhilali | 105,385 | 52,582 | 52,803 | .. | .. | .. | .. | .. | .. | 105,385 | 52,582 | 52,803 |
| Dongri | 578 | 279 | 299 | 578 | 279 | 299 | .. | .. | .. | .. | .. | .. |
| Rathavi | 36,691 | 18,237 | 18,454 | 13 | 2 | 11 | .. | .. | .. | 36,678 | 18,235 | 18,443 |
| Vagadi | 1,442 | 760 | 682 | 1,141 | 599 | 542 | .. | .. | .. | 301 | 161 | 140 |
| RAJASTHANI | **3,245,374** | **1,656,642** | **1,588,732** | **2,514,157** | **1,288,461** | **1,225,696** | **9,407** | **4,294** | **5,113** | **721,810** | **363,887** | **357,923** |
| Khichiwadi | 104,123 | 51,397 | 52,726 | 102,929 | 51,259 | 51,670 | 776 | .. | 776 | 418 | 138 | 280 |
| Malwi | 2,633,790 | 1,345,016 | 1,288,774 | 2,274,894 | 1,163,714 | 1,111,180 | 8,347 | 4,014 | 4,333 | 350,549 | 177,288 | 173,261 |
| Nimadi | 379,695 | 190,849 | 188,846 | 8,582 | 4,117 | 4,465 | 284 | 280 | 4 | 370,829 | 186,452 | 184,377 |
| Sondhi (Sundwai) | 37,018 | 22,569 | 14,449 | 37,004 | 22,560 | 14,444 | .. | .. | .. | 14 | 9 | 5 |
| Umatwadi | 90,748 | 46,811 | 43,937 | 90,748 | 46,811 | 43,937 | | | | | | |
| WESTERN HINDI | **3,666,136** | **1,927,151** | **1,738,985** | **830,433** | **441,117** | **389,316** | **2,428,794** | **1,281,133** | **1,147,661** | **406,959** | **204,901** | **202,008** |
| Bundelkhandi | 1,877,883 | 978,547 | 899,336 | 334,111 | 176,972 | 157,139 | 1,307,771 | 677,847 | 629,924 | 236,001 | 123,728 | 112,273 |
| Bhadaori | 276,047 | 160,021 | 116,026 | 6,919 | 3,031 | 3,888 | 268,919 | 156,883 | 112,036 | 209 | 107 | 102 |
| Kachhawahi | 90,002 | 44,461 | 45,541 | 834 | 255 | 579 | 89,168 | 44,206 | 44,962 | | | |
| Hindostani | 82,541 | 45,312 | 37,229 | 37,009 | 22,755 | 14,254 | 29,650 | 14,638 | 15,012 | 15,882 | 7,919 | 7,963 |
| Hindi | 1,060,582 | 556,619 | 503,963 | 305,896 | 161,839 | 144,057 | 695,805 | 369,501 | 326,304 | 58,881 | 25,279 | 33,602 |
| Jatwari | 22,310 | 9,160 | 13,150 | 3 | .. | 3 | 22,307 | 9,160 | 13,147 | .. | .. | .. |
| Urdu | 256,771 | 133,031 | 123,740 | 145,661 | 76,265 | 69,396 | 15,174 | 8,898 | 6,276 | 95,936 | 47,868 | 48,068 |
| Dravidian Family | 214,276 | 83,524 | 130,752 | 10,563 | 5,096 | 5,467 | 1,808 | 742 | 1,066 | 201,905 | 77,686 | 124,219 |
| GONDI | **214,276** | **83,524** | **130,752** | **10,563** | **5,096** | **5,467** | **1,808** | **742** | **1,066** | **201,905** | **77,686** | **124,219** |
| Unclassed Gypsy Languages | 18,267 | 10,135 | 8,132 | 5,837 | 3,263 | 2,574 | 290 | 171 | 119 | 12,140 | 6,701 | 5,439 |
| Banjari | 17,126 | 9,555 | 7,571 | 5,147 | 2,919 | 2,228 | 110 | 87 | 23 | 11,869 | 6,549 | 5,320 |
| Bargundi | 735 | 376 | 359 | 504 | 243 | 261 | | | | 231 | 133 | 98 |
| Kanjari | 277 | 139 | 138 | 97 | 55 | 42 | 180 | 84 | 96 | | | |
| Pardhi | 104 | 52 | 52 | 64 | 33 | 31 | .. | .. | .. | 40 | 19 | 21 |
| Kalbeli | 25 | 13 | 12 | 25 | 13 | 12 | .. | .. | .. | .. | .. | .. |
| *Languages not Proper to Central India* | *483,012* | *245,702* | *237,310* | *274,023* | *139,335* | *134,688* | *55,223* | *27,472* | *27,751* | *153,766* | *78,895* | *74,871* |
| Indo-European Family | 480,354 | 244,047 | 236,307 | 271,760 | 137,890 | 133,870 | 55,063 | 27,375 | 27,688 | 153,531 | 78,782 | 74,749 |
| ASSAMESE | *1* | *1* | .. | .. | .. | .. | .. | .. | .. | *1* | *1* | .. |
| BALOCHI | **95** | **57** | **38** | **88** | **51** | **37** | .. | .. | .. | **7** | **6** | **1** |
| Balochi | 1 | 1 | .. | .. | .. | .. | .. | .. | .. | 1 | 1 | .. |
| Makrani | 94 | 56 | 38 | 88 | 51 | 37 | .. | .. | .. | 6 | 5 | 1 |
| PASHTO | *1,659* | *1,200* | *459* | *1,585* | *1,151* | *434* | *23* | *19* | *4* | *51* | *30* | *21* |
| BENGALI | *894* | *289* | *605* | *340* | *117* | *223* | *317* | *79* | *238* | *237* | *93* | *144* |
| BIHARI | *78,398* | *40,681* | *37,717* | *29,294* | *15,905* | *13,389* | *6,485* | *2,973* | *3,512* | *42,619* | *21,803* | *20,816* |
| Bihari | 5 | 5 | .. | .. | .. | .. | .. | .. | .. | 5 | 5 | .. |
| Purbi | 78,381 | 40,671 | 37,710 | 29,293 | 15,904 | 13,389 | 6,479 | 2,972 | 3,507 | 42,609 | 21,795 | 20,814 |
| Magadhi | 1 | .. | 1 | .. | .. | .. | 1 | .. | 1 | | | |
| Maithili | 11 | 5 | 6 | 1 | 1 | .. | 5 | 1 | 4 | 5 | 3 | 2 |
| CENTRAL PAHADI | **5** | **1** | **4** | .. | .. | .. | .. | .. | .. | **5** | **1** | **4** |
| Gurhwali | 5 | 1 | 4 | .. | .. | .. | .. | .. | .. | 5 | 1 | 4 |
| EASTERN HINDI | **3,700** | **2,213** | **1,487** | **3** | **3** | .. | **2,956** | **1,733** | **1,223** | **741** | **477** | **264** |
| Mirzapuri | 3,618 | 2,133 | 1,485 | 3 | 3 | .. | 2,956 | 1,733 | 1,223 | 659 | 397 | 262 |
| Chhattisgarhi | 82 | 80 | 2 | | | | | | | 82 | 80 | 2 |
| GUJARATI | **71,921** | **36,628** | **35,293** | **24,516** | **13,257** | **11,259** | **1,687** | **969** | **718** | **45,718** | **22,402** | **23,316** |
| Gujarati | 61,253 | 31,160 | 30,093 | 24,385 | 13,185 | 11,200 | 1,684 | 969 | 715 | 35,184 | 17,006 | 18,178 |
| Kathiawadi | 2,396 | 1,271 | 1,125 | 123 | 65 | 58 | 3 | .. | 3 | 2,270 | 1,206 | 1,064 |
| Khandeshi | 8,272 | 4,197 | 4,075 | 8 | 7 | 1 | .. | .. | .. | 8,264 | 4,190 | 4,074 |
| KASHMIRI | **67** | **27** | **40** | **34** | **6** | **28** | **26** | **14** | **12** | **7** | **7** | .. |
| LABUDA | **59** | **31** | **28** | **59** | **31** | **28** | .. | .. | .. | .. | .. | .. |
| Multani | 50 | 22 | 28 | 50 | 22 | 28 | .. | .. | .. | .. | .. | .. |
| Peshawari | 9 | 9 | .. | 9 | 9 | .. | .. | .. | .. | .. | .. | .. |
| MARATHI | **65,913** | **32,076** | **33,837** | **39,225** | **19,117** | **20,108** | **12,503** | **5,808** | **6,695** | **14,185** | **7,151** | **7,034** |
| Marathi | 65,738 | 31,920 | 33,818 | 39,074 | 18,981 | 20,093 | 12,490 | 5,798 | 6,692 | 14,174 | 7,141 | 7,033 |
| Konkani | 11 | 9 | 2 | 10 | 8 | 2 | .. | .. | .. | 1 | 1 | .. |
| Goanese | 164 | 147 | 17 | 141 | 128 | 13 | 13 | 10 | 3 | 10 | 9 | 1 |
| NAIPALI | **60** | **32** | **28** | **3** | **3** | .. | **29** | **16** | **13** | **28** | **13** | **15** |
| ORIYA | **9** | **7** | **2** | **4** | **4** | .. | .. | .. | .. | **5** | **3** | **2** |
| PUNJABI | **19,092** | **10,754** | **8,338** | **15,005** | **8,004** | **7,001** | **782** | **537** | **245** | **3,305** | **2,213** | **1,092** |
| Jangali | 9,393 | 4,020 | 5,373 | 9,387 | 4,014 | 5,373 | 6 | 6 | .. | .. | .. | .. |
| Narnoli | 174 | 122 | 52 | 105 | 85 | 20 | 57 | 25 | 32 | 12 | 12 | .. |
| Punjabi | 9,525 | 6,612 | 2,913 | 5,513 | 3,905 | 1,608 | 719 | 506 | 213 | 3,293 | 2,201 | 1,092 |
| RAJASTHANI | **182,068** | **90,416** | **91,652** | **132,975** | **65,537** | **67,438** | **5,031** | **1,731** | **3,300** | **44,062** | **23,148** | **20,914** |
| Ajmeri | 37 | 19 | 18 | .. | .. | .. | .. | .. | .. | 37 | 19 | 18 |
| Shekhawati | 362 | 163 | 199 | 362 | 163 | 199 | .. | .. | .. | .. | .. | .. |
| Hadauti | 6,980 | 4,192 | 2,788 | 6,929 | 4,153 | 2,776 | 24 | 13 | 11 | 27 | 26 | 1 |
| Jaipuri | 5,212 | 2,797 | 2,415 | 4,542 | 2,478 | 2,064 | 44 | 22 | 22 | 626 | 297 | 329 |
| Marwadi | 85,607 | 43,119 | 42,488 | 46,795 | 22,702 | 24,093 | 3,637 | 1,584 | 2,053 | 35,175 | 18,833 | 16,342 |
| Mewadi | 73,289 | 33,930 | 39,359 | 69,321 | 32,808 | 36,513 | 1,323 | 109 | 1,214 | 2,645 | 1,013 | 1,632 |
| Mewati | 10,458 | 6,132 | 4,326 | 4,903 | 3,169 | 1,734 | 3 | 3 | .. | 5,552 | 2,960 | 2,592 |
| Thori | 123 | 64 | 59 | 123 | 64 | 59 | | | | | | |
| WESTERN HINDI | **52,808** | **28,097** | **24,711** | **27,359** | **14,349** | **13,010** | **23,151** | **12,438** | **10,713** | **2,298** | **1,310** | **988** |
| Ahirwadi | 4,754 | 3,340 | 1,414 | 4,494 | 3,295 | 1,199 | .. | .. | .. | 260 | 45 | 215 |
| Brijabhasha | 41,389 | 20,363 | 21,026 | 22,595 | 10,905 | 11,690 | 18,284 | 9,100 | 9,184 | 510 | 358 | 152 |
| Antervedi | 2,350 | 2,170 | 180 | 31 | 22 | 9 | 2,047 | 1,934 | 113 | 272 | 214 | 58 |
| Hariani (Deswali) | 1,215 | 640 | 575 | 211 | 115 | 96 | | | | 1,004 | 525 | 479 |
| Pachhabi | 2,891 | 1,475 | 1,416 | .. | .. | .. | 2,805 | 1,398 | 1,407 | 86 | 77 | 9 |
| Rohilkhandi | 201 | 109 | 92 | 28 | 12 | 16 | 7 | 6 | 1 | 166 | 91 | 75 |
| Kanouji | 8 | .. | 8 | .. | .. | .. | 8 | .. | 8 | | | |
| WESTERN PAHADI | **3,140** | **1,308** | **1,832** | **1,070** | **252** | **818** | **2,070** | **1,056** | **1,014** | .. | .. | .. |
| Bhadarwahi | 304 | 169 | 135 | .. | .. | .. | 304 | 169 | 135 | .. | .. | .. |
| Gujari | 2,836 | 1,139 | 1,697 | 1,070 | 252 | 818 | 1,766 | 887 | 879 | .. | .. | .. |
| SANSKRIT | **3** | **2** | **1** | .. | .. | .. | **3** | **2** | **1** | .. | .. | .. |
| SINDHI | **462** | **227** | **235** | **200** | **103** | **97** | .. | .. | .. | **262** | **124** | **138** |
| Sindhi | 382 | 177 | 205 | 128 | 61 | 67 | .. | .. | .. | 254 | 116 | 138 |
| Kachhi | 80 | 50 | 30 | 72 | 42 | 30 | .. | .. | .. | 8 | 8 | .. |
| Dravidian Family | 2,485 | 1,571 | 914 | 2,213 | 1,409 | 804 | 160 | 97 | 63 | 112 | 65 | 47 |
| CANARESE | *281* | *126* | *155* | *262* | *116* | *146* | *16* | *8* | *8* | *3* | *2* | *1* |
| MALAYALAM | **1** | **1** | .. | .. | .. | .. | .. | .. | .. | **1** | **1** | .. |
| TAMIL | **933** | **516** | **417** | **754** | **407** | **347** | **127** | **80** | **47** | **52** | **29** | **23** |
| TELUGU | **1,270** | **928** | **342** | **1,197** | **886** | **311** | **17** | **9** | **8** | **56** | **33** | **23** |
| Tibeto-Chinese Family | 1 | .. | 1 | 1 | .. | 1 | .. | .. | .. | .. | .. | .. |
| BURMESE | *1* | .. | *1* | *1* | .. | *1* | .. | .. | .. | .. | .. | .. |
| Austro-Asiatic Family | 89 | 32 | 57 | 4 | 4 | .. | .. | .. | .. | 85 | 28 | 57 |
| KORKU | *89* | *32* | *57* | *4* | *4* | .. | .. | .. | .. | *85* | *28* | *57* |
| Korku | 88 | 32 | 56 | 4 | 4 | .. | .. | .. | .. | 84 | 28 | 56 |
| Nihali | 1 | .. | 1 | .. | .. | .. | .. | .. | .. | 1 | .. | 1 |
| Unclassed Gypsy Languages | 83 | 52 | 31 | 45 | 32 | 13 | .. | .. | .. | 38 | 20 | 18 |
| Charain | 23 | 11 | 12 | 1 | 1 | .. | .. | .. | .. | 22 | 10 | 12 |
| Ghogari | 18 | 17 | 1 | 7 | 7 | .. | .. | .. | .. | 11 | 10 | 1 |
| Moghia | 2 | 2 | .. | 2 | 2 | .. | .. | .. | .. | .. | .. | .. |
| Sansia | 40 | 22 | 18 | 35 | 22 | 13 | .. | .. | .. | 5 | .. | 5 |
| *Asiatic Languages* | *1,405* | *888* | *517* | *1,126* | *765* | *361* | *207* | *85* | *122* | *72* | *38* | *34* |
| Indo-European Family | 787 | 422 | 365 | 521 | 311 | 210 | 195 | 73 | 122 | 71 | 38 | 33 |
| PERSIAN | *787* | *422* | *365* | *521* | *311* | *210* | *195* | *73* | *122* | *71* | *38* | *33* |
| Semitic Family | 618 | 466 | 152 | 605 | 454 | 151 | 12 | 12 | .. | 1 | .. | 1 |
| ARABIC | **618** | **466** | **152** | **605** | **454** | **151** | **12** | **12** | .. | **1** | .. | **1** |
| *European Languages* | *5,882* | *4,617* | *1,265* | *4,899* | *3,895* | *1,004* | *814* | *630* | *184* | *169* | *92* | *77* |
| Indo-European Family | 5,882 | 4,617 | 1,265 | 4,899 | 3,895 | 1,004 | 814 | 630 | 184 | 169 | 92 | 77 |
| ENGLISH | *5,850* | *4,600* | *1,250* | *4,877* | *3,885* | *992* | *810* | *627* | *183* | *163* | *88* | *75* |
| FRENCH | *16* | *10* | *6* | *11* | *7* | *4* | | | | *5* | *3* | *2* |
| GERMAN | *1* | *1* | .. | .. | .. | .. | *1* | *1* | .. | | | |
| GREEK | *2* | *2* | .. | .. | .. | .. | *2* | *2* | .. | .. | .. | .. |
| PORTUGUESE | *13* | *4* | *9* | *11* | *3* | *8* | *1* | .. | *1* | *1* | *1* | .. |

## Appendix to Table X.

1. The following dialects have been included in Baghelkhandi :—

| | Persons. | Males. | Females. | |
|---|---|---|---|---|
| (1) Jethwari . | 298 | 137 | 161 | Gwalior (290), Rajgarh (8). |
| (2) Pahadi . | 5,332 | 3,338 | 1,994 | Sailana (7), Ratlam (4), Bhopal (7), Rajgarh (7), Nagod (161), Narsinghgarh (20), Bhopawar M. S. (6), Gwalior (1,879), Jaora (2), Gwalior M. S. (10), Dewas S. B. (4), Dewas J. B. (2), Rewah (3,222), Maihar (1). |
| (3) Birgadi . | 14,746 | 7,896 | 6,850 | All in Baghelkhand M. S. |

2. The following dialects have been included in Vagadi :—

| | Persons. | Males. | Females. | |
|---|---|---|---|---|
| (1) Bagri . . | 1,141 | 599 | 542 | Narsinghgarh (330), Rajgarh (422), Dhar (3), Ratlam (188), Sailana (150), Malwa M. S. (47), Dewas S. B. (1). |
| (2) Bagdi . . | 296 | 156 | 140 | Jhabua (284), Ali Rajpur (12). |

3. The following dialects have been included in Malwi :—

| | Persons. | Males. | Females. | |
|---|---|---|---|---|
| (1) Santri . . | 50 | 29 | 21 | All in Jaora. |
| (2) Bhuyonki . | 113 | 63 | 50 | All in Sitamau. |
| (3) Bhopali . | 142 | 12 | 130 | All in Rewah. |
| (4) Kirsani . . | 108 | 108 | ... | All in Rajgarh. |
| (5) Banswadi . | 19 | 19 | ... | All in Dhar. |
| (6) Rangri . | 374,920 | 186,281 | 188,639 | Gwalior (114,708), Gwalior M. S. (187), Guna (139), Agar (31), Indore (222,393), Bhopal M. S. (339), Nimach (4), Dewas S. B. (456), Dewas J. B. (1,730), Jaora (618), Ratlam (93), Sitamau (24,359), Malwa (51), Maihar (2), Chhatarpur (11), Bhopal (287), Dhar (223), Jhabua (8,562), Ali Rajpur (4), Jobat (77), Bhopawar M. S. (566), Sirdarpur (14), Rajgarh (37), Khilchipur (3), Datia (9), Gwalior Residency Head-quarters (17). |
| (7) Rajwadi . | 417 | 193 | 224 | Dhar (99), Bhopawar M. S. (20), Gwalior (86), Nimach (4), Dewas S. B. (5), Ratlam (3), Malwa M. S. (200). |
| (8) Dhandheri . | 10,493 | 5,311 | 5,182 | Rajgarh (330), Narsinghgarh (3,178), Dhar (8), Gwalior (384), Gwalior M. S. (6,535), Khilchipur (1), Dewas J. B. (6), Ratlam (10), Sitamau (3), Sailana (1), Malwa M. S. (2), Barwani (5), Bhopawar M. S. (29), Nimach (1). |

4. The following dialects have been included in Bundelkhandi :—

| | Persons. | Males. | Females. | |
|---|---|---|---|---|
| (1) Khatola . | 8,690 | 4,337 | 4,353 | Charkhari (6,864), Chhatarpur (1,733), Datia (93). |
| (2) Banaphari . | 7,947 | 4,254 | 3,693 | Panna (408), Chhatarpur (2,065), Rewah (5), Datia (1), Charkhari (6), Ajaigarh (5,462). |
| (3) Saheri . | 922 | 502 | 420 | All in Gwalior. |
| (4) Gahohi (Gahora) . | 11,874 | 5,959 | 5,915 | Rewah (158), Baghelkhand M. S. (11,716). |

5. The following dialects have been included in Bhadaori :—

| | Persons. | Males. | Females. | |
|---|---|---|---|---|
| (1) Deshi . . | 1,508 | 808 | 700 | All in Gwalior. |
| (2) Tawarghari . | 44,216 | 35,319 | 8,897 | Rajgarh (34), Gwalior M. S. (1), Gwalior (44,181). |
| (3) Madhopuri . | 6 | ... | 6 | All in Nimach. |
| (4) Narwari . | 17 | ... | 17 | All in Gwalior M. S. |

6. The following dialect has been included in Hindostani :—

| | Persons. | Males. | Females. | |
|---|---|---|---|---|
| (1) Khadi . . | 9,878 | 4,881 | 4,992 | Bhopawar M.S. (44), Jobat (489), Ali Rajpur (2,252), Dhar (1,491), Jhabua (1,405), Barwani (4,192). |

7. The following dialects have been included in Hindi :—

| | Persons. | Males. | Females. | |
|---|---|---|---|---|
| (1) Deonagri . | 6 | 3 | 3 | All in Nagod. |
| (2) Wirwi-Hindi . | 939 | 538 | 401 | All in Gwalior. |

8. The following dialect has been included in Urdu :—

| | | | | |
|---|---|---|---|---|
| (1) Musalmani . | 117 | 101 | 16 | Dhar (115), Malwa M. S. (2). |

9. The following dialects have been included in Gondi :—

| | | | | |
|---|---|---|---|---|
| (1) Gondi Baghelkhandi | 174,305 | 62,532 | 111,773 | All in Rewah. |
| (2) Gondi Bundelkhandi | 2,060 | 2,060 | ... | All in Rewah. |

10. The following dialects have been included in Banjari :—

| | | | | |
|---|---|---|---|---|
| (1) Labhani . . | 1,874 | 907 | 967 | Ratlam (26), Sailana (70), Mhow (36), Jhabua (1,708), Ali Rajpur (34). |
| (2) Baldi . . . | 133 | 72 | 61 | All in Sitamau. |

11. The following dialects have been included in Purbi :—

| | | | | |
|---|---|---|---|---|
| (1) Benarsi . . | 6 | 3 | 3 | Nagod (3), Rewah (3). |
| (2) Gorakhpuri .. . | 13 | 13 | ... | Rewah (11), Panna (2). |
| (3) Bhojapuri . . | 45 | 33 | 12 | All in Rewah. |
| (4) Uttarkhandi . | 5 | 5 | ... | All in Ratlam. |
| (5) Unnasi . . | 20 | 11 | 9 | Rewah (17), Dhar (3). |
| (6) Deshawari . . | 366 | 278 | 88 | All in Gwalior. |

12. The following dialects have been included in Mirzapuri :—

| | | | | |
|---|---|---|---|---|
| (1) Gangapari . | 408 | 135 | 273 | Rajgarh (1), Nagod (6), Rewah (220), Baghelkhand M. S. (84), Ajaigarh (21), Nowgong (20), Maihar (52), Panna (4). |
| (2) Ayodhyapari . | 1 | 1 | ... | All in Maihar. |
| (3) Sarjupari . . | 3 | 1 | 2 | Baghelkhand M. S. (1), Rewah (2). |
| (4) Pardeshi . . | 2 | 2 | ... | All in Dhar. |
| (5) Baiswari . . | 3 | 1 | 2 | All in Bundelkhand M. S. |

13. The following dialect has been included in Punjabi :—

| | | | | |
|---|---|---|---|---|
| (1) Rohtanki . . | 2 | ... | 2 | All in Khilchipur. |

14. The following dialects have been included in Marathi :—

| | | | | |
|---|---|---|---|---|
| (1) Deccani . . | 3,903 | 2,151 | 1,752 | Bhopal M. S. (204), Bhopawar M. S. (238), Hirapur (6), Gwalior (3,343), Malwa M. S. (4), Ratlam (11), Orchha (14), Baghelkhand M. S. (10), Datia (45), Jhabua (27), Maihar (1). |
| (2) Bijapuri . . | 25 | 25 | ... | All in Rewah. |

15. The following dialects have been included in Jaipuri :—

| | | | | |
|---|---|---|---|---|
| (1) Dhundadi . . | 37 | 21 | 16 | Bhopawar M. S. (35), Gwalior (2). |
| (2) Fatehpuri . . | 4 | 4 | ... | All in Rewah. |

16. The following dialects have been included in Marwadi :—

| | | | | |
|---|---|---|---|---|
| (1) Jaisalmeri . . | 3 | ... | 3 | All in Rajgarh. |
| (2) Rewadi . . | 43 | 20 | 23 | Gwalior M. S. (32), Nagod (6), Dhar (5). |

17. The following dialect has been included in Mewati :—

| | | | | |
|---|---|---|---|---|
| (1) Alwari . . | 2 | ... | 2 | All in Jhabua. |

18. The following dialects have been included in Brijbhasha :—

| | | | | |
|---|---|---|---|---|
| (1) Bharatpuri . . | 1,120 | 774 | 346 | Rajgarh (321), Nimach (1), Dewas S. B. (95), Jaora (464), Dewas J. B. (209), Ratlam (24), Sailana (4), Malwa M. S. (2). |
| (2) Jadhomati . . | 4,276 | 2,033 | 2,243 | Rajgarh (340), Gwalior M. S. (3,936). |

| | Persons. | Males. | Females. | |
|---|---|---|---|---|
| (3) Sikarwari . | 6,071 | 2,659 | 3,412 | Bhopal (14), Gwalior (3,318), Rajgarh (1,202), Agar (1), Narsinghgarh (835), Gwalior M. S. (230), Guna (471). |
| (4) Dholpuri . | 2,534 | 1,248 | 1,286 | Rajgarh (2,061), Gwalior M. S. (74), Nimrol (399). |

19. The following dialect has been included in Hariani :—

| | | | | |
|---|---|---|---|---|
| (1) Deswali . | 1,178 | 619 | 559 | Rajgarh (119), Gwalior M. S. (14), Dewas S. B. (4), Malwa (37), Indore (1,001) Dhar (3). |

20. The following dialects have been included in Canarese :—

| | | | | |
|---|---|---|---|---|
| (1) Karnatik . | 44 | 23 | 21 | Dhar (43), Dewas S. B. (1). |
| (2) Kanadi . . | 65 | 31 | 34 | Gwalior (49), Mhow (14), Nowgong (2). |

21. The following dialects have been included in Tamil :—

| | | | | |
|---|---|---|---|---|
| (1) Madrasi . | 657 | 371 | 286 | Bhopal (8), Narsinghgarh (1), Dhar (8), Manpur (4), Gwalior (26), Nimach (43), Indore (135), Mhow (345), Indore Camp (1), Ratlam (35), Sailana (5), Nowgong (10), Panna (1), Rewah (8), Bhopal (11), Barwani (15), Sirdarpur (1). |
| (2) Nilgiri . . | 2 | 2 | ... | All in Panna. |

22. The following dialect has been included in Korku :—

| | | | | |
|---|---|---|---|---|
| (1) Mundi . . | 1 | 1 | ... | All in Bhopal M. S. |

23. The following dialects have been included in Pashto :—

| | | | | |
|---|---|---|---|---|
| (1) Kabuli . . | 1 | 1 | .. | All in Bundelkhand M. S. |
| (2) Vilayati . | 10 | 10 | ... | All in Gwalior. |
| (3) Pathani . . | 18 | 9 | 9 | Gwalior (16), Dhar (2). |
| (4) Afgani . . | 1 | 1 | ... | All in Jhabua. |

24. The following dialect has been included in Persian :—

| | | | | |
|---|---|---|---|---|
| (1) Irani . . | 5 | 5 | ... | All in Nowgong. |

25. The following dialect has been included in Gujarati :—

| | | | | |
|---|---|---|---|---|
| (1) Nagari . . | 724 | 595 | 129 | Gwalior (723), Nowgong (1). |

# TABLE XI.

## *BIRTHPLACE.*

This table is divided in two Parts. *Part A* contains the statistics of birthplace for the Agency as a whole and *Part B* gives similar information for the principal States in the Agency.

*Special Return showing the number of European British subjects born in England and Wales, Scotland and Ireland.*

| Age by annual period. | Total Population. | | | Country where born. | | | | | | | | |
|---|---|---|---|---|---|---|---|---|---|---|---|---|
| | | | | England and Wales. | | | Scotland. | | | Ireland. | | |
| | Persons. | Males. | Females. | Persons. | Males. | Females. | Persons. | Males. | Females. | Persons. | Males. | Females. |
| 1 | 2 | 3 | 4 | 5 | 6 | 7 | 8 | 9 | 10 | 11 | 12 | 13 |
| Infant | 11 | 3 | 8 | 11 | 3 | 8 | .. | .. | .. | .. | .. | .. |
| 1 | 8 | 4 | 4 | 7 | 3 | 4 | .. | .. | .. | 1 | 1 | .. |
| 2 | 9 | 3 | 6 | 8 | 3 | 5 | .. | .. | .. | 1 | .. | 1 |
| 3 | 15 | 7 | 8 | 12 | 5 | 7 | .. | .. | .. | 3 | 2 | 1 |
| 4 | 18 | 7 | 11 | 17 | 7 | 10 | .. | .. | .. | 1 | .. | 1 |
| 5 | 13 | 6 | 7 | 11 | 5 | 6 | .. | .. | .. | 2 | 1 | 1 |
| 6 | 15 | 9 | 6 | 11 | 6 | 5 | .. | .. | .. | 4 | 3 | 1 |
| 7 | 14 | 5 | 9 | 13 | 5 | 8 | .. | .. | .. | 1 | .. | 1 |
| 8 | 8 | 3 | 5 | 7 | 2 | 5 | .. | .. | .. | 1 | 1 | .. |
| 9 | 7 | 1 | 6 | 4 | .. | 4 | 1 | .. | 1 | 2 | 1 | 1 |
| 10 | 4 | .. | 4 | 4 | .. | 4 | .. | .. | .. | .. | .. | .. |
| 11 | 5 | 4 | 1 | 2 | 1 | 1 | .. | .. | .. | 3 | 3 | .. |
| 12 | 6 | 2 | 4 | 5 | 2 | 3 | .. | .. | .. | 1 | .. | 1 |
| 13 | 2 | .. | 2 | 1 | .. | 1 | 1 | .. | 1 | .. | .. | .. |
| 14 | 5 | 2 | 3 | 5 | 2 | 3 | .. | .. | .. | .. | .. | .. |
| 15 | 3 | 3 | .. | 1 | 1 | .. | 1 | 1 | .. | 1 | 1 | .. |
| 16 | 8 | 7 | 1 | 8 | 7 | 1 | .. | .. | .. | .. | .. | .. |
| 17 | 18 | 15 | 3 | 18 | 15 | 3 | .. | .. | .. | .. | .. | .. |
| 18 | 15 | 15 | .. | 15 | 15 | .. | .. | .. | .. | .. | .. | .. |
| 19 | 23 | 19 | 4 | 20 | 16 | 4 | .. | .. | .. | 3 | 3 | .. |
| 20 | 135 | 131 | 4 | 126 | 122 | 4 | 4 | 4 | .. | 5 | 5 | .. |
| 21 | 309 | 303 | 6 | 265 | 261 | 4 | 3 | 3 | .. | 41 | 39 | 2 |
| 22 | 423 | 417 | 6 | 350 | 345 | 5 | 2 | 1 | 1 | 71 | 71 | .. |
| 23 | 393 | 388 | 5 | 322 | 317 | 5 | 31 | 31 | .. | 40 | 40 | .. |
| 24 | 385 | 372 | 13 | 351 | 340 | 11 | 1 | 1 | .. | 33 | 31 | 2 |
| 25 | 213 | 194 | 19 | 175 | 157 | 18 | 4 | 4 | .. | 34 | 33 | 1 |
| 26 | 183 | 162 | 21 | 162 | 146 | 16 | 5 | 3 | 2 | 16 | 13 | 3 |
| 27 | 139 | 125 | 14 | 115 | 108 | 7 | 8 | 5 | 3 | 16 | 12 | 4 |
| 28 | 107 | 89 | 18 | 90 | 75 | 15 | 3 | 3 | .. | 14 | 11 | 3 |
| 29 | 82 | 64 | 18 | 69 | 56 | 13 | 6 | 4 | 2 | 7 | 4 | 3 |
| 30 | 91 | 68 | 23 | 78 | 59 | 19 | 3 | 2 | 1 | 10 | 7 | 3 |
| 31 | 59 | 47 | 12 | 51 | 40 | 11 | 3 | 2 | 1 | 5 | 5 | .. |
| 32 | 74 | 57 | 17 | 65 | 52 | 13 | 1 | .. | 1 | 8 | 5 | 3 |
| 33 | 37 | 31 | 6 | 33 | 27 | 6 | .. | .. | .. | 4 | 4 | .. |
| 34 | 43 | 35 | 8 | 37 | 30 | 7 | 2 | 2 | .. | 4 | 3 | 1 |
| 35 | 41 | 32 | 9 | 29 | 23 | 6 | 3 | 2 | 1 | 9 | 7 | 2 |
| 36 | 30 | 26 | 4 | 27 | 23 | 4 | 2 | 2 | .. | 1 | 1 | .. |
| 37 | 27 | 26 | 1 | 22 | 21 | 1 | 1 | 1 | .. | 4 | 4 | .. |
| 38 | 37 | 26 | 11 | 33 | 24 | 9 | .. | .. | .. | 4 | 2 | 2 |
| 39 | 24 | 19 | 5 | 22 | 17 | 5 | 1 | 1 | .. | 1 | 1 | .. |
| 40 | 28 | 16 | 12 | 23 | 13 | 10 | 1 | .. | 1 | 4 | 3 | 1 |
| 41 | 14 | 12 | 2 | 14 | 12 | 2 | .. | .. | .. | .. | .. | .. |
| 42 | 16 | 12 | 4 | 14 | 11 | 3 | .. | .. | .. | 2 | 1 | 1 |
| 43 | 9 | 7 | 2 | 6 | 5 | 1 | 1 | 1 | .. | 2 | 1 | 1 |
| 44 | 6 | 4 | 2 | 5 | 3 | 2 | 1 | 1 | .. | .. | .. | .. |
| 45 | 7 | 7 | .. | 7 | 7 | .. | .. | .. | .. | .. | .. | .. |
| 46 | 7 | 7 | .. | 6 | 6 | .. | 1 | 1 | .. | .. | .. | .. |
| 47 | 5 | 2 | 3 | 5 | 2 | 3 | .. | .. | .. | .. | .. | .. |
| 48 | 17 | 12 | 5 | 13 | 10 | 3 | 2 | 2 | .. | 2 | .. | 2 |
| 49 | 6 | 5 | 1 | 6 | 5 | 1 | .. | .. | .. | .. | .. | .. |
| 50 | 13 | 10 | 3 | 11 | 10 | 1 | 2 | .. | 2 | .. | .. | .. |
| 52 | 2 | 2 | .. | .. | .. | .. | 2 | 2 | .. | .. | .. | .. |
| 53 | 2 | 2 | .. | 2 | 2 | .. | .. | .. | .. | .. | .. | .. |
| 54 | 3 | 3 | .. | 2 | 2 | .. | .. | .. | .. | 1 | 1 | .. |
| 55 | 4 | 3 | 1 | 4 | 3 | 1 | .. | .. | .. | .. | .. | .. |
| 56 | 2 | 2 | .. | 2 | 2 | .. | .. | .. | .. | .. | .. | .. |
| 60 | 4 | 4 | .. | 4 | 4 | .. | .. | .. | .. | .. | .. | .. |
| 61 | 1 | 1 | .. | 1 | 1 | .. | .. | .. | .. | .. | .. | .. |
| 64 | 2 | .. | 2 | .. | .. | .. | 2 | .. | 2 | .. | .. | .. |
| 65 | 1 | 1 | .. | .. | .. | .. | 1 | 1 | .. | .. | .. | .. |
| 66 | 1 | .. | 1 | 1 | .. | 1 | .. | .. | .. | .. | .. | .. |
| 70 | 1 | .. | 1 | 1 | .. | 1 | .. | .. | .. | .. | .. | .. |
| 71 | 1 | 1 | .. | 1 | 1 | .. | .. | .. | .. | .. | .. | .. |
| 78 | 1 | | .. | 1 | 1 | .. | .. | .. | .. | .. | .. | .. |
| Total | 3,192 | 2,841 | 351 | 2,731 | 2,441 | 290 | 99 | 80 | 19 | 362 | 320 | 42 |

# TABLE XI.—Birthplace.

| Birthplace. | Population. | | |
|---|---|---|---|
| | Persons. | Males. | Females. |
| 1 | 2 | 3 | 4 |
| **Central India** | **9,356,980** | **4,801,459** | **4,555,521** |
| ***A.—Born in India*** | ***9,353,116*** | ***4,798,154*** | ***4,554,962*** |
| **I.—Within Central India** | **8,882,725** | **4,586,467** | **4,296,258** |
| **(i) States** | **8,877,960** | **4,584,235** | **4,293,725** |
| Ajaigarh | 80,241 | 40,968 | 39,273 |
| Alipura | 12,029 | 7,061 | 4,968 |
| Ali-Rajpur | 79,229 | 40,922 | 38,307 |
| Baoni | 13,398 | 7,919 | 5,479 |
| Barwani | 88,925 | 44,009 | 44,916 |
| Bhopal | 727,900 | 368,808 | 359,092 |
| *Nizmat-i-Janub* | *257,866* | *131,877* | *125,989* |
| *Nizmat-i-Maghrib* | *186,514* | *93,719* | *92,795* |
| *Nizmat-i-Mashrik* | *171,765* | *94,937* | *76,828* |
| *Bhopal, unspecified* | *111,755* | *48,275* | *63,480* |
| Bijawar | 123,348 | 63,177 | 60,171 |
| Bundelkhand, unspecified | 5,825 | 2,192 | 3,633 |
| Charkhari | 109,408 | 60,137 | 49,271 |
| Chhatarpur | 168,014 | 87,005 | 81,009 |
| Datia | 150,568 | 82,172 | 68,396 |
| Dewas, S. B. & J. B. | 115,482 | 60,941 | 54,541 |
| Dhar | 148,560 | 74,098 | 74,462 |
| Gwalior | 3,086,740 | 1,621,633 | 1,465,107 |
| *Zila Amjhera* | *103,080* | *51,509* | *51,571* |
| *" Bhilsa* | *147,420* | *74,198* | *73,222* |
| *" Bhind* | *374,052* | *209,822* | *164,230* |
| *" Gird Gwalior* | *460,133* | *237,045* | *223,088* |
| *" Isagarh* | *276,209* | *147,886* | *128,323* |
| *" Mandasor* | *172,572* | *97,401* | *75,171* |
| *" Narwar* | *374,680* | *189,819* | *184,861* |
| *" Shajapur* | *286,496* | *147,910* | *138,586* |
| *" Sheopur* | *122,891* | *68,517* | *54,374* |
| *" Tonwargarh* | *361,130* | *201,114* | *160,016* |
| *" Ujjain* | *298,227* | *154,020* | *144,207* |
| *Gwalior, unspecified* | *109,850* | *42,392* | *67,458* |
| Indore | 902,849 | 466,458 | 436,391 |
| *Pargana Alampur* | *10,196* | *6,713* | *3,483* |
| *Zila Indore* | *289,799* | *141,468* | *148,331* |
| *" Mehidpur* | *83,405* | *52,368* | *31,037* |
| *" Nemawar* | *77,740* | *40,248* | *37,492* |
| *" Nimar* | *271,207* | *140,451* | *130,756* |
| *" Rampura-Bhanpura* | *112,898* | *61,679* | *51,219* |
| *Indore, unspecified* | *57,604* | *23,531* | *34,073* |
| Jaora | 88,556 | 45,241 | 43,315 |
| Jhabua | 110,831 | 55,359 | 55,472 |
| Jobat | 14,454 | 7,214 | 7,240 |
| Khilchipur | 38,454 | 21,024 | 17,430 |
| Maihar | 64,784 | 32,935 | 31,849 |
| Minor States | 243,395 | 133,934 | 109,461 |
| *Gwalior Residency* | *61,086* | *34,496* | *26,590* |
| *Indore "* | *249* | *153* | *96* |
| *Bhaghelkhand Agency* | *55,717* | *29,477* | *26,240* |
| *Bhopal "* | *24,933* | *13,584* | *11,349* |
| *Bhopawar "* | *37,593* | *19,873* | *17,720* |
| *Bundelkhand "* | *44,401* | *25,385* | *19,016* |
| *Malwa "* | *19,416* | *10,966* | *8,450* |
| Nagod | 72,020 | 36,375 | 35,645 |
| Narsinghgarh | 95,677 | 49,221 | 46,456 |
| Orchha | 325,631 | 167,421 | 158,210 |
| Panna | 222,705 | 115,698 | 107,007 |
| Rajgarh | 113,362 | 59,858 | 53,504 |
| Ratlam | 78,357 | 36,428 | 41,929 |
| Rewah | 1,483,650 | 733,034 | 750,616 |
| *Tahsil Bardi* | *226,435* | *112,687* | *113,748* |
| *" Bandhogarh* | *129,547* | *65,372* | *64,175* |
| *" Beohari* | *177,645* | *87,924* | *89,721* |
| *" Huzur* | *332,144* | *163,436* | *168,708* |
| *" Mauganj* | *105,331* | *52,319* | *53,012* |
| *" Raghurajnagar* | *144,657* | *73,589* | *71,068* |
| *" Sitlaha* | *103,461* | *54,518* | *48,943* |
| *" Sohagpur* | *200,610* | *97,409* | *103,201* |
| *Rewah, unspecified* | *63,820* | *25,780* | *38,040* |
| Sailana | 25,039 | 13,408 | 11,631 |
| Samthar | 26,323 | 15,024 | 11,299 |
| Sitamau | 23,389 | 12,885 | 10,504 |
| Sohawal | 38,817 | 21,676 | 17,141 |
| **(ii) British District** | **4,765** | **2,232** | **2,533** |
| Manpur | 4,765 | 2,232 | 2,533 |
| **II.—Provinces and States in India beyond Central India.** | **470,391** | **211,687** | **258,704** |
| (a) PROVINCES AND STATES ADJACENT TO CENTRAL INDIA. | **452,929** | **200,716** | **252,213** |
| UNITED PROVINCES OF AGRA AND OUDH | **169,190** | **68,321** | **100,869** |
| **British Districts** | **168,735** | **68,129** | **100,606** |
| Agra | 9,836 | 3,906 | 5,930 |
| Aligarh | 661 | 417 | 244 |
| Allahabad | 8,285 | 4,592 | 3,693 |
| Banda | 21,375 | 7,557 | 13,818 |
| Bara-Banki | 530 | 313 | 217 |
| BRITISH DISTRICTS—*contd.* | | | |
| Benares | 1,485 | 907 | 578 |
| Cawnpore | 8,834 | 5,263 | 3,571 |
| Etawah | 5,044 | 2,013 | 3,031 |
| Farrukhabad | 1,355 | 828 | 527 |
| Fatehpur | 1,775 | 1,190 | 585 |
| Fyzabad | 730 | 514 | 216 |
| Hamirpur | 32,172 | 11,628 | 20,544 |
| Jalaun | 10,824 | 2,975 | 7,849 |
| Jhansi | 36,603 | 9,941 | 26,662 |
| Lucknow | 2,519 | 1,634 | 885 |
| Meerut | 662 | 258 | 409 |
| Mirzapur | 6,302 | 2,224 | 4,078 |
| Moradabad | 1,172 | 610 | 562 |
| Muttra | 1,230 | 724 | 506 |
| Partabgarh | 1,200 | 854 | 346 |
| Rae Bareli | 3,089 | 2,099 | 990 |
| Sultanpur | 584 | 399 | 185 |
| Unao | 1,011 | 727 | 284 |
| Other districts | 3,500 | 2,156 | 1,344 |
| United Provinces, unspecified | 7,957 | 4,405 | 3,552 |
| STATES (RAMPUR) | **455** | **192** | **263** |
| CENTRAL PROVINCES AND BERAR | **80,661** | **31,948** | **48,713** |
| BRITISH DISTRICTS | **80,657** | **31,944** | **48,713** |
| Amraoti | 793 | 459 | 334 |
| Bilaspur | 2,335 | 1,268 | 1,067 |
| Damoh | 5,716 | 1,665 | 4,051 |
| Hoshangabad | 18,567 | 6,761 | 11,806 |
| Jubbulpore | 15,479 | 5,361 | 10,118 |
| Mandla | 2,795 | 2,042 | 753 |
| Nagpur | 2,233 | 1,106 | 1,127 |
| Narsinghpur | 1,884 | 494 | 1,390 |
| Nimar (British) | 4,837 | 1,387 | 3,450 |
| Raipur | 1,277 | 882 | 395 |
| Saugor | 15,633 | 6,273 | 9,360 |
| Other districts | 631 | 350 | 281 |
| Central Provinces, unspecified | 7,877 | 3,196 | 4,681 |
| STATES (CHANGBHAKAR) | **4** | **4** | .. |
| BOMBAY INCLUDING ADEN | **54,111** | **30,584** | **23,527** |
| BRITISH DISTRICTS | **47,165** | **26,940** | **20,225** |
| Ahmedabad | 948 | 610 | 338 |
| Ahmednagar | 2,112 | 1,242 | 870 |
| Bijapur | 911 | 104 | 807 |
| Gujarat, unspecified | 3,228 | 1,893 | 1,335 |
| Khandesh, East and West | 24,363 | 14,343 | 10,020 |
| Nasik | 801 | 548 | 253 |
| Panch Mahal | 3,658 | 1,586 | 2,072 |
| Poona | 2,256 | 1,081 | 1,175 |
| Ratnagiri | 973 | 684 | 289 |
| Satara | 1,313 | 915 | 398 |
| Sholapur | 868 | 573 | 295 |
| Surat | 730 | 498 | 232 |
| Other districts | 779 | 582 | 197 |
| Bombay, unspecified | 4,225 | 2,281 | 1,944 |
| STATES | **6,946** | **3,644** | **3,302** |
| Chhota Udepur | 4,557 | 2,039 | 2,518 |
| Kathiawar | 871 | 554 | 317 |
| Kolhapur | 606 | 502 | 104 |
| Other States | 912 | 549 | 363 |
| AJMER-MERWARA | **5,226** | **3,585** | **1,641** |
| RAJPUTANA STATES | **144,401** | **66,978** | **77,423** |
| Alwar | 2,245 | 1,252 | 993 |
| Banswara | 2,414 | 1,046 | 1,368 |
| Bharatpur | 2,897 | 1,405 | 1,492 |
| Bikaner | 691 | 291 | 400 |
| Bundi | 616 | 382 | 234 |
| Dholpur | 4,443 | 2,466 | 1,977 |
| Jaipur | 26,438 | 13,876 | 12,562 |
| Jhalawar | 8,869 | 3,688 | 5,181 |
| Karauli | 1,799 | 675 | 1,124 |
| Kishangarh | 1,070 | 493 | 577 |
| Kotah | 16,205 | 6,762 | 9,443 |
| Kushalgarh | 1,059 | 586 | 473 |
| Marwar | 21,239 | 11,334 | 9,905 |
| Mewar | 20,230 | 7,828 | 12,402 |
| Partabgarh | 5,092 | 1,850 | 3,242 |
| Tonk | 15,872 | 7,304 | 8,568 |
| Other States | 618 | 299 | 319 |
| Rajputana, unspecified | 12,604 | 5,441 | 7,163 |
| (b) BORN IN OTHER PROVINCES AND STATES IN INDIA. | **17,462** | **10,971** | **6,491** |
| BARODA | **2,462** | **1,406** | **1,056** |
| PUNJAB | **8,292** | **5,418** | **2,874** |

# TABLE XI.—Birthplace—*concluded.*

| Birthplace. | Population. | | |
|---|---|---|---|
| | Persons. | Males. | Females. |
| 1 | 2 | 3 | 4 |
| **British Districts** | **7,859** | **5,118** | **2,741** |
| Amritsar | 733 | 639 | 94 |
| Delhi | 2,857 | 1,664 | 1,193 |
| Lahore | 705 | 309 | 396 |
| Other districts | 2,086 | 1,565 | 521 |
| Punjab, unspecified | 1,478 | 941 | 537 |
| **States** | **423** | **300** | **123** |
| **Kashmir** | **70** | **65** | **5** |
| **North-West Frontier Province** | **563** | **419** | **144** |
| Peshawar | 536 | 399 | 137 |
| Dera Ismail Khan and North-West Frontier Province, unspecified. | 27 | 20 | 7 |
| **Assam** | **8** | **6** | **2** |
| **Bihar and Orissa** | **1,115** | **518** | **597** |
| **British Districts** | **1,047** | **503** | **544** |
| **State (Chota-Nagpur)** | **68** | **15** | **53** |
| **Bengal, British Districts** | **1,004** | **649** | **355** |
| Calcutta | 602 | 393 | 209 |
| Other districts | 141 | 98 | 48 |
| Bengal, unspecified | 261 | 168 | 98 |
| **Madras** | **1,035** | **685** | **400** |
| **British Districts** | **1,033** | **685** | **398** |
| Madras | 789 | 504 | 285 |
| Other districts | 244 | 181 | 113 |
| **State (Travancore)** | **2** | .. | **2** |
| **Mysore State** | **491** | **233** | **258** |
| **Hyderabad State** | **2,177** | **1,437** | **740** |
| Other States | 738 | 580 | 158 |
| Hyderabad, unspecified | 1,439 | 857 | 582 |
| **Baluchistan** | **30** | **25** | **5** |
| **British District (Quetta-Pishin)** | **20** | **18** | **2** |
| **State (Makran)** | **10** | **7** | **3** |
| **Burma** | **13** | **7** | **6** |
| **French Settlement (Chandernagore).** | **15** | **12** | **3** |
| **Portuguese Settlement (Goa)** | **177** | **121** | **56** |
| ***B.—Born in other Asiatic Countries*** | ***355*** | ***248*** | ***107*** |
| Afghanistan | 178 | 144 | 34 |
| Arabia | 53 | 23 | 30 |
| Ceylon | 3 | .. | 3 |
| Japan | 4 | 2 | 2 |
| Nepal | 88 | 58 | 30 |
| Persia | 11 | 5 | 6 |
| Turkey in Asia | 18 | 16 | 2 |
| ***C.—Born in Europe*** | ***3,283*** | ***2,916*** | ***367*** |
| United Kingdom | 3,192 | 2,841 | 351 |
| *England and Wales* | *2,731* | *2,441* | *290* |
| *Scotland* | *99* | *80* | *19* |
| *Ireland* | *362* | *320* | *42* |
| France | 24 | 20 | 4 |
| Germany | 16 | 13 | 3 |
| Italy | 2 | 1 | 1 |
| Portugal | 48 | 40 | 8 |
| Russia | 1 | 1 | .. |
| ***D.—Born in Africa*** | ***129*** | ***101*** | ***28*** |
| Egypt | 127 | 99 | 28 |
| Africa, unspecified | 2 | 2 | .. |
| ***E.—Born in America*** | ***89*** | ***32*** | ***57*** |
| Canada | 74 | 25 | 49 |
| United States | 1 | .. | 1 |
| America, unspecified | 14 | 7 | 7 |
| ***F.—Born in Australia*** | ***8*** | ***8*** | .. |
| Australia, unspecified | 8 | 8 | .. |
| **Abstract.** | | | |
| **Central India Agency** | **9,356,980** | **4,801,459** | **4,555,521** |
| **A.—BORN IN INDIA** | **9,353,116** | **4,798,154** | **4,554,962** |
| **I.—Within Central India** | **8,882,725** | **4,586,467** | **4,296,258** |
| (i) States | 8,877,960 | 4,584,235 | 4,293,725 |
| (ii) British District | 4,765 | 2,232 | 2,533 |
| **II.—Provinces and States in India beyond Central India.** | **470,391** | **211,687** | **258,704** |
| (a) Provinces and States adjacent to Central India. | 452,929 | 200,716 | 252,213 |
| (b) Other Provinces and States in India. | 17,462 | 10,971 | 6,491 |
| **B.—BORN IN OTHER ASIATIC COUNTRIES.** | **355** | **248** | **107** |
| **C.—BORN IN EUROPE** | **3,283** | **2,916** | **367** |
| United Kingdom | 3,192 | 2,841 | 351 |
| Other countries in Europe | 91 | 75 | 16 |
| **D.—BORN IN AFRICA** | **129** | **101** | **28** |
| **E.—BORN IN AMERICA** | **89** | **32** | **57** |
| **F.—BORN IN AUSTRALIA** | **8** | **8** | .. |

## APPENDIX TO TABLE

*Showing the birthplaces of persons enumerated*

| Serial Number. | Birthplace. | Population. | Gwalior. | Indore. | Bhopal. | Rewah. | Orchha. | Datia. | Dhar. | Dewas, S. B. & J. B. |
|---|---|---|---|---|---|---|---|---|---|---|
| | | | PERSONS | | | | | | | |
| | 1 | 2 | 3 | 4 | 5 | 6 | 7 | 8 | 9 | 10 |
| | **Central India** | 9,356,980 | 3,092,677 | 1,004,561 | 730,383 | 1,514,843 | 330,032 | 154,603 | 154,070 | 137,395 |
| | *A.—Born in India* | 9,353,116 | 3,092,533 | 1,004,501 | 730,268 | 1,514,811 | 330,029 | 154,603 | 154,063 | 137,372 |
| 1 | I.—Within Central India | 8,882,725 | 2,979,982 | 928,717 | 700,798 | 1,480,052 | 320,805 | 147,939 | 145,936 | 130,594 |
| | (i) States | 8,877,960 | 2,979,982 | 928,717 | 700,798 | 1,479,984 | 320,805 | 147,939 | 145,884 | 130,454 |
| | (1) Ajaigarh | 80,241 | .. | .. | .. | 249 | 28 | 2 | 17 | .. |
| | (2) Alipura | 12,029 | 18 | .. | .. | .. | 17 | 1 | .. | .. |
| | (3) Ali-Rajpur | 79,229 | 1,263 | 4,245 | 15 | 144 | .. | .. | 804 | .. |
| | (4) Baoni | 13,398 | .. | .. | .. | .. | .. | .. | .. | |
| | (5) Barwani | 88,925 | 1,230 | 10,440 | .. | .. | .. | .. | 973 | 26 |
| | (6) Bhopal | 727,900 | 21,407 | 12,743 | 673,848 | 370 | 36 | 32 | 224 | 1,132 |
| | (7) Bijawar | 123,348 | .. | .. | 115 | 221 | 1,154 | 2 | 1 | .. |
| | (8) Bundelkhand (unspecified) | 5,825 | .. | 5,477 | .. | .. | 40 | .. | 93 | .. |
| | (9) Charkhari | 109,408 | .. | 187 | 13 | 45 | 576 | 28 | 1 | 2 |
| | (10) Chhatarpur | 168,014 | 246 | .. | 44 | 480 | 722 | 16 | 1 | 2 |
| | (11) Datia | 150,568 | 12,436 | 2,040 | 625 | 654 | 1,419 | 131,227 | 26 | 31 |
| | (12) Dewas, S. B. & J. B. | 115,482 | 8,458 | 8,719 | 290 | 2 | .. | 1 | 377 | 89,606 |
| | (13) Dhar | 148,560 | 13,660 | 8,157 | 41 | .. | .. | .. | 112,186 | 719 |
| | (14) Gwalior | 3,086,740 | 2,845,348 | 76,085 | 16,573 | 188 | 384 | 13,690 | 13,390 | 18,229 |
| | (15) Indore | 902,849 | 38,333 | 788,982 | 2,538 | 38 | 12 | 955 | 14,122 | 12,689 |
| | (16) Jaora | 88,556 | 7,675 | 4,126 | 64 | 36 | .. | .. | 223 | 3,355 |
| | (17) Jhabua | 110,881 | 4,066 | 1,625 | 2 | 4 | .. | .. | 921 | 22 |
| | (18) Jobat | 14,454 | 283 | 230 | .. | .. | .. | .. | 167 | .. |
| | (19) Khilchipur | 38,454 | 1,639 | .. | 158 | 88 | .. | .. | .. | 129 |
| | (20) Maihar | 64,784 | .. | .. | .. | 2,141 | .. | .. | 9 | .. |
| | (21) Minor States | 248,395 | 1,710 | .. | 1,167 | 966 | 64 | 15 | 5 | 184 |
| | (22) Nagod | 72,020 | .. | 232 | 1 | 3,892 | 315 | .. | .. | .. |
| | (23) Narsinghgarh | 95,677 | 3,418 | 1,094 | 3,478 | .. | | .. | 8 | 2,102 |
| | (24) Orchha | 325,631 | 405 | 6 | 614 | 175 | 315,530 | 866 | 228 | 3 |
| | (25) Panna | 222,705 | 256 | .. | 166 | 6,105 | 134 | 304 | 8 | .. |
| | (26) Rajgarh | 113,362 | 2,434 | 745 | 1,333 | .. | .. | 3 | 7 | 1,048 |
| | (27) Ratlam | 78,357 | 10,836 | 2,012 | 17 | 23 | .. | .. | 779 | 382 |
| | (28) Rewah | 1,483,650 | 288 | 231 | 193 | 1,460,025 | 374 | 3 | 107 | 2 |
| | (29) Sailana | 25,039 | 954 | 322 | .. | .. | .. | .. | 171 | 59 |
| | (30) Sarathar | 26,323 | 1,683 | 262 | 8 | .. | 50 | 794 | .. | .. |
| | (31) Sitamau | 23,389 | 1,986 | 756 | .. | .. | .. | .. | 26 | 739 |
| | (32) Sohawal | 38,817 | .. | .. | .. | 4,643 | .. | .. | .. | .. |
| | (ii) British Districts | 4,765 | .. | .. | .. | 68 | .. | .. | 52 | 70 |
| | (1) Manpur | 4,765 | .. | .. | .. | 68 | .. | .. | 52 | 70 |
| 2 | II.—Provinces and States in India beyond Central India. | 470,391 | 112,551 | 75,784 | 29,470 | 34,759 | 9,224 | 6,664 | 8,127 | 6,748 |
| | (a) PROVINCES AND STATES ADJACENT TO CENTRAL INDIA. | 452,929 | 109,261 | 72,233 | 28,432 | 33,723 | 9,072 | 6,621 | 7,861 | 6,464 |
| 1 | UNITED PROVINCES OF AGRA AND OUDH. | 169,130 | 40,354 | 6,641 | 5,648 | 18,239 | 8,641 | 6,366 | 2,024 | 933 |
| | (1) British Districts | 168,735 | 40,354 | 6,641 | 5,488 | 18,227 | 8,641 | 6,366 | 2,024 | 932 |
| | (2) States (Rampur) | 395 | .. | .. | 160 | 12 | .. | .. | .. | 1 |
| 2 | CENTRAL PROVINCES AND BERAR | 80,061 | 6,992 | 12,092 | 17,548 | 13,674 | 290 | 18 | 185 | 379 |
| | (1) British Districts | 80,057 | 6,992 | 12,092 | 17,548 | 13,670 | 290 | 18 | 185 | 379 |
| | (2) States (Changbhakar) | 4 | .. | .. | .. | 4 | .. | .. | .. | .. |
| 3 | BOMBAY, INCLUDING ADEN | 54,111 | 6,060 | 18,094 | 374 | 987 | 20 | 19 | 1,477 | 706 |
| | (1) British Districts | 47,165 | 5,499 | 17,664 | 344 | 905 | 8 | 2 | 1,423 | 652 |
| | (2) States | 6,946 | 561 | 430 | 30 | 82 | 12 | 17 | 54 | 54 |
| 4 | AJMER-MERWARA | 5,226 | 992 | 2,184 | 116 | 16 | 20 | 3 | 137 | 64 |
| 5 | RAJPUTANA STATES | 144,401 | 54,863 | 33,222 | 4,746 | 807 | 101 | 215 | 4,038 | 4,382 |
| | (b) BORN IN OTHER PROVINCES AND STATES IN INDIA. | 17,462 | 3,290 | 3,551 | 1,038 | 1,036 | 152 | 43 | 266 | 284 |
| 1 | BARODA | 2,492 | 315 | 1,339 | 4 | 15 | 27 | 1 | 69 | 91 |
| 2 | PUNJAB | 8,282 | 2,075 | 1,307 | 606 | 168 | 21 | 33 | 126 | 109 |
| | (1) British Districts | 7,859 | 1,936 | 1,307 | 569 | 113 | 21 | 32 | 96 | 105 |
| | (2) States | 423 | 139 | .. | 37 | 55 | .. | 1 | 30 | 4 |
| 3 | KASHMIR | 70 | 2 | 7 | 14 | 1 | .. | 3 | .. | .. |
| 4 | NORTH-WEST FRONTIER PROVINCE | 563 | 134 | .. | 88 | .. | 1 | .. | .. | 15 |
| 5 | ASSAM | 8 | 3 | .. | .. | .. | .. | .. | .. | 3 |
| 6 | BIHAR AND ORISSA | 1,115 | 190 | .. | 47 | 488 | 14 | .. | 2 | 2 |
| | (1) British Districts | 1,047 | 190 | .. | 47 | 420 | 14 | .. | 2 | 2 |
| | (2) States (Chota-Nagpur) | 68 | .. | .. | .. | 68 | .. | .. | .. | .. |
| 7 | BENGAL BRITISH DISTRICTS | 1,004 | 211 | 229 | 61 | 168 | .. | 4 | 14 | 7 |
| 8 | MADRAS | 1,035 | 110 | 390 | 23 | 41 | .. | 1 | 2 | 9 |
| | (1) British Districts | 1,033 | 108 | 390 | 23 | 41 | .. | 1 | 2 | 9 |
| | (2) States (Travancore) | 2 | 2 | .. | .. | .. | .. | .. | .. | .. |
| 9 | MYSORE STATES | 401 | 14 | .. | 6 | 7 | .. | .. | .. | .. |
| 10 | HYDERABAD STATES | 2,177 | 219 | 258 | 185 | 130 | 89 | 1 | 53 | 42 |
| 11 | BALUCHISTAN | 30 | 10 | .. | 2 | .. | .. | .. | .. | 4 |
| | (1) British Districts (Quetta Pishin) | 20 | 10 | .. | 2 | .. | .. | .. | .. | 4 |
| | (2) States (Makran) | 10 | .. | .. | .. | .. | .. | .. | .. | .. |
| 12 | BURMA | 13 | 2 | .. | 2 | 3 | .. | .. | .. | .. |
| 13 | FRENCH SETTLEMENT (CHANDERNAGORE) | 15 | .. | .. | .. | 15 | .. | .. | .. | .. |
| 14 | PORTUGUESE SETTLEMENT (GOA) | 177 | 5 | 21 | .. | .. | .. | .. | .. | 2 |
| | *B.—Born in other Asiatic countries* | 355 | 70 | 37 | 68 | 14 | 3 | .. | .. | 31 |
| | *C.—Born in Europe* | 3,383 | 74 | 22 | 44 | 18 | .. | .. | 3 | 2 |
| | *D.—Born in Africa* | 139 | .. | .. | 2 | .. | .. | .. | .. | .. |
| | *E.—Born in America* | 89 | .. | 1 | 1 | .. | .. | .. | 4 | .. |
| | *F.—Born in Australia* | 8 | .. | .. | .. | .. | .. | .. | .. | .. |

## XI.—Birthplace.

*in the main States of Central India Agency.*

ENUMERATED IN

| Jaora. | Ratlam. | Panna. | Charkhari. | Ajaigarh. | Bijawar. | Chhatarpur. | Rajgarh. | Narsinghgarh. | Nagod. | Maihar. | Jhabua. | Barwani. | Ali-Rajpur. | Other states, cantonments, and stations, etc. | Serial Number. |
|---|---|---|---|---|---|---|---|---|---|---|---|---|---|---|---|
| 11 | 12 | 13 | 14 | 15 | 16 | 17 | 18 | 19 | 20 | 21 | 22 | 23 | 24 | 25 | |
| **75,951** | **75,291** | **228,880** | **132,530** | **87,093** | **125,202** | **166,985** | **127,293** | **109,854** | **74,592** | **73,155** | **111,292** | **108,583** | **72,454** | **668,351** | |
| *75,918* | *75,259* | *228,846* | *132,530* | *87,075* | *125,200* | *166,985* | *127,287* | *109,852* | *74,591* | *73,153* | *111,264* | *108,577* | *72,447* | *666,052* | *A* |
| 72,189 | 68,504 | 217,226 | 112,200 | 83,297 | 122,424 | 160,234 | 121,051 | 104,500 | 72,401 | 68,813 | 107,222 | 90,048 | 69,341 | 578,522 | 1 |
| 72,189 | 68,504 | 217,226 | 112,200 | 83,297 | 122,424 | 160,234 | 121,051 | 104,500 | 72,401 | 68,813 | 107,222 | 90,026 | 69,339 | 573,971 | (I) |
| .. | 1 | 5,744 | 2,067 | 66,966 | 353 | 975 | .. | .. | 1,353 | 319 | .. | .. | .. | 2,167 | (1) |
| .. | .. | 31 | 81 | 1 | 38 | 215 | .. | .. | .. | .. | .. | .. | .. | 11,627 | (2) |
| .. | 5 | .. | .. | .. | .. | .. | .. | .. | .. | .. | 820 | 3,985 | 65,991 | 1,957 | (3) |
| .. | .. | .. | .. | 1 | .. | .. | .. | .. | .. | .. | .. | .. | .. | 13,397 | (4) |
| .. | 5 | .. | .. | .. | .. | .. | 11 | 1 | .. | .. | 4 | 75,658 | 383 | 194 | (5) |
| 52 | 82 | 18 | 4 | 1 | 5 | 2 | 3,364 | 4,372 | 1 | .. | 23 | 52 | 5 | 10,632 | (6) |
| .. | .. | 5,432 | 2,077 | 879 | 107,970 | 4,987 | 6 | 2 | 59 | 24 | .. | .. | .. | 419 | (7) |
| 1 | 2 | .. | .. | .. | .. | .. | .. | .. | .. | .. | .. | 3 | .. | 209 | (8) |
| .. | 2 | 1,270 | 98,383 | 1,923 | 1,558 | 2,881 | .. | .. | 25 | 17 | .. | 2 | .. | 2,550 | (9) |
| 31 | .. | 3,731 | 5,012 | 2,239 | 4,568 | 147,367 | 10 | 2 | 39 | 34 | .. | .. | .. | 3,470 | (10) |
| .. | 2 | 33 | 52 | 18 | 21 | 19 | 91 | 154 | 4 | 2 | .. | 1 | .. | 1,713 | (11) |
| 1,230 | 181 | .. | .. | .. | .. | 6 | 928 | 1,689 | .. | .. | 14 | 29 | 1 | 3,999 | (12) |
| 188 | 1,286 | 9 | .. | 1 | .. | .. | 6 | 9 | .. | .. | 509 | 2,187 | 376 | 8,281 | (13) |
| 5,221 | 6,673 | 103 | 47 | 88 | 33 | 186 | 9,014 | 8,749 | 2 | 11 | 1,431 | 1,956 | 475 | 68,914 | (14) |
| 2,751 | 1,908 | 4 | 5 | 3 | 1 | 29 | 1,036 | 1,929 | .. | 1 | 1,844 | 5,716 | 612 | 29,346 | (15) |
| 60,684 | 2,919 | 4 | .. | .. | .. | .. | 5 | 6 | .. | .. | 128 | 16 | 4 | 9,311 | (16) |
| 17 | 645 | .. | .. | .. | .. | .. | .. | .. | .. | .. | 100,525 | 154 | 558 | 2,297 | (17) |
| .. | .. | .. | .. | .. | .. | .. | .. | .. | .. | .. | 886 | 92 | 620 | 12,176 | (18) |
| 3 | .. | .. | 1 | .. | .. | .. | 2,813 | 1,754 | .. | .. | .. | .. | .. | 32,383 | (19) |
| .. | .. | 471 | 5 | 366 | 11 | 8 | .. | .. | 2,255 | 59,209 | .. | .. | .. | 309 | (20) |
| 47 | 188 | 1,240 | 1,313 | 1,117 | 117 | 380 | 103 | 166 | 1,017 | 95 | .. | 92 | 273 | 233,141 | (21) |
| .. | .. | 1,243 | 20 | 1,169 | 12 | 11 | .. | .. | 59,785 | 2,397 | .. | .. | .. | 3,442 | (22) |
| 30 | 9 | .. | .. | .. | .. | .. | 9,464 | 74,702 | .. | .. | 1 | 2 | .. | 1,374 | (23) |
| .. | 2 | 1,743 | 1,211 | 28 | 2,724 | 599 | 5 | 9 | 5 | 3 | .. | 2 | .. | 1,463 | (24) |
| .. | 4 | 192,036 | 1,828 | 7,819 | 4,995 | 2,463 | .. | 1 | 1,876 | 792 | .. | .. | .. | 3,918 | (25) |
| 2 | 16 | .. | 4 | .. | 1 | .. | 94,669 | 10,932 | .. | .. | .. | 5 | .. | 2,163 | (26) |
| 1,008 | 51,187 | .. | .. | .. | .. | .. | 21 | 12 | .. | .. | 669 | 54 | 41 | 11,321 | (27) |
| 6 | 10 | 2,665 | 134 | 560 | 21 | 106 | 5 | .. | 4,532 | 5,739 | 10 | 14 | .. | 8,625 | (28) |
| 387 | 3,273 | .. | .. | .. | .. | .. | .. | 8 | .. | .. | 339 | 6 | 2 | 19,518 | (29) |
| .. | .. | 80 | 6 | 3 | 1 | .. | .. | 1 | .. | 1 | .. | .. | .. | 23,484 | (30) |
| 591 | 164 | .. | .. | .. | .. | .. | .. | 2 | .. | .. | 19 | .. | 3 | 19,103 | (31) |
| .. | .. | 1,374 | .. | 115 | .. | .. | .. | .. | 1,448 | 169 | .. | .. | .. | 31,068 | (32) |
| .. | .. | .. | .. | .. | .. | .. | .. | .. | .. | .. | .. | 22 | 2 | 4,551 | (II) |
| .. | .. | .. | .. | .. | .. | .. | .. | .. | .. | .. | .. | 22 | 2 | 4,551 | (1) |
| 3,729 | 6,755 | 11,620 | 20,330 | 3,778 | 2,776 | 6,751 | 6,236 | 5,352 | 2,190 | 4,340 | 4,042 | 18,529 | 3,106 | 87,530 | 2 |
| **3,347** | **6,462** | **11,539** | **20,308** | **3,742** | **2,766** | **6,682** | **6,064** | **5,274** | **2,135** | **4,312** | **3,989** | **18,132** | **3,003** | **81,597** | (a) |
| **605** | **768** | **2,824** | **20,198** | **2,815** | **1,353** | **6,029** | **603** | **511** | **639** | **537** | **241** | 643 | **112** | **42,406** | 1 |
| 447 | 758 | 2,824 | 20,198 | 2,815 | 1,352 | 6,029 | 595 | 511 | 636 | 533 | 241 | 643 | 112 | 42,368 | (1) |
| 158 | 10 | .. | .. | .. | 1 | .. | 8 | .. | 3 | 4 | .. | .. | .. | 38 | (2) |
| **31** | **131** | **8,342** | **99** | **819** | **1,354** | **621** | **85** | **144** | **1,456** | **3,760** | **25** | **222** | **21** | **11,773** | 2 |
| 31 | 131 | 8,342 | 99 | 819 | 1,354 | 621 | 85 | 144 | 1,456 | 3,760 | 25 | 222 | 21 | 11,773 | (1) |
| .. | .. | .. | .. | .. | .. | .. | .. | .. | .. | .. | .. | .. | .. | .. | (2) |
| **150** | **766** | **16** | **1** | **36** | **3** | **22** | **62** | **28** | **7** | .. | **2,191** | **14,633** | **2,500** | **6,009** | 3 |
| 97 | 651 | 11 | 1 | 29 | 2 | 13 | 62 | 28 | 6 | .. | 2,135 | 11,373 | 878 | 5,382 | (1) |
| 53 | 115 | 5 | .. | 7 | 1 | 9 | .. | .. | 1 | .. | 56 | 3,260 | 1,622 | 627 | (2) |
| **88** | **165** | **1** | .. | .. | .. | .. | **14** | **44** | **3** | .. | **60** | **54** | **56** | **1,214** | 4 |
| **2,473** | **4,632** | **356** | **10** | **72** | **56** | **10** | **5,300** | **4,547** | **30** | **15** | **1,472** | **2,580** | **314** | **20,195** | 5 |
| **382** | **288** | **81** | **22** | **36** | **10** | **69** | **172** | **73** | **55** | **28** | **53** | **397** | **103** | **6,023** | (b) |
| **56** | **61** | **1** | **1** | .. | .. | .. | **20** | **3** | .. | **2** | **9** | **268** | **90** | **105** | 1 |
| **273** | **107** | **39** | .. | **18** | **6** | **50** | **135** | **48** | **26** | **4** | **21** | **45** | **2** | **3,063** | 2 |
| 273 | 95 | 39 | .. | 18 | 6 | 50 | 125 | 47 | 26 | 4 | 18 | 40 | 2 | 2,937 | (1) |
| .. | 12 | .. | .. | .. | .. | .. | 10 | 1 | .. | .. | 3 | 5 | .. | 126 | (2) |
| **17** | .. | **1** | .. | .. | **1** | **1** | **3** | .. | .. | .. | .. | **3** | .. | **17** | 3 |
| .. | **12** | **9** | **8** | .. | .. | .. | **2** | **9** | .. | .. | **7** | .. | **6** | **267** | 4 |
| .. | .. | **2** | .. | .. | .. | .. | .. | .. | .. | .. | .. | .. | .. | .. | 5 |
| .. | **2** | **1** | **13** | **17** | **2** | .. | **3** | **2** | **15** | **18** | .. | **7** | .. | **296** | 6 |
| .. | 2 | 1 | 13 | 17 | 2 | .. | 3 | 2 | 15 | 18 | .. | 7 | .. | 296 | (1) |
| .. | .. | .. | .. | .. | .. | .. | .. | .. | .. | .. | .. | .. | .. | .. | (2) |
| **4** | **11** | **17** | .. | .. | .. | **4** | **4** | **7** | **13** | **4** | **6** | **35** | .. | **295** | 7 |
| .. | **33** | **7** | .. | .. | .. | **10** | **3** | .. | .. | .. | **2** | **8** | .. | **396** | 8 |
| .. | 33 | 7 | .. | .. | .. | 10 | 3 | .. | .. | .. | 2 | 8 | .. | 396 | (1) |
| .. | .. | .. | .. | .. | .. | .. | .. | .. | .. | .. | .. | .. | .. | .. | (2) |
| 1 | 1 | .. | .. | .. | .. | .. | .. | .. | 1 | .. | .. | 1 | .. | 460 | 9 |
| 30 | 30 | 4 | .. | .. | .. | 4 | 2 | 3 | .. | 4 | 7 | 25 | 2 | 1,089 | 10 |
| .. | .. | .. | .. | .. | .. | .. | .. | .. | .. | .. | .. | .. | **2** | **12** | 11 |
| .. | .. | .. | .. | .. | .. | .. | .. | .. | .. | .. | .. | .. | .. | 4 | (1) |
| .. | .. | .. | .. | .. | .. | .. | .. | .. | .. | .. | .. | .. | 2 | 8 | (2) |
| .. | 1 | .. | .. | 1 | .. | .. | .. | 1 | .. | .. | .. | .. | .. | 3 | 12 |
| .. | .. | .. | .. | .. | .. | .. | .. | .. | .. | .. | .. | .. | .. | .. | 13 |
| 1 | 30 | .. | .. | .. | 1 | .. | .. | .. | .. | .. | 1 | 5 | 1 | 110 | 14 |
| *31* | *10* | *22* | .. | *18* | .. | .. | *6* | *2* | *1* | *2* | *23* | *4* | *2* | *4* | *B* |
| *9* | *18* | *5* | .. | .. | *9* | .. | .. | .. | .. | .. | *5* | .. | *3* | *3,085* | *C* |
| .. | .. | .. | .. | .. | .. | .. | .. | .. | .. | .. | .. | *1* | .. | *196* | *D* |
| .. | *4* | .. | .. | .. | .. | .. | .. | .. | .. | .. | .. | *1* | *2* | *76* | *E* |
| .. | .. | .. | .. | .. | .. | .. | .. | .. | .. | .. | .. | .. | .. | *8* | *F* |

## TABLE XII.

### *INFIRMITIES.*

The infirmities recorded at the census were insanity, deaf-mutism, blindness and leprosy.

This table is compiled for the Agency as a whole, showing the distribution of persons afflicted according to age.

Some persons were returned as suffering from more than one infirmity, but as the number of such persons was insignificant statistics of the principal infirmity was recorded, those of the second being ignored.

# TABLE XII.—INFIRMITIES. PART I—DISTRIBUTION BY AGE—AGENCY SUMMARY.

| AGE. | POPULATION AFFLICTED. | | | INSANE. | | | DEAF-MUTES. | | | BLIND. | | | LEPERS. | | |
|---|---|---|---|---|---|---|---|---|---|---|---|---|---|---|---|
| | Persons. | Males. | Females. | Persons. | Males. | Females. | Persons. | Males. | Females. | Persons. | Males. | Females. | Persons. | Males. | Females. |
| 1 | 2 | 3 | 4 | 5 | 6 | 7 | 8 | 9 | 10 | 11 | 12 | 13 | 14 | 15 | 16 |
| **Central India** | **15,256** | **7,934** | **7,322** | **751** | **485** | **266** | **2,159** | **1,302** | **857** | **11,858** | **5,253** | **5,965** | **1,288** | **894** | **394** |
| 0—1 | 51 | 28 | 23 | .. | .. | .. | 8 | 2 | 6 | 42 | 26 | 16 | 1 | .. | 1 |
| 1—2 | 56 | 37 | 19 | .. | .. | .. | 6 | 4 | 2 | 48 | 32 | 16 | 2 | 1 | 1 |
| 2—3 | 129 | 80 | 49 | 6 | 5 | 1 | 12 | 6 | 6 | 109 | 68 | 41 | 2 | 1 | 1 |
| 3—4 | 160 | 100 | 60 | 7 | 6 | 1 | 31 | 20 | 11 | 120 | 74 | 46 | 2 | .. | 2 |
| 4—5 | 176 | 96 | 80 | 5 | 4 | 1 | 39 | 20 | 19 | 130 | 71 | 59 | 2 | 1 | 1 |
| *Total 0—5* | *572* | *341* | *231* | *18* | *15* | *3* | *96* | *52* | *44* | *449* | *271* | *178* | *9* | *3* | *6* |
| 5—10 | 961 | 578 | 383 | 44 | 19 | 25 | 295 | 185 | 110 | 616 | 371 | 245 | 6 | 3 | 3 |
| 10—15 | 891 | 554 | 337 | 81 | 53 | 28 | 258 | 168 | 85 | 534 | 318 | 216 | 23 | 15 | 8 |
| 15—20 | 883 | 540 | 343 | 81 | 58 | 23 | 219 | 133 | 86 | 545 | 326 | 219 | 38 | 23 | 15 |
| 20—25 | 1,111 | 668 | 443 | 79 | 49 | 30 | 243 | 154 | 89 | 699 | 409 | 290 | 90 | 56 | 34 |
| 25—30 | 1,243 | 698 | 545 | 106 | 74 | 32 | 253 | 160 | 93 | 752 | 381 | 371 | 132 | 83 | 49 |
| 30—35 | 1,371 | 766 | 605 | 71 | 46 | 25 | 234 | 154 | 80 | 905 | 452 | 453 | 161 | 114 | 47 |
| 35—40 | 945 | 546 | 399 | 58 | 45 | 13 | 130 | 69 | 61 | 629 | 338 | 291 | 128 | 94 | 34 |
| 40—45 | 1,479 | 774 | 705 | 74 | 42 | 32 | 143 | 80 | 63 | 1,021 | 465 | 556 | 241 | 187 | 54 |
| 45—50 | 767 | 388 | 379 | 40 | 28 | 12 | 66 | 42 | 24 | 549 | 243 | 306 | 112 | 75 | 37 |
| 50—55 | 1,534 | 670 | 864 | 46 | 27 | 19 | 93 | 48 | 45 | 1,213 | 470 | 743 | 182 | 125 | 57 |
| 55—60 | 532 | 256 | 276 | 10 | 6 | 4 | 32 | 14 | 18 | 451 | 207 | 244 | 39 | 29 | 10 |
| 60—65 | 1,594 | 612 | 982 | 27 | 13 | 14 | 62 | 22 | 40 | 1,424 | 525 | 899 | 81 | 52 | 29 |
| 65—70 | 389 | 176 | 213 | 8 | 6 | 2 | 7 | 4 | 3 | 357 | 154 | 203 | 17 | 12 | 5 |
| 70 and over | 984 | 367 | 617 | 8 | 4 | 4 | 33 | 17 | 16 | 914 | 323 | 591 | 29 | 23 | 6 |

PART II.—Distribution by Political Charges is not published.

# TABLE XII-A.

## *INFIRMITIES BY SELECTED CASTES, TRIBES OR RACES.*

**This table shows the distribution of infirmities in selected Castes, Tribes or Races.**

# TABLE XII-A.—Infirmities by Selected Castes, Tribes or Races—Agency Summary.

| Serial Number. | Caste, Tribe or Race. | Total Population dealt with. | | | Insane. | | | Deaf-Mutes. | | | Blind. | | | Lepers. | | |
|---|---|---|---|---|---|---|---|---|---|---|---|---|---|---|---|---|
| | | Persons. | Males. | Females. | Persons. | Males. | Females. | Persons. | Males. | Females. | Persons. | Males. | Females. | Persons. | Males. | Females. |
| 1 | 2 | 3 | 4 | 5 | 6 | 7 | 8 | 9 | 10 | 11 | 12 | 13 | 14 | 15 | 16 | 17 |
| | **Central India** | **3,421,731** | **1,753,092** | **1,668,639** | **348** | **225** | **123** | **925** | **552** | **373** | **4,242** | **2,090** | **2,152** | **476** | **333** | **143** |
| 1 | Ajna | 26,465 | 15,172 | 11,293 | 2 | 2 | .. | 2 | 1 | 1 | 14 | 7 | 7 | 6 | 4 | 2 |
| 2 | Bania | 163,200 | 79,509 | 83,691 | 23 | 17 | 6 | 80 | 38 | 42 | 317 | 175 | 142 | 15 | 11 | 4 |
| | *(1) Agarwal* | *58,288* | *27,710* | *30,578* | *3* | *2* | *1* | *34* | *12* | *22* | *82* | *41* | *41* | *4* | *3* | *1* |
| | *(2) Gahoi* | *25,082* | *13,657* | *11,425* | *4* | *3* | *1* | *11* | *7* | *4* | *78* | *41* | *37* | *3* | *2* | *1* |
| | *(3) Kasaundhan* | *8,787* | *4,213* | *4,574* | .. | .. | .. | .. | .. | .. | *1* | .. | *1* | *1* | *1* | .. |
| | *(4) Kesar Bania* | *14,469* | *7,433* | *7,036* | .. | .. | .. | *3* | *3* | .. | *9* | *5* | *4* | .. | .. | .. |
| | *(5) Kharia* | *4,497* | *1,800* | *2,697* | *1* | .. | *1* | .. | .. | .. | *1* | .. | *1* | .. | .. | .. |
| | *(6) Meheshri* | *21,412* | *10,008* | *11,404* | *1* | *1* | .. | *4* | *3* | *1* | *25* | *16* | *9* | .. | .. | .. |
| | *(7) Oswal* | *14,309* | *6,072* | *8,237* | *9* | *6* | *3* | *15* | *5* | *10* | *62* | *40* | *22* | *3* | *1* | *2* |
| | *(8) Porwal, Porwad* | *16,356* | *8,616* | *7,740* | *5* | *5* | .. | *13* | *8* | *5* | *59* | *32* | *27* | *4* | *4* | .. |
| 3 | Bhat | 25,161 | 13,181 | 11,980 | 4 | 2 | 2 | 9 | 6 | 3 | 43 | 21 | 22 | 5 | 3 | 2 |
| 4 | Bhil | 25,831 | 13,693 | 12,138 | 17 | 11 | 6 | 65 | 36 | 29 | 126 | 54 | 72 | 68 | 49 | 19 |
| 5 | Bhilala | 33,764 | 16,351 | 17,413 | 18 | 11 | 7 | 55 | 24 | 31 | 120 | 63 | 57 | 40 | 31 | 9 |
| 6 | Brahman— | 577,968 | 289,803 | 288,165 | 65 | 51 | 14 | 185 | 122 | 63 | 717 | 368 | 349 | 65 | 37 | 28 |
| | *(1) Bhagor* | *32,480* | *17,035* | *15,445* | *3* | *2* | *1* | *8* | *7* | *1* | *46* | *20* | *26* | *5* | *2* | *3* |
| | *(2) Jijhotia* | *63,932* | *33,696* | *30,236* | *8* | *4* | *4* | *28* | *13* | *15* | *141* | *68* | *73* | *14* | *8* | *6* |
| | *(3) Sanadhya* | *159,124* | *81,579* | *77,545* | *21* | *16* | *5* | *51* | *37* | *14* | *289* | *155* | *134* | *20* | *16* | *4* |
| | *(4) Sarwaria* | *303,206* | *147,925* | *155,281* | *29* | *25* | *4* | *95* | *62* | *33* | *213* | *110* | *103* | *21* | *8* | *13* |
| | *(5) Shrigaud* | *15,031* | *7,780* | *7,251* | *4* | *4* | .. | *2* | *2* | .. | *25* | *13* | *12* | *5* | *3* | *2* |
| | *(6) Shrimali* | *4,195* | *1,788* | *2,407* | .. | .. | .. | *1* | *1* | .. | *3* | *2* | *1* | .. | .. | .. |
| 7 | Chamar | 859,438 | 435,873 | 423,565 | 49 | 23 | 26 | 154 | 91 | 63 | 1,101 | 502 | 599 | 108 | 72 | 36 |
| 8 | Dhangar | 5,608 | 3,027 | 2,581 | 1 | 1 | .. | 1 | .. | 1 | 5 | 3 | 2 | .. | .. | .. |
| 9 | Gond | 163,285 | 76,753 | 86,532 | 9 | 5 | 4 | 27 | 17 | 10 | 165 | 75 | 90 | 5 | 5 | .. |
| 10 | Gujar | 185,728 | 105,834 | 79,894 | 10 | 7 | 3 | 38 | 21 | 17 | 230 | 125 | 105 | 17 | 13 | 4 |
| 11 | Kachera | 6,394 | 3,197 | 3,197 | .. | .. | .. | 1 | 1 | .. | 4 | 3 | 1 | .. | .. | .. |
| 12 | Khangar | 38,443 | 20,173 | 18,270 | 3 | 2 | 1 | 11 | 4 | 7 | 33 | 21 | 12 | 3 | 3 | .. |
| 13 | Kol | 186,363 | 89,446 | 96,917 | 11 | 7 | 4 | 36 | 21 | 15 | 97 | 45 | 52 | 6 | 5 | 1 |
| 14 | Kotwal | 27,086 | 14,537 | 12,549 | 1 | .. | 1 | 3 | 2 | 1 | 13 | 2 | 11 | 1 | 1 | .. |
| 15 | Maratha | 28,008 | 14,821 | 13,187 | 1 | 1 | .. | 4 | 2 | 2 | 14 | 8 | 6 | 1 | 1 | .. |
| 16 | Mina | 71,068 | 36,632 | 34,436 | 15 | 10 | 5 | 19 | 13 | 6 | 95 | 41 | 54 | 12 | 8 | 4 |
| 17 | Pathan | 138,522 | 73,476 | 65,046 | 21 | 15 | 6 | 33 | 18 | 15 | 168 | 100 | 68 | 14 | 12 | 2 |
| 18 | Rajput— | 335,636 | 184,086 | 151,550 | 33 | 22 | 11 | 68 | 53 | 15 | 340 | 171 | 169 | 48 | 34 | 14 |
| | *(1) Baghela* | *24,852* | *12,708* | *12,144* | .. | .. | .. | *4* | *2* | *2* | *5* | *4* | *1* | .. | .. | .. |
| | *(2) Bhadauria* | *23,343* | *13,501* | *9,842* | *4* | *4* | .. | *6* | *5* | *1* | *29* | *24* | *5* | *3* | *3* | .. |
| | *(3) Bundela* | *17,362* | *8,785* | *8,577* | *6* | *3* | *3* | *4* | *2* | *2* | *27* | *8* | *19* | *5* | *5* | .. |
| | *(4) Chauhan* | *39,978* | *19,056* | *20,922* | *4* | *3* | *1* | *9* | *6* | *3* | *31* | *18* | *13* | *3* | *1* | *2* |
| | *(5) Dhandhera* | *3,759* | *1,929* | *1,830* | *1* | *1* | .. | .. | .. | .. | .. | .. | .. | *1* | *1* | .. |
| | *(6) Dikhit* | *1,330* | *784* | *546* | .. | .. | .. | .. | .. | .. | *1* | *1* | .. | .. | .. | .. |
| | *(7) Gaharwar* | *2,344* | *1,231* | *1,113* | *1* | *1* | .. | *2* | *1* | *1* | *4* | *4* | .. | .. | .. | .. |
| | *(8) Gahlot* | *23,653* | *14,288* | *9,365* | *1* | .. | *1* | *4* | *4* | .. | *59* | *11* | *48* | *7* | *4* | *3* |
| | *(9) Gaur* | *7,293* | *3,968* | *3,325* | *1* | *1* | .. | *4* | *3* | *1* | *7* | *4* | *3* | *1* | .. | *1* |
| | *(10) Kachhwaha* | *24,420* | *12,550* | *11,870* | *1* | .. | *1* | *7* | *6* | *1* | *19* | *11* | *8* | *5* | *3* | *2* |
| | *(11) Parihar* | *18,208* | *9,796* | *8,412* | *1* | *1* | .. | .. | .. | .. | *10* | *6* | *4* | *1* | .. | *1* |
| | *(12) Ponwar Maratha* | *606* | *311* | *295* | .. | .. | .. | .. | .. | .. | *1* | .. | *1* | .. | .. | .. |
| | *(13) Ponwar Rajput* | *42,696* | *24,021* | *18,675* | *4* | *3* | *1* | *13* | *11* | *2* | *62* | *24* | *38* | *4* | *2* | *2* |
| | *(14) Rathor* | *33,395* | *18,479* | *14,916* | *2* | *2* | .. | *5* | *5* | .. | *20* | *13* | *7* | *6* | *6* | .. |
| | *(15) Sengar* | *10,819* | *4,817* | *6,002* | *2* | *1* | *1* | *1* | *1* | .. | *11* | *8* | *3* | *1* | *1* | .. |
| | *(16) Sisodia* | *8,575* | *4,321* | *4,254* | *2* | .. | *2* | *1* | *1* | .. | *9* | *6* | *3* | *1* | *1* | .. |
| | *(17) Solanki* | *15,901* | *8,771* | *7,130* | .. | .. | .. | *1* | *1* | .. | *17* | *7* | *10* | *3* | *3* | .. |
| | *(18) Tonwar, Tawar* | *37,102* | *24,770* | *12,332* | *3* | *2* | *1* | *7* | *5* | *2* | *28* | *22* | *6* | *7* | *4* | *3* |
| 19 | Saharia | 49,244 | 25,373 | 23,871 | 3 | 2 | 1 | 6 | 3 | 3 | 40 | 17 | 23 | 7 | 5 | 2 |
| 20 | Saiyad | 32,197 | 17,459 | 14,738 | 7 | 3 | 4 | 11 | 6 | 5 | 29 | 15 | 14 | 4 | 3 | 1 |
| 21 | Shaikh— | 186,773 | 96,654 | 90,119 | 40 | 28 | 12 | 72 | 44 | 28 | 286 | 144 | 142 | 26 | 18 | 8 |
| | *(1) Behna* | *24,368* | *12,323* | *12,045* | .. | .. | .. | *3* | *2* | *1* | *13* | *5* | *8* | .. | .. | .. |
| | *(2) Chhipa* | *2,919* | *1,518* | *1,401* | .. | .. | .. | *2* | *1* | *1* | *5* | *2* | *3* | *1* | .. | *1* |
| | *(3) Julaha* | *12,270* | *6,554* | *5,716* | .. | .. | .. | *2* | *2* | .. | *3* | *1* | *2* | *1* | *1* | .. |
| | *(4) Shaikh* | *147,216* | *76,259* | *70,957* | *40* | *28* | *12* | *65* | *39* | *26* | *265* | *136* | *129* | *24* | *17* | *7* |
| 22 | Sondhia | 70,546 | 32,662 | 37,884 | 5 | 2 | 3 | 8 | 6 | 2 | 69 | 29 | 40 | 11 | 11 | .. |
| 23 | Teli | 185,393 | 96,168 | 89,225 | 10 | 3 | 7 | 37 | 23 | 14 | 216 | 101 | 115 | 14 | 7 | 7 |

# TABLE XIII.

## *CASTE, TRIBE OR RACE.*

This table deals with the Castes and Tribes of Hindus, Arya Samajists, Brahmos, Sikhs, Jains, Animists and Musalmans for the Agency as a whole.

The figures for Christians are omitted from this table as they are specially dealt with in Tables XVII and XVIII. The figures for Parsis and Jews are also omitted.

"Minor castes" include returns numerically insignificant.

A few castes whose proper affiliation was uncertain and cases which did not return any real caste name have been grouped under the head "Unspecified."

# TABLE XIII.—Caste, Tribe or Race. Agency Summary.

| Serial No. | Caste, Tribe or Race. | Population. Persons. | Males. | Females. |
|---|---|---|---|---|
| 1 | 2 | 3 | 4 | 5 |
| | **Central India** | **9,346,235** | **4,794,566** | **4,551,669** |
| | ***HINDU*** | ***8,262,638*** | ***4,241,694*** | ***4,020,944*** |
| 1 | Ahir | 281,425 | 143,549 | 137,876 |
| 2 | Ajna | 26,465 | 15,172 | 11,293 |
| 3 | Arakh | 2,529 | 1,360 | 1,169 |
| 4 | Bagri | 52,907 | 25,471 | 27,436 |
| 5 | Bahelia | 1,282 | 327 | 955 |
| 6 | Baiga | 23,161 | 9,430 | 13,731 |
| 7 | Bairagi | 49,106 | 28,851 | 20,255 |
| 8 | Balai | 139,885 | 65,313 | 74,572 |
| 9 | Bania | 286,446 | 139,527 | 146,919 |
| | (1) *Agarwal* | *58,288* | *27,710* | *30,578* |
| | (2) *Bhalera* | *3,189* | *1,569* | *1,641* |
| | (3) *Bijawargi* | *4,795* | *2,256* | *2,539* |
| | (4) *Chitora* | *3,353* | *1,552* | *1,801* |
| | (5) *Deshawal* | *2,394* | *1,263* | *1,131* |
| | (6) *Dhusar* | *51* | *27* | *24* |
| | (7) *Gahohi* | *25,082* | *13,657* | *11,425* |
| | (8) *Kasaundhan* | *8,787* | *4,213* | *4,574* |
| | (9) *Kesar Bania* | *14,469* | *7,433* | *7,036* |
| | (10) *Khanderwal* | *9,759* | *4,728* | *5,031* |
| | (11) *Kharia* | *4,497* | *1,800* | *2,697* |
| | (12) *Mahesri* | *21,412* | *10,008* | *11,404* |
| | (13) *Miratwal* | *2,907* | *1,569* | *1,338* |
| | (14) *Mod* | *4,671* | *2,118* | *2,553* |
| | (15) *Nima* | *2,046* | *771* | *1,275* |
| | (16) *Oswal* | *14,309* | *6,072* | *8,237* |
| | (17) *Porwal, Porwad* | *16,356* | *8,616* | *7,740* |
| | (18) *Saraogi* | *7,248* | *3,272* | *3,976* |
| | (19) *Others* | *82,842* | *40,893* | *41,949* |
| 10 | Banjara | 31,257 | 18,528 | 12,729 |
| 11 | Bansphor | 52,465 | 28,451 | 24,014 |
| 12 | Barai | 9,588 | 5,196 | 4,392 |
| 13 | Bargahi | 4,752 | 2,771 | 1,981 |
| 14 | Bari | 13,767 | 6,804 | 6,963 |
| 15 | Bargunda | 7,113 | 3,703 | 3,410 |
| 16 | Bedia | 7,998 | 3,215 | 4,783 |
| 17 | Beldar | 26,172 | 12,901 | 13,271 |
| 18 | Bemariha | 1,021 | 334 | 687 |
| 19 | Bhawaiya | 12,429 | 5,292 | 7,137 |
| 20 | Bhambhi | 7,744 | 2,885 | 4,859 |
| 21 | Bhand | 2,216 | 1,020 | 1,196 |
| 22 | Bhangi | 52,902 | 25,243 | 27,659 |
| 23 | Bhar | 844 | 407 | 437 |
| 24 | Bharbhunja | 5,673 | 2,592 | 3,081 |
| 25 | Bharewa | 22,709 | 12,961 | 9,748 |
| 26 | Bharud | 47,181 | 22,795 | 24,386 |
| 27 | Bhat | 25,161 | 13,181 | 11,980 |
| 28 | Bhil | 25,831 | 13,693 | 12,138 |
| 29 | Bhilala | 33,764 | 16,351 | 17,413 |
| 30 | Bhoi | 51,845 | 29,518 | 22,327 |
| 31 | Bhopa | 1,210 | 566 | 644 |
| 32 | Bhumia | 5,463 | 2,793 | 2,670 |
| 33 | Brahman | 986,050 | 519,389 | 466,661 |
| | (1) *Adgod, Adgaur* | *7,322* | *3,646* | *3,676* |
| | (2) *Ametha* | *1,860* | *914* | *946* |
| | (3) *Bhadauria* | *8,157* | *3,998* | *4,159* |
| | (4) *Bhagor* | *32,480* | *17,035* | *15,445* |
| | (5) *Chauvisa* | *3,475* | *1,816* | *1,659* |
| | (6) *Dakshani* | *33,813* | *18,031* | *15,782* |
| | *Deshastha* | *22,931* | *12,180* | *10,751* |
| | *Karhada* | *3,820* | *2,160* | *1,660* |
| | *Konknastha* | *7,062* | *3,691* | *3,371* |
| | (7) *Gujargaur* | *19,170* | *10,268* | *8,902* |
| | (8) *Gaur* | *8,020* | *4,502* | *3,518* |
| | (9) *Gujarathi* | *39,512* | *22,045* | *17,467* |
| | (10) *Jijhotia* | *63,932* | *33,696* | *30,236* |
| | (11) *Kanaujia* | *80,512* | *41,860* | *38,652* |
| | (12) *Kashmiri* | *631* | *338* | *293* |
| | (13) *Nagar* | *12,749* | *6,837* | *5,912* |
| | (14) *Audich* | *13,737* | *7,721* | *6,016* |
| | (15) *Audumbar* | *4,612* | *2,626* | *1,986* |
| | (16) *Palliwal* | *9,228* | *4,615* | *4,613* |
| | (17) *Rukhshara* | *9,124* | *5,459* | *3,665* |
| | (18) *Sachora* | *2,547* | *1,240* | *1,307* |
| | (19) *Sanadhya* | *159,124* | *81,579* | *77,545* |
| | (20) *Saraswat* | *10,303* | *5,058* | *5,245* |
| | (21) *Sarwa* | *303,206* | *147,925* | *155,281* |
| | (22) *Shenavi* | *5,267* | *2,846* | *2,421* |
| | (23) *Shrigaud* | *15,031* | *7,780* | *7,251* |
| | (24) *Shrimali* | *4,195* | *1,788* | *2,407* |
| | (25) *Others* | *138,043* | *85,766* | *52,277* |
| 34 | Bunkar | 8,187 | 4,060 | 4,127 |
| 35 | Chamar | 859,438 | 435,873 | 423,565 |
| 36 | Charan. See Bhat | 3,602 | 1,676 | 1,926 |
| 37 | Chhipa | 14,830 | 7,198 | 7,632 |
| 38 | Chidar | 11,695 | 6,196 | 5,499 |
| 39 | Dahayat | 2,771 | 1,274 | 1,497 |
| 40 | Dangi | 62,819 | 33,369 | 29,450 |
| 41 | Darzi, Chhipi | 58,024 | 31,165 | 26,859 |
| 42 | Deswali | 33,780 | 17,787 | 15,993 |
| 43 | Dhakad | 63,463 | 29,291 | 34,172 |
| 44 | Dhami | 634 | 319 | 315 |
| 45 | Dhangar | 5,608 | 3,027 | 2,581 |

| Serial No. | Caste, Tribe or Race. | Population. Persons. | Males. | Females. |
|---|---|---|---|---|
| 1 | 2 | 3 | 4 | 5 |
| | ***HINDU*—contd.** | | | |
| 46 | Dhanuk | 7,736 | 3,767 | 3,969 |
| 47 | Dhimar | 88,776 | 45,111 | 43,665 |
| 48 | Dhirkar | 5,413 | 2,297 | 3,116 |
| 49 | Dhobi | 81,765 | 41,569 | 40,196 |
| 50 | Dholi or Damami | 15,340 | 8,009 | 7,331 |
| 51 | Dom | 294 | 119 | 175 |
| 52 | Gadaria | 159,762 | 82,682 | 77,080 |
| 53 | Gandhi | 5,948 | 2,820 | 3,128 |
| 54 | Gaoli | 44,294 | 22,790 | 21,504 |
| 55 | Gond | 163,285 | 76,753 | 86,532 |
| 56 | Gondhali | 85 | 46 | 39 |
| 57 | Gusain | 21,443 | 11,801 | 9,642 |
| 58 | Gujar | 185,728 | 105,834 | 79,894 |
| 59 | Gurao | 257 | 98 | 159 |
| 60 | Jaga | 474 | 199 | 275 |
| 61 | Jat | 46,578 | 24,187 | 22,391 |
| 62 | Jhamral | 707 | 362 | 345 |
| 63 | Jingar | 819 | 446 | 373 |
| 64 | Jogi | 15,100 | 7,806 | 7,294 |
| 65 | Joshi | 9,581 | 5,015 | 4,566 |
| 66 | Kachera | 6,394 | 3,197 | 3,197 |
| 67 | Kachhi | 371,793 | 181,832 | 189,961 |
| 68 | Kahar | 56,835 | 29,086 | 27,749 |
| 69 | Kanghigar | 563 | 228 | 335 |
| 70 | Kalal | 63,663 | 32,766 | 30,897 |
| 71 | Kalbelia | 5,163 | 3,063 | 2,100 |
| 72 | Kalota | 22,033 | 12,378 | 9,655 |
| 73 | Kandera | 19,792 | 10,148 | 9,644 |
| 74 | Kanjar | 1,456 | 592 | 864 |
| 75 | Kasera | 3,704 | 2,166 | 1,538 |
| 76 | Kayasth | 71,392 | 38,434 | 32,958 |
| 77 | Kir | 6,370 | 3,214 | 3,156 |
| 78 | Kewat | 29,304 | 12,411 | 16,893 |
| 79 | Khangar | 38,443 | 20,173 | 18,270 |
| 80 | Kharol | 2,978 | 1,308 | 1,670 |
| 81 | Khati | 107,428 | 54,785 | 52,643 |
| 82 | Khatik | 20,566 | 11,547 | 9,019 |
| 83 | Khatri | 4,889 | 3,208 | 1,681 |
| 84 | Kirar | 86,885 | 45,547 | 41,338 |
| 85 | Kol | 186,363 | 89,446 | 96,917 |
| 86 | Koli | 173,645 | 84,956 | 88,689 |
| 87 | Komti | 1,186 | 508 | 678 |
| 88 | Korku | 19,774 | 8,674 | 11,100 |
| 89 | Koshti | 2,043 | 1,003 | 1,040 |
| 90 | Kotwal | 27,086 | 14,537 | 12,549 |
| 91 | Kunbi | 215,359 | 104,235 | 111,124 |
| 92 | Kumawat | 5,217 | 2,576 | 2,641 |
| 93 | Kumhar | 143,886 | 73,765 | 70,121 |
| 94 | Labhana | 3,505 | 1,365 | 2,140 |
| 95 | Lakhera | 8,643 | 4,715 | 3,928 |
| 96 | Loda | 13,943 | 6,822 | 7,121 |
| 97 | Lodhi | 228,235 | 120,311 | 107,924 |
| 98 | Lohar | 95,374 | 49,117 | 46,257 |
| 99 | Lunia | 1,513 | 821 | 692 |
| 100 | Mahar | 6,280 | 3,056 | 3,224 |
| 101 | Majhi | 20,611 | 13,372 | 7,239 |
| 102 | Mali | 72,462 | 37,403 | 35,059 |
| 103 | Mallah | 7,928 | 3,152 | 4,776 |
| 104 | Manihar | 1,757 | 755 | 1,002 |
| 105 | Mang | 584 | 321 | 263 |
| 106 | Mankar | 9,065 | 4,339 | 4,726 |
| 107 | Maratha | 28,008 | 14,821 | 13,187 |
| 108 | Maru | 2,903 | 1,426 | 1,477 |
| 109 | Mawasi | 5,241 | 2,569 | 2,672 |
| 110 | Mir | 8,620 | 4,212 | 4,408 |
| 111 | Mina | 71,068 | 36,632 | 34,436 |
| 112 | Minor Castes | 19,835 | 9,876 | 9,959 |
| | (1) *Barwal* | *303* | *150* | *153* |
| | (2) *Chunpach* | *58* | *44* | *14* |
| | (3) *Dadopanthi* | *60* | *47* | *13* |
| | (4) *Dakotra* | *281* | *152* | *129* |
| | (5) *Darugar* | *649* | *397* | *252* |
| | (6) *Dhadhi* | *217* | *147* | *70* |
| | (7) *Halwai* | *2,916* | *1,172* | *1,744* |
| | (8) *Harbola* | *379* | *151* | *228* |
| | (9) *Kamanigar* | *206* | *145* | *61* |
| | (10) *Kanarchi* | *248* | *134* | *114* |
| | (11) *Katia* | *686* | *451* | *235* |
| | (12) *Kherwar* | *454* | *178* | *276* |
| | (13) *Khojia* | *91* | *68* | *23* |
| | (14) *Kuchbandhia* | *260* | *128* | *132* |
| | (15) *Lilgar* | *41* | *29* | *12* |
| | (16) *Meghwal* | *1,167* | *562* | *605* |
| | (17) *Mirasi* | *597* | *347* | *250* |
| | (18) *Pal* | *710* | *395* | *315* |
| | (19) *Ruwala* | *3,377* | *1,727* | *1,650* |
| | (20) *Sansi* | *580* | *247* | *333* |
| | (21) *Silawat* | *5,959* | *2,933* | *3,026* |
| | (22) *Sonkar* | *596* | *272* | *324* |
| 113 | Mirdha | 16,936 | 11,545 | 5,391 |
| 114 | Mochi | 5,266 | 3,055 | 2,211 |
| 115 | Moghia | 11,197 | 5,927 | 5,270 |

# TABLE XIII.—Caste, Tribe or Race. Agency Summary—*continued.*

| Serial No. | Caste, Tribe or Race. | Population. Persons. | Males. | Females. |
|---|---|---|---|---|
| 1 | 2 | 3 | 4 | 5 |
| | ***HINDU*—concld.** | | | |
| 116 | Nahal | 1,055 | 473 | 582 |
| 117 | Nai | 155,538 | 76,974 | 78,564 |
| 118 | Naik | 9,776 | 5,301 | 4,475 |
| 119 | Nat | 8,347 | 4,566 | 3,781 |
| 120 | Nath | 12,309 | 6,829 | 5,480 |
| 121 | Ode | 2,124 | 1,349 | 775 |
| 122 | Panika | 26,656 | 13,732 | 12,924 |
| 123 | Parbhu | 1,587 | 818 | 769 |
| 124 | Pardhi | 24,594 | 9,749 | 14,845 |
| 125 | Pasi | 8,085 | 3,472 | 4,613 |
| 126 | Patl'a | 21,616 | 13,568 | 8,048 |
| 127 | Patwa | 3,199 | 1,794 | 1,405 |
| 128 | Pinjara | 2,943 | 1,331 | 1,612 |
| 129 | Rehewari (Rewari) | 3,741 | 1,977 | 1,764 |
| 130 | Rajput | 755,819 | 411,527 | 344,292 |
| | (1) *Badgujar* | *15,979* | *7,971* | *8,008* |
| | (2) *Baghe'a* | *24,852* | *12,708* | *12,144* |
| | (3) *Banafar* | *6,566* | *3,214* | *3,352* |
| | (4) *Bhadauria* | *23,343* | *13,501* | *9,842* |
| | (5) *Bhali* | *1,926* | *957* | *969* |
| | (6) *Bundela* | *17,362* | *8,785* | *8,577* |
| | (7) *Bundela Ponwar* | *301* | *266* | *35* |
| | (8) *Chandel* | *7,589* | *3,835* | *3,754* |
| | (9) *Chandrawat* | *5,086* | *2,675* | *2,411* |
| | (10) *Chaoda* | *3,074* | *1,553* | *1,521* |
| | (11) *Chhatri Rajput* | *61,644* | *34,732* | *26,912* |
| | (12) *Chohan (Chauhan)* | *39,978* | *19,056* | *20,922* |
| | (13) *Chorasia* | *6,838* | *3,652* | *3,186* |
| | (14) *Deora* | *11,342* | *6,178* | *5,164* |
| | (15) *Dhandhera* | *3,759* | *1,929* | *1,830* |
| | (16) *Dikhit* | *1,330* | *784* | *546* |
| | (17) *Gaharwar* | *2,344* | *1,231* | *1,113* |
| | (18) *Gahlot* | *23,653* | *14,288* | *9,365* |
| | (19) *Gaur* | *7,293* | *3,968* | *3,325* |
| | (20) *Goyal* | *3,026* | *1,714* | *1,312* |
| | (21) *Hazuri* | *6,068* | *3,173* | *2,895* |
| | (22) *Jadon* | *11,987* | *6,186* | *5,801* |
| | (23) *Kachhwaha* | *24,420* | *12,550* | *11,870* |
| | (24) *Kamar* | *4,383* | *2,056* | *2,327* |
| | (25) *Khichhi* | *2,519* | *1,386* | *1,133* |
| | (26) *Makwana* | *1,438* | *691* | *747* |
| | (27) *Nandbansi* | *1,979* | *769* | *1,210* |
| | (28) *Parihar* | *18,208* | *9,796* | *8,412* |
| | (29) *Ponwar Maratha* | *606* | *311* | *295* |
| | (30) *Ponwar Rajput* | *42,696* | *24,021* | *18,675* |
| | (31) *Parmar* | *108,760* | *61,121* | *47,639* |
| | (32) *Raghubansi* | *39,733* | *21,478* | *18,255* |
| | (33) *Rathor* | *33,395* | *18,479* | *14,916* |
| | (34) *Sendho* | *71,043* | *39,005* | *32,038* |
| | (35) *Sengar* | *10,819* | *4,817* | *6,002* |
| | (36) *Sisodia* | *8,575* | *4,321* | *4,254* |
| | (37) *Sikarwar* | *8,643* | *3,835* | *4,898* |
| | (38) *Solanki* | *15,901* | *8,771* | *7,130* |
| | (39) *Tonwar, Tawar* | *37,102* | *24,770* | *12,332* |
| | (40) *Thakur* | *5,681* | *2,852* | *2,829* |
| | (41) *Umat* | *1,980* | *1,205* | *775* |
| | (42) *Others* | *32,598* | *16,937* | *15,661* |
| 131 | Rangara | 4,475 | 2,358 | 2,117 |
| 132 | Rawat | 63,601 | 32,982 | 30,619 |
| 133 | Saharia | 49,244 | 25,373 | 23,871 |
| 134 | Salvi | 2,731 | 1,757 | 974 |
| 135 | Sanyasi | 3,411 | 1,846 | 1,565 |
| 136 | Sikligar | 1,811 | 968 | 843 |
| 137 | Sirvi | 13,645 | 6,990 | 6,655 |
| 138 | Sonar and Med Sonar | 66,612 | 34,387 | 32,225 |
| 139 | Sondhia | 70,546 | 32,662 | 37,884 |
| 140 | Sor | 13,783 | 5,924 | 7,859 |
| 141 | Sutar | 115,167 | 59,400 | 55,767 |
| 142 | Tambat | 5,743 | 3,188 | 2,555 |
| 143 | Tamboli | 15,149 | 8,736 | 6,413 |
| 144 | Teli | 185,393 | 96,168 | 89,225 |
| 145 | Vidur | 1,182 | 467 | 715 |
| 146 | Unspecified | 1,975 | 1,098 | 877 |
| | ***ARYA*** | ***139*** | ***90*** | ***49*** |
| | Arya | 189 | 90 | 49 |
| | ***BRAHMO*** | ***9*** | ***6*** | ***3*** |
| | Deshasth | 9 | 6 | 3 |
| | ***SIKH*** | ***1,384*** | ***953*** | ***431*** |
| 1 | Arora | 401 | 221 | 180 |
| 2 | Brahman | 156 | 91 | 65 |
| 3 | Jat | 582 | 474 | 108 |
| 4 | Kshatri | 128 | 87 | 41 |
| 5 | Soni | 117 | 80 | 37 |
| | ***JAIN*** | ***87,471*** | ***45,711*** | ***41,760*** |
| 1 | Agarwal | 3,135 | 1,521 | 1,614 |
| 2 | Aso | 138 | 81 | 57 |
| 3 | Bhatera | 285 | 185 | 100 |
| | ***JAIN*—contd.** | | | |
| 4 | Bijawargi | 384 | 199 | 185 |
| 5 | Bisnia | 698 | 347 | 351 |
| 6 | Choska | 392 | 222 | 170 |
| 7 | Gelora | 171 | 62 | 109 |
| 8 | Godwal | 51 | 31 | 20 |
| 9 | Golanalal | 1,487 | 787 | 700 |
| 10 | Gothwal | 234 | 125 | 103 |
| 11 | Gujarathi | 837 | 393 | 444 |
| 12 | Jaiswal | 1,981 | 1,148 | 833 |
| 13 | Jati | 94 | 46 | 48 |
| 14 | Khanderwal | 156 | 96 | 60 |
| 15 | Khariwal | 66 | 37 | 29 |
| 16 | Lad | 94 | 37 | 57 |
| 17 | Lodasa | 204 | 97 | 107 |
| 18 | Mahesri | 1,738 | 1,048 | 690 |
| 19 | Mod | 224 | 108 | 116 |
| 20 | Nima | 8,276 | 4,968 | 3,308 |
| 21 | Oswal | 32,956 | 16,764 | 16,192 |
| 22 | Palliwal | 310 | 200 | 110 |
| 23 | Porwal | 22,703 | 11,417 | 11,286 |
| 24 | Saraogi | 10,719 | 5,718 | 5,001 |
| 25 | Unspecified | 138 | 74 | 64 |
| | ***ANIMIST*** | ***483,394*** | ***239,618*** | ***243,776*** |
| 1 | Bharud | 1,669 | 812 | 857 |
| 2 | Bhil | 269,910 | 134,045 | 135,865 |
| 3 | Bhilala | 89,612 | 44,821 | 44,791 |
| 4 | Gond | 71,387 | 34,611 | 36,776 |
| 5 | Kirar | 3,037 | 1,541 | 1,496 |
| 6 | Kol | 6,284 | 3,161 | 3,123 |
| 7 | Korku | 5,597 | 2,686 | 2,911 |
| 8 | Kotwal | 523 | 254 | 269 |
| 9 | Mina | 3,568 | 1,495 | 2,073 |
| 10 | Patlia | 9 | 5 | 4 |
| 11 | Saharia | 31,798 | 16,187 | 15,611 |
| | ***MUSALMAN*** | ***511,200*** | ***266,494*** | ***244,706*** |
| 1 | Badigar | 222 | 123 | 99 |
| 2 | Banjara | 503 | 277 | 226 |
| 3 | Badhai | 1,462 | 798 | 664 |
| 4 | Bawarchi | 129 | 65 | 64 |
| 5 | Beldar | 206 | 136 | 70 |
| 6 | Bhat | 397 | 221 | 176 |
| 7 | Bhangi | 3,872 | 2,114 | 1,758 |
| 8 | Bharbhunja | 283 | 139 | 144 |
| 9 | Bhisti | 1,916 | 1,099 | 817 |
| 10 | Bohra | 15,922 | 8,473 | 7,449 |
| 11 | Dafali | 5,043 | 3,186 | 1,857 |
| 12 | Darzi | 1,297 | 759 | 538 |
| 13 | Dhobi | 640 | 372 | 268 |
| 14 | Faquir | 11,871 | 6,361 | 5,510 |
| 15 | Ghosi | 305 | 152 | 153 |
| 16 | Halwai | 294 | 112 | 182 |
| 17 | Hammal | 224 | 114 | 110 |
| 18 | Kachchi | 703 | 525 | 178 |
| 19 | Khoja | 33 | 20 | 13 |
| 20 | Kumhar | 1,388 | 677 | 711 |
| 21 | Kunjra | 2,105 | 1,100 | 1,005 |
| 22 | Lakhera | 857 | 449 | 408 |
| 23 | Lohar | 1,170 | 491 | 679 |
| 24 | Makrani | 337 | 163 | 174 |
| 25 | Manihar | 254 | 124 | 130 |
| 26 | Memar | 376 | 238 | 138 |
| 27 | Mewati | 12,786 | 6,243 | 6,543 |
| 28 | Mirasi | 416 | 168 | 248 |
| 29 | Mochi | 860 | 456 | 404 |
| 30 | Mokeri | 2,507 | 1,242 | 1,265 |
| 31 | Mughal | 18,468 | 9,973 | 8,495 |
| 32 | Nai | 857 | 490 | 367 |
| 33 | Naita | 5,553 | 2,983 | 2,570 |
| 34 | Nargir | 592 | 349 | 243 |
| 35 | Nat | 1,180 | 661 | 519 |
| 36 | Pathan | 138,522 | 73,476 | 65,046 |
| 37 | Pindara | 4,014 | 2,074 | 1,940 |
| 38 | Pinjara | 16,048 | 7,818 | 8,230 |
| 39 | Qaligar | 445 | 227 | 218 |
| 40 | Qassab | 3,770 | 1,912 | 1,858 |
| 41 | Qawwal | 141 | 76 | 65 |
| 42 | Rangrez | 1,759 | 850 | 909 |
| 43 | Rao | 235 | 145 | 90 |
| 44 | Sayad | 32,197 | 17,459 | 14,738 |
| 45 | Shaikh | 186,773 | 96,654 | 90,119 |
| | (1) *Behena* | *24,368* | *12,323* | *12,045* |
| | (2) *Chhipa* | *2,919* | *1,518* | *1,401* |
| | (3) *Julaha* | *12,270* | *6,554* | *5,716* |
| | (4) *Shaikh* | *147,216* | *76,259* | *70,957* |
| 46 | Shishgar | 387 | 276 | 111 |
| 47 | Tawaif | 239 | .. | 239 |
| 48 | Teli | 1,427 | 817 | 610 |
| 49 | Unspecified | 30,215 | 13,857 | 16,358 |

# TABLE XIV.

## *CIVIL CONDITION BY AGE FOR SELECTED CASTES, ETC.*

**This table, like Table IX, deals not with the whole population but with certain selected castes for the Agency as a whole, which are considered of local importance.**

# TABLE XIV.—Civil Condition by Age for Selected Castes.

| Serial No. | Caste, tribe or race. | Sex. | Population dealt with. | Un-married Total. | Un-married 0–5 | Un-married 5–12 | Un-married 12–15 | Un-married 15–20 | Un-married 20–40 | Un-married 40 and over. | Married Total. | Married 0–5 | Married 5–12 | Married 12–15 | Married 15–20 | Married 20–40 | Married 40 and over. | Widowed Total. | Widowed 0–5 | Widowed 5–12 | Widowed 12–15 | Widowed 15–20 | Widowed 20–40 | Widowed 40 and over. | Locality. |
|---|---|---|---|---|---|---|---|---|---|---|---|---|---|---|---|---|---|---|---|---|---|---|---|---|---|
| 1 | 2 | 3 | 4 | 5 | 6 | 7 | 8 | 9 | 10 | 11 | 12 | 13 | 14 | 15 | 16 | 17 | 18 | 19 | 20 | 21 | 22 | 23 | 24 | 25 | 26 |
| | **Central India** | Male | **1,525,962** | **687,771** | **2[illegible]5,979** | **199,209** | **85,384** | **74,917** | **91,296** | **30,996** | **693,434** | **11,552** | **27,487** | **42,908** | **83,199** | **324,294** | **203,904** | **144,057** | **904** | **1,908** | **3,516** | **7,811** | **45,823** | **84,195** | |
| | | Female | **1,458,322** | **522,133** | **215,677** | **186,[illegible]84** | **52,765** | **30,802** | **23,115** | **12,790** | **684,255** | **8,047** | **38,[illegible]49** | **55,399** | **101,941** | **337,895** | **142,[illegible]24** | **251,9[illegible]4** | **1,749** | **3,423** | **5,018** | **10,891** | **72,364** | **158,549** | |
| | ***HINDU*** | Male | *1,081,449* | *475,380* | *134,663* | *134,403* | *58,666* | *53,346* | *67,937* | *26,365* | *487,718* | *10,561* | *24,686* | *38,441* | *69,328* | *207,218* | *137,484* | *118,351* | *746* | *1,703* | *3,332* | *7,159* | *36,900* | *68,518* | |
| | | Female | *1,028,054* | *356,634* | *140,279* | *196,361* | *37,362* | *24,479* | *17,435* | *10,718* | *478,531* | *7,182* | *32,884* | *45,296* | *75,257* | *216,949* | *100,963* | *192,889* | *1,629* | *8,005* | *4,563* | *10,063* | *57,501* | *116,128* | |
| 1 | Ajna | Male | 15,172 | 6,282 | 1,762 | 1,307 | 570 | 375 | 1,424 | 844 | 6,553 | 75 | 286 | 428 | 630 | 3,137 | 1,907 | 2,337 | 14 | 33 | 22 | 355 | 502 | 1,411 | Malwa. |
| | | Female | 11,293 | 4,306 | 1,275 | 838 | 444 | 229 | 1,077 | 503 | 5,310 | 109 | 568 | 372 | 534 | 2,634 | 1,093 | 1,617 | 2 | 18 | 28 | 125 | 696 | 748 | Do. |
| 2 | Bania | Male | 70,509 | 33,606 | 8,699 | 9,606 | 4,130 | 3,582 | 5,308 | 2,131 | 36,138 | 720 | 1,761 | 2,850 | 5,083 | 15,615 | 10,109 | 9,765 | 81 | 123 | 174 | 506 | 3,992 | 4,880 | |
| | | Female | 83,691 | 26,726 | 10,092 | 8,896 | 3,597 | 2,322 | 1,194 | 625 | 38,267 | 479 | 3,235 | 4,915 | 7,332 | 14,990 | 7,316 | 18,698 | 115 | 245 | 479 | 1,029 | 5,848 | 10,982 | |
| | (1) *Agarwal* | *Male* | *27,710* | *11,794* | *3,015* | *3,285* | *1,547* | *1,283* | *1,844* | *820* | *12,679* | *113* | *413* | *886* | *1,802* | *5,629* | *3,836* | *3,237* | *57* | *17* | *43* | *140* | *1,106* | *1,874* | *General.* |
| | | *Female* | *30,578* | *9,752* | *3,786* | *3,307* | *1,393* | *501* | *455* | *310* | *13,352* | *199* | *1,364* | *1,693* | *2,367* | *5,430* | *2,299* | *7,474* | *100* | *146* | *220* | *367* | *2,350* | *4,291* | *Do.* |
| | (2) *Gahoi* | *Male* | *13,657* | *6,181* | *1,567* | *1,836* | *708* | *661* | *1,063* | *346* | *6,117* | *58* | *302* | *478* | *919* | *2,710* | *1,650* | *1,359* | *0* | *39* | *30* | *90* | *365* | *835* | *Bundelkhand.* |
| | | *Female* | *11,425* | *3,270* | *1,259* | *1,356* | *312* | *164* | *145* | *34* | *5,544* | *15* | *312* | *574* | *910* | *2,413* | *1,320* | *2,611* | *4* | *22* | *27* | *83* | *795* | *1,080* | *Do.* |
| | (3) *Kasaundhan* | *Male* | *4,213* | *1,472* | *490* | *500* | *172* | *119* | *126* | *65* | *2,324* | *121* | *188* | *268* | *239* | *999* | *509* | *417* | *2* | *5* | *14* | *40* | *181* | *175* | *Baghelkhand.* |
| | | *Female* | *4,574* | *1,430* | *745* | *415* | *205* | *20* | *37* | *8* | *2,375* | *28* | *273* | *288* | *518* | *946* | *322* | *769* | *0* | *8* | *44* | *101* | *173* | *443* | *Do.* |
| | (4) *Kesar* | *Male* | *7,433* | *3,138* | *950* | *1,111* | *349* | *245* | *320* | *163* | *3,793* | *292* | *494* | *379* | *475* | *1,324* | *829* | *502* | *9* | *20* | *24* | *38* | *158* | *253* | *Do.* |
| | | *Female* | *7,036* | *2,193* | *922* | *767* | *184* | *111* | *162* | *47* | *3,533* | *112* | *419* | *515* | *463* | *1,583* | *441* | *1,310* | *6* | *33* | *65* | *70* | *339* | *797* | *Do.* |
| | (5) *Kharia* | *Male* | *1,800* | *634* | *156* | *223* | *75* | *59* | *70* | *11* | *1,010* | *16* | *61* | *[illegible]4* | *128* | *508* | *203* | *156* | *0* | *0* | *2* | *9* | *39* | *106* | *Do.* |
| | | *Female* | *2,697* | *655* | *266* | *307* | *36* | *20* | *19* | *7* | *1,304* | *17* | *298* | *130* | *166* | *543* | *250* | *738* | *0* | *0* | *11* | *19* | *228* | *450* | *Do.* |
| | (6) *Mahesri* | *Male* | *10,008* | *4,085* | *971* | *997* | *485* | *452* | *839* | *341* | *4,322* | *60* | *121* | *343* | *700* | *1,838* | *1,260* | *1,601* | *1* | *11* | *13* | *65* | *[illegible]54* | *657* | *Malwa.* |
| | | *Female* | *11,404* | *3,523* | *1,319* | *1,164* | *705* | *195* | *11[illegible]* | *21* | *5,635* | *30* | *264* | *832* | *1,205* | *1,790* | *1,464* | *2,246* | *0* | *16* | *37* | *166* | *[illegible]28* | *1,199* | *Do.* |
| | (7) *Oswal* | *Male* | *6,072* | *2,615* | *627* | *701* | *327* | *309* | *452* | *199* | *2,335* | *24* | *7[illegible]* | *141* | *320* | *1,047* | *725* | *1,122* | *5* | *5* | *10* | *62* | *646* | *394* | *Do.* |
| | | *Female* | *8,237* | *3,268* | *960* | *763* | *415* | *921* | *115* | *94* | *3,127* | *30* | *185* | *382* | *960* | *901* | *669* | *1,842* | *2* | *7* | *34* | *67* | *595* | *1,137* | *Do.* |
| | (8) *Porwal* | *Male* | *8,616* | *3,687* | *883* | *1,013* | *467* | *454* | *684* | *186* | *3,553* | *36* | *104* | *261* | *600* | *1,560* | *1,097* | *1,371* | *7* | *26* | *38* | *62* | *643* | *595* | *Do.* |
| | | *Female* | *7,740* | *2,635* | *835* | *817* | *347* | *390* | *142* | *104* | *3,397* | *48* | *220* | *451* | *743* | *1,384* | *551* | *1,708* | *3* | *13* | *41* | *156* | *540* | *955* | *Do.* |
| 3 | Bhat | Male | 13,181 | 5,741 | 1,644 | 1,487 | 843 | 749 | 757 | 261 | 5,447 | 59 | 193 | 321 | 839 | 2,280 | 1,755 | 1,993 | 17 | 30 | 45 | 51 | 702 | 1,148 | Do. and Baghel- |
| | | Female | 11,980 | 4,506 | 1,675 | 1,444 | 771 | 323 | 208 | 85 | 5,098 | 62 | 343 | 547 | 826 | 2,128 | 1,192 | 2,376 | 10 | 6 | 41 | 108 | 763 | 1,448 | khand. |
| 4 | Bhil | Male | 13,693 | 5,890 | 2,400 | 1,641 | 442 | 533 | 565 | 309 | 6,157 | 9 | 95 | 398 | 556 | 3,411 | 1,688 | 1,646 | 0 | 1 | 1 | 30 | 919 | 695 | Hilly tracts. |
| | | Female | 12,138 | 4,216 | 2,096 | 1,384 | 347 | 225 | 123 | 41 | 5,914 | 21 | 192 | 230 | 622 | 4,136 | 713 | 2,008 | 12 | 26 | 57 | 96 | 315 | 1,502 | Do. |
| 5 | Bhilala | Male | 16,351 | 7,784 | 2,281 | 2,756 | 989 | 823 | 858 | 77 | 8,069 | 13 | 125 | 531 | 1,013 | 4,037 | 2,350 | 498 | 1 | 0 | 3 | 20 | 110 | 304 | Do. |
| | | Female | 17,413 | 8,141 | 2,890 | 2,623 | 1,186 | 941 | 466 | 35 | 7,819 | 46 | 208 | 525 | 1,252 | 3,665 | 2,123 | 1,453 | 2 | 3 | 6 | 92 | 443 | 907 | Do. |
| 6 | Brahman | Male | 289,808 | 127,408 | 31,826 | 37,127 | 14,861 | 14,501 | 20,718 | 8,375 | 129,744 | 2,416 | 6,284 | 9,144 | 17,812 | 55,933 | 38,155 | 82,651 | 133 | 260 | 970 | 2,100 | 8,270 | 20,918 | |
| | | Female | 288,165 | 88,139 | 36,233 | 35,794 | 6,839 | 3,943 | 3,253 | 2,077 | 129,503 | 2,370 | 10,083 | 13,679 | 20,760 | 59,306 | 23,305 | 70,523 | 923 | 1,202 | 1,475 | 2,556 | 21,183 | 43,184 | |
| | (1) *Bhagor* (*Bhargava*). | *Male* | *17,035* | *8,360* | *1,343* | *2,179* | *990* | *1,062* | *1,710* | *576* | *6,903* | *33* | *138* | *418* | *928* | *3,322* | *2,064* | *1,772* | *1* | *9* | *32* | *300* | *466* | *964* | *Northern Gwalior* |
| | | *Female* | *15,445* | *4,738* | *1,788* | *1,926* | *446* | *198* | *226* | *154* | *6,829* | *76* | *530* | *742* | *1,150* | *3,212* | *1,119* | *3,878* | *4* | *37* | *59* | *123* | *1,196* | *2,459* | *and Bundelkhand.* |
| | (2) *Jijhotia* | *Male* | *33,696* | *16,559* | *4,285* | *4,438* | *1,893* | *1,856* | *2,802* | *1,285* | *13,946* | *87* | *447* | *876* | *2,196* | *5,975* | *4,365* | *3,191* | *5* | *68* | *91* | *211* | *950* | *1,866* | *Bundelkhand.* |
| | | *Female* | *30,236* | *8,710* | *3,940* | *3,564* | *640* | *235* | *179* | *152* | *14,292* | *140* | *870* | *1,664* | *2,171* | *6,559* | *2,888* | *7,234* | *3* | *33* | *77* | *293* | *2,118* | *4,710* | *Do.* |
| | (3) *Sanadhya* | *Male* | *81,579* | *31,722* | *6,978* | *8,099* | *3,763* | *3,691* | *6,310* | *2,881* | *35,775* | *1,277* | *1,534* | *2,397* | *4,949* | *14,358* | *11,260* | *14,032* | *15* | *27* | *433* | *1,022* | *3,121* | *9,464* | *Northern Gwalior.* |
| | | *Female* | *77,546* | *22,198* | *10,157* | *8,182* | *1,565* | *1,229* | *740* | *325* | *32,760* | *294* | *2,163* | *3,517* | *5,577* | *14,586* | *6,623* | *22,587* | *65* | *258* | *520* | *789* | *7,333* | *13,622* | *Do.* |
| | (4) *Seruria* | *Male* | *147,925* | *66,836* | *17,790* | *21,346* | *7,777* | *7,325* | *9,214* | *3,381* | *68,667* | *1,003* | *4,050* | *5,297* | *9,268* | *30,132* | *18,917* | *12,422* | *99* | *124* | *357* | *458* | *3,348* | *8,036* | *Baghelkhand and* |
| | | *Female* | *155,281* | *48,588* | *18,935* | *20,870* | *3,752* | *1,966* | *1,835* | *1,230* | *71,467* | *1,767* | *6,305* | *7,257* | *11,005* | *33,422* | *11,711* | *35,226* | *344* | *852* | *807* | *1,230* | *9,943* | *21,550* | *Bundelkhand.* |
| | (5) *Shrigaud* | *Male* | *7,780* | *3,367* | *782* | *883* | *361* | *512* | *600* | *229* | *3,546* | *15* | *88* | *111* | *287* | *1,751* | *1,294* | *867* | *13* | *30* | *41* | *57* | *281* | *445* | *Malwa.* |
| | | *Female* | *7,251* | *2,799* | *950* | *955* | *345* | *24[illegible]* | *148* | *113* | *3,213* | *45* | *143* | *398* | *641* | *1,206* | *780* | *1,239* | *7* | *21* | *9* | *95* | *439* | *658* | *Do.* |
| | (6) *Shrimali* | *Male* | *1,788* | *564* | *148* | *182* | *77* | *55* | *82* | *20* | *907* | *1* | *27* | *45* | *184* | *395* | *256* | *317* | *0* | *2* | *16* | *52* | *104* | *143* | *Do.* |
| | | *Female* | *2,407* | *1,106* | *423* | *297* | *91* | *67* | *125* | *103* | *942* | *48* | *72* | *101* | *216* | *321* | *184* | *359* | *0* | *1* | *3* | *26* | *154* | *175* | *Do.* |
| 7 | Dhangar | Male | 3,027 | 1,654 | 414 | 486 | 424 | 134 | 120 | 76 | 1,068 | 26 | 51 | 104 | 166 | 394 | 327 | 805 | 20 | 12 | 12 | 30 | 74 | 157 | Do. |
| | | Female | 2,581 | 1,054 | 310 | 344 | 192 | 186 | 18 | 4 | 1,098 | 5 | 75 | 78 | 175 | 485 | 280 | 429 | 0 | 3 | 9 | 81 | 140 | 196 | Do. |
| 8 | Gond | Male | 76,753 | 35,975 | 11,589 | 11,083 | 4,755 | 3,399 | 3,359 | 1,790 | 35,656 | 1,866 | 3,968 | 2,731 | 4,103 | 14,384 | 8,604 | 5,122 | 17 | 175 | 285 | 512 | 1,375 | 2,808 | Baghelkhand. |
| | | Female | 86,532 | 36,457 | 14,672 | 12,757 | 3,693 | 2,624 | 1,569 | 1,142 | 38,081 | 600 | 2,805 | 3,311 | 5,996 | 15,259 | 10,110 | 11,994 | 29 | 185 | 270 | 571 | 3,678 | 7,261 | Do. |

| | | | | | | | | | | | | | | | | | | | | | | | | | |
|---|---|---|---|---|---|---|---|---|---|---|---|---|---|---|---|---|---|---|---|---|---|---|---|---|---|
| 9 | Gujar | Male | 105,834 | 46,281 | 11,970 | 11,184 | 5,375 | 5,248 | 9,846 | 2,658 | 47,828 | 1,346 | 2,240 | 2,857 | 6,492 | 20,944 | 13,949 | 11,725 | 91 | 145 | 277 | 358 | 3,787 | 7,067 | Northern Gwalior. |
| | | Female | 79,894 | 28,159 | 10,398 | 9,957 | 3,299 | 1,486 | 2,244 | 775 | 39,965 | 478 | 2,245 | 2,953 | 5,579 | 19,045 | 9,665 | 11,770 | 31 | 99 | 267 | 483 | 3,218 | 7,722 | Do. |
| 10 | Kachera | Male | 3,197 | 1,382 | 429 | 465 | 151 | 224 | 82 | 31 | 1,483 | 4 | 115 | 136 | 263 | 684 | 281 | 332 | 3 | 3 | 8 | 22 | 78 | 223 | Malwa and Bundelkhand. |
| | | Female | 3,197 | 1,151 | 401 | 444 | 124 | 132 | 19 | 31 | 1,473 | 13 | 55 | 99 | 178 | 617 | 511 | 573 | 3 | 8 | 27 | 32 | 155 | 348 | |
| 11 | Khangar | Male | 20,173 | 9,028 | 2,712 | 2,645 | 1,268 | 842 | 850 | 711 | 9,443 | 521 | 376 | 484 | 693 | 4,351 | 3,018 | 1,702 | 101 | 112 | 77 | 160 | 534 | 718 | Northern Gwalior and Bundelkhand. |
| | | Female | 18,270 | 5,516 | 2,241 | 2,130 | 600 | 387 | 110 | 48 | 9,376 | 47 | 689 | 1,292 | 1,430 | 4,148 | 1,770 | 3,378 | 14 | 80 | 98 | 289 | 856 | 2,041 | |
| 12 | Kirar | Male | 45,547 | 18,332 | 7,542 | 6,220 | 2,671 | 1,154 | 525 | 220 | 19,278 | 18 | 1,694 | 4,524 | 6,580 | 2,880 | 3,582 | 7,937 | 2 | 32 | 62 | 181 | 3,248 | 4,412 | Hilly tracts. |
| | | Female | 41,338 | 17,846 | 7,536 | 6,239 | 2,926 | 778 | 246 | 121 | 18,613 | 101 | 3,080 | 2,294 | 3,542 | 7,353 | 2,298 | 4,879 | 0 | 22 | 61 | 379 | 1,576 | 2,841 | Do. |
| 13 | Kol | Male | 89,446 | 38,255 | 13,875 | 12,980 | 4,429 | 3,322 | 2,472 | 1,777 | 42,650 | 984 | 2,515 | 2,775 | 4,296 | 20,250 | 11,830 | 7,941 | 47 | 236 | 352 | 482 | 2,101 | 4,728 | Do. |
| | | Female | 96,917 | 35,365 | 13,674 | 12,271 | 3,603 | 2,938 | 1,616 | 1,263 | 47,895 | 1,237 | 3,620 | 3,560 | 5,795 | 24,237 | 9,446 | 13,657 | 109 | 401 | 290 | 478 | 3,349 | 9,030 | Do. |
| 14 | Kotwal | Male | 14,537 | 6,621 | 1,882 | 2,254 | 930 | 674 | 490 | 391 | 6,904 | 334 | 465 | 578 | 768 | 3,114 | 1,745 | 1,012 | 30 | 86 | 74 | 110 | 289 | 423 | Do. |
| | | Female | 12,549 | 3,958 | 1,597 | 1,455 | 284 | 460 | 86 | 76 | 6,474 | 92 | 518 | 414 | 813 | 3,558 | 1,079 | 2,117 | 48 | 52 | 187 | 88 | 511 | 1,281 | Do. |
| 15 | Maratha | Male | 14,821 | 5,435 | 1,588 | 1,490 | 590 | 680 | 880 | 207 | 6,661 | 30 | 125 | 353 | 1,059 | 3,198 | 1,896 | 2,725 | 2 | 26 | 38 | 114 | 996 | 1,549 | Northern Gwalior. |
| | | Female | 13,187 | 3,782 | 1,385 | 1,221 | 516 | 318 | 244 | 98 | 5,802 | 62 | 261 | 651 | 1,016 | 2,463 | 1,349 | 3,603 | 7 | 42 | 57 | 154 | 1,209 | 2,134 | Do. |
| 16 | Mina | Male | 36,632 | 13,305 | 3,916 | 2,738 | 2,194 | 2,600 | 1,610 | 247 | 18,589 | 50 | 205 | 2,639 | 5,065 | 5,898 | 4,732 | 4,738 | 11 | 27 | 90 | 296 | 1,423 | 2,891 | Hilly tracts. |
| | | Female | 34,436 | 10,896 | 4,496 | 3,338 | 857 | 950 | 982 | 273 | 17,962 | 173 | 313 | 1,133 | 2,955 | 7,373 | 6,015 | 5,578 | 110 | 50 | 97 | 258 | 1,398 | 3,670 | Do. |
| 17 | Rajput | Male | 185,738 | 84,729 | 20,453 | 21,458 | 11,538 | 11,886 | 14,075 | 5,819 | 80,847 | 1,920 | 3,596 | 6,306 | 11,538 | 32,661 | 24,826 | 20,162 | 167 | 315 | 678 | 1,498 | 6,656 | 10,848 | |
| | | Female | 152,718 | 56,017 | 20,355 | 18,733 | 6,075 | 4,885 | 3,024 | 2,945 | 68,336 | 1,097 | 3,473 | 6,063 | 11,534 | 30,965 | 15,204 | 28,365 | 150 | 367 | 670 | 2,204 | 8,343 | 16,631 | |
| | *(1) Baghela* | *Male* | *12,708* | *5,787* | *1,536* | *1,735* | *650* | *811* | *905* | *160* | *5,954* | *45* | *139* | *286* | *718* | *2,634* | *2,132* | *967* | *29* | *12* | *16* | *43* | *349* | *518* | *Baghelkhand.* |
| | | *Female* | *12,144* | *4,260* | *1,567* | *1,741* | *344* | *287* | *198* | *123* | *5,404* | *56* | *210* | *311* | *604* | *3,177* | *1,046* | *2,450* | *20* | *33* | *24* | *360* | *633* | *1,410* | *Do.* |
| | *(2) Bhadauria* | *Male* | *13,601* | *6,390* | *594* | *1,421* | *450* | *2,473* | *1,301* | *151* | *6,285* | *1,062* | *1,181* | *1,222* | *1,403* | *794* | *623* | *826* | *15* | *6* | *80* | *115* | *220* | *390* | *Northern Gwalior.* |
| | | *Female* | *9,842* | *5,182* | *890* | *1,505* | *262* | *1,289* | *215* | *1,021* | *3,604* | *139* | *360* | *447* | *466* | *1,483* | *659* | *1,056* | *30* | *94* | *71* | *90* | *256* | *615* | *Do.* |
| | *(3) Bundela* | *Male* | *8,785* | *4,070* | *980* | *1,002* | *538* | *465* | *652* | *433* | *3,989* | *19* | *156* | *309* | *878* | *1,681* | *946* | *726* | *10* | *33* | *26* | *37* | *189* | *431* | *Bundelkhand.* |
| | | *Female* | *8,577* | *2,769* | *991* | *1,084* | *407* | *156* | *96* | *35* | *4,177* | *24* | *188* | *422* | *652* | *2,121* | *770* | *1,631* | *4* | *18* | *26* | *115* | *447* | *1,021* | *Do.* |
| | *(4) Bun. Ponwar* | *Male* | *266* | *149* | *48* | *40* | *10* | *17* | *29* | *5* | *96* | *0* | *0* | *6* | *4* | *58* | *28* | *21* | *0* | *0* | *0* | *0* | *5* | *16* | *Do.* |
| | | *Female* | *35* | *11* | *4* | *6* | *0* | *1* | *0* | *0* | *9* | *0* | *2* | *0* | *0* | *7* | *0* | *15* | *0* | *0* | *0* | *0* | *3* | *12* | *Do.* |
| | *(5) Chauhan (Chohan)* | *Male* | *19,056* | *8,715* | *2,555* | *2,303* | *1,122* | *972* | *1,210* | *653* | *3,257* | *126* | *264* | *479* | *1,100* | *3,761* | *2,527* | *2,084* | *20* | *95* | *96* | *179* | *574* | *1,120* | *Northern Gwalior and Malwa.* |
| | | *Female* | *20,922* | *8,123* | *2,847* | *2,412* | *1,110* | *721* | *490* | *543* | *3,558* | *179* | *442* | *852* | *1,230* | *3,827* | *2,028* | *4,241* | *34* | *56* | *73* | *236* | *1,153* | *2,689* | |
| | *(6) Dhandera* | *Male* | *1,929* | *827* | *196* | *272* | *129* | *93* | *99* | *38* | *850* | *0* | *2* | *40* | *122* | *446* | *240* | *252* | *0* | *0* | *4* | *10* | *75* | *163* | *Bundelkhand.* |
| | | *Female* | *1,830* | *733* | *265* | *281* | *112* | *30* | *40* | *5* | *774* | *6* | *27* | *53* | *107* | *351* | *230* | *323* | *0* | *7* | *8* | *11* | *97* | *193* | *Do.* |
| | *(7) Dikhit* | *Male* | *784* | *393* | *89* | *106* | *43* | *51* | *73* | *32* | *299* | *1* | *8* | *12* | *29* | *148* | *101* | *92* | *0* | *1* | *0* | *10* | *29* | *82* | *Baghelkhand and Bundelkhand.* |
| | | *Female* | *546* | *186* | *59* | *81* | *21* | *18* | *3* | *3* | *225* | *1* | *11* | *19* | *30* | *121* | *43* | *136* | *5* | *3* | *5* | *6* | *27* | *90* | |
| | *(8) Gaharwar* | *Male* | *1,231* | *585* | *153* | *210* | *75* | *60* | *83* | *14* | *556* | *1* | *15* | *30* | *102* | *248* | *160* | *90* | *1* | *1* | *3* | *8* | *35* | *42* | *Baghelkhand.* |
| | | *Female* | *1,113* | *351* | *129* | *149* | *35* | *13* | *16* | *9* | *545* | *1* | *96* | *40* | *66* | *274* | *68* | *217* | *2* | *2* | *11* | *5* | *54* | *143* | *Do.* |
| | *(9) Gahalot* | *Male* | *14,288* | *5,580* | *2,065* | *1,588* | *794* | *489* | *461* | *183* | *6,955* | *12* | *86* | *529* | *775* | *2,814* | *2,739* | *1,753* | *0* | *0* | *4* | *93* | *624* | *1,032* | *Malwa and Baghelkhand.* |
| | | *Female* | *9,365* | *3,247* | *1,825* | *1,001* | *320* | *134* | *77* | *90* | *4,321* | *7* | *109* | *629* | *1,051* | *1,025* | *1,500* | *1,797* | *2* | *6* | *42* | *128* | *638* | *981* | |
| | *(10) Gaur* | *Male* | *3,968* | *1,685* | *483* | *531* | *194* | *190* | *211* | *76* | *1,871* | *10* | *64* | *106* | *174* | *886* | *641* | *412* | *0* | *1* | *2* | *20* | *84* | *305* | *Bhopal.* |
| | | *Female* | *3,325* | *1,135* | *527* | *381* | *130* | *49* | *46* | *8* | *1,587* | *9* | *80* | *107* | *185* | *797* | *409* | *603* | *0* | *4* | *30* | *55* | *151* | *363* | *Do.* |
| | *(11) Kachhwaha* | *Male* | *12,550* | *6,469* | *866* | *532* | *1,871* | *791* | *2,264* | *155* | *3,664* | *146* | *252* | *512* | *510* | *1,307* | *937* | *2,417* | *20* | *50* | *198* | *212* | *757* | *1,180* | *Northern Gwalior.* |
| | | *Female* | *11,870* | *6,027* | *1,275* | *1,365* | *575* | *656* | *594* | *562* | *5,349* | *223* | *412* | *508* | *926* | *2,204* | *1,076* | *1,494* | *7* | *8* | *45* | *262* | *427* | *746* | *Do.* |
| | *(12) Khichhi* | *Male* | *1,386* | *509* | *210* | *190* | *51* | *96* | *161* | *61* | *499* | *0* | *2* | *8* | *27* | *291* | *171* | *78* | *0* | *0* | *2* | *4* | *22* | *50* | *Do.* |
| | | *Female* | *1,133* | *350* | *161* | *150* | *20* | *10* | *5* | *4* | *564* | *2* | *26* | *44* | *85* | *278* | *129* | *219* | *0* | *0* | *0* | *14* | *71* | *134* | |
| | *(13) Parihar* | *Male* | *9,796* | *5,179* | *1,185* | *1,567* | *719* | *641* | *622* | *445* | *3,850* | *32* | *102* | *231* | *463* | *1,738* | *1,284* | *767* | *6* | *10* | *25* | *57* | *206* | *463* | *Baghelkhand and Bundelkhand.* |
| | | *Female* | *8,412* | *3,142* | *1,142* | *1,127* | *420* | *203* | *204* | *46* | *3,633* | *93* | *156* | *325* | *611* | *1,636* | *763* | *1,637* | *5* | *22* | *55* | *110* | *480* | *965* | |
| | *(14) Ponwar* | *Male* | *24,021* | *10,515* | *2,946* | *2,492* | *1,251* | *1,386* | *1,437* | *1,003* | *10,054* | *137* | *307* | *479* | *1,466* | *4,393* | *3,272* | *3,452* | *13* | *25* | *50* | *142* | *1,423* | *1,769* | *Malwa.* |
| | | *Female* | *18,675* | *5,806* | *2,384* | *2,016* | *735* | *332* | *280* | *119* | *8,826* | *33* | *294* | *622* | *1,384* | *4,450* | *2,143* | *4,043* | *11* | *25* | *47* | *280* | *1,187* | *2,493* | *Do.* |
| | *(15) Ponwar Maratha* | *Male* | *311* | *108* | *23* | *34* | *27* | *15* | *8* | *1* | *159* | *0* | *1* | *4* | *30* | *72* | *62* | *44* | *0* | *0* | *0* | *11* | *14* | *19* | *Do.* |
| | | *Female* | *295* | *107* | *43* | *39* | *19* | *3* | *2* | *1* | *136* | *0* | *1* | *15* | *27* | *37* | *56* | *52* | *0* | *0* | *3* | *8* | *18* | *23* | *Do.* |
| | *(16) Rathor* | *Male* | *18,479* | *8,068* | *2,270* | *1,954* | *963* | *961* | *1,339* | *681* | *8,613* | *168* | *462* | *607* | *1,143* | *3,774* | *2,559* | *1,798* | *21* | *29* | *40* | *145* | *604* | *959* | *Do.* |
| | | *Female* | *14,916* | *4,879* | *2,112* | *1,636* | *456* | *497* | *335* | *144* | *6,968* | *86* | *531* | *673* | *1,302* | *2,930* | *1,541* | *3,074* | *17* | *26* | *91* | *198* | *998* | *1,744* | *Do.* |
| | *(17) Sengar* | *Male* | *4,817* | *2,341* | *532* | *659* | *295* | *256* | *443* | *156* | *1,991* | *28* | *57* | *138* | *254* | *904* | *610* | *485* | *5* | *6* | *23* | *77* | *145* | *239* | *Malwa and Northern Gwalior.* |
| | | *Female* | *6,002* | *2,255* | *551* | *832* | *370* | *215* | *155* | *132* | *2,764* | *71* | *129* | *287* | *598* | *1,228* | *451* | *983* | *3* | *7* | *13* | *48* | *338* | *574* | |
| | *(18) Sisodia* | *Male* | *4,321* | *1,880* | *564* | *472* | *202* | *249* | *300* | *93* | *2,061* | *2* | *20* | *86* | *154* | *1,038* | *761* | *380* | *2* | *3* | *6* | *35* | *111* | *223* | *Baghelkhand.* |
| | | *Female* | *4,254* | *1,379* | *630* | *444* | *212* | *60* | *22* | *11* | *2,056* | *5* | *45* | *131* | *318* | *959* | *598* | *819* | *9* | *9* | *20* | *53* | *252* | *484* | *Do.* |
| | *(19) Solanki* | *Male* | *8,771* | *3,397* | *838* | *815* | *341* | *356* | *582* | *625* | *4,359* | *36* | *81* | *346* | *474* | *1,336* | *2,038* | *1,016* | *8* | *10* | *36* | *112* | *307* | *542* | *Malwa.* |
| | | *Female* | *7,130* | *2,164* | *970* | *672* | *201* | *134* | *139* | *48* | *3,280* | *70* | *155* | *269* | *487* | *1,646* | *753* | *1,686* | *5* | *27* | *46* | *159* | *507* | *942* | *Do.* |

# TABLE XIV.—Civil Condition by Age for Selected Castes—*continued.*

| Serial No. | Caste, tribe or race. | Sex. | Population dealt with. | Unmarried. Total. | 0–5 | 5–12 | 12–15 | 15–20 | 20–40 | 40 and over. | Married. Total | 0–5 | 5–12 | 12–15 | 15–20 | 20–40 | 40 and over. | Widowed. Total. | 0–5 | 5–12 | 12–15 | 15–20 | 20–40 | 40 and over. | Locality. |
|---|---|---|---|---|---|---|---|---|---|---|---|---|---|---|---|---|---|---|---|---|---|---|---|---|---|
| 1 | 2 | 3 | 4 | 5 | 6 | 7 | 8 | 9 | 10 | 11 | 12 | 13 | 14 | 15 | 16 | 17 | 18 | 19 | 20 | 21 | 22 | 23 | 24 | 25 | 26 |
| | ***HINDU—contd.*** | | | | | | | | | | | | | | | | | | | | | | | | |
| | *(20) Tonwar* | *Male* | *24,770* | *11,782* | *2,330* | *3,536* | *1,773* | *1,584* | *1,966* | *664* | *10,485* | *95* | *407* | *976* | *1,712* | *4,338* | *2,957* | *2,503* | *17* | *33* | *37* | *138* | *883* | *1,345* | *Northern Gwalior.* |
| | | *Female* | *12,333* | *4,912* | *2,183* | *1,912* | *326* | *277* | *173* | *41* | *5,561* | *42* | *200* | *509* | *1,405* | *2,464* | *941* | *1,859* | *5* | *20* | *60* | *66* | *603* | *1,105* | *Do.* |
| 18 | Saharia | Male | 25,373 | 12,341 | 5,020 | 3,640 | 1,141 | 1,229 | 1,036 | 275 | 10,976 | 19 | 102 | 788 | 1,072 | 6,990 | 2,005 | 2,056 | 1 | 74 | 185 | 165 | 306 | 1,325 | Hilly tracts. |
| | | Female | 23,871 | 9,973 | 4,998 | 3,395 | 836 | 559 | 178 | 7 | 11,839 | 42 | 312 | 1,018 | 2,129 | 6,563 | 1,775 | 2,059 | 11 | 40 | 51 | 347 | 1,068 | 547 | Do. |
| 19 | Sondhia | Male | 32,662 | 14,731 | 4,661 | 3,776 | 1,365 | 1,391 | 2,872 | 666 | 14,227 | 151 | 490 | 594 | 1,300 | 7,057 | 4,635 | 3,704 | 8 | 13 | 29 | 162 | 1,543 | 1,949 | Malwa. |
| | | Female | 37,884 | 10,366 | 3,955 | 3,098 | 1,173 | 793 | 778 | 569 | 19,706 | 148 | 859 | 2,162 | 2,789 | 8,024 | 5,724 | 7,812 | 53 | 156 | 443 | 743 | 2,762 | 3,655 | Do. |
| | ***JAIN*** | Male | ***28,181*** | ***12,468*** | ***3,456*** | ***3,629*** | ***1,615*** | ***1,332*** | ***1,811*** | ***639*** | ***11,943*** | ***53*** | ***258*** | ***461*** | ***1,407*** | ***6,248*** | ***3,516*** | ***3,770*** | ***5*** | ***24*** | ***18*** | ***62*** | ***1,247*** | ***2,414*** | |
| | | Female | ***27,478*** | ***9,493*** | ***4,347*** | ***3,588*** | ***942*** | ***144*** | ***359*** | ***113*** | ***12,147*** | ***78*** | ***457*** | ***1,069*** | ***2,021*** | ***6,121*** | ***2,401*** | ***5,838*** | ***19*** | ***37*** | ***65*** | ***190*** | ***2,147*** | ***3,380*** | |
| 1 | Bania | Male | 28,181 | 12,468 | 3,456 | 3,622 | 1,615 | 1,332 | 1,811 | 632 | 11,943 | 53 | 258 | 461 | 1,407 | 6,248 | 3,516 | 3,770 | 5 | 24 | 18 | 62 | 1,247 | 2,414 | |
| | | Female | 27,478 | 9,493 | 4,347 | 3,588 | 942 | 144 | 359 | 113 | 12,147 | 78 | 457 | 1,069 | 2,021 | 6,121 | 2,401 | 5,838 | 19 | 37 | 65 | 190 | 2,147 | 3,380 | |
| | *(1) Oswal* | *Male* | *16,764* | *7,546* | *2,093* | *2,094* | *954* | *866* | *1,180* | *449* | *6,849* | *31* | *131* | *266* | *709* | *3,648* | *2,064* | *2,369* | *3* | *14* | *9* | *43* | *816* | *1,484* | *Malwa.* |
| | | *Female* | *16,192* | *6,732* | *2,698* | *2,229* | *601* | *120* | *105* | *29* | *6,764* | *37* | *184* | *627* | *1,189* | *3,467* | *1,270* | *3,646* | *9* | *20* | *34* | *157* | *1,338* | *2,038* | *Do.* |
| | *(2) Porwal* | *Male* | *11,417* | *4,922* | *1,463* | *1,528* | *661* | *466* | *631* | *183* | *5,094* | *22* | *127* | *196* | *698* | *2,600* | *1,452* | *1,401* | *2* | *10* | *9* | *19* | *431* | *930* | *Northern Gwalior and Bundelkhand.* |
| | | *Female* | *11,286* | *3,711* | *1,849* | *1,359* | *341* | *24* | *254* | *84* | *5,383* | *41* | *273* | *442* | *832* | *2,564* | *1,131* | *2,192* | *10* | *17* | *31* | *33* | *759* | *1,342* | |
| | ***MUSALMAN*** | Male | ***179,517*** | ***78,168*** | ***22,985*** | ***24,344*** | ***9,347*** | ***8,795*** | ***10,472*** | ***9,395*** | ***86,693*** | ***423*** | ***1,836*** | ***2,184*** | ***7,301*** | ***43,386*** | ***31,493*** | ***14,726*** | ***31*** | ***151*** | ***128*** | ***448*** | ***5,115*** | ***8,853*** | |
| | | Female | ***163,786*** | ***55,477*** | ***23,207*** | ***20,906*** | ***5,627*** | ***2,414*** | ***2,167*** | ***1,156*** | ***79,810*** | ***486*** | ***3,139*** | ***5,470*** | ***12,119*** | ***42,064*** | ***16,532*** | ***27,499*** | ***70*** | ***311*** | ***201*** | ***431*** | ***7,000*** | ***19,396*** | |
| 1 | Pathan | Male | 73,476 | 31,886 | 8,658 | 10,200 | 3,851 | 3,653 | 4,494 | 1,030 | 35,487 | 194 | 602 | 1,019 | 3,157 | 18,388 | 12,132 | 6,103 | 11 | 65 | 54 | 127 | 2,044 | 3,802 | Northern Gwalior and Bhopal. |
| | | Female | 65,046 | 22,675 | 9,273 | 8,840 | 2,172 | 1,039 | 899 | 452 | 31,962 | 191 | 1,149 | 2,171 | 4,518 | 17,639 | 6,294 | 10,409 | 15 | 98 | 98 | 131 | 2,609 | 7,463 | |
| 2 | Saiyad | Male | 17,450 | 7,895 | 2,382 | 2,142 | 1,024 | 959 | 1,129 | 259 | 8,099 | 23 | 178 | 354 | 958 | 3,744 | 2,842 | 1,465 | 3 | 8 | 14 | 60 | 488 | 892 | Northern Gwalior, Indore and Bhopal. |
| | | Female | 14,738 | 5,553 | 2,278 | 2,006 | 718 | 296 | 181 | 74 | 7,036 | 55 | 227 | 382 | 1,419 | 3,297 | 1,656 | 2,149 | 7 | 48 | 18 | 71 | 472 | 1,533 | |
| 3 | Shaikh | Male | 88,582 | 38,387 | 11,945 | 12,002 | 4,372 | 4,183 | 4,849 | 1,036 | 43,037 | 206 | 1,056 | 811 | 3,186 | 21,259 | 16,519 | 7,158 | 17 | 78 | 55 | 261 | 2,583 | 4,164 | |
| | | Female | 83,002 | 27,249 | 11,656 | 10,060 | 2,737 | 1,079 | 1,087 | 630 | 40,812 | 240 | 1,763 | 2,917 | 6,182 | 21,128 | 8,582 | 14,941 | 48 | 170 | 175 | 229 | 3,919 | 10,400 | |
| | *(1) Behna* | *Male* | *12,323* | *5,176* | *1,703* | *1,653* | *614* | *616* | *541* | *150* | *6,048* | *65* | *254* | *357* | *685* | *3,017* | *1,670* | *1,099* | *3* | *27* | *13* | *161* | *484* | *421* | *Bhopal and Baghelkhand.* |
| | | *Female* | *12,045* | *3,803* | *1,767* | *1,403* | *258* | *139* | *192* | *44* | *6,150* | *54* | *402* | *416* | *1,066* | *3,240* | *973* | *2,092* | *6* | *41* | *39* | *113* | *476* | *1,417* | |
| | *(2) Shaikh* | *Male* | *76,259* | *33,211* | *10,242* | *10,349* | *3,758* | *3,668* | *4,308* | *886* | *36,989* | *141* | *802* | *454* | *2,501* | *18,242* | *14,849* | *6,059* | *14* | *51* | *42* | *110* | *2,099* | *3,743* | *Northern Gwalior, Indore, Bhopal, Ratlam.* |
| | | *Female* | *70,957* | *23,446* | *9,889* | *8,557* | *2,479* | *940* | *895* | *586* | *34,662* | *186* | *1,361* | *2,501* | *6,117* | *17,888* | *7,609* | *12,849* | *42* | *129* | *136* | *116* | *3,443* | *8,983* | |
| | ***ANIMIST*** | Male | ***236,115*** | ***121,755*** | ***44,875*** | ***36,840*** | ***15,856*** | ***11,444*** | ***11,066*** | ***1,674*** | ***107,150*** | ***515*** | ***707*** | ***1,919*** | ***5,163*** | ***67,442*** | ***31,411*** | ***7,210*** | ***29*** | ***30*** | ***43*** | ***149*** | ***2,561*** | ***4,405*** | |
| | | Female | ***240,004*** | ***100,529*** | ***47,844*** | ***36,129*** | ***8,834*** | ***3,765*** | ***3,154*** | ***803*** | ***113,767*** | ***301*** | ***2,169*** | ***3,564*** | ***12,544*** | ***72,761*** | ***22,428*** | ***25,708*** | ***31*** | ***70*** | ***99*** | ***207*** | ***5,656*** | ***19,645*** | |
| 1 | Bhil | Male | 134,045 | 69,602 | 25,850 | 21,083 | 9,845 | 6,311 | 6,185 | 328 | 62,311 | 236 | 385 | 673 | 1,720 | 42,372 | 16,925 | 2,132 | 6 | 12 | 20 | 61 | 750 | 1,283 | Hilly tracts. |
| | | Female | 135,865 | 55,798 | 27,220 | 21,067 | 4,790 | 1,265 | 1,298 | 158 | 65,361 | 187 | 1,198 | 1,648 | 6,622 | 42,114 | 13,592 | 14,706 | 23 | 39 | 59 | 92 | 3,079 | 11,414 | Do. |
| 2 | Bhilala | Male | 44,821 | 25,859 | 9,687 | 8,208 | 2,904 | 2,522 | 2,247 | 291 | 17,619 | 36 | 23 | 427 | 836 | 10,750 | 5,547 | 1,343 | 0 | 1 | 0 | 11 | 473 | 858 | Do. |
| | | Female | 44,791 | 23,001 | 10,018 | 7,632 | 2,564 | 1,561 | 1,023 | 203 | 18,563 | 12 | 213 | 480 | 2,121 | 12,517 | 3,220 | 3,227 | 0 | 4 | 18 | 21 | 618 | 2,566 | Do. |
| 3 | Gond | Male | 34,611 | 15,718 | 5,485 | 4,065 | 2,022 | 1,816 | 1,515 | 815 | 16,178 | 127 | 118 | 381 | 1,519 | 8,687 | 5,351 | 2,715 | 14 | 8 | 16 | 35 | 986 | 1,656 | Do. |
| | | Female | 36,776 | 13,480 | 6,244 | 4,578 | 918 | 678 | 691 | 371 | 17,747 | 56 | 343 | 660 | 1,964 | 10,943 | 3,781 | 5,549 | 3 | 17 | 11 | 63 | 1,803 | 4,152 | Do. |
| 4 | Kirar | Male | 1,541 | 556 | 223 | 170 | 64 | 42 | 52 | 5 | 809 | 5 | 35 | 58 | 91 | 394 | 231 | 176 | 0 | 1 | 0 | 5 | 76 | 94 | Do. |
| | | Female | 1,496 | 378 | 197 | 136 | 18 | 14 | 13 | 0 | 878 | 3 | 77 | 60 | 98 | 617 | 23 | 240 | 0 | 2 | 4 | 5 | 73 | 156 | Do. |
| 5 | Kol | Male | 3,161 | 1,817 | 489 | 577 | 108 | 86 | 45 | 12 | 1,691 | 5 | 29 | 63 | 122 | 989 | 483 | 153 | 0 | 2 | 1 | 4 | 72 | 74 | Do. |
| | | Female | 3,123 | 1,188 | 534 | 492 | 68 | 48 | 19 | 27 | 1,556 | 12 | 75 | 55 | 137 | 987 | 290 | 379 | 0 | 4 | 0 | 5 | 72 | 298 | Do. |
| 6 | Kotwal | Male | 254 | 123 | 34 | 38 | 28 | 18 | 8 | 2 | 98 | 0 | 0 | 12 | 7 | 47 | 32 | 33 | 0 | 0 | 0 | 2 | 15 | 16 | Do. |
| | | Female | 269 | 77 | 40 | 31 | 5 | 0 | 1 | 0 | 164 | 0 | 3 | 9 | 40 | 89 | 23 | 28 | 0 | 0 | 0 | 1 | 6 | 21 | Do. |
| 7 | Mina | Male | 1,495 | 656 | 120 | 254 | 80 | 54 | 118 | 30 | 782 | 21 | 32 | 11 | 37 | 401 | 280 | 107 | 0 | 2 | 0 | 0 | 51 | 54 | Do. |
| | | Female | 2,073 | 638 | 327 | 247 | 33 | 14 | 13 | 4 | 1,048 | 1 | 32 | 67 | 115 | 644 | 189 | 387 | 4 | 1 | 3 | 6 | 124 | 249 | Do. |
| 9 | Saharia | Male | 13,187 | 7,924 | 2,987 | 2,445 | 805 | 600 | 896 | 191 | 7,712 | 85 | 90 | 292 | 831 | 3,802 | 2,612 | 551 | 2 | 4 | 6 | 31 | 138 | 370 | Do. |
| | | Female | 15,611 | 5,969 | 3,264 | 1,946 | 438 | 185 | 96 | 40 | 8,450 | 30 | 228 | 585 | 1,447 | 4,850 | 1,310 | 1,192 | 1 | 3 | 4 | 14 | 381 | 789 | Do. |

# TABLE XV.

## *OCCUPATION OR MEANS OF LIVELIHOOD,*

The statistics of occupation are comprised in four Tables as follows :—

Table XV-A.—General Table of occupation or means of livelihood for the Agency as a whole.

„ XV B.—Subsidiary occupation of Agriculturists (Actual workers only) :—
(1) Rent receivers (Landlords).
(2) Rent payers (Actual cultivators).
(3) Farm servants and field labourers.

„ XV C.—Showing for certain mixed occupations the number of persons who returned each as their (*a*) principal, (*b*) subsidiary means of livelihood.

„ XV D.—Occupations by Religions showing actual workers and dependents together for both sexes.

„ XV E.—*Statistics of Industries*—These are based on the information collected on a separate Industrial Schedule filled in by the owner or manager of each factory, etc., where more than 20 persons were employed. This Table is divided into four parts :—

Part I shows for the Agency as a whole the *number of persons* employed in each kind of factory dealt with; Part II gives for each *Political charge* the *number of persons* employed in each industry with the names of States where situated; Part III gives particulars as to ownership of factories, etc., and Part IV the *caste* and *race* of manager of factory, etc.

The last two throw light on the extent to which the different castes and races have taken part in the *establishment* or *management* of the various industrial undertakings.

Groups Nos. 29, 34, 61, 75, 85, 94, 95 and 141 have been omitted from Tables XV-A and D as there were no entries.

# TABLE XV-A.—OCCUPATION OR MEANS OF LIVELIHOOD.

| Class. | Sub-class. | Order. | Group No. | Occupation or Means of Livelihood. | Total Workers and Dependents. | ACTUAL WORKERS. Total. Males. | Total. Females. | Partially Agriculturists. Males. | Partially Agriculturists. Females. | Dependents. |
|---|---|---|---|---|---|---|---|---|---|---|
| 1 | 2 | 3 | 4 | 5 | 6 | 7 | 8 | 9 | 10 | 11 |
| | | | | **Central India** | **9,356,980** | **3,288,363** | **2,032,029** | **140,411** | **28,144** | **4,036,588** |
| A.—Production of raw materials. | | | | **A.—Production of raw materials** | **5,953,423** | **2,067,030** | **1,356,994** | **30,804** | **7,949** | **2,529,399** |
| | I. Exploitation of the Surface of the Earth. | | | ***I.—EXPLOITATION OF THE SURFACE OF THE EARTH.*** | ***5,949,356*** | ***2,065,646*** | ***1,356,540*** | ***30,751*** | ***7,949*** | ***2,597,170*** |
| | | 1.—Pasture and Agriculture. | | ***1.—Pasture and Agriculture.*** | ***5,936,785*** | ***2,059,905*** | ***1,355,300*** | ***30,169*** | ***7,794*** | ***2,521,580*** |
| | | | | *(a) Ordinary cultivation* | *5,660,991* | *1,925,526* | *1,307,190* | *21,600* | *5,509* | *2,428,275* |
| | | | 1 | Income from rent of agricultural land | 123,516 | 43,762 | 10,279 | .. | .. | 69,475 |
| | | | 2 | Ordinary cultivators | 4,038,048 | 1,425,548 | 711,868 | .. | .. | 1,900,632 |
| | | | 3 | Agents, managers of landed estates (not planters), clerks, rent collectors, etc. | 11,024 | 3,921 | 824 | 288 | 46 | 6,279 |
| | | | 4 | Farm servants and field labourers | 1,488,403 | 452,295 | 584,219 | 21,312 | 5,463 | 451,889 |
| | | | | *(b) Growers of special products and market gardening* | *14,290* | *5,466* | *2,935* | *624* | *204* | *5,889* |
| | | | 5 | Tea, coffee, cinchona and indigo plantations | 150 | 91 | .. | .. | .. | 59 |
| | | | 6 | Fruit, flower, vegetable, betel, vine, arecanut, etc., growers. | 14,140 | 5,375 | 2,935 | 624 | 204 | 5,830 |
| | | | | *(c) Forestry* | *40,139* | *15,643* | *10,904* | *441* | *82* | *13,589* |
| | | | 7A | Forest officers, rangers, guards, etc. (Government) | 27 | 14 | .. | .. | .. | 13 |
| | | | 7B | Forest officers, rangers, guards, etc. (Native States) | 2,824 | 1,265 | 123 | 36 | 13 | 1,436 |
| | | | 8 | Wood-cutters, fire-wood, lac, catechu, rubber, etc., collectors and charcoal burners. | 37,288 | 14,357 | 10,781 | 405 | 69 | 12,140 |
| | | | | *(d) Raising of farm stock* | *221,276* | *113,231* | *34,263* | *7,495* | *1,999* | *73,782* |
| | | | 9 | Cattle and buffalo breeders and keepers | 17,745 | 8,617 | 2,296 | 202 | 61 | 6,832 |
| | | | 10 | Sheep, goat and pig breeders | 3,366 | 1,341 | 691 | 55 | 19 | 1,334 |
| | | | 11 | Breeders of other animals (horses, camels, mules, asses, etc.). | 17,402 | 10,113 | 1,568 | 261 | 34 | 5,721 |
| | | | 12 | Herdsmen, shepherds, goatherds, etc. | 182,763 | 93,160 | 29,708 | 6,977 | 1,885 | 59,895 |
| | | | | *(e) Raising of small animals* | *89* | *36* | *8* | *2* | .. | *45* |
| | | | 13 | Birds, bees, silk worms, etc. | 89 | 36 | 8 | 2 | .. | 45 |
| | | 2.—Fishing and Hunting. | | ***2.—Fishing and Hunting*** | ***12,571*** | ***5,741*** | ***1,240*** | ***589*** | ***155*** | ***5,590*** |
| | | | 14 | Fishing | 10,687 | 5,066 | 1,190 | 551 | 155 | 4,431 |
| | | | 15 | Hunting | 1,884 | 675 | 50 | 38 | .. | 1,159 |
| | II.—Extraction of Minerals. | | | ***II.—EXTRACTION OF MINERALS*** | ***4,067*** | ***1,384*** | ***454*** | ***53*** | .. | ***2,229*** |
| | | 3.—Mines. | | ***3.—Mines*** | ***3,039*** | ***1,104*** | ***375*** | ***10*** | .. | ***1,560*** |
| | | | 16 | Coal mines and petroleum wells | 2,411 | 852 | 186 | 10 | .. | 1,373 |
| | | | 17 | Mines and metallic minerals (gold, iron, manganese, etc.) | 628 | 252 | 189 | .. | .. | 187 |
| | | 4.—Quarries of hard rocks. | | ***4.—Quarries of hard rocks*** | ***110*** | ***25*** | ***1*** | .. | .. | ***84*** |
| | | | 18 | Other minerals (jade, diamonds, limestone, etc.) | 110 | 25 | 1 | .. | .. | 84 |
| | | 5.—Salt, etc. | | ***5.—Salt, etc.*** | ***918*** | ***255*** | ***78*** | ***43*** | .. | ***585*** |
| | | | 19 | Rock, sea and marsh salt | 785 | 203 | 78 | 42 | .. | 504 |
| | | | 20 | Extraction of saltpetre, alum and other substances, soluble in water. | 133 | 52 | .. | 1 | .. | 81 |
| B.—Preparation and supply of material substances. | | | | **B.—Preparation and supply of material substances.** | **1,711,417** | **616,879** | **271,787** | **81,455** | **16,496** | **822,751** |
| | III.—Industry. | | | ***III.—INDUSTRY*** | ***1,145,073*** | ***416,117*** | ***187,117*** | ***59,109*** | ***11,568*** | ***541,839*** |
| | | 6.—Textiles. | | ***6.—Textiles*** | ***168,094*** | ***56,373*** | ***40,065*** | ***6,056*** | ***1,677*** | ***71,586*** |
| | | | 21 | Cotton ginning, cleaning and pressing | 26,587 | 9,817 | 3,769 | 1,281 | 278 | 13,001 |
| | | | 22 | Cotton spinning, sizing and weaving | 106,726 | 34,117 | 29,922 | 3,384 | 883 | 42,687 |
| | | | 23 | Jute spinning, pressing and weaving | 265 | 97 | 17 | 11 | .. | 151 |
| | | | 24 | Rope, twine and string | 1,541 | 622 | 312 | 7 | .. | 607 |
| | | | 25 | Other fibres (cocoanut, aloes, palmleaf, flax, hemp, straw, etc.). | 387 | 125 | 103 | 21 | 3 | 159 |
| | | | 26 | Wool carders and spinners, weavers of woollen blankets, carpets, etc. | 11,198 | 4,520 | 1,919 | 938 | 403 | 4,759 |
| | | | 27 | Silk spinners and weavers | 551 | 258 | 8 | 7 | .. | 285 |
| | | | 28 | Hair, camel and horse hair, bristles work, brush-makers, etc. | 265 | 69 | 73 | .. | .. | 123 |
| | | | 30 | Dyeing, bleaching, printing, preparation and sponging of textiles. | 17,746 | 5,794 | 3,358 | 349 | 94 | 8,594 |
| | | | 31 | Other (lace, crape, embroideries, fringes, etc.) and insufficiently described textile industries. | 2,758 | 954 | 584 | 58 | 16 | 1,220 |
| | | 7.—Hides, skins and hard materials from the animal kingdom. | | ***7.—Hides, skins and hard materials from the animal kingdom.*** | ***23,670*** | ***11,171*** | ***1,369*** | ***1,362*** | ***50*** | ***11,130*** |
| | | | 32 | Tanners, curriers, leather dressers and dyers, etc. | 11,036 | 5,423 | 793 | 832 | 40 | 4,820 |
| | | | 33 | Makers of leather articles, such as trunks, water bags, etc. | 12,630 | 5,746 | 576 | 530 | 10 | 6,308 |
| | | | 35 | Bone, ivory, horn, shell, etc., workers | 4 | 2 | .. | .. | .. | 2 |

# TABLE XV-A.—Occupation or Means of Livelihood—*continued.*

| Class. | Sub-class. | Order. | Group No. | Occupation or Means of Livelihood. | Total Workers and Dependents. | Actual Workers. Total. Males. | Actual Workers. Total. Females. | Actual Workers. Partially Agriculturists. Males. | Actual Workers. Partially Agriculturists. Females. | Dependents. |
|---|---|---|---|---|---|---|---|---|---|---|
| 1 | 2 | 3 | 4 | 5 | 6 | 7 | 8 | 9 | 10 | 11 |
| B.—Preparation and supply of material substances—*contd.* | III.—Industry. | 8.—Wood. | | ***8.—Wood*** | ***133,102*** | ***49,369*** | ***29,303*** | ***6,215*** | ***612*** | ***61,430*** |
| | | | 36 | Sawyers, carpenters, turners and joiners, etc. | 64,075 | 26,391 | 1,693 | 5,111 | 183 | 35,991 |
| | | | 37 | Basket makers and other industries of woody material, including leaves. | 69,027 | 22,978 | 20,610 | 1.104 | 429 | 25,439 |
| | | 9.—Metals. | | ***9.—Metals*** | ***70,801*** | ***25,595*** | ***6,794*** | ***3,549*** | ***558*** | ***38,412*** |
| | | | 38 | Forging and rolling of iron and other metals | 706 | 351 | 5 | 69 | .. | 350 |
| | | | 39 | Plough and agricultural implement makers | 1,767 | 779 | 22 | 104 | .. | 966 |
| | | | 40 | Makers of arms, guns, etc. | 1,218 | 537 | 50 | 16 | .. | 631 |
| | | | 41 | Other workers in iron and makers of implements and tools principally or exclusively of iron. | 51,851 | 19,073 | 4,948 | 3,139 | 450 | 27,830 |
| | | | 42 | Workers in brass, copper and bell metal | 12,036 | 3,590 | 1,601 | 122 | 99 | 6,845 |
| | | | 43 | Workers in other metals (tin, zinc, lead, quick-silver, etc.) | 3,097 | 1,190 | 167 | 84 | 9 | 1,740 |
| | | | 44 | Workers in mints, die-sinkers, etc. | 126 | 75 | 1 | 8 | .. | 50 |
| | | 10.—Ceramics. | | ***10.—Ceramics*** | ***100,011*** | ***36,587*** | ***21,935*** | ***6,586*** | ***1,375*** | ***41,4[illegible]*** |
| | | | 45 | Makers of glass and crystal ware | 9,544 | 2,758 | 2,718 | 132 | 57 | 4,063 |
| | | | 46 | Makers of porcelain and crockery | 6 | 2 | .. | .. | .. | 4 |
| | | | 47 | Potters and earthen pipe and bowl makers | 86,035 | 32,052 | 18,122 | 6,383 | 1,314 | 35,861 |
| | | | 48 | Brick and tile makers | 4,418 | 1,775 | 1,085 | 71 | 4 | 1,558 |
| | | | 49 | Others (mosaic, talc, mica, alabaster, etc., workers) | 8 | .. | .. | .. | .. | 8 |
| | | 11.—Chemical products properly so called and analogous. | | ***11.—Chemical products properly so called, and analogous.*** | ***71,493*** | ***21,581*** | ***16,334*** | ***4,528*** | ***1,685*** | ***33,578*** |
| | | | 50 | Manufacture of matches and explosive materials | 1,490 | 503 | 172 | 36 | 26 | 809 |
| | | | 51 | Manufacture of aerated and mineral waters | 38 | 19 | .. | .. | .. | 19 |
| | | | 52 | Manufacture of dyes, paint and ink | 336 | 173 | 2 | 1 | .. | 161 |
| | | | 53 | Manufacture and refining of vegetable and mineral oils. | 66,063 | 19,649 | 15,237 | 4,397 | 1,590 | 31,177 |
| | | | 54 | Manufacture of paper card-board and papier mache. | 60 | 23 | 2 | .. | .. | 35 |
| | | | 55 | Others (soap, candles, lac, cutch, perfumes and miscellaneous drugs). | 3,506 | 1,208 | 921 | 94 | 69 | 1,377 |
| | | 12.—Food industries. | | ***12.—Food industries*** | ***65,028*** | ***19,506*** | ***16,307*** | ***917*** | ***555*** | ***29,215*** |
| | | | 56 | Rice pounders and huskers and flour grinders | 18,470 | 1,853 | 9,751 | 27 | 46 | 6,366 |
| | | | 57 | Bakers and biscuit makers | 945 | 281 | 140 | 2 | 3 | 524 |
| | | | 58 | Grain parchers, etc. | 7,894 | 2,537 | 2,467 | 213 | 264 | 2,890 |
| | | | 59 | Butchers | 14,179 | 5,423 | 1,427 | 306 | 103 | 7,329 |
| | | | 60 | Fish curers | 372 | 142 | 50 | 6 | .. | 180 |
| | | | 62 | Makers of sugar, molasses and gur | 287 | 41 | 90 | .. | .. | 156 |
| | | | 63 | Sweetmeat makers, preparers of jam and condiments, etc. | 17,599 | 6,739 | 1,943 | 132 | 30 | 8,917 |
| | | | 64 | Brewers and distillers | 2,709 | 1,146 | 439 | 231 | 109 | 1,124 |
| | | | 65 | Toddy drawers | 7 | 7 | .. | .. | .. | .. |
| | | | 66 | Manufacturers of tobacco, opium and ganja | 2,566 | 1,337 | .. | .. | .. | 1,229 |
| | | 13.—Industries of dress and the toilet. | | ***13.—Industries of dress and the toilet*** | ***391,413*** | ***149,756*** | ***45,756*** | ***27,675*** | ***4,794*** | ***195,901*** |
| | | | 67 | Hat, cap and turban makers | 324 | 166 | 16 | 1 | .. | 142 |
| | | | 68 | Tailors, milliners, dress makers and darners, embroiderers on linen. | 59,027 | 21,927 | 9,624 | 3,034 | 483 | 27,476 |
| | | | 69 | Shoe, boot, and sandal makers | 189,695 | 72,071 | 20,299 | 12,938 | 2,381 | 97,325 |
| | | | 70 | Other industries pertaining to dress, gloves, socks, gaiters, belts, buttons, umbrellas, canes, etc. | 2,253 | 649 | 515 | 34 | 8 | 1,089 |
| | | | 71 | Washing, cleaning and dyeing | 55,605 | 19,418 | 14,055 | 3,396 | 839 | 22,137 |
| | | | 72 | Barbers, hairdressers and wig makers | 84,441 | 35,513 | 1,214 | 8,272 | 513 | 47,714 |
| | | | 73 | Other industries connected with the toilet (tattooers, shampooers, bath-houses, etc.) | 68 | 17 | 33 | .. | .. | 18 |
| | | 14.—Furniture industries. | | ***14.—Furniture industries*** | ***363*** | ***158*** | ***54*** | .. | .. | ***151*** |
| | | | 74 | Cabinet makers, carriage painters, etc. | 363 | 158 | 54 | .. | .. | 151 |
| | | 15.—Building industries. | | ***15.—Building industries*** | ***28,566*** | ***11,412*** | ***2,780*** | ***616*** | ***70*** | ***14,374*** |
| | | | 76 | Lime-burners, cement workers | 3,182 | 1,059 | 744 | 66 | 15 | 1,379 |
| | | | 77 | Excavators, plinth builders and well sinkers | 469 | 267 | 2 | 3 | .. | 200 |
| | | | 78 | Stone and marble workers, masons and brick layers | 17,683 | 7,084 | 1,064 | 342 | 32 | 9,535 |
| | | | 79 | Others (thatchers, building contractors, house painters, tilers, plumbers, lock smiths, etc.) | 7,232 | 3,002 | 970 | 205 | 28 | 3,260 |
| | | 16.—Construction of means of transport. | | ***16.—Construction of means of transport*** | ***1,443*** | ***713*** | ***61*** | ***124*** | .. | ***669*** |
| | | | 80 | Cart, carriage, palki, etc., makers and wheel-wrights | 69 | 33 | .. | .. | .. | 36 |
| | | | 81 | Saddlers, harness makers, whip and lash makers | 1,367 | 680 | 60 | 124 | .. | 627 |
| | | | 82 | Ship and boat builders. | 7 | .. | 1 | .. | .. | 6 |
| | | 17.—Production and transmission of physical forces (heat, light, electricity, etc.) | | ***17.—Production and transmission of physical forces (heat, light, electricity, motive power, etc.)*** | ***95*** | ***58*** | ***1*** | .. | .. | ***36*** |
| | | | 83 | Gas works, electric light and ice factories | 95 | 58 | 1 | .. | .. | 36 |

# TABLE XV-A.—Occupation or Means of Livelihood—*continued.*

| Class. | Sub-Class. | Order. | Group No. | Occupation or Means of Livelihood. | Total Workers and Dependents. | Actual Workers. Total. Males. | Actual Workers. Total. Females. | Actual Workers. Partially Agriculturists. Males. | Actual Workers. Partially Agriculturists. Females. | Dependents. |
|---|---|---|---|---|---|---|---|---|---|---|
| 1 | 2 | 3 | 4 | 5 | 6 | 7 | 8 | 9 | 10 | 11 |
| B.—Preparation and supply of material substances—*contd.* | III.—Industry—*contd.* | 18.—Industries of luxury and those pertaining to literature and the arts and sciences. | | ***18.—Industries of luxury and those pertaining to literature and the arts and sciences.*** | ***59,450*** | ***19,702*** | ***3,318*** | ***1,491*** | ***935*** | ***29,430*** |
| | | | 84A | Printers, lithographers, engravers, etc. (Government). | 19 | 5 | .. | .. | .. | 14 |
| | | | 84B | Printers, lithographers, engravers, etc. (Native States). | 330 | 133 | .. | .. | .. | 197 |
| | | | 86 | Bookbinders and stitchers, envelope makers, etc. | 219 | 102 | 2 | .. | .. | 115 |
| | | | 87 | Makers of musical instruments | 128 | 59 | 6 | 6 | .. | 65 |
| | | | 88 | Makers of watches and clocks and optical, photographic and surgical instruments. | 322 | 138 | 2 | .. | .. | 182 |
| | | | 89 | Workers in precious stones and metals, enamellers, imitation jewellery makers and gilders, etc. | 46,592 | 17,598 | 2,295 | 1,381 | 228 | 26,699 |
| | | | 90 | Makers of bangles, rosaries, bead and other necklaces, spangles, lingams and sacred threads. | 4,207 | 1,448 | 865 | 30 | 5 | 1,894 |
| | | | 91 | Toy, kite, cage, fishing tackle, etc., makers, taxidermists, etc. | 389 | 85 | 144 | 2 | 2 | 160 |
| | | | 92 | Others including managers, persons other than performers employed in the theatres and other places of public entertainment, employés of public societies, race course service, huntsmen, etc. | 244 | 134 | 4 | 2 | .. | 10[illegible] |
| | | 19.—Industries concerned with refuse matter. | | ***19.—Industries concerned with refuse matter*** | ***38,614*** | ***14,136*** | ***10,050*** | ***67*** | ***27*** | ***14,428*** |
| | | | 93 | Sweepers, scavengers, dust and sweeping contractors | 38,614 | 14,136 | 10,050 | 67 | 27 | 14,428 |
| | IV.—Transport. | | | ***IV.—TRANSPORT*** | ***52,412*** | ***23,611*** | ***3,130*** | ***1,694*** | ***234*** | ***25,671*** |
| | | 20.—Transport by water. | | ***20.—Transport by water*** | ***1,393*** | ***562*** | ***238*** | ***127*** | ***4*** | ***593*** |
| | | | 96B | Persons employed on the maintenance of streams, rivers and canals (including construction) (Native States). | 56 | 35 | 2 | .. | .. | 19 |
| | | | 97 | Boat owners, boat men and towmen | 1,337 | 527 | 236 | 127 | 4 | 574 |
| | | 21.—Transport by road. | | ***21.—Transport by road*** | ***37,800*** | ***17,371*** | ***2,780*** | ***1,460*** | ***226*** | ***17,649*** |
| | | | 98A | Persons employed on the construction and maintenance of roads and bridges (Government). | 385 | 198 | 54 | .. | .. | 133 |
| | | | 98B | Persons employed on the construction and maintenance of roads and bridges (Native States). | 5,735 | 2,098 | 1,354 | 74 | 25 | 2,283 |
| | | | 99 | Cart owners, and drivers, coachmen, stable boys, tramway, mail carriage, etc., managers and employés (excluding private servants). | 22,858 | 10,971 | 1,024 | 884 | 152 | 10,863 |
| | | | 100 | Palki, etc., bearers and owners | 993 | 428 | 1 | 29 | 1 | 564 |
| | | | 101 | Pack elephant, camel, mule, ass and bullock owners and drivers. | 5,518 | 2,739 | 314 | 463 | 7 | 2,465 |
| | | | 102 | Porters and messengers | 2,311 | 937 | 33 | 10 | 1 | 1,341 |
| | | 22.—Transport by rail. | | ***22.—Transport by rail*** | ***10,923*** | ***4,689*** | ***112*** | ***67*** | ***4*** | ***6,122*** |
| | | | 103 | Railway employés of all kinds other than construction coolies. | 10,194 | 4,309 | 95 | 65 | 4 | 5,790 |
| | | | 104 | Labourers employed on railway construction | 729 | 380 | 17 | 2 | .. | 332 |
| | | 23.—Post Office, Telegraph and Telephone services. | | ***23.—Post Office, Telegraph and Telephone services.*** | ***2,296*** | ***989*** | .. | ***40*** | .. | ***1,307*** |
| | | | 105A | Post Office, Telegraph and Telephone services (Government). | 1,506 | 620 | .. | 18 | .. | 886 |
| | | | 105B | Post Office, Telegraph and Telephone services (Native States). | 790 | 369 | .. | 22 | .. | 421 |
| | V.—Trade. | | | ***V.—TRADE*** | ***513,932*** | ***177,151*** | ***81,540*** | ***20,652*** | ***4,604*** | ***255,241*** |
| | | 24.—Banks, establishments of credit, exchange and insurance. | | ***24.—Banks, establishments of credit, exchange and insurance.*** | ***36,093*** | ***12,065*** | ***2,642*** | ***1,779*** | ***288*** | ***21,386*** |
| | | | 106 | Bank managers, money lenders, exchange and insurance agents, money changers and brokers and their employés. | 36,093 | 12,065 | 2,642 | 1,779 | 288 | 21,386 |
| | | 25.—Brokerage, commission and export. | | ***25.—Brokerage, commission and export*** | ***5,195*** | ***1,874*** | ***39*** | ***35*** | ***3*** | ***3,282*** |
| | | | 107 | Brokers, commission agents, commercial travellers, warehouse owners and employés. | 5,195 | 1,874 | 39 | 35 | 3 | 3,282 |
| | | 26.—Trade in textiles. | | ***26.—Trade in textiles*** | ***27,121*** | ***11,161*** | ***1,810*** | ***494*** | ***50*** | ***14,150*** |
| | | | 108 | Trade in piece goods, wool, cotton, silk, hair and other textiles. | 27,121 | 11,161 | 1,810 | 494 | 50 | 14,150 |

# TABLE XV-A.—Occupation or Means of Livelihood—*continued.*

| Class. | Sub-class. | Order. | Group No. | Occupation or Means of Livelihood. | Total Workers and Dependents. | Actual Workers. Total. Males. | Actual Workers. Total. Females. | Actual Workers. Partially Agriculturists. Males. | Actual Workers. Partially Agriculturists. Females. | Dependents. |
|---|---|---|---|---|---|---|---|---|---|---|
| 1 | 2 | 3 | 4 | 5 | 6 | 7 | 8 | 9 | 10 | 11 |
| B.—Preparation and supply of material substances—*contd.* | V.—Trade—*contd.* | 27.—Trade in skins, leather and furs. | | ***27.—Trade in skins, leather and furs*** | *2,095* | *807* | *109* | *107* | *4* | *1,179* |
| | | | 109 | Trade in skins, leather, furs, feathers, horns, etc. | 2,095 | 807 | 109 | 107 | 4 | 1,179 |
| | | 28.—Trade in wood. | | ***28.—Trade in wood*** | *1,750* | *343* | *879* | *8* | *4* | *528* |
| | | | 110 | Trade in wood (not firewood) cork, bark, etc. | 1,750 | 343 | 879 | 8 | 4 | 528 |
| | | 29.—Trade in metals. | | ***29.—Trade in metals*** | *3,159* | *1,194* | *15* | *143* | *5* | *1,950* |
| | | | 111 | Trade in metals, machinery, knife, tool, etc., sellers | 3,159 | 1,194 | 15 | 143 | 5 | 1,950 |
| | | 30.—Trade in pottery. | | ***30.—Trade in pottery*** | *18* | *9* | *1* | .. | .. | *8* |
| | | | 112 | Trade in pottery | 18 | 9 | 1 | .. | .. | 8 |
| | | 31.—Trade in chemical products. | | ***31.—Trade in chemical products*** | *6,945* | *2,718* | *988* | *141* | *7* | *3,239* |
| | | | 113 | Trade in chemical products (drugs, dyes, paints, petroleum, explosives, etc.) | 6,945 | 2,718 | 988 | 141 | 7 | 3,239 |
| | | 32.—Hotels, cafes, restaurants, etc. | | ***32.—Hotels, cafes, restaurants, etc.*** | *24,152* | *8,504* | *2,725* | *1,101* | *220* | *12,928* |
| | | | 114 | Vendors of wine, liquors and aerated waters, etc. | 22,330 | 7,941 | 2,159 | 1,100 | 220 | 12,230 |
| | | | 115 | Owners and managers of hotels, cookshops, sarais, etc., and their emyloyés | 1,822 | 563 | 566 | 1 | .. | 698 |
| | | 33.—Other trade in food stuffs. | | ***33.—Other trade in food stuffs*** | *294,305* | *96,745* | *56,789* | *12,463* | *2,956* | *140,771* |
| | | | 116 | Fish dealers | 655 | 292 | 68 | 8 | .. | 295 |
| | | | 117 | Grocers and sellers of vegetable oil, salt and other condiments. | 62,100 | 19,106 | 13,016 | 4,204 | 759 | 29,978 |
| | | | 118 | Sellers of milk, butter, ghee, poultry, eggs, etc. | 29,194 | 9,115 | 7,852 | 1,816 | 539 | 12,227 |
| | | | 119 | Sellers of sweetmeats, sugar, gur and molasses | 10,488 | 4,640 | 957 | 16 | 14 | 4,891 |
| | | | 120 | Cardamom, betel-leaf, vegetables, fruit and areca-nut sellers. | 38,752 | 11,120 | 11,439 | 1,631 | 651 | 16,193 |
| | | | 121 | Grain and pulse dealers | 130,110 | 45,718 | 17,107 | 4,286 | 732 | 67,285 |
| | | | 122 | Tobacco, opium, ganja, etc., sellers | 6,973 | 2,039 | 951 | 97 | 18 | 3,983 |
| | | | 123 | Dealers in sheep, goats and pigs | 2,881 | 1,188 | 738 | 45 | 16 | 1,005 |
| | | | 124 | Dealers in hay, grass and fodder | 13,152 | 3,577 | 4,661 | 360 | 227 | 4,914 |
| | | 34.—Trade in clothing and toilet articles. | | ***34.—Trade in clothing and toilet articles.*** | *9,614* | *6,373* | *164* | *329* | *3* | *3,077* |
| | | | 125 | Trade in ready made clothing and other articles of dress and toilet (hats, umbrellas, socks, ready made shoes, perfumes, etc.). | 9,614 | 6,373 | 164 | 329 | 3 | 3,077 |
| | | 35.—Trade in furniture. | | ***35.—Trade in furniture*** | *626* | *293* | *25* | .. | *2* | *308* |
| | | | 126 | Trade in furniture, carpets, curtains and bedding | 187 | 71 | 2 | .. | .. | 114 |
| | | | 127 | Hardware, cooking utensils, porcelain, crockery, glassware, bottles, articles for gardening, the cellar, etc. | 439 | 222 | 23 | .. | 2 | 194 |
| | | 36.—Trade in building materials. | | ***36.—Trade in building materials*** | *485* | *197* | *37* | *6* | .. | *251* |
| | | | 128 | Trade in building materials (stones, bricks, plaster, cement, sand, tiles, thatch, etc.) | 485 | 197 | 37 | 6 | .. | 251 |
| | | 37.—Trade in means of transport. | | ***37.—Trade in means of transport*** | *4,296* | *1,654* | *324* | *152* | *37* | *2,318* |
| | | | 129 | Dealers and hirers of elephants, camels, horses, cattle, asses, mules, etc., sellers (not makers) of carriages, saddlery, etc. | 4,296 | 1,654 | 324 | 152 | 37 | 2,318 |
| | | 38.—Trade in fuel. | | ***38.—Trade in fuel*** | *12,797* | *3,807* | *3,336* | *603* | *200* | *5,651* |
| | | | 130 | Dealers in firewood, charcoal, coal, cowdung, etc. | 12,797 | 3,807 | 3,336 | 603 | 200 | 5,654 |
| | | 39.—Trade in articles of luxury and those pertaining to letters and arts and sciences. | | ***39.—Trade in articles of luxury and those pertaining to letters and the arts and sciences.*** | *17,938* | *5,669* | *3,734* | *562* | *114* | *8,535* |
| | | | 131 | Dealers in precious stones, jewellery (real and imitation), clocks, optical instruments, etc. | 3,614 | 1,231 | 135 | 38 | 10 | 2,248 |
| | | | 132 | Dealers in common bangles, bead, necklaces, fans, small articles, toys, hunting and fishing tackle, flowers, etc. | 14,021 | 4,317 | 3,597 | 494 | 104 | 6,107 |
| | | | 133 | Publishers, booksellers, stationers, dealers in music, pictures, musical instruments and curiosities. | 303 | 121 | 2 | 30 | .. | 180 |

# TABLE XV-A.—Occupation or Means of Livelihood—*continued.*

| Class. | Sub-class. | Order. | Group No. | Occupation or Means of Livelihood. | Total Workers and Dependents. | Actual Workers. Total. Males. | Actual Workers. Total. Females. | Actual Workers. Partially Agriculturists. Males. | Actual Workers. Partially Agriculturists. Females. | Dependents. |
|---|---|---|---|---|---|---|---|---|---|---|
| 1 | 2 | 3 | 4 | 5 | 6 | 7 | 8 | 9 | 10 | 11 |
| B.—Preparation and supply of material substances—*concld.* | V.—Trade—*concld.* | 40.—Trade in refuse matter. | | *40.—Trade in refuse matter* | *4* | *3* | .. | .. | .. | *1* |
| | | | 134 | Dealers in rags, stable refuse, etc. | 4 | 3 | .. | . | .. | 1 |
| | | 41.—Trade of other sorts. | | *41.—Trade of other sorts* | *67,339* | *23,735* | *7,923* | *2,729* | *711* | *35,681* |
| | | | 135 | Shop-keepers otherwise unspecified | 62,447 | 21,824 | 7,427 | 2,682 | 673 | 33,196 |
| | | | 136 | Itinerant traders, pedlars, hawkers, etc. | 2,245 | 828 | 101 | 5 | 37 | 1,316 |
| | | | 137 | Conjurors, acrobats, fortune tellers, reciters, exhibitors of curiosities, and wild animals. | 2,192 | 758 | 363 | 25 | .. | 1,071 |
| | | | 138 | Other trades (including farmers of pounds, tolls and markets). | 455 | 325 | 32 | 17 | 1 | 98 |
| C.—Public administration and liberal arts. | | | | **C.—Public administration and liberal arts** | **490,986** | **201,939** | **17,866** | **19,946** | **815** | **271,187** |
| | VI.—Public force. | | | *VI.—PUBLIC FORCE* | *181,938* | *90,182* | *2,321* | *6,764* | *169* | *89,435* |
| | | 42.—Army. | | *42. Army* | *89,551* | *48,815* | .. | *2,160* | .. | *40,736* |
| | | | 139 | Army (Government) | 11,474 | 8,498 | .. | 108 | .. | 2,976 |
| | | | 140A | Imperial Service | 8,425 | 5,062 | .. | .. | .. | 3,363 |
| | | | 140B | Army (Native States) | 69,652 | 35,255 | .. | 2,052 | .. | 34,397 |
| | | 44.—Police. | | *44.—Police* | *92,387* | *41,367* | *2,321* | *4,604* | *169* | *48,699* |
| | | | 142A | Police (Government) | 2,488 | 993 | .. | 51 | .. | 1,495 |
| | | | 142B | Police (Native States) | 38,219 | 17,785 | | 846 | .. | 20,434 |
| | | | 143 | Village watchmen | 51,680 | 22,589 | 2,321 | 3,707 | 169 | 26,770 |
| | VII.—Public administration. | | | *VII.—PUBLIC ADMINISTRATION* | *139,485* | *54,282* | *2,056* | *3,778* | *38* | *83,147* |
| | | 45.—Public administration. | | *45.—Public administration* | *139,485* | *54,282* | *2,056* | *3,778* | *38* | *83,147* |
| | | | 144 | Service of the State | 4,836 | 1,903 | .. | 66 | .. | 2,933 |
| | | | 145A | Rulers of Native States and their families | 443 | 121 | 1 | .. | .. | 321 |
| | | | 145B | Darbar officials | 69,194 | 28,796 | .. | 1,480 | .. | 40,398 |
| | | | 145C | Menials | 38,506 | 14,411 | 2,037 | 624 | 38 | 22,058 |
| | | | 146 | Municipal and other local (not village) service | 2,411 | 961 | 11 | 10 | .. | 1,439 |
| | | | 147 | Village officials and servants other than watchmen. | 24,095 | 8,090 | 7 | 1,598 | .. | 15,998 |
| | VIII.—Professions and liberal arts. | | | *VIII.—PROFESSIONS AND LIBERAL ARTS* | *138,390* | *49,169* | *9,121* | *9,095* | *585* | *80,107* |
| | | 46.—Religion. | | *46.—Religion* | *94,629* | *33,161* | *3,087* | *8,168* | *380* | *58,381* |
| | | | 148 | Priests, ministers, etc. | 54,227 | 19,677 | 875 | 5,786 | 274 | 33,675 |
| | | | 149 | Religious mendicants, inmates of monasteries, etc. | 32,827 | 9,886 | 1,990 | 2,039 | 79 | 20,451 |
| | | | 150 | Catechists, readers, church and mission service | 496 | 286 | 50 | .. | .. | 160 |
| | | | 151 | Temple, burial or burning ground service, pilgrim conductors, circumcisers. | 7,579 | 3,312 | 172 | 343 | 27 | 4,095 |
| | | 47.—Law. | | *47.—Law* | *3,663* | *1,335* | .. | *21* | .. | *2,328* |
| | | | 152 | Lawyers of all kinds including kazis, law agents and mukhtiars. | 2,342 | 780 | .. | 10 | .. | 1,562 |
| | | | 153 | Lawyer's clerks, petition writers, etc. | 1,321 | 555 | .. | 11 | .. | 766 |
| | | 48.—Medicine. | | *48.—Medicine* | *5,954* | *1,543* | *1,281* | *77* | *24* | *3,130* |
| | | | 154A | Medical practitioners of all kinds (including dentists, oculists and veterinary surgeons (Government) ). | 202 | 93 | .. | 3 | .. | 109 |
| | | | 154B | Medical practitioners of all kinds (including dentists, oculists and veterinary surgeons (Native States)). | 2,454 | 883 | 47 | 66 | 1 | 1,524 |
| | | | 155A | Midwives, vaccinators, compounders, nurses, masseurs, etc. (Government). | 172 | 46 | 25 | .. | .. | 101 |
| | | | 155B | Midwives, vaccinators, compounders, nurses, masseurs, etc. (Native States). | 3,126 | 521 | 1,209 | 8 | 23 | 1,396 |
| | | 49.—Instruction. | | *49.—Instruction* | *6,951* | *2,761* | *515* | *165* | *6* | *3,675* |
| | | | 156 | Professors and teachers of all kinds (except law, medicine, music, dancing and drawing) and clerks and servants connected with education. | 6,951 | 2,761 | 515 | 165 | 6 | 3,675 |
| | | 50.—Letters and arts and sciences. | | *50.—Letters and arts and sciences* | *27,193* | *10,362* | *4,238* | *664* | *175* | *12,593* |
| | | | 157 | Public scribes, stenographers, etc. | 15 | 6 | .. | .. | .. | 9 |
| | | | 158A | Architects, surveyors, engineers, and their employés (Government). | 75 | 27 | .. | .. | .. | 48 |
| | | | 158B | Architects, surveyors, engineers, and their employés (Native States). | 1,921 | 912 | .. | 17 | .. | 1,009 |
| | | | 159 | Others (authors, photographers, artists, sculptors, astronomers, meteorologists, botanists, astrologers, etc.) | 2,476 | 1,100 | 83 | 84 | 11 | 1,293 |
| | | | 160 | Music composers and masters, players on all kinds of musical instruments (not military), singers, actors and dancers. | 22,706 | 8,317 | 4,155 | 563 | 164 | 110,234 |
| | IX.—Persons living on their income. | | | *IX.—PERSONS LIVING ON THEIR INCOME.* | *31,173* | *8,313* | *4,362* | *309* | *23* | *18,498* |
| | | 51.—Persons living principally on their income. | | *51.—Persons living principally on their income.* | *31,173* | *8,313* | *4,362* | *309* | *23* | *18,498* |
| | | | 161 | Proprietors (other than of agricultural land), fund and scholarship holders and pensioners. | 31,173 | 8,313 | 4,362 | 309 | 23 | 18,498 |

## TABLE XV-A.—OCCUPATION OR MEANS OF LIVELIHOOD—*concluded.*

| Class. | Sub-class. | Order. | Group No. | Occupation or Means of Livelihood. | Total Workers and Dependents. | ACTUAL WORKERS. | | | | Dependents. |
|---|---|---|---|---|---|---|---|---|---|---|
| | | | | | | TOTAL. | | PARTIALLY AGRICULTURISTS. | | |
| | | | | | | Males. | Females. | Males. | Females. | |
| 1 | 2 | 3 | 4 | 5 | 6 | 7 | 8 | 9 | 10 | 11 |
| D.—Miscellaneous. | | | | **D.—Miscellaneous** . . . . | **1,201,154** | **402,515** | **385,388** | **8,206** | **2,974** | **413,251** |
| | X.—Domestic service. | | | ***X.—DOMESTIC SERVICE*** . . | ***214,177*** | ***81,543*** | ***43,565*** | ***4,415*** | ***1,503*** | ***89,069*** |
| | | 52.—Domestic service. | | ***52.—Domestic Service*** . . . . . . | ***214,177*** | ***81,543*** | ***43,565*** | ***4,415*** | ***1,503*** | ***89,069*** |
| | | | 162 | Cooks, water carriers, door keepers, watch men and other indoor servants. | 204,889 | 77,503 | 43,032 | 4,391 | 1,499 | 84,354 |
| | | | 163 | Private grooms, coachmen, dog boys, etc. . . | 9,288 | 4,040 | 533 | 24 | 4 | 4,715 |
| | XI.—Insufficiently described occupations. | | | ***XI.—INSUFFICIENTLY DESCRIBED OCCUPATIONS.*** | ***754,480*** | ***223,103*** | ***275,887*** | ***2,422*** | ***881*** | ***255,490*** |
| | | 53.—General terms which do not indicate a definite occupation. | | ***53.—General terms which do not indicate a definite occupation.*** | ***754,480*** | ***223,103*** | ***275,887*** | ***2,422*** | ***881*** | ***255,490*** |
| | | | 164 | Manufacturers, business men and contractors otherwise unspecified. | 6,025 | 2,131 | 182 | 131 | 6 | 3,712 |
| | | | 165 | Cashiers, accountants, book-keepers, clerks and other employés in unspecified offices, ware houses and shops. | 5,160 | 2,120 | 64 | 158 | 2 | 2,976 |
| | | | 166 | Mechanics otherwise unspecified . . . . | 1,567 | 603 | .. | .. | .. | 964 |
| | | | 167 | Labourers and workmen otherwise unspecified . | 741,728 | 218,249 | 275,641 | 2,133 | 873 | 247,838 |
| | XII.—Unproductive. | | | ***XII.—UNPRODUCTIVE*** . . . | ***232,497*** | ***97,869*** | ***65,936*** | ***1,369*** | ***590*** | ***68,692*** |
| | | 54.—Inmates of jails and asylums and hospitals. | | ***54.—Inmates of jails and asylums and hospitals.*** | ***4,148*** | ***3,004*** | ***501*** | ***44*** | .. | ***643*** |
| | | | 168 | Inmates of jails, asylums and hospitals . . . | 4,148 | 3,004 | 501 | 44 | .. | 643 |
| | | 55.—Beggars, vagrants, prostitutes. | | ***55.—Beggars, vagrants, prostitutes*** . . . | ***228,349*** | ***94,865*** | ***65,435*** | ***1,325*** | ***590*** | ***68,049*** |
| | | | 169 | Beggars, vagrants, procurers, prostitutes, receivers of stolen goods, cattle poisoners, etc. | 228,349 | 94,865 | 65,435 | 1,325 | 590 | 68,049 |

# TABLE XV.—Occupation or Means of Livelihood.

## PART B.—Subsidiary occupations of Agriculturists—Actual workers only.
### (1) Rent receivers—(Landlords).

| Occupations. | Population. | | |
|---|---|---|---|
| | Persons. | Males. | Females. |
| 1 | 2 | 3 | 4 |
| **Total number of rent receivers (actual workers).** | **54,041** | **43,762** | **10,279** |
| ***Number of actual workers who returned subsidiary occupations.*** | ***25,540*** | ***22,320*** | ***3,220*** |
| (a) *Agricultural* | *16,278* | *14,318* | *1,960* |
| Rent payers | 12,503 | 11,062 | 1,441 |
| Agricultural labourers | 3,775 | 3,256 | 519 |
| (b) *Non-agricultural* | *9,262* | *8,002* | *1,260* |
| Government employés of all kinds | 473 | 469 | 4 |
| Money lenders and grain dealers | 1,824 | 1,498 | 326 |
| Other traders of all kinds | 791 | 614 | 177 |
| Priests | 1,288 | 1,015 | 273 |
| Clerks of all kinds (not Government) | 414 | 407 | 7 |
| School masters | 133 | 129 | 4 |
| Lawyers | 26 | 22 | 4 |
| Estate agents and managers | 61 | 61 | ... |
| Medical practitioners | 63 | 55 | 8 |
| Artisans | 271 | 217 | 54 |
| Others | 3,918 | 3,515 | 403 |

## PART B.—Subsidiary occupations of Agriculturists—Actual workers only.
### (2) Rent payers (actual cultivators).

| Occupations. | Population. | | |
|---|---|---|---|
| | Persons. | Males. | Females. |
| 1 | 2 | 3 | 4 |
| **Total number of rent payers (actual workers)** | **2,137,416** | **1,425,548** | **711,868** |
| ***Number of actual workers who returned subsidiary occupations*** | ***138,348*** | ***104,078*** | ***34,270*** |
| (a) *Agricultural* | *36,881* | *27,460* | *9,421* |
| Rent receivers | 16,874 | 13,442 | 3,432 |
| Agricultural labourers | 20,007 | 14,018 | 5,989 |
| (b) *Non-agricultural* | *101,467* | *76,618* | *24,849* |
| General labourers | 19,960 | 11,935 | 8,025 |
| Government employés of all kinds | 61 | 61 | ... |
| Money lenders and grain dealers | 6,990 | 5,965 | 1,025 |
| Other traders of all kinds | 7,281 | 6,017 | 1,264 |
| Fishermen and boatmen | 2,091 | 1,849 | 242 |
| Cattle breeders and milkmen | 7,254 | 5,472 | 1,782 |
| Village watchmen | 2,795 | 2,441 | 354 |
| Weavers | 1,544 | 1,286 | 258 |
| Barbers | 3,124 | 2,656 | 468 |
| Oil-pressers | 4,690 | 3,736 | 954 |
| Washermen | 2,542 | 1,705 | 837 |
| Potters | 2,321 | 1,562 | 759 |
| Blacksmiths and carpenters | 3,592 | 3,035 | 557 |
| Others | 37,222 | 28,898 | 8,324 |

# TABLE XV.—OCCUPATION OR MEANS OF LIVELIHOOD.

## PART B.—**Subsidiary occupations of Agriculturists—Actual workers only.**
## **(3) Farm servants and field labourers.**

| Occupations. | Population. | | |
|---|---|---|---|
| | Persons. | Males. | Females. |
| 1 | 2 | 3 | 4 |
| **Total number of farm servants and field labourers (actual workers)** | **1,036,514** | **452,295** | **584,219** |
| ***Number of actual workers who returned subsidiary occupations*** | ***60,907*** | ***38,771*** | ***22,136*** |
| (a) *Agricultural* | *9,379* | *6,889* | *2,490* |
| Rent receivers | 2,983 | 2,839 | 144 |
| Rent payers | 6,396 | 4,050 | 2,346 |
| (b) *Non-agricultural* | *51,528* | *31,882* | *19,646* |
| General labourers | 17,182 | 6,887 | 10,295 |
| Village watchmen | 1,272 | 1,089 | 183 |
| Cattle breeders and milkmen | 3,659 | 2,673 | 986 |
| Mill hands | 1,665 | 892 | 773 |
| Fishermen and boatmen | 833 | 608 | 225 |
| Rice pounders | 232 | 89 | 143 |
| Traders of all kinds | 1,673 | 1,300 | 373 |
| Oil pressers | 859 | 672 | 187 |
| Weavers | 1,895 | 1,327 | 568 |
| Potters | 989 | 744 | 245 |
| Leather workers | 4,644 | 4.233 | 411 |
| Placksmiths and carpenters | 1,261 | 1,049 | 212 |
| Washermen | 2,212 | 1,799 | 413 |
| Others | 13,152 | 8,520 | 4,632 |

# TABLE XV.—Occupation or Means of Livelihood.

PART C.—**Showing for certain mixed occupations the number of persons who returned each as their (a) Principal and (b) subsidiary means of Livelihood.**

| Serial No. | Occupations. A. | Occupations. B. | Total. Persons. | Total. Males. | Total. Females. | Number of persons (actual workers) who returned (occupation A) as their principal occupation. Males. | Females. | Number of persons in preceding column who returned (occupation B) as their subsidiary occupation. Males. | Females. | Number of persons (actual workers) who returned (occupation B) as their principal occupation. Males. | Females. | Number of persons in preceding column who returned (occupation A) as their subsidiary occupation. Males. | Females. |
|---|---|---|---|---|---|---|---|---|---|---|---|---|---|
| 1 | 2 | 3 | 4 | 5 | 6 | 7 | 8 | 9 | 10 | 11 | 12 | 13 | 14 |
| | **Central India** | | **512,011** | **278,128** | **233,883** | **215,666** | **205,071** | **13,192** | **8,699** | **46,771** | **19,022** | **2,499** | **1,091** |
| 1 | Field labourers | Village watchmen | 373,321 | 179,286 | 194,035 | 165,806 | 185,292 | 7,975 | 7,116 | 4,734 | 1,486 | 771 | 141 |
| 2 | Grain dealers | Money lenders | 26,025 | 19,134 | 6,891 | 13,972 | 5,571 | 1,441 | 370 | 3,058 | 781 | 663 | 169 |
| 3 | Cattle breeders | Milkmen | 36,966 | 26,104 | 10,862 | 19,718 | 4,930 | 770 | 221 | 5,132 | 5,130 | 489 | 581 |
| 4 | Basket makers | Drummers | 12,942 | 7,187 | 5,755 | 4,570 | 4,423 | 1,360 | 685 | 1,078 | 583 | 159 | 114 |
| 5 | Fishermen | Boatmen | 2,497 | 1,698 | 799 | 1,065 | 609 | 217 | 87 | 349 | 146 | 47 | 7 |
| 6 | Shepherds | Blanket weavers | 16,643 | 12,243 | 4,400 | 8,970 | 3,684 | 1,195 | 223 | 1,743 | 431 | 335 | 62 |
| 7 | Chamari (tanners) | General labourers | 16,342 | 6,721 | 9,621 | 1,023 | 289 | 66 | 54 | 5,620 | 9,274 | 12 | 4 |
| 8 | Priests | Beggars | 1,736 | 1,453 | 283 | 252 | .. | 94 | ... | 1,088 | 283 | 19 | ... |
| 9 | Prostitutes | Singers and dancers | 144 | 3 | 141 | ... | 66 | ... | 31 | 3 | 36 | ... | 8 |
| 10 | Midwives | Scavengers | 412 | 179 | 233 | ... | 61 | ... | 12 | 179 | 155 | ... | 5 |
| 11 | Scavengers | Drummers | 165 | 94 | 71 | 74 | 71 | 20 | ... | ... | ... | ... | ... |
| 12 | Oil-sellers | Grain dealers | 374 | 278 | 96 | 99 | 75 | 14 | ... | 165 | 21 | ... | ... |
| 13 | Patwari (Village accountant) | Cultivators | 24,444 | 23,748 | 696 | 102 | ... | 20 | ... | 23,622 | 696 | 4 | ... |

# TABLE XV.—Occupation or Means of Livelihood. Part D.—Distribution by Religion.

| Class. | Sub-class. | Order. | Group No. | Occupation or means of livelihood. | Total number of workers and dependents. | Hindu. | Jain. | Animist. | Musalman. | Christian. | Others. |
|---|---|---|---|---|---|---|---|---|---|---|---|
| 1 | 2 | 3 | 4 | 5 | 6 | 7 | 8 | 9 | 10 | 11 | 12 |
| | | | | **Central India** . | **9,356,980** | **8,262,638** | **87,471** | **463,394** | **511,290** | **9,358** | **2,919** |
| A.—Production of raw materials. | | | | **A.—Production of raw materials** | **5,953,423** | **5,391,165** | **12,895** | **408,541** | **139,995** | **777** | **50** |
| | I.—Exploitation of the surface of the earth. | | | ***I.—EXPLOITATION OF THE SURFACE OF THE EARTH.*** | ***5,949,356*** | ***5,388,039*** | ***12,876*** | ***408,539*** | ***139,087*** | ***774*** | ***48*** |
| | | 1.—Pasture and agriculture. | | ***1.—Pasture and agriculture*** . . | ***5,936,785*** | ***5,376,846*** | ***12,876*** | ***408,291*** | ***137,950*** | ***774*** | ***48*** |
| | | | | *(a) Ordinary cultivation* . . . . | *5,660,991* | *5,125,204* | *12,798* | *391,833* | *130,397* | *716* | *43* |
| | | | 1 | Income from rent of agricultural land . | 123,516 | 116,098 | 697 | 1,194 | 5,515 | 7 | 5 |
| | | | 2 | Ordinary cultivators . . . . . | 4,038,048 | 3,646,841 | 11,412 | 290,086 | 88,982 | 691 | 36 |
| | | | 3 | Agents, managers of landed estates (not planters), clerks, rent collectors, etc. | 11,024 | 6,704 | 54 | 23 | 4,242 | .. | 1 |
| | | | 4 | Farm servants and field labourers . | 1,488,403 | 1,355,561 | 635 | 100,530 | 31,658 | 18 | 1 |
| | | | | *(b) Growers of special products and market gardening.* | *14,290* | *13,410* | *16* | *57* | *770* | *37* | .. |
| | | | 5 | Tea, coffee, cinchona and indigo plantations. | 150 | .. | .. | .. | 150 | .. | .. |
| | | | 6 | Fruit, flower, vegetable, betel, vine, areca nut, etc., growers. | 14,140 | 13,410 | 16 | 57 | 620 | 37 | .. |
| | | | | *(c) Forestry* . . . . . . | *40,139* | *31,901* | *12* | *6,516* | *1,694* | *11* | *5* |
| | | | 7A | Forest officers, rangers, guards, etc. (Government) | 27 | 14 | .. | 1 | 12 | .. | .. |
| | | | 7B | Forest officers, rangers, guards, etc. (Native States). | 2,824 | 1,843 | 11 | 96 | 858 | 11 | 5 |
| | | | 8 | Wood cutters, fire wood, lac, catechu, rubber, etc., collectors and charcoal burners. | 37,288 | 30,044 | 1 | 6,419 | 824 | .. | .. |
| | | | | *(d) Raising of farm stock* . . . | *221,276* | *206,245* | *50* | *9,884* | *5,087* | *10* | .. |
| | | | 9 | Cattle and buffalo breeders and keepers | 17,745 | 16,905 | 19 | 51 | 770 | .. | .. |
| | | | 10 | Sheep, goat and pig breeders . . | 3,366 | 2,500 | .. | .. | 866 | .. | .. |
| | | | 11 | Breeders of other animals (horses, camels, mules, asses, etc.) | 17,402 | 15,846 | 10 | 1,277 | 269 | .. | .. |
| | | | 12 | Herdsmen, shepherds, goatherds, etc. | 182,763 | 170,994 | 21 | 8,556 | 3,182 | 10 | .. |
| | | | | *(e) Raising of small animals* . . . | *89* | *86* | .. | *1* | *2* | .. | .. |
| | | | 13 | Birds, bees, silkworms, etc. . . | 89 | 86 | .. | 1 | 2 | .. | .. |
| | | 2.—Fishing and hunting. | | ***2.—Fishing and hunting*** . . | ***12,571*** | ***11,193*** | .. | ***241*** | ***1,137*** | .. | .. |
| | | | 14 | Fishing . . . . . . . | 10,687 | 9,625 | .. | 23 | 1,039 | .. | .. |
| | | | 15 | Hunting . . . . . . . | 1,884 | 1,568 | .. | 218 | 98 | .. | .. |
| | II.—Extraction of Minerals. | | | ***II.—EXTRACTION OF MINERALS.*** | ***4,067*** | ***3,196*** | ***19*** | ***9*** | ***908*** | ***3*** | ***9*** |
| | | 3.—Mines. | | ***3.—Mines*** . . . . . . . | ***3,039*** | ***2,445*** | ***12*** | ***9*** | ***568*** | ***3*** | ***9*** |
| | | | 16 | Coal mines and petroleum wells . . | 2,411 | 1,842 | 1 | .. | 566 | 2 | .. |
| | | | 17 | Mines and metallic minerals (gold, iron, manganese, etc.). | 628 | 603 | 11 | 9 | 2 | 1 | 2 |
| | | 4.—Quarries of hard rocks. | | ***4.—Quarries of hard rocks*** . . | ***110*** | ***107*** | .. | .. | ***3*** | .. | .. |
| | | | 18 | Other minerals (jade, diamond, limestone, etc.) | 110 | 107 | .. | .. | 3 | .. | .. |
| | | 5.—Salt, etc. | | ***5.—Salt, etc.*** . . . . . | ***918*** | ***574*** | 7 | .. | ***337*** | .. | .. |
| | | | 19 | Rock, sea and marsh salt . . . | 785 | 507 | 7 | .. | 271 | .. | .. |
| | | | 20 | Extraction of saltpetre, alum and other substances soluble in water. | 133 | 67 | .. | .. | 66 | .. | .. |
| B.—Preparation and supply of material substances. | | | | **B.—Preparation and supply of material substances.** | **1,711,417** | **1,477,847** | **67,963** | **7,972** | **156,004** | **1,071** | **500** |
| | III.—Industry. | | | ***III.—INDUSTRY*** . . . . | ***1,145,073*** | ***1,047,099*** | ***4,391*** | ***9,990*** | ***91,046*** | ***214*** | ***103*** |
| | | 6.—Textiles. | | ***6.—Textiles*** . . . . . | ***168,094*** | ***134,758*** | ***419*** | ***895*** | ***31,989*** | ***10*** | ***13*** |
| | | | 21 | Cotton ginning, cleaning and pressing . | 26,587 | 15,347 | 48 | 1 | 11,181 | .. | 10 |
| | | | 22 | Cotton spinning, sizing and weaving . | 106,726 | 95,594 | 292 | 820 | 10,010 | 10 | .. |
| | | | 23 | Jute spinning, pressing and weaving . | 265 | 222 | 20 | .. | 23 | .. | .. |
| | | | 24 | Rope, twine and string . . | 1,541 | 1,440 | .. | 65 | 36 | .. | .. |
| | | | 25 | Other fibres (cocoanut, aloes, palm leaf, flax, hemp, straw, etc.) | 387 | 377 | .. | .. | 10 | .. | .. |
| | | | 26 | Wool carders and spinners, weavers of woollen blankets, carpets, etc. | 11,198 | 10,869 | .. | 6 | 323 | .. | .. |
| | | | 27 | Silk spinners and weavers . . . | 551 | 451 | 12 | .. | 88 | .. | .. |
| | | | 28 | Hair, camel and horse hair, bristles work, brush-makers, etc. | 265 | 242 | .. | .. | 23 | .. | .. |
| | | | 30 | Dying, bleaching, printing, preparation and sponging of textiles. | 17,746 | 7,618 | 22 | 3 | 10,100 | .. | 3 |
| | | | 31 | Other (lace, crape, embroideries, fringes, etc.) and insufficiently described textile industries. | 2,758 | 2,596 | 25 | .. | 135 | .. | .. |

## TABLE XV.—Occupation or Means of Livelihood. Part D.—Distribution by Religion —*continued*

| Class. | Sub-class. | Order. | Group No. | Occupation or means of livelihood. | Total number of workers and dependents. | Hindu. | Jain. | Animist. | Musalman. | Christian. | Others. |
|---|---|---|---|---|---|---|---|---|---|---|---|
| 1 | 2 | 3 | 4 | 5 | 6 | 7 | 8 | 9 | 10 | 11 | 12 |
| B.—Preparation and supply of material substances—*contd.* | III.—Industry—*contd.* | 7.—Hides, skins, etc. | | ***7.—Hides, skins, and hard materials from the animal kingdom.*** | ***23,670*** | ***23,236*** | .. | ***9*** | ***425*** | .. | .. |
| | | | 32 | Tanners, curriers, leather dressers and dyers, etc. | 11,036 | 10,813 | .. | .. | 223 | .. | .. |
| | | | 33 | Makers of leather articles, such as trunks, water bags, etc. | 12,630 | 12,423 | .. | 5 | 202 | .. | .. |
| | | | 35 | Bone, ivory, horn, shell, etc., workers . | 4 | .. | .. | 4 | .. | .. | .. |
| | | 8.—Wood. | | ***8.—Wood*** . . . . . . . | ***133,102*** | ***131,372*** | ***38*** | ***482*** | ***1,201*** | ***6*** | ***3*** |
| | | | 36 | Sawyers, carpenters, turners and joiners, etc. | 64,075 | 63,005 | 30 | 125 | 909 | 6 | .. |
| | | | 37 | Basket makers and other industries of woody material including leaves. | 69,027 | 68,367 | 8 | 357 | 292 | .. | 3 |
| | | 9.—Metals. | | ***9.—Metals*** . . . . . . | ***70,801*** | ***61,716*** | ***126*** | ***91*** | ***8,865*** | .. | ***3*** |
| | | | 38 | Forging and rolling of iron and other metals. | 706 | 683 | .. | .. | 23 | .. | .. |
| | | | 39 | Plough and agricultural implement makers. | 1,767 | 1,763 | .. | .. | 4 | .. | .. |
| | | | 40 | Makers of arms, guns, etc. . . . . | 1,218 | 857 | .. | .. | 361 | .. | .. |
| | | | 41 | Other workers in iron and makers of implements and tools principally or exclusively of iron. | 51,851 | 45,493 | 14 | 90 | 6,252 | .. | 2 |
| | | | 42 | Workers in brass, copper and bell metal. | 12,036 | 11,252 | 84 | 1 | 698 | .. | 1 |
| | | | 43 | Workers in other metals (tin, zinc, lead, quick-silver, etc.) | 3,097 | 1,660 | 28 | .. | 1,409 | .. | .. |
| | | | 44 | Workers in mints and die-sinkers, etc.. | 126 | 8 | .. | .. | 118 | .. | .. |
| | | 10.—Ceramics. | | ***10.—Ceramics*** . . . . | ***100,011*** | ***96,922*** | ***12*** | ***64*** | ***3,013*** | .. | .. |
| | | | 45 | Makers of glass and crystal ware . | 9,544 | 6,805 | 11 | .. | 2,728 | .. | .. |
| | | | 46 | Makers of porcelain and crockery . | 6 | 4 | .. | .. | 2 | .. | .. |
| | | | 47 | Potters and earthen pipe and bowl makers. | 86,035 | 85,740 | 1 | 41 | 253 | .. | .. |
| | | | 48 | Brick and tile makers . . . . | 4,418 | 4,365 | .. | 23 | 30 | .. | .. |
| | | | 49 | Others (mosaic, talc, mica, alabaster, etc., workers). | 8 | 8 | .. | .. | .. | .. | .. |
| | | 11.—Chemical products, etc. | | ***11.—Chemical products properly so called and analogous.*** | ***71,493*** | ***69,410*** | ***8*** | ***81*** | ***1,994*** | .. | .. |
| | | | 50 | Manufacture of matches and explosive materials. | 1,490 | 462 | .. | .. | 1,028 | .. | .. |
| | | | 51 | Manufacture of aerated and mineral waters. | 38 | 36 | .. | .. | 2 | .. | .. |
| | | | 52 | Manufacture of dyes, paint and ink . | 336 | 123 | .. | .. | 213 | .. | .. |
| | | | 53 | Manufacture and refining of vegetable and mineral oils. | 66,063 | 65,571 | 8 | 30 | 454 | .. | .. |
| | | | 54 | Manufacture of papers, cardboard and papier mache. | 60 | 2 | .. | .. | 58 | .. | .. |
| | | | 55 | Others (soap, candles, lac, cutch, perfumes and miscellaneous drugs). | 3,506 | 3,216 | .. | 51 | 239 | .. | .. |
| | | 12.—Food industries. | | ***12.—Food industries*** . . . | ***65,028*** | ***49,475*** | ***3,388*** | ***372*** | ***11,758*** | ***15*** | ***20*** |
| | | | 56 | Rice pounders and huskers and flour grinders. | 18,470 | 14,715 | 462 | 286 | 3,006 | 1 | .. |
| | | | 57 | Bakers and biscuit makers . . . | 945 | 505 | .. | 12 | 414 | 14 | .. |
| | | | 58 | Grain parchers, etc. . . . . | 7,894 | 6,504 | 2 | 13 | 1,375 | .. | .. |
| | | | 59 | Butchers . . . . . . . | 14,179 | 7,638 | .. | 7 | 6,534 | .. | .. |
| | | | 60 | Fish curers . . . . . . | 372 | 372 | .. | .. | .. | .. | .. |
| | | | 62 | Makers of sugar, molasses and gur . | 287 | 280 | 1 | .. | 6 | .. | .. |
| | | | 63 | Sweetmeat makers, preparers of jam and condiments, etc. | 17,599 | 14,674 | 2,558 | 39 | 328 | .. | .. |
| | | | 64 | Brewers and distillers . . . | 2,709 | 2,589 | .. | 8 | 92 | .. | .. |
| | | | 65 | Toddy drawers . . . . . | 7 | .. | .. | 7 | .. | .. | 20 |
| | | | 66 | Manufacturers of tobacco, opium and ganja. | 2,566 | 2,198 | 365 | .. | 3 | .. | .. |
| | | 13.—Industries of dress and the toilet. | | ***13.—Industries of dress and toilet.*** | ***391,413*** | ***378,359*** | ***180*** | ***100*** | ***12,643*** | ***86*** | ***52*** |
| | | | 67 | Hat, cap and turban makers . . | 324 | 168 | 2 | .. | 154 | .. | .. |
| | | | 68 | Tailors, milliners, dress makers and darners, embroiderers on linen. | 59,027 | 54,142 | 178 | 80 | 4,550 | 72 | 5 |
| | | | 69 | Shoe, boot and sandle makers . . | 189,695 | 187,377 | .. | 8 | 2,257 | 6 | 47 |
| | | | 70 | Other industries pertaining to dress, gloves, socks, gaiters belts, buttons, umbrellas, canes, etc. | 2,253 | 1,877 | .. | .. | 376 | .. | .. |
| | | | 71 | Washing, cleaning and dyeing . . | 55,605 | 51,780 | .. | 1 | 3,816 | 8 | .. |
| | | | 72 | Barbers, hair-dressers and wig makers . | 84,441 | 82,951 | .. | 11 | 1,479 | .. | .. |
| | | | 73 | Other industries connected with the toilet (tattooers, shampooers, bath houses, etc.) | 68 | 57 | .. | .. | 11 | .. | .. |
| | | 14.—Furniture. | | ***14.—Furniture industries*** . . | ***363*** | ***137*** | .. | .. | ***226*** | .. | .. |
| | | | 74 | Cabinet makers, carriage painters, etc.. | 363 | 137 | .. | .. | 226 | .. | .. |
| | | 15.—Building industries. | | ***15.—Building industries*** . . | ***28,566*** | ***22,573*** | ***40*** | ***79*** | ***5,873*** | ***1*** | .. |
| | | | 76 | Lime burners, cement workers . . | 3,182 | 2,972 | .. | 8 | 202 | .. | .. |
| | | | 77 | Excavators, plinth builders and well sinkers. | 469 | 293 | .. | .. | 176 | .. | .. |
| | | | 78 | Stone and marble workers, masons, and brick layers. | 17,683 | 13,777 | 2 | 44 | 3,860 | .. | .. |
| | | | 79 | Others (thatchers, building contractors, house-painters, tilers, plumbers, lock-smiths, etc.) | 7,232 | 5,531 | 38 | 27 | 1,635 | 1 | .. |

## TABLE XV.—Occupation or Means of Livelihood. Part D.—Distribution by Religion —*continued.*

| Class. | Sub-class. | Order. | Group No. | Occupation or means of livelihood. | Total number of workers and dependents | Hindu. | Jain. | Animist. | Musalman. | Christian. | Others. |
|---|---|---|---|---|---|---|---|---|---|---|---|
| 1 | 2 | 3 | 4 | 5 | 6 | 7 | 8 | 9 | 10 | 11 | 12 |
| B.—Preparation and supply of material substances—*contd.* | III.—Industry—*contd.* | 16.—Construction of means of transport. | | ***16.—Construction of means of transport.*** | ***1,443*** | ***1,403*** | ***3*** | ***7*** | ***29*** | ***1*** | .. |
| | | | 80 | Cart, carriage, palki, etc., makers and wheel wrights. | 69 | 63 | .. | .. | 5 | 1 | .. |
| | | | 81 | Saddlers, harness makers, whip and lash makers | 1,367 | 1,340 | 3 | .. | 24 | .. | .. |
| | | | 82 | Ship and boat builders . . . | 7 | .. | .. | 7 | .. | .. | .. |
| | | 17.—Production and transmission of physical forces, heat, light, etc. | | ***17.—Production and transmission of physical forces (heat, light, electricity, motive powers, etc.)*** | ***95*** | ***55*** | .. | .. | ***33*** | ***7*** | .. |
| | | | 83 | Gas works, electric light and ice factories. | 95 | 55 | .. | .. | 33 | 7 | .. |
| | | 18.—Industries of luxury and those pertaining to literature and the arts and sciences. | | ***18.—Industries of luxury and those pertaining to literature and the arts and sciences.*** | ***59,450*** | ***44,136*** | ***174*** | .. | ***8,090*** | ***45*** | ***5*** |
| | | | 84A | Printers, lithographers engravers, etc. (Government). | 19 | 4 | .. | .. | 8 | 7 | .. |
| | | | 84B | Printers, lithographers, engravers, etc. (Native States). | 330 | 264 | 4 | .. | 35 | 26 | 1 |
| | | | 86 | Book-binders and stitchers, envelope makers, etc. | 219 | 153 | .. | .. | 66 | .. | .. |
| | | | 87 | Makers of musical instruments . . | 128 | 113 | .. | .. | 15 | .. | .. |
| | | | 88 | Makers of watches and clocks and optical, photographic and surgical instruments. | 322 | 258 | .. | .. | 54 | 10 | .. |
| | | | 89 | Workers in precio·s stones and metals, enamellers, imitation jewellery makers, and gilders, etc. | 46,592 | 40,318 | 164 | .. | 6,110 | .. | .. |
| | | | 90 | Makers of bangles, rosaries, bead, and other necklaces, spangles, lingams and sacred threads. | 4,207 | 2,562 | 6 | .. | 1,633 | 2 | 4 |
| | | | 91 | Toy, kite, cage, fishing tackle, etc., makers, taxidermists, etc. | 389 | 296 | .. | .. | 93 | .. | .. |
| | | | 92 | Others including managers, persons other than performers employed in the theatres and other places of public entertainment, employés of public societies, race course service, huntsmen, etc. | 244 | 168 | .. | .. | 76 | .. | .. |
| | | 19.—Industries concerned with refuse matter. | | ***19.—Industries concerned with refuse matter.*** | ***38,614*** | ***33,554*** | ***3*** | ***40*** | ***4,967*** | ***43*** | ***7*** |
| | | | 93 | Sweepers, scavengers, dust and sweeping contractors. | 38,614 | 33,554 | 3 | 40 | 4,967 | 43 | 7 |
| | IV.—Transport. | | | ***IV.—TRANSPORT . . .*** | ***52,419*** | ***38,615*** | ***183*** | ***837*** | ***11,685*** | ***768*** | ***394*** |
| | | 20.—Transport by water. | | ***20.—Transport by water . .*** | ***1,393*** | ***1,307*** | ***4*** | ***5*** | ***77*** | .. | .. |
| | | | 96B | Persons employed on the maintenance of streams, rivers and canals (including construction), Native States. | 56 | 2 | 4 | .. | 50 | .. | .. |
| | | | 97 | Boat owners, boatmen and towmen . | 1,337 | 1,305 | .. | 5 | 27 | .. | .. |
| | | 21.—Transport by road. | | ***21.—Transport by road . .*** | ***37,800*** | ***28,386*** | ***134*** | ***524*** | ***8,709*** | ***15*** | ***32*** |
| | | | 98A | Persons employed on the construction and maintenance of roads and bridges (Government). | 385 | 253 | .. | 5 | 127 | .. | .. |
| | | | 98B | Persons employed on the construction and maintenance of roads and bridges (Native States). | 5,735 | 5,103 | .. | 86 | 544 | .. | 2 |
| | | | 99 | Cart owners and drivers, coachmen, stable boys, tramway, mail carriage, etc., managers and employés (excluding private servants). | 22,858 | 15,435 | 107 | 433 | 6,849 | 15 | 19 |
| | | | 100 | Palki, etc., bearers and owners . . | 993 | 991 | .. | .. | 2 | .. | .. |
| | | | 101 | Pack elephant, camel, mule, ass, bullock owners and drivers. | 5,518 | 4,804 | 17 | .. | 687 | .. | 10 |
| | | | 102 | Porters and messengers . . | 2,311 | 1,800 | 10 | .. | 500 | .. | 1 |
| | | 22.—Transport by rail. | | ***22.—Transport by Rail . .*** | ***10,923*** | ***7,223*** | ***43*** | ***192*** | ***2,460*** | ***721*** | ***284*** |
| | | | 103 | Railway employés of all kinds other than construction coolies. | 10,194 | 6,641 | 43 | 81 | 2,434 | 718 | 277 |
| | | | 104 | Labourers employed on railway construction. | 729 | 582 | .. | 111 | 26 | 3 | 7 |
| | | 23.—Post office, etc. | | ***23.—Post office, telegraph and telephone services.*** | ***2,296*** | ***1,699*** | ***2*** | ***116*** | ***439*** | ***32*** | ***8*** |
| | | | 105A | Post office, telegraph and telephone services (Government). | 1,506 | 1,021 | 1 | 78 | 366 | 32 | 8 |
| | | | 105B | Post office, telegraph and telephone services (Native States). | 790 | 678 | 1 | 38 | 73 | .. | .. |

# TABLE XV.—Occupation or Means of Livelihood. Part D.—Distribution by Religion —*continued.*

| Class. | Sub-class. | Order. | Group No. | Occupation or means of livelihood. | Total number of workers and dependents. | Hindu. | Jain. | Animist. | Musalman. | Christian. | Others. |
|---|---|---|---|---|---|---|---|---|---|---|---|
| 1 | 2 | 3 | 4 | 5 | 6 | 7 | 8 | 9 | 10 | 11 | 12 |
| B.—Preparation and supply of material substances—*contd.* | V.—Trade. | | | ***V.—TRADE*** | ***513,932*** | ***393,133*** | ***63,389*** | ***4,915*** | ***53,273*** | ***89*** | ***133*** |
| | | 24.—Banks, establishments of credit, etc. | | ***24.—Banks, establishments of credit, exchange and insurance.*** | ***36,093*** | ***23,994*** | ***10,793*** | ***14*** | ***1,276*** | .. | ***16*** |
| | | | 106 | Bank managers, money lenders, exchange and insurance agents, money changers and brokers and their employés. | 36,093 | 23,994 | 10,793 | 14 | 1,276 | .. | 16 |
| | | 25.—Brokerage, commission, etc. | | ***25.—Brokerage, commission and export.*** | ***5,195*** | ***3,694*** | ***1,085*** | ***7*** | ***403*** | ***6*** | .. |
| | | | 107 | Brokers, commission agents, commercial travellers, warehouse owners and employés. | 5,195 | 3,694 | 1,085 | 7 | 403 | 6 | .. |
| | | 26.—Trade in textiles. | | ***26.—Trade in textiles*** | ***27,121*** | ***17,732*** | ***5,787*** | ***5*** | ***3,562*** | ***33*** | ***2*** |
| | | | 108 | Trade in piece goods, wool, cotton, silk, hair, and other textiles. | 27,121 | 17,732 | 5,787 | 5 | 3,562 | 33 | 2 |
| | | 27.—Trade in skins, etc. | | ***27.—Trade in skins, leather and furs.*** | ***2,095*** | ***1,510*** | ***297*** | ***3*** | ***284*** | ***1*** | .. |
| | | | 109 | Trade in skins, leather, furs, feathers, horns, etc. | 2,095 | 1,510 | 297 | 3 | 284 | 1 | .. |
| | | 28.—Trade in wood. | | ***28.—Trade in wood*** | ***1,750*** | ***1,312*** | ***59*** | ***135*** | ***244*** | .. | .. |
| | | | 110 | Trade in wood (not firewood), cork, bark, etc. | 1,750 | 1,312 | 59 | 135 | 244 | .. | .. |
| | | 29.—Trade in metals. | | ***29.—Trade in metals*** | ***3,159*** | ***2,178*** | ***15*** | ***26*** | ***940*** | .. | .. |
| | | | 111 | Trade in metals, machinery, knife, tool, etc., sellers. | 3,159 | 2,178 | 15 | 26 | 940 | .. | .. |
| | | 30.—Trade in pottery. | | ***30.—Trade in pottery*** | ***18*** | ***9*** | ***5*** | .. | ***4*** | .. | .. |
| | | | 112 | Trade in pottery | 18 | 9 | 5 | .. | 4 | .. | .. |
| | | 31.—Trade in chemical products. | | ***31.—Trade in chemical products*** | ***6,945*** | ***4,552*** | ***21*** | ***20*** | ***2,343*** | ***3*** | ***6*** |
| | | | 113 | Trade in chemical products (drugs, dyes, paints, petroleum, explosives, etc.) | 6,945 | 4,552 | 21 | 20 | 2,343 | 3 | 6 |
| | | 32.—Hotels, cafes, etc. | | ***32.—Hotels, cafes, restaurants, etc.*** | ***24,152*** | ***22,383*** | ***165*** | ***104*** | ***1,424*** | ***22*** | ***54*** |
| | | | 114 | Vendors of wine, liquors, and aerated waters. | 22,330 | 21,063 | 165 | 102 | 939 | 7 | 54 |
| | | | 115 | Owners and managers of hotels, cook shops, sarais, etc., and their employés | 1,822 | 1,320 | .. | 2 | 485 | 15 | .. |
| | | 33.—Other trade in food stuffs. | | ***33.—Other trade in food stuffs*** | ***294,305*** | ***234,661*** | ***32,435*** | ***2,999*** | ***24,195*** | ***10*** | ***12*** |
| | | | 116 | Fish dealers | 655 | 651 | .. | .. | 4 | .. | .. |
| | | | 117 | Grocers and sellers of vegetable oil, salt and other condiments. | 62,100 | 48,644 | 6,312 | 180 | 6,958 | 6 | .. |
| | | | 118 | Sellers of milk, butter, ghee, poultry, eggs, etc. | 29,194 | 27,977 | 286 | 10 | 918 | 3 | .. |
| | | | 119 | Sellers of sweetmeats, sugar, gur, and molasses. | 10,488 | 9,752 | 554 | 2 | 180 | .. | .. |
| | | | 120 | Cardamom, betel leaf, vegetables, fruit and areca nut sellers. | 38,752 | 33,933 | 55 | 211 | 4,553 | .. | .. |
| | | | 121 | Grain and pulse dealers | 130,110 | 97,460 | 24,467 | 65 | 8,111 | 1 | 6 |
| | | | 122 | Tobacco, opium, ganja sellers | 6,973 | 5,069 | 761 | .. | 1,137 | .. | 6 |
| | | | 123 | Dealers in sheep, goats and pigs | 2,881 | 2,533 | .. | 1 | 347 | .. | .. |
| | | | 124 | Dealers in hay, grass and fodder | 13,152 | 8,642 | .. | 2,523 | 1,987 | .. | .. |
| | | 34.—Trade in clothing and toilet articles. | | ***34.—Trade in clothing and toilet articles.*** | ***9,614*** | ***4,655*** | ***383*** | .. | ***4,576*** | .. | .. |
| | | | 125 | Trade in ready-made clothing and other articles of dress and toilet (hats, umbrellas, socks, ready-made shoes, perfumes, etc). | 9,614 | 4,655 | 383 | .. | 4,576 | .. | .. |
| | | 35.—Trade in furniture. | | ***35.—Trade in furniture*** | ***626*** | ***527*** | ***14*** | .. | ***85*** | .. | .. |
| | | | 126 | Trade in furniture, carpets, curtains and bedding. | 187 | 166 | .. | .. | 21 | .. | .. |
| | | | 127 | Hardware, cooking utensils, porcelain, crockery, glassware, bottles, articles for gardening, the cellar, etc. | 439 | 361 | 14 | .. | 64 | .. | .. |

## TABLE XV.—Occupation or Means of Livelihood. Part D.—Distribution by Religion —*continued.*

| Class. | Sub-class. | Order. | Group No. | Occupation or means of livelihood. | Total number of workers and dependents. | Hindu. | Jain. | Animist. | Musalman. | Christian. | Others. |
|---|---|---|---|---|---|---|---|---|---|---|---|
| 1 | 2 | 3 | 4 | 5 | 6 | 7 | 8 | 9 | 10 | 11 | 12 |
| B.—Preparation and supply of material substances—*contd.* | V.—Trade—*contd.* | 36.—Trade in building materials. | | *36.—Trade in building materials* . | *485* | *387* | .. | .. | *98* | .. | .. |
| | | | 128 | Trade in building materials (stones, bricks, plaster, cement, sand, tiles, thatch, etc.) | 485 | 387 | .. | .. | 98 | .. | .. |
| | | 37.—Trade in means of transport. | | *37.—Trade in means of transport.* | *4,296* | *3,489* | *42* | *87* | *678* | .. | .. |
| | | | 129 | Dealers and hirers of elephants, camels, horses, cattle, asses, mules, etc., sellers (not makers) of carriages, saddlery, etc. | 4,296 | 3,489 | 42 | 87 | 678 | .. | .. |
| | | 38.—Trade in fuel. | | *38.—Trade in fuel* . . . . | *12,797* | *9,893* | *39* | *1,495* | *1,367* | .. | *3* |
| | | | 130 | Dealers in firewood, charcoal, coal, cow-dung, etc. | 12,797 | 9,893 | 39 | 1,495 | 1,367 | .. | 3 |
| | | 39.—Trade in articles of luxury and those pertaining to letters and arts and sciences. | | *39.—Trade in articles of luxury and those pertaining to letters and arts and sciences.* | *17,938* | *13,040* | *921* | .. | *3,973* | .. | *4* |
| | | | 131 | Dealers in precious stone, jewellery (real and imitation), clocks, optical instruments, etc. | 3,614 | 2,630 | 888 | .. | 92 | .. | 4 |
| | | | 132 | Dealers in common bangles, bead necklaces, fans, small articles, toys, hunting and fishing tackle, flowers, etc. | 14,021 | 10,247 | 19 | .. | 3,755 | .. | .. |
| | | | 133 | Publishers, booksellers, stationers, dealers in music, pictures, musical instruments, curiosities. | 303 | 163 | 14 | .. | 126 | .. | .. |
| | | 40.—Trade in refuse matters. | | *40.—Trade in refuse matters* . . | *4* | *4* | .. | .. | .. | .. | .. |
| | | | 134 | Dealers in rags, stable refuse, etc. . | 4 | 4 | .. | .. | .. | .. | .. |
| | | 41.—Trade in other sorts. | | *41.—Trade in other sorts* . . | *67,339* | *48,113* | *11,328* | *27* | *7,891* | *14* | *36* |
| | | | 135 | Shopkeepers otherwise unspecified . | 62,447 | 44,663 | 11,269 | 27 | 6,439 | 14 | 35 |
| | | | 136 | Itinerant traders, pedlers, hawkers, etc. | 2,245 | 1,488 | 22 | .. | 785 | .. | .. |
| | | | 137 | Conjurers, acrobats, fortune tellers, reciters, exhibitors of curiosities and wild animals. | 2,192 | 1,550 | .. | .. | 641 | .. | 1 |
| | | | 138 | Other traders (including farmers of pounds, tolls and markets). | 455 | 412 | 37 | .. | 6 | .. | .. |
| C.—Public administration and liberal arts. | | | | **C.—Public administration and liberal arts.** | **409,986** | **369,197** | **1,383** | **6,200** | **106,059** | **5,028** | **2,019** |
| | VI.—Public force. | | | *VI.—PUBLIC FORCE* . . . | *181,938* | *128,543* | *96* | *4,361* | *43,673* | *3,938* | *1,327* |
| | | 42.—Army. | | *42.—Army* . . . . . . | *89,551* | *60,375* | *26* | *610* | *23,444* | *3,891* | *1,205* |
| | | | 139 | Army (Government) . . . . | 11,474 | 3,838 | .. | 158 | 2,869 | 3,818 | 791 |
| | | | 140A | Imperial Service . . . . | 8,425 | 4,255 | .. | .. | 3,825 | 2 | 343 |
| | | | 140B | Army (Native States) . . . | 69,652 | 52,282 | 26 | 452 | 16,750 | 71 | 71 |
| | | 44.—Police. | | *44.—Police* . . . . . . | *92,387* | *68,168* | *70* | *3,751* | *20,229* | *47* | *122* |
| | | | 142A | Police (Government) . . . . | 2,488 | 796 | .. | 794 | 862 | 12 | 24 |
| | | | 142B | Police (Native States) . . . . | 38,219 | 20,880 | 12 | 653 | 16,541 | 35 | 98 |
| | | | 143 | Village watchmen . . . . | 51,680 | 46,492 | 58 | 2,304 | 2,826 | .. | .. |
| | VII.—Public administration. | | | *VII.—PUBLIC ADMINISTRATION.* | *139,485* | *97,349* | *897* | *1,451* | *38,846* | *483* | *459* |
| | | 45.—Public administration. | | *45.—Public administration* . . | *139,485* | *97,349* | *897* | *1,451* | *38,846* | *483* | *459* |
| | | | 144 | Service of the State . . . . | 4,836 | 3,150 | .. | .. | 1,311 | 227 | 148 |
| | | | 145A | Rulers of Native States and their families. | 443 | 408 | .. | .. | 35 | .. | .. |
| | | | 145B | Darbar officers . . . . . | 69,194 | 49,293 | 748 | .. | 18,775 | 238 | 140 |
| | | | 145C | Menials . . . . . . | 38,506 | 21,201 | 72 | 52 | 17,008 | 17 | 156 |
| | | | 146 | Municipal and other local (not village) service. | 2,411 | 1,501 | 1 | .. | 893 | 1 | 15 |
| | | | 147 | Village officials and servants other than watchmen. | 24,095 | 21,796 | 76 | 1,399 | 824 | .. | .. |
| | VIII.—Professions and liberal arts. | | | *VIII.—PROFESSIONS AND LIBERAL ARTS.* | *138,390* | *123,585* | *571* | *315* | *13,059* | *692* | *168* |
| | | 46.—Religion. | | *46.—Religion* . . . . . | *94,629* | *91,188* | *436* | *169* | *2,366* | *400* | *70* |
| | | | 148 | Priests, ministers, etc. . . . | 54,227 | 52,950 | 220 | 31 | 906 | 58 | 62 |
| | | | 149 | Religious mendicants, inmates of monasteries, etc. | 32,327 | 31,173 | 206 | 130 | 799 | 17 | 2 |
| | | | 150 | Catechists, readers, church mission service. | 496 | 85 | 5 | .. | 75 | 325 | 6 |
| | | | 151 | Temple, burial or burning ground service. | 7,579 | 6,960 | 5 | 8 | 586 | .. | .. |
| | | 47.—Law. | | *47.—Law* . . . . . . | *3,663* | *2,617* | *42* | .. | *988* | .. | *16* |
| | | | 152 | Lawyers of all kinds including Kazis, law agents and mukhtiars. | 2,342 | 1,535 | 32 | .. | 761 | .. | 14 |
| | | | 153 | Lawyer's clerks, petition writers, etc. . | 1,321 | 1,082 | 10 | .. | 227 | .. | 2 |

## TABLE XV.—Occupation or Means of Livelihood. Part D.—Distribution by Religion —*concluded*.

| Class. | Sub-class. | Order. | Group No. | Occupation or Means of Livelihood. | Total number of workers and dependents. | Hindu. | Jain. | Animist. | Musalman. | Christian. | Others. |
|---|---|---|---|---|---|---|---|---|---|---|---|
| 1 | 2 | 3 | 4 | 5 | 6 | 7 | 8 | 9 | 10 | 11 | 12 |
| C.—Public administration and liberal arts—*contd.* | VIII.—Professions and liberal arts—*contd.* | 48.—Medicine. | | ***48.—Medicine*** | ***5,954*** | ***4,350*** | ***32*** | ***17*** | ***1,435*** | ***105*** | ***15*** |
| | | | 154A | Medical practitioners of all kinds including dentists, oculists and veterinary surgeons (Government). | 202 | 99 | .. | .. | 73 | 30 | .. |
| | | | 154B | Medical practitioners of all kinds including dentists, oculists and veterinary surgeons (Native States). | 2,454 | 1,625 | 23 | .. | 729 | 63 | 14 |
| | | | 155A | Midwives, vaccinators, compounders, nurses, masseurs, etc. (Government). | 172 | 130 | .. | .. | 41 | 1 | .. |
| | | | 155B | Midwives, vaccinators, compounders, nurses, masseurs (Native States). | 3,126 | 2,496 | 9 | 17 | 592 | 11 | 1 |
| | | 49.—Instruction. | | ***49.—Instruction*** | ***6,951*** | ***5,590*** | ***44*** | ***8*** | ***1,944*** | ***91*** | ***44*** |
| | | | 156 | Professors and teachers of all kinds (except law, medicine, music, dancing, and drawing) and clerks and servants connected with education. | 6,951 | 5,520 | 44 | 8 | 1,244 | 91 | 44 |
| | | 50.—Letters and arts and sciences. | | ***50.—Letters and arts and sciences*** | ***27,193*** | ***19,910*** | ***17*** | ***121*** | ***7,026*** | ***96*** | ***23*** |
| | | | 157 | Public scribes, stenographers | 15 | 10 | .. | .. | 5 | .. | .. |
| | | | 158A | Architects, surveyors, engineers, and other employés (Government). | 75 | 30 | .. | .. | 16 | 23 | 6 |
| | | | 158B | Architects, surveyors, engineers, and other employés (Native States). | 1,921 | 1,462 | 1 | 5 | 387 | 53 | 13 |
| | | | 159 | Others (authors, photographers, artists, sculptors, astronomers, meteorologists, botanists, astrologers, etc.). | 2,476 | 2,207 | .. | .. | 260 | 5 | 4 |
| | | | 160 | Music composers and masters, players on all kinds of musical instruments (not military), singers, actors and dancers. | 22,706 | 16,201 | 16 | 116 | 6,358 | 15 | .. |
| | IX.—Persons living on their income. | 51.—Persons living principally on their income. | | ***IX.—PERSONS LIVING ON THEIR INCOME.*** | ***31,173*** | ***19,790*** | ***319*** | ***73*** | ***10,481*** | ***515*** | ***65*** |
| | | | | ***51.—Persons living principally on their income.*** | ***31,173*** | ***19,790*** | ***319*** | ***73*** | ***10,481*** | ***515*** | ***65*** |
| | | | 161 | Proprietors (other than of agricultural land), fund and scholarship holders and pensioners. | 31,173 | 19,720 | 319 | 73 | 10,481 | 515 | 65 |
| D.—Miscellaneous. | | | | **D.—Miscellaneous** | **1,201,154** | **1,024,429** | **4,730** | **60,681** | **109,142** | **1,882** | **290** |
| | X.—Domestic service. | 52.—Domestic service. | | ***X.—DOMESTIC SERVICE*** | ***214,177*** | ***170,491*** | ***1,858*** | ***3,053*** | ***36,886*** | ***1,801*** | ***88*** |
| | | | | ***52.—Domestic service*** | ***214,177*** | ***170,491*** | ***1,858*** | ***3,053*** | ***36,886*** | ***1,801*** | ***88*** |
| | | | 162 | Cooks, water carriers, door-keepers, watchmen and other indoor servants. | 204,889 | 163,933 | 1,846 | 2,874 | 34,707 | 1,470 | 59 |
| | | | 163 | Private grooms, coachmen, dog boys, etc. | 9,288 | 6,558 | 12 | 179 | 2,179 | 331 | 29 |
| | XI.—Insufficiently described occupations. | 53.—General terms which do not indicate a definite occupation. | | ***XI.—INSUFFICIENTLY DESCRIBED OCCUPATIONS.*** | ***754,480*** | ***650,314*** | ***2,591*** | ***56,919*** | ***45,191*** | ***40*** | ***202*** |
| | | | | ***53.—General terms which do not indicate a definite occupation.*** | ***754,480*** | ***650,314*** | ***2,591*** | ***56,919*** | ***45,191*** | ***40*** | ***202*** |
| | | | 164 | Manufacturers, business men and contractors otherwise unspecified. | 6,025 | 4,764 | 63 | 203 | 854 | 1 | 140 |
| | | | 165 | Cashiers, accountants, book-keepers, clerks, and other employés in unspecified offices, ware-houses and shops. | 5,160 | 4,082 | 396 | 47 | 594 | 3 | 38 |
| | | | 166 | Mechanics otherwise unspecified | 1,567 | 1,076 | .. | .. | 487 | .. | 4 |
| | | | 167 | Labourers and workmen otherwise unspecified. | 741,728 | 640,392 | 2,132 | 55,962 | 43,186 | 36 | 20 |
| | XII.—Unproductive. | 54.—Inmates of jails, etc. | | ***XII.—UNPRODUCTIVE*** | ***232,497*** | ***203,624*** | ***281*** | ***1,416*** | ***27,135*** | ***41*** | .. |
| | | | | ***54.—Inmates of jails and asylums and hospitals.*** | ***4,148*** | ***3,399*** | ***4*** | ***291*** | ***417*** | ***37*** | .. |
| | | | 168 | Inmates of jails, asylums and hospitals | 4,148 | 3,399 | 4 | 291 | 417 | 37 | .. |
| | | 55.—Beggars, vagrants, etc. | | ***55.—Beggars, vagrants, prostitutes*** | ***228,349*** | ***200,225*** | ***277*** | ***1,125*** | ***26,718*** | ***4*** | .. |
| | | | 169 | Beggars, vagrants, procurers, prostitutes, receivers of stolen goods, cattle poisoners, etc. | 228,349 | 200,225 | 277 | 1,125 | 26,718 | 4 | .. |

## TABLE XV-E.

***STATISTICS OF INDUSTRIES***

## TABLE XV-E.—Statistics of Industries.

| Description of factory, mine, etc. | Classification of factory, etc., according to number of persons employed. | Number of factories. | Total number of persons employed. Males. | Females. |
|---|---|---|---|---|
| 1 | 2 | 3 | 4 | 5 |
| **Central India—** | **Total** | **144** | **12,198** | **3,974** |
| *I.—Mines—* | ***Total*** | ***4*** | ***1,540*** | ***358*** |
| Diamond mines in which mechanical power is used | From 100 to 200 persons | 1 | 44 | 61 |
| Manganese ore mine in which mechanical power is used | " 200 to 400 " | 1 | 224 | 104 |
| Colliery works in which mechanical power is used | " 200 to 400 " | 1 | 209 | .. |
| Coal mine in which mechanical power is used | " 400 and over | 1 | 1,063 | 193 |
| *II.—Textile industries—* | ***Total*** | ***105*** | ***7,378*** | ***2,827*** |
| Cotton ginning factories— | **Total** | **81** | **3,356** | **2,278** |
| Factories in which mechanical power is used | From 20 to 50 persons | 28 | 664 | 407 |
| | " 50 to 100 " | 41 | 1,716 | 1,205 |
| | " 100 to 200 " | 11 | 878 | 539 |
| | " 200 to 400 " | 1 | 98 | 127 |
| Cotton presses— | **Total** | **10** | **524** | **110** |
| Presses in which mechanical power is used | From 20 to 50 persons | 4 | 160 | 16 |
| | " 50 to 100 " | 5 | 256 | 82 |
| | " 100 to 200 " | 1 | 108 | 12 |
| Cotton ginning and oil mill in which mechanical power is used | From 20 to 100 persons | 1 | 25 | 11 |
| Cotton spinning and weaving mills— | **Total** | **5** | **2,955** | **401** |
| Mills in which mechanical power is used | From 20 to 50 persons | 1 | 24 | 12 |
| | " 50 to 100 " | 1 | 52 | 7 |
| | " 400 and over | 3 | 2,879 | 382 |
| Cotton carpet and rug manufacture factories— | **Total** | **6** | **458** | **27** |
| Factories in which mechanical power is used | From 100 to 200 persons | 1 | 141 | 8 |
| Factories in which mechanical power is not used | **Total** | **5** | **317** | **19** |
| | From 20 to 50 persons | 4 | 154 | 4 |
| | " 100 to 200 " | 1 | 163 | 15 |
| Dari, etc., weaving factory and litho press in which mechanical power is not used | From 20 to 50 persons | 1 | 32 | .. |
| Textile institute in which mechanical power is not used | " 20 to 50 " | 1 | 28 | .. |
| *III.—Leather industries—* | ***Total*** | ***3*** | ***215*** | ***1*** |
| Leather factory in which mechanical power is used | From 50 to 100 persons | 1 | 99 | .. |
| Tanneries in which mechanical power is not used | " 50 to 100 " | 2 | 116 | 1 |
| *IV.—Metal industries—* | ***Total*** | ***2*** | ***383*** | .. |
| Repairing and workshops in which mechanical power is used | From 20 to 50 persons | 1 | 36 | .. |
| | " 200 to 400 " | 1 | 347 | .. |
| *V.—Glass and earthen ware industries—* | ***Total*** | ***3*** | ***294*** | ***23*** |
| Glass factory in which mechanical power is not used | From 50 to 100 persons | 1 | 89 | .. |
| Tile factory in which mechanical power is not used | " 100 to 200 " | 1 | 128 | .. |
| Brick factory in which mechanical power is not used | " 100 to 200 " | 1 | 77 | 23 |
| *VI.—Industries connected with chemical products—* | ***Total*** | ***2*** | ***240*** | ***84*** |
| Gunpowder and miscellaneous factory in which mechanical power is used | From 100 to 200 persons | 1 | 138 | .. |
| Shellac factory in which mechanical power is used | " 100 to 200 " | 1 | 102 | 84 |
| *VII.—Food industries—* | ***Total*** | ***12*** | ***467*** | ***101*** |
| | **Total** | **6** | **254** | **51** |
| Factories in which mechanical power is used | From 20 to 50 persons | 1 | 22 | 7 |
| Hay press | " 20 to 50 " | 1 | 40 | 4 |
| Flour and ice manufacture factory | " 50 to 100 " | 1 | 38 | 14 |
| Flour manufacture factory | " 50 to 100 " | 1 | 55 | 6 |
| Dairy | " 50 to 100 " | 2 | 99 | 20 |
| Sugar factories | **Total** | **6** | **213** | **50** |
| Factories in which mechanical power is not used | From 20 to 50 persons | 3 | 87 | 11 |
| Country liquor distillery | " 20 to 50 " | 1 | 26 | 5 |
| Sugar factories | " 50 to 100 " | 2 | 100 | 34 |
| *VIII.—Furniture industries—* | ***Total*** | ***4*** | ***217*** | ***25*** |
| Furniture making factories— | **Total** | **4** | **217** | **25** |
| Factories in which mechanical power is used | From 20 to 50 persons | 1 | 44 | .. |
| | " 100 to 200 " | 1 | 97 | 25 |
| Factories in which mechanical power is not used | " 20 to 50 " | 2 | 76 | .. |
| *IX.—Industries connected with buildings—* | ***Total*** | ***4*** | ***1,003*** | ***542*** |
| Lime works in which mechanical power is not used | From 50 to 100 persons | 1 | 51 | .. |
| Stone works in which mechanical power is not used | " 50 to 100 " | 2 | 102 | .. |
| Stone quarrying and lime burning in which mechanical power is not used. | " 400 and over | 1 | 850 | 542 |
| *X.—Production and transmission of physical forces—* | ***Total*** | ***3*** | ***110*** | ***13*** |
| Electric light works in which mechanical power is used | From 20 to 50 persons | 2 | 73 | .. |
| | " 50 to 100 " | 1 | 37 | 13 |
| *XI.—Industries of luxury—* | ***Total*** | ***2*** | ***261*** | .. |
| Printing press in which mechanical power is used | From 200 to 400 persons | 1 | 202 | .. |
| Printing press in which mechanical power is not used | " 50 to 100 " | 1 | 59 | .. |

## PART I.—PROVINCIAL SUMMARY.

| CLASSIFICATION OF PERSONS EMPLOYED. | | | | | | | | | | | | Remarks. | |
|---|---|---|---|---|---|---|---|---|---|---|---|---|---|
| DIRECTION, SUPERVISION AND CLERICAL WORK. | | | | SKILLED WORKMEN. | | | | UNSKILLED LABOURERS. | | | | N.B.—The state of business is indicated thus in figures :—<br>(1) Much brisker than usual.<br>(2) Brisker than usual.<br>(3) Somewhat brisker than usual.<br>(4) Normal.<br>(5) Somewhat slacker than usual.<br>(6) Slacker than usual.<br>(7) Much slacker than usual. | |
| Europeans and Anglo-Indians. | | Indians. | | Europeans and Anglo-Indians. | | Indians. | | Age 14 and over. | | Age under 14. | | | |
| Males. | Females. | Males. | Females. | Males. | Females. | Males. | Females. | Males. | Females. | Males. | Females. | | |
| 6 | 7 | 8 | 9 | 10 | 11 | 12 | 13 | 14 | 15 | 16 | 17 | 18 | |
| 35 | 2 | 759 | 24 | 34 | .. | 5,386 | 715 | 5,313 | 3,069 | 581 | 173 | Power. | State of business. |
| 5 | .. | 31 | .. | .. | .. | 1,138 | 195 | 332 | 144 | 34 | 19 | Steam 4 | |
| .. | .. | 5 | .. | .. | .. | 1 | 2 | 35 | 56 | 3 | 3 | | (2) 2 |
| .. | .. | 6 | .. | .. | .. | 2 | .. | 185 | 88 | 31 | 16 | | (5) 1 |
| 1 | .. | .. | .. | .. | .. | 207 | .. | 1 | .. | .. | .. | | (6) 1 |
| 4 | .. | 20 | .. | .. | .. | 928 | 193 | 111 | .. | .. | .. | | 4 |
| 13 | 2 | 505 | 24 | 26 | .. | 3,109 | 430 | 3,295 | 2,961 | 437 | 110 | | |
| 5 | 2 | 354 | 24 | 26 | .. | 666 | 123 | 2,163 | 2,029 | 142 | 100 | Steam 79 | (4) 3 |
| .. | .. | 80 | 20 | .. | .. | 138 | 49 | 407 | 310 | 39 | 28 | Oil 1 | (5) 36 |
| .. | .. | 215 | 2 | 6 | .. | 379 | 74 | 1,039 | 1,077 | 77 | 52 | Water 1 | (6) 1 |
| 1 | .. | 56 | 2 | .. | .. | 149 | .. | 649 | 517 | 23 | 20 | 81 | (7) 41 |
| 4 | 2 | 3 | .. | 20 | .. | .. | .. | 68 | 125 | 3 | .. | | 81 |
| .. | .. | 27 | .. | .. | .. | 97 | 14 | 387 | 95 | 13 | 1 | Steam 10 | (2) 1 |
| .. | .. | 13 | .. | .. | .. | 15 | .. | 131 | 15 | 1 | 1 | | (6) 9 |
| .. | .. | 10 | .. | .. | .. | 74 | 14 | 168 | 68 | 4 | .. | | 10 |
| .. | .. | 4 | .. | .. | .. | 8 | .. | 88 | 12 | 8 | .. | | |
| .. | .. | .. | .. | .. | .. | 6 | .. | 18 | 11 | 1 | .. | Steam 1 | (6) 1 |
| 3 | .. | 94 | .. | .. | .. | 1,961 | 274 | 626 | 118 | 271 | 9 | Steam 5 | (2) 1 |
| .. | .. | 4 | .. | .. | .. | 10 | 12 | 10 | .. | .. | .. | | (4) 4 |
| .. | .. | 2 | .. | .. | .. | 50 | 7 | .. | .. | .. | .. | | 5 |
| 3 | .. | 88 | .. | .. | .. | 1,901 | 255 | 616 | 118 | 271 | 9 | | |
| 5 | .. | 25 | .. | .. | .. | 354 | 19 | 64 | 8 | 10 | .. | | |
| 3 | .. | 4 | .. | .. | .. | 123 | .. | 11 | 8 | .. | .. | Oil 1 | (4) 1 |
| 2 | .. | 21 | .. | .. | .. | 231 | 19 | 53 | .. | 10 | .. | *Nil.* | (2) 1 |
| .. | .. | 12 | .. | .. | .. | 91 | 4 | 41 | .. | 10 | .. | | (3) 1 |
| 2 | .. | 9 | .. | .. | .. | 140 | 15 | 12 | .. | .. | .. | | (4) 2 |
| | | | | | | | | | | | | | (6) 1 |
| | | | | | | | | | | | | | 5 |
| .. | .. | 2 | .. | .. | .. | .. | .. | 39 | .. | .. | .. | *Nil.* | (4) 1 |
| .. | .. | 3 | .. | .. | .. | 18 | .. | 7 | .. | .. | .. | *Nil.* | (4) 1 |
| 3 | .. | 21 | .. | 1 | .. | 148 | .. | 34 | 1 | 8 | .. | | |
| 1 | .. | 8 | .. | .. | .. | 74 | .. | 12 | .. | 4 | .. | Steam 1 | (2) 1 |
| 2 | .. | 13 | .. | 1 | .. | 74 | .. | 22 | 1 | 4 | .. | Manual 2 | (4) 2 |
| | | | | | | | | | | | | 3 | 3 |
| 3 | .. | 32 | .. | 2 | .. | 230 | .. | 116 | .. | .. | .. | Electricity 2 | (1) 1 |
| 1 | .. | .. | .. | .. | .. | 14 | .. | 21 | .. | .. | .. | | (3) 1 |
| 2 | .. | 32 | .. | 2 | .. | 216 | .. | 95 | .. | .. | .. | | 2 |
| .. | .. | 5 | .. | .. | .. | 87 | .. | 190 | 23 | 12 | .. | *Nil.* | (2) 1 |
| .. | .. | 4 | .. | .. | .. | 15 | .. | 70 | .. | .. | .. | | (4) 2 |
| .. | .. | .. | .. | .. | .. | 64 | .. | 64 | .. | .. | .. | | 3 |
| .. | .. | 1 | .. | .. | .. | 8 | .. | 56 | 23 | 12 | .. | | |
| .. | .. | 8 | .. | .. | .. | 205 | 84 | 20 | .. | 7 | .. | Steam and manual 2 | (2) 1 |
| .. | .. | 5 | .. | .. | .. | 109 | .. | 17 | .. | 7 | .. | | (4) 1 |
| .. | .. | 3 | .. | .. | .. | 96 | 84 | 3 | .. | .. | .. | | 2 |
| 4 | .. | 51 | .. | 4 | .. | 60 | 6 | 324 | 74 | 24 | 21 | | |
| 3 | .. | 21 | .. | 4 | .. | 33 | 6 | 177 | 30 | 16 | 6 | Steam 5 | (2) 1 |
| .. | .. | 2 | .. | .. | .. | 10 | .. | 10 | 7 | .. | .. | | (3) 3 |
| .. | .. | 2 | .. | .. | .. | .. | .. | 28 | 2 | 10 | 2 | | |
| .. | .. | 6 | .. | .. | .. | 12 | 6 | 20 | 8 | .. | .. | Steam and oil 1 | (4) 2 |
| 3 | .. | 4 | .. | 4 | .. | .. | .. | 43 | 6 | 1 | .. | | |
| .. | .. | 7 | .. | .. | .. | 11 | .. | 76 | 16 | 5 | 4 | 6 | 6 |
| 1 | .. | 30 | .. | .. | .. | 27 | .. | 147 | 35 | 8 | 15 | *Nil.* | (3) 2 |
| 1 | .. | 22 | .. | .. | .. | 22 | .. | 42 | 11 | .. | .. | | (4) 3 |
| .. | .. | 2 | .. | .. | .. | 2 | .. | 22 | 4 | .. | 1 | | (5) 1 |
| .. | .. | 6 | .. | .. | .. | 3 | .. | 63 | 20 | 8 | 14 | | 6 |
| .. | .. | 26 | .. | .. | .. | 99 | .. | 61 | 22 | 31 | 3 | | |
| .. | .. | 26 | .. | .. | .. | 99 | .. | 61 | 22 | 31 | 3 | | |
| .. | .. | 7 | .. | .. | .. | 32 | .. | 5 | .. | .. | .. | Steam and oil 1 | (4) 1 |
| .. | .. | 8 | .. | .. | .. | 46 | .. | 38 | 22 | 5 | 3 | Electricity 1 | (4) 1 |
| .. | .. | 11 | .. | .. | .. | 21 | .. | 18 | .. | 26 | .. | *Nil.* | (2) 2 |
| | | | | | | | | | | | | | 4 |
| 3 | .. | 44 | .. | 1 | .. | 113 | .. | 815 | 522 | 27 | 20 | *Nil.* | (2) 1 |
| 2 | .. | 5 | .. | .. | .. | .. | .. | 36 | .. | 8 | .. | | (6) 3 |
| .. | .. | 7 | .. | .. | .. | 95 | .. | .. | .. | .. | .. | | 4 |
| 1 | .. | 32 | .. | 1 | .. | 18 | .. | 779 | 522 | 19 | 20 | | |
| 3 | .. | 5 | .. | .. | .. | 15 | .. | 86 | 13 | 1 | .. | Steam 3 | |
| 2 | .. | 4 | .. | .. | .. | 13 | .. | 54 | .. | .. | .. | | (3) 2 |
| 1 | .. | 1 | .. | .. | .. | 2 | .. | 32 | 13 | 1 | .. | | (4) 1 |
| | | | | | | | | | | | | | 3 |
| 1 | .. | 31 | .. | .. | .. | 189 | .. | 40 | .. | .. | .. | | |
| 1 | .. | 25 | .. | .. | .. | 155 | .. | 21 | .. | .. | .. | Electricity 1 | (2) 2 |
| .. | .. | 6 | .. | .. | .. | 34 | .. | 19 | .. | .. | .. | *Nil.* | |

# TABLE XV-E.—Statistics of Industries.

| Description of factory, mine, etc. | Political Charge. | Number of factories. | Total number of persons employed. | |
|---|---|---|---|---|
| | | | Males. | Females. |
| 1 | 2 | 3 | 4 | 5 |
| *Central India* | *Total* | *144* | *12,108* | *3,974* |
| | **Gwalior Residency** | **44** | **3,777** | **1,018** |
| Cotton ginning factories | „ „ | 28 | 1,244 | 784 |
| Cotton presses | „ „ | 5 | 296 | 42 |
| Cotton spinning and weaving mill | „ „ | 1 | 645 | 138 |
| Textile institute | „ „ | 1 | 28 | .. |
| Cotton carpet factory | „ „ | 1 | 163 | 15 |
| Leather factory | „ „ | 1 | 99 | .. |
| Tannery | „ „ | 1 | 59 | 1 |
| Workshop | „ „ | 1 | 847 | .. |
| Glass factory | „ „ | 1 | 89 | .. |
| Sugar factory | „ „ | 1 | 27 | 34 |
| Electric light work | „ „ | 1 | 38 | .. |
| Printing press | „ „ | 1 | 202 | .. |
| Hay press | „ „ | 1 | 40 | 4 |
| | **Indore Residency** | **42** | **3,385** | **1,133** |
| Cotton ginning factories | „ „ | 27 | 960 | 763 |
| Cotton spinning and weaving mills | „ „ | 2 | 2,234 | 244 |
| Cotton presses | „ „ | 5 | 228 | 68 |
| Rug making factory | „ „ | 1 | 141 | 8 |
| Repairing shop | „ „ | 1 | 36 | .. |
| Dairy | „ „ | 1 | 55 | 6 |
| Flour and ice manufacture factory | „ „ | 1 | 22 | 7 |
| Flour manufacture factory | „ „ | 1 | 38 | 14 |
| Brick manufacture factory | „ „ | 1 | 77 | 23 |
| Electric light work | „ „ | 1 | 85 | .. |
| Printing press | „ „ | 1 | 59 | .. |
| | **Baghelkhand Agency** | **17** | **2,968** | **864** |
| Coal mine | „ „ | 1 | 1,063 | 193 |
| Colliery works | „ „ | 1 | 209 | .. |
| Cotton spinning and weaving mill | „ „ | 1 | 24 | 12 |
| Cotton carpet and rug making factory | „ „ | 1 | 47 | .. |
| Tannery | „ „ | 1 | 57 | .. |
| Gunpowder and miscellaneous factory | „ „ | 1 | 138 | .. |
| Shellac factory | „ „ | 1 | 102 | 84 |
| Sugar factories | „ „ | 3 | 146 | 8 |
| Furniture moulding and water works | „ „ | 1 | 97 | 25 |
| Furniture making factories | „ „ | 2 | 82 | .. |
| Stone quarrying and lime burning factory | „ „ | 1 | 850 | 542 |
| Stone works | „ „ | 2 | 102 | .. |
| Lime works | „ „ | 1 | 51 | .. |
| | **Bhopal Agency** | **12** | **701** | **257** |
| Cotton ginning factories | „ „ | 4 | 289 | 209 |
| Cotton spinning and weaving mill | „ „ | 1 | 52 | 7 |
| Cotton carpet and rug manufacture factory | „ „ | 1 | 38 | 4 |
| Dari, etc., weaving factory and litho press | „ „ | 1 | 32 | .. |
| Tile factory | „ „ | 1 | 128 | .. |
| Sugar factory | „ „ | 1 | 52 | 17 |
| Country liquor distillery | „ „ | 1 | 35 | 7 |
| Furniture making factory | „ „ | 1 | 38 | .. |
| Electric light works | „ „ | 1 | 37 | 13 |
| | **Bhopawar Agency** | **10** | **622** | **359** |
| Manganese ore mine | „ „ | 1 | 224 | 104 |
| Cotton ginning factories | „ „ | 9 | 398 | 255 |
| | **Bundelkhand Agency** | **2** | **90** | **61** |
| Diamond mine | „ „ | 1 | 44 | 61 |
| Cotton carpet weaving factory | „ „ | 1 | 46 | .. |
| | **Malwa Agency** | **17** | **565** | **282** |
| Cotton ginning factories | „ „ | 13 | 465 | 267 |
| Cotton ginning and oil mill | „ „ | 1 | 25 | 11 |
| Cotton carpet and rug making factory | „ „ | 1 | 23 | .. |
| Country liquor distilleries | „ „ | 2 | 52 | 4 |

## PART II.—DISTRIBUTION BY POLITICAL CHARGES.

| CLASSIFICATION OF PERSONS EMPLOYED. | | | | | | | | | | | | Remarks showing States where situated. |
|---|---|---|---|---|---|---|---|---|---|---|---|---|
| DIRECTION, SUPERVISION AND CLERICAL WORK. | | | | SKILLED WORKMEN. | | | | UNSKILLED LABOURERS. | | | | |
| Europeans and Anglo-Indians. | | Indians. | | Europeans and Anglo-Indians. | | Indians. | | Age 14 and over. | | Age under 14. | | |
| Males. | Females. | Males. | Females. | Males. | Females. | Males. | Females. | Males. | Females. | Males. | Females. | |
| 6 | 7 | 8 | 9 | 10 | 11 | 12 | 13 | 14 | 15 | 16 | 17 | 18 |
| *35* | *9* | *759* | *24* | *34* | .. | *5,386* | *715* | *5,313* | *3,060* | *581* | *173* | |
| **8** | .. | **283** | .. | **2** | .. | **1,365** | **181** | **1,533** | **804** | **86** | **33** | |
| .. | .. | 160 | .. | .. | .. | 305 | 84 | 742 | 684 | 37 | 16 | Gwalior. |
| .. | .. | 14 | .. | .. | .. | 42 | 2 | 227 | 39 | 13 | 1 | Do. |
| .. | .. | 15 | .. | .. | .. | 346 | 80 | 274 | 58 | 10 | .. | Do. |
| .. | .. | 3 | .. | .. | .. | 18 | .. | 7 | .. | .. | .. | Do. |
| 2 | .. | 9 | .. | .. | .. | 140 | 15 | 12 | .. | .. | .. | Do. |
| 1 | .. | 8 | .. | .. | .. | 74 | .. | 12 | .. | 4 | .. | Do. |
| 1 | .. | 6 | .. | .. | .. | 42 | .. | 6 | 1 | 4 | .. | Do. |
| 2 | .. | 32 | .. | 2 | .. | 216 | .. | 95 | .. | .. | .. | Do. |
| .. | .. | 4 | .. | .. | .. | 15 | .. | 70 | .. | .. | .. | Do. |
| .. | .. | 2 | .. | .. | .. | 2 | .. | 15 | 20 | 8 | 14 | Do. |
| 1 | .. | 3 | .. | .. | .. | 10 | .. | 24 | .. | .. | .. | Do. |
| 1 | .. | 25 | .. | .. | .. | 155 | .. | 21 | .. | .. | .. | Do. |
| .. | .. | 2 | .. | .. | .. | .. | .. | 28 | 2 | 10 | 2 | Do. |
| **11** | .. | **220** | **23** | **10** | .. | **1,946** | **232** | **1,383** | **824** | **315** | **54** | |
| .. | .. | 110 | 23 | 6 | .. | 132 | 39 | 671 | 656 | 41 | 45 | Indore. |
| 3 | .. | 73 | .. | .. | .. | 1,555 | 175 | 342 | 60 | 261 | 9 | Do. |
| .. | .. | 13 | .. | .. | .. | 55 | 12 | 160 | 56 | .. | .. | Do. |
| 3 | .. | 4 | .. | .. | .. | 123 | .. | 11 | 8 | .. | .. | Do. |
| 1 | .. | .. | .. | .. | .. | 14 | .. | 21 | .. | .. | .. | Do. |
| 3 | .. | 4 | .. | 4 | .. | .. | .. | 43 | 6 | 1 | .. | Mhow Cantonment. |
| .. | .. | 2 | .. | .. | .. | 10 | .. | 10 | 7 | .. | .. | Ditto. |
| .. | .. | 6 | .. | .. | .. | 12 | 6 | 20 | 8 | .. | .. | Indore. |
| .. | .. | 1 | .. | .. | .. | 8 | .. | 56 | 23 | 12 | .. | Mhow Cantonment. |
| 1 | .. | 1 | .. | .. | .. | 3 | .. | 30 | .. | .. | .. | Indore. |
| .. | .. | 6 | .. | .. | .. | 34 | .. | 19 | .. | .. | .. | Do. |
| **9** | .. | **116** | .. | **2** | .. | **1,634** | **289** | **1,167** | **551** | **45** | **24** | |
| 4 | .. | 20 | .. | .. | .. | 928 | 193 | 111 | .. | .. | .. | Rewah. |
| 1 | .. | .. | .. | .. | .. | 207 | .. | 1 | .. | .. | .. | Do. |
| .. | .. | 4 | .. | .. | .. | 10 | 12 | 10 | .. | .. | .. | Do. |
| .. | .. | 5 | .. | .. | .. | 32 | .. | 10 | .. | .. | .. | Do. |
| 1 | .. | 7 | .. | 1 | .. | 32 | .. | 16 | .. | .. | .. | Do. |
| .. | .. | 5 | .. | .. | .. | 109 | .. | 17 | .. | 7 | .. | Do. |
| .. | .. | 3 | .. | .. | .. | 96 | 84 | 3 | .. | .. | .. | Do. |
| .. | .. | 10 | .. | .. | .. | 8 | .. | 128 | 7 | .. | 1 | Do. |
| .. | .. | 8 | .. | .. | .. | 46 | .. | 38 | 22 | 5 | 3 | Do. |
| .. | .. | 10 | .. | .. | .. | 53 | .. | 18 | .. | 6 | .. | Do. |
| 1 | .. | 32 | .. | 1 | .. | 18 | .. | 779 | 522 | 19 | 20 | Do. |
| .. | .. | 7 | .. | .. | .. | 95 | .. | .. | .. | .. | .. | Do. |
| 2 | .. | 5 | .. | .. | .. | .. | .. | 36 | .. | 8 | .. | Maihar. |
| **6** | **2** | **47** | .. | **20** | .. | **191** | **11** | **399** | **239** | **38** | **5** | |
| 4 | 2 | 17 | .. | 20 | .. | 22 | .. | 214 | 206 | 12 | 1 | Bhopal 1<br>Narsinghgarh 1<br>Rajgarh 1<br>Khilchipur 1 |
| .. | .. | 2 | .. | .. | .. | 50 | 7 | .. | .. | .. | .. | Bhopal. |
| .. | .. | 2 | .. | .. | .. | 36 | 4 | .. | .. | .. | .. | Narsinghghar. |
| .. | .. | 2 | .. | .. | .. | .. | .. | 30 | .. | .. | .. | Rajgarh. |
| .. | .. | .. | .. | .. | .. | 64 | .. | 64 | .. | .. | .. | Bhopal. |
| .. | .. | 3 | .. | .. | .. | 6 | .. | 38 | 13 | 5 | 4 | Narsinghgarh, |
| 1 | .. | 12 | .. | .. | .. | 11 | .. | 11 | 7 | .. | .. | Bhopal. |
| .. | .. | 8 | .. | .. | .. | .. | .. | 10 | .. | 20 | .. | Do. |
| 1 | .. | 1 | — | .. | .. | 2 | .. | 32 | 13 | 1 | .. | Do. |
| **1** | .. | **28** | .. | .. | .. | **81** | .. | **465** | **333** | **47** | **26** | |
| .. | .. | 6 | .. | .. | .. | 2 | .. | 185 | 88 | 31 | 16 | Jhabua. |
| 1 | .. | 22 | .. | .. | .. | 79 | .. | 280 | 245 | 16 | 10 | Jhabua 1<br>Barwani 3<br>Dhar 5 |
| .. | .. | **9** | .. | .. | .. | **10** | **2** | **58** | **56** | **13** | **3** | |
| .. | .. | 5 | .. | .. | .. | 1 | 2 | 35 | 56 | 3 | 3 | Charkhari. |
| .. | .. | 4 | .. | .. | .. | 9 | .. | 23 | .. | 10 | .. | Do. |
| .. | .. | **56** | **1** | .. | .. | **159** | .. | **313** | **253** | **37** | **28** | |
| .. | .. | 45 | 1 | .. | .. | 128 | .. | 256 | 238 | 36 | 28 | Sitamau 1<br>Piploda 1<br>Ratlam 3<br>Dewas 4<br>Jaora 4 |
| . | .. | .. | .. | .. | .. | 6 | .. | 18 | 11 | 1 | .. | Sailana. |
| . | .. | 1 | .. | .. | .. | 14 | .. | 8 | .. | .. | .. | Ratlam. |
| . | .. | 10 | .. | .. | .. | 11 | .. | 31 | 4 | .. | .. | Ratlam 1<br>Jaora 1 |

## TABLE XV-E.—STATISTICS OF INDUSTRIES. PART III.—

| Description of Factory, etc. | Number of factories. | Number owned by States. | Number owned by Companies of which the Directors are | | |
|---|---|---|---|---|---|
| | | | Europeans and Anglo-Indians. | Indians. | Of both races. |
| 1 | 2 | 3 | 4 | 5 | 6 |
| *Total* | *119* | *16* | *2* | *29* | ... |
| Diamond mine | 1 | .. | .. | .. | .. |
| Manganese ore mine | 1 | .. | 1 | .. | .. |
| Colliery works | 1 | 1 | .. | .. | .. |
| Coal mine | 1 | 1 | .. | .. | .. |
| Cotton ginning factories | 81 | 1 | .. | 23 | .. |
| Cotton presses | 10 | 1 | .. | 4 | .. |
| Cotton ginning and oil mill | 1 | .. | .. | 1 | .. |
| Cotton spinning and weaving mills | 5 | 3 | .. | 1 | .. |
| Cotton carpet and rug manufacture factories | 6 | 4 | 1 | .. | .. |
| Dari, etc., weaving factory and litho press | 1 | 1 | .. | .. | .. |
| Textile institute | 1 | 1 | .. | .. | .. |
| Leather factory | 1 | 1 | .. | .. | .. |
| Tanneries | 2 | 2 | .. | .. | .. |

## TABLE XV-E.—STATISTICS OF INDUSTRIES. PART IV.—

| Description of Factory, etc. | Number of factories. | Europeans and Anglo-Indians. | | | | | | |
|---|---|---|---|---|---|---|---|---|
| | | | Total. | Bania Agarwal. | Bania Bijawargi. | Bania Chitora. | Bania Kapol. | Bania Mahesri. |
| 1 | 2 | 3 | 4 | 5 | 6 | 7 | 8 | 9 |
| *Total* | *119* | *11* | *101* | *23* | *1* | *1* | *1* | *11* |
| Diamond mine | 1 | .. | 1 | .. | .. | .. | .. | .. |
| Manganese ore mine | 1 | 1 | .. | .. | .. | .. | .. | .. |
| Colliery works | 1 | 1 | .. | .. | .. | .. | .. | .. |
| Coal mine | 1 | 1 | .. | .. | .. | .. | .. | .. |
| Cotton ginning factories | 81 | 1 | 80 | 21 | .. | 1 | 1 | 11 |
| Cotton presses | 10 | .. | 10 | 1 | 1 | .. | .. | .. |
| Cotton ginning and oil mill | 1 | .. | 1 | .. | .. | .. | .. | .. |
| Cotton spinning and weaving mills | 5 | 2 | 3 | .. | .. | .. | .. | .. |
| Cotton carpet and rug manufacture factories | 6 | 2 | 4 | .. | .. | .. | .. | .. |
| Dari, etc., weaving factory and litho press | 1 | .. | 1 | .. | .. | .. | .. | .. |
| Textile institute | 1 | .. | 1 | 1 | .. | .. | .. | .. |
| Leather factory | 1 | 1 | .. | .. | .. | .. | .. | .. |
| Tanneries | 2 | 2 | .. | .. | .. | .. | .. | .. |

## Particulars as to Ownership of Factories, etc.

| Number privately owned by | | | | | | | | | | | | | | |
|---|---|---|---|---|---|---|---|---|---|---|---|---|---|---|
| Europeans and Anglo-Indians. | Indians. | | | | | | | | | | | | | |
| | Total. | Bania Agarwal. | Bania Bhatera. | Bania Khanderwal. | Bania Mahesri. | Bania Oswal. | Bania Saravgi. | Kayasth. | Luhana. | Maratha. | Musalman Pathan. | Musalman Sayad. | Bohra. | Parsi. |
| 7 | 8 | 9 | 10 | 11 | 12 | 13 | 14 | 15 | 16 | 17 | 18 | 19 | 20 | 21 |
| *1* | *64* | *18* | *1* | *3* | *8* | *1* | *1* | *5* | *1* | *2* | *1* | *1* | *20* | *2* |
| .. | 1 | .. | .. | .. | .. | .. | .. | .. | .. | .. | .. | 1 | .. | .. |
| .. | .. | .. | .. | .. | .. | .. | .. | .. | .. | .. | .. | .. | .. | .. |
| .. | .. | .. | .. | .. | .. | .. | .. | .. | .. | .. | .. | .. | .. | .. |
| .. | .. | .. | .. | .. | .. | .. | .. | .. | .. | .. | .. | .. | .. | .. |
| .. | 57 | 17 | 1 | 2 | 7 | 1 | 1 | 4 | 1 | 2 | .. | .. | 19 | 2 |
| .. | 5 | 1 | .. | 1 | 1 | .. | .. | 1 | .. | .. | 1 | .. | .. | .. |
| .. | .. | .. | .. | .. | .. | .. | .. | .. | .. | .. | .. | .. | .. | .. |
| .. | 1 | .. | .. | .. | .. | .. | .. | .. | .. | .. | .. | .. | 1 | .. |
| 1 | .. | .. | .. | .. | .. | .. | .. | .. | .. | .. | .. | .. | .. | .. |
| .. | .. | .. | .. | .. | .. | .. | .. | .. | .. | .. | .. | .. | .. | .. |
| .. | .. | .. | .. | .. | .. | .. | .. | .. | .. | .. | .. | .. | .. | .. |
| .. | .. | .. | .. | .. | .. | .. | .. | .. | .. | .. | .. | .. | .. | .. |
| .. | .. | .. | .. | .. | .. | .. | .. | .. | .. | .. | .. | .. | .. | .. |

## Caste or Race of Managers of Factories, etc.

| Number managed by | | | | | | | | | | | | | | | | | | | | | |
|---|---|---|---|---|---|---|---|---|---|---|---|---|---|---|---|---|---|---|---|---|---|
| Indians. | | | | | | | | | | | | | | | | | | | | | |
| Bania Nima. | Bania Oswal. | Bania Porwal. | Bania Saravgi. | Bania Shrimali. | Bhatia. | Brahman Audich. | Brahman Dakshani. | Brahman Kanujia. | Brahman Malwi. | Brahman Naramdeo. | Dhangar. | Gujarati. | Kayasth. | Khatri. | Lohar. | Luhana. | Parbhu. | Musalman Pathan. | Musalman Sayad. | Bohra. | Parsi. |
| 10 | 11 | 12 | 13 | 14 | 15 | 16 | 17 | 18 | 19 | 20 | 21 | 22 | 23 | 24 | 25 | 26 | 27 | 28 | 29 | 30 | 31 |
| *1* | *4* | *2* | *2* | *2* | *1* | *1* | *4* | *5* | *1* | *1* | *1* | *1* | *6* | *1* | *1* | *1* | *1* | *2* | *2* | *18* | *6* |
| .. | .. | .. | .. | .. | .. | .. | .. | .. | .. | .. | .. | .. | .. | .. | .. | .. | .. | .. | 1 | .. | .. |
| .. | .. | .. | .. | .. | .. | .. | .. | .. | .. | .. | .. | .. | .. | .. | .. | .. | .. | .. | .. | .. | .. |
| .. | .. | .. | .. | .. | .. | .. | .. | .. | .. | .. | .. | .. | .. | .. | .. | .. | .. | .. | .. | .. | .. |
| .. | .. | .. | .. | .. | .. | .. | .. | .. | .. | .. | .. | .. | .. | .. | .. | .. | .. | .. | .. | .. | .. |
| 1 | 3 | 1 | 1 | 1 | 1 | 1 | 3 | 4 | 1 | 1 | .. | 1 | 2 | 1 | 1 | 1 | 1 | .. | .. | 17 | 4 |
| .. | 1 | 1 | 1 | .. | .. | .. | .. | 1 | .. | .. | 1 | .. | 1 | .. | .. | .. | .. | 1 | .. | .. | 1 |
| .. | .. | .. | .. | 1 | .. | .. | .. | .. | .. | .. | .. | .. | .. | .. | .. | .. | .. | .. | .. | .. | .. |
| .. | .. | .. | .. | .. | .. | .. | .. | .. | .. | .. | .. | .. | 1 | .. | .. | .. | .. | .. | .. | 1 | 1 |
| .. | .. | .. | .. | .. | .. | .. | 1 | .. | .. | .. | .. | .. | 2 | .. | .. | .. | .. | 1 | .. | .. | .. |
| .. | .. | .. | .. | .. | .. | .. | .. | .. | .. | .. | .. | .. | .. | .. | .. | .. | .. | .. | 1 | .. | .. |
| .. | .. | .. | .. | .. | .. | .. | .. | .. | .. | .. | .. | .. | .. | .. | .. | .. | .. | .. | .. | .. | .. |
| .. | .. | .. | .. | .. | .. | .. | .. | .. | .. | .. | .. | .. | .. | .. | .. | .. | .. | .. | .. | .. | .. |
| .. | .. | .. | .. | .. | .. | .. | .. | .. | .. | .. | .. | .. | .. | .. | .. | .. | .. | .. | .. | .. | .. |

## TABLE XVI.

### *OCCUPATION.*

BY SELECTED CASTES, TRIBES OR RACES.

This Table gives statistics for the occupations of certain selected castes, tribes and races. The occupations are arranged under 12 main heads corresponding to the sub-classes of the scheme of classification given in Table XV-A; these heads have been sub-divided, where necessary, in order to distinguish between occupations of persons in the service of Government and those of Native States. Columns 6 and 7 throw light on the extent to which traditional caste occupations are followed, while column 8 is intended to make it possible to discount the tendency of functional castes to return their traditional occupations as their principal means of livelihood. The figures in column 9 onward are exclusive of those shown in column 6. Asterisks have been placed against the figures in those columns which are affected by this arrangement.

## TABLE XVI.—Occupation by

| Serial Number. | Caste, Tribe or Race. | Sex. | Traditional occupation. | Population dealt with: Actual workers. | Population dealt with: Dependants. | Number of actual workers whose traditional caste occupation was returned as their: Principal means of livelihood. | Number of actual workers whose traditional caste occupation was returned as their: Subsidiary means of livelihood. | Number of actual workers returned their traditional occupation as their principal means of livelihood who had some subsidiary occupation. | RECORDED — I. Exploitation of the surface of the soil: Income from rent of land. | Cultivators of all kinds. | Agents and managers of landed estates, planters, forest officers and their clerks, rent collectors, etc. | Field labourers, wood cutters, etc. | Raisers of livestock, milkmen and herdsmen. | Fishing and hunting. |
|---|---|---|---|---|---|---|---|---|---|---|---|---|---|---|
| | 1 | 2 | 3 | 4 | 5 | 6 | 7 | 8 | 9 | 10 | 11 | 12 | 13 | 14 |
| | **Central India** | Males | .. | 1,277,941 | 837,723 | 471,965 | 60,359 | 15,533 | 29,969 | 334,367 | 2,383 | 162,119 | 27,388 | 2,427 |
| | | Females | | 758,298 | 1,260,786 | 199,553 | 18,141 | 4,039 | 6,952 | 160,625 | 197 | 182,482 | 5,493 | 173 |
| | *HINDU* | Males | .. | *1,004,413* | *663,426* | *346,645* | *54,992* | *13,971* | *19,798* | *307,721* | *1,940* | *126,175* | *20,682* | *2,095* |
| | | Females | | *596,894* | *990,787* | *140,742* | *17,583* | *3,784* | *6,480* | *148,099* | *66* | *140,939* | *3,617* | *11* |
| 1 | Ajna | Males | Agriculture | 9,256 | 5,916 | 7,362 | 644 | 24 | ..* | ..* | .. | 461 | 42 | .. |
| | | Females | | 5,760 | 5,533 | 3,516 | 356 | 16 | ..* | ..* | .. | 652 | 1 | .. |
| 2 | Bania | Males | .. | *47,998* | *32,981* | *31,087* | *4,256* | *812* | *339* | *7,904* | *58* | .. | *208* | .. |
| | | Females | | *23,414* | *60,977* | *13,281* | *2,995* | *214* | *1,367* | *3,990* | *9* | .. | *54* | .. |
| | (1) Agarwal | Males | Trade | 16,675 | 11,035 | 11,784 | 1,493 | 207 | 102 | 2,511 | 6 | .. | 37 | .. |
| | | Females | | 6,899 | 23,679 | 3,767 | 2,032 | 67 | 629 | 598 | .. | .. | 8 | .. |
| | (2) Gahohi | Males | Ditto | 8,361 | 5,296 | 5,945 | 908 | 110 | 28 | 1,470 | .. | .. | 30 | .. |
| | | Females | | 3,744 | 7,681 | 2,354 | 66 | 26 | 28 | 782 | .. | .. | 6 | .. |
| | (3) Kasaundhan | Males | Ditto | 2,624 | 1,589 | 1,588 | 345 | 143 | 15 | 656 | .. | .. | 30 | .. |
| | | Females | | 2,015 | 2,559 | 1,193 | 70 | 32 | 217 | 338 | .. | .. | 3 | .. |
| | (4) Kesar Bania | Males | Ditto | 4,222 | 3,211 | 2,301 | 239 | 74 | 41 | 1,413 | 22 | .. | 30 | .. |
| | | Females | | 2,946 | 4,090 | 1,681 | 73 | 31 | 110 | 888 | 9 | .. | 4 | .. |
| | (5) Kharia | Males | Ditto | 1,201 | 599 | 859 | 123 | 45 | 17 | 135 | 25 | .. | 16 | .. |
| | | Females | | 682 | 2,015 | 524 | 33 | 47 | 40 | 61 | .. | .. | 1 | .. |
| | (6) Mahesri | Males | Ditto | 6,000 | 4,008 | 3,641 | 412 | 116 | 63 | 542 | 1 | .. | 18 | .. |
| | | Females | | 2,869 | 8,535 | 1,664 | 389 | 5 | 126 | 255 | .. | .. | 2 | .. |
| | (7) Oswal | Males | Ditto | 3,305 | 2,767 | 2,105 | 320 | 20 | 23 | 464 | 4 | .. | 7 | .. |
| | | Females | | 2,205 | 6,032 | 1,302 | 324 | 3 | 134 | 216 | .. | .. | .. | .. |
| | (8) Porwal | Males | Ditto | 4,840 | 3,776 | 2,864 | 416 | 97 | 50 | 718 | .. | .. | 40 | .. |
| | | Females | | 2,054 | 5,686 | 796 | 8 | 3 | 83 | 152 | .. | .. | 30 | .. |
| 3 | Banjara | Males | Carriers by pack animals. | 11,484 | 7,044 | 3,738 | 313 | 41 | 83 | 3,215 | .. | 1,790 | 409 | 7 |
| | | Females | | 4,212 | 8,517 | 999 | 23 | 26 | 1 | 1,024 | .. | 1,057 | 66 | .. |
| 4 | Bhat | Males | Legend singers. | 7,672 | 5,509 | 1,803 | 208 | 61 | 357 | 2,419 | .. | 765 | 173 | .. |
| | | Females | | 4,891 | 7,089 | 686 | 89 | 28 | 61 | 1,224 | 9 | 888 | 54 | .. |
| 5 | Bhil | Males | Agriculture | 7,526 | 6,167 | 3,785 | 336 | 122 | ..* | ..* | 15 | 1,383 | 365 | 146 |
| | | Females | | 5,061 | 7,077 | 1,725 | 10 | 1 | ..* | ..* | .. | 1,922 | 73 | .. |
| 6 | Bhilala | Males | Ditto | 9,374 | 6,977 | 7,157 | 62 | 81 | ..* | ..* | 10 | 1,293 | 313 | 9 |
| | | Females | | 9,396 | 8,017 | 7,844 | .. | 3 | ..* | ..* | .. | 1,045 | 91 | .. |
| 7 | Brahman | Males | .. | *179,467* | *110,336* | *17,176* | *4,989* | *1,974* | *6,818* | *109,079* | *1,033* | *8,357* | *1,896* | .. |
| | | Females | | *80,976* | *207,189* | *6,114* | *2,060* | *296* | *1,927* | *46,096* | .. | *7,988* | *395* | .. |
| | (1) Bhagor (Bhargava) | Males | Priests | 10,259 | 6,776 | 1,692 | 557 | 107 | 294 | 4,989 | 10 | 394 | 178 | .. |
| | | Females | | 5,480 | 9,965 | 642 | .. | 18 | 517 | 2,708 | .. | 869 | 18 | .. |
| | (2) Jijhotia | Males | Ditto | 20,885 | 12,811 | 3,909 | 242 | 136 | 2,244 | 8,441 | 57 | 1,161 | 192 | .. |
| | | Females | | 8,912 | 21,324 | 771 | 362 | 52 | 334 | 3,282 | .. | 1,552 | 17 | .. |
| | (3) Sanadhya | Males | Ditto | 48,089 | 33,490 | 5,308 | 2,863 | 284 | 1,639 | 26,414 | 56 | 2,476 | 463 | .. |
| | | Females | | 20,719 | 56,826 | 739 | 213 | 86 | 352 | 12,677 | .. | 1,256 | 51 | .. |
| | (3) Sarwaria | Males | Ditto | 94,541 | 53,384 | 5,267 | 1,060 | 698 | 2,558 | 67,792 | 890 | 4,080 | 959 | .. |
| | | Females | | 43,297 | 111,984 | 2,862 | 762 | 48 | 680 | 26,988 | .. | 3,340 | 236 | .. |
| | (5) Shrigaud | Males | Ditto | 4,669 | 3,111 | 859 | 238 | 39 | 40 | 1,178 | 19 | 201 | 31 | .. |
| | | Females | | 1,967 | 5,284 | 794 | 531 | 10 | 25 | 296 | .. | 266 | 3 | .. |
| | (6) Shrimali | Males | Ditto | 1,024 | 764 | 141 | 22 | 10 | 48 | 258 | 1 | 45 | 3 | .. |
| | | Females | | 601 | 1,806 | 306 | 192 | 12 | 19 | 145 | .. | 5 | .. | .. |

## CASTES, TRIBES OR RACES.

PRINCIPAL OCCUPATION OF ACTUAL WORKERS.

| II Extraction of minerals. | | III Industries. | | IV Transport. | | V Trade. | VI Public Force. | | | | VII Public—Administration. | | | | VIII Arts and Professions. | | | IX Persons living on their own income. | X Domestic service. | XI Labourers unspecified. | XII Beggars, prostitutes, criminals and inmates of jails and asylums. |
|---|---|---|---|---|---|---|---|---|---|---|---|---|---|---|---|---|---|---|---|---|---|
| | | | | | | | Commissioned and gazetted officers. | | Others. | | Gazetted officers. | | Others. | | | | | | | | |
| Owners, managers, clerks, etc. | Labourers. | Owners, managers, clerks, etc. | Artisans and other workmen. | Owners, managers, ship's officers, etc. | Labourers, boatmen, carters, palki-bearers, etc. | | Government. | Native States. | Government. | Native States. | Government. | Native States. | Government. | Native States. | Religious. | Lawyers, doctors and teachers. | Others. | | | | |
| 15 | 16 | 17 | 18 | 19 | 20 | 21 | 22 | 23 | 24 | 25 | 26 | 27 | 28 | 29 | 30 | 31 | 32 | 33 | 34 | 35 | 36 |
| 81 | 1,179 | 580 | 14,423 | 482 | 4,135 | 18,424 | 146 | 399 | 3,744 | 5,699 | 21 | 381 | 823 | 9,882 | 547 | 1,096 | 4,990 | 7,475 | 37,555 | 190,727 | 24,331 |
| 3 | 402 | 2 | 10,155 | 8 | 960 | 9,652 | .. | .. | .. | 3 | .. | .. | .. | .. | 78 | 68 | 1,123 | 3,646 | 10,141 | 153,253 | 13,960 |
| *59* | *976* | *335* | *7,196* | *173* | *9,399* | *10,383* | *1* | *395* | *409* | *4,479* | .. | *283* | *334* | *5,933* | *198* | *555* | *2,015* | *5,156* | *25,190* | *94,093* | *18,910* |
| *3* | *378* | *1* | *4,070* | *6* | *594* | *6,092* | .. | .. | .. | *3* | .. | .. | .. | .. | *23* | *35* | *429* | *2,604* | *7,043* | *125,124* | *11,949* |
| .. | 20 | .. | 142 | .. | 16 | 4 | .. | .. | .. | 12 | .. | .. | .. | 1 | .. | .. | 3 | 75 | 121 | 829 | 168 |
| .. | 3 | .. | .. | .. | .. | .. | .. | .. | .. | .. | .. | .. | .. | .. | .. | .. | .. | 19 | 82 | 1,454 | 33 |
| *4* | *139* | *15* | *268* | *9* | *198* | .. | .. | *36* | *1* | *48* | .. | *25* | *34* | *263* | *27* | *77* | *421* | *1,178* | *2,545* | *2,263* | *158* |
| *3* | *89* | *1* | *133* | .. | *41* | .. | .. | .. | .. | .. | .. | .. | .. | .. | .. | *3* | *70* | *706* | *505* | *3,646* | *216* |
| 1 | 64 | 13 | 73 | 9 | 30 | ..* | .. | 8 | .. | 10 | .. | 1 | 30 | 175 | 12 | 32 | 34 | 212 | 814 | 671 | 46 |
| .. | 15 | 1 | 35 | .. | 2 | ..* | .. | .. | .. | .. | .. | .. | .. | .. | .. | 1 | 13 | 374 | 158 | 1,257 | 46 |
| .. | 6 | .. | 9 | .. | 5 | ..* | .. | 3 | .. | 6 | .. | 6 | .. | 30 | 1 | 7 | 8 | 129 | 222 | 441 | 15 |
| .. | 8 | .. | 15 | .. | .. | ..* | .. | .. | .. | .. | .. | .. | .. | .. | .. | .. | 3 | 44 | 70 | 413 | 21 |
| .. | 4 | .. | .. | .. | 23 | ..* | .. | .. | .. | .. | .. | .. | .. | 3 | .. | 1 | 3 | 4 | 84 | 210 | 3 |
| .. | .. | .. | .. | .. | 22 | ..* | .. | .. | .. | .. | .. | .. | .. | .. | .. | .. | 3 | 3 | 21 | 210 | 5 |
| .. | 2 | .. | .. | .. | 49 | ..* | .. | 19 | .. | 1 | .. | .. | .. | .. | .. | 1 | 78 | 90 | 27 | 147 | 1 |
| 3 | 57 | .. | 11 | .. | 13 | ..* | .. | .. | .. | .. | .. | .. | .. | .. | .. | .. | .. | .. | 4 | 111 | 55 |
| .. | .. | .. | .. | .. | .. | ..* | .. | .. | .. | .. | .. | 10 | .. | 1 | 10 | .. | 25 | 15 | 49 | 29 | 10 |
| .. | .. | .. | .. | .. | .. | ..* | .. | .. | .. | .. | .. | .. | .. | .. | .. | .. | .. | 20 | 23 | 13 | .. |
| .. | 11 | 1 | 103 | .. | 12 | ..* | .. | .. | .. | 26 | .. | 5 | 2 | 18 | 8 | 10 | 111 | 403 | 756 | 221 | 58 |
| .. | 3 | .. | 42 | .. | 4 | ..* | .. | .. | .. | .. | .. | .. | .. | .. | .. | .. | 15 | 74 | 121 | 552 | 11 |
| 1 | 15 | .. | 57 | .. | 3 | ..* | .. | 4 | 1 | 1 | .. | .. | .. | 14 | 1 | 15 | 100 | 84 | 282 | 110 | 14 |
| .. | 5 | .. | 11 | .. | .. | ..* | .. | .. | .. | .. | .. | .. | .. | .. | .. | .. | 7 | 101 | 28 | 353 | 48 |
| *2 | 30 | 1 | 26 | .. | 6 | ..* | .. | 2 | .. | 4 | .. | 3 | 2 | 22 | .. | 11 | 62 | 241 | 311 | 434 | 16 |
| .. | 1 | .. | 19 | .. | .. | ..* | .. | .. | .. | .. | .. | .. | .. | .. | .. | 2 | 29 | 90 | 85 | 787 | 30 |
| .. | 33 | 1 | 183 | .. | 21 | 423 | 1 | .. | 17 | 13 | .. | .. | .. | 4 | .. | .. | 18 | 257 | 180 | 1,055 | 86 |
| .. | 6 | .. | 70 | .. | .. | 225 | .. | .. | .. | .. | .. | .. | .. | .. | .. | .. | 3 | 7 | 58 | 664 | 32 |
| .. | 6 | 5 | 86 | .. | 60 | 103 | .. | .. | .. | 115 | .. | 2 | 1 | 77 | 1 | 3 | 101 | 30 | 280 | 506 | 779 |
| .. | 1 | .. | 66 | .. | 31 | 25 | .. | .. | .. | .. | .. | .. | .. | .. | 1 | .. | 7 | 71 | 55 | 1,096 | 706 |
| .. | 4 | 5 | 24 | 7 | 75 | 30 | .. | .. | .. | 195 | .. | .. | 5 | 78 | .. | .. | 28 | .. | 384 | 918 | 84 |
| .. | 8 | .. | 12 | .. | 4 | 122 | .. | .. | .. | 1 | .. | .. | .. | .. | 1 | .. | 6 | 4 | 44 | 997 | 142 |
| .. | .. | 46 | 25 | .. | 26 | 11 | .. | .. | .. | 43 | .. | .. | .. | 13 | .. | .. | 1 | 2 | 165 | 258 | 2 |
| .. | 7 | .. | 15 | .. | .. | 7 | .. | .. | .. | 2 | .. | .. | .. | .. | .. | .. | 2 | 2 | 65 | 312 | 4 |
| *17* | *103* | *198* | *529* | *68* | *555* | *2,719* | .. | *349* | *17* | *2,960* | .. | *81* | *907* | *3,666* | .. | *341* | *446* | *1,307* | *4,988* | *7,584* | *9,050* |
| .. | *79* | .. | *176* | *3* | *190* | *801* | .. | .. | .. | .. | .. | .. | .. | .. | .. | *11* | *57* | *630* | *1,180* | *9,911* | *6,965* |
| .. | .. | .. | 21 | .. | 11 | 218 | .. | 24 | 5 | 277 | .. | 7 | 111 | 250 | ..* | 20 | 51 | 19 | 317 | 372 | 999 |
| .. | 3 | .. | 25 | .. | .. | 59 | .. | .. | .. | .. | .. | .. | .. | .. | ..* | 1 | 1 | 63 | 57 | 277 | 240 |
| 1 | .. | 20 | 169 | .. | 32 | 298 | .. | 10 | 12 | 469 | .. | 29 | 27 | 557 | ..* | 45 | 48 | 190 | 654 | 1,199 | 1,181 |
| .. | 7 | .. | 38 | .. | 3 | 71 | .. | .. | .. | .. | .. | .. | .. | .. | ..* | 2 | 14 | 90 | 288 | 1,525 | 918 |
| 10 | 16 | 39 | 233 | 30 | 141 | 845 | .. | 73 | .. | 1,448 | .. | 14 | 25 | 1,115 | ..* | 86 | 101 | 644 | 1,630 | 2,815 | 2,466 |
| .. | 8 | .. | 61 | 3 | 2 | 233 | .. | .. | .. | .. | .. | .. | .. | .. | ..* | 6 | 11 | 132 | 221 | 4,246 | 721 |
| 5 | 75 | 134 | 35 | 13 | 345 | 1,060 | .. | 239 | .. | 516 | .. | 8 | 20 | 1,347 | ..* | 84 | 79 | 298 | 1,888 | 2,827 | 4,012 |
| .. | 53 | .. | 17 | .. | 108 | 427 | .. | .. | .. | .. | .. | .. | .. | .. | ..* | 1 | 25 | 196 | 416 | 3,621 | 4,327 |
| 1 | 12 | 2 | 69 | 22 | 6 | 229 | .. | 3 | .. | 283 | .. | 22 | 22 | 284 | ..* | 76 | 158 | 141 | 439 | 269 | 353 |
| .. | .. | .. | 9 | .. | 3 | 7 | .. | .. | .. | .. | .. | .. | .. | .. | ..* | 1 | 6 | 140 | 172 | 198 | 47 |
| .. | .. | 3 | 2 | 3 | 20 | 49 | .. | .. | .. | 17 | .. | 1 | 2 | 113 | ..* | 28 | 9 | 30 | 60 | 104 | 29 |
| .. | 1 | .. | 26 | .. | 4 | 4 | .. | .. | .. | .. | .. | .. | .. | .. | ..* | .. | .. | 9 | 26 | 44 | 12 |

# TABLE XVI.—Occupation by

| Serial Number. | Caste, Tribe or Race. | Sex. | Traditional occupation. | Population dealt with | | Number of actual workers whose traditional caste occupation was returned as their | | Number of actual workers returned their traditional occupation as their principal means of livelihood who had some subsidiary occupation. | Recorded — I Exploitation of the surface of the soil. | | | | | |
|---|---|---|---|---|---|---|---|---|---|---|---|---|---|---|
| | | | | Actual Workers. | Dependants. | Principal means of livelihood. | Subsidiary means of livelihood. | | Income from rent of land. | Cultivators of all kinds. | Agents and managers of landed estates, planters, forest officers and their clerks, rent collectors, etc. | Field labourers, wood cutters, etc. | Raisers of livestock, milkmen and herdsmen. | Fishing and hunting. |
| | 1 | 2 | 3 | 4 | 5 | 6 | 7 | 8 | 9 | 10 | 11 | 12 | 13 | 14 |
| 8 | Chamar | Males | Leather workers | 254,057 | 181,816 | 63,679 | 19,675 | 5,884 | 2,846 | 73,636 | 3 | 57,566 | 3,820 | 60 |
| | | Females | | 174,699 | 248,866 | 15,167 | 4,566 | 982 | 216 | 46,871 | .. | 66,956 | 778 | .. |
| 9 | Dhangar | Males | Military and dominant. | 1,707 | 1,320 | 693 | 94 | 14 | 5 | 287 | .. | 137 | 29 | .. |
| | | Females | | 1,270 | 1,811 | 70 | .. | .. | .. | 95 | .. | 170 | 35 | .. |
| 10 | Gond | Males | Agriculture and hunting. | 49,036 | 27,717 | 38,000 | 1,410 | 132 | ..* | ..* | .. | 4,379 | 545 | 296* |
| | | Females | | 47,267 | 39,265 | 32,830 | 606 | 23 | ..* | ..* | .. | 5,264 | 181 | ..* |
| 11 | Gujar | Males | Agriculture | 62,645 | 43,189 | 43,132 | 5,931 | 458 | ..* | ..* | 7 | 5,231 | 5,295 | 17 |
| | | Females | | 23,660 | 56,234 | 13,859 | 2,920 | 420 | ..* | ..* | .. | 3,052 | 481 | .. |
| 12 | Kachera | Males | Glass and lac workers. | 1,872 | 1,325 | 1,095 | 114 | 33 | 8 | [illegible] | 135 | 248 | 4 | .. |
| | | Females | | 1,233 | 1,961 | 739 | 48 | 8 | 1 | 144 | .. | 101 | 1 | .. |
| 13 | Kalal | Males | Distillers and toddy drawers. | 18,946 | 13,820 | 6,002 | 1,175 | 622 | 160 | 7,526 | 19 | 2,064 | 340 | 48 |
| | | Females | | 11,240 | 19,657 | 2,315 | 357 | 179 | 13 | 4,048 | 1 | 2,181 | 59 | 1 |
| 14 | Khangar | Males | Watchmen | 11,580 | 8,593 | 3,056 | 1,215 | 85 | 71 | 3,828 | 360 | 1,012 | 265 | 5 |
| | | Females | | 7,315 | 10,955 | 76 | .. | .. | 18 | 2,486 | 2 | 1,986 | 70 | .. |
| 15 | Kirar | Males | Agriculture and hunting. | 25,349 | 20,198 | 16,994 | 2,239 | 200 | ..* | ..* | .. | 2,091 | 79 | 315* |
| | | Females | | 14,328 | 27,010 | 6,535 | 5 | .. | ..* | ..* | 9 | 3,456 | 88 | ..* |
| 16 | Kol | Males | Hunting and collecting jungle produce. | 56,541 | 32,905 | 15,738 | 1,234 | 113 | 262 | 7,328 | .. | 16,739 | 1,919 | 10* |
| | | Females | | 58,041 | 38,876 | 15,838 | 286 | 179 | 12 | 2,982 | .. | 18,763 | 675 | 8* |
| 17 | Kotwal | Males | Watchmen. | 8,917 | 5,620 | 2,363 | 381 | 134 | 302 | 1,193 | .. | 1,334 | 403 | .. |
| | | Females | | 6,716 | 5,833 | 162 | .. | .. | 3 | 795 | .. | 2,469 | 75 | .. |
| 18 | Maratha | Males | Military and dominant. | 9,004 | 5,817 | 5,044 | 94 | 140 | 46 | 1,294 | 6 | 413 | 66 | 1 |
| | | Females | | 4,354 | 8,833 | 369 | .. | .. | 158 | 972 | 2 | 594 | 18 | 2 |
| 19 | Mina | Males | Hunting and robbery. | 25,013 | 11,619 | 13,737 | 367 | 83 | 30 | 3,452 | 12 | 3,063 | 208 | 726* |
| | | Females | | 15,152 | 19,284 | 105 | 6 | 12 | .. | 1,976 | .. | 3,892 | 13 | ..* |
| 20 | Mochi | Males | Shoe-makers and leather workers. | 1,748 | 1,307 | 1,155 | 77 | 33 | 61 | 116 | 8 | 120 | 2 | ..* |
| | | Females | | 989 | 2,222 | 397 | 71 | 9 | 75 | 80 | 2 | 63 | .. | .. |
| 21 | Rajput | Males | .. | *113,437* | *79,301* | *20,195* | *9,779* | *765* | *7,835* | *60,114* | *248* | *9,869* | *9,176* | *139* |
| | | Females | | *89,437* | *113,281* | .. | .. | .. | *9,558* | *20,196* | *39* | *7,403* | *905* | .. |
| | (1) Baghela | Males | Military and dominant. | 8,508 | 4,205 | 2,614 | 193 | 51 | 1,329 | 3,146 | 50 | 366 | 88 | 11 |
| | | Females | | 2,420 | 9,724 | .. | .. | .. | 322 | 1,380 | 1 | 140 | 19 | .. |
| | (2) Bhadauria | Males | Ditto | 8,039 | 5,462 | 510 | 468 | 117 | 1,515 | 5,336 | 3 | 280 | 59 | 2 |
| | | Females | | 2,662 | 7,180 | .. | .. | .. | 299 | 1,244 | .. | 402 | .. | .. |
| | (3) Bundela | Males | Ditto | 4,871 | 3,914 | 1,121 | 62 | 17 | 622 | 2,269 | 18 | 368 | 58 | .. |
| | | Females | | 1,586 | 6,991 | .. | .. | .. | 194 | 796 | .. | 396 | 4 | .. |
| | (4) Bundela Ponwar. | Males | Ditto | 143 | 123 | 42 | 12 | 2 | 16 | 48 | .. | 13 | .. | .. |
| | | Females | | 7 | 28 | .. | .. | .. | 1 | 6 | .. | .. | .. | .. |
| | (5) Chohan (Chauhan). | Males | Ditto | 11,717 | 7,339 | 2,759 | 172 | 77 | 471 | 4,920 | 20 | 1,384 | 278 | 13 |
| | | Females | | 5,531 | 15,391 | .. | .. | .. | 247 | 2,545 | .. | 1,218 | 27 | .. |
| | (6) Dhandhera | Males | Ditto | 921 | 1,008 | 393 | 7 | 8 | 120 | 307 | 2 | 24 | 27 | .. |
| | | Females | | 420 | 1,410 | .. | .. | .. | 19 | 214 | .. | 143 | 1 | .. |
| | (7) Dikhit | Males | Ditto | 455 | 299 | 42 | 6 | .. | 8 | 293 | .. | 95 | 1 | .. |
| | | Females | | 134 | 412 | .. | .. | .. | 2 | 69 | 1 | 32 | .. | .. |
| | (8) Gaharwar | Males | Ditto | 766 | 465 | 104 | 15 | 4 | 95 | 487 | 10 | 19 | 9 | .. |
| | | Females | | 140 | 973 | .. | .. | .. | 4 | 102 | .. | 12 | 1 | .. |

CASTES, TRIBES OR RACES.

PRINCIPAL OCCUPATION OF ACTUAL WORKERS.

| II Extraction of minerals: Owners, managers, clerks, etc. | II Extraction of minerals: Labourers. | III Industries: Owners, managers, clerks, etc. | III Industries: Artisans and other workmen. | IV Transport: Owners, managers, ship's officers, etc. | IV Transport: Labourers, boatmen, carters, palki-bearers, etc. | V Trade. | VI Public Force: Commissioned and gazetted officers: Government. | VI Public Force: Commissioned and gazetted officers: Native States. | VI Public Force: Others: Government. | VI Public Force: Others: Native States. | VII Public—Administration: Gazetted officers: Government. | VII Public—Administration: Gazetted officers: Native States. | VII Public—Administration: Others: Government. | VII Public—Administration: Others: Native States. | VIII Arts and Professions: Religion. | VIII Arts and Professions: Lawyers, doctors and teachers. | VIII Arts and Professions: Others. | XI Persons living on their own income. | X Domestic Service. | XI Labourers unspecified. | XII Beggars, prostitutes, criminals and inmates of jails and asylums. |
|---|---|---|---|---|---|---|---|---|---|---|---|---|---|---|---|---|---|---|---|---|---|
| 15 | 16 | 17 | 18 | 19 | 20 | 21 | 22 | 23 | 24 | 25 | 26 | 27 | 28 | 29 | 30 | 31 | 32 | 33 | 34 | 35 | 36 |
| .. | 85 | 2 | 2,557 | 8 | 352 | 1,914 | .. | .. | 200 | 264 | .. | .. | .. | .. | 15 | 1 | 212 | 230 | 7,316 | 37,359 | 1,932 |
| .. | 36 | .. | 1,399 | .. | 59 | 750 | .. | .. | .. | .. | .. | .. | .. | .. | .. | .. | 38 | 176 | 1,017 | 40,147 | 1,089 |
| .. | 3 | .. | 8 | .. | 5 | 78 | .. | .. | .. | .. | .. | 20 | .. | 45 | .. | 1 | 34 | 16 | 48 | 275 | 23 |
| .. | 4 | .. | 132 | .. | .. | 43 | .. | .. | .. | .. | .. | .. | .. | .. | .. | .. | .. | 3 | 337 | 367 | 14 |
| .. | 70 | .. | .. | .. | 48 | 275 | .. | .. | .. | 61 | .. | .. | .. | 31 | 15 | .. | 18 | 25 | 348 | 4,595 | 321 |
| .. | 11 | .. | .. | .. | .. | 100 | .. | .. | .. | .. | .. | .. | .. | .. | .. | .. | 30 | 3 | 42 | 8,363 | 443 |
| .. | 12 | 5 | 414 | 6 | 165 | 342 | .. | 10 | 156 | 533 | .. | 1 | 11 | 205 | 43 | 1 | 54 | 198 | 976 | 5,551 | 285 |
| .. | 3 | .. | 39 | .. | 187 | 194 | .. | .. | .. | .. | .. | .. | .. | .. | .. | .. | 4 | 56 | 154 | 5,526 | 105 |
| .. | 3 | .. | 4 | .. | .. | 15 | .. | .. | .. | 1 | .. | .. | .. | 3 | .. | 1 | 9 | 3 | 46 | 62 | 7 |
| .. | 10 | .. | 8 | .. | .. | 12 | .. | .. | .. | .. | .. | .. | .. | .. | .. | .. | 1 | 4 | 6 | 117 | 92 |
| 5 | 5 | 12 | 75 | 24 | 141 | 832 | .. | .. | 3 | 37 | .. | .. | 3 | 69 | 12 | 2 | 17 | 129 | 322 | 1,036 | 63 |
| .. | 6 | .. | 41 | .. | 3 | 695 | .. | .. | .. | .. | .. | .. | .. | .. | 1 | .. | 1 | 102 | 148 | 1,516 | 109 |
| 1 | 7 | 1 | 22 | .. | 9 | 61 | .. | .. | .. | .. | .. | .. | 13 | 423 | .. | 7 | 55 | 170 | 386 | 1,768 | 60 |
| .. | 2 | .. | 47 | 1 | 1 | 10 | .. | .. | .. | .. | .. | .. | .. | .. | 3 | 1 | 21 | 27 | 462 | 1,824 | 278 |
| .. | 99 | .. | 92 | .. | 1 | 9 | .. | .. | 1 | .. | .. | .. | 1 | .. | .. | .. | .. | .. | 154 | 2,936 | 2,577 |
| .. | 9 | .. | .. | .. | .. | .. | .. | .. | .. | .. | .. | .. | .. | .. | .. | .. | .. | .. | 4 | 3,896 | 331 |
| .. | 87 | 2 | 6 | .. | 16 | 191 | .. | .. | .. | 120 | .. | .. | .. | 23 | 1 | .. | 31 | 377 | 1,512 | 10,970 | 1,209 |
| .. | 4 | .. | 1 | .. | .. | 127 | .. | .. | .. | .. | .. | .. | .. | .. | 17 | .. | 84 | 27 | 456 | 18,673 | 374 |
| 6 | .. | 2 | 2 | .. | 7 | 22 | .. | .. | .. | .. | .. | .. | .. | 118 | .. | .. | 110 | .. | 555 | 2,470 | 30 |
| .. | .. | .. | 4 | .. | .. | 13 | .. | .. | .. | .. | .. | .. | .. | .. | .. | .. | 2 | .. | 92 | 3,055 | 46 |
| 2 | .. | 4 | 170 | 20 | 153 | 171 | .. | .. | .. | .. | .. | 48 | 13 | 243 | 13 | 64 | 113 | 144 | 481 | 370 | 125 |
| .. | 9 | .. | 719 | .. | 9 | 78 | .. | .. | .. | .. | .. | .. | .. | .. | .. | 17 | 3 | 139 | 565 | 670 | 30 |
| .. | 19 | .. | 135 | 1 | 53 | 15 | .. | .. | .. | 27 | .. | .. | 3 | 31 | 31 | .. | 1 | 2 | 339 | 2,330 | 798 |
| .. | 11 | .. | 2 | .. | 7 | .. | .. | .. | .. | .. | .. | .. | .. | .. | .. | .. | 3 | .. | 90 | 8,913 | 140 |
| .. | 25 | .. | 43 | .. | 12 | 30 | .. | .. | 6 | 2 | .. | 2 | 1 | 5 | .. | 4 | 20 | 5 | 40 | 58 | 33 |
| .. | 4 | .. | 14 | 2 | 2 | 13 | .. | .. | .. | .. | .. | .. | .. | .. | .. | .. | 4 | 2 | 53 | 268 | 10 |
| *16* | *179* | | *906* | *30* | *226* | *992* | .. | .. | .. | .. | .. | *103* | *30* | *475* | *34* | *48* | *969* | *539* | *2,697* | *4,678* | *693* |
| .. | *79* | .. | *799* | .. | *80* | *378* | .. | .. | .. | .. | .. | .. | .. | .. | .. | *2* | *68* | *546* | *1,379* | *5,381* | *344* |
| .. | 9 | .. | 13 | 4 | 9 | 10' | .. | .. | .. | .. | .. | 3 | .. | 20 | .. | .. | 15 | 49 | 379 | 275 | 23 |
| .. | 2 | .. | .. | .. | .. | 8 | .. | .. | .. | .. | .. | .. | .. | .. | .. | .. | 1 | 77 | 175 | 283 | 12 |
| .. | 16 | .. | .. | .. | 1 | 14 | .. | .. | .. | .. | .. | .. | .. | 5 | .. | 1 | 3 | 25 | 61 | 191 | 17 |
| .. | 1 | .. | .. | .. | 1 | 29 | .. | .. | .. | .. | .. | .. | .. | .. | .. | .. | .. | 93 | 48 | 527 | 13 |
| .. | 4 | .. | 6 | .. | 10 | 44 | .. | .. | .. | .. | .. | 18 | 2 | 47 | 2 | 3 | 19 | 29 | 69 | 115 | 47 |
| .. | 16 | .. | 9 | .. | 1 | 6 | .. | .. | .. | .. | .. | .. | .. | .. | .. | .. | 1 | 24 | 32 | 57 | 50 |
| .. | .. | .. | .. | .. | .. | 9 | .. | .. | .. | .. | .. | 1 | .. | .. | .. | .. | .. | 3 | 4 | 6 | 1 |
| .. | .. | .. | .. | .. | .. | .. | .. | .. | .. | .. | .. | .. | .. | .. | .. | .. | .. | .. | .. | .. | .. |
| 4 | 7 | 11 | 154 | 9 | 26 | 155 | .. | .. | .. | .. | .. | 12 | 8 | 117 | 1 | 6 | 90 | 98 | 559 | 547 | 68 |
| .. | 6 | .. | 168 | .. | 28 | 57 | .. | .. | .. | .. | .. | .. | .. | .. | .. | .. | 3 | 29 | 127 | 998 | 83 |
| .. | 1 | .. | .. | .. | .. | 6 | .. | .. | .. | .. | .. | 1 | .. | 13 | .. | .. | .. | 1 | 12 | 13 | 1 |
| .. | .. | .. | .. | .. | .. | 1 | .. | .. | .. | .. | .. | .. | .. | .. | .. | .. | .. | 8 | 7 | 17 | 5 |
| .. | .. | .. | .. | .. | .. | .. | .. | .. | .. | .. | .. | .. | .. | .. | .. | .. | .. | .. | 13 | 31 | 2 |
| .. | 1 | .. | 1 | .. | .. | .. | .. | .. | .. | .. | .. | .. | .. | .. | .. | .. | .. | 1 | 4 | 23 | .. |
| .. | 5 | .. | .. | .. | .. | 4 | .. | .. | .. | .. | .. | .. | .. | 3 | .. | .. | .. | 1 | 19 | 8 | 2 |
| .. | 1 | .. | 1 | .. | .. | 3 | .. | .. | .. | .. | .. | .. | .. | .. | .. | .. | 2 | .. | 4 | 4 | 6 |

## TABLE XVI.—Occupation by

| Serial Number. | Caste, Tribe or Race. | Sex. | Traditional occupation. | Population dealt with: Actual workers. | Population dealt with: Dependants. | Number of actual workers whose traditional caste occupation was returned as their: Principal means of livelihood. | Number of actual workers whose traditional caste occupation was returned as their: Subsidiary means of livelihood. | Number of actual workers returned their traditional occupation as their principal means of livelihood who had some subsidiary occupation | Recorded — I. Exploitation of the surface of the soil: Income from rent of land. | Cultivators of all kinds. | Agents and managers of landed estates, planters, forest officers and their clerks, rent collectors, etc. | Field labourers, wood cutters, etc. | Raisers of livestock, milkmen and herdsmen. | Fishing and hunting. |
|---|---|---|---|---|---|---|---|---|---|---|---|---|---|---|
| | 1 | 2 | 3 | 4 | 5 | 6 | 7 | 8 | 9 | 10 | 11 | 12 | 13 | 14 |
| | Rajput—*contd.* | | | | | | | | | | | | | |
| | (9) Gahlot | Males. | Military and dominant. | 9,073 | 5,215 | 1,695 | 100 | 25 | 61 | 5,323 | 9 | 887 | 267 | .. |
| | | Females | | 3,407 | 5,958 | .. | .. | .. | 7 | 1,880 | .. | 770 | 24 | .. |
| | (10) Gaur | Males. | Ditto | 2,667 | 1,301 | 240 | 24 | .. | 89 | 1,364 | .. | 535 | 104 | .. |
| | | Females | | 1,255 | 2,070 | .. | .. | .. | 45 | 360 | 2 | 560 | 3 | .. |
| | (11) Kachhwaha. | Males. | Ditto | 8,749 | 3,801 | 1,637 | 225 | 14 | 171 | 5,357 | 58 | 563 | 145 | 1 |
| | | Females | | 2,619 | 9,251 | .. | .. | .. | 146 | 1,510 | .. | 207 | 10 | .. |
| | (12) Khichhi | Males. | Ditto | 871 | 515 | 77 | 12 | 1 | 209 | 409 | 4 | 8 | 55 | 2 |
| | | Females | | 266 | 867 | .. | .. | .. | 42 | 101 | 2 | 54 | 2 | .. |
| | (13) Parihar | Males. | Ditto | 5,719 | 4,077 | 994 | 156 | 101 | 580 | 2,968 | 11 | 456 | 109 | 2 |
| | | Females | | 1,631 | 6,781 | .. | .. | .. | 89 | 824 | .. | 248 | 4 | .. |
| | (14) Ponwar Maratha | Males. | Ditto | 144 | 167 | 36 | 14 | 4 | 6 | 34 | .. | 15 | .. | .. |
| | | Females | | 28 | 267 | .. | .. | .. | .. | 6 | .. | .. | .. | .. |
| | (15) Ponwar Rajput | Males. | Ditto | 14,663 | 9,358 | 2,769 | 219 | 66 | 790 | 7,140 | 11 | 1,578 | 390 | 91 |
| | | Females | | 4,247 | 14,428 | .. | .. | .. | 87 | 2,006 | 6 | 764 | 5 | .. |
| | (16) Rathor | Males. | Ditto | 10,836 | 7,643 | 2,018 | 426 | 209 | 442 | 5,067 | 26 | 1,162 | 194 | 6 |
| | | Females | | 5,337 | 9,579 | .. | .. | .. | 503 | 2,896 | 6 | 762 | 40 | .. |
| | (17) Sengar | Males. | Ditto | 2,819 | 1,998 | 509 | 164 | 5 | 411 | 1,551 | 2 | 126 | 9 | 1 |
| | | Females | | 1,328 | 4,674 | .. | .. | .. | 64 | 920 | .. | 198 | 7 | .. |
| | (18) Sisodia | Males. | Ditto | 2,722 | 1,599 | 259 | 44 | 21 | 62 | 1,558 | 4 | 339 | 115 | 1 |
| | | Females | | 1,289 | 2,965 | .. | .. | .. | 79 | 441 | .. | 502 | 25 | .. |
| | (19) Solanki | Males. | Ditto | 5,761 | 3,010 | 1,085 | 241 | 30 | 80 | 2,694 | 20 | 561 | 172 | .. |
| | | Females | | 2,176 | 4,954 | .. | .. | .. | 122 | 957 | 2 | 673 | 14 | .. |
| | (20) Tonwar | Males. | Ditto | 13,968 | 10,802 | 1,221 | 219 | 13 | 758 | 9,843 | .. | 1,083 | 96 | 2 |
| | | Females | | 2,954 | 9,378 | .. | .. | .. | 286 | 1,939 | 12 | 317 | 14 | .. |
| 22 | Saharia | Males. | Hunting and collecting jungle produce. | 13,426 | 11,947 | 3,597 | 1,424 | 101 | 3 | 5,608 | .. | 1,175 | 37 | [illegible]* |
| | | Females | | 9,089 | 14,782 | 225 | .. | .. | .. | 2,968 | .. | 2,420 | .. | ..* |
| 23 | Sondhia | Males. | Agriculture and dacoity. | 21,691 | 10,971 | 16,456 | 246 | 96 | ..* | ..* | 1 | 2,485 | 986 | .. |
| | | Females | | 10,186 | 27,698 | 5,349 | 45 | 6 | ..* | ..* | .. | 3,913 | 161 | .. |
| 24 | Teli | Males. | Oil-pressers | 57,437 | 38,731 | 23,662 | 5,736 | 1,968 | 572 | 20,501 | 25 | 4,207 | 1,172 | .. |
| | | Females | | 38,205 | 51,020 | 12,541 | 3,140 | 1,452 | 70 | 12,852 | .. | 4,697 | 113 | .. |
| | ***JAIN*** | Males. | .. | ***16,873*** | ***11,308*** | ***13,355*** | ***1,339*** | ***289*** | ***104*** | ***1,436*** | ***14*** | .. | ***8*** | .. |
| | | Females | | ***5,073*** | ***22,405*** | ***2,727*** | ***178*** | ***84*** | ***59*** | ***894*** | ***7*** | .. | ***6*** | .. |
| 1 | Bania | Males. | .. | *16,873* | *11,308* | *13,355* | *1,339* | *289* | *104* | *1,436* | *14* | .. | *8* | .. |
| | | Females | | *5,073* | *22,405* | *2,727* | *176* | *84* | *59* | *824* | *7* | .. | *6* | .. |
| | (1) Oswal | Males. | Trade | 9,992 | 6,772 | 7,918 | 890 | 165 | 54 | 733 | 7 | .. | 5 | .. |
| | | Females | | 2,821 | 13,371 | 1,406 | 103 | 25 | 34 | 423 | .. | .. | 1 | .. |
| | (2) Porwal | Males. | Ditto | 6,881 | 4,536 | 5,437 | 442 | 117 | 50 | 703 | 7 | .. | 3 | .. |
| | | Females | | 2,252 | 9,034 | 1,321 | 75 | 59 | 25 | 401 | 7 | .. | 5 | .. |
| | ***MUSALMAN*** | Males. | .. | ***112,953*** | ***66,564*** | ***31,178*** | ***2,118*** | ***767*** | ***1,057*** | ***22,875*** | ***369*** | ***8,981*** | ***1,463*** | ***314*** |
| | | Females | | ***42,176*** | ***120,610*** | ***660*** | ***44*** | ***31*** | ***413*** | ***9,758*** | ***194*** | ***7,425*** | ***245*** | ***160*** |
| 1 | Pathan | Males. | Military service. | 47,036 | 26,440 | 14,754 | 1,057 | 354 | 484 | 10,128 | 118 | 3,279 | 490 | 137 |
| | | Females | | 16,006 | 49,040 | .. | .. | .. | 174 | 4,301 | 8 | 2,863 | 102 | 76 |
| 2 | Saiyad | Males. | Ditto | 10,628 | 6,881 | 3,705 | 181 | 94 | 146 | 2,159 | 54 | 522 | 121 | 60 |
| | | Females | | 3,873 | 11,865 | .. | .. | .. | 90 | 635 | .. | 699 | 8 | 25 |

## Castes, Tribes or Races.

PRINCIPAL OCCUPATION OF ACTUAL WORKERS.

| II Extraction of minerals. | | III Industries. | | IV Transport. | | V Trade. | VI Public force. | | | | VII Public—Administration. | | | | VIII Arts and Professions. | | | IX Persons living on their own income. | X Domestic service. | XI Labourers unspecified. | XII Beggars, prostitutes, criminals and inmates of jails and asylums. |
|---|---|---|---|---|---|---|---|---|---|---|---|---|---|---|---|---|---|---|---|---|---|
| | | | | | | | Commissioned and gazetted officers. | | Others. | | Gazetted officers. | | Others. | | | | | | | | |
| Owners, managers, clerks, etc. | Labourers. | Owners, managers, clerks, etc. | Artisans and other workmen. | Owners, managers, ship's officers, etc. | Labourers, boatmen, carters, palki-bearers, etc. | | Government. | Native States. | Government. | Native States. | Government. | Native States. | Government. | Native States. | Religious. | Lawyers, doctors and teachers. | Others. | | | | |
| 15 | 16 | 17 | 18 | 19 | 20 | 21 | 22 | 23 | 24 | 25 | 26 | 27 | 28 | 29 | 30 | 31 | 32 | 33 | 34 | 35 | 36 |
| .. | 21 | .. | 41 | .. | 22 | 96 | .. | .. | .. | ..* | .. | .. | .. | 18 | .. | 1 | .. | 16 | 87 | 480 | 49 |
| .. | 1 | .. | 18 | .. | 1 | 23 | .. | .. | .. | .. | .. | .. | .. | .. | .. | .. | 1 | 7 | 123 | 516 | 36 |
| 1 | 5 | .. | 3 | .. | 1 | 43 | .. | .. | ..* | ..* | .. | .. | 7 | 14 | 1 | .. | 18 | 6 | 51 | 151 | 34 |
| .. | 7 | .. | 13 | .. | 1 | 10 | .. | .. | .. | .. | .. | .. | .. | .. | .. | .. | 2 | 2 | 38 | 181 | 31 |
| 4 | 8 | .. | 222 | .. | 14 | 19 | .. | ..* | ..* | ..* | .. | 10 | 3 | 19 | .. | 5 | .. | 52 | 180 | 232 | 49 |
| .. | .. | .. | 105 | .. | 2 | 87 | .. | .. | .. | .. | .. | .. | .. | .. | .. | .. | 24 | 86 | 188 | 282 | 22 |
| .. | 3 | .. | 5 | .. | .. | 7 | .. | .. | .. | .. | .. | 5 | .. | 2 | .. | .. | .. | .. | 50 | 24 | 11 |
| .. | .. | .. | .. | .. | 1 | 1 | .. | .. | .. | .. | .. | .. | .. | .. | .. | .. | .. | .. | 37 | 26 | .. |
| .. | 7 | .. | 55 | .. | 9 | 32 | ..* | ..* | ..* | ..* | .. | 2 | 1 | 16 | 4 | 6 | 9 | 29 | 85 | 268 | 76 |
| .. | 4 | .. | 15 | .. | .. | 9 | .. | .. | .. | .. | .. | .. | .. | .. | .. | .. | 4 | 59 | 120 | 251 | 4 |
| .. | 2 | .. | .. | 1 | .. | 10 | .. | ..* | .. | ..* | .. | 6 | .. | 5 | .. | .. | 8 | 3 | 9 | 13 | 1 |
| .. | .. | .. | .. | .. | .. | .. | .. | .. | .. | .. | .. | .. | .. | .. | .. | .. | 3 | 1 | 2 | 16 | .. |
| 6 | 27 | 16 | 415 | 11 | 28 | 73 | .. | ..* | ..* | ..* | .. | 4 | 2 | 75 | 13 | 8 | 20 | 58 | 347 | 726 | 65 |
| .. | 25 | .. | 348 | .. | 4 | 11 | .. | .. | .. | .. | .. | .. | .. | .. | .. | 2 | .. | 24 | 91 | 847 | 27 |
| .. | 24 | 1 | 416 | 2 | 77 | 201 | .. | ..* | ..* | ..* | .. | 26 | 4 | 29 | 4 | 8 | 30 | 56 | 343 | 569 | 131 |
| .. | 4 | .. | 48 | .. | 40 | 117 | .. | .. | .. | .. | .. | .. | .. | .. | .. | 1 | 7 | 76 | 216 | 589 | 32 |
| 1 | .. | .. | 2 | .. | .. | 10 | .. | ..* | .. | ..* | .. | 1 | 3 | 13 | .. | 2 | 1 | 19 | 41 | 108 | 14 |
| .. | .. | .. | 16 | .. | .. | 1 | .. | .. | .. | .. | .. | .. | .. | .. | .. | .. | .. | 15 | 28 | 78 | 1 |
| .. | 13 | 3 | 29 | 1 | 6 | 59 | .. | ..* | ..* | ..* | .. | 7 | .. | 20 | 2 | 2 | 26 | 11 | 67 | 115 | 23 |
| .. | .. | .. | 11 | .. | .. | .. | .. | .. | .. | .. | .. | .. | .. | .. | .. | .. | 13 | 13 | 55 | 149 | 1 |
| .. | 15 | 3 | 401 | .. | 11 | 48 | .. | ..* | .. | ..* | .. | 7 | .. | 44 | 1 | 1 | 28 | 37 | 208 | 303 | 42 |
| .. | .. | .. | 20 | .. | 6 | 5 | .. | .. | .. | .. | .. | .. | .. | .. | .. | .. | 7 | 13 | 97 | 258 | 2 |
| .. | 12 | 3 | 144 | 2 | 12 | 62 | .. | .. | .. | ..* | .. | .. | .. | 15 | 6 | 5 | .. | 46 | 113 | 508 | 37 |
| .. | 4 | .. | 19 | .. | .. | 10 | .. | .. | .. | .. | .. | .. | .. | .. | .. | .. | .. | 18 | 87 | 279 | 19 |
| .. | 15 | .. | 80 | .. | .. | 8 | .. | .. | .. | 1 | .. | .. | .. | 19 | 1 | .. | .. | .. | 85 | 2,393 | 81 |
| .. | 3 | .. | 1 | .. | .. | 2 | .. | .. | .. | .. | .. | .. | .. | .. | .. | .. | 1 | .. | 1 | 3,256 | 212 |
| .. | 2 | .. | 231 | .. | 17 | 22 | .. | .. | .. | 27 | .. | 1 | 5 | 69 | .. | 1 | 17 | 170 | 324 | 712 | 165 |
| .. | 3 | .. | 33 | .. | .. | 13 | .. | .. | .. | .. | .. | .. | .. | .. | .. | .. | 11 | 11 | 44 | 564 | 84 |
| 1 | 67 | .. | 244 | .. | 318 | 2,015 | .. | .. | 1 | 20 | .. | .. | 7 | 72 | 5 | 4 | 44 | 304 | 898 | 3,122 | 181 |
| .. | 5 | .. | 366 | .. | 50 | 2,484 | .. | .. | .. | .. | .. | .. | .. | .. | .. | .. | 6 | 69 | 204 | 4,598 | 150 |
| 9 | 10 | 9 | 133 | 3 | 50 | ..* | .. | .. | 3 | 99 | .. | 1 | 5 | 133 | 95 | 96 | 46 | 198 | 910 | 341 | 39 |
| .. | .. | .. | 248 | .. | 9 | ..* | .. | .. | .. | .. | .. | .. | .. | .. | 6 | .. | 15 | 89 | 193 | 788 | 109 |
| 9 | 10 | 9 | 133 | 3 | 50 | ..* | .. | .. | 3 | 99 | .. | 1 | 5 | 133 | 95 | 96 | 46 | 198 | 910 | 341 | 39 |
| .. | .. | .. | 248 | .. | 9 | ..* | .. | .. | .. | .. | .. | .. | .. | .. | 6 | .. | 15 | 89 | 193 | 788 | 109 |
| .. | 7 | 8 | 122 | 1 | 19 | ..* | .. | .. | 2 | 22 | .. | .. | 2 | 117 | 15 | 19 | 16 | 93 | 666 | 150 | 16 |
| .. | .. | .. | 241 | .. | 2 | ..* | .. | .. | .. | .. | .. | .. | .. | .. | 5 | .. | 13 | 65 | 116 | 465 | 50 |
| 2 | 3 | 1 | 11 | 2 | 31 | ..* | .. | .. | 1 | 7 | .. | 1 | 3 | 16 | 10 | 7 | 30 | 105 | 244 | 191 | 16 |
| .. | .. | .. | 7 | .. | .. | ..* | .. | .. | .. | .. | .. | .. | .. | .. | 1 | .. | 2 | 24 | 77 | 323 | 59 |
| 24 | 190 | 211 | 6,495 | 71 | 1,504 | 7,843 | .. | .. | 1 | 59 | .. | 78 | 468 | 3,223 | 967 | 455 | 2,060 | 2,088 | 10,478 | 6,543 | 4,735 |
| .. | 94 | 1 | 5,476 | 1 | 908 | 3,273 | .. | .. | .. | .. | .. | .. | .. | .. | 16 | 13 | 641 | 940 | 2,072 | 3,214 | 2,512 |
| 7 | 24 | 115 | 2,312 | 24 | 664 | 2,407 | .. | ..* | ..* | ..* | .. | 29 | 126 | 1,519 | 99 | 187 | 741 | 906 | 3,763 | 2,812 | 1,916 |
| .. | 13 | .. | 2,246 | .. | 127 | 1,049 | .. | .. | .. | .. | .. | .. | .. | .. | 5 | 5 | 275 | 420 | 903 | 2,720 | 719 |
| 9 | 5 | 18 | 877 | 6 | 96 | 540 | .. | ..* | ..* | ..* | .. | 28 | 55 | 272 | 78 | 75 | 116 | 333 | 668 | 334 | 848 |
| .. | .. | .. | 389 | 1 | 7 | 189 | .. | .. | .. | .. | .. | .. | .. | .. | 1 | 2 | 29 | 149 | 224 | 245 | 680 |

# TABLE XVI.—OCCUPATION BY

| Serial Number. | Caste, Tribe or Race. | Sex. | Traditional occupation. | Population dealt with: Actual workers. | Population dealt with: Dependants. | Number of actual workers whose traditional caste occupation was returned as their: Principal means of livelihood. | Number of actual workers whose traditional caste occupation was returned as their: Subsidiary means of livelihood. | Number of actual workers returned their traditional occupation as their principal means of livelihood who had some subsidiary occupation. | RECORDED — I. Exploitation of the surface of the soil: Income from rent of land. | Cultivators of all kinds. | Agents and managers of landed estates, planters, forest officers and their clerks, rent collectors, etc. | Field labourers, wood cutters, etc. | Raisers of live stock, milkmen and herdsmen. | Fishing and hunting. |
|---|---|---|---|---|---|---|---|---|---|---|---|---|---|---|
| | 1 | 2 | 3 | 4 | 5 | 6 | 7 | 8 | 9 | 10 | 11 | 12 | 13 | 14 |
| | Musalman—*contd.* | | | | | | | | | | | | | |
| 3 | Shaikh | Males | .. | *55,989* | *33,393* | *19,716* | *880* | *819* | *497* | *10,593* | *197* | *5,180* | *859* | *117* |
| | | Females | | *22,797* | *60,905* | *660* | *44* | *31* | *149* | *4,392* | *116* | *8,863* | *185* | *59* |
| | (1) Behena | Males | Cotton cleaners. | 7,462 | 4,861 | 1,478 | 214 | 114 | 21 | 2,055 | 12 | 865 | 198 | 45 |
| | | Females | | 5,374 | 6,671 | 660 | 44 | 31 | 54 | 1,163 | 102 | 937 | 19 | 38 |
| | (2) Shaikh | Males | Military service. | 47,827 | 28,432 | 11,238 | 666 | 205 | 406 | 8,538 | 185 | 4,315 | 659 | 72 |
| | | Females | | 17,423 | 53,534 | .. | .. | .. | 95 | 3,659 | 14 | 2,928 | 116 | 21 |
| | *ANIMIST* | Males | .. | *140,201* | *95,914* | *80,787* | *1,908* | *1,913* | *1* | *9,335* | *55* | *26,963* | *5,933* | *18* |
| | | Females | | *114,055* | *125,949* | *55,494* | *336* | *140* | .. | *1,344* | .. | *34,895* | *1,695* | *2* |
| 1 | Bhil | Males | Agriculture. | 76,330 | 57,715 | 48,009 | 1,254 | 147 | ..* | ..* | 28 | 13,647 | 2,851 | 6 |
| | | Females | | 59,122 | 76,743 | 26,010 | 245 | 41 | ..* | ..* | .. | 21,667 | 1,057 | .. |
| 2 | Bhilala | Males | Ditto | 26,156 | 18,665 | 22,876 | 268 | 691 | ..* | ..* | 27 | 1,192 | 510 | .. |
| | | Females | | 24,583 | 20,208 | 22,122 | 48 | 21 | ..* | ..* | .. | 1,508 | 216 | .. |
| 3 | Gond | Males | Agriculture and hunting. | 24,064 | 10,547 | 7,669 | 198 | 126 | ..* | ..* | .. | 8,663 | 1,446 | .. |
| | | Females | | 20,468 | 16,308 | 5,704 | 5 | 37 | ..* | ..* | .. | 9,383 | 271 | .. |
| 4 | Kirar | Males | Ditto | 1,091 | 450 | 704 | 27 | 9 | ..* | ..* | .. | 111 | 97 | ..* |
| | | Females | | 441 | 1,055 | 191 | 6 | .. | ..* | ..* | .. | 133 | .. | ..* |
| 5 | Kol | Males | Hunting and collecting jungle produce. | 2,146 | 1,015 | 370 | 77 | 4 | .. | 185 | .. | 513 | 123 | 12* |
| | | Females | | 1,910 | 1,213 | 865 | .. | 4 | .. | 102 | .. | 294 | 25 | 2* |
| 6 | Kotwal | Males | Watchmen | 166 | 88 | 29 | 3 | 7 | .. | 69 | .. | 13 | 3 | .. |
| | | Females | | 130 | 139 | 4 | .. | .. | .. | 23 | .. | 24 | 4 | .. |
| 7 | Mina | Males | Hunters and robbers. | 1,087 | 408 | 110 | 21 | 6 | 1 | 580 | .. | 187 | 75 | ..* |
| | | Females | | 792 | 1,281 | 76 | 15 | .. | .. | 294 | .. | 395 | .. | ..* |
| 8 | Saharia | Males | Hunting and collecting of jungle produce. | 9,161 | 7,026 | 1,020 | 60 | 223 | .. | 1,501 | .. | 2,636 | 128 | ..* |
| | | Females | | 6,609 | 9,002 | 452 | 17 | 37 | .. | 925 | .. | 1,421 | 59 | ..* |
| | *CHRISTIAN* | Males | .. | *3,501* | *511* | .. | .. | .. | .. | .. | *5* | .. | *2* | .. |
| | | Females | | *100* | *1,035* | .. | .. | .. | .. | .. | .. | .. | .. | .. |
| 1 | Anglo-Indians | Males | .. | 174 | 122 | .. | .. | .. | .. | .. | .. | .. | .. | .. |
| | | Females | | 39 | 230 | .. | .. | .. | .. | .. | .. | .. | .. | .. |
| 2 | Europeans. | Males | .. | 3,327 | 389 | .. | .. | .. | .. | .. | 5 | .. | 2 | .. |
| | | Females | | 61 | 805 | .. | | .. | .. | .. | .. | .. | .. | .. |

## Castes, Tribes or Races.

PRINCIPAL OCCUPATION OF ACTUAL WORKERS.

| II Extraction of Minerals. Owners, managers, clerks, etc. | II Extraction of Minerals. Labourers. | III Industries. Owners, managers, clerks, etc. | III Industries. Artisans and other workmen. | IV Transport. Owners, managers, ship's officers, etc. | IV Transport. Labourers, boatmen, carters, palki-bearers, etc. | V Trade. | VI Public Force. Commissioned and gazetted officers. Government. | VI Public Force. Commissioned and gazetted officers. Native States. | VI Public Force. Others. Government. | VI Public Force. Others. Native States. | VII Public—Administration. Gazetted officers. Government. | VII Public—Administration. Gazetted officers. Native States. | VII Public—Administration. Others. Government. | VII Public—Administration. Others. Native States. | VIII Arts and Professions. Religious. | VIII Arts and Professions. Lawyers, doctors and teachers. | VIII Arts and Professions. Others. | IX Persons living on their own income. | X Domestic service. | XI Labourers unspecified. | XII Beggars, prostitutes, criminals and inmates of jails and asylums. |
|---|---|---|---|---|---|---|---|---|---|---|---|---|---|---|---|---|---|---|---|---|---|
| 15 | 16 | 17 | 18 | 19 | 20 | 21 | 22 | 23 | 24 | 25 | 26 | 27 | 28 | 29 | 30 | 31 | 32 | 33 | 34 | 35 | 36 |
| 3 | 161 | 78 | 8,736 | 41 | 744 | 4,896 | .. | .. | 1 | 53 | .. | 91 | 987 | 1,439 | 90 | 193 | 1,903 | 849 | 6,047 | 3,397 | 1,971 |
| .. | 11 | 1 | 9,841 | .. | 74 | 9,035 | .. | .. | .. | .. | .. | .. | .. | .. | 10 | 6 | 337 | 371 | 945 | 5,249 | 1,113 |
| 1 | 63 | 1 | 340 | 3 | 78 | 670 | .. | .. | 1 | 52 | .. | .. | 1 | 64 | 4 | 5 | 97 | 50 | 206 | 1,060 | 97 |
| .. | 9 | 1 | 442 | .. | 4 | 353 | .. | .. | .. | .. | .. | .. | .. | .. | 8 | .. | 6 | 22 | 95 | 1,344 | 117 |
| 7 | 98 | 77 | 3,396 | 38 | 666 | 4,226 | .. | ..* | ..* | ..* | .. | 21 | 286 | 1,368 | 86 | 188 | 1,106 | 799 | 5,841 | 2,337 | 1,874 |
| .. | 2 | .. | 2,399 | .. | 70 | 1,682 | .. | .. | .. | .. | .. | .. | .. | .. | 2 | 6 | 331 | 349 | 850 | 3,905 | 996 |
| .. | 3 | 6 | 669 | .. | 189 | 298 | 8 | .. | 434 | 1,139 | .. | 11 | 9 | 598 | 7 | 9 | 55 | 19 | 970 | 19,750 | 654 |
| .. | .. | .. | 361 | .. | 105 | 985 | .. | .. | .. | .. | .. | .. | .. | .. | .. | .. | 34 | 9 | 804 | 19,197 | 110 |
| .. | .. | 6 | 448 | .. | 133 | 82 | 7 | .. | 396 | 118 | .. | .. | 8 | 489 | 7 | 1 | 44 | .. | 428 | 9,384 | 288 |
| .. | .. | .. | 162 | .. | 24 | 87 | .. | .. | .. | .. | .. | .. | .. | .. | .. | .. | 34 | .. | 314 | 9,810 | 7 |
| .. | .. | .. | 39 | .. | 7 | 17 | 1 | .. | 16 | .. | .. | 11 | .. | 90 | .. | 1 | .. | 4 | 181 | 1,165 | 18 |
| .. | .. | .. | 27 | .. | 2 | 4 | .. | .. | .. | .. | .. | .. | .. | .. | .. | .. | .. | .. | 75 | 570 | 59 |
| .. | .. | .. | 142 | .. | 8 | 133 | .. | .. | .. | 26 | .. | .. | .. | 22 | .. | .. | 9 | 8 | 79 | 5,672 | 187 |
| .. | .. | .. | 156 | .. | 76 | 152 | .. | .. | .. | .. | .. | .. | .. | .. | .. | .. | .. | 5 | 84 | 4,620 | 17 |
| .. | .. | .. | .. | .. | 25 | 10 | .. | .. | .. | .. | .. | .. | .. | .. | .. | .. | .. | 7 | 27 | 95 | 15 |
| .. | .. | .. | .. | .. | .. | 2 | .. | .. | .. | .. | .. | .. | .. | .. | .. | .. | .. | 4 | 21 | 89 | 1 |
| .. | .. | .. | .. | .. | .. | 16 | .. | .. | .. | .. | .. | .. | .. | 16 | .. | .. | 2 | .. | 96 | 808 | 5 |
| .. | .. | .. | .. | .. | .. | 36 | .. | .. | .. | .. | .. | .. | .. | .. | .. | .. | .. | .. | 8 | 576 | 2 |
| .. | .. | .. | 28 | .. | .. | .. | .. | .. | .. | ..* | .. | .. | 1 | .. | .. | .. | .. | .. | 6 | 17 | .. |
| .. | .. | .. | 10 | .. | .. | .. | .. | .. | .. | .. | .. | .. | .. | .. | .. | .. | .. | .. | .. | 65 | .. |
| .. | 3 | .. | .. | .. | 9 | 28 | .. | .. | .. | 1 | .. | .. | .. | 1 | .. | .. | .. | .. | 18 | 65 | 9 |
| .. | .. | .. | .. | .. | .. | .. | .. | .. | .. | .. | .. | .. | .. | .. | .. | .. | .. | .. | 3 | 16 | 8 |
| .. | .. | .. | 12 | .. | .. | 12 | .. | .. | 22 | 994 | .. | .. | .. | 25 | .. | .. | .. | .. | 135 | 2,544 | 132 |
| .. | .. | .. | 6 | .. | 3 | 54 | .. | .. | .. | .. | .. | .. | .. | .. | .. | .. | .. | .. | 290 | 3,381 | 16 |
| 3 | .. | 19 | .. | 235 | .. | 1 | 137 | 4 | 2,904 | .. | 21 | 8 | 7 | .. | 50 | 60 | 34 | 14 | 7 | .. | .. |
| .. | .. | .. | .. | 1 | .. | 9 | .. | .. | .. | .. | .. | .. | .. | .. | 33 | 20 | 11 | 4 | 29 | .. | .. |
| .. | .. | 8 | .. | 95 | .. | .. | 12 | .. | .. | .. | .. | .. | 4 | .. | 25 | 17 | 1 | 5 | 7 | .. | .. |
| .. | .. | .. | .. | .. | .. | .. | .. | .. | .. | .. | .. | .. | .. | .. | 12 | 7 | 5 | 2 | 18 | .. | .. |
| 3 | .. | 11 | .. | 140 | .. | 1 | 125 | 4 | 2,904 | .. | 21 | 8 | 3 | .. | 25 | 43 | 23 | 9 | .. | .. | .. |
| .. | .. | .. | .. | 1 | .. | 2 | .. | .. | .. | .. | .. | .. | .. | .. | 21 | 13 | 6 | 2 | 16 | .. | .. |

## TABLE XVII.

### *TERRITORIAL DISTRIBUTION OF THE CHRISTIAN POPULATION BY SECT AND RACE.*

This Table shews denominations of Christians of all races.

The term "Anglo-Indian" has been used for those who returned themselves as "Eurasians," in accordance with the decision of the Government of India conveyed by the Census Commissioner for India. This term includes all persons of mixed blood formerly known as "Eurasians" and is not confined to those of British origin.

## TABLE XVII.—DISTRIBUTION OF THE CHRISTIAN POPULATION BY SECT AND RACE.

| Denominations. | Total. | | | Distribution by Race. | | | | | |
|---|---|---|---|---|---|---|---|---|---|
| | | | | European and allied races. | | Anglo-Indian. | | Native. | |
| | Persons. | Males. | Females. | Males. | Females. | Males. | Females. | Males. | Females. |
| 1 | 2 | 3 | 4 | 5 | 6 | 7 | 8 | 9 | 10 |
| **Central India** | **9,358** | **6,170** | **3,188** | **3,716** | **866** | **296** | **269** | **2,158** | **2,053** |
| Anglican communion | 3,663 | 2,877 | 786 | 2,682 | 514 | 77 | 70 | 118 | 202 |
| Armenian | 2 | 2 | ... | 2 | ... | ... | ... | ... | ... |
| Baptist | 75 | 59 | 16 | 32 | 1 | ... | ... | 27 | 15 |
| Greek | 2 | 2 | ... | 1 | ... | 1 | ... | ... | ... |
| Lutheran | 2 | 1 | 1 | 1 | ... | ... | 1 | ... | ... |
| Methodist | 124 | 113 | 11 | 100 | ... | ... | ... | 13 | 11 |
| Presbyterian | 1,470 | 687 | 783 | 145 | 36 | 5 | 7 | 537 | 740 |
| Protestant | 473 | 330 | 143 | 21 | 8 | 4 | 4 | 305 | 131 |
| Quaker | 48 | 21 | 27 | 1 | 2 | ... | ... | 20 | 25 |
| Roman Catholic | 3,241 | 1,928 | 1,313 | 655 | 271 | 183 | 169 | 1,090 | 873 |
| Salvationists | 2 | 2 | ... | 2 | ... | ... | ... | ... | ... |
| Sect not returned | 249 | 141 | 108 | 67 | 34 | 26 | 18 | 48 | 56 |
| Indefinite Beliefs | 7 | 7 | ... | 7 | ... | ... | ... | ... | ... |

NOTE.—Th Sect "Indefinite Beliefs" consists of 3 Agnostic, 1 Atheist, 1 Freethinker and 2 Unitarians.

# TABLE XVIII.

## *EUROPEANS, ARMENIANS AND ANGLO-INDIANS BY RACE AND AGE.*

**This table shews the distribution of Christians in the Agency as a whole.**

# TABLE XVIII.—Europeans, Armenians and Anglo-Indians by Race and Age.

| TOTAL. | | | EUROPEANS AND ALLIED RACES. | | | | | | | | | | | | | | | | | | | | | | | | | | ARMENIANS. | | | | | | | | | | | | | ANGLO-INDIANS (EURASIANS). | | | | | | | | | | | | |
|---|---|---|---|---|---|---|---|---|---|---|---|---|---|---|---|---|---|---|---|---|---|---|---|---|---|---|---|---|---|---|---|---|---|---|---|---|---|---|---|---|---|---|---|---|---|---|---|---|---|---|---|---|---|---|
| Persons. | Males. | Females. | British Subjects. | | | | | | | | | | | | | Others. | | | | | | | | | | | | | All ages. | | | 0-12 | | 12-15 | | 15-30 | | 30-50 | | 50 and over. | | All ages. | | | 0-12 | | 12-15 | | 15-30 | | 30-50 | | 50 and over. | |
| | | | All ages. | | | 0-12 | | 12-15 | | 15-30 | | 30-50 | | 50 and over. | | All ages. | | | 0-12 | | 12-15 | | 15-30 | | 30-50 | | 50 and over. | | | | | | | | | | | | | | | | | | | | | | | | | | |
| | | | Persons. | Males. | Females. | Males. | Females. | Males. | Females. | Males. | Females. | Males. | Females. | Males. | Females. | Persons. | Males. | Females. | Males. | Females. | Males. | Females. | Males. | Females. | Males. | Females. | Males. | Females. | Persons. | Males. | Females. | Males. | Females. | Males. | Females. | Males. | Females. | Males. | Females. | Males. | Females. | Persons. | Males. | Females. | Males. | Females. | Males. | Females. | Males. | Females. | Males. | Females. | Males. | Females. |
| 1 | 2 | 3 | 4 | 5 | 6 | 7 | 8 | 9 | 10 | 11 | 12 | 13 | 14 | 15 | 16 | 17 | 18 | 19 | 20 | 21 | 22 | 23 | 24 | 25 | 26 | 27 | 28 | 29 | 30 | 31 | 32 | 33 | 34 | 35 | 36 | 37 | 38 | 39 | 40 | 41 | 42 | 43 | 44 | 45 | 46 | 47 | 48 | 49 | 50 | 51 | 52 | 53 | 54 | 55 |
| **Central India**— 5,147 | 4,012 | 1,135 | 3,968 | 3,414 | 554 | 120 | 113 | 39 | 81 | 2,673 | 188 | 528 | 198 | 44 | 29 | 612 | 300 | 312 | 67 | 121 | 10 | 10 | 119 | 107 | 87 | 66 | 17 | 8 | 2 | 2 | .. | | ... | ... | ... | ... | ... | ... | ... | 2 | ... | 565 | 206 | 269 | 101 | 72 | 11 | 23 | 76 | 91 | 85 | 78 | 23 | 10 |

**Table showing the adjustments of different Political Charges of Central India Agency in 1901.**

| ADJUSTMENT. | POPULATION. | | | | | |
|---|---|---|---|---|---|---|
| | Persons. | | Males. | | Females. | |
| 1 | 2 | | 3 | | 4 | |
| **Gwalior Residency.** | | | | | | |
| Imperial Table II in 1901 | | 2,187,612 | | 1,160,245 | | 1,027,367 |
| *Add—* | | | | | | |
| Gwalior portion from Malwa Agency | 614,540 | | 314,634 | | 299,906 | |
| Gwalior portion from Bhopal Agency | 118,542 | | 59,483 | | 59,059 | |
| Gwalior portion from Indore Residency (Agency) | 23,710 | | 12,051 | | 11,659 | |
| Minor Estates of Kalukhera, Narwar and Lalgarh from Malwa Agency. | 4,175 | | 2,039 | | 2,136 | |
| Minor Estate of Karaudia from Indore Agency | 1,469 | | 724 | | 745 | |
| Minor Estates of Kamalpur, Kheri-Rajpura, Pathari and Tappa from Bhopal Agency. | 2,542 | | 1,263 | | 1,279 | |
| Minor Estate of Maksudangarh from Bhopal Agency | 14,284 | | 7,351 | | 6,933 | |
| Nimach Cantonment and Agar Station from Malwa Agency | 18,614 | | 10,538 | | 8,076 | |
| Gwalior Railway portion from Bhopal Agency | 186 | | 105 | | 81 | |
| Gwalior Railway portion from Malwa Agency | 2,579 | | 1,691 | | 888 | |
| | | +800,641 | | 409,879 | | 390.762 |
| | | 2,988,253 | | 1,570,124 | | 1,418,129 |
| *Deduct—* | | | | | | |
| Chhabra Pargana of Tonk transferred to Rajputana Agency | 36,046 | | | | | |
| Chhabra Railway station transferred to Rajputana Agency | 66 | | 18,744 | | 17,302 | |
| Fatehabad Railway station transferred to Indore Agency | 141 | | 40 | | 26 | |
| | | —36,253 | 90 | | 51 | |
| | | | | 18,874 | | 17,379 |
| TOTAL GWALIOR RESIDENCY | | 2,952,000 | | 1,551,250 | | 1,400,750 |
| **Indore Residency.** | | | | | | |
| Imperial Table II in 1901 | | 285,905 | | 150,533 | | 135,372 |
| *Add—* | | | | | | |
| Late Indore Agency | 104,770 | | 53,493 | | 51,286 | |
| Indore portion from Malwa Agency | 204,224 | | 105,314 | | 98,910 | |
| Indore portion from Bhopawar Agency | 235,210 | | 121,247 | | 113,963 | |
| Indore portion from Bhopal Agency | 115,818 | | 59,029 | | 56,789 | |
| Minor Estate of Bhatkheri from Malwa Agency | 1,878 | | 901 | | 977 | |
| Minor Estate of Hirapur from Bhopal Agency | 448 | | 205 | | 243 | |
| Portion of Rajgarh state transferred to Indore Residency in exchange of Talen from Bhopal Agency | 467 | | 243 | | 224 | |
| Railway portion from Bhopawar Agency | 319 | | 215 | | 104 | |
| Railway portion from Malwa Agency | 89 | | 63 | | 26 | |
| Fatehabad Railway station from Gwalior Residency | 141 | | 90 | | 51 | |
| | | +663,373 | | 340,800 | | 322,573 |
| | | 949,278 | | 491,333 | | 457,945 |
| *Deduct—* | | | | | | |
| Gwalior portion } of old Indore Agency. | 23,710 | | 12,051 | | 11,659 | |
| Minor Estate of Karaudia } of old Indore Agency. | 1,469 | | 724 | | 745 | |
| Dewes S. B. and J. B., Bagli, Pathari, and Uni } of old Indore Agency. | 79,600 | | 40,718 | | 38,882 | |
| Talen transferred to Bhopal Agency | 2,392 | | 1,160 | | 1,232 | |
| | | —107,171 | | 54,653 | | 52,518 |
| TOTAL INDORE RESIDENCY | | 842,107 | | 436,680 | | 405,427 |
| **Baghelkhand Agency.** | | | | | | |
| Imperial Table II in 1901 | | 1,555,024 | | 771,301 | | 783,723 |
| *Add*—Population of Rewah villages in Allahabad district | | +1,040 | | 557 | | 483 |
| | | 1,556,064 | | 771,858 | | 784,206 |
| *Deduct*—Population of Allahabad villages in Rewah State | | —2,079 | | 1,016 | | 1,063 |
| TOTAL BAGHELKHAND AGENCY | | 1,553,985 | | 770,842 | | 783,143 |

**Table showing the adjustments of different Political Charges of Central India Agency in 1901**—*contd.*

| ADJUSTMENT. | Population. Persons. | | Males. | | Females. | |
|---|---|---|---|---|---|---|
| 1 | 2 | | 3 | | 4 | |
| **Bhopal Agency.** | | | | | | |
| Imperial Table II in 1901 | | 1,267,526 | | 641,704 | | 625,822 |
| *Add*—Talen transferred from Indore Residency | | +2,392 | | 1,160 | | 1,232 |
| | | 1,269,918 | | 642,864 | | 627,054 |
| *Deduct*— | | | | | | |
| Sironj Pargana of Tonk transferred to Rajputana Agency | 68,539 | | 35,181 | | 33,358 | |
| Dewas S. B. and J. B. portions | 21,058 | | 10,707 | | 10,351 | |
| Dhar portion | 1,415 | | 747 | | 668 | |
| Indore portion | 115,818 | | 59,029 | | 56,789 | |
| Gwalior portion | 118,542 | | 59,483 | | 59,059 | |
| Minor Estate of Hirapur | 448 | | 205 | | 243 | |
| Minor Estates of Kamalpur, Kheri-Rajpura, Pathari and Tappa | 2,542 | | 1,263 | | 1,279 | |
| Minor Estate of Maksudangarh | 14,284 | | 7,351 | | 6,933 | |
| Portion of Rajgarh State transferred to Indore Residency | 467 | | 243 | | 224 | |
| Gwalior Railway portion | 186 | | 105 | | 81 | |
| | | −343,299 | | 174,314 | | 168,985 |
| TOTAL BHOPAL AGENCY | | 926,619 | | 468,550 | | 458,069 |
| **Bhopawar Agency.** | | | | | | |
| Imperial Table II in 1901 | | 782,808 | | 397,321 | | 385,487 |
| *Add*—Dhar portion from Bhopal Agency | | +1,415 | | 747 | | 668 |
| *Deduct*— | | 784,223 | | 398,068 | | 386,155 |
| Indore portion | 235,210 | | 121,247 | | 113,963 | |
| Railway portion of Indore except Bamania | 319 | | 215 | | 104 | |
| | | −235,529 | | 121,462 | | 114,067 |
| TOTAL BHOPAWAR AGENCY | | 548,694 | | 276,606 | | 272,088 |
| **Bundelkhand Agency.** | | | | | | |
| Imperial Table II in 1901 (no changes) | | 1,308,326 | | 671,285 | | 637,041 |
| **Malwa Agency.** | | | | | | |
| Imperial Table II in 1901 | | 1,136,801 | | 582,908 | | 553,893 |
| *Add*— | | | | | | |
| Dewas S. B. and J. B. portions from late Indore Agency | 63,621 | | 32,620 | | 31,001 | |
| Bagli from late Indore Agency | 14,049 | | 7,122 | | 6,927 | |
| Pathari from late Indore Agency | 1,436 | | 710 | | 726 | |
| Uni ditto | 494 | | 266 | | 228 | |
| Dewas S. B. and J. B portions from Bhopal Agency | 21,058 | | 10,707 | | 10,351 | |
| | | +100,658 | | 51,425 | | 49,233 |
| *Deduct*— | | 1,237,459 | | 634,333 | | 603,126 |
| Pirawa Pargana of Tonk transferred to Rajputana Agency | 25,286 | | 13,230 | | 12,056 | |
| Gwalior portion | 614,540 | | 314,634 | | 299,906 | |
| Indore portion | 204,224 | | 105,314 | | 98,910 | |
| Nimach Cantonment and Agar Station | 18,614 | | 10,538 | | 8,076 | |
| Minor Estates of Kalukhera, Narwar, and Lalgarh | 4,175 | | 2,039 | | 2,136 | |
| Minor Estate of Bhatkheri | 1,878 | | 901 | | 977 | |
| Railway portion of Gwalior except Fatehabad | 2,438 | | 1,601 | | 837 | |
| Fatehabad Railway station | 141 | | 90 | | 51 | |
| Railway portion of Indore | 89 | | 63 | | 26 | |
| | | −871,385 | | 448,410 | | 422,975 |
| TOTAL MALWA AGENCY | | 366,074 | | 185,923 | | 180,151 |

## Table showing the adjustments of different Political Charges of Central India Agency in 1891.

| ADJUSTMENT. | POPULATION. | | | | | |
|---|---|---|---|---|---|---|
| | Persons. | | Males. | | Females. | |
| 1 | 2 | | 3 | | 4 | |
| **Gwalior Residency.** | | | | | | |
| Imperial Table II in 1891 | | 1,757,509 | | 948,805 | | 808,704 |
| *Add—* | | | | | | |
| Late Guna Agency | 337,973 | | 180,117 | | 157,856 | |
| Gwalior portion from late Indore Agency | 33,747 | | 17,829 | | 15,918 | |
| Gwalior portion from Bhopal Agency | 426,195 | | 225,238 | | 200,957 | |
| Gwalior portion from Malwa Agency | 830,868 | | 438,156 | | 392,712 | |
| Nimach Cantonment and Agar Station | 19,322 | | 11,295 | | 8,027 | |
| Agra-Barkhera from Bhopal Agency | 7,440 | | 3,922 | | 3,518 | |
| Maksudangarh from Bhopal Agency | 14,422 | | 7,751 | | 6,671 | |
| | | +1,669,967 | | 884,308 | | 785,659 |
| | | 3,427,476 | | 1,833,113 | | 1,594,363 |
| *Deduct—* | | | | | | |
| Chhabra Pargana of Tonk transferred to Rajputana Agency | 46,473 | | 24,290 | | 22,183 | |
| Minor Estates of Dariakheri, Dhabla Dhir and Dhabla Ghosi | 3,081 | | 1,515 | | 1,566 | |
| | | −49,554 | | 25,805 | | 23,749 |
| TOTAL GWALIOR RESIDENCY | | 3,377,922 | | 1,807,308 | | 1,570,614 |
| **Indore Residency (Agency.)** | | | | | | |
| Imperial Table II in 1891 | | 372,792 | | 201,944 | | 170,848 |
| *Add—* | | | | | | |
| Indore portion from Bhopal Agency | 151,913 | | 80,213 | | 71,700 | |
| Indore portion from Malwa Agency | 395,598 | | 207,886 | | 187,712 | |
| Indore portion from Bhopawar Agency | 261,126 | | 135,539 | | 125,587 | |
| | | +808,637 | | 423,638 | | 384,999 |
| *Deduct—* | | 1,181,429 | | 625,582 | | 555,817 |
| Gwalior portion | 33,747 | | 17,829 | | 15,918 | |
| Dewas, S. B. do. | 38,708 | | 20,377 | | 18,331 | |
| Dewas, J. B. do. | 33,505 | | 17,838 | | 15,667 | |
| Bagli Estate | 14,675 | | 7,579 | | 7,096 | |
| | | −120,635 | | 63,623 | | 57,012 |
| TOTAL INDORE RESIDENCY | | 1,060,794 | | 561,959 | | 498,835 |
| **Baghelkhand Agency.** | | | | | | |
| Imperial Table II in 1891 | | 1,737,606 | | 872,222 | | 865,384 |
| *Add—* | | | | | | |
| Population of Rewah villages in Allahabad district | 1,224 | | 619 | | 605 | |
| Minor States of Baraunda, Paldeo, Jaso, Bhaisonda, Pahara Taraon and Kamta-Rajaula | 50,726 | | 26,018 | | 24,708 | |
| | | +51,950 | | 26,637 | | 25,313 |
| *Deduct—* | | 1,789,556 | | 898,859 | | 890,697 |
| Population of Allahabad villages in Rewah state | | −2,498 | | 1,208 | | 1,290 |
| TOTAL BAGHELKHAND AGENCY | | 1,787,058 | | 897,651 | | 889,407 |
| **Bhopal Agency.** | | | | | | |
| Imperial Table II in 1891 | | 2,006,859 | | 1,052,777 | | 954,082 |
| *Add—* | | | | | | |
| Minor Estates of Dariakheri, Dhabla Dhir, and Dhabla Ghosi | | +3,081 | | 1,515 | | 1,566 |
| | | 2,009,940 | | 1,054,292 | | 955,648 |
| *Deduct—* | | | | | | |
| Dewas S. B. portion | 15,909 | | 8,612 | | 7,297 | |
| Dewas J. B. portion | 13,891 | | 7,266 | | 6,625 | |
| Indore portion | 151,913 | | 80,213 | | 71,700 | |
| Dhar portion | 1,945 | | 1,080 | | 865 | |
| Gwalior portion | 426,195 | | 225,238 | | 200,957 | |
| Agra Barkhera | 7,440 | | 3,922 | | 3,518 | |
| Maksudangarh | 14,422 | | 7,751 | | 6,671 | |
| Sironj Pargana of Tonk transferred to Rajputana Agency | 93,856 | | 50,488 | | 43,368 | |
| | | −725,571 | | 384,570 | | 341,001 |
| TOTAL BHOPAL AGENCY | | 1,284,369 | | 669,722 | | 614,647 |

**Table showing the adjustments of different Political Charges of Central India Agency in 1891—*contd.***

| ADJUSTMENT. | Population. | | | | | |
|---|---|---|---|---|---|---|
| | Persons. | | Males. | | Females. | |
| 1 | 2 | | 3 | | 4 | |
| **Bhopawar Agency.** | | | | | | |
| Imperial Table II in 1891 | | 978,652 | | 502,832 | | 475,820 |
| *Add*— | | | | | | |
| Dhar portion from Bhopal Agency | 1,945 | | 1,080 | | 865 | |
| Dhar portion from Malwa Agency | 24 | +1,969 | 16 | 1,096 | 8 | 873 |
| | | 980,621 | | 503,928 | | 476,693 |
| *Deduct*— | | | | | | |
| Indore portion | 261,126 | | 135,539 | | 125,587 | |
| Dewas S. and J. B. portions | 5,900 | −267,026 | 3,064 | 138,603 | 2,836 | 128,423 |
| TOTAL BHOPAWAR AGENCY | | 713,595 | | 365,325 | | 348,270 |
| **Bundelkhand Agency.** | | | | | | |
| Imperial Table II in 1891 | | 1,508,053 | | 784,906 | | 723,147 |
| *Deduct*— | | | | | | |
| Minor states of Baraunda, Paldeo, Jaso, Bhaisonda, Pahara, Taraon and Kamta-Rajaula. | | −50,726 | | 26,018 | | 24,708 |
| TOTAL BUNDELKHAND AGENCY | | 1,457,327 | | 758,888 | | 698,439 |
| **Malwa Agency.** | | | | | | |
| Imperial Table II in 1891 | | 1,619,968 | | 851,933 | | 767,435 |
| *Add*— | | | | | | |
| Dewas S. B. porton from late Indore Agency | 38,708 | | 20,377 | | 18,331 | |
| Dewas S. B. portion from Bhopal Agency | 15,909 | | 8,612 | | 7,297 | |
| Dewas S. B. portion from Bhopawar Agency | 2,950 | | 1,532 | | 1,418 | |
| Dewas J. B. portion from late Indore Agency | 33,505 | | 17,838 | | 15,667 | |
| Dewas J. B. portion from Bhopal Agency | 13,891 | | 7,266 | | 6,625 | |
| Dewas J. B portion from Bhopawar Agency | 2,950 | | 1,532 | | 1,418 | |
| Bagli from late Indore Agency | 14,675 | +122,588 | 7,579 | 64,736 | 7,096 | 57,852 |
| | | 1,741,956 | | 916,669 | | 825,287 |
| *Deduct*— | | | | | | |
| Pirawa Pargana of Tonk transferred to Rajputana Agency | 40,806 | | 21,567 | | 19,239 | |
| Gwalior portion | 830,868 | | 438,156 | | 392,712 | |
| Indore portion | 395,598 | | 207,886 | | 187,712 | |
| Nimach Cantonment and Agar Station | 19,322 | | 11,295 | | 8,027 | |
| Dhar portion | 24 | −1,286,618 | 16 | 678,920 | 8 | 607,698 |
| TOTAL MALWA AGENCY | | 455,338 | | 237,749 | | 217,589 |

# PROVINCIAL TABLE I.

## *AREA AND POPULATION OF STATES.*

This table and the next gives for each State of any size leading statistics, *viz.*, total population, density, variation since 1901, distribution by religion and the number of literate persons.

The figures in the Provincial Tables I and II represent the actuals for entire States, Gangapur Pargana of Gwalior and Nandwai of Indore which lie in the Rajputana Agency having been included in their respective States. The totals for Central India will, therefore, necessarily not agree with those given in the corresponding Imperial Tables.

The following table will explain the difference.

| | Area. | Occupied houses. | POPULATION. | | | | | |
|---|---|---|---|---|---|---|---|---|
| | | | 1911. | | | 1901. | | |
| | | | Persons. | Males. | Females. | Persons. | Males. | Females. |
| 1 | 2 | 3 | 4 | 5 | 6 | 7 | 8 | 9 |
| As shown in Imperial Tables I and II | 77,367 | 2,039,955 | 9,356,980 | 4,801,459 | 4,555,521 | 8,497,805 | 4,361,136 | 4,136,669 |
| *Add*— | | | | | | | | |
| Gangapur Pargana of Gwalior . | 26 | 1,834 | 9,197 | 4,783 | 4,414 | 9,003 | 4,606 | 4,397 |
| Nandwai Pargana of Indore . . | 37 | 848 | 3,295 | 1,680 | 1,615 | 2,404 | 1,261 | 1,143 |
| Total . | 77,430 | 2,042,637 | 9,369,472 | 4,807,922 | 4,561,550 | 8,509,212 | 4,367,003 | 4,142,209 |

# PROVINCIAL TABLE I.—AREA AND POPULATION OF STATES.

| Serial No. | States. | Area in square miles. | Number of Towns. | Number of Villages. | Number of occupied houses. | Population 1911 Persons. | Population 1911 Males. | Population 1911 Females. | Population 1901 (Both sexes). | Percentage of variation 1901 to 1911. | Percentage of variation 1891 to 1901. | Number of persons in square mile in 1911. | Revenue. |
|---|---|---|---|---|---|---|---|---|---|---|---|---|---|
| 1 | 2 | 3 | 4 | 5 | 6 | 7 | 8 | 9 | 10 | 11 | 12 | 13 | 14 |
| | **Central India** | **77,430** | **77** | **33,065** | **2,042,637** | **9,369,472** | **4,807,922** | **4,561,550** | **8,509,212** | **+ 10** | **— 16** | **121** | Rs. **4,18,21,700** |
| 1 | GWALIOR STATE | **25,133** | **25** | **10,379** | **661,339** | **3,102,279** | **1,630,327** | **1,471,952** | **2,949,596** | **+ 5** | **— 10** | **123** | **1,40,00,000** |
| | Gwalior Gird (including Lashkar) | 1,713 | 5 | 800 | 72,860 | 312,675 | 167,084 | 145,591 | 332,514 | — 18 | .. | 183 | |
| | Tonwarghar | 2,001 | 2 | 921 | 64,926 | 376,659 | 205,854 | 170,805 | 374,530 | + 1 | .. | 188 | |
| | Bhind (including Nimrol) | 1,720 | 2 | 849 | 69,729 | 399,924 | 216,298 | 183,626 | 418,698 | — 4 | .. | 233 | |
| | Sheopur | 2,365 | 2 | 570 | 28,855 | 124,671 | 65,786 | 58,885 | 134,046 | — 7 | .. | 53 | |
| | Narwar | 3,763 | 2 | 1,342 | 83,583 | 408,129 | 213,638 | 194,491 | 364,554 | + 12 | .. | 108 | |
| | Bhilsa | 1,781 | 1 | 862 | 37,633 | 180,411 | 93,193 | 87,218 | 130,370 | + 38 | .. | 101 | |
| | Isagarh | 3,761 | 2 | 1,486 | 71,778 | 333,169 | 173,377 | 159,792 | 279,516 | + 19 | .. | 89 | |
| | Ujjain | 2,557 | 3 | 1,029 | 77,913 | 321,603 | 165,249 | 156,354 | 290,061 | + 11 | .. | 126 | |
| | Shajapur | 2,398 | 3 | 1,040 | 71,500 | 300,538 | 154,677 | 145,861 | 277,395 | + 8 | .. | 125 | |
| | Mandasor (including Gangapur) | 1,773 | 3 | 944 | 56,102 | 224,725 | 115,357 | 109,368 | 201,486 | + 12 | .. | 127 | |
| | Amjhera | 1,301 | .. | 536 | 26,460 | 119,775 | 59,814 | 59,961 | 96,426 | + 24 | .. | 92 | |
| 2 | INDORE STATE | **9,506** | **9** | **3,727** | **236,061** | **1,007,856** | **517,501** | **490,355** | **853,012** | **+ 18** | **— 22** | **106** | **70,00,000** |
| | Indore (including city and Petlawad) | 1,570 | 1 | 737 | 60,787 | 235,283 | 121,873 | 113,410 | 256,384 | — 8 | .. | 150 | |
| | Mehidpur | 840 | 2 | 447 | 28,736 | 121,243 | 62,718 | 58,525 | 91,885 | + 32 | .. | 144 | |
| | Nemawar | 1,059 | .. | 343 | 22,537 | 94,600 | 47,808 | 46,792 | 74,568 | + 27 | .. | 89 | |
| | Nimar (including Nisarpur and Lawani) | 3,871 | 4 | 1,270 | 73,182 | 348,450 | 177,677 | 170,773 | 257,429 | + 35 | .. | 90 | |
| | Rampura-Bhanpura (including Nandwai) | 2,129 | 2 | 905 | 47,744 | 192,521 | 99,358 | 93,163 | 156,035 | + 23 | .. | 90 | |
| | Alampur | 37 | .. | 25 | 3,075 | 15,759 | 8,067 | 7,692 | 16,711 | — 6 | .. | 426 | |
| 3 | BHOPAL STATE | **6,902** | **6** | **2,985** | **168,629** | **730,383** | **370,560** | **359,823** | **667,350** | **+ 9** | **— 30** | **106** | **30,00,000** |
| | Nizamat-i-Maghrib | 2,226 | 4 | 1,005 | 52,995 | 225,069 | 115,102 | 109,967 | 196,423 | + 15 | .. | 101 | |
| | Nizamat-i-Junub | 2,704 | .. | 1,014 | 58,535 | 271,829 | 136,760 | 135,069 | 245,640 | + 11 | .. | 101 | |
| | Nizamat-i-Mashriq | 1,972 | 2 | 966 | 57,099 | 233,485 | 118,698 | 114,787 | 225,287 | + 4 | .. | 118 | |
| 4 | REWAH STATE | **13,000** | **4** | **5,403** | **304,839** | **1,514,843** | **752,297** | **762,546** | **1,326,802** | **+ 14** | **— 12** | **117** | **53,86,000** |
| | Huzur Tahsil | 1,201 | 2 | 942 | 70,286 | 338,775 | 167,749 | 171,026 | 316,139 | + 7 | .. | 282 | |

| | | | | | | | | | | | | | |
|---|---|---|---|---|---|---|---|---|---|---|---|---|---|
| | Raghurajnagar | 977 | 1 | 479 | 33,019 | 154,893 | 76,385 | 78,508 | 144,336 | + 7 | .. | 159 | |
| | Sitlaha | 816 | .. | 500 | 24,254 | 113,858 | 57,367 | 56,491 | 103,604 | + 10 | .. | 140 | |
| | Mauganj | 784 | .. | 655 | 21,966 | 108,204 | 53,521 | 54,683 | 99,534 | + 9 | .. | 138 | |
| | Bardi | 2,912 | .. | 835 | 42,838 | 231,739 | 115,878 | 115,861 | 198,921 | + 16 | .. | 80 | |
| | Beohari | 1,872 | .. | 600 | 37,649 | 183,893 | 90,156 | 93,737 | 222,515 | + 49 | .. | 98 | |
| | Bandhogarh | 1,797 | 1 | 569 | 29,869 | 147,925 | 73,388 | 74,537 | | | | 82 | |
| | Sohagpur | 2,641 | .. | 823 | 44,968 | 235,556 | 117,853 | 117,703 | 241,753 | — 3 | .. | 89 | |
| 5 | ORCHHA | 2,079 | 1 | 763 | 73,322 | 330,032 | 168,633 | 161,399 | 321,678 | + 3 | — 3 | 159 | 10,96,400 |
| 6 | DATIA | 911 | 2 | 450 | 29,603 | 154,603 | 80,175 | 74,428 | 173,905 | — 11 | — 8 | 170 | 9,46,000 |
| 7 | DHAR | 1,783 | 2 | 528 | 35,491 | 154,070 | 77,257 | 76,813 | 142,115 | + 8 | — 16 | 86 | 9,30,200 |
| 8 | DEWAS S. B. | 441 | 1 | 242 | 17,203 | 74,290 | 38,100 | 36,190 | 62,730 | + 18 | — 24 | 168 | 3,71,400 |
| 9 | DEWAS J. B. | 417 | 1 | 224 | 14,603 | 63,015 | 32,222 | 30,793 | 55,097 | + 14 | — 21 | 151 | 3,74,100 |
| 10 | SAMTHAR | 180 | 1 | 87 | 7,495 | 31,908 | 16,291 | 15,617 | 33,472 | — 5 | — 17 | 177 | 4,23,500 |
| 11 | JAORA | 568 | 1 | 291 | 18,574 | 75,951 | 39,054 | 36,897 | 77,040 | — 1 | — 34 | 134 | 8,24,000 |
| 12 | RATLAM | 643 | 1 | 224 | 19,083 | 75,291 | 38,277 | 37,014 | 79,336 | — 5 | — 5 | 117 | 9,00,000 |
| 13 | PANNA | 2,596 | 1 | 1,013 | 51,629 | 228,880 | 114,936 | 113,944 | 192,986 | + 19 | — 19 | 88 | 5,00,000 |
| 14 | CHARKHARI | 880 | 1 | 277 | 27,889 | 132,530 | 67,516 | 65,014 | 123,954 | + 7 | — 11 | 151 | 5,00,000 |
| 15 | AJAIGARH | 802 | .. | 344 | 18,223 | 87,093 | 44,286 | 42,807 | 78,236 | + 11 | — 15 | 109 | 2,20,300 |
| 16 | BIJAWAR | 973 | 1 | 318 | 28,980 | 125,202 | 64,233 | 60,969 | 110,500 | + 13 | — 10 | 129 | 2,79,000 |
| 17 | BAONI | 121 | .. | 52 | 3,989 | 20,121 | 10,342 | 9,779 | 19,780 | + 2 | + 7 | 166 | 1,00,000 |
| 18 | CHHATARPUR | 1,118 | 3 | 308 | 39,291 | 166,985 | 85,967 | 81,018 | 156,139 | + 7 | — 10 | 149 | 4,75,900 |
| 19 | SITAMAU | 185 | 1 | 92 | 6,499 | 26,484 | 13,646 | 12,838 | 23,863 | + 11 | — 28 | 143 | 3,00,000 |
| 20 | SAILANA | 279 | 1 | 96 | 6,468 | 26,885 | 13,678 | 13,207 | 24,286 | + 11 | — 23 | 96 | 3,89,000 |
| 21 | RAJGARH | 962 | 2 | 728 | 28,868 | 127,293 | 66,070 | 61,223 | 94,924 | + 34 | — 24 | 132 | 4,77,500 |
| 22 | NARSINGHGARH | 734 | 1 | 412 | 24,030 | 109,854 | 56,706 | 53,148 | 92,093 | + 19 | — 21 | 150 | 4,86,000 |
| 23 | JHABUA | 1,336 | .. | 758 | 22,602 | 111,292 | 55,458 | 55,834 | 81,145 | + 37 | — 32 | 83 | 2,26,700 |
| 24 | BARAUNDHA | 218 | .. | 72 | 3,905 | 16,982 | 8,666 | 8,316 | 15,724 | + 8 | .. | 78 | 15,000 |
| 25 | NAGOD | 501 | 2 | 338 | 16,376 | 74,592 | 36,382 | 38,210 | 62,806 | + 19 | — 25 | 149 | 1,82,000 |
| 26 | MAIHAR | 407 | 1 | 205 | 16,890 | 73,155 | 35,565 | 37,590 | 63,908 | + 14 | — 18 | 180 | 1,21,500 |
| 27 | BARWANI | 1,178 | 1 | 352 | 20,869 | 108,583 | 54,488 | 54,095 | 76,136 | + 43 | — 5 | 92 | 4,60,000 |
| 28 | ALI-RAJPUR | 836 | .. | 324 | 12,030 | 72,454 | 36,326 | 36,128 | 50,185 | + 44 | — 28 | 87 | 1,65,000 |
| 29 | KHILCHIPUR | 273 | 1 | 290 | 8,800 | 40,075 | 20,990 | 19,085 | 31,143 | + 29 | — 14 | 147 | 1,14,000 |
| 30 | OTHER STATES AND BRITISH CANTONMENTS AND STATIONS.* | 2,468 | 7 | 1,783 | 119,057 | 506,491 | 261,973 | 244,518 | 469,271 | + 8 | — 16 | 205 | 15,58,200 |

* For details see Appendix A.

# PROVINCIAL TABLE I.—APPENDIX A.

| Serial No. | States, Estates, British Cantonments and Stations. | Area in square miles. | Number of Towns. | Number of Villages. | Number of occupied houses. | Population 1911 Persons. | Population 1911 Males. | Population 1911 Females. | Population 1901 (Both sexes). | Variation, Increase (+) Decrease (—) 1901 to 1911. | Variation 1891 to 1901. | Revenue. |
|---|---|---|---|---|---|---|---|---|---|---|---|---|
| 1 | 2 | 3 | 4 | 5 | 6 | 7 | 8 | 9 | 10 | 11 | 12 | 13 |
| | | | | | | | | | | | | Rs. |
| | **OTHER STATES AND BRITISH CANTONMENTS AND STATIONS.** | **2,468** | **7** | **1,783** | **119,057** | **506,491** | **261,973** | **244,518** | **469,271** | **+ 37,220** | ... | **15,58,200** |
| | **GWALIOR RESIDENCY MINOR STATES AND BRITISH CANTONMENTS, ETC.** | **578** | **3** | **477** | **28,379** | **117,491** | **61,851** | **55,640** | **107,833** | **+ 9,658** | ... | ...... |
| | **MINOR STATES** | **571** | ... | **476** | **21,824** | **96,283** | **50,138** | **46,145** | **81,791** | **+ 14,492** | ... | **2,42,900** |
| 1 | Agra-Barkhera | 31 | ... | 34 | 1,564 | 7,178 | 3,611 | 3,567 | 5,258 | + 1,920 | — 2,182 | 19,000 |
| 2 | Bhadaura | 50 | ... | 15 | 704 | 2,902 | 1,577 | 1,325 | 2,275 | + 627 | — 855 | 5,000 |
| 3 | Dharnaoda | 41 | ... | 36 | 1,265 | 5,509 | 2,858 | 2,651 | 4,366 | + 1,143 | — 562 | 10,000 |
| 4 | Garha | 44 | ... | 70 | 2,754 | 12,402 | 6,484 | 5,918 | 9,481 | + 2,921 | — 1,378 | 22,000 |
| 5 | Kalukheda | 6 | ... | 4 | 245 | 1,112 | 552 | 560 | 932 | + 180 | — 90 | 7,000 |
| 6 | Karaudia | 10 | ... | 2 | 335 | 1,358 | 701 | 657 | 1,469 | — 111 | + 55 | 8,000 |
| 7 | Kathaun | 5 | ... | 2 | 850 | 3,546 | 1,859 | 1,687 | 3,505 | + 41 | — 20 | 7,000 |
| 8 | Khaniadhana | 68 | ... | 53 | 3,846 | 17,582 | 9,091 | 8,491 | 15,532 | + 2,050 | + 661 | 22,000 |
| 9 | Kheri-Rajpura | 6 | ... | 2 | 140 | 655 | 346 | 309 | 630 | + 25 | — 13 | 4,000 |
| 10 | Khiaoda | 10 | ... | 8 | 268 | 1,128 | 592 | 536 | 857 | + 271 | — 150 | 2,000 |
| 11 | Lalgarh | 14 | ... | 6 | 476 | 2,070 | 1,077 | 993 | 1,838 | + 232 | — 116 | 18,000 |
| 12 | Narwar | 16 | ... | 3 | 387 | 1,817 | 938 | 879 | 1,405 | + 412 | — 206 | 21,000 |
| 13 | Paron | 60 | ... | 34 | 1,426 | 6,199 | 3,190 | 3,009 | 5,557 | + 642 | — 2,427 | 25,000 |
| 14 | Patharia | 7 | ... | 2 | 246 | 955 | 485 | 470 | 441 | + 514 | — 257 | 4,500 |
| 15 | Raghugarh | 116 | ... | 122 | 5,041 | 22,010 | 11,503 | 10,507 | 19,446 | + 2,564 | + 1,314 | 52,000 |
| 16 | Tappa-Suklie | 15 | ... | 12 | 330 | 1,324 | 659 | 665 | 882 | + 442 | — 221 | 3,400 |
| 17 | Sirsi | 12 | | 36 | 1,106 | 4,907 | 2,648 | 2,259 | 5,448 | — 541 | + 770 | 7,000 |
| 18 | Umri | 60 | ... | 35 | 841 | 3,629 | 1,967 | 1,662 | 2,469 | + 1,160 | — 588 | 6,000 |
| | **BRITISH CANTONMENTS AND STATIONS.** | **750** | **3** | **1** | **6,555** | **21,208** | **11,713** | **9,495** | **26,042** | **— 4,834** | ... | ...... |
| 19 | Agar Station | 1 | 1 | ... | 1,087 | 3,487 | 1,981 | 1,506 | 3,990 | — 503 | — 41 | ...... |

| | | | | | | | | | | | | |
|---|---|---|---|---|---|---|---|---|---|---|---|---|
| 20 | Guna Station | 2 | 1 | ... | 1,437 | 5,099 | 2,766 | 2,331 | 6,037 | — 938 | + 1,344 | ...... |
| 21 | Nimach Cantonment | 4 | 1 | .. | 3,906 | 12,318 | 6,741 | 5,577 | 14,624 | — 2,306 | — 667 | ...... |
| 22 | Residency Head-quarters | 0·50 | ... | 1 | 125 | 304 | 223 | 81 | 1,391 | — 1,087 | ... | ...... |
| | INDORE RESIDENCY MINOR STATES AND BRITISH CANTONMENTS, ETC. | 13 | 2 | 3 | 10,731 | 39,658 | 23,398 | 16,260 | 47,657 | — 7,999 | ... | ... .. |
| | MINOR STATES | 6 | ... | 3 | 172 | 643 | 313 | 330 | 500 | + 143 | ... | 8,000 |
| 1 | Hirapur | 6 | ... | 3 | 172 | 643 | 313 | 330 | 500 | + 143 | ... | 8,000 |
| | BRITISH CANTONMENTS AND STATIONS. | 7 | 2 | ... | 10,609 | 39,015 | 23,085 | 15,930 | 47,157 | — 8,142 | ... | ...... |
| 2 | Indore Residency | 1 | 1 | ... | 2,715 | 9,195 | 5,362 | 3,833 | 11,118 | — 1,923 | + 1,778 | ...... |
| 3 | Mhow Cantonment | 6 | 1 | ... | 7,894 | 29,820 | 17,723 | 12,097 | 36,039 | — 6,219 | — 1,734 | ..... |
| | BAGHELKHAND AGENCY MINOR STATES AND BRITISH CANTONMENTS, ETC. | 580 | ... | 394 | 20,523 | 93,002 | 46,180 | 46,822 | 84,745 | + 8,257 | ... | ... .. |
| | MINOR STATES | 580 | ... | 393 | 20,388 | 92,608 | 45,923 | 46,685 | 84,363 | + 8,245 | ... | 1,55,500 |
| 1 | Bhaisaunda | 32 | ... | 18 | 1,063 | 4,599 | 2,353 | 2,246 | 4,168 | + 431 | — 587 | 9,000 |
| 2 | Jaso | 72 | ... | 68 | 1,731 | 8,086 | 3,964 | 4,122 | 7,209 | + 877 | — 1,621 | 23,000 |
| 3 | Kamta-Rajaula | 13 | ... | 2 | 262 | 1,123 | 627 | 496 | 1,232 | — 109 | — 353 | 2,500 |
| 4 | Kothi | 169 | ... | 80 | 4,610 | 21,303 | 10,502 | 10,801 | 19,143 | + 2,160 | — 3,513 | 26,000 |
| 5 | Pahra | 27 | ... | 17 | 805 | 3,529 | 1,826 | 1,703 | 3,535 | — 6 | — 615 | 18,000 |
| 6 | Paldeo | 28 | ... | 20 | 1,848 | 8,990 | 4,549 | 4,441 | 8,598 | + 392 | — 785 | 26,000 |
| 7 | Sohawal | 213 | ... | 177 | 9,303 | 41,828 | 20,542 | 21,286 | 37,268 | + 4,560 | — 6,585 | 46,000 |
| 8 | Taraon | 26 | ... | 11 | 766 | 3,150 | 1,560 | 1,590 | 3,210 | — 60 | — 217 | 10,000 |
| | BRITISH CANTONMENTS AND STATION | 0·14 | ... | 1 | 135 | 394 | 257 | 137 | 382 | + 12 | + 129 | ... |
| 9 | Satna Agency Head-quarters | 0·14 (Included in Rewah) | ... | 1 | 135 | 394 | 257 | 137 | 382 | + 12 | + 129 | ... |
| | BHOPAL AGENCY MINOR STATES AND BRITISH CANTONMENTS, ETC. | 284 | 1 | 164 | 10,863 | 43,130 | 22,132 | 20,998 | 41,109 | + 2,021 | ... | ... |
| | MINOR STATES | 283 | ... | 164 | 8,681 | 35,389 | 17,976 | 17,413 | 29,406 | + 5,983 | ... | 1,11,900 |
| 1 | Basoda (Nawab) | 40 | ... | 27 | 1,180 | 4,630 | 2,355 | 2,275 | 4,897 | — 267 | — 1,813 | 19,000 |
| 2 | Dariakheri | 6 | ... | 2 | 157 | 534 | 265 | 269 | 442 | + 92 | ... | 7,500 |
| 3 | Dhabla-Dhir | 12 | ... | 3 | 525 | 1,777 | 874 | 903 | 1,778 | — 1 | ... | 10,000 |
| 4 | Dhabla-Ghosi | 6 | ... | 1 | 162 | 590 | 286 | 304 | 668 | — 78 | ... | 9,500 |
| 5 | Dugri | 3 | ... | 1 | 56 | 164 | 78 | 86 | 144 | + 20 | ... | 1,500 |
| 6 | Jabria-Bhil | 5 | ... | 2 | 245 | 844 | 435 | 409 | 903 | — 59 | ... | 5,000 |

# PROVINCIAL TABLE I.—APPENDIX A—*contd.*

[The area figures bracketed have already been included in the area of the parent state.]

| Serial No. | States, Estates, British Cantonments and Stations. | Area in square miles. | Number of Towns. | Number of Villages. | Number of occupied houses. | Population 1911 Persons. | Population 1911 Males. | Population 1911 Females. | Population 1901 (Both sexes.) | Variation, Increase (+) Decrease (—). 1901 to 1911. | Variation, Increase (+) Decrease (—). 1891 to 1901. | Revenue. |
|---|---|---|---|---|---|---|---|---|---|---|---|---|
| 1 | 2 | 3 | 4 | 5 | 6 | 7 | 8 | 9 | 10 | 11 | 12 | 13 |
| | **BHOPAL AGENCY MINOR STATES AND BRITISH CANTONMENTS, ETC.—*contd.*** | | | | | | | | | | | Rs. |
| 7 | Khajuri | 1 | ... | 1 | 178 | 533 | 256 | 277 | 520 | + 13 | ... | 2,400 |
| 8 | Korwai | 144 | ... | 88 | 4,258 | 18,456 | 9,453 | 9,003 | 13,705 | + 4,751 | — 8,082 | 37,000 |
| 9 | Muhammadgarh | 29 | ... | 16 | 677 | 2,863 | 1,450 | 1,413 | 2,944 | — 81 | — 1,776 | 7,000 |
| 10 | Pathari (Nawab) | 29 | ... | 21 | 880 | 3,866 | 1,924 | 1,942 | 2,704 | + 1,162 | — 2,112 | 9,000 |
| 11 | Piplianagar | 2 | ... | 1 | 277 | 836 | 433 | 403 | 701 | + 135 | — 135 | 2,000 |
| 12 | Sadankheri | 6 | ... | 1 | 91 | 296 | 167 | 129 | (179) In 1901 was in Gwalior. | + (117) | | 2,000 |
| | **BRITISH CANTONMENTS AND STATIONS.** | **1** | **1** | ... | **2,182** | **7,741** | **4,156** | **3,585** | **11,703** | **— 3,962** | **+ 579** | ... |
| 13 | Sehore Station | 1 (included in Bhopal State.) | 1 | ... | 2,182 | 7,741 | 4,156 | 3,585 | 11,703 | — 3,962 | + 579 | ... |
| | **BHOPAWAR AGENCY MINOR STATES AND BRITISH CANTONMENTS, ETC.** | **398** | ... | **474** | **17,911** | **83,181** | **41,717** | **41,464** | **63,240** | **+ 19,941** | ... | ... |
| | **MINOR STATES** | **390** | ... | **441** | **15,885** | **74,922** | **37,421** | **37,501** | **55,567** | **+ 19,355** | ... | **3,21,800** |
| 1 | Bada-Barkhera | (51) | ... | 25 | 1,518 | 7,258 | 3,589 | 3,669 | 6,027 | + 1,231 | ... | 46,000 |
| 2 | Bakhatgarh | (66) | ... | 30 | 1,914 | 7,876 | 3,875 | 4,001 | 6,774 | + 1,102 | ... | 60,000 |
| 3 | Bharudpura | (32) | ... | 15 | 524 | 2,405 | 1,208 | 1,197 | 1,542 | + 863 | ... | 6,000 |
| 4 | Chhota-Barkhera | (28) | ... | 12 | 519 | 2,582 | 1,271 | 1,311 | 1,929 | + 653 | ... | 7,800 |
| 5 | Dhotria | (18) | ... | 9 | 715 | 3,205 | 1,611 | 1,594 | 3,040 | + 165 | ... | 12,000 |
| 6 | Garhi (Bhaisakho) | (4) | ... | 6 | 211 | 947 | 494 | 453 | 564 | + 383 | ... | 4,300 |
| 7 | Jamnia | (31) | ... | 42 | 754 | 3,154 | 1,572 | 1,582 | 2,877 | + 277 | ... | 24,500 |
| 8 | Jobat | 140 | ... | 61 | 2,784 | 15,560 | 7,722 | 7,838 | 9,443 | + 6,117 | — 5,604 | 21,000 |
| 9 | Kachhi-Baroda | (34) | ... | 18 | 897 | 3,638 | 1,815 | 1,823 | 2,783 | + 855 | ... | 30,000 |
| 10 | Kali-Baori | (11) | ... | 8 | 525 | 2,744 | 1,387 | 1,357 | 1,646 | + 1,098 | ... | 7,000 |
| 11 | Kathiwara | 90 | ... | 50 | 736 | 3,837 | 1,949 | 1,888 | 3,425 | + 412 | ... | 4,000 |
| 12 | Kotidah | (6) | ... | 5 | 129 | 522 | 271 | 251 | 328 | + 194 | ... | 1,400 |
| 13 | Mathwar | 129 | ... | 33 | 398 | 1,905 | 985 | 920 | 1,022 | + 883 | ... | 4,000 |

| | | | | | | | | | | | | |
|---|---|---|---|---|---|---|---|---|---|---|---|---|
| 14 | Multhan | (99) | ... | 27 | 2,368 | 10,061 | 5,033 | 5,028 | 7,644 | + 2,417 | ... | 60,000 |
| 15 | Nimkhera (Tirla) | (90) | ... | 76 | 1,510 | 6,840 | 3,407 | 3,433 | 4,641 | + 2,199 | ... | 22,300 |
| 16 | Rajgarh | (30) | ... | 8 | 170 | 856 | 452 | 404 | 682 | + 174 | ... | 6,509 |
| 17 | Rataomal | 31 | ... | 16 | 278 | 1,532 | 780 | 752 | 1,200 | + 332 | ... | 5,000 |
| | **BRITISH CANTONMENTS AND STATIONS.** | **8** | ... | **33** | **2,026** | **8,259** | **4,296** | **3,963** | **7,673** | **+ 586** | ... | ... |
| 18 | Manpur (British Pargana) | 7 | ... | 32 | 1,577 | 6,609 | 3,445 | 3,164 | 4,890 | + 1,719 | − 542 | ... |
| 19 | Sardarpur Station | 1 | ... | 1 | 449 | 1,650 | 851 | 799 | 2,783 | − 1,133 | − 352 | ... |
| | **BUNDELKHAND AGENCY MINOR STATES AND BRITISH CANTONMENTS, ETC.** | **420** | **1** | **131** | **18,991** | **82,204** | **42,596** | **39,608** | **80,965** | **+ 1,239** | ... | ... |
| | **MINOR STATES** | **413** | ... | **130** | **16,455** | **72,109** | **36,703** | **35,406** | **69,458** | **+ 2,651** | ... | **2,72,000** |
| 1 | Alipura | 73 | ... | 27 | 3,642 | 16,146 | 8,448 | 7,698 | 14,654 | + 1,492 | ... | 30,000 |
| 2 | Banka-Pahari | 5 | ... | 1 | 231 | 1,357 | 660 | 697 | 1,056 | + 301 | − 42 | 4,000 |
| 3 | Beri | 32 | ... | 6 | 982 | 4,219 | 2,232 | 1,987 | 4,279 | − 60 | − 246 | 21,000 |
| 4 | Bihat | 16·16 | ... | 8 | 1,096 | 5,387 | 2,657 | 2,730 | 3,984 | + 1,403 | − 455 | 13,000 |
| 5 | Bijna | 7·50 | ... | 3 | 343 | 1,326 | 656 | 670 | 1,578 | − 252 | − 748 | 10,000 |
| 6 | Bilheri | 4·70 | ... | 2 | 735 | 2,860 | 1,410 | 1,450 | 3,073 | − 213 | − 242 | 7,000 |
| 7 | Dhurwai | 15 | ... | 9 | 350 | 1,530 | 794 | 736 | 1,826 | − 296 | + 52 | 8,000 |
| 8 | Garrauli | 39 | ... | 17 | 1,279 | 5,222 | 2,680 | 2,542 | 5,231 | − 9 | − 298 | 25,000 |
| 9 | Gaurihar | 71·25 | ... | 15 | 1,829 | 8,451 | 4,279 | 4,172 | 7,760 | + 691 | − 2,388 | 27,000 |
| 10 | Jigni | 20·48 | ... | 6 | 795 | 3,597 | 1,802 | 1,795 | 3,838 | − 241 | − 64 | 13,000 |
| 11 | Lughasi | 45·33 | ... | 12 | 1,477 | 6,738 | 3,452 | 3,286 | 6,285 | + 453 | − 663 | 20,000 |
| 12 | Naigawan-Rebai | 12·25 | ... | 4 | 628 | 2,393 | 1,178 | 1,215 | 2,497 | − 104 | − 876 | 11,000 |
| 13 | Sarila | 35·28 | ... | 9 | 1,525 | 6,712 | 3,403 | 3,309 | 6,298 | + 414 | + 676 | 59,000 |
| 14 | Tori-Fatehpur | 36 | ... | 11 | 1,543 | 6,171 | 3,052 | 3,119 | 7,099 | − 928 | − 2,496 | 24,000 |
| | **BRITISH CANTONMENTS AND STATIONS.** | **7·50** | **1** | **1** | **2,536** | **10,095** | **5,893** | **4,202** | **11,507** | **− 1,412** | ... | ... |
| 15 | Nowgong Cantonment | 7·50 | 1 | ... | 2,352 | 9,421 | 5,454 | 3,967 | 11,507 | − 1,412 | ... | ... |
| 16 | Agency Head-quarters | Included in Nowgong Cantonment. | ... | 1 | 184 | 674 | 439 | 235 | | | | |
| | **MALWA AGENCY MINOR STATES.** | | | | | | | | | | | |
| | **MINOR STATES** | **195** | ... | **141** | **11,609** | **47,825** | **24,099** | **23,726** | **43,722** | **+ 4,103** | .. | **4,46,100** |
| 1 | Bagli | 135 | ... | 53 | 4,058 | 16,498 | 8,401 | 8,097 | 14,049 | + 2,449 | ... | 1,00,000 |
| 2 | Biland | (2) | ... | 1 | 30 | 317 | 161 | 156 | 202 | + 115 | ... | 6,500 |
| 3 | Borkheda | (2) | ... | 2 | 235 | 969 | 506 | 463 | 900 | + 69 | ... | 18,900 |
| 4 | Gularkheda | (10) | ... | 3 | 117 | 474 | 235 | 239 | 634 | − 160 | ... | 7,700 |

## PROVINCIAL TABLE I.—APPENDIX A—*concld.*

| Serial No. | States, Estates, British Cantonments and Stations. | Area in square miles. | Number of | | Number of occupied houses. | Population. | | | | Variation, Increase (+) Decrease (–). | | Revenue. |
|---|---|---|---|---|---|---|---|---|---|---|---|---|
| | | | | | | 1911. | | | 1901. | | | |
| | | | Towns. | Villages. | | Persons. | Males. | Females. | (Both sexes). | 1901 to 1911. | 1891 to 1901. | |
| 1 | 2 | 3 | 4 | 5 | 6 | 7 | 8 | 9 | 10 | 11 | 12 | 13 |
| | MALWA AGENCY MINOR STATES —*contd.* | | | | | | | | | | | Rs. |
| 5 | **Jawasia** | **(4)** | ... | **3** | **125** | **512** | **276** | **236** | **418** | **+ 94** | ... | **11,500** |
| 6 | Kerwasa | (5) | ... | 2 | 171 | 653 | 317 | 336 | 900 | – 247 | ... | 11,000 |
| 7 | Khojankhera | (5) | ... | 2 | 93 | 378 | 198 | 180 | 600 | – 222 | ... | 6,000 |
| 8 | Panth-Piploda | 25 | ... | 11 | 1,019 | 4,483 | 2,282 | 2,201 | 3,544 | + 939 | ... | 32,000 |
| 9 | Pathari | (15) | ... | 12 | 397 | 1,777 | 936 | 841 | 1,436 | + 341 | ... | 18,000 |
| 10 | Piploda | 35 | ... | 24 | 1,941 | 8,033 | 3,950 | 4,083 | 9,529 | – 1,496 | ... | 95,000 |
| 11 | Sajaota (Shajaota) | (7) | ... | 3 | 94 | 367 | 193 | 174 | 300 | + 67 | ... | 10,000 |
| 12 | Sarwan | (71) | ... | 12 | 1,265 | 5,064 | 2,480 | 2,584 | 4,000 | + 1,064 | ... | 42,000 |
| 13 | Sheogarh | (60) | ... | 7 | 1,245 | 5,217 | 2,603 | 2,614 | 4,000 | + 1,217 | ... | 42,000 |
| 14 | Sidri | (1) | ... | 1 | 75 | 338 | 167 | 171 | 200 | + 138 | ... | 3,000 |
| 15 | Sirsi | (15) | ... | 3 | 213 | 794 | 408 | 386 | 1,352 | – 558 | ... | 25,000 |
| 16 | Tal | (10) | ... | 3 | 317 | 1,334 | 688 | 646 | 1,000 | + 334 | ... | 14,000 |
| 17 | **Uni** | **(5)** | ... | **1** | **136** | **641** | **345** | **296** | **494** | **+ 147** | ... | **1,800** |
| 18 | Uparwara | (10) | ... | 2 | 289 | 1,129 | 574 | 555 | 1,076 | + 53 | ... | 20,000 |

The figures for Jawasia and Uni have also been included in those of Dewas Senior and Junior respectively.

## PROVINCIAL TABLE II.

***POPULATION OF STATES BY RELIGION AND EDUCATION.***

# PROVINCIAL TABLE II.—Population of States by Religion and Education.

| Serial No. | States. | Total population. | Hindu. Males. | Hindu. Females. | Jains. Males. | Jains. Females. | Animists. Males. | Animists. Females. | Musalmans. Males. | Musalmans. Females. | Christians. Males. | Christians. Females. | Others. Males. | Others. Females. | Number of literate persons. Total. | 0—15. Males. | 0—15. Females. | 15—20. Males. | 15—20. Females. | 20 and over. Males. | 20 and over. Females. |
|---|---|---|---|---|---|---|---|---|---|---|---|---|---|---|---|---|---|---|---|---|---|
| 1 | 2 | 3 | 4 | 5 | 6 | 7 | 8 | 9 | 10 | 11 | 12 | 13 | 14 | 15 | 16 | 17 | 18 | 19 | 20 | 21 | 22 |
|  | **Central India** | **9,369,472** | **4,247,410** | **4,026,290** | **46,024** | **42,048** | **239,772** | **243,928** | **266,774** | **244,949** | **6,170** | **3,188** | **1,772** | **1,147** | **244,074** | **27,924** | **2,235** | **24,524** | **1,671** | **180,004** | **7,716** |
| 1 | **GWALIOR STATE** | **3,102,279** | **1,491,773** | **1,346,479** | **20,243** | **18,132** | **29,966** | **29,983** | **87,889** | **78,021** | **326** | **284** | **130** | **103** | **87,891** | **10,665** | **746** | **8,733** | **467** | **64,762** | **2,518** |
|  | Gwalior Gird (including Lashkar) | *312,675* | 148,707 | 130,303 | 919 | 810 | 790 | 771 | 16,463 | 13,517 | 146 | 136 | 59 | 54 | *18,490* | 2,164 | 131 | 1,578 | 87 | 14,004 | 526 |
|  | Tonwarghar | *376,659* | 198,401 | 164,707 | 1,306 | 1,116 | 208 | 189 | 5,933 | 4,791 | 6 | 2 | .. | .. | *5,738* | 797 | 17 | 662 | 9 | 4,217 | 36 |
|  | Bhind (including Nimrol) | *399,994* | 207,172 | 175,968 | 3,214 | 2,650 | .. | 2 | 5,905 | 4,997 | 7 | 9 | .. | .. | *6,944* | 1,166 | 43 | 1,068 | 47 | 4,483 | 137 |
|  | Sheopur | *124,671* | 62,367 | 55,728 | 123 | 94 | 768 | 765 | 2,527 | 2,295 | .. | .. | 1 | 3 | *2,921* | 315 | 33 | 280 | 19 | 2,186 | 79 |
|  | Narwar | *408,129* | 201,603 | 183,202 | 1,694 | 1,597 | 5,313 | 5,269 | 5,016 | 4,318 | 2 | 1 | 10 | 4 | *6,576* | 794 | 47 | 729 | 31 | 4,846 | 129 |
|  | Bhilsa | *180,411* | 87,529 | 81,990 | 632 | 625 | 401 | 393 | 4,616 | 4,202 | 6 | 4 | 9 | 4 | *4,330* | 734 | 27 | 530 | 17 | 2,938 | 84 |
|  | Isagarh | *333,169* | 161,145 | 148,767 | 2,471 | 2,187 | 2,847 | 2,790 | 6,894 | 6,033 | 16 | 12 | 4 | 3 | *6,846* | 888 | 14 | 720 | 8 | 5,118 | 98 |
|  | Ujjain | *321,603* | 145,194 | 138,171 | 2,462 | 2,138 | 1,361 | 1,311 | 16,120 | 14,668 | 79 | 53 | 24 | 13 | *14,999* | 1,664 | 216 | 1,258 | 134 | 10,909 | 818 |
|  | Shajapur | *300,538* | 139,156 | 130,954 | 2,162 | 1,965 | 1,392 | 1,409 | 11,961 | 11,533 | 1 | .. | 5 | .. | *6,374* | 790 | 42 | 606 | 28 | 4,768 | 142 |
|  | Mandasor (including Gangapur) | *224,725* | 98,974 | 93,946 | 4,121 | 3,859 | 2,860 | 2,679 | 9,331 | 8,809 | 58 | 63 | 13 | 12 | *11,332* | 1,014 | 104 | 943 | 58 | 8,883 | 330 |
|  | Amjhera | *119,775* | 41,525 | 41,643 | 1,139 | 1,091 | 14,026 | 14,355 | 3,114 | 2,858 | 5 | 4 | 5 | 10 | *3,341* | 339 | 72 | 350 | 29 | 2,412 | 139 |
| 2 | **INDORE STATE** | **1,097,856** | **452,169** | **428,065** | **5,653** | **5,227** | **22,187** | **22,414** | **36,247** | **34,360** | **341** | **154** | **304** | **175** | **39,900** | **4,741** | **263** | **4,143** | **185** | **29,729** | **839** |
|  | Indore (including city and Petlawad) | *235,283* | 102,553 | 96,080 | 1,450 | 1,278 | 4,279 | 4,243 | 13,075 | 11,574 | 307 | 130 | 209 | 105 | *13,101* | 1,421 | 54 | 1,081 | 62 | 10,266 | 217 |
|  | Mehidpur | *121,943* | 58,308 | 54,412 | 686 | 622 | 113 | 77 | 3,605 | 3,411 | 1 | 1 | 5 | 2 | *2,748* | 357 | 9 | 314 | 9 | 2,007 | 52 |
|  | Nemawar | *94,600* | 39,732 | 38,672 | 522 | 518 | 2,978 | 3,221 | 4,576 | 4,381 | .. | .. | .. | .. | *2,976* | 441 | 16 | 614 | 18 | 1,845 | 42 |
|  | Nimar (including Nisarpur and Lawani.) | *348,450* | 153,271 | 146,909 | 1,018 | 984 | 13,576 | 13,602 | 9,708 | 9,202 | 19 | 14 | 85 | 62 | *12,588* | 1,653 | 108 | 1,285 | 51 | 9,207 | 284 |
|  | Rampura-Bhanpura (including Nandwai). | *199,591* | 90,460 | 84,532 | 1,971 | 1,824 | 1,241 | 1,271 | 5,667 | 5,521 | 14 | 9 | 5 | 6 | *8,213* | 851 | 74 | 808 | 42 | 6,200 | 238 |
|  | Alampur | *15,759* | 7,845 | 7,480 | 6 | 1 | .. | .. | 216 | 211 | .. | .. | .. | .. | *274* | 18 | 2 | 41 | 3 | 204 | 6 |
| 3 | **BHOPAL STATE** | **730,383** | **297,218** | **286,884** | **2,573** | **2,516** | **28,039** | **30,572** | **42,388** | **39,668** | **139** | **94** | **203** | **149** | **12,965** | **1,283** | **115** | **1,204** | **83** | **9,806** | **444** |
|  | Nizamat-i-Maghrib | *225,069* | 102,842 | 98,599 | 745 | 716 | 1,404 | 1,873 | 10,103 | 9,278 | 4 | .. | 4 | 1 | *2,290* | 256 | 19 | 205 | 10 | 1,734 | 66 |
|  | Nizamat-i-Junub | *271,829* | 112,718 | 110,052 | 556 | 515 | 15,126 | 16,766 | 8,327 | 7,721 | 5 | 2 | 28 | 13 | *3,443* | 434 | 9 | 354 | 5 | 2,606 | 35 |
|  | Nizamat-i-Mashriq | *233,485* | 81,658 | 78,233 | 1,272 | 1,285 | 11,509 | 12,433 | 23,958 | 22,609 | 130 | 92 | 171 | 135 | *7,202* | 593 | 87 | 645 | 68 | 5,466 | 343 |
| 4 | **REWAH STATE** | **1,514,843** | **734,892** | **745,469** | **299** | **307** | **9** | **1** | **17,010** | **16,754** | **76** | **69** | **11** | **6** | **18,225** | **2,636** | **162** | **2,159** | **119** | **12,662** | **487** |
|  | Huzur Tahsil | *338,775* | 162,483 | 165,402 | 34 | 31 | .. | .. | 5,229 | 5,588 | 3 | 3 | 7 | 2 | *7,050* | 826 | 48 | 749 | 39 | 5,191 | 197 |
|  | Raghurajnagar | *154,893* | 74,414 | 76,596 | 98 | 82 | .. | .. | 1,861 | 1,820 | 12 | 10 | .. | .. | *3,041* | 299 | 82 | 376 | 52 | 2,122 | 110 |
|  | Sitlaha | *113,858* | 56,389 | 55,583 | .. | .. | .. | .. | 978 | 908 | .. | .. | .. | .. | *1,083* | 173 | 7 | 120 | .. | 770 | 13 |
|  | Mauganj | *108,204* | 51,947 | 53,251 | .. | .. | .. | .. | 1,574 | 1,432 | .. | .. | .. | .. | *1,300* | 124 | 1 | 152 | 6 | 1,003 | 14 |
|  | Bardi | *231,739* | 113,222 | 113,482 | .. | 5 | .. | .. | 2,654 | 2,374 | 2 | .. | .. | .. | *968* | 73 | .. | 92 | 2 | 797 | 4 |
|  | Beohari | *183,893* | 89,127 | 92,633 | 28 | 27 | .. | .. | 1,001 | 1,077 | .. | .. | .. | .. | *1,769* | 194 | 3 | 213 | 4 | 1,311 | 44 |
|  | Bandhogarh | *147,925* | 71,609 | 72,838 | 6 | 14 | .. | .. | 1,746 | 1,656 | 28 | 28 | .. | .. | *1,179* | 171 | 7 | 206 | 8 | 748 | 39 |
|  | Sohagpur | *235,556* | 115,701 | 115,624 | 133 | 148 | 9 | .. | 1,974 | 1,899 | 31 | 28 | 4 | 4 | *1,835* | 776 | 14 | 251 | 8 | 720 | 56 |

| | | | | | | | | | | | | | | | | | | | | | |
|---|---|---|---|---|---|---|---|---|---|---|---|---|---|---|---|---|---|---|---|---|---|
| 5 | ORCHHA | 330,032 | 156,016 | 149,091 | 3,127 | 2,952 | 5,235 | 5,273 | 4,253 | 4,076 | 1 | 1 | 1 | 6 | 3,790 | 450 | 8 | 337 | 11 | 2,929 | 61 |
| 6 | DATIA | 154,603 | 76,815 | 71,457 | 341 | 332 | .. | .. | 3,016 | 2,637 | 3 | 2 | .. | .. | 3,865 | 313 | 18 | 336 | 25 | 3,070 | 103 |
| 7 | DHAR | 154,070 | 58,459 | 58,384 | 1,341 | 1,204 | 11,155 | 11,148 | 6,186 | 5,944 | 74 | 117 | 42 | 16 | 6,114 | 719 | 48 | 703 | 67 | 4,402 | 175 |
| 8 | DEWAS S. B. | 74,290 | 33,216 | 31,530 | 393 | 355 | 84 | 80 | 4,399 | 4,151 | 8 | 5 | .. | .. | 3,205 | 431 | 33 | 312 | 23 | 2,288 | 118 |
| 9 | DEWAS J. B. | 63,015 | 28,667 | 27,550 | 415 | 333 | 135 | 116 | 2,994 | 2,788 | 8 | 6 | 3 | .. | 2,673 | 349 | 27 | 279 | 5 | 1,943 | 70 |
| 10 | SAMTHAR | 31,908 | 15,176 | 14,475 | 14 | 16 | .. | .. | 1,099 | 1,125 | 2 | 1 | .. | .. | 630 | 57 | .. | 77 | .. | 496 | .. |
| 11 | JAORA | 75,951 | 30,111 | 28,380 | 1,092 | 940 | 857 | 810 | 6,956 | 6,730 | 8 | 11 | 30 | 17 | 3,533 | 425 | 52 | 451 | 14 | 2,462 | 129 |
| 12 | RATLAM | 75,231 | 23,186 | 22,556 | 2,430 | 2,219 | 7,483 | 7,447 | 4,942 | 4,570 | 197 | 187 | 39 | 35 | 6,832 | 773 | 159 | 589 | 120 | 4,665 | 596 |
| 13 | PANNA | 228,880 | 103,067 | 101,788 | 1,198 | 1,188 | 8,133 | 8,493 | 2,562 | 2,458 | 16 | 10 | 20 | 7 | 4,236 | 574 | 31 | 523 | 13 | 3,012 | 83 |
| 14 | CHARKHARI | 132,530 | 64,608 | 62,053 | 177 | 186 | .. | .. | 2,729 | 2,771 | 2 | 4 | .. | .. | 2,085 | 170 | 6 | 210 | 3 | 1,666 | 30 |
| 15 | AJAIGARH | 87,093 | 42,371 | 41,036 | 274 | 252 | 323 | 306 | 1,314 | 1,239 | .. | .. | 4 | 4 | 1,036 | 75 | 3 | 72 | 5 | 849 | 32 |
| 16 | BIJAWAR | 125,202 | 61,856 | 58,713 | 1,050 | 1,000 | .. | .. | 1,323 | 1,254 | 4 | 2 | .. | .. | 1,511 | 167 | 3 | 167 | 1 | 1,161 | 12 |
| 17 | BAONI | 20,121 | 9,148 | 8,579 | 19 | 26 | .. | .. | 1,175 | 1,174 | .. | .. | .. | .. | 421 | 61 | .. | 55 | .. | 365 | .. |
| 18 | CHHATARPUR | 166,985 | 82,800 | 78,935 | 320 | 265 | .. | .. | 2,837 | 2,714 | 10 | 4 | .. | .. | 2,471 | 333 | 18 | 212 | 13 | 1,859 | 36 |
| 19 | SITAMAU | 26,484 | 12,350 | 11,626 | 402 | 348 | 16 | 14 | 872 | 845 | 4 | 4 | 2 | 1 | 1,788 | 184 | 30 | 175 | 27 | 1,258 | 114 |
| 20 | SAILANA | 26,885 | 9,365 | 9,054 | 410 | 359 | 3,186 | 3,154 | 716 | 640 | .. | .. | 1 | .. | 1,310 | 92 | 17 | 123 | 19 | 971 | 88 |
| 21 | RAJGARH | 127,293 | 62,548 | 58,004 | 148 | 146 | .. | .. | 3,370 | 3,070 | .. | .. | 4 | 3 | 2,841 | 246 | 13 | 242 | 12 | 2,259 | 69 |
| 22 | NARSINGHGARH | 109,854 | 53,967 | 50,703 | 189 | 167 | 34 | 35 | 2,512 | 2,238 | .. | .. | 4 | 5 | 3,009 | 257 | 19 | 289 | 13 | 2,353 | 78 |
| 23 | JHABUA | 111,292 | 13,812 | 13,617 | 912 | 824 | 39,545 | 40,254 | 1,066 | 1,031 | 114 | 95 | 9 | 13 | 1,636 | 152 | 17 | 156 | 10 | 1,225 | 76 |
| 24 | BARAUNDHA | 16,982 | 8,361 | 8,024 | .. | .. | 195 | 203 | 110 | 89 | .. | .. | .. | .. | 189 | 40 | 2 | 57 | 3 | 83 | 4 |
| 25 | NAGOD | 74,592 | 34,250 | 36,074 | 31 | 29 | 860 | 884 | 1,239 | 1,223 | .. | .. | 2 | .. | 2,243 | 271 | 14 | 240 | 9 | 1,617 | 92 |
| 26 | MAIHAR | 73,155 | 34,448 | 36,483 | 14 | 16 | .. | .. | 1,102 | 1,087 | 1 | 1 | .. | .. | 1,758 | 212 | 5 | 179 | 4 | 1,330 | 22 |
| 27 | BARWANI | 108,583 | 21,832 | 21,150 | 244 | 177 | 29,603 | 30,020 | 2,764 | 2,725 | 13 | 2 | 42 | 21 | 3,358 | 348 | 17 | 414 | 17 | 2,490 | 72 |
| 28 | ALI-RAJPUR | 72,454 | 9,922 | 9,575 | 70 | 66 | 24,974 | 25,139 | 1,159 | 1,142 | 195 | 203 | 6 | 3 | 1,222 | 117 | 15 | 112 | 10 | 887 | 81 |
| 29 | KHILCHIPUR | 40,075 | 20,207 | 18,459 | | 25 | 4 | 5 | 680 | 596 | .. | .. | .. | .. | 747 | 61 | 10 | 66 | 7 | 528 | 75 |
| 30 | OTHER STATES AND BRITISH CANTONMENTS AND STATIONS.* | 506,491 | 204,780 | 193,985 | 2,636 | 2,441 | 27,749 | 27,627 | 21,265 | 17,949 | 4,628 | 1,932 | 915 | 583 | 22,620 | 1,722 | 390 | 1,909 | 386 | 16,937 | 1,276 |

* For details see Appendix B.

# PROVINCIAL TABLE II.—APPENDIX B.

| Serial No. | States, Estates, British Cantonments and Stations. | Population. | Distribution by Religion. Hindu. Males. | Hindu. Females. | Jains. Males. | Jains. Females. | Animists. Males. | Animists. Females. | Musalmans. Males. | Musalmans. Females. | Christians. Males. | Christians. Females. | Others. Males. | Others. Females. | Number of Literate Persons. Persons. | Literate Males. | Literate Females. |
|---|---|---|---|---|---|---|---|---|---|---|---|---|---|---|---|---|---|
| 1 | 2 | 3 | 4 | 5 | 6 | 7 | 8 | 9 | 10 | 11 | 12 | 13 | 14 | 15 | 16 | 17 | 18 |
| | **OTHER STATES AND BRITISH CANTONMENTS AND STATIONS.** | **506,491** | **204,780** | **193,986** | **2,636** | **2,441** | **27,749** | **27,627** | **21,265** | **17,949** | **4,628** | **1,932** | **915** | **583** | **22,620** | **20,568** | **2,052** |
| | **GWALIOR RESIDENCY MINOR STATES AND BRITISH CANTONMENTS, ETC.** | **117,491** | **48,904** | **44,596** | **1,014** | **886** | **5,629** | **5,439** | **5,071** | **4,213** | **758** | **311** | **475** | **195** | **4,895** | **4,459** | **436** |
| | **MINOR STATES** | **96,283** | **41,813** | **38,283** | **827** | **737** | **5,583** | **5,386** | **1,911** | **1,733** | ... | ... | **4** | **6** | **1,718** | **1,633** | **85** |
| 1 | Agra-Barkhera | 7,178 | 3,394 | 3,820 | 27 | 31 | ... | ... | 190 | 216 | ... | ... | ... | ... | 61 | 57 | 4 |
| 2 | Bhadaura | 2,902 | 1,526 | 1,289 | 18 | 11 | ... | ... | 32 | 25 | ... | ... | 1 | ... | 76 | 74 | 2 |
| 3 | Dharnaoda | 5,509 | 2,469 | 2,260 | 68 | 61 | 177 | 166 | 149 | 144 | ... | ... | ... | ... | 119 | 113 | 6 |
| 4 | Garha | 12,402 | 5,699 | 5,201 | 108 | 85 | 457 | 451 | 220 | 181 | ... | ... | ... | ... | 203 | 194 | 9 |
| 5 | Kalukheda | 1,112 | 502 | 510 | 17 | 21 | ... | ... | 33 | 29 | ... | ... | ... | ... | 45 | 38 | 7 |
| 6 | Karaudia | 1,358 | 631 | 599 | 23 | 15 | ... | ... | 47 | 43 | ... | ... | ... | ... | 18 | 18 | ... |
| 7 | Kathaun | 3,546 | 1,506 | 1,330 | ... | ... | 314 | 264 | 39 | 43 | ... | ... | ... | ... | 46 | 38 | 8 |
| 8 | Khaniadhana | 17,582 | 7,847 | 7,249 | 269 | 239 | 779 | 824 | 196 | 179 | ... | ... | ... | ... | 365 | 356 | 9 |
| 9 | Kheri-Rajpura | 655 | 320 | 287 | 13 | 8 | ... | ... | 13 | 14 | ... | ... | ... | ... | 17 | 11 | 6 |
| 10 | Khiaoda | 1,128 | 526 | 458 | ... | ... | 66 | 78 | ... | ... | ... | ... | ... | ... | 14 | 14 | ... |
| 11 | Lalgarh | 2,070 | 1,025 | 947 | 33 | 30 | ... | ... | 19 | 16 | ... | ... | ... | ... | 36 | 28 | 8 |
| 12 | Narwar | 1,817 | 714 | 692 | 5 | 8 | ... | ... | 219 | 179 | ... | ... | ... | ... | 88 | 87 | 1 |
| 13 | Paron | 6,189 | 2,825 | 2,650 | 3 | 3 | 308 | 313 | 54 | 43 | ... | ... | ... | ... | 86 | 84 | 2 |
| 14 | Patharia | 965 | 472 | 454 | ... | ... | ... | ... | 13 | 16 | ... | ... | ... | ... | 13 | 10 | 3 |
| 15 | Raghugarh | 22,010 | 8,350 | 7,598 | 223 | 207 | 2,363 | 2,221 | 566 | 481 | ... | ... | 1 | ... | 363 | 348 | 15 |
| 16 | Tappa-Suklia | 1,324 | 638 | 643 | 2 | 1 | ... | ... | 19 | 21 | ... | ... | ... | ... | 64 | 64 | ... |
| 17 | Sirsi | 4,907 | 1,770 | 1,461 | ... | ... | 848 | 779 | 80 | 19 | ... | ... | ... | ... | 57 | 57 | ... |
| 18 | Umri | 3,629 | 1,599 | 1,285 | 23 | 17 | 271 | 270 | 72 | 84 | ... | ... | 2 | 6 | 47 | 42 | 5 |
| | **BRITISH CANTONMENTS AND STATIONS.** | **21,208** | **7,091** | **6,313** | **187** | **149** | **46** | **53** | **3,160** | **2,480** | **758** | **311** | **471** | **189** | **3,177** | **2,826** | **351** |
| 19 | Agar Station | 3,487 | 1,156 | 1,063 | 51 | 27 | 6 | 9 | 560 | 368 | 23 | 9 | 165 | 80 | 511 | 490 | 21 |

| | | | | | | | | | | | | | | | | | |
|---|---|---|---|---|---|---|---|---|---|---|---|---|---|---|---|---|---|
| 20 | Guna Station | 5,099 | 1,829 | 1,687 | 54 | 46 | 35 | 40 | 632 | 463 | 19 | 23 | 199 | 72 | 433 | 413 | 19 |
| 21 | Nimach Cantonment | 12,318 | 3,972 | 3,502 | 82 | 76 | 5 | 4 | 1,898 | 1,632 | 711 | 278 | 73 | 85 | 2,172 | 1,863 | 309 |
| 22 | Residency Head-quarters | 304 | 134 | 61 | ... | ... | ... | ... | 70 | 17 | 5 | 1 | 14 | 2 | 63 | 60 | 3 |
| | **INDORE RESIDENCY MINOR STATES AND BRITISH CANTONMENTS, ETC.** | **39,658** | **13,711** | **9,748** | **175** | **155** | **528** | **427** | **5,554** | **4,310** | **3,074** | **1,259** | **356** | **361** | **7,432** | **6,418** | **1,014** |
| | **MINOR STATES** | **643** | **250** | **255** | ... | ... | **53** | **68** | **10** | **7** | ... | ... | ... | ... | **5** | **5** | ... |
| 1 | Hirapur | 643 | 250 | 255 | ... | ... | 53 | 68 | 10 | 7 | ... | ... | ... | ... | 5 | 5 | ... |
| | **BRITISH CANTONMENTS AND STATIONS.** | **39,015** | **13,461** | **9,493** | **175** | **155** | **475** | **359** | **5,544** | **4,303** | **3,074** | **1,259** | **356** | **361** | **7,427** | **6,413** | **1,014** |
| 2 | Indore Residency | 9,195 | 3,374 | 2,201 | 20 | 5 | 465 | 352 | 1,011 | 716 | 367 | 434 | 125 | 125 | 2,410 | 1,877 | 533 |
| 3 | Mhow Cantonment | 29,820 | 10,087 | 7,292 | 155 | 150 | 10 | 7 | 4,533 | 3,587 | 2,707 | 825 | 231 | 236 | 5,017 | 4,536 | 481 |
| | **BAGHELKHAND AGENCY MINOR STATES AND BRITISH CANTONMENTS, ETC.** | **93,002** | **44,241** | **44,978** | **2** | **2** | **868** | **895** | **1,043** | **939** | **8** | **8** | **18** | ... | **2,160** | **2,071** | **89** |
| | **MINOR STATES** | **92,698** | **44,093** | **44,902** | **2** | **2** | **868** | **895** | **957** | **882** | **3** | **4** | ... | ... | **2,105** | **2,020** | **85** |
| | Bhaisaunda | 4,599 | 2,314 | 2,218 | ... | ... | ... | ... | 39 | 28 | ... | ... | ... | ... | 173 | 162 | 11 |
| 2 | Jaso | 8,086 | 3,780 | 3,922 | ... | ... | 118 | 150 | 66 | 50 | ... | ... | ... | ... | 161 | 161 | ... |
| 3 | Kamta-Rajaula | 1,123 | 620 | 491 | ... | ... | ... | ... | 7 | 5 | ... | ... | ... | ... | 130 | 128 | 2 |
| 4 | Kothi | 21,303 | 10,305 | 10,611 | 1 | 2 | ... | ... | 193 | 184 | 3 | 4 | ... | ... | 559 | 530 | 29 |
| 5 | Pahra | 3,529 | 1,762 | 1,656 | ... | ... | ... | ... | 64 | 47 | ... | ... | ... | ... | 87 | 87 | ... |
| 6 | Paldeo | 8,990 | 4,490 | 4,390 | 1 | ... | ... | ... | 58 | 51 | ... | ... | ... | ... | 241 | 240 | 1 |
| 7 | Sohawal | 41,828 | 19,292 | 20,049 | ... | ... | 750 | 745 | 500 | 492 | ... | ... | ... | ... | 672 | 632 | 40 |
| 8 | Taraon | 3,150 | 1,530 | 1,565 | ... | ... | ... | ... | 30 | 25 | ... | ... | ... | ... | 82 | 80 | 2 |
| | **BRITISH CANTONMENTS AND STATIONS.** | **394** | **148** | **76** | ... | ... | ... | ... | **86** | **57** | **5** | **4** | **18** | ... | **55** | **51** | **4** |
| 9 | Satna Agency Head-quarters | 394 | 148 | 76 | ... | ... | ... | ... | 86 | 57 | 5 | 4 | 18 | ... | 55 | 51 | 4 |
| | **BHOPAL AGENCY MINOR STATES AND BRITISH CANTONMENTS, ETC.** | **43,130** | **18,517** | **17,547** | **322** | **330** | **41** | **45** | **3,184** | **3,028** | **55** | **43** | **13** | **5** | **1,774** | **1,658** | **116** |
| | **MINOR STATES** | **35,389** | **15,384** | **14,859** | **281** | **286** | **41** | **45** | **2,269** | **2,221** | ... | **1** | **1** | **1** | **807** | **756** | **51** |
| 1 | Basoda (Nawab) | 4,630 | 1,974 | 1,851 | 31 | 37 | ... | ... | 350 | 387 | ... | ... | ... | ... | 94 | 86 | 8 |
| 2 | Dariakheri | 534 | 263 | 266 | ... | ... | ... | ... | 2 | 3 | ... | ... | ... | ... | 8 | 6 | 2 |
| 3 | Dhabla-Dhir | 1,777 | 836 | 868 | ... | ... | 24 | 24 | 14 | 11 | ... | ... | ... | ... | 64 | 60 | 4 |
| 4 | Dhabla Ghosi | 590 | 280 | 297 | ... | ... | 1 | 2 | 5 | 5 | ... | ... | ... | ... | 30 | 26 | 4 |
| 5 | Dugri | 164 | 27 | 47 | ... | ... | ... | ... | 51 | 39 | ... | ... | ... | ... | 3 | 3 | ... |
| 6 | Jabria-Bhil | 844 | 389 | 377 | ... | ... | ... | ... | 46 | 32 | ... | ... | ... | ... | 16 | 16 | ... |

# PROVINCIAL TABLE II.—Appendix B—*contd.*

| Serial No | States, Estates, British Cantonments and Stations. | Population. | DISTRIBUTION BY RELIGION. | | | | | | | | | | | | Number of Literate Persons. | | |
|---|---|---|---|---|---|---|---|---|---|---|---|---|---|---|---|---|---|
| | | | Hindu. | | Jains. | | Animists. | | Musalmans. | | Christians. | | Others. | | | | |
| | | | Males | Females. | Males. | Females. | Males. | Females. | Males. | Females. | Males. | Females. | Males. | Females. | Persons. | Males. | Females. |
| 1 | 2 | 3 | 4 | 5 | 6 | 7 | 8 | 9 | 10 | 11 | 12 | 13 | 14 | 15 | 16 | 17 | 18 |
| | MINOR STATES—*contd.* | | | | | | | | | | | | | | | | |
| 7 | Khajuri | 533 | 189 | 207 | ... | ... | ... | ... | 67 | 70 | ... | ... | ... | ... | 17 | 17 | ... |
| 8 | Korwai | 18,456 | 8,096 | 7,721 | 148 | 146 | 16 | 19 | 1,193 | 1,116 | ... | 1 | ... | ... | 361 | 346 | 15 |
| 9 | Muhammadgarh | 2,863 | 1,213 | 1,148 | 38 | 42 | ... | ... | 199 | 223 | ... | ... | ... | ... | 80 | 71 | 9 |
| 10 | Pathari (Nawab) | 3,866 | 1,679 | 1,693 | 54 | 48 | ... | ... | 190 | 200 | ... | ... | 1 | 1 | 98 | 91 | 7 |
| 11 | Piplianagar | 836 | 271 | 255 | 10 | 13 | ... | ... | 152 | 135 | ... | ... | ... | ... | 28 | 28 | ... |
| 12 | Sadankheri | 296 | 167 | 129 | ... | ... | ... | .. | ... | ... | ... | ... | ... | ... | 8 | 6 | 2 |
| | **BRITISH CANTONMENTS AND STATIONS.** | **7,741** | **3,133** | **2,688** | **41** | **44** | ... | ... | **915** | **807** | **55** | **42** | **12** | **4** | **967** | **902** | **65** |
| 13 | Sehore Cantonment | 7,741 | 3,133 | 2,688 | 41 | 44 | ... | .. | 915 | 807 | 55 | 42 | 12 | 4 | 967 | 902 | 65 |
| | **BHOPAWAR AGENCY MINOR STATES AND BRITISH CANTONMENTS, ETC.** | **83,181** | **21,340** | **21,195** | **440** | **412** | **18,247** | **18,254** | **1,556** | **1,471** | **129** | **129** | **5** | **3** | **1,883** | **1,808** | **75** |
| | **MINOR STATES** | **74,922** | **19,177** | **19,320** | **418** | **384** | **16,513** | **16,557** | **1,302** | **1,232** | **9** | **8** | **2** | ... | **1,457** | **1,411** | **46** |
| 1 | Bada-Barkhera | 7,258 | 2,745 | 2,844 | 17 | 12 | 601 | 641 | 166 | 172 | ... | ... | ... | ... | 138 | 134 | 4 |
| 2 | Bakhatgarh | 7,876 | 2,481 | 2,603 | 110 | 109 | 1,023 | 1,027 | 260 | 262 | ... | ... | 1 | ... | 266 | 257 | 9 |
| 3 | Bharudpura | 2,405 | 545 | 529 | ... | ... | 657 | 660 | 6 | 8 | ... | ... | ... | ... | 30 | 30 | ... |
| 4 | Chhota-Barkhera | 2,582 | 552 | 551 | 5 | 3 | 704 | 745 | 10 | 12 | ... | ... | ... | ... | 24 | 22 | 2 |
| 5 | Dhotria | 3,205 | 983 | 993 | 70 | 71 | 555 | 528 | 3 | 2 | ... | ... | ... | ... | 70 | 69 | 1 |
| 6 | Garhi | 947 | 185 | 155 | 1 | 2 | 306 | 296 | 2 | ... | ... | ... | ... | ... | 14 | 14 | ... |
| 7 | Jamnia | 3,154 | 877 | 886 | 2 | 2 | 626 | 609 | 67 | 65 | ... | ... | ... | ... | 71 | 71 | ... |
| 8 | Jobat | 15,560 | 766 | 708 | 15 | 14 | 6,657 | 6,815 | 275 | 293 | 9 | 8 | ... | ... | 141 | 137 | 4 |
| 9 | Kachhi-Baroda | 3,638 | 1,371 | 1,394 | 22 | 19 | 321 | 318 | 101 | 92 | ... | ... | ... | ... | 96 | 93 | 3 |
| 10 | Kali-Baori | 2,744 | 1,077 | 1,050 | ... | .. | 225 | 240 | 85 | 67 | ... | ... | ... | ... | 50 | 50 | ... |
| 11 | Kathiwada | 3,837 | 1,892 | 1,861 | ... | .. | .. | ... | 57 | 27 | ... | ... | ... | ... | 41 | 41 | ... |
| 12 | Kotidah | 522 | 36 | 24 | ... | .. | 223 | 222 | 7 | 5 | ... | ... | ... | ... | 10 | 10 | ... |

| No. | Name | | | | | | | | | | | | | | | | |
|---|---|---|---|---|---|---|---|---|---|---|---|---|---|---|---|---|---|
| 13 | Mathwad . . . . . | 1,905 | 84 | 67 | ... | ... | 894 | 847 | 7 | 6 | ... | ... | ... | ... | 12 | 12 | ... |
| 14 | Multhan . . . . | 10,061 | 3,185 | 3,180 | 144 | 125 | 1,676 | 1,614 | 128 | 109 | ... | ... | ... | ... | 353 | 335 | 18 |
| 15 | Nimkhera . . . . | 6,840 | 1,803 | 1,902 | 32 | 27 | 1,503 | 1,443 | 69 | 61 | ... | ... | ... | ... | 114 | 111 | 3 |
| 16 | Rajgarh . . . . . | 856 | 186 | 162 | ... | ... | 224 | 217 | 41 | 25 | ... | ... | 1 | ... | 15 | 15 | ... |
| 17 | Ratanmal . . . . | 1,532 | 409 | 411 | ... | ... | 353 | 335 | 18 | 6 | ... | ... | ... | ... | 12 | 10 | 2 |
| | **BRITISH CANTONMENTS AND STATIONS.** | **8,259** | **2,163** | **1,875** | **22** | **28** | **1,734** | **1,697** | **254** | **239** | **120** | **121** | **3** | **3** | **426** | **397** | **29** |
| 18 | Manpur (British Pargana) . . | 6,609 | 1,643 | 1,434 | 12 | 7 | 1,530 | 1,474 | 142 | 129 | 118 | 120 | ... | ... | 221 | 212 | 9 |
| 19 | Sardarpur . . . . . | 1,650 | 520 | 441 | 10 | 21 | 204 | 223 | 112 | 110 | 2 | 1 | 3 | 3 | 205 | 185 | 20 |
| | **BUNDELKHAND AGENCY MINOR STATES AND BRITISH CANTONMENTS, ETC.** | **82,204** | **38,041** | **36,294** | **79** | **63** | **51** | **45** | **3,789** | **3,025** | **588** | **162** | **48** | **19** | **3,010** | **2,802** | **208** |
| | **MINOR STATES . . . .** | **72,109** | **34,847** | **33,617** | **57** | **47** | **48** | **45** | **1,734** | **1,686** | **16** | **11** | **1** | ... | **1,381** | **1,335** | **46** |
| 1 | Alipura . . . . . | 16,146 | 7,887 | 7,216 | 15 | 4 | ... | ... | 533 | 467 | 13 | 11 | ... | ... | 296 | 272 | 24 |
| 2 | Banka-Pahari . . . . | 1,357 | 577 | 612 | 13 | 13 | 48 | 45 | 22 | 27 | ... | ... | ... | ... | 18 | 18 | ... |
| 3 | Beri . . . . . . | 4,219 | 2,128 | 1,889 | ... | ... | ... | ... | 104 | 98 | ... | ... | ... | ... | 106 | 105 | 1 |
| 4 | Bihat . . . . . | 5,387 | 2,461 | 2,548 | ... | ... | ... | ... | 195 | 182 | ... | ... | 1 | ... | 73 | 73 | ... |
| 5 | Bijna . . . . . | 1,326 | 634 | 643 | 4 | 2 | ... | ... | 18 | 25 | ... | ... | ... | ... | 36 | 35 | 1 |
| 6 | Bilheri . . . . . | 2,860 | 1,301 | 1,274 | ... | ... | ... | ... | 109 | 176 | ... | ... | ... | .. | 113 | 111 | 2 |
| 7 | Dhurwai . . . . . | 1,530 | 772 | 719 | ... | .. | ... | ... | 22 | 17 | .. | ... | ... | ... | 39 | 39 | ... |
| 8 | Garranti . . . . . | 5,222 | 2,590 | 2,484 | ... | ... | ... | ... | 87 | 58 | 3 | ... | ... | ... | 80 | 80 | ... |
| 9 | Gaurihar . . . . . | 8,451 | 4,140 | 4,054 | 3 | ... | ... | ... | 136 | 118 | ... | ... | ... | ... | 136 | 131 | 5 |
| 10 | Jigni . . . . . | 3,597 | 1,727 | 1,728 | ... | ... | ... | ... | 75 | 67 | ... | ... | ... | ... | 108 | 104 | 4 |
| 11 | Lughasi . . . . . | 6,738 | 3,410 | 3,240 | 1 | ... | .. | ... | 41 | 16 | ... | ... | ... | ... | 87 | 87 | ... |
| 12 | Naigawan-Rebai . . . | 2,393 | 1,126 | 1,168 | ... | ... | ... | ... | 52 | 47 | | ... | ... | ... | 37 | 37 | ... |
| 13 | Sarila . . . . . | 5,712 | 3,194 | 3,098 | ... | ... | ... | ... | 209 | 211 | ... | ... | ... | ... | 141 | 134 | 7 |
| 14 | Tori-Fatehpur . . . . | 6,171 | 2,900 | 2,944 | 21 | 28 | ... | ... | 131 | 147 | ... | ... | ... | ... | 111 | 109 | 2 |
| | **BRITISH CANTONMENTS AND STATIONS.** | **10,095** | **3,194** | **2,677** | **22** | **16** | **3** | ... | **2,055** | **1,339** | **572** | **151** | **47** | **19** | **1,629** | **1,467** | **162** |
| 15 | Nowgong Cantonment . . | 9,421 | 2,906 | 2,555 | 22 | 16 | 1 | ... | 1,956 | 1,284 | 522 | 97 | 47 | 15 | 1,488 | 1,362 | 126 |
| 16 | Agency Head-quarters . . | 674 | 288 | 122 | ... | ... | 2 | ... | 99 | 55 | 50 | 54 | ... | 4 | 141 | 105 | 36 |

# PROVINCIAL TABLE II.—Appendix B—*concld.*

| Serial No. | States, Estates, British Cantonments and Stations. | Population. | DISTRIBUTION BY RELIGION. | | | | | | | | | | | | Number of Literate Persons. | | |
|---|---|---|---|---|---|---|---|---|---|---|---|---|---|---|---|---|---|
| | | | Hindu. | | Jains. | | Animists. | | Musalmans. | | Christians. | | Others. | | | | |
| | | | Males. | Females. | Males. | Females. | Males. | Females. | Males. | Females. | Males. | Females. | Males. | Females. | Persons. | Males. | Females. |
| 1 | 2 | 3 | 4 | 5 | 6 | 7 | 8 | 9 | 10 | 11 | 12 | 13 | 14 | 15 | 16 | 17 | 18 |
| | MALWA AGENCY MINOR STATES | | | | | | | | | | | | | | | | |
| | MINOR STATES— | **47,825** | **20,026** | **19,628** | **604** | **593** | **2,385** | **2,522** | **1,068** | **963** | **16** | **20** | ... | ... | **1,466** | **1,352** | **114** |
| 1 | Bagli | 16,498 | 7,690 | 7,419 | 248 | 228 | 29 | 34 | 432 | 415 | 2 | 1 | ... | ... | 653 | 617 | 36 |
| 2 | Biland | 317 | 123 | 123 | 16 | 13 | ... | ... | 22 | 20 | ... | ... | ... | ... | 26 | 26 | ... |
| 3 | Borkheda | 969 | 431 | 398 | 33 | 26 | 21 | 22 | 21 | 17 | ... | ... | ... | ... | 26 | 23 | 3 |
| 4 | Gudarkheda | 474 | 222 | 229 | 12 | 9 | ... | ... | 1 | 1 | ... | ... | ... | ... | 26 | 25 | 1 |
| 5 | Jawasia | **512** | **259** | **224** | **5** | **1** | ... | ... | **12** | **11** | ... | ... | ... | ... | ... | ... | ... |
| 6 | Kerwasa | 653 | 289 | 304 | 16 | 19 | 12 | 13 | ... | ... | ... | ... | ... | ... | 30 | 30 | ... |
| 7 | Khojankhera | 378 | 196 | 180 | ... | ... | ... | ... | 2 | ... | ... | ... | ... | ... | 7 | 6 | 1 |
| 8 | Panth-Piploda | 4,483 | 2,188 | 2,132 | 1 | ... | ... | ... | 82 | 51 | 11 | 18 | ... | ... | 120 | 109 | 20 |
| 9 | Pathari | 1,777 | 922 | 827 | 9 | 9 | ... | ... | 5 | 5 | ... | ... | ... | ... | 47 | 47 | ... |
| 10 | Piploda | 8,033 | 3,303 | 3,401 | 117 | 144 | 270 | 304 | 260 | 234 | ... | ... | ... | ... | 130 | 101 | 29 |
| 11 | Sajaota (Shajaota) | 367 | 189 | 171 | ... | ... | ... | ... | 4 | 3 | ... | ... | ... | ... | 2 | 2 | ... |
| 12 | Sarwan | 5,064 | 1,323 | 1,353 | 33 | 28 | 1,036 | 1,120 | 88 | 83 | ... | ... | ... | ... | 152 | 142 | 10 |
| 13 | Sheogarh | 5,217 | 1,471 | 1,467 | 64 | 75 | 985 | 598 | 80 | 73 | 3 | 1 | ... | ... | 129 | 121 | 8 |
| 14 | Sidri | 338 | 166 | 170 | ... | ... | ... | ... | 1 | 1 | ... | ... | ... | ... | 9 | 9 | ... |
| 15 | Sirsi | 794 | 382 | 365 | 10 | 8 | ... | ... | 16 | 13 | ... | ... | ... | ... | 23 | 23 | ... |
| 16 | Tal | 1,334 | 660 | 611 | ... | ... | 3 | 7 | 25 | 28 | ... | ... | ... | ... | 12 | 12 | ... |
| 17 | Uni | **641** | **330** | **286** | **2** | ... | ... | ... | **13** | **10** | ... | ... | ... | ... | ... | ... | ... |
| 18 | Uparwara | 1,129 | 471 | 478 | 45 | 34 | 29 | 24 | 29 | 19 | ... | ... | ... | ... | 65 | 59 | 6 |

The figures for Jawasia and Uni have also been included in those of Dewas Senior and Junior respectively.

# PROVINCIAL TABLE III.

## *Railway Stations in Central India Agency by States, Political Charges and Railway Lines.*

The figures embodied in this Table for Stations on different Railways have been included in the totals of the States to which they refer. The figures are separately shown here merely for reference in future should necessity arise in case of territorial changes.

The figures for Stations on the Gwalior Light Railway have been included in those of the villages within whose boundaries they lie. They all belong to the Gwalior State.

The Station of Pachpahar on the Bombay, Baroda and Central India Railway lies partly in Gwalior and partly in Jhalawar State so as also Mehidpur Road in Indore and Dewas S. B. The population of these Stations were equally shared by the States concerned.

The town of Alot belongs to the Dewas State S. B. but the land occupied by the Railway Station of this name forms part of the Gadgucha Pargana of the Junior Branch State.

# PROVINCIAL TABLE III.—Railway Stations in Central India Agency by States, Political Charges and Railway Lines.

| Political charge. | State. | Station (with Railway line). | No. of Occupied Houses. | Population. Persons. | Population. Males. | Population. Females. |
|---|---|---|---|---|---|---|
| 1 | 2 | 3 | 4 | 5 | 6 | 7 |
| Gwalior Residency | Gwalior | R. M. R.—Kesarpura | 19 | 51 | 30 | 21 |
| | | Nimach | 200 | 629 | 351 | 278 |
| | | Harkia Khal | 15 | 35 | 23 | 12 |
| | | Mandsaur | 31 | 209 | 137 | 72 |
| | | Dalauda | 14 | 118 | 81 | 37 |
| | | Dhodhar | 15 | 68 | 44 | 24 |
| | | Runija | 21 | 81 | 46 | 35 |
| | | Barnagar | 44 | 134 | 84 | 50 |
| | | Sipra Bridge | 17 | 57 | 38 | 19 |
| | | ***Total*** | ***376*** | ***1,382*** | ***834*** | ***548*** |
| | | B. B. & C. I. R.—Ujjain | 125 | 556 | 364 | 192 |
| | | Aslaoda | 12 | 34 | 20 | 14 |
| | | Unhal | 16 | 46 | 27 | 19 |
| | | Nagda | 82 | 395 | 254 | 141 |
| | | Suvasra | 12 | 47 | 34 | 13 |
| | | Pachpahar (half) | 14 | 45 | 27 | 18 |
| | | Khachraud | 20 | 82 | 54 | 28 |
| | | ***Total*** | ***281*** | ***1,205*** | ***780*** | ***425*** |
| | | G. I. P. R.—Mungavali | 8 | 53 | 41 | 12 |
| | | Pipraigaon | 6 | 25 | 19 | 6 |
| | | Tumain | 17 | 42 | 30 | 12 |
| | | Shadoragaon | 6 | 16 | 10 | 6 |
| | | Pagara | 7 | 28 | 17 | 11 |
| | | Guna | 89 | 282 | 172 | 110 |
| | | Bhilsa | 24 | 97 | 72 | 25 |
| | | Sojna | 17 | 76 | 52 | 24 |
| | | Sumer | 14 | 62 | 34 | 28 |
| | | Gulabganj | 10 | 27 | 14 | 13 |
| | | Pabai | 15 | 43 | 26 | 17 |
| | | Basoda | 14 | 57 | 39 | 18 |
| | | Kalhar | 24 | 102 | 60 | 42 |
| | | Tajpur | 6 | 22 | 14 | 8 |
| | | Maksi | 22 | 69 | 39 | 20 |
| | | Beroha | 8 | 33 | 21 | 12 |
| | | Kali Sindh | 7 | 26 | 16 | 10 |
| | | Akodia | 14 | 39 | 24 | 15 |
| | | Shujaulpur | 18 | 52 | 33 | 19 |
| | | Kala Pipal | 15 | 40 | 22 | 18 |
| | | Parbati | 8 | 25 | 15 | 10 |
| | | Sank | 7 | 31 | 17 | 14 |
| | | Dabra | 15 | 35 | 24 | 11 |
| | | Autpeth | 14 | 34 | 22 | 12 |
| | | Antri | 16 | 67 | 40 | 27 |
| | | Sandalpur | 4 | 14 | 9 | 5 |
| | | Sithouli | 13 | 34 | 25 | 9 |
| | | Gwalior | 107 | 388 | 268 | 120 |
| | | Morar Road | 15 | 44 | 31 | 13 |
| | | Banmor | 9 | 48 | 35 | 13 |
| | | Nurabad | 2 | 11 | 4 | 7 |
| | | Morena | 17 | 81 | 55 | 26 |
| | | Hetampur | 11 | 42 | 20 | 22 |
| | | ***Total*** | ***579*** | ***2,045*** | ***1,320*** | ***725*** |
| | | **Total Gwalior State** | **1,236** | **4,632** | **2,934** | **1,698** |
| | Dharnaoda | G. I. P. R.—Dharnaoda | 7 | 23 | 15 | 8 |
| | | Rothiai | 6 | 17 | 7 | 10 |
| | | **Total Dharnaoda** | **13** | **40** | **22** | **18** |
| | Khaniadhana | G. I. P. R.—Basai | 9 | 33 | 17 | 16 |
| | | **Total Gwalior Residency** | **1,258** | **4,705** | **2,973** | **1,732** |

## PROVINCIAL TABLE III.—Railway Stations in Central India Agency by States, Political Charges and Railway Lines—*contd.*

| Political charge. | State. | Station (with Railway line). | No. of Occupied Houses. | Population. | | |
|---|---|---|---|---|---|---|
| | | | | Persons. | Males. | Females. |
| 1 | 2 | 3 | 4 | 5 | 6 | 7 |
| Indore Residency . | Indore . . | R. M. R.—Piplia . . . . . . | 13 | 42 | 28 | 14 |
| | | Tharod . . . . . | 15 | 44 | 29 | 15 |
| | | Chambal . . . . . | 17 | 46 | 28 | 18 |
| | | Fatehabad . . . . . | 56 | 270 | 175 | 95 |
| | | Ajnod . . . . . . | 17 | 57 | 31 | 26 |
| | | Palia . . . . . . | 25 | 78 | 37 | 41 |
| | | Indore . . . . . . | 80 | 562 | 368 | 194 |
| | | Rao . . . . . . | 17 | 86 | 50 | 36 |
| | | Mhow . . . . . . | 423 | 1,489 | 836 | 653 |
| | | Patalpani . . . . . | 47 | 144 | 84 | 60 |
| | | Kalakund . . . . . | 51 | 170 | 100 | 70 |
| | | Choral . . . . . . | 24 | 81 | 52 | 29 |
| | | Mukhtiara . . . . . | 15 | 60 | 33 | 27 |
| | | Barwaha . . . . . | 27 | 134 | 91 | 43 |
| | | Sanawad . . . . . | 24 | 80 | 53 | 27 |
| | | ***Total*** . | ***851*** | ***3,343*** | ***1,995*** | ***1,348*** |
| | | B. B. & C. I. R.—Garoth . . . . . | 24 | 71 | 40 | 31 |
| | | Shamgarh . . . . . | 101 | 299 | 199 | 100 |
| | | Mehidpur Road (half) . . | 10 | 32 | 20 | 12 |
| | | ***Total*** . | ***135*** | ***402*** | ***259*** | ***143*** |
| | | G. I. P. R.—Tarana Road . . . . . | 15 | 48 | 25 | 23 |
| | | **Total Indore State portion** . . | **1,001** | **3,793** | **2,279** | **1,514** |
| | | **Total Indore Residency** . . . | **1,001** | **3,793** | **2,279** | **1,514** |
| Baghelkhand Agency . | Rewah . . | E. I. R.—Dabhaura . . . . . | 11 | 39 | 28 | 11 |
| | | Satna . . . . . | 129 | 392 | 231 | 161 |
| | | ***Total*** . | ***140*** | ***431*** | ***259*** | ***172*** |
| | | B. N. R.—Chandia Road . . . . | 17 | 55 | 39 | 16 |
| | | Umaria . . . . . . | 106 | 218 | 141 | 77 |
| | | Karkeli . . . . . . | 9 | 31 | 17 | 14 |
| | | Birsinghpur . . . . . | 33 | 144 | 72 | 72 |
| | | Ghunghuti . . . . . | 11 | 29 | 18 | 11 |
| | | Sahdol . . . . . . | 109 | 407 | 218 | 189 |
| | | Burhar . . . . . . | 10 | 69 | 50 | 19 |
| | | Anuppur . . . . . | 12 | 36 | 24 | 12 |
| | | Jaithari . . . . . | 21 | 74 | 38 | 36 |
| | | Venkat Nagar . . . . | 12 | 50 | 31 | 19 |
| | | ***Total*** . | ***340*** | ***1,113*** | ***648*** | ***465*** |
| | | **Total Rewah State** . . . . | **480** | **1,544** | **907** | **637** |
| | Maihar . . | E. I. R. —Amdara . . . . . | 22 | 42 | 31 | 11 |
| | | Maihar . . . . . | 15 | 40 | 23 | 17 |
| | | Jukehi . . . . . | 10 | 24 | 16 | 8 |
| | | Bhadanpur . . . . . | 15 | 28 | 20 | 8 |
| | | **Total Maihar State** . . . . | **62** | **134** | **90** | **44** |
| | Sohawal . . | E. I. R.—Jaitwar . . . . . . | 11 | 31 | 18 | 13 |
| | Nagod . . | E. I. R.—Unchehra . . . . . | 17 | 37 | 23 | 14 |
| | Kothi . . | E. I. R.—Majhgawan . . . . . | 13 | 32 | 21 | 11 |
| | Taraon . . | G. I. P. R.—Chitrakot . . . . . | 10 | 30 | 24 | 6 |
| | | **Total Baghelkhand Agency** . | **593** | **1,808** | **1,083** | **725** |

# PROVINCIAL TABLE III.—Railway Stations in Central India Agency by States, Political Charges and Railway Lines—*contd.*

| Political charge. | State. | Station (with Railway line). | No. of Occupied Houses. | Population. Persons. | Males. | Females. |
|---|---|---|---|---|---|---|
| 1 | 2 | 3 | 4 | 5 | 6 | 7 |
| Bhopal Agency | Bhopal | G. I. P. R.—Budni | 15 | 72 | 49 | 23 |
| | | Midghat | 13 | 36 | 22 | 14 |
| | | Choka | 9 | 15 | 12 | 3 |
| | | Barkhera | 81 | 283 | 153 | 130 |
| | | Hirania | 15 | 67 | 43 | 24 |
| | | Kamkhera | 9 | 30 | 17 | 13 |
| | | Dip | 20 | 75 | 53 | 22 |
| | | Misrod | 18 | 66 | 37 | 29 |
| | | Habibganj | 9 | 25 | 18 | 7 |
| | | Bhopal | 207 | 1,001 | 626 | 375 |
| | | Sukhi-Siwania | 7 | 13 | 8 | 5 |
| | | Bhadbhada Ghat | 9 | 31 | 18 | 13 |
| | | Dewanganj | 17 | 71 | 46 | 25 |
| | | Salamatpur | 11 | 40 | 26 | 14 |
| | | Sanchi | 9 | 24 | 17 | 7 |
| | | Sehore | 19 | 40 | 26 | 14 |
| | | Phanda | 7 | 11 | 8 | 3 |
| | | Beragarh | 12 | 30 | 16 | 14 |
| | | **Total Bhopal State** | **487** | **1,930** | **1,195** | **735** |
| | Kurwai | G. I. P. R.—Bareth | 15 | 49 | 27 | 22 |
| | | Kethora | 15 | 47 | 23 | 24 |
| | | **Total Kurwai State** | **30** | **96** | **50** | **46** |
| | | **Total Bhopal Agency** | **517** | **2,026** | **1,245** | **781** |
| Bhopawar Agency | Jhabua | B. B. & C. I. R.—Bhairongarh | 21 | 61 | 33 | 28 |
| | | Amargarh | 38 | 138 | 89 | 49 |
| | | Bajranggarh | 17 | 61 | 39 | 22 |
| | | Meghnagar | 16 | 39 | 25 | 14 |
| | | **Total Jhabua State** | **92** | **299** | **186** | **113** |
| | Indore | B. B. & C. I. R.—Bamnia | 21 | 57 | 31 | 26 |
| | | Panchpiplia | 12 | 26 | 17 | 9 |
| | | **Total Indore State portion** | **33** | **83** | **48** | **35** |
| | | **Total Bhopawar Agency** | **125** | **382** | **234** | **148** |
| Bundelkhand Agency | Orchha | G. I. P. R.—Orchha | 7 | 25 | 14 | 11 |
| | | Arjar | 12 | 36 | 29 | 7 |
| | | Teharka | 6 | 29 | 21 | 8 |
| | | **Total Orchha State** | **25** | **90** | **64** | **26** |
| | Datia | G. I. P. R.—Datia | 15 | 59 | 40 | 19 |
| | | Govindpur | 12 | 30 | 24 | 6 |
| | | Sonagir | 19 | 85 | 68 | 17 |
| | | Kotra | 16 | 43 | 35 | 8 |
| | | **Total Datia State** | **62** | **217** | **167** | **50** |
| | Samthar | G. I. P. R.—Nandkhas | 8 | 81 | 62 | 19 |
| | Alipura | G. I. P. R.—Harpalpur | 20 | 63 | 41 | 22 |
| | | **Total Bundelkhand Agency** | **115** | **451** | **334** | **117** |

## PROVINCIAL TABLE III.—Railway Stations in Central India Agency by States, Political Charges and Railway Lines—*concld.*

| Political charge. | State. | Station (with Railway line). | No of Occupied Houses. | Population. Persons. | Males. | Females. |
|---|---|---|---|---|---|---|
| 1 | 2 | 3 | 4 | 5 | 6 | 7 |
| Malwa Agency | Ratlam | R. M. R.—Namli | 12 | 99 | 72 | 27 |
| | | Naigawan | 15 | 50 | 31 | 19 |
| | | *Total* | *27* | *149* | *103* | *46* |
| | | B. B. & C. I. R.—Ratlam | 400 | 1,315 | 797 | 518 |
| | | Marwani | 22 | 50 | 33 | 17 |
| | | *Total* | *422* | *1,365* | *830* | *535* |
| | | **Total Ratlam State** | **449** | **1,514** | **933** | **581** |
| | Jaora | R. M. R.—Jaora | 29 | 177 | 118 | 59 |
| | | Malhargarh | 18 | 91 | 62 | 29 |
| | | **Total Jaora State** | **47** | **268** | **180** | **88** |
| | Sailana | B. B. & C. I. R.—Raoti | 17 | 43 | 31 | 12 |
| | | Bangrod | 15 | 106 | 77 | 29 |
| | | **Total Sailana State** | **32** | **149** | **108** | **41** |
| | Dewas S. B. | B. B. & C. I. R.—Mehidpur Road (half) | 11 | 32 | 21 | 11 |
| | Dewas J. B. | B. B. & C. I. R.—Alot | 25 | 58 | 44 | 14 |
| | | **Total Malwa Agency** | **564** | **2,021** | **1,286** | **735** |
| Central India | All parts | Stations on R. M. R. (28) | 1,301 | 5,142 | 3,112 | 2,030 |
| | | Do. B. B. & C. I. R. (20½) | 1,031 | 3,593 | 2,276 | 1,317 |
| | | Do. G. I. P. R. (67) | 1,258 | 4,673 | 2,987 | 1,686 |
| | | Do. E. I. R. (9) | 243 | 665 | 411 | 254 |
| | | Do. B. N. R. (10) | 340 | 1,113 | 648 | 465 |
| | | **Total Central India (134½)** | **4,173** | **15,186** | **9,434** | **5,752** |